UNIVERSITY OF NOTTINGHAM
10 0065767 5
WITHDRAWN
FROM THE LIBRARY

FRESHWATER QUALITY

Additional Reports undertaken for the
Royal Commission on Environmental Pollution

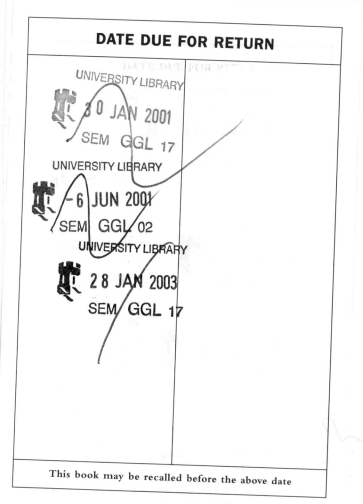

DATE DUE FOR RETURN

UNIVERSITY LIBRARY

3 0 JAN 2001

SEM GGL 17

UNIVERSITY LIBRARY

-6 JUN 2001

SEM GGL 02

UNIVERSITY LIBRARY

2 8 JAN 2003

SEM GGL 17

This book may be recalled before the above date

90014

LONDON: HMSO

D1421794

© Crown copyright 1992
    Applications for reproduction should be made to HMSO

First published 1992

ISBN 0 11 701678 0

1000657675

Foreword

By Lord Lewis of Newnham, FRS

Chairman

Royal Commission on Environmental Pollution

The studies in this volume were undertaken at the request of the Royal Commission to assist it in the preparation of its sixteenth report on Freshwater Quality (Cm 1966). The views expressed are those of the authors to whom any enquiries should be directed. Two other studies carried out for the report are reproduced as appendices 5 & 6 to the sixteenth report. On behalf of the Royal Commission I am grateful for the efforts of each of our consultants and the contribution they made to our work.

Lewis of Newnham

Contents

The Potential Pollution Impact of Domestic Chemical Use on Fresh Water Quality

Report No: CO 2672-M/1

April 1991

Authors: S Hedgecott and H R Rogers

Contract Manager: A J Dobbs

Contract No: 8157

Contract duration: 10 August 1990 to 1 March 1991

Any enquiries relating to this report should be referred to the Contract Manager at the following address:

WRc plc, Henley Road, Medmenham, PO Box 16, Marlow, Buckinghamshire SL7 2HD.
Telephone: Henley (0491) 571531

Summary

I Objectives

To investigate the potential impact on the freshwater aquatic environment of the release of chemicals used in domestic situations by a short review of available information.

II Reasons

Although many studies have investigated the potential impact of the diffuse release of contaminants on the aquatic environment, few have considered domestic sources as a specific case. In addition, current regulations do not usually take domestic releases specifically into account. This study provides an initial assessment of the potential effects of such chemicals on sewage treatment, water quality, and aquatic organisms.

III Conclusions

This preliminary study suggests that normal usage of domestic products does not appear to result in significant acute hazards to sewage treatment or the aquatic environment. However, where sewage treatment is carried out locally (ie cesspits and septic tanks) some problems have been reported. The potential for chronic effects is not clear cut. Improper disposal of a number of domestic chemicals down drains or sewers could potentially cause local problems.

On the basis of this preliminary study, those chemicals released in the most significant amounts from homes are a number of metals, nitrogen and phosphorus-based nutrients, and cleaning products. Although there is little current evidence of water pollution problems resulting from domestic chemical use a number of recommendations are made regarding their testing, usage and disposal.

IV Recommendations

- Chemicals used domestically, such as cosmetics and toiletries, should all be tested for adverse environmental effects.

- Further consideration should be given to the contribution of domestic premises to heavy metal contaminants in sewage sludge. In the long term the copper and zinc levels may be critical to continued use of sewage sludge in agriculture.

- Clearer guidance is needed for householders on the disposal of chemicals used domestically, eg paints, solvents, oils etc.

- Use of priority chemicals in domestic formulations should be studied and eliminated if possible.

V Resume of Contents

Chemicals are grouped according to the types of products in which they are found. Metals are considered as a special case because of the wide variety of sources contributing to their presence in wastewaters. For each group a consideration is made, where possible, of the amounts that might be expected to be lost or released in domestic wastewater and the effects that they might have on sewage treatment and the environment. Within the constraints of this study, it has only been possible to make a brief assessment of the potential for environmental effects.

Contents

1 Introduction

A great number of chemicals are used in homes for a variety of purposes. For existing chemicals use is largely unregulated and even for new chemicals once approved, or at least once the products are suitably labelled under the new chemicals regulations, such use is largely unregulated and uncontrolled. Clearly domestic use is either small scale or very diffuse in contrast with industrial use but with increasing concern about environmental impact and increased control of point source pollution it is timely to consider in more detail domestic sources. It should be remembered that the domestic use of hard detergents a few decades ago produced extreme environmental effects in the guise of foaming of rivers. Detergents are not considered in this report, being the subject of another study commissioned by the Royal Commission on Environmental Pollution. This report has pulled together available data for a range of consumer products and attempted to put that into context in order to establish the relative importance of domestic sources of these products for freshwater pollution.

It is well recognised that homes constitute diffuse sources of hazardous wastes such as used oils, waste paint, solvents and batteries. For example, Stanek *et al* (1987) estimated that about 4% by weight of the total hazardous waste disposed of in Massachusetts, USA, arose from domestic sources, released principally to landfill, the ground or sewers. Because these sources are less well regulated than industrial sources it could be argued that their impact on the environment may be more significant than this figure suggests.

The potential for harmful effects of hazardous materials in diffuse wastewaters (rather than solid waste), such as from residences, is less clear. Nearly every chemical substance used by man can potentially occur in domestic wastewaters, largely as the result of the vast range of chemical products available for use in the home. The aim of this report is to collate information on the hazardous substances which may be present in domestic wastewaters and attempt to identify those substances which have the potential to cause problems at sewage treatment works or in the aquatic environment.

1.1 Scale of the problem

The OECD (1986) identified five main diffuse sources of hazardous waste, namely:

– agriculture;

– business activities;

– educational and service laboratories;

– households; and

– hazardous components contained in products.

Of these the first three may be considered as 'industrial' sources and are not considered in any detail here, although it should be noted that certain activities (such as car washes or cottage industries) can contribute to influent at supposed 'domestic only' sewage treatment works. Also, many of the substances arising from these sources are the same as those arising from domestic sources, although the relative volumes appear to be very different. For example, a survey in Vermont, USA, identified the volumes of hazardous waste produced by small businesses such as car dealers, undertakers, machine shops and photographic processors (Anonymous 1990). The bulk of the hazardous waste generated was accounted for by waste oils (54%) and solvents and degreasers (27%). Antifreeze (10%), paint thinner (7%), and photographic chemicals (2%) made up most of the remainder. By contrast, in a domestic hazardous waste collection scheme in Massachusetts, USA, waste oils (3% of liquid waste) and solvents (11%) were less important than substances such as paints (58%) and pesticides (16%) (Blackmar *et al* 1984). The results of this domestic collection are presented in more detail in Tables 1.1 and 1.2.

Assuming that non-participants held the same amount of hazardous materials as participants, ie nearly 11 litres per person, and assuming that a similar pattern would be seen in the UK, a total of about 600 000 m^3 of hazardous liquid wastes may currently be in UK residences (based on a population of 55 million (MRS 1990)). This is more likely to be an over-estimate rather than an under-estimate because non-participants may not have taken part because they had little or no waste to dispose of.

The OECD (1986) estimated the amounts of hazardous substances disposed of from diffuse sources in West Germany in 1982, as shown in Table 1.3. Their findings indicate a totally different ranking compared to Blackmar *et al* (1984). For example, motor oils were much more important in the West German study, and paints much less

Table 1.1 Quantities of liquid domestic chemicals collected in a hazardous waste collection scheme[1] (Blackmar *et al* 1984)

Product	Volume collected (1)	% Contribution to total	Amount per person[2] (1)
Paints	9 459	59%	6.3
Pesticides[3]	2 582	16%	1.7
Solvents	1 748	11%	1.2
Fertilisers	579	4%	0.4
Corrosives	560	3%	0.4
Waste oils	548	3%	0.4
Flammables	350	2%	0.2
Corrosive oxidisers	350	2%	0.2
Paint strippers	67	0.4%	0.04
Total	**16 243**	**100**	**10.8**

Notes

[1] A one-off collection lasting 3 days.

[2] About 1% of population participated.

[3] An additional 531 kg of solid pesticides was collected.

Table 1.2 Types of liquid domestic chemicals collected in a hazardous waste collection scheme (Blackmar *et al* 1984)

Product	Major compounds
Paints	Household paints
Pesticides	Arsenic, Lead arsenate, Chlordane, Creosote, DDT, Dieldrin Malathion, Methoxychlor, Parathion, 2,4,5-T, Strychnine, 2,4-D
Solvents	Acetone, o-Dichlorobenzene, Formaldehyde, Methylene, 1,1,1-Trichloroethylene, Toluene
Fertilisers	Inorganic nutrients
Corrosives	Sulphuric acid, Hydrochloric acid
Waste Oils	Motor oil
Flammables	Kerosene, Petrol
Corrosive Oxidisers	Photographic chemicals
Paint Strippers	not specified
Others	Lead acetate, Lead pigments, Mercury

Table 1.3 Hazardous substances disposed of at diffuse sites in West Germany, 1982 (figures from OECD 1986)

Product	Rate of disposal (tonnes/year)[1]	Percentage contribution	Release in wastewater (incl. drains)	Release via runoff/leaching (excl. landfill)
Motor oils	8 000	38	Likely	Likely
Batteries	7 000	33	No	No
Paints, dyes	2 200	10.5	Yes	Possible
Pharmaceuticals	1 050	5	Yes	No
Lacquers, varnish	615	2.9	Likely	Possible
Solvents	580	2.8	Likely	Possible
Fertilisers	579	2.7	Possible	Yes
Shoe-care mixtures	300	1.4	No	No
Adhesives	191	0.9	No	No
Polishes	170	0.8	No	No
Carpet/fabric cleaners	161	0.8	Possible	No
Pesticides	113	0.5	Possible	Yes

Notes

[1] Total release of 20 959 tonnes/year; of this 13 298 tonnes/year has the potential for release to water.

important. However, since the OECD considered all diffuse sources (rather than just domestic) this is perhaps not surprising.

Figures provided by the Central Statistical Office (CSO 1988) for production industries in the UK indicate that domestic and office chemicals, such as pharmaceuticals, soaps and toiletries, account for about 2.6% of production output in the UK (based on their 'index of output'), whilst industrial chemicals account for about 4%. These figures must be considered very tentative but they demonstrate the relative importance of domestic chemicals. Studies in the USA have revealed that between 1 and 20% of the hazardous waste materials present in homes may be disposed of down the drains (Brown 1987). This is in addition to the quantities released to sewers in the course of normal usage. On this basis it would appear that domestic premises could potentially be an important source of hazardous chemicals in sewers and the environment.

1.2 Rural areas as a specific case

There may be particular problems associated with rural areas, particularly where tourism is important. Such areas often have small sewage works which may not be adequate to handle the increased demand incurred during holiday seasons, resulting in their processing capacity being exceeded. The converse, where sewage works are capable of handling high-season loads, can result in problems from underloading in the off-season, which may lead to operational difficulties and decreased treatment efficiency. Additional problems can arise from caravan and camping sites, which may have no sewage or wastewater treatment

facilities, and from the discharge of the contents of chemical toilets, which can present difficulties at sewage treatment works (Rangeley 1983). For example, some chemical toilets contain sodium o-phenylphenate as an antimicrobial agent, and this can inhibit the activity of sewage sludge bacteria (Voets et al 1976, Klecka et al 1985).

The main pollutants in wastewater from tourist areas are organic matter, organic nitrogen and oil and grease (Galil and Rebhun 1990). Many of the chemicals regularly used in the maintenance and cleaning of domestic premises are not used in caravans or other holiday accommodation. Therefore, although there may be particular problems associated with rural areas these are likely to be localised and may not be a major problem when compared to other sources of contaminated domestic wastewaters.

Another feature of rural areas is that a lower percentage of dwellings are connected to mains sewerage. This is most notable in the area served by South-West Water plc, which has a sewer connection rate of 88% compared to the national rate of over 96% (WSA 1990). In place of mains sewerage, domestic wastewaters are disposed of to septic tanks (where the effluent is finally disposed of to groundwater) or cesspits, (which are periodically emptied and the contents disposed of to sewage treatment works). Assuming that 136 l of water is released per person per day (ie the same as the amount supplied; WSA 1990) and that 2 million people are not connected to mains sewerage, then 270 000 m^3 of wastewater may be released via these routes every day.

In a study of the final effluent of domestic septic tanks from households in Australia (all with washing machines, none with dishwashers) Whelan and Titamnis (1982) measured a wide range of contaminants including pH, conductivity, redox potential, BOD5, cations, metals, suspended solids, nitrogen (N) and phosphorus (P). They concluded that N and P were the major chemical contaminants of domestic septic tank effluent, and all other chemical components were insignificant provided the effluent was not released directly to water. (N and P are discussed further in Section 6.) In addition there were no problems associated with plugs of contaminants in the effluent because there was almost complete mixing of the wastewaters within the septic tank. Reviewing the available literature, Montgomery et al (1988) also concluded that dilution of domestic wastewaters in septic tanks or septic tank effluent would be adequate to ensure that any chemical contaminants would have no harmful effects, with the possible exception of nitrate. A study in the USA investigated contamination of groundwater by effluents from 17 septic tank systems (each serving more than one household) (Chen 1988). Concentrations of nitrate, nitrite, and ammoniacal nitrogen were up to 3, 80 and 4 times higher, respectively, in groundwater receiving septic tank effluents. Concentrations of ortho-phosphate were up to 25 times higher.

1.3 Conclusions

The limited information available suggests that in gross terms households are important sources of certain potentially problematic substances. These substances can be broadly categorised as hazardous chemicals (such as solvents) and non-hazardous chemicals (such as nutrients), and the amounts of each which may be released will depend on the catchment in question. In addition, the same types of substances may be released from their domestic-type usage in non-domestic situations (eg toilet cleaners used in office complexes). However, most of the available information relates to waste materials, rather than wastewaters, for which the situation is less clear. The following sections of this report will attempt to elucidate the situation for domestic wastewaters.

References

ANONYMOUS (1990) How much unregulated hazardous waste? *BioCycle* **47**, April 1990.

BLACKMAR D S, HORSELY S W, SEGALL L and WOOLF A (1984) Results of a regional household hazardous waste collection program in Barnstable Count, Massachusetts. *Hazardous Waste* **1**, 111-122.

CSO (CENTRAL STATISTICAL OFFICE) (1988) Annual abstract of statistics No. 124, 1988 edition. HMSO, London.

GALIL N and REBHUN M (1990) Best treatment sequence for small communities. *Water Quality International*, No. **1**, 30-31 (1990).

KLECKA G M, LANDI L P and BODNER K M (1985) Evaluation of the OECD activated sludge, respiratory inhibition test. *Chemosphere* **14**, 1239-1251.

MONTGOMERY H A C, SHAW P J and CHEESEMAN R V (1988) Water quality changes in a septic tank effluent discharged to the chalk. *Journal of the Institution of Water and Environmental Management*, 2nd August, 361-364.

MRS (MARKET RESEARCH SOCIETY) (1990) Personal communication.

OECD (1986) Fate of small quantities of hazardous waste. OECD Environment Monograph No. 6. OECD, Paris, August 1986.

RANGELEY J (1983) Discharges from small sewage treatment works: a river inspector's view. *Public Health Enqineer* **11**, 1 January, 31-33.

STANEK E J III, TUTHILL R W, WILLIS C and MOORE G S (1987) Household hazardous waste in Massachusetts. *Archives of Environmental Health* **42**, 83-86.

VOETS J P, PIPYN P, VAN LUNCKER P and VERSTRAETE W (1976) The degradation of microbicides under different environmental conditions. *Journal of Applied Bacteriology* **40**, 67-72.

WHELAN B R and TITMANI Z V (1982) Daily chemical variability of domestic septic tank effluent. *Water, Air and Soil Pollution* **17**, 131-139.

WSA (WATER SERVICES ASSOCIATION) (1990) Waterfacts 1990. WSA, London.

2 Cleaners and deodorisers

2.1 Household cleaners

The use of domestic cleaning products in the UK is widespread. Household cleaners are regularly used in an estimated 96.1% of households, domestic bleaches in 92.8%, floor and furniture polishes in 92.4% and scouring powders in 60.8% (Keynote Report 1989). The market for domestic powdered cleaners steadily declined from 27 900 t in 1983 to 12 000 t in 1986, whilst that for domestic liquid cleaners increased from 29 300 t in 1983 to 37 800 t in 1986.

A large number of different cleaners are available for use in the home, containing a variety of active chemicals. Some of the major active ingredients are listed below in Table 2.1.

Table 2.1 Major active ingredients of some household cleaners

Cleaner type	Contact with water	Common active ingredients
Toilet cleaner	Extensive	1. Solid cleaners Sodium acid sulphate Sodium sulphate Sodium carbonate 2. Liquid cleaners Phosphoric acid (6.4% aqueous solution) Hydrochloric acid Oxalic acid Sodium metasilicate Zinc chloride Sodium nitrate Potassium dichromate Sodium tripolyphosphate Sodium fluoride Also ancillary ingredients such as colourant, perfume, rust inhibitor, thickening agent, ammonium-based bactericide.
Bleaches and drain cleaners	Extensive	1. Liquid cleaners Sodium hydroxide Sodium hypochlorite Sodium carbonate Potassium hydroxide Calcium hypochlorite Hydrogen peroxide Hydrochloric acid Petroleum distillates 2. Powdered cleaners Sodium silicate Sodium sulphate Sodium tripolyphosphate
Ammonia-based cleaners	Varies	Ammonia Ethanol
Abrasive cleaners	Varies	Ammonia Ethanol Phosphates (eg trisodiumphosphate) Silica Sodium sulphate Potassium persulphate

Table 2.1 continued

Cleaner type	Contact with water	Common active ingredients
Disinfectants Methylene glycol	Varies	Diethylene glycol
		Sodium hypochlorite (and various other sodium compounds)
		Phenol
		2,4-Dichlorophenol
Floor/furniture polish	Limited	Diethylene glycol
		Petroleum distillates
		Nitrobenzene
Rug and upholstery cleaners	Limited	Naphthalene
		Perchloroethylene
		Oxalic acid
		Diethylene glycol
Septic tank and cesspit cleaners	Extensive	Sodium hydroxide
		Potassium hydroxide
		Aluminium
		Sodium carbonate
		Sodium bisulphate
		Sodium chloride
		Copper sulphate
		Aluminium sulphate

Many of the chemicals listed are priority pollutants or have regulated industrial use. At high concentrations many of them would have an impact on sewage treatment plant operation or have a direct environmental impact. One common ingredient, sodium hypochlorite, is considered in more detail below as an example, in order to assess the potential for such acute effects.

2.1.1 Sodium hypochlorite

Sodium hypochlorite is a major component of domestic cleaners. It is the most common hypochlorite used in the home, as a bleach and disinfectant, and it is effective against a wide variety of micro-organisms (Windholz 1976). Household products usually comprise aqueous solutions with between 5 and 5.5% sodium hypochlorite (about 50 g/l) (Gosselin *et al* 1984). It is an oxidising agent and has no BOD or COD.

The activity of activated sludge is inhibited by as little as 0.3 mg/l sodium hypochlorite, with 50% inhibition seen at 3 mg/l, but recovery taking less than a week (Raff *et al* 1987). On the basis of these data and the concentration data for sodium hypochlorite in household products it would appear that about 200-fold dilution is necessary to ensure no adverse effects on sewage treatment. If it is assumed that the same amount of water supplied to households (136 l/person/day) (WSA 1990) is released as wastewater, it can be calculated that a total of 0.7 litres of sodium hypochlorite cleaner can be used per person per day with this 200-fold dilution still being achieved almost immediately in the sewer.

(Although the cleaner will probably be used as a 'plug' rather than continuously this will be compensated for in the sewer by the presence of 'clean' wastewater from other households.) With an average 2.5 persons per household (CSO 1988) this equates to 1.75 litres per household per day, or almost an entire large bottle. Therefore it is envisaged that there will be very few, if any, situations in which normal use of this type of cleaner will result in potentially hazardous levels in sewage works influent.

The reported acute LC50s for annelids, crustaceans and fish typically fall between 2 and 60 mg/l sodium hypochlorite (Environment Canada 1985, Ewell *et al* 1986, Curtis *et al* 1979, Linden and Bengttson 1979). Thus it would seem that a dilution factor of up to 2000 will be necessary to ensure household products have no significant adverse effects on aquatic biota (assuming a 100-fold difference between the LC50 and the no effect concentration). Using the same calculation as above this suggests that 0.175 litres (or 175 ml) of cleaner per household per day will be adequately diluted almost immediately. *Ad hoc* testing conducted at WRc has indicated that a 'typical' drain cleaning operation can use anything between about 100 and 300 ml of cleaner, but such cleaning operations are not carried out daily. This suggests that the required dilution should again be achieved almost immediately within the sewer.

2.2 Disinfectants

A number of compounds from a variety of classes of chemicals are incorporated as active ingredients in proprietary disinfectants, such as alcohols, aldehydes, phenols, carboxylic acids and quaternary ammonium salts. There are some concerns regarding disinfectants' reported biorecalcitrance in sewage treatment works and the environment (Janicke 1987), and since they function as antimicrobial agents it is possible that their release to sewers or water could have detrimental effects on sewage works or the environment.

A number of investigations into the biodegradability of chemicals used as disinfectants have been carried out (Gerike *et al* 1978, Gerike and Fischer 1979, Boethling 1984, Guhl and Gode 1989). In general it would appear that most of these substances are readily biodegradable, although this depends understandably on their concentration. Some of the results from a study of biodegradability and microbial toxicity are summarised below in Table 2.2.

Table 2.2 Biodegradability of disinfectant chemicals and levels at which they inhibit microbial activity (Gerike and Gode 1990)

	Inhibitory threshold mg/l
Alcohols – readily biodegradable	
ethanol	> 1000
1-propanol	10000
2-propanol	> 1000
benzyl alcohol	–
Aldehydes – readily biodegradable	
formaldehyde	30
ethanedial	500
pentanedial	90 – 130
1,3,5-tris(2-hydroxy-ethyl)hexahydrotriazine	360
acrolein diacetate	–
Carboxylic Acids – biodegradable to readily biodegradable	
peracetic acid	25 – 90
chloroacetic acid	750 – > 1000
bromoacetic acid	750 – > 1000
Phenols – readily to extremely biodegradable	
phenol	110
o-phenylphenol	16
p-chloro-m-cresol	30 – 32
2,3,6-trichlorophenol	–
Quaternary Ammonium Compounds – slowly to readily biodegradable	
benzyldimethyldodecylammonium chloride (BDMDAC)	3 – 22
dichlorobenzyldimethyldodecylammonium chloride (DCBDMDAC)	16
cetyltrimethylammonium bromide (CTAB)	15
didecyldimethylammonium chloride (DDDMAC)	–
laurylpyridinium methosulfate (LPMS)	> 8
Miscellaneous – readily biodegradable	
condensation product of cocosaminopropylamine + caprolactum	3
condensation product of cocosaminopropylenediamine + glutamic acid	> 8
2-(3-iodo-2-propynyloxy)ethanol, N-phenylcarbamate	v. high

These results show that most of these disinfectants are readily biodegraded and have quite high threshold inhibition concentrations. For example, it has been concluded for quaternary ammonium compounds (QACs) that they are unlikely to have any adverse effects on sewage treatment at the relatively low and constant concentrations which will arise from any domestic discharge (Gerike *et al* 1978, Boethling 1984). The same will probably also be true of the other disinfectants.

Boethling (1984) estimated for the USA that the average concentration of QACs in sewage would be approximately 1 mg/l, but only about 0.3 mg/l of this would be of alkyldimethylbenzylammonium-based compounds used in domestic products such as disinfectants and hair conditioners. Such compounds have been shown to be toxic to algae, molluscs, crustaceans, echinoderms, fish and other aquatic organisms at the mg/l level. However, considering the apparent effectiveness of sewage treatment in degrading these compounds it is unlikely that they will be released to the environment in such high concentrations. Where domestic wastewaters are released directly to surface waters concentrations may be higher, so there may be the potential for adverse effects. River die-away studies with a number of different QACs (mostly synthetic detergents) at concentrations at the mg/l level or higher have demonstrated half-lives of less than one to several days (Baleux and Caumette 1977, Dean-Raymond and Alexander 1977, Larson and Perry 1981). In addition sorption to suspended solids and sediments removes QACs and may enhance biodegradation (Boethling 1984). Therefore it seems unlikely that there will be problems even in watercourses receiving untreated domestic effluent containing QAC-based disinfectants.

2.3 Deodorisers (1,4-Dichlorobenzene)

In the UK most space deodorisers for use in toilets contain 1,4-dichlorobenzene (1,4-DCB) as the active ingredient. Together with use as a moth repellent this accounts for 90% of 1,4-DCB use (Belin 1985); most of the remaining 10% is used as a chemical intermediate in industry (Jori *et al* 1982). All of the 1,4-DCB content of space deodorisers is released by volatilisation or dissolution, and it has been assumed that 50% is released by each process (Yoshida *et al* 1987). Crane *et al* (1989) estimated an annual release to water of about 1500 t/y of 1,4-DCB in the UK from all uses, equivalent to about half the production. The pattern of usage above suggests that much of this release will arise from space deodorisers dissolved in domestic-type wastewaters.

1,4-DCB appears to be readily biodegraded under aerobic conditions (Topping 1987), and degradation by sewage sludge organisms has been demonstrated (Spain and Nishino 1987). It has been shown to have adverse effects on sewage sludge activity only at concentrations of the order of 1 g/l or above (Liu and Thomson 1983, Swanwick and Foulkes 1971), and it is considered very unlikely that domestic sources could result in such high concentrations. Studies in Switzerland have indicated that the main input of 1,4-DCB into rivers is from treated sewage (Ahel *et al* 1983), indicating that although sewage treatment may not be adversely affected it may permit passage of 1,4-DCB into the aquatic environment.

A partitioning model for 1,4-DCB based on a 'unit world' indicated that about 50% will be found in the aqueous environment; mostly dissolved but some associated with solids and biota (Yoshida *et al* 1987). A mean residence time in water of about four days was estimated. Schwarzenbach *et al* (1979) estimated that 68% of the input of 1,4-DCB to Lake Zurich ultimately volatilises, but the residence time was as long as five months. Theoretical or experimental half-lives of 8 and 72 hours have been estimated for 1,4-DCB in surface waters (Cadena *et al* 1984, Rippen *et al* 1984), and 10 to 18 days in sea water (Wakeham *et al* 1983) with volatilisation responsible for most losses. A review of the reported concentrations of 1,4-DCB in UK surface waters (Crane *et al* 1989) included concentrations in the range 0.1 to 13 µg/l, but values of 1 µg/l or less were reported as typical, when detected at all. Investigations by WRc into the concentrations of 1,4-DCB in UK rivers and estuaries have found levels from below the detection limit (2 ng/l) to 110 ng/l, with the higher concentrations being associated with sewage outfalls (Moore and Watts 1988, Rogers *et al* 1989). Reported concentrations of <0.5 to 10 µg/l in raw sewage and 0.1 to 2.2 µg/l in sewage effluent appear to be typical (Crane *et al* 1989).

Reviewing the toxicity of 1,4-DCB to fresh- and salt-water life, Crane *et al* (1989) concluded that certain invertebrates are the most sensitive species. Acute lethality is seen at concentrations around 1 to 2 mg/l for the most sensitive species such as the water flea, *Daphnia magna*, and the mysid shrimp, *Mysidopsis bahia*. The highest concentration reported as having no adverse effects is 0.22 mg/l in freshwater, but no equivalent value has been reported for saltwater organisms. Comparing these values with the reported concentrations in surface waters suggests that aquatic biota are unlikely to be adversely affected by 1,4-DCB arising from diffuse, domestic sources, with the highest reported concentrations in UK surface waters being an order of magnitude below the lowest reported no effect concentration.

Considering human health, a suggested no adverse response level (SNARL) of 64 µg/l of 1,4-DCB in drinking water has been estimated, (based on an acceptable daily intake of 10.71 µg/kg day for a 60 kg adult drinking 2 litres of water per day, and allocating 20% of the ADI to water) (Crane *et al* 1989). Therefore domestic sources of 1,4-DCB in waters abstracted for drinking water are not likely to result in a problem. However, the reported odour thresholds for 1,4-DCB in water range from 0.3 to 30 µg/l, with values around 1 to 3 µg/l most often reported (Crane *et al* 1989). Levels approaching or equal to this mid-range have on occasion been reported for waters in the UK and elsewhere.

2.4 Industrial sources of domestic-type chemicals

At a number of power stations the amount of sewage produced per member of staff per day has been estimated at approximately 130 litres, with about 76 l being foul water and 54 l urinal flushing (CEGB 1980). These figures were

12

obtained from studies at power stations operating shifts and with primarily male staff and do not necessarily apply to all working environments. In comparison the amount of water supplied to households is estimated at 136 1 per person per day (WSA 1990). Assuming the volume of domestic effluent equals the volume of influent, and based on a population of 55 million (MRS 1990) this suggests a domestic wastewater output of about 7.5 million m³ per day. If it is assumed that about 20 million people are in employment in some sort of workplace (based on a working population of 28 million, 3 million unemployed, 3 million self-employed and 2 million or more working outdoors (CSO 1988)) then the total domestic-type sewage effluent from workplaces could be around 2.6 million m³ per day. Thus the industrial sources of domestic-type wastewater may account for about a quarter of the total. (However, this estimate makes no account of additional non-domestic sources such as shops, schools, public toilets and so forth, so any calculation can only be considered as very approximate.) Therefore any assessment of the market size or potential impact of domestic cleaning products may need to be revised to take account of these non-domestic sources.

2.5 Conclusions

The generally reassuring picture relating to acute effects from cleaning products is not unexpected. Such products are used so widely that adverse effects are almost certain to have been noted and action taken if these effects were significant. The two aspects which seem to have received insufficient study are those related to:

a.   the use and occurrence of priority or otherwise controlled substances in domestic products, eg zinc chloride in toilet cleaners;

b.   the use or generation of chlorinated substances which are priorities for pollution control, eg the continued use of dichlorobenzenes and the production of a range of chlorinated organic substances resulting from hypochlorite bleach use.

These aspects will be considered again in Section 13.

Routine use of most domestic cleaning products means that their entry into wastewater is unavoidable. However, concentrations of potentially hazardous active ingredients are quite low and dilution in sewers seems to be sufficient to ensure dilution to harmless levels almost instantaneously, with no acute adverse effects on biota in sewage works or surface waters. It has not been possible to assess the likelihood of chronic effects at this stage. Effects on on-site sewerage systems (septic tanks and cesspits) are less clear. It would seem that normal usage of cleaning products does not result in any adverse effects (Kampf and Heide 1989), and levels in their effluents are low and probably not harmful to groundwater. However, adverse effects of, for example solid toilet cleaners, on septic tank operation have been noted (Kampf and Bral 1989).

A proposed hazardous waste awareness scheme in the USA (Robertson et al 1987) approved the disposal down the drains of unwanted products such as ammonia-based cleaners, chlorine bleaches, scourers, drain cleaners, toilet cleaners, and disinfectants, as long as they were well flushed with water. However, the authorities noted that for the final three categories this option should only be adopted when the premises were connected to mains sewerage because of potential detrimental effects on septic tank systems.

References

AHEL M, GIGER W, MOLNAR-KUBICA E and SCHAFFNER C (1983) Organic micropollutants in surface waters of the Glatt Valley, Switzerland. *Proc. Conf. Analysis of Organic Micropollutants in Water*, Oslo, 280–288.

BALEUX B and CAUMETTE P (1977) Biodegradation of some cationic surface-active agents. *Water Research* **11**, 833–841.

BELIN C B (1985) Aspects technico-économiques des mesures de réduction de la pollution des eaux par les rejets de certains derivés chlorés du benzène. CEGOS report number C05/729.

BOETHLING R S (1984) Environmental fate and toxicity in wastewater treatment of quaternary ammonium surfactants. *Water Research* **18**, 1061–1076.

CADENA F, EICEMAN G A and VANDIVER V J (1984) Removal of volatile organic pollutants from rapid streams. *Journal of the Water Pollution Control Federation* **56**, 460–463.

CEGB (1980) Report on investigation of quantities of sewage effluent discharged by 2000 MW power stations. Central Electricity Generating Board, Planning Department, Generation and Transmission Development Board, London.

CRANE R I, FAWELL J K and ZABEL T F (1989) Proposed environmental quality standards for dichlorobenzenes. WRc report number DoE 2084–M.

CSO (CENTRAL STATISTICAL OFFICE) (1988) Annual abstract of statistics no. 124, 1988 edition. HMSO, London.

CURTIS M W, COPELAND T L and WARD C H (1979) Acute toxicity of 12 industrial chemicals to freshwater and salt-water organisms. *Water Research* **13**, 137–141.

DEAN-RAYMOND D and ALEXANDER M (1977) Bacterial metabolism of quaternary ammonium compounds. *Applied and Environmental Microbiology* **33**, 1037–1041.

ENVIRONMENT CANADA (1985) Environmental and technical information for problem spills: sodium hypochlorite.

EWELL W S, GORSUCH J W, KRINGLE R O, ROBILLARD K A and SPIEGAL R C (1986) Simultaneous evaluation of the acute effects of chemicals on seven aquatic species. *Environmental Toxicology and Chemistry* **5**, 831–840.

GERIKE P and FISCHER W K (1979) A correlation study of biodegradability determinations with various chemicals in various tests. *Ecotoxicology and Environmental Safety* **3**, 159–173.

GERIKE P, FISCHER W K and JASIAK W (1978) Surfactant quaternary ammonium salts in aerobic sewage digestion. *Water Research* **12**, 1117–1122.

GERIKE P and GODE P (1990) The biodegradability and inhibitory threshold concentration of some disinfectants. *Chemosphere* **21**, 799–812.

GOSSELINE R E, SMITH R P and HODGE H C (1984) Clinical toxicology of commercial products. 5th edition. Williams and Wilkins, 1984.

GUHL W and GODE P (1989) Interference in the function of biological sewage plants by chemicals: comparison of tolerance limits with results obtained in the oxygen consumption test with bacteria. *Vom Wasser* **72**, 165–173.

HASEGAWA R, TAKAHASHI M, KOKUBO T, FURUKAWA F, TOYODA K, SATO H, KUROKAWA Y and HAYASHI Y (1986) Carcinogenicity study of sodium hypochlorite in F344 rats. *Food and Chemical Toxicology* **12**, 1295–1302.

JANICKE W (1987) Wasch- und Reinigungsmittel als Haushaltschemikalien und Gewässerschutz. (Domestic washing products and cleaning agents as household chemicals, with regard to water quality protection.) *Korrespondenz Abwasser* **34**, 43–46.

JORI A, CALAMARI D, CATTABENI F, DI DOMENICO A, GALLI C L, GALLI E and RAMUNDO A (1982) Ecotoxicological profile of p-dichlorobenzene. *Ecotoxicology and Environmental Safety* **6**, 413–432.

KAMPF R and BRAL E A M A (1989) De ontwikkeling van een testmethode om de invloed van stoffengebruik in de huishouding op de biologische werking van septic tanks, vast te stellen (Test to assess the influence of household products on small scale wastewater treatment plants. *H₂0* **22**, 554–557.

KAMPF R and HEIDE B A (1989) De invloed van bijzondere stoffen op idividuele zuiveringsystemen (The effects of household products on individual on-site sewage treatment plants). *H₂0* **22**, 550–553, 567.

KEYNOTE REPORT (1989) An industry sector overview: household cleaning products. 2nd edition. Keynote Publications Ltd., 1989.

LARSON R J and PERRY R L (1981) Use of the electrolytic respirometer to measure biodegradation in natural waters. *Water Research* **15**, 697–702.

LINDEN E and BENGTTSON B E (1979) The acute toxicity of 78 chemicals and pesticide formulations against the two brackish water organisms, the bleak and the harpacticoid. *Chemosphere* **8**, 843–851.

LIU D and THOMSON K (1983) Toxicity assessment of chlorobenzenes using bacteria. *Bulletin of Environmental Contamination and Toxicology* **31**, 105–111.

MRS (MARKET RESEARCH SOCIETY) (1990) Personal communication.

MOORE K and WATTS C D (1988) Fate and transport of organic compounds in rivers. Pages 154–168 in: Organic micropollutants in the aquatic environment. Ed G Angeletti and A Bjorseth, Dordrecht, Kluwer Academic Publishers.

RAFF J, HEGEMANN W and WEIL L (1987) Experiments on the behaviour of microbicides in sewage treatment plants. *GWF – Wasser/Abwasser* **128**, 319–323.

RIPPEN G, KLÖPFFER W, FRISCHE R and GUNTHER K-O (1984) The environmental model segment approach for estimating potential environmental concentrations. *Ecotoxicology and Environmental Safety* **8**, 363–377.

ROBERTSON D K, AKAGHA J, BELASCO J, BULLIS J, BYRNE G, DI PATRIA J, FISHER W, FONZINO J, HSU J, MERCHAN L, OSTER D, ROSENBERG J, VON AULOCK S and VROEGINDAY B (1987) Liquid household hazardous wastes in the United States: identification, disposal, and management plan. *Environmental Management* **11**, 735–742.

ROGERS H R, CRATHORNE B and LEATHERLAND T M (1989) Occurrence of chlorobenzene isomers in the water column of a UK estuary. *Marine Pollution Bulletin* **20**, 276–281.

SCHWARZENBACH R P, MOLNAR-KUBICA E, GIGER W and WAKEHAM S G (1979) Distribution, residence times and fluxes of tetrachloroethylene and 1,4-dichlorobenzene in Lake Zurich, Switzerland. *Environmental Science and Technology* **13**, 1367–1373.

SPAIN J C and NISHINO S F (1987) Degradation of 1,4-dichlorobenzene by a *Pseudomonas* sp. *Applied and Environmental Microbiology* **53**, 1010–1019.

SWANWICK J D and FOULKES M (1971) Inhibition of anaerobic digestion of sewage sludge by chlorinated hydrocarbons. *Water Pollution Control* **70**, 58–70.

TOPPING B (1987) The biodegradability of para-dichlorobenzene and its behaviour in model activated sludge plants. *Water Research* **21**, 295–300.

WAKEHAM S G, DAVIS A C and KARAS J L (1983) Mesocosm experiments to determine the fate and persistence of volatile organic compounds in coastal seawater. *Environmental Science and Technology* **17**, 611–617.
WINDHOLZ M (Ed) (1976) The Merck Index. 9th edition. Merck and Co. Publishers.

WSA (WATER SERVICES ASSOCIATION) (1990) Waterfacts 1990. WSA, London.

YOSHIDA K, SHIGEOKA T and YAMAUCHI F (1987) Multi-phase non-steady state equilibrium model for evaluation of environmental fate of organic chemicals. *Toxicological and Environmental Chemistry* **15**, 159–183.

3 Cosmetics and toiletries

There is no detailed information available either to quantify the inputs of cosmetic preparations and toiletries to domestic sewage, or to assess the behaviour of component residues during sewage treatment processes. However, although a wide range of different chemicals are used in cosmetic and toiletry preparations (Table 3.1), residues entering sewers are almost certainly very diluted. These chemicals receive extensive toxicity testing by manufacturers, which suggests that their general mammalian toxicity is likely to be low, but this does not necessarily apply to ecotoxicity as well, and persistence is not usually evaluated.

Table 3.1   Chemicals used in cosmetics and toiletries (Atkins and Hawley 1978)

Product type	Constituents
Skin creams	sodium lauryl sulphate
	aluminium chlorhydroxide
	zinc oxide
Bath salts/bubble bath	sodium bicarbonate
	trisodium phosphate
	sodium chloride
	sodium hexametaphosphate
	sodium lauryl sulphate
	sodium chloride
	sodium sulphate
	sodium tripolyphosphate
Dentifrices	sodium alginate
	sodium lauryl sulphate
	dicalcium phosphate
	sodium lauryl sulphate
	alumina hydrate
	titanium dioxide
	tricalcium phosphate
	sodium metaphosphate
	stannous fluoride
	ammonium phosphate
	calcium carbonate
	calcium pyrophosphate
	calcium sulphate
	magnesium carbonate
	magnesium oxide
	magnesium phosphate
	potassium chlorate
	sodium benzoate
	sodium bicarbonate
	sodium fluoride
Deodorants and antiperspirants	aluminium chlorhydroxide
	aluminium chloride
	aluminium sulphate
	magnesium oxide
	sodium lauryl sulphate
	aluminium phenolsulphonate
	sodium stearate
	zinc oxide
	zinc phenol sulphonate
	boric acid
	hexachlorophene

Table 3.1 continued

Product type	Constituents
Hair dyes/neutralisers/hair lotions	pyrogallol
	paraphenylene diamine
	resorcinol
	salicylic acid
	potassium bromate
	2,5-diaminotoluene
	thioglycolate
Depilatories	calcium thioglycolate
	barium sulphide
	zinc oxide
	calcium hydroxide
	sodium lauryl sulphate
Eye make-up	sodium benzoate
	calcium carbonate
	lithium stearate
	titanium dioxide
	aluminium powder
	iron oxide
Face make-up	zinc stearate
	zinc oxide
	magnesium carbonate
	titanium oxide
Shaving creams/lotions	sodium alginate
	sodium salicylate
	coconut oil soap
	ammonium stearates
	aluminium chlorhydroxy
	allantoinate
	zinc phenolsulfonate

Yamagishi *et al* (1981 and 1983) reported that residues of two synthetic musks, musk xylene (5-t-butyl-2,4,6-trinitroxylene) and musk ketone (2-acetyl-5-t-butyl-4,6-dinitroxylene) were present at 4 to 10 ng/l in river water, and 30 to 54 ug/kg in freshwater fish. These synthetic chemicals are used as fragrances in soaps, creams and lotions, and originate from sewage effluent inputs. Musk ketone is also used in commercial herbicide formulations and this may be another source. There is little known about the environmental fate and effects of synthetic musks.

Recently there has been an upsurge in the use of natural products in cosmetics and toiletries. Some of the natural materials incorporated in cosmetic and toiletry products include vitamins, fruit acids, amino acids, sugars, glycosides, essential oils, gums, phytosterol emulsions, algal extracts and dyestuffs (Marderosian 1983). However, it should be noted that the argument that 'natural' equals 'safe' is not scientifically justified.

3.1 Conclusions

It seems unlikely that chemicals used in cosmetics and toiletries would be likely to have a direct, acute effect on sewage treatment plants or receiving waters. However, the presence of synthetic odour constituents in river waters (such as the musks noted above) highlights the necessity to question whether such products should continue to be introduced onto the market without some form of ecotoxicity testing. This is equally true for novel 'natural' chemicals. If 'natural' can be assumed to equal safe it can only be so when the chemical is used in the same location and at the same concentration as it occurs naturally, because the ability to pollute is not intrinsic to a chemical structure but is due to a combination of property, location and concentration. Another feature that should be considered further is the contribution that bath salts and foams may be making to phosphorous loads. It may be insignificant but we have not had time to follow this further.

References

ATKINS E D and HAWLEY J R (1978) Sources of metals and metal levels in municipal wastewaters. Research program for the abatement of municipal pollution under provisions of the Canada-Ontario agreement on Great Lakes water quality. Environment Canada research report no. 80.

MARDEROSIAN A D (1983) Overview of pharmacognostical research and cosmetic formulation. *Cosmetics and Toiletries* **98**, 47–70.

YAMAGISHI T, MIYAZAKI T, HORII S and KANEKO S (1981) Identification of musk xylene and musk ketone in freshwater fish collected from the Tama river, Tokyo. *Bulletin of Environmental Contamination and Toxicolology* **26**, 656–662.

YAMAGISHI T, MIYAZAKI T, HORII S and AKIYAMA K (1983) Synthetic musk residues in biota and water from Tama River and Tokyo Bay. *Archives of Environmental Contamination and Toxicology* **12**, 83–89.

4 Water treatment chemicals

This section briefly considers the chemicals used in the treatment of domestic water supplies and for the disinfection of swimming pools and spas (jacuzzis and whirlpool baths).

4.1 Domestic water treatment

Treatment of domestic water supplies is carried out on an industrial scale by the water undertakings and on a domestic scale by individual householders. Although the former introduces larger volumes and more substances to the water supply, some of which are presented in Table 4.1, they can be considered as coming from an industrial source and therefore for the purposes of this report the emphasis here is on the small-scale treatment of supplied water.

There is little relevant information available to assess the potential effects of domestic water filters and softeners. Most of the current concern surrounding their use in the home is associated with potential health problems resulting, for example, from possible increases in bacterial contaminants. Potential chemical effects are less clear. Domestic water softeners can decrease water's aggressivity and so decrease corrosion of metal pipes and joints, leading to lower levels of metals such as copper in wastewaters (De Jong *et al* 1984) (see Section 10). Water softening products such as 'Calgon' contain polyphosphoric acids, which are metabolised in sewage treatment to phosphates and so can add to the total phosphate load of wastewaters. Other products, such as some filters, can increase the concentration of salts in the treated water. However, it is suggested that compared to the industrial use of similar substances by the water industry domestic sources are probably insignificant at present.

Table 4.1 Chemicals used for the industrial treatment of domestic water

Type/function (higher volume usage first)	Compounds use
pH adjusters/softeners	Caustic soda, soda ash Bases Acids Lime Sodium chloride
Oxidisers/disinfectants	Chlorine and derivatives (eg chlorine dioxide, sodium hypochlorite, calcium hypochlorite) Bromine and derivatives Potassium permanganate Hydrogen peroxide Ozone
Coagulants/flocculants	Aluminium sulphate Ferric chloride Ferric sulphate Sodium aluminate Polyacrylamide-based polyelectrolytes
Corrosion inhibitors	Chromate salts Inorganic and organic phosphates Polyphosphates
Filter media/adsorbents	Activated carbon Polystyrene-based ion-exchange resins
Fluoridation	Fluorides
Pesticides	Permethrin

4.2 Recreational water treatment – swimming pools and spas

Treated water from swimming pools and spas is released both continually, resulting from replenishment of the pool, and intermittently, when pools are emptied. Although the individual volumes involved are considerably smaller for spas than pools the numbers of public and private spas has rapidly increased in recent years and will probably continue to do so.

Traditionally swimming pools have been disinfected by treatment with chlorine, often as sodium hypochlorite. In the presence of ammonia (or amines in general) present in swimming pools from sweat and urine, chlorine forms chloramines (mostly monochloramine) which are very slow-acting disinfectants. Consequently swimming pool operators try to achieve 'chlorination breakpoint', ie a chlorine-to-ammonia ratio greater than 10:1 above which free residual chlorine (HOCl) will be present.

To achieve chlorination breakpoint a chlorine dose of up to 5 mg/l may be required (Sobotka and Krzysztofik 1984, Lahl *et al* 1981), although actual concentrations of chlorine added will vary according to how heavily used the pool is and how well it is operated. In the UK the DoE recommend that a free residual chlorine level of 1 to 3 mg/l is maintained at all times, with combined residual chlorine remaining below 1 mg/l (Price and Smith 1985). When cyanuric chloride is used as a chlorine stabiliser (Sommerfeld and Adamson 1982) the free residual chlorine level should be maintained at 1.5 to 3 mg/l, and the cyanuric acid should not normally exceed 200 mg/l, but may be as high as 400 mg/l in exceptional circumstances (DoE 1984).

Hamence (1980) presented data for eleven separate public pools in the UK with a mean free chlorine concentration of 0.6 mg/l but a mean total chlorine concentration of 3.86 mg Cl_2/l when combined chlorine species (monochloramine, dichloramine, and nitrogen trichloride) were included. The highest concentrations were of nitrogen trichloride. Lahl *et al* (1981) reported a similar mean value of 0.5 mg/l free chlorine but a lower level of 1.2 mg/l total chlorine for seven pools in Germany .

At chlorine doses above about 6.5 mg/l nitrogen trichloride (an irritant with an unpleasant odour) is reported to be formed (Powick 1989). However, Hamence (1980) found that what he originally identified (using a standard analytical method) as nitrogen trichloride was actually chlorinated compounds from urine, particularly creatinine. He suggested that other reports of nitrogen trichloride were similarly incorrect, and therefore that its reported presence in swimming pools was probably exaggerated. The formation of other undesirable chlorinated species is more certain. For example, trihalomethanes (mostly chloroform $CHCl_3$, but also some $CHCl_2Br$, $CHClBR_2$, $CHBr_3$) may be produced by the reaction of chlorine with nitrogenous compounds in urine (and bromide ions in the water). The production of trihalomethanes is catalysed by copper, which is often used as an algicide in swimming pools (Barnes *et al* 1989). Lahl *et al* (1981) reported a mean chloroform concentration of about 200 µg/l generated by chlorination of swimming pools, whereas Barnes *et al* (1989) reported a lower range of concentrations from 5 to 163 µg/l. Other trihalomethanes were detected less frequently and at considerably lower concentrations (maximum level 56 µg/l).

It might be expected that the higher temperatures (40 °C) associated with spas would accelerate the production of trihalomethanes. Benoit and Jackson (1987) analysed for trihalomethanes in 25 spas (commercial and domestic) of which 16 were treated with chlorine and 9 with bromine. Trihalomethane levels were equivalent to levels in swimming pools, with a mean of 292 µg/l (range 35 to 674 µg/l), compared to the mean of 200 µg/l found by Lahl *et al* (1981) and cited levels of 50 to 980 µg/l in swimming pools. The mean bromoform concentration was somewhat higher at 1253 µg/l (range 37 to 3600 µg/l). Benoit and Jackson (1987) also observed that other organohalides besides trihalomethanes were not formed to any significant extent, despite the intensive loadings and high sweat input associated with spas.

Although chloroform concentrations of 200 µg/l have been reported in pool water its volatility should result in lower concentrations in pool wastewater. A review of the effects of chloroform on bacteria, including sewage flora, indicates that they are not usually affected below 1 mg/l (Oakley and Zabel 1988), and chloroform present in pool wastewater should therefore have no adverse affects on sewage treatment. In addition chloroform concentrations are greatly reduced during sewage treatment, and combined with dilution in sewers and receiving waters this should ensure that concentrations in sewage works effluent are below the level of 5 µg/l considered to be harmless to aquatic life (CEC 1978, Oakley and Zabel 1988).

Besides chlorine a number of other disinfectants are available for treating swimming pools. These are briefly outlined below.

i   Chlorine dioxide

Has only limited use because of concerns regarding hazards to human health, such as the formation of chlorite, which is a potential cause of methaemoglobinaemia (Powick 1984) and a suspected carcinogen (EPA 1981), and chlorate, which is also a suspected carcinogen (EPA 1981).

ii   Ozone

Has little residual disinfectant power (because of its short half-life) and is therefore used in conjunction with a residual disinfectant (such as chlorine or bromine). Free residual chlorine in ozonated pools can be reduced to

0.5 to 1 mg/l (from 1 to 3 mg/l), and as a result chloroform concentrations are typically reduced from 200 to 60 µg/l (Lahl *et al* 1981). It can also result in the production of aldehydes and hydro- and other peroxides.

iii UV radiation

Has no residual effect, needs clear water to be effective, and is usually only used in small pools (<10 m^3) (Powick 1984).

iv Bromine

Can be used in liquid form, which appears to result in few problems, or in the solid form as bromides (Price and Smith 1985). The concentration of free residual bromine should be between 4 and 6 mg/l (DoE 1984), with bromide being kept below a maximum of 500 mg/l as bromine (Price and Smith 1985). However, in the UK bromine treatment is only used in some private pools and spas (Powick 1984).

Ozonation is the only one of these that is used to a significant extent in the UK, and because of the potential health hazard for bathers this is strictly controlled and there are not likely to be any environmental problems.

In addition to these disinfectants further chemicals are added, most notably algicides. Various commercial algicide preparations are used, typically containing quaternary ammonium compounds, copper or a polyoxyethylene alkyliminio compound, and a number are presented in Table 4.2 (Adamson and Sommerfeld 1980).

Table 4.2   Active ingredients of some proprietary swimming pool algicides

Algicide	Active ingredients	Recommended dose of active ingredient
Padicide	n-Alkyl dimethyl benzyl ammonium chlorides	1.8 mg/l
	n-Alkyl dimethyl ethylbenzyl ammonium chlorides	1.8 mg/l
Algimycin	Poly[oxyethylene-(dimethylimino)-ethylene-(di-methylimino)-ethylene-dichloride]	5.4 mg/l
	Simazine	0.63 mg/l
Bio-Gard	Copper triethanolamine complex, copper as elemental	0.43 mg/l
Algaedyn	Colloidal silver as elemental	0.19 mg/l
Pad Algae Kill	Sodium trichloro-s-triazinetrione	24 mg/l

In the UK the use of algicides based on quaternary ammonium compounds or polyoxyethylene compounds is limited such that the concentration of these active chemicals is less than 0.05 mg/l at the point of discharge, if discharged to water (DoE 1984). Therefore there should be no environmental problems arising from the use of such algicides. Maximum permitted levels for the other algicides in pools are also set, ranging from 10 to 150 mg/l, and based principally on human health considerations.

Considering one of these other algicides as an example, if Algimycin is applied at the recommended dose of 1.36 kg per 20 000 gallons (75 700 l) this would result in a simazine concentration of 0.63 mg/l in the pool. Because of the high persistence of simazine in water, with reported half-lives of the order of months (Hedgecott and Zabel 1990), levels in any wastewater are unlikely to be greatly reduced. Repeated application of 0.25 to 0.5 mg/l simazine has been shown to cause damage to turf (Hiltibran and Turgeon 1977), and repeated dosing of soil with the similar herbicide atrazine may adversely affect the microflora (Eisler 1989). It is therefore possible that if an Algimycin-treated pool is emptied to land or a soakaway there may be some detrimental effects on local flora, but fauna are less likely to be affected. Bacteria do not appear to be adversely affected by simazine below about 1 mg/l (Hedgecott and Zabel 1990), and sewage treatment processes are unlikely to be affected. Although conventional treatment probably reduces simazine by only about 30% (Donnez 1986) dilution of any swimming pool wastewater in the sewers and receiving waters should ensure that simazine levels in surface waters are below a concentration of 10 µg/l, which is considered to be acceptable for the protection of aquatic life (Hedgecott and Zabel 1990).

4.3 Conclusions

Domestic treatment of water is becoming more popular and in general it seems unlikely to give rise to any adverse surface water quality changes. However two aspects may require further consideration.

i   The increased use of silver impregnated carbon filters. Silver in sewage sludge could be a problem for application to agricultural land, but for economic reasons this seems unlikely to be a significant factor.

ii   Increased salt concentrations arising from regeneration of ion exchange units. On their own this is unlikely to be significant but together with other changes resulting in more salt usage it could become significant, particularly in areas with high water re-use.

In conclusion it appears that the regulations and maximum permitted levels of pool treatment chemicals for public pools should prevent any adverse effects on sewage treatment or the environment resulting from routine operation of the pool or from pool emptying. However, less control is exercised over private swimming pools or spas. If these are operated correctly there should be no major problems arising from regular wastewater release or from emptying. The one area where there is potentially a problem is where pools are pumped out onto land or small watercourses, but it has not been possible to ascertain how common an occurrence this is.

References

ADAMSON R P and SOMMERFIELD M R (1980) Laboratory comparison of the effectiveness of several algicides on isolated swimming pool algae. *Applied and Environmental Microbiology* **39**, 348–353.

BARNES D, FITZGERALD P A and SWAN H B (1989) Catalysed formation of chlorinated organic materials in water. *Water Science and Technology* **21**, 59–63.

BENOIT F M and JACKSON R (1987) Trihalomethane formation in whirlpool spas. *Water Research* **21**, 353–357.

CEC (COUNCIL OF THE EUROPEAN COMMUNITIES) (1978) Directive on the quality of freshwaters needing protection or improvement in order to support fish life, 18 July 1978 (78/659/EEC). *Official Journal* **L222**, 14 August.

DE JONG J W, HARING B J A, HOOGSTEIN K and VANNES A W (1984) The influence of the quality of drinking water on the copper content of sewage sludge in the provinces of Friesland, Groningen and Drenthe. H_2O **17**, 556–560.

DoE (DEPARTMENT OF THE ENVIRONMENT) (1984) Committee on chemicals and materials of construction for use in public water supply and swimming pools. Fourteenth statement. July 1984.

DONNEZ P (1986) Study of the discharges of certain dangerous substances into the aquatic environment and the best technical means for the reduction of water pollution from such discharges in application of the Directive 76/464/EEC. EXCOSER SC report for the EEC.

EISLER R (1989) Atrazine hazards to fish, wildlife, and invertebrates: a synoptic review. US Department of the Interior, Fish and Wildlife Service, Contaminant Hazard Reviews report number 18.

EPA (1981) Chlorine, is there a better alternative? *Science of the Total Environment* **18**, 235–243.

HAMENCE J H (1980) The chlorination of swimming pools and the presence of apparent nitrogen trichloride. *Journal of Association of Public Analysts* **18**, 125–128.

HEDGECOTT S and ZABEL T F (1990) Proposed environmental quality standards for atrazine and simazine in water. WRc report to the Department of the Environment, number DoE 2316–M, August 1990.

HILTIBRAN R C and TURGEON A J (1977) Creeping bentgrass response to aquatic herbicides in irrigation water. *Journal of Environmental Quality* **6**, 263–267.

LAHL U, BÄTJER K, DÜSZELN J V, GABEL B, STACHEL B and THIEMANN W (1981) Distribution and balance of volatile halogenated hydrocarbons in the water and air of covered swimming pools using chlorine for water disinfection. *Water Research* **15**, 803–814.

OAKLEY S D and ZABEL T F (1988) Proposed environmental quality standards for chloroform in water. WRc report to the Department of the Environment, number DoE 1580–M/2, March 1988.

POWICK D E J (1989) Swimming pools – brief outline of water treatment and management. *Water Science and Technology* **21**, 151–160.

PRICE T J and SMITH J M (1985) Swimming pool waters; the new blue book appreciated and discussed. *Environmental Health* **93**, 31–35.

SOBOTKA J and KRZYSZTOFIK B (1984) Biochemical changes occurring in swimming pool water during ultraviolet radiation disinfection. *Aqua* (1984), No.3, 170–172.

SOMMERFIELD M R and ADAMSON R P (1982) Influence of stabiliser concentration on effectiveness of chlorine as an algicide. *Applied and Environmental Microbiology* **43**, 497–499.

5 Food and drink

Potentially hazardous substances in food include additives (preservatives, colourings, flavourings, fragrances, flavour enhancers), residues of pesticides of growth promoters, and other contaminants (eg metals, DEHP). The undesirable contaminants will normally only be present in small quantities and their release in domestic wastewaters will be minimal compared to releases from the use that resulted in them being present in food in the first place. Therefore, only food additives are considered here. In addition a brief consideration is made of nutrients (nitrogen and phosphorus derivatives), in order to give an indication of the importance of domestic sources of these materials, both in kitchen wastewater (eg from washing up) and human urine and faeces.

5.1 Food additives

Because food additives are generally consumed their use is regulated. The FAO/WHO recommend tolerable weekly and short-term intakes for those considered to be potentially hazardous to human health. For example, proposed FAO/WHO acceptable daily intakes (ADIs) include 0-0.5 mg/kg bodyweight for butylated hydroxyanisole (an antioxidant), 0-1.2 mg/kg bodyweight for trans-anethole (a flavouring) and 0-0.05 mg/kg bodyweight for erythrosine (a colouring) (FAO/WHO 1989). These ADIs mean that the concentrations of additives in foodstuffs are generally limited and consequently amounts reaching domestic wastewaters via kitchen wastewaters or urine and faeces should be small and unlikely to cause environmental problems.

5.2 Nitrogen- and phosphorus-based nutrients

Ukita *et al* (1986) developed a mass balance model for total nitrogen (N) and total phosphorus (P) in foodstuffs in Japan. The average diet contained 13.3 g N/person/day of which 0.6 g N/person/day was released in kitchen wastewater, 0.7 g N/person/day in bathwater (via sweat) and 10 g N/person/day in faeces and urine. Thus a total of 11.3 g N/person/day was released in domestic wastewater. For P the food content was 1.37 g P/person/day and losses to sewers in kitchen wastewater, bathwater and faeces were 0.18, 0.05 and 1 g P/person/day, respectively, totalling 1.23 g P/person/day. Goda (1986) provided very similar estimates of the N and P loads in domestic wastewaters, with 11 to 13 g N/person/day and 1.8 g P/person/day. In a UK study conducted during 1985-86 the mean loadings of Kjeldahl nitrogen (contributions from nitrite and nitrate were negligible) in an almost entirely domestic catchment was 12.5 g/person/day (Petts and Stiff 1987), which compares well with the figures of 11 to 13 and 11.3 g N/person/day reported in the Japanese studies.

Based on these *per capita* loadings and a UK population of 55 million it can be estimated that domestic wastewaters release approximately 250 000 t/y of N to sewers. In the UK 80% of domestic sewage is treated, but the rate of removal of inorganic nitrogen during conventional treatment is low; if it is assumed to be 10% then the release of N from domestic sources to the environment will be of the order of 230 000 t/y. The total aqueous input of N to UK waters in 1985 has been estimated at about 319 000 t/y (Anonymous 1990), suggesting that domestic sources may be responsible for about 70% of the aqueous input of N.

Domestic sources of P have been estimated as contributing 53% of the total amount of P released to waters in the UK (Lund and Moss 1990), as compared to a mean of 37% for Europe as a whole. In a study in the USA, Alhajjar *et al* (1989) estimated that detergents accounted for about 46% of the total phosphorus content of domestic effluents. Additional American studies have demonstrated that detergent phosphorus bans can result in significant decreases in the phosphorus loadings of municipal sewage works influents and effluents. In Michigan average total phosphorus concentrations in sewage works influent and effluent were decreased by 23% and 24%, respectively, and in Washington DC influent concentrations were reduced by 32% (Hartig *et al* 1990).

Whelan and Titamnis (1982) investigated the composition of final effluents from domestic septic tanks in Australia. They concluded that N and P were the major chemical contaminants, and all other chemical components (such as metals) were insignificant provided the effluent was not released directly to water. Total nitrogen averaged about 130 mg/l and was almost all present as dissolved ammonium, with only 0.01 to 0.03 mg/l nitrate. Total phosphorus averaged about 17 mg/l, almost all as dissolved orthophosphate. Comparison with other studies, conducted in Canada, the USA and New Zealand, suggested that the nitrogen levels were high in this study (more typical values being below 100 mg/l) but the phosphorus levels were typical. The dissolved loads were equivalent to 3.8 kg/person/year N and 0.6 kg/person/year P.

Reneau *et al* (1989) reported for the USA that the average septic tank effluent contained 40 to 80 mg/l N, of which about 75% was as ammonium. P concentrations were typically 11 to 31 mg/l with a mean of 16 mg/l, and

85% of this was as orthophosphate.

Although there is some variability in these results they all indicate that most of the N and P in domestic effluents are in the dissolved form, meaning that they will be mobile and more prone to transport to groundwater.

Chen (1988) investigated the effects of 17 multi-dwelling septic tank systems in the USA on groundwater quality. Elevated concentrations of nitrate, nitrite, ammoniacal nitrogen and orthophosphate were detected in most samples of groundwater near septic tanks. The results are summarised in Table 5.1.

Table 5.1 Groundwater contamination by N and P from septic tank effluents (Chen 1988)

Groundwater type	Concentrations (µg/l) (as N or P)			
	NO_3	NO_2	NH_4	ortho-P
Control	<100 – 1100	<1 – 2	140 – 4200	<1 – 34
Near septic tank effluent	<100 – 3700	<1 – 170	100 – 12000	<1 – 850

These results indicate that domestic effluents can greatly influence local groundwater nutrient concentrations, with levels of the more soluble nitrate and ortho-phosphate apparently being increased as much as 3-fold and 25-fold, respectively.

5.3 Conclusions

It is suggested that food additives derived from domestic food consumption are unlikely to have any significant adverse effects on the environment because their levels are controlled by their acceptability for human consumption.

Domestic releases of nitrogen-based and phosphorus-based nutrients appear to be major sources of these substances in the aquatic environment. The major source of nitrogenous materials is food, either as food waste or as human excreted waste. Major sources of phosphates are detergents and food, but few studies have differentiated between these sources when assessing overall release. Groundwater nutrient levels have consistently been shown to be elevated in aquifers receiving domestic septic tank effluent, and eutrophication of surface waters resulting (in part) from the release of sewage effluents has been well documented. Clearly domestic sources of these substances, such as food and faecal waste, make a significant contribution to their environmental loads.

References

ALHAJJAR B J, HARKIN J M and CHESTERS G (1989) Detergent formula and characteristics of wastewater in septic tanks. *Journal of the Water Pollution Control Federation* **61**, 605–613

ANONYMOUS (1990) The implementation of the ministerial declaration of the second international conference on the protection of the North Sea. Ministry of Transport and Public Works, The Netherlands, February 1990.

CHEN M (1988) Pollution of ground water by nutrients and faecal coliforms from lakeshore septic tank systems. *Water, Air and Soil Pollution* **37**, 407–417.

FAO/WHO (1989) Evaluation of certain food additives and contaminants. 33rd report of the joint FAO/WHO Expert Committee on Food Additives. *Technical Report Series* 776, WHO, Geneva.

GODA T (1986) General review and new concepts regarding the development of human wastewater treatment in Japan. *Water Science and Technology* **18** (7/8), 137–145.

HARTIG J H, TRAUTRIM C, DOLAN D M and RATHKE D E (1990) The rationale for Ohio's detergent phosphorus ban. *Water Resources Bulletin* **26**, 201–207.

LUND J W G and MOSS B (1990) Eutrophication in the United Kingdom – trends in the 1980s. The Soap and Detergent Industry Association 1990.

PETTS K W and STIFF M J (1987) An assessment of *per capita* loads of a domestic sewage. An interim report. WRc report number 525–S, March 1987.

RENEAU R B Jr, HAGEDORN C and DEGEN M J (1989) Fate and transport of biological and inorganic contaminants from on-site disposal of domestic wastewater. *Journal of Environmental Quality* **18**, 135–144.

UKITA M, NAKANISHI H and SEKINE M (1986) The pollutant load factor of household wastewater in Japan. *Water Science and Technology* **18**, 157–167.

WHELAN B R and TITAMNI Z V (1982) Daily chemical variability of domestic septic tank effluent. *Water, Air and Soil Pollution* **17**, 131–139.

6 Paints and varnishes

A 1980 US census estimated that about 11% of households disposed of 2.4 litres of paint products per annum, mainly to landfill (Stanek *et al* 1987). A small proportion of waste paint products will also be discharged to domestic sewers following brush and roller washing, but it is difficult to estimate the magnitude of this input.

Flammability and user inhalation are the main hazards associated with the use of paint and paint products and are due to solvent constituents. White spirit (a mixture of petroleum hydrocarbons with a boiling range of 152-210 °C; about 48% straight and branched C9-C12 paraffinic hydrocarbons; about 38% cycloparaffins; about 14% alkylbenzene; traces of benzene) and xylene are the main organic solvents used in paint formulations. Toxicological data for white spirit is sparse, but xylene is moderately toxic to fish (the 96-hour LC50 for the guppy is 38 mg/l (Verschueren 1983) and is biodegradable in activated sludge (Weber *et al* 1987).

The UK sales of paint products are summarised in Table 6.1, and information on the major components of paint formulations are shown in Table 6.2.

The very significant move away from solvent based paints to water based is likely to lead to increased paint residues going into domestic wastewater. Brushes can now be washed out in the sink directly whereas previously white spirit washing was needed. Amounts are likely to be small and infrequent and could be balanced by reductions in white spirit residues going down the drain. Statistics relating to this change or general consideration of the freshwater environmental impacts do not appear to be available. Impacts seem likely to be slight but worthy of further consideration.

Table 6.1   UK sales of paints, varnishes and fillers 1989 (HMSO 1990)

Product	1989 Sales
Emulsion paints	218 million litres
Thinners	18 million litres
Spirit based lacquers, varnishes, and stains	5.9 million litres
Cellulose based lacquers, varnishes, and stains	18 million litres
Paint removers and strippers	13 million litres
Linseed oil putties, bedding compounds and resinous materials	15 000 tonnes

Table 6.2   Chemical components of paint formulations (ICI 1990)

Product type	Chemical components	% Component
Emulsion paint	acrylic/alkyd resins polyvinyl acetate styrene-butadiene polymers silicone polymers	
Gloss/exterior paint/ woodstains/varnish	white spirit (petroleum distillate b.pt. 150-200 C)	10->20
	aromatic hydrocarbons xylene polyurethanes	1-10
	dichlofluanid	~1
	carbendazim	<2
	tri(hexylene glycol)biborate	1-10
	zinc naphthenate	1-10
	dodecylamine salicylate	1-10
	dodecylamine lactate	2

Table 6.2   Continued

Product type	Chemical components	% Component
Brush cleaner/renovator	aromatic hydrocarbons	>20
Thinners(various)	white spirit	>20
	butanol	>20
	xylene	>20
	diacetone alcohol	>20
Tinters(various)	ethylene glycol	1->20
	methyl dipropoxol	1-10

6.1 Conclusions

Large amounts of paint are used domestically and no doubt a considerable amount is unused and needs to be disposed of. There does not appear to be any evidence of freshwater or other pollution arising from paint use or disposal of residues. However, in general there appears to be an absence of advice on the best ways to dispose of paint residues or other wastes arising from redecorating (eg waste wall paper paste, which can contain fungicides such as organotins, excess paint stripper and white spirit residues). Do-it-yourself chain stores and improved labelling would appear to be good ways to disseminate information and encourage waste collection for recycling or disposal.

References

HMSO (1990) Business monitor, quarterly statistics. Paints, varnishes and painter's fillings. Central Statistical Office, PQ2551, Q2 1990.

ICI (1990) Dulux decorative products – substances content paper. March 1990 issue. ICI Paints, Slough, UK.

STANEK E J, TUTHILL R W, WILLIS C, MOORE G S (1987) Household hazardous waste in Massachusetts. *Archives of Environmental Health* **42**, 83–86.

VERSCHUEREN K (1983) Handbook of environmental data on organic chemicals 2nd edition. Van Nostrand Reinhold Publishers.

WEBER W J, JONES B E and KATZ L E (1987) Fate of toxic organic compounds in activated sludge and integrated PAC systems. *Water Science and Technology* **19**, 471–482.

7 Pharmaceutical chemicals, medicines and disposable medical products

The discharges of pharmaceutical chemicals to sewage treatment works from manufacturing sources is likely to be small when compared to chemical discharges from other industries because of the greater attention paid to careful handling and sterile packaging processes for high cost pharmaceutical chemicals (Richardson and Bowron 1985). Other sources of pharmaceuticals besides production losses are therefore expected to be relatively important. Most pharmaceutical chemicals are administered in hospitals, clinics, or in the home and will be released from these same sources. There are two routes to sewers from these sources:

1. via excreta or urine containing residues or metabolites flushed down WCs;

2. from the deliberate disposal of unwanted proprietary and expired prescription medicines down WCs.

   The Working Group on the Disposal of Awkward Household Wastes (HMSO 1974) recommended that surplus pills and drugs could be disposed of by flushing down the WC or by return to agreed collection points. The sluicing away of lotions, antiseptics and drugs to sewers in liquid, capsule or solid form is assumed to be an acceptable disposal method as many drugs are non-toxic and those that are toxic are assumed to be diluted to low levels in crude sewage. However, the subsequent fate of residues in sewage treatment works depends on their biodegradability and partitioning behaviour during sewage treatment processes. Although pharmaceutical chemicals receive considerable pharmacological and clinical testing, information on their environmental behaviour and ecotoxicity is generally not available. Richardson and Bowron (1985) suggested that a large number of pharmaceutical chemicals will undergo microbial transformations during sewage treatment processes (Table 7.1). However, the extent of biodegradation and the possibility that partial degradation of residues occurs to produce chemically different metabolites has not received detailed investigation. Since these substances may be biologically active at very low concentrations such investigation was considered to be desirable (Richardson and Bowron 1985).

Table 7.1   Biodegradation test results for selected pharmaceutical chemicals (Richardson and Bowron 1985)

Compound	Test result[1]
Amitriptyline	non-biodegradable
Ampicillin	biodegradable
Aspirin	readily biodegradable
Caffeine	readily biodegradable
Chlorhexidine	non-biodegradable
Clofibrate	non-biodegradable
Codeine phosphate	non-biodegradable
Dextropropoxyphene	non-biodegradable
Ephedrine	readily biodegradable after acclimatisation
Erythromycin	non-biodegradable
Ibuprofen	biodegradable
Menthol	readily degradable
Meprobamate	non-biodegradable
Methyldopa	non-biodegradable
Metronidazole	non-biodegradable
Naproxen	non-biodegradable
Nicotinamide	readily biodegradable
Paracetamol	readily biodegradable after acclimatisation
Phenylpropanolamine	readily biodegradable after acclimatisation
Sulphamethoxazole	non-biodegradable
Sulphasalazine	non-biodegradable
Tetracycline	non-biodegradable
Theobromine	readily biodegradable after acclimatisation
Theophylline	readily biodegradable
Tolbutamide	non-biodegradable

Notes
[1] as defined by DoE (1981)

Recent work has considered concern over the presence of trace concentrations of pharmaceutical chemicals in sewage effluent discharged to rivers which may later be abstracted for potable water supply (Richardson and Bowron 1985), although information on the typical concentrations of pharmaceutical chemicals in sewage and river waters are sparse. Watts *et al* (1983) identified the pharmaceuticals, erythromycin, tetracycline and theophylline at the μg/l level in river water. Concentration data for a range of pharmaceutical chemicals in sewage and sewage effluent are shown in Table 7.2.

Table 7.2 Pharmaceutical chemicals identified in sewage and sewage effluent

Chemical	Sample	Concentration, μg/l	
Aspirin	sewage effluent[1]	~	1
Caffeine	sewage effluent[1]	~	1
Diazepam	sewage effluent[2]	<	1
Methaqualone	sewage[1]	~	1
Methotrexate	sewage[1]	~	1
Oral contraceptives (unspecified)	sewage[1]	<	0.1

Notes
[1] Richardson and Bowron (1985)
[2] Waggott (1981)

Particular concerns have been expressed about the presence of contraceptive steroids in waters in areas of re-use. However, Rathner and Sonneborn (1979) estimated that in the sewage of a large city (West Berlin) the amounts of oestrogens arising from contraceptives were several orders of magnitude less than the amounts of natural steroid hormones excreted by the population. Thus any potential problems associated with such hormones may be considered to arise from water re-use rather than from contraceptive use. Aherne *et al* (1985) detected norethisterone in two and progesterone in one of eight UK rivers, and progesterone in one of six potable supplies (detection limits 10 and 5 μg/l, respectively). However, they found no evidence for adverse effects resulting from contamination following normal use of such agents in areas of water re-use.

7.1 Conclusions

Release of pharmaceuticals in domestic wastewater is probably one of the main sources of these substances in surface waters. However, information on their typical concentrations in sewage and river waters, and on their environmental behaviour and ecotoxicity, is limited, and so their hazard potential is uncertain. Since they are biologically active substances in humans, often at very low concentrations, it might be expected that their presence in the aquatic environment could have some adverse effects. However, although pharmaceuticals have been detected in river water there are no recognised problems associated with them, and present information does not suggest that domestic sources of these substances are environmentally significant. However, the need for ecotoxicity testing for pharmaceuticals with high production volumes should be considered.

References

AHERNE G W, ENGLISH J and MARKS V (1985) The role of immunoassay in the analysis of microcontaminants in water samples. *Ecotoxicology and Environmental Safety* **9**, 79–83.

DoE (DEPARTMENT OF THE ENVIRONMENT) (1981) Standard committee of analysts assessment of biodegradability. In: Methods for the examination of waters and associated materials. HMSO, London.

HMSO (1974) Disposal of awkward household wastes. Report of the Working Group on the Disposal of Awkward Household Wastes.

RATHNER M and SONNEBORN M (1979) Biologically active oestrogens in potable water and effluents. *Forum Stadte-Hygiene* **30**, 45–49.

RICHARDSON M L and BOWRON J M (1985) The fate of pharmaceutical chemicals in the aquatic environment. Journal of Pharmacy and Pharmacology **37**, 1–12.

WAGGOTT A (1981) Trace organic substances in the River Lee. Pages 55–99 in: Chemistry in water reuse. Ed. W J Cooper. Ann Arbor Publishers.

WATTS C D, CRATHBORNE B, FIELDING M and STEEL C P (1983) Identification of non-volatile organics in water using field desorption mass spectrometry and high performance liquid chromatography. Pages 120–131 in: Analysis of organic micropollutants in water. Eds G Angeletti and A Bjorseth. Report of the 3rd European Symposium on Organic Micropollutants, Oslo, Norway, September 19-21, 1983. D Reidel Publ. Co., Dordrecht.

8 Pesticides

8.1 Home, garden and path pesticides

The total UK sales of active ingredients of herbicides and plant growth regulators varied between 15,563 and 24,300 t/year over the period 1983 to 1988, whilst sales of insecticides varied between 997 and 1,300 t/year (Keynote Report 1990). However, no estimates of the proportion of the market occupied by domestic (amateur) products have been made. The non-agricultural, non-domestic use of herbicides in England and Wales in 1989 is summarised in Table 8.1. The major users were industry (34%), local authorities (including road maintenance) (33%), railway, airport and port authorities (21%), water companies (7%) and the leisure industry (5%). Unfortunately there are no equivalent figures concerning the domestic use of pesticides in the UK, but it is considered likely that the domestic market for most active ingredients will be small compared to the agricultural, industrial and amenity markets. Figures reported by Savage *et al* (1980) for a survey of 24 common pesticides in the USA indicate that domestic use accounted for about 12.5% of fungicide and wood preservative usage, 8% of insecticide usage and only 2.5% of herbicide usage.

Table 8.1   Herbicide usage (1989) in non-agricultural situations (excluding domestic) (PSL 1990)

Active ingredient	Tonnage used	%
Atrazine	137.5	25
Simazine	77	14
Diuron	66	12
2,4-D	49.5	9
Mecoprop	44	8
Amitrole	38.5	7
Glyphosate	27.5	5
Sodium chlorate	22	4
MCPA	22	4
Others	[1]	11
Total	**550**	**99**

Notes
[1] 250 kg or more of each of the following: Asulam, Bromacil, Chloramben, Chlorthal, Dalapon, Dicamba, Dichlobenil, Dichlorprop, Dikegulac, Diquat, Ferrous sulphate, Imazapyr, Ioxynil, Maleic hydrazide, Mefluidide, Paclobutrazol, Paraquat, Picloram, Tebuthiuron, Terbutryn, Triclopyr.

The best available data on domestic pesticides come from a national study conducted in the USA in the 1970s (Savage *et al* 1980). In this it was found that about 91% of households surveyed used pesticides in either the home or the garden. This compared to figures from earlier, smaller-scale studies of 71.7%, 89% and 92.5%. However, in Savage's survey the pesticides used in the home included fly sprays, flea collars for pets, timber and masonry treatments, mothballs, and insecticides used for termite control, all of which have limited relevance to UK wastewaters. The rate of pesticide use outdoors was much lower, at up to 60.1% of households. Old pesticides were stored for at least a year in 20.6% of households. Assuming this rate of use in the UK implies that pesticides are used in about 13 million households and stored in about 4.5 million, but no estimate of quantities used and stored can be made.

In a survey of the use and disposal of hazardous wastes by residents in Massachusetts it was found that 10% of households disposed of waste or excess pesticides and 1% of herbicides (Stanek *et al* 1987). The average amounts disposed of are unknown, being given as 'two cans' for each. Of the pesticides, 94% was disposed of directly in landfill and only 4% down the sewers or in the ground. For herbicides 80% was disposed of via these three routes, but no break-down was provided, largely because the small sample size (five households) means that such an analysis would be unreliable.

Savage *et al* (1980) also investigated the methods of pesticide disposal. Of the households that responded, the reported rate of disposal of unused pesticides down toilets, domestic drains or road drains was only 1.5%. The equivalent figure for 'made-up' pesticides in excess of requirements was 2.4%, but the pesticides would have been much more dilute. These figures should be viewed with some caution, however, because a high proportion of the households (43.4% for unused pesticides and 70.6% for excess pesticides) did not provide the relevant information. These figures imply that in the UK about 330 000 households may dispose of unused pesticides down the sewers and about 530 000 may dispose of excess diluted pesticides down the sewers.

There are more than 300 combinations of pesticide active ingredients approved for use in amateur products in the UK (MAFF/HSE 1990). The most common active ingredients are listed in Table 8.2.

Some supposedly non-hazardous pesticide products are available, based on 'natural' ingredients. The British Organic Standards Committee approves the use of a number of natural pesticides in non-agricultural situations (Maguire 1990):

derris	– insecticide, acaricide
quassid	– fungicide, insecticide, acaricide
metaldehyde tape	– molluscicide
potassium permanganate	– lumbricide
pyrethrum (natural)	– insecticide
cuprous oxide	– for leaf and fruit diseases

Table 8.2   Active ingredients most commonly found in amateur pesticide products (MAFF/HSE 1990)

Pesticide active ingredient	Use
Amitrole	herbicide
Carbaryl	insecticide
Creosote products	wood preservative
2,4-D	herbicide
Dicamba	herbicide
Dichlofluanid	wood preservative
Dichlorprop	herbicide
Ferrous sulphate	herbicide
Lindane	insecticide, wood preservative
Malathion	insecticide
MCPA	herbicide
Mecoprop	herbicide
Metaldehyde	slug killer
Pentachlorophenol (PCP) + PCP-laurate	wood preservative
Permethrin	insecticide
Pyrethrins	insecticide
Tetramethrin	insecticide, wood preservative
Tributyltin oxide (TBTO)	wood preservative

These substances are considered less hazardous because generally they are less toxic to non-target organisms and less persistent.

Pesticides approved for sale on the domestic market are generally less hazardous to man than many of those used in commercial situations (agricultural or industrial), and therefore are also normally less toxic and less environmentally hazardous.

The DoE's Working Group on the Disposal of Awkward Household Wastes (DoE 1974) reviewed the options for disposal of small quantities of domestic pesticides. They recommended that if disposal was unavoidable solid preparations should be placed in sealed containers in the dustbin, and liquid preparations should be emptied into an outside drain or a toilet, or poured onto soil. They concluded that 'in the quantities and concentrations normally encountered, disposal into sewers is unlikely adversely to affect treatment processes at sewage works'. In contrast in a proposed hazardous waste awareness scheme in New Jersey, USA, Robertson *et al* (1987) considered that such disposal of any pesticides (even head-lice shampoos) was unacceptable, and that they should only be disposed of via hazardous waste collection schemes.

8.2 Veterinary and medicinal pesticides

In addition to pesticides used in the garden there are a number of pesticides used for control of parasites of humans and pets, such as head lice and dog fleas. The most commonly-used of these are briefly considered below.

8.2.1 Lindane (gamma-hexachlorocyclohexane)

In general lindane is not as effectively removed during sewage treatment as many other priority pollutants. Experimental studies have shown that removal by conventional wastewater treatment ranges from 1.9 to 50%, and quite significant proportions may therefore be present in effluent (Petrasek et al 1983, Gutierrez *et al* 1984, van Luin and van Starkenburg 1984, Buisson *et al* 1988). However, Hill and McCarty (1967) reported that diluted sewage degraded lindane at a rate of 0.3 mg/l/day at 35 °C (but not at 20 °C), and Verschueren (1983) reported a study in which anaerobic bacteria degraded 90% of lindane over four days.

Petrasek *et al* (1983) calculated a concentration factor of 4 for lindane in return activated sludge. For influents with lindane concentrations of 0.07 to 0.52 µg/l the mean concentrations in sewage sludge were below 0.05 mg/kg (dry weight) in five of six samples, and 0.08 mg/kg in the sixth (van Luin and van Starken-burg 1984). Rogers (1987) quoted mean concentrations of 0.2 to 0.4 mg/kg for lindane in sewage sludge .

8.2.2 Carbaryl

Carbaryl in wastewaters can be rapidly degraded by activated sludge, with a removal efficiency of about 99% (Rybinski and Niemirycz 1984). Kanazawa (1987) similarly found 'appreciable' degradation of 20 µg/l carbaryl by activated sludge. At concentrations up to 100 mg/l it poses no threat to sewage micro-organisms, although some inhibition of nitrification at 14 mg/l has been noted (Lieberman and Alexander 1981).

8.2.3 Permethrin

Studies suggest that about 99% of permethrin is removed during conventional sewage treatment (Abram *et al* 1980, Woodhead 1983). However, at an influent concentration of 10 µg/l permethrin a concentration of 3.5 µg/l would be expected in digested sludge (Abram *et al* 1980), which is sufficiently high to potentially have some insecticidal properties.

A high rate of removal, about 99%, has also been recorded over five to six days when 15 µg/l permethrin was added to artificial ponds (Rawn *et al* 1980). Removal was brought about by biodegradation and photo-oxidation.

8.2.4 Malathion

Malathion appears to be readily degraded under aerobic or anaerobic conditions, and is not detectable in most sewage sludges (Rogers 1987). A concentration of 10 mg/l does not affect the nitrification or denitrification activity of activated sludge (Knoetze 1979, Lieberman and Alexander 1981), but levels above 200 mg/l inhibit the growth of micro-organisms (Singh and Seth 1989).

8.3 Wood preservatives

The wood preserving industry uses more pesticides than any other industry world-wide, principally pentachlorophenol, creosote and CCA (copper, chrome and arsenate) (Mueller *et al* 1989). These can be released by misuse, accidental spillage and improper disposal, leading to contamination of surface waters, surface soils, and underlying groundwaters.

A wide range of active ingredients is approved for use in amateur wood preserving products in the UK, and a number are listed in Table 8.3. The major ones are coal tar creosote, tributyltin oxide, lindane, dichlofluanid, naphthenates and pentachlorophenol (often as pentachlorophenyl laurate). Pentachlorophenol and creosote are considered below.

8.3.1 Pentachlorophenol

In addition to extensive use as a wood preserver pentachlorophenol (PCP) is used as a herbicide, fungicide, algicide, insecticide, defoliant, mossicide, disinfectant and antimicrobial agent. As these uses suggest it is toxic to most biota. Acute LC50s for fish are typically below 1 mg/l, with a lowest reported value of 0.23 mg/l for rainbow trout (Verschueren 1983). Sub-lethal effects under chronic exposure have been observed at concentrations as low as 19 µg/l. For invertebrates acute EC50s as low as 0.55 mg/l (for immobilisation of *Daphnia magna*) have been reported (Kuhn *et al* 1989), whilst in chronic tests a no effect level of 0.18 mg/l has been determined for survival of *Daphnia* (Adema 1978). However, the most sensitive aquatic organisms appear to be algae, with adverse effects resulting from exposure to as little as 1 µg/l PCP (Verschueren 1983).

PCP also bioaccumulates in fish, with reported bioaccumulation factors (ie concentration in tissue compared to concentration in water) of 500 to 1000. It is also persistent in some soils, with reported half-lives of up to 5 years, but is less persistent in water, with most half-lives of the order of days to weeks. Its persistence in soils may increase the likelihood of contamination of ground- or surface waters following spillages or disposal to land in a domestic

Table 8.3 Some active ingredients approved for use in amateur wood preserving products (MAFF/HSE 1990)

Acypetacs-zinc
Alkyldimethylbenzyl ammonium chloride
Carbendazim
* Coal tar creosote
Copper naphthenate
Cypermethrin
* Dichlofluanid
Disodium octaborate
Dodecylbenzyltrimethyl ammonium chloride
Furmecyclox
* Lindane (gamma-hexachlorocyclohexane)
* Pentachlorophenol/Pentachlorophenyl laurate
Permethrin
Sodium 2-phenylphenoxide
* Tributyltin oxide
Tri(hexylene glycol) biborate
Zinc naphthenate
Zinc octoate

Notes
* signifies major usage

context, but there is insufficient information available to enable the hazard potential to be elucidated.

Acclimated sewage sludge can readily degrade PCP at concentrations up to 20 mg/l (Moss *et al* 1983), but the activity of unacclimated sludge is inhibited at this level. PCP in sewage works influent arising from domestic sources is likely to be well below this level. For example Melcer and Bedford (1988) found PCP in 29% of sewage treatment work influents in America at concentrations of 1 to 640 µg/l, and it is likely that much of this was from commercial rather than domestic sources.

Although there are many data on the effects of pentachlorophenol on biota there is no information on which to assess the potential for its release from domestic usage. It is suggested that during application, much of which will be indoors, there is little likelihood of large losses by dripping or spillage. Therefore the only likely significant releases to water would be those resulting from cleaning of equipment or disposal of excess pesticides down drains.

8.3.2 Creosote

Coal tar creosote is obtained by the destructive distillation of coal tar or wood tar, and there are therefore two types. Wood tar creosote is composed mostly of phenols and phenol derivatives, and is used therapeutically as an antiseptic and expectorant, but not a wood preserver. Coal tar creosote is a complex mixture of about 150 to 200 chemicals, mostly polycyclic aromatic hydrocarbons (PAH) (85%), phenolics (10%) and heterocyclics (5%). The major ingredients are usually naphthalene, 2-methylnaphthalene, phenanthrene and anthracene. In the domestic situation coal tar creosote is used for timber preservation (eg fences) and in roofing pitch.

Creosote is only slowly degraded in the environment. There is little information on its sewage treatability, but in general it appears to be biorecalcitrant. Some removal from wastewater can be achieved using carbon or surfactants. Because of its persistence any spillages of creosote or wash-off from new applications may result in runoff into surface waters or penetration of groundwater. Complete elimination or degradation from these may take 3 to 12 months (Sax 1989). Amounts present in domestic wastewater resulting from disposal down sewers and brush washing have not been assessed, and so the potential for adverse effects on sewage works cannot be fully considered. However, its biorecalcitrance suggests there is at least the potential for adverse effects on sewage biota.

Aquatic organisms are quite sensitive to creosote. Sax (1989) reported acute LC50s for freshwater fish such as rainbow trout and goldfish of 0.56 to 4.4 mg/l, with no effect levels of 0.25 to 0.75 mg/l. Marine arthropods appear to be more sensitive, with a lowest acute LC50 of 0.02 mg/l for American lobster larvae. Creosote is not expected to bioaccumulate from water into aquatic organisms (Sax 1989). Also, many aquatic organisms are able to eliminate PAHs, the major constituents of commercial coal tar creosote, and therefore these are not significantly biomagnified up food chains (US Public Health Service 1989).

On the basis of these data it is considered unlikely that the small amounts of creosote released from domestic spillages or disposal will result in any detrimental effects on surface waters, especially when viewed in the light of the actual and potential losses from creosote production and industrial timber treatment. There is, however, the possibility of local effects on groundwater. Although it is unlikely that the volumes involved in domestic situations will cause any extensive or long-term effects, private water supplies may potentially be affected, but more information is necessary before this can be considered fully.

8.4 Conclusions

No figures on the size of the amateur market for pesticides in the UK are available but it is likely to be small compared to agricultural and industrial markets. If used properly in the home and garden most pesticide products should be released in only small quantities to sewers, for example following the rinsing of equipment. Dilution should therefore be adequate to preclude any acute adverse effects on sewage treatment or aquatic organisms. Similar considerations apply to veterinary and medical pesticide use. Application of herbicides to paths and drives is also likely to be small in comparison with industrial use although no reliable statistics are available. However, since domestic use is less controlled and less controllable than other uses, it is desirable that more care and consideration be given to the ingredients selected and the formulation strength allowed for amateur products. This is done at present but possibly should be encouraged.

Disposal of residues or old material seems unlikely to cause an acute problem but as with some of the other areas clearer guidance would be desirable, possibly through improved labelling or dissemination of information at retail outlets.

References

ABRAM F S H, EVINS C and HOBSON J A (1980) Pemethrin for the control of animals in water mains. Water Research Centre technical report TR 145.

ADEMA D M M (1978) *Daphnia magna* as a test animal in acute and chronic toxicity tests. *Hydrobiologia* **59**, 125–134.

BUISSON R S K, KIRK P W W and LESTER J N (1988) The behaviour of selected chlorinated organic micropollutants in the activated sludge process: a pilot plant study. *Water, Air and Soil Pollution* **37**, 419–432.

DoE (DEPARTMENT OF THE ENVIRONMENT) (1974) Disposal of awkward household wastes. Report of the Working Group on the Disposal of Awkward Household Wastes. HMSO, London.

GUTIERREZ A G, McINTYRE A E, PERRY R and LESTER J N (1984) Behaviour of persistent organochlorine micropollutants during primary sedimentation of waste water. *The Science of the Total Environment* **39**, 27–47.

HILL D W and McCARTY P I (1967) Anaerobic degradation of selected chlorinated hydrocarbon pesticides. *Journal of the Water Pollution Control Federation* **39**, 1259–1277.

KANAZAWA J (1987) Biodegradability of pesticides in water by microbes in activated sewage, soil and sediment. *Environmental Monitoring and Assessment* **9**, 57–70.

KEYNOTE REPORT (1990) An industry sector overview: pesticides. 7th edition. Keynote publications Ltd., 1990.

KNOETZE C (1979) *Water Report* **9**, 5–6.

KUHN R, PATTARD M, PERNAK K and WINTER A (1989) Results of the harmful effects of selected water pollutants (anilines, phenols, aliphatic compounds) to *Daphnia magna. Water Research* **23**, 495–499.

LIEBERMAN M T and ALEXANDER M (1981) Effects of pesticides on decomposition of organic matter and nitrification in sewage. *Bulletin of Environmental Contamination and Toxicology* **26**, 554–560.

MAFF/HSE (1990) Pesticides 1990. Pesticides approved under the Control of Pesticides Regulations 1986. MAFF/HSE reference book 500, HMSO, London.

MAGUIRE K (1990) The use of pesticides by local authorities. *Environmental Health* July 1990, 191–194.

MELCER H and BEDFORD W (1988) Removal of pentachlorophenol in municipal activated sludge systems. *Journal of the Water Pollution Control Federation* **60**, 622–626

MOSS L, KIRSCH R, WUKASCH R and GRADY C (1983) Pentachlorophenol biodegradation – I. *Water Research* **17**, 1575–1584.

MUELLER J G, CHAPMAN P J and HAP PRITCHARD P (1989) Creosote-contaminated sites. Their potential for bioremediation. *Environmental Science and Technology* **23**, 1197–1201.

PETRASEK A C, KUGELMAN I J, AUSTERN B M, PRESSLEY T A, WINSLOW L A and WISE R H (1983) Fate of toxic organic compounds in wastewater treatment plants. *Journal of the Water Pollution Control Federation* **55**, 1286–1296.

PSL (PRODUCE STUDIES LIMITED) (1990) The use of herbicides in non-agricultural situations in England and Wales. PSL, Newbury, report number PSL 5813/DJC/DKP, September 1990.

RAWN G P, WEBSTER G P B and MUIR D C G (1980) Bioactivity and degradation of permethrin in artificial pools. *Canadian Technical Report, Fisheries and Aquatic Science* **975**, 140–149.

ROBERTSON D K, AKAGHA J, BELASCO J, BULLIS J, BYRNE G, DI PATRIA J, FISHER W, FONZINO J, HSU J, MERCHAN L, OSTER D, ROSENBERG J, VON AULOCK S and VROEGINDAY B (1987) Liquid household hazardous wastes in the United States: identification, disposal, and management plan. *Environmental Management* **11**, 735–742.

ROHERS H R (1987) Organic contaminants in sewage sludge; occurrence and fate of synthetic organic compounds in sewage sludge – a review. Water Research Centre report no. PRD 1539–M.

RYBINSKI J and NIEMIRYCZ E (1984) Carbaryl and propoxur in an activated sludge medium. *Arch. Ochr. Srodowiska* **1**, 105–113. (Abstract)

SAVAGE E P, KEEFE T J, WHEELER H W and MOUNCE L (1980) National household pesticide usage study, 1976–1977. US EPA report no. 54/9–80–002, Washington DC, USA.

SAX I (1989) Dangerous properties of industrial materials. Report 9, (4), 51–63. Van Nostrand Reinhold Publishers.

SINGH A K and SETH P K (1989) Degradation of malathion by micro-organisms isolated from industrial effluents. *Bulletin of Environmental Contamination and Toxicology* **43**, 28–35.

US PUBLIC HEALTH SERVICE (1989) Draft toxicological profile for creosote. Agency for toxic substances and disease registry, US public health service.

van LUIN A B and van STARKENBURG W (1984) Hazardous substances in waste water. *Water Science and Technology* **17**, 843–853.

VERSCHUEREN K (1983) Handbook of environmental data on organic chemicals. 2nd edition. Van Nostrand Reinhold Publishers.

WOODHEAD D (1983) Permethrin trials in the Meltham sewage catchment area. *Water Services* **87**, 198–202.

9 Water distribution systems

A number of chemicals with different functions and types of activity are added to potable water supplies as part of the treatment processes, such as flocculating agents, disinfectants and pesticides. These may be considered as being of industrial origin, stemming as they do from the water industry. In addition to these it is possible for various chemicals to arise in the water during distribution to domestic premises and during use there. Substances entering water during distribution to households may be leached or dissolved from the pipes and joints, or may enter the pipes from surrounding groundwater. For example, Van Beek (1981) recorded concentrations of 47 µg/l toluene, 56 µg/l xylene, 21 µg/l benzene in drinking water in the Netherlands which arose from penetration of the distribution pipes by contaminated groundwater. However, although this could lead to contaminating substances being present in domestic wastewater they cannot really be considered as being of domestic origin, and are not considered further here. Within the home further substances may enter by leaching or dissolution from pipes and joints, and by reaction of water contaminants with components of the pipes and joints.

9.1 Materials used in distribution and plumbing networks

In the UK distribution mains are normally made from asbestos cement, iron, polyethylene or uPVC; these are connected to plumbing within buildings by communication pipes made of lead, copper, polythene or PVC, usually with brass or gun-metal fittings (Goodman 1984). Pipes and storage tanks in plumbing systems may be made of lead, copper, galvanised iron or a variety of plastics (uPVC, polythene, propylene, glass-reinforced plastic or acrylobutadiene styrene (ABS)).

The constraints placed on materials used are usually based on the DoE's Model Water Byelaws, which aim to prevent wastage (following corrosion) and biological contamination. Certain organic contaminants can be leached from plastics (such as antioxidants, plasticisers and dyes), or plastics can be attacked and degraded by micro-organisms, leading to contamination from their metabolites. The levels of plastic-component chemicals likely to be leached are small, and are not considered to pose a threat to sewage treatment or surface waters, particularly when compared to other origins of plastic components. In addition, although the Byelaws do not really consider chemical contamination, they do consider contamination by organic substances that might promote microbiological growth. Therefore, some of the potential problems arising from the use of plastics can be averted by appropriate application of the Byelaws. However, there are no such controls over metals, and the potential problems associated with them are discussed below and in Section 12.

Investigating the presence of metals in tap water in Finland, Hisvirta *et al* (1985) found that copper, zinc and lead were those most often found at high levels, originating from contaminated water used for abstraction and from materials used for distribution pipes. The losses of metals from distribution pipes into water supplies has been widely studied, particularly with reference to the health problems arising from corrosion of lead pipes or lead solder. For example, in a study in Scotland water boilers containing lead-based solder were found to have mean lead concentrations of 14 µg/l at the inlet and 150 µg/l at the outlet (Harold *et al* 1990), which is above the EC guideline of 50 µg/l for drinking water. Additional concerns include iron from water mains, and zinc and copper from domestic plumbing. About 28,000 km, or 80%, of the water mains in the UK are made of cast iron (R J Oliphant, WRc) and many of these are heavily corroded and approaching the end of their useful lives. Zinc is released from the corrosion of galvanised iron domestic plumbing with particularly high losses occurring over the first 100 days of use of new systems, but with only a gradual decline over time (Kumpera 1985).

A number of studies have investigated the input of metals into water supplies from domestic distribution systems. The specific metals that are identified vary according to the particular characteristics of the study area. For example, in a study in Oregon, USA, iron and copper were the major contaminants (Treweek *et al* 1984) whereas in a similar study in Lausanne, Switzerland, zinc was the most important metal (Ammann *et al* 1981). Reviewing data for about 300 sewage treatment works sludges in purely residential areas in the UK, the USA, Canada and Sweden, Page (1974) commonly found concentrations of copper in excess of 500 mg/kg and zinc in excess of 1000 mg/kg (dry weights), with domestic plumbing being proposed as the major source. In general it would appear that copper and zinc are the principal metal contaminants from domestic plumbing.

Most concern over metals in domestic water have related to human health or aesthetic effects, with copper, zinc, lead and iron being of particular note. Recommended maximum levels of 3 mg/l copper and 5 mg/l zinc have been suggested for standing water at the point where it is made available to the consumer (CEC 1980). For lead and iron maximum concentrations of 50 µg/l and 200 µg/l, respectively, have been set.

9.1.1 Lead

Lead piping was regularly used throughout the UK until the 1940s, and in some areas until the 1960s (Goodman 1984). The characteristics of water that increase plumbosolvency have been widely studied, and generally speaking acidic soft waters are more of a problem. Following Governmental proposals the water undertakings identified the water supply areas where there were problems and modifications to treatment processes to reduce lead levels have been adopted, such as addition of alkali. Coupled with programmes of replacement of old lead piping the incidence of high lead levels in domestic water has been steadily reduced.

An additional source of lead is galvanic corrosion of lead/tin-based solder used to join copper pipes. Problems have been reported in particular in large institutional buildings with extensive pipe runs and intermittent water use, but even in these cases lead levels fall significantly within a few weeks (Goodman 1984). Although the extent of this problem is uncertain Goodman (1984) considers it to be at least an order of magnitude less than that of lead piping, (although he does not state whether he means in terms of lead concentrations or numbers of incidences).

9.1.2 Copper

In the UK copper is the main metal used in domestic plumbing. Copper is attacked by waters having a high bicarbonate concentration but insoluble copper deposits usually form quite quickly and limit further attack. Dissolution is greater in hot water, in particular in copper hot water cylinders. Most water undertakings are well aware of the problems aggressive water may cause and public water supplies are generally controlled to limit copper attack. Therefore, in most cases the only occasions on which high levels of copper will occur after an initial period of attack will be where the water is particularly aggressive and has been standing in the pipes for a long time, such as when properties are left empty. A possible exception to this is where untreated private water supplies are used.

9.1.3 Iron

As mentioned above, iron pipes are commonly used for water mains, and there is no available information on the relative contributions of water mains and domestic plumbing to the total iron load in domestic wastewater. The main problem in the domestic context is likely to arise where iron and copper pipes are connected, resulting in galvanic corrosion of the iron. However, because iron contamination leads to discoloration of the water at relatively low concentrations most problems are likely to be noticed and addressed by the consumer or water undertaker, and sewage treatment or surface water quality are unlikely to be affected.

9.1.4 Zinc

Most zinc in domestic waters arises from galvanised iron, with losses being particularly associated with newly-installed pipes and tanks (Goodman 1984, Kumpera 1985), although high levels can persist over a number of years (Ammann *et al* 1981). When zinc concentrations are elevated it can appear at the tap in a gritty particulate form, and is therefore obvious to the consumer.

9.2 Conclusions

Domestic plumbing adds significantly to the overall metal concentrations in waste waters. The implications of this are discussed in Section 13 which considers the whole area of metals in more detail.

References

AMMANN P, SCHWEIZER C and WYSS C (1981) Balance sheet of heavy metal contamination in the catchment of a sewage-treatment plant. Pages 274–283 in: Characterisation, treatment and use of sewage sludge. Proceedings of 2nd European Symposium, Vienna, 1980. Publ. CEC, Brussels, 1981. Ed. L'Hermite and Ott.

CEC (COUNCIL OF THE EUROPEAN COMMUNITIES) (1980) EC Directive relating to the quality of water intended for human consumption (80/778/EEC). *Official Journal* **L229/11**, 30th August.

GOODMAN A H (1984) Contamination of water within buildings. *Public Health Engineer* **12**, 1 January, 23–25.

HISVIRTA L, LEHTO J, KUMPULAINEN J, KOIVISTOINEN P and PITKANEN L (1985) Vesijohtoveden metallit (Metals in mains water). *Vesitalous* **26**, 12–14 and 30.

KUMPERA F (1985) Korrosionsprobleme in der Hausinstallation (Corrosion problems in domestic plumbing systems). *Gas/Wasser/Wärme* **39**, 14–16.

PAGE A L (1974) Fate and effects of trace elements in sewage sludge when applied to agricultural lands. A literature review study. US EPA report number EPA–670/2–74–005.

TREWEEK G P, CHOW B, GLICKER J and SPRINKER M (1984) Water quality changes from corrosion of distribution and consumer plumbing systems. Pages 1429–1445 in Proceedings AWWA Annual Conference, Dallas, Texas, 1984.

VAN BEEK C G E M (1981) Soil pollution, consequences for the water works. *H₂0* **14**, 269–274.

10 Photographic chemicals

10.1 Film processing chemicals

A wide range of chemicals is used in the processing of photographic films, and because they usually need to be present in excess a large proportion of the amount used is released unchanged to sewers. Substances used include a number of potentially hazardous chemicals such as hydroquinone, acetic acid, sulphuric acid, p-toluene sulphonic acid, triethanolamine and sodium sulphite (Hobbs 1988, EHMI 1990), but these tend to be used in relatively small quantities. Those substances used, and therefore released, in the highest quantities are shown in Table 10.1, along with an indication of their biodegradability and thus their potential for release to surface waters.

Table 10.1 The main photographic processing chemicals

	Biodegraded	Potential for release to water
Benzyl alcohol	Yes	Limited
EDTA	No	Yes
Ethylene glycol	Yes	Limited
Formaldehyde	Yes	Limited
Hydroxylamine sulphate	No	Yes
Maleic acid	Yes	Limited
l-Phenyl-3-pyrazolidone	No	Yes
Sulphite	Yes	Limited
Thiosulphite	Yes	Limited

There is little information available on the use of photographic chemicals in the home. Annually about 80 to 90 million rolls of colour film are used by amateur photographers and processed by professional printers and developers (Harris 1987). Equivalent figures for black and white films are not available. No reliable estimate of the number of films processed by amateurs has been made but a random 'straw-poll' survey conducted by WRc indicated that only one out of 76 regular camera users processed films at home.

An additional 'domestic' source of photographic chemicals is the processing of x-ray film in hospitals and dentist's surgeries, which account for 80% and 3%, respectively, of all x-rays in the UK (excluding Northern Ireland) (Hobbs 1988). Processing is carried out at an estimated 950 hospitals and an unknown number of dentist's surgeries throught the UK, but the contribution from dentistry to the load of processing chemicals reaching sewers is considered to be unimportant (Hobbs 1988), and is presumably below 3% because of the small size of dentistry x-rays compared to medical and industrial x-rays.

As indicated in Table 10.1 most of the higher volume chemicals are readily biodegraded during biological sewage treatment. Investigations into the biodegradability of a range of 45 photographic waste chemicals indicated that about half were readily biodegraded during sewage treatment (NAPM/H 1974). Of the rest only a few were inhibitory to sewage bacteria, ie sodium selenite, potassium dichromate and some p-phenylenediamine based colour developers, and these only had an effect at concentrations comparable to the maxima in effluent from a commercial processing plant. Therefore risk from domestic use and disposal is considered to be minimal.

An indication of the toxicity of some of the more recalcitrant chemicals is given in Table 10.2. Only those chemicals with the highest usage are likely to be released in anything like significant amounts from domestic sources, and it is considered extremely unlikely that such release would lead to concentrations in the environment approaching those at which toxic effects have been seen, ie 1 mg/l or higher.

In conclusion it appears that the domestic release of photographic processing chemicals will not have any significant effect on sewage treatment or the environment. However, a related area that may be of concern and warrants further investigation is the increasing use of unplumbed mini-processors in shops, airports etc. In these the used solutions are collected in tanks for a number of days before being disposed of manually down the sewer. There is therefore considerably less dilution and a much higher potential for a 'plug' of photographic chemicals reaching a sewage treatment works or the environment. Such mini-labs currently account for an estimated 20% of the amateur film market and are increasing (Green 1987).

Table 10.2 Toxicity of some potentially hazardous photographic chemicals (data presented by Hobbs 1988)

EDTA (relatively high volume use)	Signif. effect on *Daphnia*	1 - 10 mg/l
	NOEC for fathead minnow	> 100 mg/l
	NOEC for green alga (*Selenastrum capricornutum*)	> 100 mg/l
1-Phenyl-3-pyrazolidone (relatively high volume use)	Signif. effect on *Daphnia*	1 - 10 mg/l
	Signif. effect on fathead minnow	1 - 10 mg/l
Hydroxylamine sulphate (relatively high volume use)	No data	
p-Phenylenediamine derivatives (relatively low volume use)	Signif. effect on *Daphnia*	0.1 - 1 mg/l
	Signif. effect on fathead minnow	0.1 - 1 mg/l
	Fathead minnow 96 hr LC50	3.4 mg/l

10.2 Silver and its compounds

Discharge consents for industrial photographic effluents usually consider pH (acidity), silver, suspended solids and oxygen demand to be of concern (Kodak Ltd 1977). Clearly the small volume of domestic photographic effluent will mean that acidity, suspended solids and oxygen demand will be negligible by the time the waste has been diluted in the sewer. However, some consideration of silver is necessary because it is highly toxic to both invertebrates (acute lethal levels of 0.25 µg/l or above) and fish (acute lethal levels of 3.9 µg/l or above) (EPA 1980).

Production of photographic materials accounts for about 30 to 35% of all silver consumption (Taylor *et al* 1980, Mason 1983). During film processing much of the silver present in film emulsions is solubilised and will be released with the liquid waste, usually in the form of very stable silver-thiosulphate complexes. Most commercial processors make some effort to recover this silver, with between 12 and 95% efficiency depending on the type of waste (Mason 1983). Overall only about 9% of that solubilised is released in commercial photographic effluent (Degenkolb and Scobey 1977). Therefore the relative contribution from amateur sources to the amount in sewers is likely to be larger than for other photo-processing chemicals, which are not recovered by commercial processors.

Although silver is toxic to bacteria, silver-thiosulphate complexes have been reported as having no effect on sewage flora activity at concentrations as high as 10 mg/l, and are not considered a hazard to sewage treatment (Bard *et al* 1976). During sewage treatment silver-thiosulphates are converted to silver sulphide and a small amount of pure silver which are both insoluble and therefore tend to be removed in sewage sludge rather than discharged. About 70 to 80% of the influent silver is removed in this way (Bard *et al* 1976, Lytle 1984), with reported concentrations in sludge usually between 0.1 and 10 mg/kg, dry weight (Mason 1983). Although there are no specific limitations on incineration or agricultural use of sewage sludge containing silver, it is envisaged that such controls for other metals (such as cadmium) will ensure that no hazard will result from the presence of silver, particularly as it is not readily leached from sludges or soils (Hobbs 1988).

The figures given above for use and release suggest that commercial processing releases a maximum of about 3% of silver production to sewers or surface waters. MRI (1975) proposed that 10% of silver production was released via photographic use; 2.5% directly to water and 7.5% in sewage sludge. These figures are not widely disparate. However, the contribution from domestic sources has not been estimated. Lytle (1984) investigated silver concentrations in sewage treatment works influent of three types, containing: (1) a high proportion of wastewater from photo-processing; (2) a high proportion of wastewater from other industrial silver usage; and (3) no wastewater from any major silver user, Table 10.3.

Table 10.3 Silver concentrations in sewage treatment works influent (Lytle 1984)

Source of influent	Silver conc. µg/l (mean value)	Flow m³/d	Silver load kg/d (mean of 2)
Municipal + no silver sources	6	45 420	0.29
	8	37 850	
Municipal + industrial silver sources (not photo-processing)	26	189 250	3.1
	10	121 120	
Municipal + photo-processing	2 000	150	0.41
	713	720	

These findings indicate that photo-processing wastes represented about 11% of the influent silver load at the six plants, whilst 82% came from other industrial sources. It is possible that the 8% coming from minor silver sources could similarly be separated into photo-processing and other uses, and this rough calculation suggests that a maximum of 1% of silver reaching sewage works may arise from amateur photo-processing.

Lytle (1984) also measured silver concentrations in the river water receiving treated effluent. Municipal wastewaters with no major silver sources had no effect on silver concentrations in the receiving water, with levels of 0.07 µg/l upstream of the discharge and 0.03 µg/l downstream. Taylor *et al* (1980) reported maximum silver concentrations in North American surface waters of 38 µg/l in industrialised areas and 0.2 µg/l in non-industrialised areas. Considering the toxicity data given above these data indicate that toxic effects could potentially be seen in surface waters receiving industrial effluent. However, although these values came from separate studies in separate areas and are therefore not directly comparable, they support the suggestion above that non-industrial sources of silver are minor compared to industrial sources.

10.3 Conclusions

It is difficult to assess the volumes of photographic processing chemicals used in the home and released in domestic wastewater, but it would appear that they will be small compared with the volumes released by commercial photo-processors. Because of this and the fact that most of those used in the greatest quantities are readily biodegraded during sewage treatment, the release of chemicals from amateur film processing is not considered to present a hazard to sewage treatment or the aquatic environment. Silver is recovered by most commercial processors and consequently the relative contribution of amateur sources to the total release from film processing will be higher than for the other chemicals. However, such releases still appear to be very minor.

One area that may be of concern is the increasing occurrence of mini-processors, where waste processing chemicals are allowed to accumulate and then tend to be emptied down the drains, resulting in a comparatively high volume and high concentration plug of chemicals entering the sewer.

References

BARD C C, MURPHY J J, STONE D L and TERHAAR C J (1976) Silver in photoprocessing effluents. *Journal of the Water Pollution Control Federation* **48**, 389–394.

DEGENKOLB D J and SCOBEY F J (1977) Silver recovery from photographic wash waters by ion exchange. *Journal of the Society of Motion Picture and Television Engineers* **86**, 65–68.

EHMI (ENVIRONMENTAL HAZARDS MANAGEMENT INSTITUTE) (1990) Household hazardous waste wheel (TM). EHMI, Durham, New Hampshire.

EPA (1980) Ambient water quality criteria for silver. US EPA report 440/5–80–071, October 1980.

GREEN R (1987) Mini-lab guide. *The British Journal of Photography*, **29** May 1987, 627–632.

HARRIS K (1987) *Photographic Processor*, October 1987, p13.

HOBBS S J (1988) Industry category document: the UK photographic industry. Building Research Establishment Client Report, Building Research Establishment, Princes Risborough.

KODAK LTD (1977) Disposal of photographic waste. Towards a cleaner environment no. 2. Kodak Ltd, Hemel Hempstead, Bucks.

MASON L F A (1983) Silver and the environment. A literature survey with particular reference to the photographic industry. CEFIC, Brussels.

MRI (1975) Silver. An appraisal of environmental exposure. Midwest Research Institute technical report number 3.

NAPM/H (NATIONAL ASSOCIATION OF PHOTOGRAPHIC MANUFACTURERS/HYDROSCIENCE) (1974) Environmental effect of photoprocessing chemicals. Volume 1. NAPM Inc., New York.

TAYLOR M C, DEMAYO A and REEDER S (1980) Guidelines for surface water quality. Vol 1 Inorganic chemical substances. Silver. Environment Canada, Inland Waters Directorate, Water Quality Branch.

11   Motor vehicle products

Do-it-yourself (DIY) motor vehicle maintenance results in the discharge of significant amounts of chemical waste to sewers. Motor car sump oil is probably the most common household waste disposed to sewers and inputs have been estimated to be about 0.5 litre per year per household using data from a US survey (Stanek *et al* 1987). UK sales of antifreeze for internal combustion engines were estimated to be about 51 300 tonnes in 1989 (HMSO 1990) and a US survey estimated that about 3 litres of antifreeze or radiator fluid are discharged to sewers by about 7% of households per annum. Propylene glycol, propan-2-ol, ethylene glycol and methanol, which are the main components of antifreeze products, show low toxicity to aquatic organisms and are probably readily degraded during sewage treatment processes provided they are present at residual levels in influent sewage (Mayes *et al* 1983, Dwyer and Tiedje 1983, Kaplan *et al* 1982, Novak *et al* 1985, Dalouche *et al* 1987). Other chemicals that are used in DIY motor maintenance are shown in Table 11.1.

11.1   Conclusions

Significant amounts of motor vehicle related chemicals appear to be discharged to sewers, particularly oils and coolants. It seems that many of these substances are readily biodegraded during sewage treatment (provided they are not present at high concentrations) and are of low toxicity to aquatic organisms. However, quite high levels of mineral oil have been detected in UK sewage effluents and sludges (Britcher and Waggott 1983), and persistent components of oils (such as PAH) have been widely reported in the aquatic environment. Better guidance on the disposal of fluids associated with motor vehicle use and maintainance is desirable.

Table 11.1   Chemicals used in DIY motor car maintenance products (Atkins and Hawley 1978)

Product	Chemical components
Antifreeze	Methanol Ethylene glycol Rust inhibitors – Zinc chloride, chromates, sodium mercaptobenzothiazole
Carburettor cleaners	Potassium hydroxide Sodium chromate Ammonium oxalate
Transmission fluids	Zinc dialkyl dithiophosphate, Barium and calcium petroleum sulphonates, Barium and calcium alkyl phenolates
Corrosion inhibitors	Sodium chromate, nitrate, carbonate, metasilicate and phosphate. Potassium dichromate
Chassis lubricants	Aluminium soap Molybdenum disulphide
Engine and motor cleaners	Potassium hydroxide

References

ATKINS E D and HAWLEY J R (1978) Sources of metals and metal levels in municipal wastewaters. Research program for the abatement of municipal pollution under provisions of the Canada-Ontario agreement on Great Lakes water quality. Environment Canada research report no. 80.

BRITCHER H and WAGGOTT A (1983) Determination of pollutants in effluents. A survey of concentrations of mineral oils in UK sewages, effluents and sludges. WRc report no. 233-S.

DALOUCHE A, VENIEN F and MARTIN G (1987) Chemical oxidation and biodegradation of aliphatic compounds. *Environmental Technology Letters* **8**, 297–306.

DWYER D F and TIEDJE J M (1983) Degradation of ethylene glycol and polyethylene glycols by methanogenic consortia. *Applied and Environmental Microbiology* **46**, 185–190.

HMSO (1990) Business monitor, quarterly statistics. Antifreeze for internal combustion engines. Central Statistical Office, PAS2582

KAPLAN D L, WALSH J T and KAPLAN A M (1982) Gas chromatographic analysis of glycols to determine biodegradability. *Environmental Science and Technology* **16**, 723–725.

NOVAK J T, GOLDSMITH C D, BENOIT R E and O'BRIEN J H (1985) Biodegradation of methanol and tertiary butyl alcohol in subsurface systems. *Water Science and Technology* **17**, 71–85.

MAYES M A, ALEXANDER H C and DILL D C (1983) A study to assess the influence of age on the response of fathead minnows in static acute toxicity tests. *Bulletin of Environmental Contamination and Toxicology* **31**, 139–147.

STANEK E J, TUTHILL R W, WILLIS C and MOORE G S (1987) Household hazardous waste in Massachusetts. *Archives of Environmental Health* **42**, 83–86.

12   Metals

12.1   Introduction

Elsewhere in this study the release of chemicals from domestic sources has been considered in terms of the products being used, largely because there is a direct link between the type of product and the type of chemical being released. A major exception to this is the release of metals, for which the sources are many and diverse; major ones include building materials, water distribution systems, food and faecal waste, toilet paper, detergents and soaps, household cleaners, cosmetics, medicines, and sweat and dust. Other sources may be less obvious; for example tin fluoride is used in toothpaste, selenium compounds in dandruff shampoos and aluminium compounds in deodorants. As an example of the varied sources of metals in the domestic environment, some domestic products containing zinc or its compounds and which may enter domestic wastewater are listed below (Atkins and Hawley 1978):

Zinc	pesticides
	soil nutrient
	oils
Zinc caprylate	fungicidal ointments
Zinc carbonate	skin creams
Zinc chloride	rust inhibitor in antifreeze
	toilet cleaners
	mouthwash
Zinc chromate	paints, pigments
Zinc dialkyl dithiophosphate	transmission fluids
	motor oils
Zinc oxide	baby powder, talcum powder
	skin creams, make-up
	deodorants
	mouthwash
	suppositories
	paints, pigments
Zinc phenolsulfonate	aftershave, deodorants
	suppositories, medicines
Zinc peroxide	skin creams
Zinc pytithione	shampoo
Zinc silicofluoride	pesticides
Zinc stearate	floor cleaners
	skin creams, make-up
	baby powder, foot powder, talcum powder
	polishes
Zinc sulfocarbolate	face packs
Zinc sulphate	skin creams
	pesticides
	suppositories, medicines
Zinc sulphide	skin creams
	pigments
Zinc undecyclenate	foot powder
Copper zinc chromate	pesticides

Some of the sources of metals have been touched upon elsewhere in this report, most notably under water distribution systems (Section 9), but this section assesses the general potential impact of metals arising from diverse sources.

The total heavy metal burden in the UK's sewers has been estimated at approximately 13 000 t, arising from industrial and domestic sources and from runoff. Estimates of the contributions from these different sources are not available, but some indication of the relative importance of domestic sources is provided in the following sections.

12.2 Domestic sources of metals

Moriyama *et al* (1989) estimated the contribution of the different domestic sources of metals to the total load in domestic effluent in two cities in Japan, by sampling wastewaters as they left houses. There were large differences between the different locations but also some consistencies. For example, in both cases the largest single source of lead (44 and 82%) was bath water, of copper (78 and 33%) was also bath water and of manganese (60 and 94%) was faeces. Overall, bath water and faeces were the major source of metals, tap water was intermediate, and the contribution from laundry and kitchen wastewaters was minimal. Table 12.1 summarises these data and indicates the percentage contribution from each of the five sources to the total load of each metal.

Table 12.1 Domestic sources of metals in wastewater

	Major sources (% contribution)[1]	Intermediate sources (% contribution)[1]	Minor sources (% contribution)[1]
Cadmium	Bath (38 15) Faeces (20 61)	Tap (22 18) Laundry (14 3)	Kitchen (6 3)
Nickel	Faeces (12 61)	Tap (23 21) Bath (41 5)	Kitchen (9 9) Tap (23 21)
Lead	Bath (44 82) Tap (47 11)		Kitchen (1 1) Laundry (7 5) Faeces (1 1)
Chromium	Bath (25 33) Laundry (37 28)	Tap (28 17)	Kitchen (8 8) Faeces (2 14)
Manganese	Faeces (60 94)	Tap (20 2)	Kitchen (7 1) Laundry (8 2) Bath (5 1)
Copper	Bath (78 33)	Tap (15 11) Faeces (3 45)	Kitchen (1 4) Laundry (3 7)
Zinc	Bath (62 16) Faeces (20 59)	Tap (7 13)	Kitchen (4 3) Laundry (7 9)
Iron	Bath (43 7) Faeces (8 56)	Tap (23 9) Laundry (22 22)	Kitchen (4 6)

Notes

[1] Numbers in parentheses refer to two separate study areas

These data indicate that tap water accounts for about 20 to 30% of the domestic loads of most of the metals, but as much as 50% of the nickel load and as little as 10% of the manganese and zinc loads. Obviously the contribution from tap water will vary geographically depending on the quality of the domestic supply, and the varying influence of additional sources such as water treatment and distribution systems. As mentioned in Section 9 water treatment and distribution has been considered as an industrial source of contaminants for the purposes of this report, and no attempt was made by Moriyama *et al* (1989) to distinguish between contributions from these 'industrial' sources and from domestic water systems.

An investigation of the origins of metals in domestic wastewater in the United States identified foodstuffs as a major source (in faecal matter), accounting for about 50% of cadmium, copper and zinc, and about 30% of chromium and mercury, but only a small proportion of lead and nickel (Gurnham *et al* 1979). The bulk of the remainder was contributed by detergents and related washing products.

12.3 Metal loads in domestic wastewaters

Table 12.2 presents the estimated loads in ug/person/day for each of the metals arising from each of the sources identified by Moriyama *et al* (1989) in Japan, DeWaal (1982) in the Netherlands, Bischofsberger (1981) in Germany (Munich) and Hellstrom and Knutsson (1983) in Sweden (Stockholm).

Table 12.2 Amounts of metals in domestic wastewater[1] (µg/person.day)

Tap Water	Moriyama[2]	DeWaal		Bath Water	Moriyama[2]	DeWaal
Iron	13 550	–		Iron	25 400	–
Copper	4 435	548		Copper	22 385	–
Zinc	2 950	2 740		Zinc	15 500	–
Lead	1 708	110		Lead	2 643	–
Manganese	891	–		Nickel	347	–
Nickel	237	219		Manganese	223	–
Chromium	141	110		Chromium	163	–
Cadmium	28	14		Cadmium	42	–

Laundry	Moriyama[2]	DeWaal		Pipe Corrosion		DeWaal
Iron	15 050	–		Copper		16 685
Zinc	2 450	–		Zinc		9 507
Copper	985	–		Lead		2 932
Manganese	417	–		Cadmium		55
Lead	310	–				
Chromium	197	–				
Nickel	141	–				
Cadmium	15					

Kitchen	Moriyama[2]	DeWaal		Faeces	Moriyama[2]	DeWaal
Iron	2 650	–		Iron	11 050	–
Zinc	1 250	–		Zinc	10 800	12 000
Copper	425	–		Manganese	5 886	–
Manganese	339	–		Copper	1 715	2 493
Nickel	83	–		Nickel	226	342
Lead	68	–		Lead	65	178
Chromium	49	–		Cadmium	41	55
Cadmium	7	–		Chromium	35	68

Totals

	Moriyama[3]	DeWaal		Bischofsberger[4]	Hellstrom & Knutsson
Iron	55 300	–		–	–
Zinc	30 100	24 247		137 808	71 000 – 125 000
Copper	21 000	19 726		14 521	21 000 – 39 000
Manganese	7 300	–		–	52 000 – 57 000
Lead	3 364	3 220		7 589	6 000 – 6 200
Nickel	837	561		2 192	3 000 – 3 600
Chromium	466	178		2 329	2 300 – 3 000
Cadmium	118	124		233	400 – 900

Tap Water				Bath Water		
Moriyama[2]	DeWaal			Moriyama[2]	DeWaal	
	Sewage works influent[3] Moriyama				Sewage works effluent + sludge[3] Moriyama	
Iron	283 000				295 000	
Zinc	37 500				29 500	
Copper	8 000				5 400	
Manganese	16 300				15 100	
Lead	2 467				2 084	

Table 12.2 Continued

	Sewage works influent[3] Moriyama	Sewage works effluent + sludge[3] Moriyama
Nickel	941	970
Chromium	852	717
Cadmium	135	116

Notes
[1] Values are mean estimates for discharge in μg/person.day.
[2] Mean values from two study areas.
[3] Mean values from three study areas.
[4] Mean values from seven residential estates in Munich.

Where the results from the studies of Moriyama *et al* (1989) and DeWaal (1982) are directly comparable they are in good agreement except for the *per capita* loadings of copper and lead in tap water. Since these are both so dependent on the type of plumbing used it is perhaps not surprising that large differences are seen between the Netherlands and Japan. The total loads in domestic wastewater also agree reasonably well for these two studies. The loads reported by Hellstrom and Knutsson (1983) for Stockholm, Sweden, agree well with those reported by Bischofsberger (1981) for Munich, Germany, but these are notably higher for most of the metals when compared to the other two studies (eg manganese, chromium and zinc). Hellstrom and Knutsson (1983) did not identify their source wastewaters and so no explanation for the high loads in the Stockholm study can be offered. The wastewater in the Munich study was purely of domestic origin, with metals being measured in sewers receiving no industrial input and no surface runoff. The volume of wastewater was assumed to be equal to 90% of the metered water supplied to the households. It is possible that the apparently high metal loadings result from this being an overestimate of actual wastewater volumes, but this cannot be ascertained. Other possible causes of the differences between the studies include different degrees of infiltration or leakage in the sewers, or simply inherent variation between locations.

12.4 Domestic v other sources of metals

12.4.1 Domestic metals in sewage treatment works influents

Using the data presented by Moriyama *et al* (1989) it is possible to estimate the contribution from domestic wastewaters to the influent metal loads at the wastewater treatment plants studied, which received no industrial effluent. These estimates are presented in Table 12.4, along with some equivalent estimates cited by Elliott (1984) for New York.

No details of the catchments were provided by Moriyama *et al* (1989) except that the sewage treatment works 'accepted only domestic wastewater', but additional sources of metals may have included precipitation (and leaching of atmospheric metals), runoff (particularly from roads), and possibly small industries. The domestic loads of lead and copper were 136% and 263% of the loads in treatment works influent and no process can be proposed to explain this except leakage or deposition in sewers, but these would presumably result in loss of other metals too. It is possible that these high values are the result of sampling or analytical errors. Although there are large differences between the two sets of data they suggest that domestic wastewater may be a significant source of metals released to the aquatic environment or sewage sludge, particularly for copper, lead, cadmium and zinc. Gurnham *et al* (1979) reported levels as high as 2 μg/l cadmium and 200 μg/l zinc in purely domestic wastewater in the USA.

Data provided in ENDS (1991) indicate that domestic sources contribute 87% of the copper load in UK sewers, 63% of zinc, 46% of lead, 30% of nickel, 21% of cadmium, 5% of chromium and 5% of mercury. The source of these data is not provided, but they suggest a similar pattern to that in the studies above.

DeWaal (1982) also compared the contribution made by domestic sources with contributions from other diffuse sources and from industrial sources in the Netherlands. Domestic sources of metals (cadmium, chromium, copper, lead, nickel and zinc) totalled 48 mg/person/day as compared to equivalents of 104 mg/person/day from other diffuse sources (road runoff, precipitation) and about 220 mg/person/day from industry (in 1980). On this basis, domestic sources contributed about 13% of the total. However, the intention in the Netherlands at that time was to reduce industrial metal releases to a level equivalent to about 75 mg/person/day by 1985, and if this was achieved then the domestic contribution could be more like 20%.

Table 12.3 Contribution of domestic sources to total metal loads at city sewage treatment works

Metal	Domestic contribution, %	
	Moriyama *et al* (1989) Japan	Elliott (1984) New York
Copper	>100	47
Lead	>100	–
Nickel	89	25
Cadmium	87	49
Zinc	80	42
Chromium	55	28
Manganese	45	–
Iron	20	–

12.4.2 Domestic metals in sewage sludge

Moriyama *et al's* (1989) results also demonstrate that treatment works influent loads and effluent loads (including sludge) are the same, because metals cannot be degraded. In fact in most cases the bulk of the metals ends up in sludge, with some percentage removals shown in Table 12.4.

Table 12.4 Percentage removal of some metals into sludge (data from Foess and Ericson (1980)[1] and Elliott (1984)[2])

	Primary sludge[1]		Activated sludge[1]		Combined[2]
	range	mean	range	mean	
Cadmium	0 – 76	8	0 – 88	17	16 – >50
Chromium	0 – 80	26	0 – 98	46	54 – 91
Copper	0 – 77	26	0 – 95	57	49 – 80
Iron	0 – 89	40	8 – 98	63	68 – 87
Lead	0 – 88	24	0 – 95	39	46 – 88
Manganese	0 – 81	15	0 – 93	38	48 – 67
Mercury	0 – 75	27	0 – 99	39	61 – 93
Nickel	0 – 92	6	0 – 80	20	41 – 55
Zinc	0 – 88	31	0 – 99	58	54 – 74

Griepink *et al* (1984) investigated the concentrations of metals in sewage sludge from three European treatment works: one in a rural area with no industry, one receiving mostly industrial effluent, and one receiving mixed effluents. Their results are presented in Figure 12.1. These data can be used as an indication of the importance of non-industrial sources of each of these metals, although it should be noted that this assumes that the three treatment works had no differences in partitioning of metal between effluent and sludge. For example, the fact that the concentrations recorded in rural sludges were mostly higher than those in mixed sludges indicates the variability that can occur between catchments. It has been assumed that the rural treatment works received only domestic effluent, but without further information on the catchment this must be viewed with some caution.

Non-industrial sources of nickel and cobalt in particular, but also of zinc, copper and manganese, appear to be quite important. Nickel concentrations in rural sludge were over three times as high as those in industrially-derived sludge. Comparing these findings with those of Moriyama *et al* (1989) shows some differences, but some variability is expected. Nickel, copper and zinc had major non-industrial sources in both studies, lead, cadmium and manganese in one or the other. Cobalt was found to be high by Griepink *et al* (1984) but was not investigated by Moriyama *et al* (1989). Other authors have also observed high levels of some of these metals in sewage sludges from treatment plants receiving no industrial wastewater, as shown in Table 12.5.

Schmidt and Schöcke (1983) proposed that the cadmium they detected (see Table 12.5) arose largely from old galvanised guttering or roofing materials, particularly when the rain-water was acidic. Nickel, and possibly chromium, was found to be mostly of mineral origin rather than domestic, arising from local soils and rock (basalt), and possibly also abstracted river water. Sources of the other metals were not investigated.

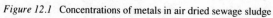

Figure 12.1 Concentrations of metals in air dried sewage sludge

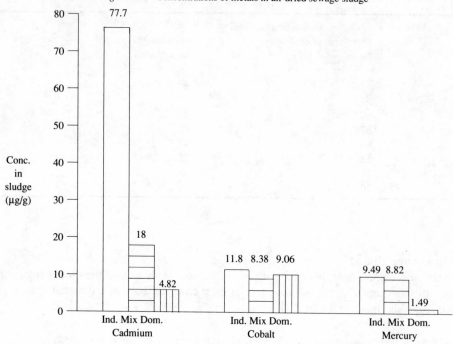

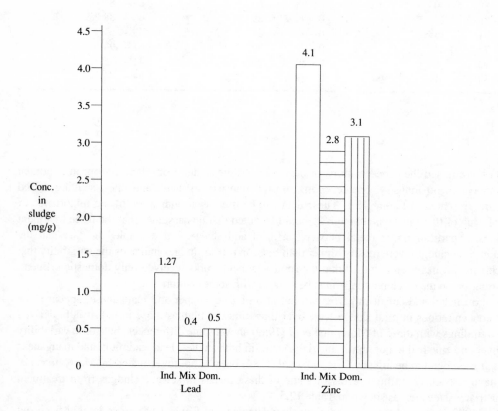

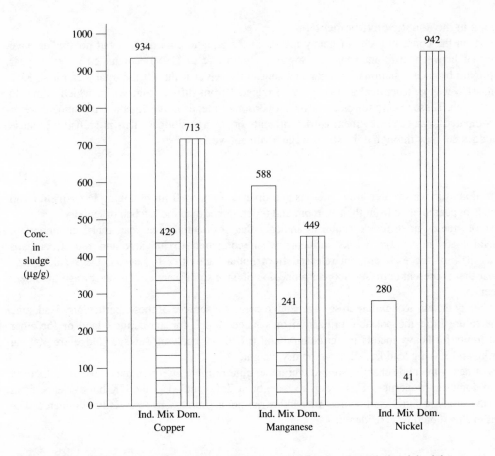

Table 12.5 Reported ranges of metal concentrations in sewage sludges of non-industrial origin

	Conc. in sludge		Location	Ref
	mg/kg	dry w't		
Cadmium	4 –	10	FRG	3
	<2 –	432	UK	4
Chromium	83		FRG	1
	4 –	10 095	UK	4
Copper	200		FRG	1
	>500		UK, Sweden, USA, Canada	2
	150 –	300	FRG	3
	69 –	2 190	UK	4
Iron	10 000 –	15 000	FRG	3
	2 480 –	92 435	UK	4
Lead	198		FRG	1
	150 –	500	FRG	3
	43 –	2 434	UK	4
Nickel	94		FRG	1
	40 –	60	FRG	3
	9 –	936	UK	4
Zinc	1 300		FRG	1
	>1 000		UK, Sweden, USA, Canada	2
	1 000 –	2 000	FRG	3
	279 –	27 600	UK	4

References
1. Schmidt and Schöcke (1983)
2. Page (1974)
3. Gutenkunst (1989)
4. Sleeman (1984)

12.4.3 Domestic metals in the aquatic environment

There are very many data on the concentrations of heavy metals in the aquatic environment but no studies have identified and distinguished between different sources. However, Imhoff *et al* (1980) conducted an eight year investigation to develop mass balance equations for metals present in the River Ruhr. Of the total metal load 55% was of industrial origin, 41% was geochemical and only 4% originated from diffuse sources, of which domestic wastewaters would be only one. These results suggest a lower proportion of metals in the aquatic environment are of domestic origin when compared to sewage treatment works influents or sewage sludges. This is probably because much industrial effluent does not pass through domestic sewage treatment works.

12.5 Conclusions

The sources of metals in domestic wastewater are numerous and diverse, ranging from plumbing to cosmetics and human faeces. Most metals appear to arise from the bathroom and toilet, rather than the kitchen or laundry.

Data from a number of studies in different countries indicate that residential areas can make an important contribution to the metal loads in sewage works influents when compared to industry and runoff, perhaps contributing as much as 20% of the total amount released from human activities to sewers, De Waal (1982). However, it would appear that at present domestic sources alone do not have significant effects on sewage treatment or the aquatic environment.

Because many of the heavy metals accumulate in sewage sludge domestic sources of these, particularly lead, zinc and copper, may in the future limit the possible utilization of sewage sludge for agricultural land or for other purposes. Some current limits for heavy metals in agricultural soil (pH 6–7) receiving sewage sludge are 300 mg zinc/kg, 135 mg copper/kg and 300 mg lead/kg, all based on dry weight.

As industrial sources of heavy metal discharges are brought under control more attention may have to be focused on the contribution from domestic properties. This seems to have been little studied in the UK but evidence from elsewhere indicates it may remain a significant source after industrial point sources are essentially eliminated. The longer term implications of this should be considered.

References

ATKINS E D and HAWLEY J R (1978) Sources of metals and metal levels in municipal wastewaters. Research program for the abatement of municipal pollution under provisions of the Canada-Ontario agreement on Great Lakes water quality. Environment Canada research report no. 80.

BISCHOFSBERGER W (1981) Herkunft und Verbleib von Schwermetallen im Abwasser und Klärschlamm. Berichte aus Wassergütewirtschaft und Gesundheitsingenieurwesen. Institut für Bauingenieurwesen V, Technische Universität München, report number 34.

DeWAAL A J W (1982) Cadmium, chroom, koper, lood, nikkel en zink in huishoudelijk afvalwater en in af te voeren neerslag. (Cadmium, chromium, copper, lead, nickel and zinc in domestic sewage and in stormwater runoff). H_2O **15**, 355–361.

ELLIOTT G E P (1984) Toxic elements in wastewater sludge. *The Public Health Engineer* **12**, 3 July, 165–166.

ENDS (1991) Sludge disposal problems focus attention on metal inputs from homes. *ENDS Report* **192**, January 1991, 9.

FOESS G W and ERICSON W A (1980) Toxic control – the trend for the future. *Water and Wastes Engineering*, Feb. 1980, 21–27.

GRIEPINK B, MUNTAU H and COLINET E (1984) Certification of the contents of some heavy metals (Cd, Co, Cu, Mn, Hg, Ni, Pb and Zn) in three types of sewage sludge. *Fresenius' Zeitschrift für Analytische Chemie* **318**, 490–494.

GURNHAM C F, ROSER B A, RITCHIE H R, FETHERSTON W T and SMITH A W (1979) Control of heavy metal content of municipal wastewater sludge. US Department of Commerce NTIS report no. PB–295 917.

GUTENKUNST B (1989) Praktische Erfahrungen und Ergebnisse aus Sielhautuntersuchungen zur Ermittlung schwermetallhaltiger Einleitungen. (Practical experiences and results of the detection of heavy metals in discharges by analysis of sewer slime). *Korrespondenz Abwasser* **36**, 1367–1375.

HAROLD E, HAMPTON E and McKIRDY K (1990) Lead levels in drinking water from water boilers in Glasgow District Council premises. *Environmental Health*, February 1990, 32–33.

HELLSTROM B G and KNUTSSON P (1983) Pollution levels in domestic wastewater from the Stockholm region. *Vatten* **39**, 265–271.

IMHOFF K R, KOPPE P and DIETZ F (1980) Resultate der mehrjährigen Untersuchungen über Herkunft, Verhalten und Verleib von Schwermetallen in der Ruhr (Results of investigations lasting several years into the origin, behaviour and persistence of heavy metals in the Ruhr). *GWF–Wasser/Abwasser* **121**, 383–391.

KUMPERA F (1985) Korrosionsprobleme in der Hausinstallation (Corrosion problems in domestic plumbing systems). *Gas/Wasser/Wärme* **39**, 14–16.

MORIYAMA K, MORI T, ARAYASHIKA H, SAITO H and CHINO M (1989) The amount of heavy metals derived from domestic wastewater. *Water Science and Technology* **21**, 1913–1916.

PAGE A L (1974) Fate and effects of trace elements in sewage sludge when applied to agricultural lands. A literature review study. US EPA report number EPA–670/2–74–005.

SCHMIDT H and SCHÖCKE K (1983) Untersuchungen zur Herkunft der Schwermetalle Nickel und Cadmium in Klärschlammen aus nichtgewerblichen Quellen (Studies of the origin of the heavy metals nickel and cadmium in sewage sludges from non-industrial sources). *Korrespondenz Abwasser* **30**, 622–624.

SLEEMAN P (1984) Determination of pollutants in effluents. Detailed analysis of the trace element contents of UK sewage sludges. WRc report number 280–S/1, April 1984.

13 Conclusions

It would have been very surprising if this rapid review of domestic chemical use and its impact on freshwater pollution revealed major problems. It is clear that despite the large volume usage of chemicals in people's houses our sewage treatment works continue to operate and our rivers and lakes do not show adverse effects that cannot be accounted for by point or non-domestic diffuse pollution sources. This review has, however, revealed some aspects of domestic chemical use which could be modified to produce a smaller environmental impact and other areas where further thought should be given to quantify and perhaps avert future problems. Most of these are not novel. The major points are as follows.

1. While many chemicals used domestically are tested before use, this testing does not include an assessment of ecotoxicity. It is certainly possible for a chemical to be essentially harmless to man but to have a dramatic environmental impact. At the very least, therefore, there should be an assessment of their persistence. There already exists a Directive to ensure that non-ionic surfactants present in detergents are at least 80% biodegradable (using a specified reference method) (CEC 1982). Similar regulations for other chemicals may be desirable.

2. 'Natural' chemicals can only be considered to be safe if they are being used in a similar environment to that where they occur naturally and at similar concentrations. If this is not the case they should be tested in the same way as any other new chemical.

3. Many chemicals or preparations are used domestically and give rise to waste residuals, such as paints, oils, adhesives, solvents and pharmaceuticals. There is a need for clearer guidance on the best way to dispose of such materials. Possibilities include more informative labelling or dissemination of information at retail outlets. Retailers might also be encouraged to accept waste returns.

4. Priority chemicals can in some cases be used domestically (eg lindane in hair shampoo for lice treatment, herbicides for path clearance). More thought should be given to domestic use of such chemicals which act as a very diffuse source, making them difficult to control. Examples of actions which could be taken include restrictions on use where suitable alternatives exist and changes in packaging, for example by selling smaller quantities or more dilute formulations.

5. Increased affluence is leading to increased attention to water quality which in turn is leading to increased salt use (eg ion exchange treatment, dishwashers and bath salts). In areas of high water re-use this may become significant in the future and more consideration is recommended.

6. Various sources contribute to the significant amount of heavy metals in domestic wastewater. Because these metals tend to concentrate in sewage sludge their residues tend not to be a problem for receiving waters. However, as industrial sources come under better control domestic sources may become the dominant and, perhaps, the limiting factor in the use of sewage sludge. This is not an immediate problem but thought should be given now to the future implications.

Reference

COUNCIL OF THE EUROPEAN COMMUNITIES (CEC) (1982) Council Directive of 31 March 1982 on the approximation of the laws of the Member States relating to methods of testing the biodegradability of non-ionic surfactants and amending Directive 73/404/EEC. *Official Journal* L109, 22 April 1982.

The Impact of the Waste Management Industry on Freshwater Quality

Report No: CO 2720-M/2

January 1992

Author: C P Young

Contract Manager: A J Dobbs

Contract No: 8157

Any enquiries relating to this report should be referred to the Contract Manager at the following address:

WRc plc, Henley Road, Medmenham, PO Box 16, Marlow, Buckinghamshire SL7 2HD.
Telephone: Henley (0491) 571531

Summary

I   **Objectives**

To review past and present information on the arisings and disposals of wastes in Britain and to assess their impacts on the aquatic environment. To consider the probable future trends in waste management practice and their implications for environmental quality.

II   **Reasons**

The Royal Commission on Environmental Pollution are reviewing the effect of waste disposal on environmental quality.

III   **Conclusions**

Past disposal practices have allowed contaminants to move freely into the environment. However, although substantial volumes of municipal and industrial wastes have been deposited in landfills, no clear case has been reported in Britain of deterioration of a public water supply to the point where it was unusable. It is concluded that in future a high proportion, if not all landfills will be operated on a containment principle, with control and treatment of leachates and landfill gas. The improvement in waste management standards will require a higher degree of professionalism amongst waste management practitioners than in the past, and is likely to lead to substantial increases in the costs of waste disposal.

IV   **Recommendations**

Areas of uncertainty regarding the specification of loading rates for the codisposal of industrial and other wastes, or the means of specifying the conditions under which a Certificate of Completion may be issued for a landfill and on the behaviour and degradation of organic wastes in landfills, soils and aquifers have been identified and recommended as topics for further study.

V   **Resume of contents**

The legal framework for waste disposal in Britain, since the 1950s, is reviewed and consideration given to the implications for the future organisation of waste disposal of proposed European Community Directives. The volumes of waste arisings and disposals are examined and compared with the number of licensed facilities for waste management. Alternative waste disposal methods are considered. The observed impact of landfill disposal of wastes on water resources is discussed, leading to an overview which identifies areas for further investigation.

Contents

1 Introduction

The objectives of this report are to:

- assess the extent to which past waste management practices have led to, and past monitoring practices have allowed the recognition of contamination of, water resources, especially groundwaters;

- recognise probable future trends in waste disposal practices and to suggest their possible effects on environmental protection;

- identify needs for future research.

2 Legislative framework and administration of waste disposal

2.1 Pre 1972

Before the Public Health Act 1936 there was no legislation giving specific powers to local authorities to control the collection and disposal of wastes. However, certain aspects of pollution control, especially towards water supplies, were embodied in earlier legislation. As an example, Sections 20 and 22 of the Cemeteries Clauses Act 1847 made it an offence to allow polluted liquid draining from burial grounds to contaminate freshwater resources, with an initial fine of £50, and an additional £10 per day for each day, after the first 24 hours, during which the polluting discharge was allowed to continue. These provisions were incorporated into the Public Health Act 1875, which also specified that no new burial grounds should be established within 200 yards of housing, with the presumption that, at that time, the majority of houses relied on their own wells for water supply. The minimum distance between burial grounds and housing was reduced to 100 yards in the Burial Act 1906, and this figure would appear to remain in force via the 1936 and subsequent Public Health Acts.

In addition to the powers to control waste disposal given to local authorities by the 1936 Act, the Water Act 1945 enabled statutory water undertakings to make byelaws and to acquire land in order to protect from pollution any water which the undertaking was authorised to take. Additional control over the disposal of liquid wastes was given to the river authorities by the Water Resources Act 1963, in which direct discharge of such waste to groundwaters via wells or boreholes was prohibited. The ban did not apply to the discharge of liquid wastes to the surface.

Although legal controls over wastes were very limited before 1936, and incomplete after that date, the management exercised by local authorities and communities appears generally to have taken account of the vital importance of reliable water supplies. The apparent lack of large numbers of confirmed examples of extensive freshwater contamination resulting from pre-1970 waste disposals may indicate that the objections against developments and activities, which were likely to lead to contamination of water supplies, were considered seriously and acted upon.

2.2 The Deposit of Poisonous Waste Act 1972 and the Control of Pollution Act 1974

Following pioneering experimental studies, during the 1950s, of the pollution potential of municipal wastes (Ministry of Housing and Local Government 1961) working parties were set up by the government to report on possible environmental impacts of toxic wastes and municipal refuse disposal (Ministry of Housing and Local Government 1970). The need to review waste control and improve environmental protection was already apparent when, in the early 1970s (eg Sunday Times, No 7826, 10 June 1973), newspaper articles reported the disposal of wastes containing cyanide and polychlorinated biphenyls (PCBs) to landfills in situations where water pollution appeared possible. In response to the public concern, the Deposit of Poisonous Wastes Act 1972 was enacted. This Act made it unlawful to deposit poisonous, noxious or polluting wastes on land in such a way that an environmental hazard would be created. In order to control the disposal, notification of removal or deposit of wastes considered to be poisonous had to be given both to the local authority in whose area the waste arose and, if different, the local authority whose area the waste would be deposited, and to the relevant river authorities or river purification boards. The classes of mainly industrial wastes which were controlled by this Act became known colloquially as 'Notifiable Wastes' and, although the Deposit of Poisonous Wastes Act was repealed in 1981 following implementation of the relevant parts of the Control of Pollution Act, the terminology remains in frequent usage.

The Control of Pollution Act 1974 (COPA) has provided the framework for pollution control over the last 16 years, and embodies the UKs response to requirements of European Community Directives. Part 1 of the Act deals with the disposal of waste on land via a system of licensing waste disposal facilities for the deposit of controlled wastes. Controlled wastes are defined in Section 30 of the Act as household, industrial and commercial or any such waste, but specifically excluding agricultural wastes and the wastes from mines and quarries.

The Act was designed to provide a structure in which local environmental and amenity needs could be taken into account when consideration is given to proposals for waste disposal. In order to achieve this, the licensing of disposal facilities was placed in the hands of Waste Disposal Authorities (WDAs), and the organisation of collection into the hands of Waste Collection Authorities (WCAs). As originally enacted in 1974, the WDAs comprised the Shire and Metropolitan counties of England, the District Councils of Wales, and the District and Island Councils in Scotland. Following the dismemberment of the Metropolitan Counties under the Local Government Act 1985, the functions of the WDAs have been carried out by one of the constituent district or borough councils acting as a 'lead' authority. In the cases of London, Greater Manchester and Merseyside Waste Regulatory or Waste Disposal bodies were established by Orders after abolition of the Metropolitan Counties, but in the other cases, voluntary arrangements were encouraged, which subsequently led to criticism on the grounds of differing standards of performance (Department of the Environment 1988a).

The Waste Collection Authorities are the District or Borough Councils. A high proportion of industrial wastes are collected and deposited by specialist private sector operators, whilst the majority of municipal solid waste (household refuse and trade wastes) are handled directly by the WCA, with the WDAs acting as public sector disposal operators. The arrangements for the collection, disposal, licensing and regulation of wastes are summarised in Table 2.1.

Table 2.1 Organisation of waste management under Control of Pollution Act 1974

	Type of wastes	Collection	Disposal	Regulation	Planning matters	Consultees
England	Domestic	District Council	County Council or Private Sector	County Council or Lead Authority	County Council	NRA, WCA
	Commercial and non-hazardous	District Council or Private Sector	County Council or Private Sector	County Council or Lead Authority	County Council	NRA, WCA
	Hazardous	Private Sector	Dominantly Private Sector	County Council or Lead Authority	County Council	NRA, WCA
Wales	Domestic	District Council	District Coucil	District	County Council	NRA
	Commcerial and non-hazardous industrial	District Council or Private Sector	District Council or Private Sector	District	County Council	NRA
	Hazardous	Private Sector	Predominantly Private Sector	District	County Council	NRA
Scotland	Domestic	District Council	District Council	District	Regional Council	River Purification Board
	Commercial and non-hazardous industrial	District Council or Private Sector	District Council or Private Sector	District	Regional Council	River Purification Board
	Hazardous	Private Sector	Predominantly Private Sector	District	Regional Council	River Purification Board

Licensing of a facility for the disposal of controlled wastes cannot be granted unless the area in question has consent under the Town and Country Planning Acts. However, if a planning consent exists a WDA cannot reject an application for a license unless it is satisfied that rejection is necessary to prevent water pollution or danger to public health. Both the National Rivers Authority (previously the appropriate Regional Water Authority) and the WCA in whose area the application for a disposal licence falls are statutory consultees on both the planning and licensing matters. In Scotland the appropriate River Purification Board is a statutory consultee. The consultations may lead to the incorporation of conditions aimed at safeguarding environmental and amenity interests in both the planning and licensing. If agreement cannot be achieved between the planning and licensing bodies and the statutory consultees regarding the inclusion of conditions the matter may be referred to the Secretary of State for determination.

During the first ten years or so of operation of COPA, some tension developed between the technical requirements of landfilling, for example by doming sites to encourage run-off and limit leachate production, and broad planning objectives, for example, the prevention of the visual intrusion that doming might cause. However, in July 1988, the Town and Country Planning (Assessment of Environmental Effects) Regulations 1988 were brought into effect, fulfilling the requirements of European Community Directive 85/337. The Regulations provide that Environmental Assessments should be mandatory for waste disposal and treatment facilities handling special wastes (see below for Definition of Special Wastes) but at the discretion of the planning authority for sites accepting any other controlled waste at a rate of 75 000 tonnes per year or more, or smaller sites in environmentally sensitive locations. The list of areas which may need consideration in the assessment and the subsequent production of an Impact Statement includes not only matters such as visual amenity and traffic, which are traditional planning concerns, but also impacts on water, vegetation and wildlife. Each assessment is required to describe existing conditions, provide estimates of the probable impact of the proposed development on these conditions and to specify mitigation measures that would be undertaken to ameliorate predicted impacts. Although many proposed disposal facilities may not fall within either the mandatory or discretionary requirement of the Regulations, it appears that a systematic application of the approach to planning consent/site licensing embodied in the Regulations is being widely applied. It is anticipated that the closer linking of planning and site licensing considerations at an early stage should lead to more effective environmental protection and fewer disputes over license or planning conditions.

Once issued, a site licence may only be revoked by a WDA if it is considered that water pollution, danger to public health or serious detriment to local amenities cannot be avoided by modifying the licence conditions (Section 7, COPA). Normally, a site licence would be for a specified period of time, after which it would lapse (Section 6, COPA). However, at any time within that period the licence holder may transfer the licence to another person, or relinquish the licence (Section 8, COPA). The provisions have been seen as a weakness in the existing legislation on a number of counts,

1. that a licence could be transferred to an inexperienced operator,

2. that an unscrupulous operator could avoid responsibility for imminent environmental impairment originating in a landfill by relinquishing the licence before any effects were noted, and

3. that because the licences expire on completion of landfilling, there is no procedure under the pollution control legislation to enforce aftercare and monitoring responsibility at completed landfills.

This latter objection has been seen widely as the most serious flaw in the existing legislation, and it has been addressed in the recently enacted Environmental Protection Act 1990. In order to overcome this deficiency, the most commonly applied procedure has been to seek agreements under Section 52 of the Town and Country Planning Act 1971 (Section 50 of the Town and Country Planning (Scotland) Act 1972) to ensure proper aftercare and monitoring. However, it is not lawful for a planning authority to make granting of planning consent conditional upon entering into an agreement, so that unless they are entered into freely they cannot be imposed.

The class of hazardous wastes defined by the Deposit of Poisonous Wastes Act 1972 (Notifiable Wastes) was superseded in 1980 by definition of a class of Special Wastes under Section 17 of COPA (The Control of Pollution (Special Waste) Regulations 1980). The wastes included are those which are believed to represent the greatest hazard, particularly with respect to their inflammability, corrosivity and toxicity to human life.

The schedules attached to the Regulations list 31 elements and compounds which, if present in a waste such that the waste may then pose a threat to human life, classify the wastes as Special. The existing definition of Special Wastes relies heavily on potential effects on human life and does not take account of wider environmental impacts. However, recent European Community proposals for revisions of existing Directives, or for new Directives, have indicated that a broadening of definition to encompass environmental damage will be required. This view was also expressed in the second report of the House of Commons Environment Committee (1989) and a consultative paper on the review of the Special Wastes Regulations was circulated in January 1990 by the Department of the Environment and Welsh Office. Importantly, the proposed redefinition of Special Wastes included material that could be infectious to man and other organisms, and substances with ecotoxic effects on animals, plants, soil, water and via the food chains. The existing, and proposed, Special Waste Regulations embody a consignment note system, allowing potentially hazardous wastes to be traced from 'cradle to grave' and also enabling relatively accurate estimates to be made of arisings of this group of wastes.

Overall, the management of wastes and control of pollution is regulated through a complex network of laws and regulations, some enacted specifically for the purposes of environmental protection. The situation is dynamic, with new UK legislation superseding established systems and anticipated European Community requirements providing continued change. Although not complete, the listings in Table 2.2 illustrate the complexity and overlap of laws and regulations concerned with the disposal of wastes to land and the protection of water resources.

Table 2.2   UK and European Community Legislation relevant to Waste Disposal and Freshwater Pollution Control

Area of Control	UK Legislation	EC Directives
Waste to land	Control of Pollution Act 1974 (Pt 1)	75/442/EEC – Wastes
		75/439/EEC – Waste oils
	Litter Act 1958	76/403/EEC – PCBs and PCTs
	Town and Country	78/319/EEC – Toxic wastes
	Planning Acts 1970, 1980	84/631/EEC – transfrontier shipments
	Town and Country	
	Planning (Scotland) Act 1972	87/101/EEC – Waste oils
	Town and Country Planning	
	(Assessment of Environmental	85/337/EEC – assessment of effects
	Effects) Regulations 1988	

Table 2.2   continued

Area of Control	UK Legislation	EC Directives
	Health & Safety at Work Act 1974 Special Waste Regulations 1980 The Collection and Disposal of Waste Regulations 1988	
Freshwasters	Public Health Acts 1936, 1961 Control of Pollution Act 1974 (Pt 2)	75/440/EEC – surface waters
	Water Act 1945 Water Resources Act 1963	80/778/EEC – water for human consumption
	Water Act 1989	80/68/EEC – protection of groundwater against pollution

2.3   The Environmental Protection Act 1990, and prospective developments

The Environmental Protection Act 1990 marks the most importance advance in pollution control legislation in the UK since the Control of Pollution Act 1974, and is expected to make good the shortcomings which became apparent in past legislation, especially with respect to responsibilities for aftercare of waste disposal facilities. The Act is in nine parts, of which Parts 1, 2, 3 and 8 are seen as having the greatest impact on waste management and freshwater pollution control.

Part 1 introduces the concept of Integrated Pollution Control (IPC), that is a multimedia approach to the control of pollution, covering discharges to air, water and land of prescribed substances from scheduled processes. The Act enables the Secretary of State to prescribe industrial processes for which authorisation is required, either from Her Majesty's Inspectorate of Pollution (HMIP) or, in the case of emissions only to the air, by Local Authority Air Pollution Control Inspectors. It has recently been suggested (Hawkins 1991) that up to 5000 industrial processes will require authorisation by HMIP and about 27 000 industrial emissions to the atmosphere will need licensing by Local Authority Inspectors. In those cases where both types of emissions occur at the same site, enforcement could be transferred completely to HMIP, who would be responsible for setting conditions such that the Best Practicable Environmental Option (BPEO) is achieved, but having regard to economic factors (Best Available Technique Not Entailing Excessive Cost – BATNEEC). This part gives the Secretary of State the power to set environmental quality objectives (EQOs) and to plan for their improvement. Authorisation for discharges to the environment cannot be granted if the NRA objects that such releases would lead to the failure of water quality objectives. On the basis of encouraging application of the 'polluter pays' principle, operators of scheduled processes are to be charged for authorisations and may be fined or imprisoned if they fail to keep within the provisions of their authorisations, or to prove that the abatement methods in use are the best available. Registers of information are required to be maintained by the enforcing authorities and these registers are to be available for public inspection, free of charge, at all reasonable times. However, certain information may be excluded from the registers if it is considered that its inclusion would be contrary to the interests of national security, or unreasonably prejudicial to a commercial interest.

Part II of the Act, Waste on Land, repeals but at the same time replaces and expands COPA Part I. The most important change results from the separation of the regulatory and operational functions of waste disposal, by creating Waste Regulatory Authorities and by arranging for the local authority operational functions either to be carried out by 'arms length' Local Authority Waste Disposal Companies (LAWDCs) or to be undertaken entirely by the private sector, following competitive tendering. This separation of 'poacher and gamekeeper' functions parallels that undergone by the water industry in 1989 with the division of the multipurpose Regional Water Authorities into regulatory units (National Rivers Authority) and operational companies (Water Utilities plcs).

The Waste Regulation Authorities (WRAs) are defined as the county councils of non-metropolitan counties in England, the district or island councils in Wales and Scotland and the 'lead districts' or Waste Authorities constituted by order in the areas previously metropolitan counties. The Waste Disposal Authorities (WDAs) will be formed by essentially the same bodies as the WRAs and will have the duty to plan waste disposals and to arrange for this to occur by co-ordinating the efforts of waste collection authorities with waste disposal contractors. The WDAs will not act as waste disposal contractors.

The Waste Collection Authorities (WCAs) remain the district and borough councils, as under COPA, but they, and the WDAs, will be responsible for preparing plans and making arrangements for the recovery and recycling of wastes. An important change from the conditions under COPA will be that annual reports by WRAs to the Secretary of State will be required, in order to assist in monitoring the performance of the WRAs, and if necessary, in direct intervention and the imposition of conditions on waste management licences. In order to encourage uniformity of standards the Waste Management Paper Series published by the Department of the Environment is undergoing revision and will become statutory instruments. Local authorities are expected to have created 'ghost' LAWDCs by 1 April 1991 and as from that time the institutional arrangements for the collection, disposal and regulation of wastes will be as summarised in Table 2.3.

Table 2.3   Organisation of Waste Management under Environmental Protection Act 1990

Waste type	Collection	Disposal arrangements	Disposal operations	Regulation	Planning	Consultees
Domestic	WCA or LAWDC or Private Sector	WDA	LAWDC/Private	WRA	County/Region	NRA
Commercial and non-hazardous indusrial	WCA or LAWDC or Private Sector	WDA	LAWDC/Private	WRA	County/Region	NRA
Hazardous	LAWDC or Private Sector	WDA	LAWDC/Private	WRA	County/Region	NRA

Part II imposes a 'Duty of Care' on all disposers, carriers, holders, importers and producers of waste not to permit the waste to be deposited, released to the environment or transported in an illegal manner. Although the draft code on the Duty of Care anticipates that all waste producers at a scale larger than that of private domestic premises will be subject to the requirements, strict liability is not intended in the case of defaults by others to whom the waste has been legally passed, but over which the original holder no longer exercises control. However, it is possible that this will be at variance with a recently submitted proposal for a Directive on civil liability for damage caused by waste (89/C251/04) which appears to seek strict liability. Should such a requirement become embodied in UK legislation it would be expected to lead to a significant increase in auditing the performance of waste handlers and disposers by the producers of waste, which would tend to accelerate the rate of improvement in waste disposal standards.

The 'waste disposal licences' issued under Part II cover a wider remit than the 'site licences' under COPA, but may only be issued to 'fit and proper' persons, which appears to mean people who are technically competent to undertake the work required, who have not been convicted of relevant offences and who are in a position to make adequate financial provisions to discharge obligations under the licence. The requirements for grant of a licence remain similar to those under COPA, that is that planning consent is received before a licence can be granted, that proposals to grant licences must be referred to the NRA for comment and the refusal of grant of a licence by a WRA can only be on the grounds that its rejection is necessary to prevent either pollution of the environment, or harm to human health or severe detriment to the amenities of the locality. In view of the collaborative working arrangements that have grown up between WDAs, the NRA and waste disposal operators under COPA, and particularly since the introduction of the Town and Country Planning (Assessment of Environmental Effects) Regulations 1988, it would be hoped that few, if any, proposals for disposal licences would require outright rejection under the provisions of Section 28 of the 1990 Act. Auditing of the performance of the WRAs will be carried out by HMIP, both via the annual reports prepared by the WRAs and as a result of field visits.

Perhaps the most important innovation in Part II is the extension of the disposal licence into the aftercare period, removing the need for separate agreements under the Town and Country Planning Acts. At the same time, the ability of a licence holder to surrender a licence at will, which was contained on the Control of Pollution Act 1974, has now been stopped. Under Section 31 of EPA a licence may only be accepted for surrender by the RWA if they, in consultation with the NRA, are satisfied that the site no longer poses any environmental threat and that a 'certificate of completion' may be issued (Section 31(a)).

In addition to the proposed EC Directive on civil liability for damage caused by wastes, a proposal for a directive on the landfill of waste (Commission of the European Communities 1991) is under consideration. The proposal recognises four classes of waste, similar to those incorporated in the Environmental Protection Act 1990 (Table 2.4) but specifies only three types of landfill (inert wastes, municipal and other compatible wastes, hazardous waste). It is proposed that classification of the wastes into one or other category should be on the basis of leaching (eluate) tests and reference to trigger values for specific contaminants. Although the proposal generally requires wastes of different categories to be kept separate, provision is made for the codisposal (joint disposal) of different wastes where it can be shown that they are compatible and that the codisposal would give rise to synergistic effects between the wastes in terms of environmental protection (ENDS 1991). Although earlier drafts contained a blanket prohibition on the disposal of liquid wastes to landfills, this provision is retained only for liquids which are incompatible with the solid wastes and the operating procedures at the site. The draft makes it clear that containment of wastes and the collection, and safe disposal of leachate would be required at all classes of site, and standards are given for containment by natural strata (maximum hydraulic conductivities and minimum thicknesses of strata), and it is noted that the same degree of containment is required for sites taking municipal and compatible wastes as those receiving hazardous wastes. If the containment criteria cannot be met by the natural strata at a site the installation of lining membranes to achieve the same degree of containment would be permitted. An active aftercare period with site maintenance of 10 years is proposed, with monitoring extending to 30 years after completion of the site. The proposed draft includes provisions for the standardisation of sampling procedures for wastes, both in terms of frequency and number of samples to be taken, and the analyses to be carried out. The provisions apply to all types of waste and it is considered likely that such a position would be regarded as unnecessarily wasteful of valuable resources by the UK, especially if applied to inert and domestic wastes at a similar frequency to that for hazardous waste (ENDS 1991). The draft includes provisions to oblige landfill operators to carry financial guarantees to cover both the potential costs of environmental liability and the costs of aftercare maintenance and monitoring.

Landfills operational at the time at which the Directive comes into force would be required to submit 'conditioning plans' to bring them up to the standards demanded by the Directive. Any landfills which were unable to meet the new standards within 5 years of entry into force of the Directive would be closed.

Table 2.4 Comparison of waste classifications between Environmental Proctection Act 1990 and EC Proposals for Directive on Waste Disposal to Landfill

EPA '90	EC Proposal
Household waste (S 62(7))	Municipal Waste (Article 3(a))
Commercial waste (S 62 (9))	
Industrial waste (S 62 (8))	Industrial waste (Article 3 (c))
Special Waste (S 52)	Hazardous waste (Article 3 (c))
(No equivalent classification in UK)	Inert waste (Article 3 (d))

3 Review of waste arisings

3.1 Introduction

Accurate data on both the rate of waste arisings and in their final disposal routes (Section 4) are not generally available. The proportion of waste arisings that are quantified by weighing is small, although possibly increasing, and the majority of quoted values are estimates based on volume related measurements, for example number of truck loads. In addition, changes in the definitions of classes of wastes (Special Waste Regulations 1980, Collection and Disposal of Waste Regulations 1988) introduces uncertainties into comparisons made between recent and older surveys. However, there appears to be a general agreement (Department of the Environment 1989) that during the late 1980s a total of about 2,500 million tonnes of wastes, excluding radioactive waste, were being produced annually in the United Kingdom. In addition to the indigenous arisings, a small, but possibly increasing quantity of wastes is imported (about 0.06 million tonnes/yr). Examination of the table shows that, although attracting considerable attention in both the technical and popular press, the controlled wastes that are typically deposited in landfills represents less than 5% of the total annual arisings in Britain. Close to 80% of all waste arisings are accounted for by discharges of industrial effluents, subject to discharge consent conditions imposed by the National Rivers Authority. In particular, the wastes produced by agriculture (10% of total) and mines and quarrying (5% of total) are not generally deposited in landfills, whilst the small quantity of low level radioactive wastes sent to landfill (about 0.001% of total arisings) is controlled by legislation separate from the Control of Pollution Act 1974.

Annual arisings of wastes are conventionally reported on an 'as delivered' basis, that is including the weight attributable to moisture content. Sludge and effluents typically possess high moisture contents (>90%), whilst mines and quarry waste may be essentially dry, with household, commercial and many industrial waste characteristically containing between 25 and 35% moisture content on a dry weight basis (Blakey and Craft 1986). Re-estimation of the annual rate of arisings in terms of dry solids, which includes substances dissolved in effluents as well as suspended solids, suggests that about 90% of all waste arisings are composed of water (Table 3.1).

Table 3.1   Estimates of annual waste arisings in the United Kingdom, excluding radioactive wastes (million tonnes/year)

Waste classification	Type	Weight as delivered	Weight dry matter
Controlled wastes	Household & commercial	30	22
	Industrial solids	80	60
	Sewage sludge	20	2
	Industrial effluents	2000	20
	Agricultural	250	15
Other Wastes	Mines and quarry	130	130
Totals		**say 2500**	**say 250**

(Based on data in Department of the Environment 1989)

The rates of arisings of the different classes of controlled wastes are not uniform across the United Kingdom, especially in the case of the more hazardous industrial waste (Table 3.2).

3.2 Controlled Wastes

3.2.1 Household and commercial wastes

These are wastes arising from private dwellings and residential homes, prisons etc and probably represent the most accurately surveyed group of wastes, with the possible exception of Special Wastes. It has been recently estimated (Department of the Environment 1989) that half of the household waste collection are weighed, rather than estimated on a volume basis.

The overall composition of household waste has changed significantly during the past 50 years (Table 3.3), reflecting the changing life-style of a high proportion of the population. The principal change took place some 25 to

Table 3.2 Estimates of controlled waste arisings, excluding industrial effluents, in the United Kingdom countries (million tonnes/yr, as delivered)

Type of waste	England	Wales	Scotland	Northern Ireland	United Kingdom
Household and commercial	25	1.5	2.7	0.8	30
Industrial, non-hazardous	63	4	7	2	76
Industrial, hazardous	2.25	0.12	0.025	0.005	2.4
Industrial, special	16.5	0.9	2.0	0.6	20
Totals	**108.25**	**6.6**	**11.74**	**3.41**	**130**

(Based on data in Department of the Environment, 1988a, 1989)

30 years ago with the rapid decline in coal fired domestic heating in favour of less atmospherically polluting sources (gas, oil, electricity, smokeless fuels). As a result, the high proportion of ashes and fines which characterised household wastes of the 1930s, 40s and 50s declined progressively through the 1960s and 70s. A notable feature of waste compositions during the earlier period was the significant increase in ash content during the winter months, with a general decline in combustible materials, including paper and cardboard at the same time, reflecting a widespread habit of burning wastes on the fire or stove during the winter, rather than consigning them to the waste bin. At the same time that the ash content of waste has declined, the proportions of vegetables and putrescible materials, and of paper and cardboard have risen significantly, the former probably reflecting the decline in home production of composts for garden use and the latter the increase in sale of prepacked goods. In general, the proportions of the materials used for packaging (glass, metals, paper etc) have increased over the last few decades, with plastics first appearing in the 1960s and now forming about 7% of the waste stream.

Recent data no longer suggest a seasonal fluctuation in composition of wastes. However, regional differences which reflect social and economic factors may be present. Comparison of average *per capita* waste arisings from the Department of the Environment regions of England, Wales and Scotland (Table 3.4) suggests that a higher proportion of heavy wastes, possibly ashes, is found in the arisings in the Northern, North-eastern and Welsh regions, than in the Southern and Midlands areas. The low *per capita* arisings in Scotland cannot be explained on the basis of the information available. The *per capita* arisings are based on the quantities collected by the waste authorities.

Estimation of the *per capita* annual average weight of waste collected by waste authorities have been made since 1976 by the Department of the Environment (1980, 1985, 1989). The weight of all wastes collected has shown no significant change over a 10-year period (Table 3.5).

The apparent discrepancy between the average *per capita* arisings estimated in Table 3.3 (about 0.47 tonnes/year) and that in Table 3.4 (about 0.36 tonnes/year) is because only about 75% of domestic and commercial wastes are

Table 3.3 Changes in composition of household wastes 1936–1980 (as % by weight)

Waste type	1936	1955 summer	Year 1955/6 winter	1973	1980
Fines and ashes	56	32	56	20	14
Vegetable and putrescrible	14	20	18	18	26
Paper and carboard	15	20	13	33	28
Metals	4	7	4	9	8
Textiles	2	3	1	3	3
Glass	3	9	6	11	10
Plastics	0	0	0	2	7
Miscellaneous	6	9	2	4	4

(Data from 11th Report of Royal Commission on Environmental Pollution; Pollution of Water by Tipped Refuse, Ministry of Housing and Local Government 1961, Digest of Environmental Pollution and Water Statistics, No 3, Department of the Environment 1980).

collected by waste authorities, the remainder of such wastes arising from the activities of private sector waste collection and disposal companies, particularly with respect to the commercial wastes (trade wastes). The total annual production of household and commercial wastes (probably synonymous with the term 'municipal solid wastes') in England and Wales is therefore estimated to be about 30 million tonnes (Department of the Environment 1989) of which about half are household wastes. Commercial wastes are collected from businesses, including restaurants and shops, and the mixture of packaging and putrescible food wastes is basically similar to that from households, and the overall composition is considered to be that indicated in Table 3.2.

Table 3.4   Estimates of average *per capita* waste arisings, 1986/87

Region	Total wastes (million tonnes)	Population (millions)	Average waste per capita (tonnes)
North	1.696	3.087	0.549
Yorks and Humberside	2.312	4.878	0.474
East Midlands	1.708	3.766	0.454
East Anglia	0.861	1.863	0.462
South East	7.637	16.857	0.453
South West	2.027	4.316	0.470
West Midlands	2.255	5.152	0.438
North West	3.288	6.476	0.508
(Totals, England)	**21.784**	**46.395**	**0.470**
Wales	1.443	2.755	0.524
(Totals, England and Wales)	**23.227**	**49.150**	**0.473**
Scotland	1.800	5.167	0.348
(Totals, Great Britain)	**25.027**	**54.317**	**0.461**

Table 3.5   Average *per capita* waste collections, by waste authorities

England and Wales (as tonnes)									
Year	1976/7	1978/9	1979/80	1980/1	1981/2	1982/3	1983/4	1984/5	1985/6	1986/7
All wastes	0.334	0.329	0.346	0.333	0.327	0.332	0.337	0.337	0.348	0.356
Household waste	0.288	0.262	0.268	0.277	0.273	0.276	0.282	0.273	0.276	0.278

3.2.2   Non-hazardous industrial wastes

The major part of industrial wastes do not possess characteristics which lead to their being classified either as hazardous or notifiable wastes under the categorisation incorporated in the Deposit of Poisonous Wastes Act 1972, or as Special Wastes under Section 17 of COPA 1974. Such wastes may be potentially biodegradable or inflammable, for example cardboard, plastic scrap etc, or non-flammable or inert, for example slags and ashes or demolition rubble. Overall some 80 to 90 million tonnes arise annually (Table 3.1), although perhaps less than 50% of that total are deposited annually to landfills (see Section 4).

3.2.3   Industrial effluents

The Department of the Environment (1989) have estimated that about 2,000 million tonnes (m^3) of industrial effluents are produced annually, varying in composition from essentially clean water at elevated temperatures (cooling water) to contaminated water requiring special treatment. The control of such discharges is exercised through a system of discharge consents, set by the National Rivers Authority under provisions of Part II of the Control of Pollution Act 1974 and the appropriate sections of the Water Act 1989. The discharge consents may specify limits on both volumes and composition to either receiving waters (rivers, lakes, estuaries etc) or to sewage systems. Where discharge to sewers is authorised, the industrial waste will be treated in admixture with municipal sewage and the producer of the effluent is charged by the sewage treatment plant operator on the basis of composition and volume of the effluents. Where this is done the responsibility for the quality of the final effluent produced by the treatment works lies with the works operator. A proportion of the sludge produced by sewage treatment plants may be deposited in landfills and, therefore, a small fraction of the material contained in the large volume of industrial effluents may go to landfill (see Section 4).

3.2.4 Hazardous and special wastes

There is no clear definition in UK regulations of the meaning of Hazardous Wastes. However, the usage, and the apparent synonyms of 'toxic' and 'notifiable' stems from lists associated with the now defunct Deposit of Poisonous Wastes Act 1972 and is generally accepted as referring to wastes which pose a definite risk to the environment, including threats to the life or health of animals and plants. In practice, two main groups of waste are recognised:

- inorganic solids, sludges and liquids such as solid materials from metal refining and manufacturing, sludges from wastewater treatment and pickling acids, and

- organic solids, sludges and liquid such as tarry residues, scrap plastics for ends or beginnings of runs, spent solvents and oils, biological sludges and oily aqueous mixes.

In a few parts of the United Kingdom waste disposal authorities collect data relating to the arisings of 'hazardous' or 'notifiable' wastes separately from Special Wastes, and direct comparison of the quantities of the two types is possible. Elsewhere direct evidence is not collected and it is assumed by Her Majesty's Inspectorate of Pollution that the combined weight of hazardous and special waste arising is about 2.5 times that of Special Wastes.

Special Wastes are specified by the Control of Pollution (Special Waste) Regulations 1980, with their technical definition being described in Waste Management Paper No 23 (Department of the Environment 1981). Schedules attached to the Regulations list 31 substances, including alkalis, acids, heavy metals and drugs that are characteristic of Special Wastes, and which are dangerous to human life by virtue of their corrosivity, toxicity or flammability. As has been noted (Section 2.3), a review of the definition of Special Wastes is in hand, and it is probable that a wider range of wastes, including many of these currently considered 'hazardous' will in future be classified as Special.

Special wastes are subject to a consignment note system and detailed records of their arisings and disposal routes are therefore available on a regular basis. The Third Report of the Hazardous Waste Inspectorate (Department of the Environment 1988a) indicated that a total of 1.6 million tonnes were produced in England and Wales in 1986/87, with the highest rates of arisings being concentrated around the urbanised areas of the Midlands, Merseyside and Lancashire, the North-east and the London area in England, West Glamorgan in Wales, the Midland Valley of Scotland and the Belfast area of Northern Ireland (Figure 1).

3.2.5 Imported wastes

In addition to waste arisings in Britain, wastes are imported for disposal by landfill or other treatments. The imports include both hazardous/special wastes and non-hazardous industrial wastes. Slightly more than half (55%) of hazardous imports originates in Holland, with a further 25% coming from Eire and Belgium, and the remainder from other European countries, North America, Australia and the Far East. Prior to 1985 the annual import of hazardous wastes was generally below 10,000 tonnes, but increased to 25,000 tonnes in 1985/86, 53,000 tonnes in 1986/87 and 80,000 tonnes in 1987/88, before reducing to 52,000 tonnes in 1988/89 (Department of the Environment 1989). Imports of non-hazardous wastes have also shown considerable variations, with pre-1986 levels generally less than 200 tonnes per year, followed by a massive increase to 130,000 tonnes in 1986, but declining to 10,000 tonnes in 1987/88 and 5,000 tonnes in 1988/89.

The substantial increase in imported wastes during the mid and late 1980s give rise to considerable concern that the United Kingdom was looked upon as a cheap disposal site for hazardous wastes. It is noted that sections 109 and 110 of Part VIII of the Environmental Protection Act 1990 empower the Secretary of State for the Environment to prevent the import (or export) of wastes or specified substances into or out of the United Kingdom if those actions are considered likely to cause pollution of the environment.

3.2.6 Radioactive wastes

Radioactive wastes are excluded from the provisions of the Control of Pollution Act 1974 because they have their own legislation. High and medium level wastes are not deposited in landfills. However, low level wastes, defined as materials with a maximum alpha activity of 20 millicuries per m^3 and a maximum beta activity of 60 millicuries per m^3, are deposited at a small number of specially licensed sites, most particularly at Drigg, near Sellafield, but also at Dounreay and Clifton Marsh. The materials in question are lightly contaminated cleaning materials, bags and sacks, bottles, protective clothing, electrical and building wastes from sites handling radioactive material and soils. In the late 1970s (Department of the Environment 1980) an annual total of about 50,000 m^3 of low level radioactive wastes were deposited in the licensed landfills.

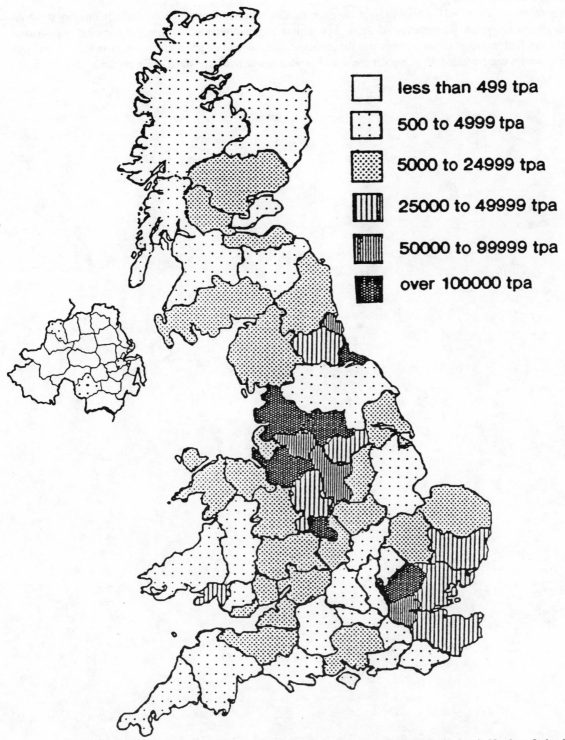

less than 499 tpa

500 to 4999 tpa

5000 to 24999 tpa

25000 to 49999 tpa

50000 to 99999 tpa

over 100000 tpa

Figure 1 Special waste arisings 1986/7, by counties in England and Wales, by districts in Northern Ireland.

3.3   Other wastes

3.3.1   Agricultural wastes

Four categories of agricultural waste are normally recognised, silage liquors, animal slurries, straw and chemical wastes and used pesticide containers. Since the onset of bovine spongiform encephalitis problems have arisen over the disposal of the 1.0 to 1.5 million farm animals that die annually on British farms, and it is estimated that up to 500 000 carcases per year are disposed of by burial on farmland, rather than via the traditional fellmongering route (Observer, No 10402, 24 February 1991, p6). The greater proportion of agricultural wastes is faecal matter dropped on fields as slurries and liquids, totalling an estimated 200 to 250 million tonnes per year (Table 3.1).

3.3.2   Mines and quarry wastes

The residues from machinery and quarrying, including China clay (kaolinite) production currently amount to about 130 million tonnes per year. A proportion of these wastes may be employed as fill material for civil engineering projects, especially if transport distances between the points of arisings and disposal are small. However, if no local usage for the wastes can be found deposition at the site of production remains the most common option for disposal.

4 The disposal of wastes to landfill

4.1 Quantities of wastes deposited annually in landfills

Setting aside agricultural wastes, mines and quarry wastes and industrial effluents discharged under National River Authority consents, it is estimated that the total arisings of controlled wastes in the United Kingdom is about 130 million tonnes (Table 3.2). Of this total a high proportion of inert industrial wastes such as PFA, slag wastes and building wastes are used as fill materials or aggregates in civil engineering applications, whilst only about 15% of the sewage sludge, containing 0.2 million tonnes of dry solids, is deposited in landfills.

Of the types of waste classified as household, commercial and industrial non-hazardous, over 90% are deposited in landfills, with between 5 and 8% being subjected to municipal incineration. The ashes from incineration, representing about 20% of the bulk of the original wastes, are dominantly landfilled.

The proportion of hazardous and special waste arisings landfilled is lower than that for municipal and non-hazardous industrial wastes, and recent figures (Department of the Environment 1988a) indicated 83% landfilled, 8% marine disposal, 7% chemical or physical treatment and 2% high temperature incineration. Although it is sometimes alleged that hazardous wastes are transported long distances prior to disposal, a comparison of the distribution of disposals, by counties (Figure 2), with arisings (Figure 1), shows that the majority are deposited close to their source. Because Special Wastes are closely documented, a mass-balance between arisings, imports, exports and disposal may be achieved (Table 4.1), which shows that in the late 1980s the United Kingdom was a net importer of Special Wastes.

Table 4.1   Special Wastes Arisings and Disposals in the United Kingdom, late 1980s (values in 1000 tonnes/year)

	Arisings	Imports	Exports	Disposals
England	1477	887	741	1623
Wales	83	32	72	43
Scotland	30	0	13	17
Northern Ireland	4.6	6.7	7.7	3.6
United Kingdom (rounded value)	**1595**	**926**	**834**	**1687**

Based on these proportions, it is estimated that a total of about 103 million tonnes/year of controlled wastes are deposited in landfills in the United Kingdom (Table 4.2). This figure is similar to the annual 90 million tonnes suggested for the whole United Kingdom in Waste Management Paper No 26 (Department of the Environment 1986) but only about 70% of the total suggested by Croft and Campbell (1990).

4.2 The distribution of licensed waste disposal facilities

Prior to the resurgence of interest in the early 1970s of the fate of wastes deposited in landfills, little information was available on the number or location of landfills in Britain. The report of the Key committee on solid toxic wastes (Department of the Environment 1970) recorded that in the late 1960s 1,186 landfills for the disposal of industrial wastes were registered. However, during the period 1971 to 1974 a survey of waste disposal sites was carried out, based on questionnaires sent to the then extant 1,332 local authorities in England and Wales. Approximately two thirds of the local authorities had responded by mid 1973 (Gray, Mather and Harrison 1974), recording a total of 2,494 disposal sites, of which 25 were considered to pose a serious risk to surface waters and 26 to threaten aquifers. The total number of sites considered to be posing threats to water resources was subsequently increased to 53 (Department of the Environment 1975).

The completed survey was not published, although the results remained available from the Department of the Environment. In 1990, the results were reported in the Observer (Lean and Ghazi 1990) and showed that the total number of sites surveyed in England and Wales in the early 1970s was 3,055, of which 1,241 were classified as posing potential risks to water supplies, and 59 as posing serious risks. The distribution of sites located before the end of the 1971/74 survey, for England and Wales, is shown in Figure 3. The 1971/74 survey did not include landfills in Scotland and Northern Ireland, but more recently (Department of the Environment 1988a) it has been

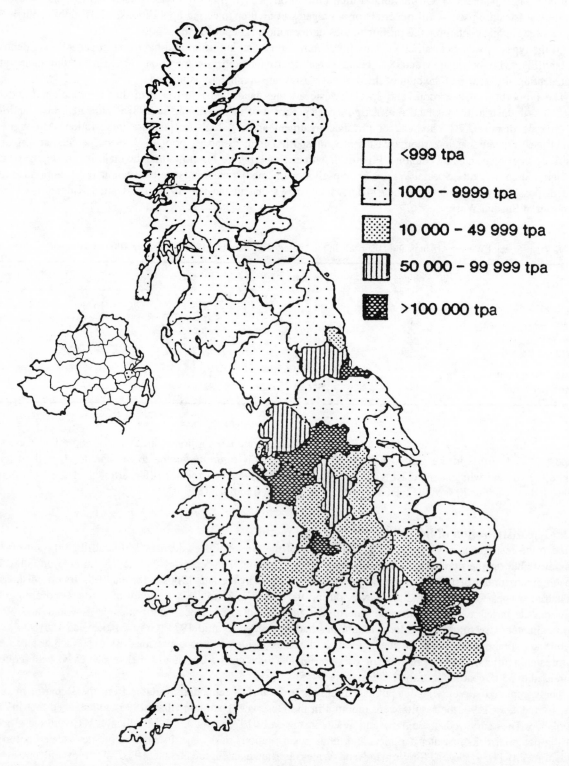

Figure 2 Special waste deposits 1986/7, by county in England and Wales, by region in Scotland and by district in Northern Ireland.

Table 4.2 Estimate of disposals to landfill in the United Kingdom (million tonnes/year)

Class of waste	Annual arisings weight	% to landfill	% incinerated	Weight direct landfill	Weight incinerator residues [1]	Total weight
Household and commercial	30	90	6	27	0.5	27.5
Non-hazardous industrial	76	90	6	68.5	1.0	69.5
Sewage sludge (dry soilds)	20	15	small	3.0	–	3.0
Hazardous and specials	4.0	83	2	3.3	0.02	3.32
Totals	**130**			**101.8**	**1.52**	**103.32**

Note [1] Assumes 20% of original weight as ashes

reported that about 500 landfills were located in Scotland during the late 1900s, of which 32% were public sector landfills and the remainder are private sector, with the majority being located in the Central Region (approximately coincident with the Central Valley of Scotland).

A further survey of waste disposal facilities in England and Wales was carried out during 1982/83 (Department of the Environment 1984). The survey returns were more complete than the previous study, and indicated a total of 5,094 disposal facilities, of which 4,008 were landfills. An overall increase in numbers of sites appears to be present, but it should be noted that some 36% of the sites recorded in 1984 were described as being for inert or construction wastes, and it is possible that many such disposal facilities were omitted from the returns on which the 1971–74 survey was based.

The 1982/83 survey of waste disposal facilities (Department of the Environment 1984) has led to the regular publication of summarised details of waste treatment and disposal facilities in England, Scotland and Wales, under the title Sitefile. The most recent version (Aspinwall and Co 1991) records 2,718 active landfills in England, 205 in Wales and 383 in Scotland. Within the limits of the data available, no significant change in the overall distribution of landfill sites appears to have occurred between the 1973/4 survey (Figure 3, also Gray, Mather and Harrison 1974) and the most recent compilation (Aspinwall and Co Ltd 1991).

Overall, the progressive decrease on the number of active sites is not unexpected and reflects the concentration of disposal facilities into fewer, but larger and better engineered and managed disposal sites, whilst the significant increase in the number of completed sites which the current survey seems to indicate is consistent with both the accelerated closure of small, inefficient sites, and the location and recording of previously forgotten disposal facilities.

A recent survey of 100 landfills receiving controlled wastes (Croft and Campbell 1990) suggested that they received annually about 13 million tonnes of waste, or between 10 and 20% of the total arisings. If it is indeed true that there are about 2,500 active landfills accepting controlled wastes, then it appears that less than 5% of the sites may account for up to 20% of waste disposals. There are 83 waste disposal authorities in England and Wales and a sample of 100 sites represents only slightly more than one per area. It would, therefore, seem possible that up to 50% of all disposal take place to a relatively small number of sites, perhaps less than 400, so that a high proportion of active sites are small, with annual waste inputs of less than 20,000 tonnes.

Comparison of the distribution of landfill sites with the extent of outcrop of the principal and regional aquifers (Figure 4) suggests that unless geotechnical engineering works are carried out to prevent the escape of leachate by percolation through permeable strata, between 30 and 40% of sites would be expected to threaten the quality of groundwaters. The total annual water abstraction for all purposes in England and Wales is about 9,350 million m³, of which 6,290 million m³ are for public water supply (Water Services Association 1989). Thirty-one per cent of the public supply in England and Wales is derived from groundwater sources, but in Scotland (Robins and Harrison 1986) and Northern Ireland (Commission of the European Communities 1982), the proportion of groundwater use is less than 5% of the total public supply.

In addition to the principal and regional aquifers shown in Figure 4, local aquifers yielding sufficient water for supplies for single houses or small groups of dwellings are present in many areas. Data on the amount and geographical distribution of small private supplies is poor. The majority of such supplies are groundwater derived, in the form of springs or wells. In has been estimated that less than 2% of the national domestic water supply comes from such sources (Department of the Environment 1984). However, the same survey suggested that up to 3.5% of

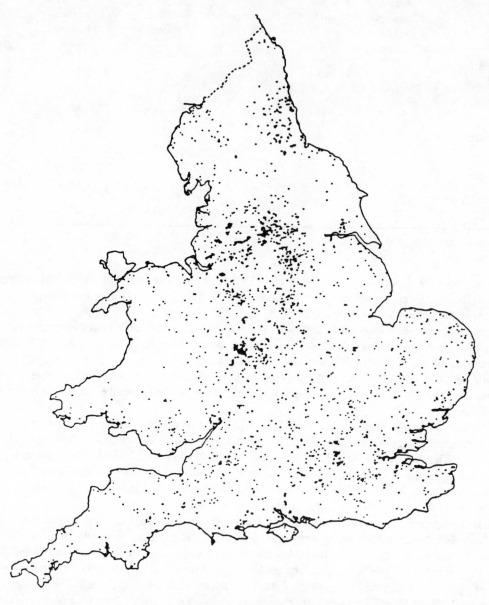

(after Gray, Mather and Harrison, 1974)

Figure 3   Distribution of active landfills in England and Wales 1971/3.

the population (2 million people) may consume such water during the course of a year. Private well supplies are predominantly based on shallow, often highly permeable aquifers (gravel and sand beds etc) which are poorly protected against surface derived pollution and concern has been expressed over their quality by the Department of the Environment (1984), who reported that in the early 1980s less than 20% by volume of private supplies met the standards laid down in the community directive on water for human consumption. The responsibilities of Environmental Health Officers with respect to such supplies have been strengthened by the 1989 Water Act and further data on the quality of such supplies may become available in the future.

The sources of groundwater used in the United Kingdom are summarised in Table 4.3.

4.3   Changes in landfill site management practices

Prior to the enactment of specific waste regulation and pollution control legislation in the early 1970s, regulation of waste disposal relied on elements of the Public Health Act 1936, the Water Act 1945 and the Planning Acts (Ministry of Housing and Local Government 1970). Municipal solid wastes were predominantly collected by district

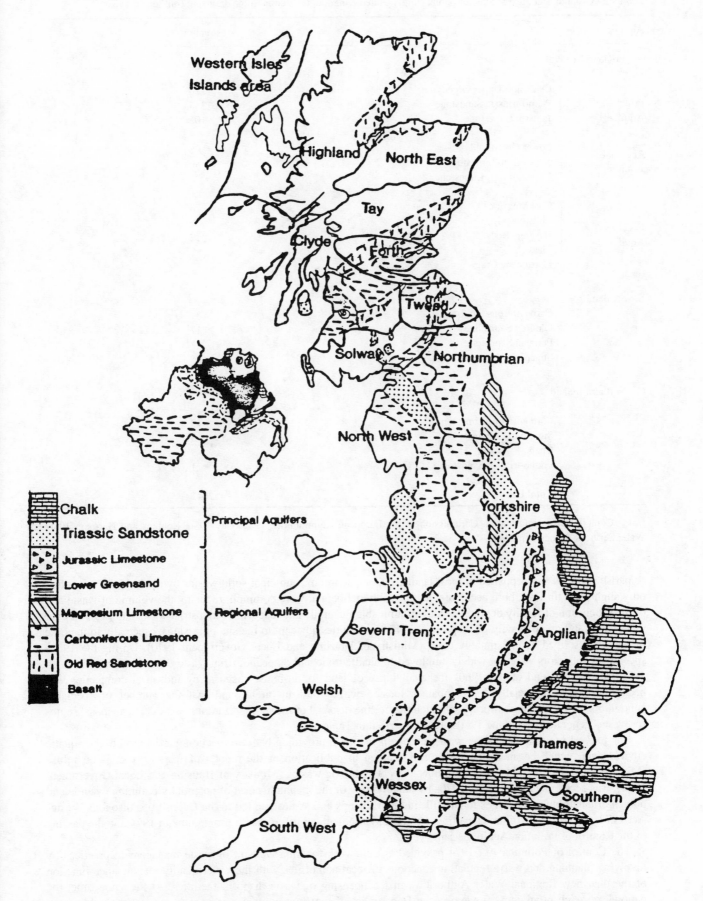

Figure 4   Outcrops of the principal aquifers, the National Rivers Authority regions in England and Wales, River Purification Authority regions in Scotland.

Table 4.3 Groundwater abstractions for public suppy, United Kingdom (excluding mine drainage) (millions m³/year)

Aquifer		Abstraction
A England and Wales		
Principal Aquifers	Chalk and Upper Greensand	1110
	Permo-triassic Sandstones	345
	Jurassic Limestone	105
Regional Aquifers	Lower Greensand	98
	Magnesium Limestone	80
	Carboniferous Limestone	78
Local Aquifers	Coal Measures	78
	Millstone Grit	19
	Hastings Beds	12
	Liassic	2
	Pleistocene Crag	13
B Scotland		
	Carboniferous Sandstones	31
	Old Red Sandstones	17
	Permian Sandstone	7
	Superficial Deposits	5
C Northern Ireland		
	Carboniferous Limestone	19
	Superficial Deposits	13
	Chalk	8
	Premo-triassic Sandstone	1
Total UK		**2041**

Note   Compiled from information Commission of the European Communities 1982. Day 1986, Robbins and Harrison 1986, Water Services Association, 1989.

or parish councils and deposited at local landfills. Compaction of municipal solid wastes by site vehicles was often only slight, and tip fires, both accidental and possibly deliberate, were common, reducing the volume of waste and of the proportion of readily degradable and inflammable material. The disposal of industrial waste had evolved over many years and relied heavily on disposal at in-house facilities adjacent to the site of arisings, especially in the case of wastes described as indisputably toxic (Ministry of Housing and Local Government 1970). During the 1960s specialist contractors were not widely employed to handle toxic and other industrial wastes, but it was noted (op cit 1970) that by the end of the 1960s the availability of land for in-house disposal by industrial companies was becoming scarce, especially for companies located within built-up areas, and that the number of specialist contractors was increasing, offering safe facilities for the disposal of the more hazardous wastes. The disposal routes for wastes generated during the 1960s are summarised in Table 4.4.

The interest in promoting better waste management and in providing better protection, particularly to the aquatic environment, which began in the 1960s and resulted in publication of the reports of working parties on refuse (Ministry of Housing and Local Government 1971) and toxic wastes (Ministry of Housing and Local Government 1970), was accelerated in the early 1970s by the reporting of the illegal disposal of potentially polluting cyanide and polychlorinated biphenyl wastes to landfills in the Midlands and Wales and led to the Deposit of Poisonous Wastes Act 1972, the setting up of the Department of the Environment landfill research programme in 1974 and the passing of the Control of Pollution Act in the same year.

The Control of Pollution Act 1974 provided a framework for improvement of waste management practices by involving planning and waste regulating functions of local authorities with the water quality maintenance function of the then new Regional Water Authorities, in the licensing of waste disposal facilities. At the same time, the national research programme funded by the Department of the Environment was seen as a way of providing the technical input needed to ensure the publication of Waste Management Papers and other reports.

Table 4.4   Disposal of wastes to landfills, 1960s (as percentages)

Waste type	Local authority landfill	Specialist contractors landfill	In-house landfill
Municipal solid waste (domesic and commercial)	100	0	0
Non-hazardous industrial	11	22	67
Hazardous and special	4	28	68

An important criterion for assessing the potential threat to water supplies of landfills located by the 1971–75 survey (Gray, Mather and Harrison 1974) was the presence or absence of a low permeability natural lining which would prevent the escape of polluting leachate. The field and laboratory studies that formed an important element of the first phase of the national research programme (Department of the Environment 1978) were, in part, directed at reviewing the efficiency of natural processes in rocks and sediments in attenuating leachate pollution.

Evidence was brought forward to suggest that at suitably selected sites, known generally as 'dilute and disperse' sites, these processes were sufficient to prevent contamination of water resources by leachates. Nevertheless, the work of the late 1970s recognised that not all sites were suitable for such practices, especially those on highly fissured strata where rapid groundwater flows were anticipated. In such cases, conversion to semi-containment sites by laying a bed of engineered material, with high attenuating properties, was pursued as one option (Robinson and Lucas 1984, Robinson and Blackley 1987), whilst at other sites lining with effectively impermeable natural or synthetic membranes was advocated. Creation of sealed containment sites by lining would lead to the accumulation of leachate within the wastes, giving rise to a need to collect and treat the leachate prior to final disposal (Robinson and Maris 1979, Robinson and Davies 1985, Robinson 1987).

Recognition of the importance of controlling liquid inputs to landfills, and hence the rate of leachate production (Blakey and Craft 1986), encouraged the widespread adoption of cellular filling of waste sites, and by the mid 1980s the technical and scientific basis of landfill waste management had progressed to such an extent that a major technical memorandum for waste disposal operators was published as Waste Management Paper No 26 (Department of the Environment 1986).

The potential problems associated with the generation and migration of potentially dangerous and explosive concentrations of landfill gas, a mixture of methane and carbon dioxide, were recognised in Waste Management Paper No 26. The increasing size of landfills and the increased proportion of putrescible wastes was seen as enlarging the threat. Shortly after publication of WMP 26 an explosion due to landfill gas damaged a bungalow at Loscoe in Derbyshire (Williams and Aitkenhead 1989). A subsequent survey mounted by Her Majesty's Inspectorate of Pollution suggested that landfill gas poses a problem at a significant number of landfills. As a result, Waste Management Paper No 27, on landfill gas, was published (Her Majesty's Inspectorate of Pollution 1989) in which stringent procedures, including site lining, were recommended to minimise gas migration. A revised update of Waste Management Paper No 27 was published in November 1991. At the same time, codes of practice covering many aspects of wastes and landfill management have been prepared by the professional body of the private sector waste disposal companies (National Association of Waste Disposal Contractors 1989) and on the geotechnical engineering aspects of landfill design and construction by the National Rivers Authority (1989).

As a result, effectively all landfill proposals, with the possible exception of sites for inert wastes only, now require lining with natural or synthetic material, leachate collection and disposal and landfill gas monitoring and control. In the past the available evidence suggests that between 30 and 45% of all sites were designed and operated on the dilute and disperse principle. Although there have been no recorded incidents of public supply boreholes being taken out of use due to landfill leachate in the United Kingdom (Parsons 1990), it appears that a combination of the requirements for landfill gas control, and anticipated conditions that may be incorporated in a proposed EC Directive on the landfilling of wastes (see Section 2.3), mean that only a very small proportion, if any, of new landfills in Britain will be licensed as dilute and disperse sites in the future.

Although the latest revision of the draft proposal for a Directive on the landfilling of wastes does not exclude the codisposal of hazardous industrial wastes with other waste (see Section 2.3), it remains true that the United Kingdom is the only member of the European Community that actively supports this disposal route. General guidelines for the codisposal of wastes were incorporated in Waste Management Paper No 26 (Department of the Environment 1986) and suggestions for enhancing them have been made more recently by Knox (1990).

5 Alternative disposal options

5.1 Introduction

Approximately 10% of solid controlled wastes in England and Wales are not deposited directly to landfills. The exception to the rule is sewage sludge, of which between 80 and 85% is committed to disposal routes other than landfill (Table 5.1).

In practice, disposal by incineration, solidification, other forms of chemical treatment and the separation of usable and reusable components recycling schemes produces material and residues which may be landfilled as a final disposal option. Of the options shown in Table 5.1, only disposal to sea may not possess some element of final landfilling.

Table 5.1   Fate of annual controlled waste arisings in England and Wales (millions of tonnes)

Description of wastes	Incineration	Chemical treatment	Solidification	Recycle/ reclamation/ recovery	Disposal to sea	Landfill	Total arisings
Domestic and commercial	1.7	–	–	2.9[1]	–	25.2	28
Non-hazardous industrial	2.8	–	–		–	41.4	46
Sewage sludge (wet weight)	1.2	–	–	12.5[2]	6.0	4.3	24
Special and hazardous	0.1	0.2	0.1	0.3[3]	0.2	3.1	4.0

Notes

[1] Additional between 9 and 10 million tonnes of metals are recovered commercially via scrap yards

[2] Spread on farmland

[3] Principally solvents and oils

5.2 Disposal to sea

Disposal to sea was until recently the second most used route for disposal of hazardous waste (c 8% of total arisings) and sewage sludge (c 25% of arisings). However, the Second International North Sea Conference, London, in November 1987 recommended that disposal of potentially polluting materials to the North Sea should be stopped at the earliest possible date. As a result, the direct disposal of industrial waste by this route has declined and the disposal of sewage sludge will be progressively phased out over the next decade. The additional load of hazardous wastes which requires redirection is moderate, but the increase in sewage sludge volumes that will require land based treatment and disposal is significant and is likely to lead to increased demands for landfill space and incineration capacity.

5.3 Composting

Past experiences of composting materials such as screened municipal solid waste or sewage sludge and straw have not been commercially successful and at the present only an insignificant volume of waste is treated by this method. However, pilot schemes, using fine screenings from the Byker waste sorting facility are again producing compost and a commercial operation is being started in Birmingham, with a target production of between 40,000 and 50,000 tonnes of compost per year (Johnson 1990).

5.4 Treatment and solidification

Simple treatments of municipal solid wastes such as pulverisation (shredding) and baling may be used to encourage ease of handling and compaction of the materials prior to landfilling. In the case of hazardous wastes, chemical or physical treatment may be given prior to final disposal by neutralisation of acidic or alkaline materials, dewatering or phase separation of immiscible or poorly soluble liquid wastes, and by oxidation or reduction reactions. The available capacity for chemical treatment to the UK has been estimated to be about 600,000 tonnes per year, of which perhaps less than half is utilised.

Solidification or stabilisation processes, principally dependent on pozzolanic reactions based on the addition of portland cement, sodium silicate, lime and similar materials to sludges or slurries of hazardous wastes has been practised for many years.

Mixing and reaction of the wastes and additives normally takes place at the point of disposal, with the slurry being pumped into excavations and allowed to set. The early investigations of sites containing solidified waste (Department of the Environment 1978) suggested that the processes acted to effectively immobilise metallic ions. The national capacity for solidification is believed to be about 350,000 tonnes per year, of which less than half is used. However, recent investigations (ENDS 1989) have suggested that certain of these processes may not adequately retain organic compounds within the solidification matrix, and that the solidified materials may not be of sufficient mechanical strength and of higher permeability than previously understood.

5.5 Incineration

In 1989, some 37 municipal waste incinerators, four of which are equipped with energy recovery facilities, were operating in the UK, and treating an estimated 4.5 million tonnes per year of wastes (Table 5.1) (Holmes 1989). None of the plants was fitted with acid emission control devices (scrubbers). Control of the incineration process is essential in order to prevent the formation of dioxins in the exhaust gases, but the age of some of the plant may lead to difficulties (see Table 5.2).

Table 5.2   Characteristics of incineration plants

Type	Operating temperature °C	Critical operational control	Problems
Municipal, for domestic, commercial and non-hazardous wastes	800–1100	Exhaust emissions must be cooled rapidly to 300 °C	Rapid cooling essential, dioxins may form at 400 to 600 °C
High temperature, for hazardous wastes, including clinical wastes	>1200	i requires excess oxygen ii residence time of gas in burner important iii combustion temperature iv good mixing of gases in burner (turbulence)	Quality of emissions difficult to maintain if operating conditions depart from optimal

High temperature incineration of hazardous and special wastes lies entirely within the private sector. At the present time there are four merchant incinerators in operation, capable of handling up to 100,000 tonnes per year of waste, including liquids and sludges. The high temperatures at which these incinerators operate are necessary in order to destroy many potentially hazardous compounds, but depend critically on maintaining the correct conditions within the furnace (Table 5.2).

The prospect of closure of the sea disposal route to sewage sludge, and the possible limitations of the additional volumes of sludge that would be acceptable to either farmland or landfill has rekindled interest in sludge incineration amongst Water Utilities and a number of new facilities are being constructed, with emission control equipment that satisfies current and probable future European Community emission control standards. The ashes that result from incineration of the sludge represent less than 20% of the dry bulk of the sludge and, with suitable handling and transport, are likely to be more acceptable to landfill than the raw sludge. As an alternative, methods for conversion of the ashes to a stable, lightweight material suitable for concrete aggregate, by sintering at high temperatures (1400–1600 °C) have been developed (Bhatty and Reid 1989, Robbins 1990) and may find application in the United Kingdom.

5.6 Recycling, reclamation and recovery

A significant reduction both on the volumes of waste requiring disposal to landfill and in the need to consume raw materials may accompany an increase in the proportion of wastes that are reclaimed or recycled, and it has become the UK target that 50% of the recoverable portion of municipal solid wastes should be recycled by the year 2000 (Newell 1990). The proportion of recycled material used by certain industries is already quite high (Table 5.3), but for certain waste, for example paper, glass and plastics the extent to which a higher proportion of waste may be separated and recycled is dependent on economic factors (Bell 1990, Newell 1990). As an example, the cost of cleaning 1 tonne of waste polythene (used sacks), shredding and preparing for reuse by injection moulding on modern equipment is between £150 and £200. Therefore, unless the product made from the recycled material can be sold for well in excess of £200 per tonne the process becomes unviable.

The recovery and reuse of certain liquid wastes, particularly solvents and oils, is an established industry. A recent survey (Department of the Environment 1988a) of 23 solvent recovery companies has estimated that the annual recovery is about 112,000 tonnes, made up of the types and quantities of solvents shown in Table 5.4.

Table 5.3 Recycled scrap materials as a percentage of total consumption

Material	1976	1979	1983	1986	1988
Paper	29	29	26	27	26
Glass	25	nd	9	13	16
Aluminium	28	25	20	15	13
Copper	39	31	40	42	45
Lead	66	74	65	65	70
Tin	13	23	70	60	60
Zinc	22	23	23	23	21
Ferrous metals	67	nd	59	50	44

Disposal of the residues that arise from recovery of the solvents may take several routes. Oily residues may be blended with other waste oils, or non-recoverable solvent streams and burnt as boiler fuel. Flammable residues which are unsuitable for boiler fuel, but which remain liquid at normal temperatures, are typically sent for incineration, together with any sludges or solids that cannot be landfilled. Residues which are solid at normal temperatures may be

Table 5.4 Annual recovery of solvent (1986/7)

Group	Typical compounds	Quantity (tonne)
Chlorinated	Methylene dichloride Ethylene dichloride Trichloroethylene 1,1,1-trichloroethane Perchloroethylene Chloroform Freons Chlorobenzene	14 000
Non-chlorinated, mixed	Petrol distillate low flash-point fuels	11 000
Single solvents	Alcohols Ketones Esters Hydrocarbons etc	63 000
Thinners	Alcohols Ketones Esters Hydrocarbons	24 000
Total		**112 000**

poured into drums and allowed to solidify prior to landfilling. Steam distillation of the wastes tends to produce a very wet residue, unsuitable for direct burning, and this material is normally removed to landfill by tanker.

The recovery of waste oils is carried out by about 130 companies (Department of the Environment 1988a) with an annual reuse or recovery of approximately 300,000 tonnes. The oil treated is collected from many sources, both commercial (eg motor trade garages, transport companies) industrial (cutting oils, lubricating oils) and via civic amenity sites, and includes transformer oils which may contain PCBs. The oil is processed to provide predominantly light fuel oil, although a small proportion is produced as heavy fuel oil. The fuel oil is used mainly for stone drying at quarries and in asphalt coating plants, with minor usage in metal smelters.

Because the fuels may include oils derived from many sources, including oils which have become accidentally or deliberately contaminated with solvents, the composition is variable. In particular the chlorine and PCB content may be elevated, as may also lead and vanadium. Closer quality control during final production from waste oils will be necessary to ensure compliance with air emission standards. About 10% of the oils recovered are industrial oils (rolling and drawing oils, hydraulic oil) which are reprocessed to a level where they may be used again for their original purposes.

The residues from oil recovery includes materials such as acid tars, for which specific disposal routes are recommended in the appropriate Waste Management Papers.

5.7 Recovery of energy from wastes

The energy content of wastes may be recovered by three principal methods:

—   incineration

—   production of waste derived fuel (wdf)

—   combustion of landfill gas.

The incineration of solid wastes has been considered in Section 5.5 and the production and use of fuels from waste oils and solvents in Section 5.6. However, it is noted that only 10% of the municipal incinerators in Britain (Nottingham, Coventry, Sheffield and Edmonton) have energy recovery systems, whereas in Europe over 80% of municipal incineration plants are so equipped. The Edmonton plant produces about £10 of energy per tonne of waste incinerated against an estimated nett disposal cost of £12 per tonne.

It is reported by Holmes (1989) that at least 10 waste derived fuel plants have been built in Britain since the early 1970s. Pilot schemes set up in the early 1980s at Byker, Eastbourne and Doncaster were not entirely successful, because the fuel pellets were made from waste that had been pulverised prior to sorting and pelletisation, as a result of which contamination by undesirable materials was common, leading to corrosion and encrustation in certain types of boilers (Johnson 1990). Recent developments in sorting wastes have overcome some of the problems of cross-contamination and pellets of a consistent composition and with a heating value about two thirds that of coal (18.5 megajoules per kg cf 28 megajoules per kg) may be produced. The most recent wdf plant completed is on the Isle of Wight, and is capable of producing 15,000 tonnes per year of high grade fuel pellets at about £30 per tonne. The market value of the pellets is probably not more than £5 per tonne, and the Council of the Isle of Wight is considering using the pellets for fueling an on-site power generator project. A further problem which has beset the Isle of Wight plant during late 1990 has been the accusation that aerial emissions from the wdf process have exceeded EC standards. More generally, the tightening of European Commission emission standards, due to become effective in 1996 (Johnson 1990), may require that all burners using wdf fit flue gas scrubbers and filters to control emissions of hydrogen chloride and heavy metals. Such increases in cost may make wdf even less economically attractive.

The extraction and utilisation of landfill gas has been pursued to a limited extent in Britain for at least the last 10 years, starting with studies of the use of the gas in brick kilns at the London Brick Company's site at Stewartby, in Bedfordshire. A recent review of the situation (Richards 1988) has shown that in late 1988 there were some 24 active gas utilisation schemes, with a further 8 being constructed and 18 at advanced planning stages, representing energy savings in the range £8M to £16M per year. Although apparently modest, the number of schemes to exploit landfill gas as a renewable energy source in the United Kingdom is greater than other European countries, and is exceeded only by the United States.

Within Britain nearly half the gas extracted is burned in motors linked to electricity generating plant, the largest of which is probably the gas turbine powered generator at Packington, near Birmingham, which produces up to 3.5MW of exportable power (Biddle 1988). Approximately one third of the gas is employed in kilns, with the remainder acting as a boiler fuel.

At the present time, all landfill gas utilisation is based on direct extraction from the landfills, followed by appropriate pretreatment before use. However, landfills represent relatively uncontrolled anaerobic biological reactors, which may lead to undesirable fluctuations in gas production rates and gas composition. As a result, interest is being taken in both digestion of leachate which has been pumped from the landfills (Young, Mosey and Maris 1988, Blakey and Maris 1990) and the digestion in the solid state of the putrescible fraction of Municipal Solid Wastes, following sorting and reclamation (Coombs and Alston 1988).

Control of landfill gas migration is a requisite of landfill management (Waste Management Paper No 27, Her Majesty's Inspectorate of Pollution 1989; 1991). At the same time estimates that direct emissions of landfill gas may account for 20% of the UK methane load (Reeds 1990) suggest that gas flaring, linked, where economically viable, to energy recovery systems, is likely to increase at landfill sites.

6 The effects of landfilling on water quality

6.1 Records of contamination due to landfilling

Information about cases where actual water pollution had occurred as a result of toxic wastes (and related products) landfilling was obtained from local, water supply and river authorities and reported by the Technical Committee on Solid Toxic Waste Disposal (Ministry of Housing and Local Government 1970). The following points were observed:

– there had been no significant pollution of groundwater used for public supply

– stream pollution was more common than groundwater pollution

– small shallow groundwater sources were more susceptible to contamination than deeper sources.

Seventeen named sites were cited to demonstrate the range of pollution instances encountered. These included ten cases of surface water pollution (eg from pesticides, cyanide, sludges from tar distillation and other processes, oily, acid or alkali wastes) contamination of shallow wells, private supplies or investigation boreholes (eg with phenolic or chrome wastes) and actual or potential pollution of public supply boreholes by iron, phenols (2 cases) and unspecified, drummed wastes.

During the 1970s a number of conferences addressing groundwater contamination and the protection of groundwater resources were held. At the WRA Conference, Reading held in 1972, methods for preventing groundwater contamination by correct landfill design were discussed, with tracer techniques for defining potential flowpaths (Cole 1974). However, no instances of actual contamination from waste disposal sites in England and Wales were presented. Similarly, at the 1976 Water Research Centre conference and the 1977 International Association of Hydrogeologists Conference at Birmingham, North American and European experiences were discussed but no UK case studies were presented (WRc 1976, IAH 1977), although WRc techniques for identifying groundwater pollution at landfill sites were presented (Barber, Naylor and Maris 1976).

However, during the mid-1970s detailed investigations were being carried out at twenty sites receiving hazardous wastes, as part of the Department of the Environment's research programme. The results published in the 'Brown Book' (Department of the Environment 1978) are summarised in Table 6.1. The data compiled for the DoE report demonstrated that hazardous waste disposal did not necessarily cause deterioration in surface or groundwater quality.

– No surface water quality deterioration. Where groundwater quality was not investigated, surface water concentrations of potential contaminants were not enhanced above background levels at Leoch, Maendy and Shaw (Site number 12, 13 and 16 (see Table 6.1).

– Containment sites. Thick natural clays at Hooton, Mitco and Tanfield Lea (Sites 9, 14, 17) provided a barrier against groundwater pollution, and where minor seepages did occur, a surface for effective attenuation processes (adsorption, ion exchange etc).

– Contamination restricted to within 50 metres of site perimeter. This was observed at Haigh Quarry (7) and Eastfield Quarry (3) although at the latter the potential problems of a migrating unattenuated oil phase into the sandstone was recognised. At Ewelme (4) local contamination was restricted to a zone of increased bicarbonate concentrations, known as a 'hardness halo' around the site (Mather and Parker 1978) and at Tythgeston (18) and Wildmoor (20), only enhanced chloride levels were observed immediately beyond the site perimeter. Other sites where contamination was observed up to 30 m from the site were Brofiskin (1) where TOC, phenols and barium were enhanced at depths greater than 61.5 m, Rainham (15) where groundwater contained up to 1% leachate, and Flitwick (5) where cutting oil disposal had raised TOC and phenol levels to 570 mg/l and 43 mg/l respectively, downgradient of the site. At Ingham (10) trace halogenated solvent and copper contamination was recorded, although phenols, oils and heavy metals appeared to be successfully attenuated before reaching the saturated zone.

Table 6.1 Summary of 20 detailed invesigations carried out for DoE Hazardous Waste Research Programme (DoE 1978)

Site No	Site	Geology	Groundwater flow	Waste types	Groundwater contaminants	Extent of pollution
1	Brofiskin, Mid Glamorgan	Carboniferous limestone	Fissure	Petrochemical wastes PCBs, solvents, metal-bearing wastes etc. plus non-notifiable industrial solid waste	TOC, phenols, organic N, Ba, Mn	Greatest >61.5 m below ground level, <30 m from site
2	Coatham Stob	Dolerite dyke in Sandstone	Dyke-fissure sandstone - intergranular plus minor fissures	Chromite-ore processing wastes, liquid sodium thiosulphate wastes etc	Cr V Na	Cr to 250 m from site. Dispersion and dilution main attenuation processes plus Cr(VI) – Cr (III) reduction and adsorption/ precipitation
3	Eastfield Quarry, Midland Valley, Scotland	Coal measures sandstone	Intergranular and fissures and by mine workings	Industrial solid wastes plus liquid wastes. Lagoon oil phase = aliphatic hydrocarbons, creosote, white spirit	PCBs, oil, metal cations	Minor migration of relatively unattenuated discrete oil phase into sandstone a potential problem
4	Ewelme, Oxon	Gravels Clay Horizons, Chalk Marl	Complex	Phospate and paint sludges, solvents etc	SO_4, Na, K, TOC, Cl, NO_3–Ca Mg	Hardness 'halo' around site, no evidence of organic contamination
5	Flitwick, Beds	Greensand	Intergranular	'Soluble' cutting oils, metal finishing wastes etc plus solid wastes – metal turnings, abrasives etc.	TOC, Na phenols	TOC to 570 mg/l + phenols to 43 mg/l downgradient of site
6	Green Oakhill Sand Quarry, Nr Glasgow	Superficial Sands	Intergranular	Industrial and domestic solid plus treatment sludges, acid and alkali wastes, oils and oily sludges etc.	TOC, phenols, Do, Cl, SO_4, NH_4, Na, K	Minor plume downgradient of site
7	Haigh Quarry	Middle Coal Measures, Sandstones and Shales	Fissure	Metal treatment, tannery and woolcombing wastes	Potentially – Cl. Cu, phenol, Zn, Cr, thiocyanate	Very minor attenuation of phenols by evaporation biodegradation etc. Cr and other metals low.

Table 6.1 continued

Site No	Site	Geology	Groundwater flow	Waste types	Groundwater contaminants	Extent of pollution
8	Hammerwich, Staffs	Sandpit in Bunter sandstone	Intergranular	50 tonnes drummed cyanide and barium heat-treatment process waste below incinerator ash, domestic refuse and rubble	Cyanide, phenols, Fe, Mn, Cd	Initially highly contaminated, major attenuation of all contaminants except thiocyanate after 1975
9	Hooton, Cheshire	Boulder clay overlying triassic sandstone	Containment site – very minor intergranular flow in sandstone lenses to trias	Oils, dyes, waxes, resins, general solid industrial waste plus elemental mercury	TOC, SO_4, Cl	No groundwater contamination
10	Ingham, Suffolk	Chalk	Fissure	Oils, sludges, liquid industrial waste and general solid industrial waste	TOC, phenols, Cl, carboxylic acids	Trace halogenated solvents and copper contamination. No phenol, oils or heavy metal contamination
11	Kingskettle Gas Works, Fife	Boulder Clay and sands and gravels. Upper Old Red Sandstone	Sandy gravels and ORS intergranular	Coal gas treatment oxide wastes (Fe, sulphide and cyanide bearing)	phenols, cyanide	Phenol detected 400 m from site
12	Leoch Quarries, Nr Dundee	Lower Old Red Sanstone Freestone cut by olivine basalt dyke	Surface water studied	Domestic and commercial plus mercuric chloride waste	–	Surface water concentrations not enhanced above background levels
13	Maendy, South Glamorgan	Carboniferous Sandstone	Fissures	Petrochemical and distillation residues, phenols, PCBs, solvents, metal wastes and industrial solid wastes	Springwaters – TOC, Zn, PCBs	None. Indicators not above background levels
14	Mitco, West Midlands	Eiruria Marl (Coal measures)	Effectively non-marl impermeable	Sewage sludge, domestic waste plus industrial liquid lagoon	Potentially phenols plus Zn, Ni, Cu, Cr	Rapid attenuation of contaminants, only minor seepage out of clay
15	Rainham, Essex	Alluvial clay over gravels over tertiary sands over upper chalk	Gravels, sand and chalk probably in hydraulic continuity	Solid pharmaceutical waste, metal slag, incinerator ash etc and oil, paint, solvents, gas liquour, tar etc	Potentially heavy metals, PCBs and chlorinated solvents, cyanide, phenols	Up to 1% leachate contamination at some boreholes beyond site

Table 6.1 continued

Site No	Site	Geology	Groundwater flow	Waste types	Groundwater contaminants	Extent of pollution
16	Shaw, Greater Manchester	Peat, glacial sands over lower coal measures sandstones and shales	Surface water studied	Domestic plus broken fluorescent tubes and glass waste. 90–180 kgg Hg (elemental)	Potentially Hg in surface Water	No surface water contamination by mercury
17	Tanfield Lea, Co Durham	24.5 m alluvial clays and silts over 7.5m boulder clay over middle coal measures	Waste in brick pit in alluvial clays unlikely to be in hydraulic continuity with coal measures groundwater	Battery cells (mercury, zinc ammonium, manganese compounds) and colliery spoil	Zn, Mn, NH_3, Cl	Perched water in waste
18	Tythgeston, mid Glamorgan	Carboniferous limestone	Fissure	Domestic waste, 2 million tyres, and drums of solvents, resins and chemical residues, oils, sludges and organic sulphides (many drums removed on discovery) extensive tyre fire 1972	Potentially TOC, carboxylic acids, phenols Ni and Zn, Cl	Cl only indicator of leachate contamination of groundwater beyond site perimeter
19	Villa Farm, West Midlands	4 m Boulder clay above Wolston Sand above 44 m further interbedded glacial sands above Keuper Marl	Wolston Sand principal local groundwater source lagoons in hydraulic continuity with the formulation	Oil-separation lagoons receive cutting oils, metallic sludges metal finishing wastes, waste acids and solvents	TOC, phenol, Na, Cl, SO_4	High degree of contamination of Wolston Sand groundwater up to c 100 m from lagoons
20	Wildmoor, West Midlands	Bunter pebble beds (glacial sands and gravels removed)	Intergranular and fissure (recharge mound below landfill?)	Solid industrial and oil wastes, liquid sludges, acid and alkali wastes etc	Cl, Zn, TOC	Cl only indicator of leachate contamination beyond perimeter of site also partially due to contamination from nearby domestic landfil

– Contaminated at greater distances from site. Kingskettle gas works (11) contaminated groundwater 400 m from the site. It was thought that the nearby public supply borehole could be in jeopardy if the abstraction regime was altered. Initial severe contamination of groundwater by cyanide, phenols and heavy metals was observed at Hammerwich (8); however, the levels diminished considerably after 1975 to leave thiocyanate as the sole detectable pollutant.

– Acute groundwater contamination. Coatham Stob (2), a quarry within a fissured dolerite dyke, was used for the disposal of chromite ore processing wastes and liquid sodium thiosulphate containing wastes. Groundwater up to 250 m from the site was contaminated with vanadium, sodium and hexavalent chromium, the only attenuation mechanism for chromium apparently being dispersion and dilution (Barber, Young, Blakey, Ross and Williams 1981).

At Villa Farm (19), liquid organic wastes (cutting oils, metallic sludges and metal finishing wastes) were shown to be in direct hydraulic continuity with the Wolston Sands, a local source of groundwater, resulting in contamination by phenolic compounds, TOC etc over one hundred metres from the lagoons.

The policy review committee recognised that groundwater contamination was present at the site which had been examined, but concluded that pollution plumes around the landfills were often restricted in extent, and that the attenuation mechanisms within the waste and unsaturated zone (including dilution) were beneficial, and that 'sensible landfill is realistic' (Department of the Environment 1978).

However, confidence in the unsaturated zone to attenuate organic components in leachates was not universal. Results of investigations at two 'dilute and disperse' sites in the Triassic Sandstone, Nottinghamshire, were reported by Harris and Parry (1982). The groundwater levels at the Gorsethorpe and Burntstump landfills were 6 and 47 m below the sites respectively, and data indicated that leachate was migrating through the unsaturated zone at rates of 1 to 2 m per year with little or no attenuation of the major contaminants (TOC, ammonia, sulphate and chloride). The presence of a 1-m colliery shale cap at Gorsethorpe appeared to make no difference. Later work (Harris and Lowe 1984, Blakey and Towler 1988) indicated that the lack of buffering capacity of the sandstone against the low pH of the organic leachates and the disappearance of microbial colonies in the aggressive leachate front led to only restricted biodegradation of organic compounds in the unsaturated zone.

The public profile of the impact of waste disposal on water quality was raised by the publication of a joint Friends of the Earth (FOE) and Observer investigation (Lean and Ghazi 1990). However many of the criticisms were answered by Parsons (1990) who drew attention to the Halcrow report (DoE 1988) also cited by FOE, that 'there are few examples of sources actually being lost through landfill pollution problems'. Parsons also reported that 'according to DoE, to date, no groundwater source has ever been lost through landfill contamination'.

Until the mid 1980s literature on landfill monitoring was often biased towards leachate quality and quantity and the prevention of groundwater contamination. In March 1986 a house at Loscoe, Derbyshire, was completely destroyed by a methane gas explosion, badly injuring the three occupants. Evidence given at the Public Inquiry demonstrated that the explosion was due to the migration of landfill gas from a nearby brick pit (Williams and Aitkenhead 1989).

Following the Inquiry, Her Majesty's Inspectorate of Pollution (HMIP) issued a letter (1987) requiring waste disposal authorities to identify potentially gassing landfills. This was followed in 1989 by the publication of Waste Management Paper No 27, The Control of Landfill Gas, with an updated version being issued in November 1991.

6.2 Monitoring landfill sites

Early guidance on landfill site investigations including techniques for monitoring solid, gaseous and liquid samples in the landfill, unsaturated and saturated zones, was provided by Naylor, Rowland, Young and Barber (1989). Points considered includes:

– the need for base line surveys against which monitoring data can be compared;

– the need for representative samples collected using the correct borehole construction, sampling and sample storage techniques;

– groundwater level measurements;

– monitoring frequency;

– appropriate determinands (eg chloride, a good conservative 'marker' species).

Much of the information was repeated in Department of the Environment (1978), with greater emphasis on sampling techniques for specific determinands, and the monitoring frequencies employed during the DoE research programme. Waste Management Papers 26 and 27 (Department of the Environment 1986, Her Majesty's Inspectorate of Pollution 1989) also addressed leachate and landfill gas monitoring techniques and requirements.

Despite detailed advice published by consultants and government departments, it is clear that very little monitoring is in fact carried out. In 1988 Sir William Halcrow and Partners Limited reported that routine groundwater monitoring was primarily carried out on treated public supply water to confirm compliance with EC directives or was carried out for research purposes, eg by BGS and WRc, (Department of the Environment 1988b).

Croft and Campbell (1990) carried out a study of 100 UK landfills. Although there was a self-confessed bias towards the larger and better-management sites, only approximately 33% of sites undertook gas and/or groundwater monitoring and a further 10% of sites were known to have either gas or leachate problems that were left unresolved.

However, the proposed EC Landfill Directive specifies that 'a landfill must meet the necessary conditions, naturally or artificially achieved, to prevent pollution of the soil or groundwater', 'appropriate measures shall be taken in order to control the accumulation and migration of landfill gas' and that leachate, gas and groundwater quality monitoring must be undertaken at specific intervals.

6.3 Summary

Since the 1970s landfill gas, leachate and groundwater quality monitoring has been undertaken by research organisations and consultancies, primarily for the DoE. There has been no obligation on individual contractors to undertake any monitoring unless specified in the waste disposal license. Where monitoring has been carried out very few cases of severe groundwater contamination have been recorded and frequently such information has been largely ignored.

Monitoring is expensive in terms of man power and analytical costs, but the costs of remedial work to prevent further contamination far exceed those of monitoring.

When the EC Landfill Directive is implemented it is probable that there will be a legal obligation not only to take measures to control gas and leachate migration, but to monitor gas, leachate and groundwater at regular intervals.

7 Overview

7.1 The current situation

The data on the current and past wastes arisings, disposal routes and impacts on environmental quality have been found to be incomplete, so that confident interpretation and subsequent prediction is not always possible. However, the evidence that has been examined points to a number of tentative conclusions which may be used to suggest future scenarios and to identify information and research requirements.

On the available evidence, the annual volume of municipal solid waste arisings does not appear to have changed significantly since the enactment of the Control of Pollution Act in 1974, but an increase in the plastics content of the wastes from 2% to about 7% has occurred over the same time. Arisings of hazardous and special wastes account for less than 5% of all waste arisings. In excess of 90% of household, commercial and non-hazardous industrial wastes, and over 80% of hazardous and special wastes are deposited in landfills, amounting to an estimated 60 or 70 million tonnes per year.

The number of landfills in England and Wales appears to have decreased from about 4,200 in the early 1970s, to an estimated 3,800 in 1990, with between 300 and 400 landfills in Scotland. The landfill surveys of the 1970s (Gray *et al* 1974) and the 1980s (Department of the Environment 1984) did not record the size of the sites, nor their anticipated operational lives. The 1980 survey recorded only about 200 sites as being closed or completed, whilst Lean and Ghazi (1990) suggested that 1,630 sites in England and Wales had closed between 1974 and 1990. The rate of licensing of new landfills was relatively steady at between 500 and 600 per year between 1977/8 and 1986/7 (Department of the Environment 1989a). In view of the relative stability of numbers of landfills it is suggested that the annual rates of licensing new sites and completion and closure of exhausted sites are approximately balanced, and it is noted that the estimate of 8,000 recorded closed sites would be consistent with a closure rate of 500 per year over the time since the Control of Pollution Act. In reality, there are probably many more than 8,000 completed sites in the country, but prior to the Control of Pollution Act complete recording of landfills via a licensing system did not take place and evidence of previous disposal sites may not exist.

A detailed study of 100 landfills receiving controlled wastes in the late 1980s (Croft and Campbell 1990) has shown that although the sites examined represented less than 3% of the total stock of licensed landfills, they received about 20% of all controlled waste disposals to landfills. The operation lives of the sites examined was typically between 10 and 20 years. The dominance of the waste management scene by a small percentage of the licensed sites suggests that a large number of the other sites are small with possibly short operational lives.

The leachates produced by wastes in landfills may threaten both surface waters and groundwaters. Approximately one third of the surface of England and Wales is underlain by outcropping aquifer materials, and landfills located in these areas could affect groundwater quality. An early cataloguing of pollution incidents attributable to waste disposal (Ministry of Housing and Local Government 1970) recorded 17 examples of which 29% related to groundwaters. The more complete survey carried out by the British Geological Survey in the early 1970s (Gray *et al* 1974) considered the hydrogeological characteristics of the sites to be of high importance when assessing the risk of environmental damage and it is suggested that between 30 and 50% of landfills recorded in that survey were on or adjacent to aquifers.

Although the number of sites sampled represented only a small proportion of the total number, the recent survey by Croft and Campbell (1990) showed that 45% of the sites were located in areas with high permeability strata. In the survey, only 15% of the sites located on aquifers were reported to have been fully lined to prevent leachate escape. In the past, it would be expected that an even smaller proportion of sites would have been lined. It is frequently asserted that inadequately contained sites may threaten groundwater quality (Department of the Environment 1988b) and it is therefore, perhaps, surprising that there is no recorded example in Britain of a public groundwater supply having been lost through contamination by landfill leachate. The past lack of requirements for private well supplies to be subject to routine quality monitoring (Department of the Environment 1984) may explain the lack of information regarding pollution of such sources.

The apparent lack of recorded incidents may be, in part, due to the efficacy of natural attenuating processes in aquifers limiting the spread of contaminants in groundwater. The results of studies of 20 sites carried out during the first phase of the Department of the Environment national research programme (Department of the Environment 1978) found evidence of relatively restricted groundwater contamination and were cited in support of the continued use of dilute and disperse landfills, subject to the presence of suitable hydrogeological conditions.

However, it is equally possible that the paucity of published, documented examples of groundwater contamination attributable to the landfill disposal of wastes in the United Kingdom is a reflection of the very limited monitoring of groundwater around landfills that occurred in the past, or at the present time. Although current and proposed legislation is expected to improve the frequency and adequacy of monitoring at landfills there is a serious lack of historic data on the effects of past landfill practices on either surface water or groundwater resources. In the past the problem was compounded by the lack of any mechanism for the collection, collation and analysis of such data, even on a regional basis. There also exists the problem that past information on the overall quality of groundwaters was based almost entirely on analyses of samples taken from boreholes, wells and springs providing public, or occasionally, private water supplies. Few, if any, observation boreholes were established, and monitored, within the recharge zones of aquifers, but remote from supply sources, and it has not been generally possible to describe adequately the overall quality of aquifer systems, nor their responses to quality changes attributable to landfill disposal of wastes, or other man-made causes. Unfortunately, this situation still persists with the National Rivers Authority reliant on the result of analyses of samples taken from supply boreholes to assess the overall quality of groundwaters. This surveillance protocol is basically unable to detect significant changes in groundwater quality until such time as they become apparent in the water pumped to supply. In this context it should be stated that, in addition to the study of the effects of landfill disposal of waste on groundwater being carried out for the Department of the Environment, WRc is also engaged on an assessment of the adequacy of past and present groundwater resource quality monitoring on behalf of the National Rivers Authority, in which the problem outlined above is to be addressed.

The difficulty of assessing the impact of past landfilling practices on the quality of the groundwater resources of the United Kingdom may be increased by the incompleteness of records of the locations and other characteristics (size, rates of waste disposal, types of waste etc) of many completed landfills. It has been noted that the more recent surveys appear to identify an increased number of completed sites, but it is considered likely that many will remain unidentified. In mitigation it may be argued that such sites are likely to be small and may have contained only domestic waste which had been allowed or encouraged to burn, thereby reducing the ultimate pollution potential. Nonetheless, it is considered that the persistence of old sites, very few of which were containment landfills, must continue to pose a potential threat to groundwater, possibly at unexpected locations, into the future, and particularly if redevelopment of the land, on adjacent areas, allows reactivation of leaching of the wastes.

7.2 Potential future problems related to past and current disposal practices

It is accepted that landfills containing putrescible wastes are likely to continue to degrade actively for many years, possibly decades, after completion of tipping, and to produce significant quantities of both leachates and landfill gas during that time (Department of the Environment 1986, Her Majesty's Inspectorate of Pollution 1989).

Only a small proportion of sites located on aquifers in the past were effectively lined, and, in many cases, completion did not include the construction of capping layers designed to minimise leachate formation. The potential for these sites to continue to contaminate both groundwaters and surface waters, and to allow uncontrolled migration of landfill gas will remain for a considerable time yet. Warnings of both leachate and gas problems around such sites may not be given at an early stage because of both the small proportion of past sites with adequate monitoring systems, and the imprecision of the Control of Pollution Act in defining responsibilities for site management and maintenance in the post closure period. For those past sites at which containment was provided by the installation of synthetic lining membranes, possible problems may arise from the lack of enforceable post closure monitoring and because of uncertainties over the long term reliability of liners (Reeds 1990, Arnot 1990).

Uncertainties will therefore remain over the extent to which continued leakage of pollutants from unlined sites, or by sudden failure of lining membranes, may occur. The uncertainty may be compounded by the lack of suitable monitoring facilities (groundwater observation boreholes, gas monitoring wells etc) in and around a constantly increasing number of completed, but biologically active landfills, and by uncertainties over responsibilities for monitoring and remedial actions. The unpredictability of incidents arising from the releases of pollutants outlined above implies that in many cases significant contamination of ground and water will take place before the problem is recognised (Rivett, Lerner, Lloyd and Clark 1990) and remedial actions can begin. The need for a pool of experienced hydrologists and hydrogeologists able to predict the evolution of contaminant dispersion patterns, to devise methods of controlling the migration of contaminants, and to monitor the behaviour of such systems will remain. In some cases the only viable option may be to prevent further spread of contamination by installing physical or hydraulic barriers, but it is considered probable that increasing use will be made of chemical engineering methods, or those related to biotechnology to detoxify the ground and water *in situ* (Reina 1990).

The recent increase in concern over landfill gas migration (Her Majesty's Inspectorate of Pollution 1989) and the accelerated interest in the possible use of landfill gas as a renewable energy source (Richards 1988), together with the separation of the regulatory functions from operations in the water industry and the anticipated requirements of future European Community directives for containment of all waste disposal sites, has led to a situation where nearly all new landfills are designed as containment sites, with provision for collocation, treatment and disposal of leachates. The same uncertainties over the long term performance and integrity of the lining materials which apply to older sites are likely to remain, together with a lack of data on which to judge the long-term reliability of leachate collection and treatment systems, whether by recirculation (Barber and Maris 1984) aerobic treatment (Robinson and Grantham 1988) or anaerobic digestion (Blakey and Maris 1990). The very large (> 1,000,000 m³) landfills begun during the last decade may require protracted periods before the wastes are stabilised, in terms of continued surface settlement, and cease to actively produce leachates or landfill gases. Problems of the suitability of the restored landfill areas for after uses may therefore occur for a considerable period of time after site closure, making it difficult for the land owners to realise the potential value of the restored land.

7.3 Trends in waste management and their implications for environmental protection

A number of trends in waste management have been emerging over the last several years, in response both to the increasing stringency of European Community legislation, and to the rise of environmental issues in the public's consciousness.

The principal thrusts of change may be summarised as:

– more stringent definition of waste types;

– greater isolation of wastes from the environment until rendered innocuous;

– increased professionalism within the waste management industry;

– reduction in volumes of waste at source;

– greater sorting, recycling and reclamation of wastes.

In the United Kingdom, these changes conform with the requirements of the new Environmental Protection Act 1990 and incorporate the conditions that are likely to be imposed on implementation of the draft Community Directives on the landfilling of wastes and on civil liability for damage caused by waste.

It is possible that categorisation of wastes will increasingly depend on the application of standardised leaching tests (called eluate tests in the draft EC Directive on landfilling wastes) and comparison with lists of 'trigger level' concentrations. A significant increase in sampling and analytical costs would be anticipated, which will result in increased disposal charges.

Allied to the use of prescribed methods for categorising wastes, the proposed Directive will, if implemented in its present form, effectively prevent any future 'dilute and disperse' landfills being created. Instead, all sites, even those licensed only for inert wastes, will be required to collect and treat all leachates generated within the wastes and to manage and control the landfill gas. At the same time adequate facilities for monitoring leachate and landfill gas will be required at all new sites, together with means of monitoring the impact of activities on surrounding water resources.

The management of future landfills will require high levels of technical and management skills, and the United Kingdom is responding to the need to ensure a professional body of managers by pursuing protocols that will lead to the authorisation of Certificates of Technical Competence for those engaged in waste management activities (Baker 1989, Moss 1990).

In parallel with the move to create certificates of professional competence for workers in the industry, the Environmental Protection Act 1990 will require a Certificate of Completion to be issued by the relevant Waste Regulatory Authority before a disposal licence can be handed in and the responsibility for the completed site passed from the operator to the Waste Regulatory Authority. This section of the new Act is in accord with conditions that are likely to be incorporated in the draft Directive. Before issuing a certificate of completion a WRA will be expected to take account of the views of the National Rivers Authority and other bodies. No guidance has been provided by the Department of the Environment, or Her Majesty's Inspectorate of Pollution, as to how 'completion' is to be recognised and there is concern that considerable delays may occur in the issue of certificates (Stone and Wilson 1991).

A further problem which may arise if the proposed landfill Directive is enacted in its present form concerns the fate of landfills operating before the date of implementation, and of the responsibility for their subsequent operation. The draft Directive would require that a 'conditioning plan' be prepared, giving details of the ways in which operational landfills could be brought into line with the requirements of the Directive. If the landfills are unable to be upgraded to the new standards, they must be closed within 5 years. If the site in question is large and at an early stage in filling, premature closure may lead to conditions under which the risk of environmental impairment is increased because the final design form of the site cannot be achieved.

Increasing public pressure for actions that encourage individuals to contribute to good husbandry of resources is likely to lead to a greater segregation of different waste types, and the reclamation and recycling of many parts of the waste stream. At the same time waste minimisation programmes by industry may lead to the production of new, and possibly more concentrated wastes, but in smaller quantities. Such wastes may encourage the development of new methods of chemical and physical treatment methods (Bryan 1990) as viable alternatives to landfill. It is considered possible that the moves towards greater reuse of materials currently considered waste may change the overall composition of final waste streams towards an even higher proportion of putrescible materials. If this is the case, greater opportunities will exist for further recovery of energy in the form of landfill gas (Richards 1988), possibly including the use of solid phase anaerobic digestion technology and the controlled digestion of leachates removed from the wastes. The use of large, permanent reactor cells in which anaerobic digestion of solid wastes is encouraged by techniques such as leachate recirculation and sewage effluent additions, followed by aerobic maturation of the residues to produce an inert fill or soil substitute material, has recently been proposed by the West Yorkshire Joint Waste Committee. Two prototype reactors are being constructed, under the title Landfill 2000, and this methodology may be a pointer to one way forward over the next decade.

7.4   Areas of uncertainty

The changing legislative framework and evolving public attitudes to environmental matters presupposes more sophisticated control of the waste management process. The increased site preparation, management and monitoring requirements of increasing regulations are likely to result in substanitally higher disposal costs which, in an industry becoming rapidly dominated by the private sector, are likely to be passed onto the consumer. However, setting aside economic problems, the direction of progress of waste management suggests that there are a number of areas in which additional technical information will be required.

–   Extent of impact of waste disposals on the aquatic environment and the efficacy of monitoring protocols

It is unlikely that the true extent of contamination of either surface waters or groundwaters by older landfills will ever be fully established because of the general lack of observation facilities and routine sampling surveys in the past. However, it is hoped that completion of the survey of landfill monitoring being carried out by WRc on behalf of HMIP will not only provide a better overview of the current influence of the landfill disposal of wastes on water quality, but also enable the suitability and adequacy of the existing monitoring programmes to be assessed and revised protocols formulated.

–   Clarification of requirements for Certificates of Completion

Continued uncertainty over those requirements to be fulfilled before a Certificate of Completion can be issued may make it exceedingly difficult for prospective site operators to obtain the necessary financial guarantees (environmental impairment assurance) with respect to the aftercare of sites. An unnecessary increase in costs may result and it would be urged that consultation on the probable requirements for Certification between HMIP, the NRA, representatives of the waste management industry and other interested bodies should begin at an early stage, to prevent subsequent confrontations.

–   Enlarged technical basis for codisposal

In order for codisposal to be acceptable under the probable terms of the proposed Directive on landfilling wastes, evidence will be required of the compatibility of the wastes, the loading rate limits and any synergistic or antagonistic effects. The studies required include further investigations on a laboratory scale of the fate of specific groups of organic compounds, in landfills, of the speciation of metals and metal-waste interactions, as well as the development of improved monitoring method to control landfills as anaerobic reactors (Knox 1990). Most importantly, the laboratory scale work should be linked to full-scale field studies and all work must be directed at defining quantified loading rates for the codisposal of industrial wastes.

–   Measurement and control of landfill gas flux

The potential for recovery of energy from wastes in the form of landfill gas has led to interest in the development of methods of enhancing gas production. At the same time, future changes in wastes composition may increase the potential for gas production, even at small sites, with consequent risks of environmental damage due to gas migration. Current methods of measurement of gas flux are not sufficiently sensitive to measure low flux rates. Development of reliable, robust equipment and techniques for low flux measurement is required.

–   The role of micro-organisms in waste management

Many of the processes that lead to leachate formation from wastes are microbially mediated and, similarly, many natural attenuating mechanisms are attributed to microbial activity. However, detailed knowledge of the types of bacteria present in the various environments that may be present, and their adaptabilities, resilience and requirements for optimal activity are poorly known. The encouragement of more rapid, controlled degradation of wastes in the next generation of containment landfills, and the potential for microbially mediated enhanced biorestoration of contaminated soil and water due to past practices, or future accidents, both require a more complete understanding of the microbiology of the respective systems.

– Improvement in estimation of hydraulic characteristics of landfills

The completion of water balance calculations as an aid to landfill site design and operation has long been recommended and may become obligatory under the proposed landfill Directive. Improved techniques for estimating and monitoring the effectiveness of engineering methods to restrict infiltration to wastes, for determining the way in which fluids pass through waste masses (including rapid by-passing flows) and the dispersion of contaminated liquids into the environment should be developed. Whilst the initial impetus for development may come from requirements associated with disposal licence requirements the same techniques and equipment will be essential management tools during the operational and aftercare phases of landfill development.

– Improved monitoring of landfills and groundwater resources

It is anticipated that completion of the programmes of study being made by WRc on behalf of the Department of the Environment with respect to, inter alia, the monitoring of groundwater at landfill sites and for the National Rivers Authority on the monitoring of the quality of the nation's groundwater resources will lead to recommendations for complimentary monitoring protocols. Without prejudicing the outcome of the work referred to above, it would be anticipated that the monitoring programme required for landfill sites would be not less vigorous than that implied in Waste Management Paper No 26, (Department of the Environment 1986) or in the draft European Community directive on landfills, and would follow a format similar to that shown in Tables 7.1, 7.2 and 7.3. In order to provide comparability, it would seem logical that the groundwater resource quality protocol should include analyses for the same lists of determinands, as a minimum requirement, at a frequency sufficient to be able to properly define natural seasonal variations in groundwater quality.

Table 7.1   Monitoring prior to deposit of wastes (investigation and preparatory phase)

Monitoring type	Frequency of measurements	Number/location of sampling points	Parameters to measure	Comments	Source of recommendation
Meteorological	Daily	Local met. station; or on-site measurements	Not specified	Presume sufficient data to complete water balance. Minimum of 12 months data prior to operational phase	WMP26, sect. 3.118 EC Prop. Annex II, 4
Surfaces waters	Not specified	Upstream and downstream of each possible discharge	pH, conductivity temperature, DO.	Water also to be monitored for ecological status. 12 months data required.	NAWDC8, sections 4.2, 4.3, 4.5
Groundwater	Weekly (first 4 weeks). Monthly thereafter.	Minimum 3 boreholes, 1 upgradient, 2 down-gradient	pH, conductivity, NH_4–N, COD. Water level.	Recommend minimum of 12 months data prior to operational phase.	NAWDC8, sections 3.1, 3.5, 3.6, 3.7. EC Prop. Annex II, 4.
Gas	Not specified	Numbers not specified	Not specified	Minimum 12 months period	WMP27, sections 6.6, 6.15

Note: Source or recommendations listed after *Table 7.3*

Table 7.2   Monitoring during operation phase including final capping

Monitoring type	Frequency of measurements	Number/location of sampling points	Parameters to measure	Comments	Source of recommendation
Control of Wastes (Industrial, homogenous)	Per delivery	1 kg or 1 litre	List of 21 determinands under eluate criteria	The proposed waste acceptance criteria are primarily aimed at industrial wastes	EC Prop Annex III, 3
(Industrial, heterogeneous)	Per 5 tonnes waste	1 kg			EC Prop Annex III, 3
(Industrial, in containers)	Per delivery, if in containers	Bulked sample of between 1 and 2.5 kg$\sqrt{N+1}$ containers		Monitoring of municipal wastes is to evaluate changes in composition	EC Prop Annex III, 3
(Municipal waste)	Not stated, but 'regular'	not specified	To include percentage composition (putrescibles, metals etc), calorific value etc.		
Stabilization of wastes	Annually	Not specified	Void space utilized Settlement		WMP4, Appendix D. EC Prop, Annex IV, 3.
Prevention of nuisance	Weekly	Not specified	Effects on vegetation Presence of vermin	Visual inspections	WMP4, Appendix D
Meteorlogical	Daily	Not specified	Volume & intensity precipitation. Max. & min temp. Wind direction and speed. Evaporation Humidity	On-site measurements may be replaced by 'effective' rainfall estimates provided by local meteorological network	EC Prop. Annex IV, 1
Water balance	Six monthly (April & October)	Not specified	Estimates of 1 (total liquid input) E (evapotranspiration) a (absorptive capacity of wastes) W (weight of wastes deposited).	Calculation of Lo (free leachate in site) from: $$L_o = 1 - E - aW$$	EC Prop, Annex IV, 4
Surface waters	Monthly	Upstream and downstream of each potential discharge, 10 litre bulk sample from each location	Ph and Cl and others related to types of wastes. Flows	On site determinations of pH, temperature, conductivity and dissolved oxygen.	WMP4, Appendix D NAWDC8, section 4 EC Prop, Annex IV, 2.
	Six monthly	As monthly	pH, Cl, NH_4-N, COD/ BOD/TOC, conductivity and others related to types of waste. Flows	As monthly	WMP4, Appendix D NAWDC8, section 4 EC Prop, Annex IV, 2.
Groundwater	Monthly	Minimum of 3 boreholes, upgradient, 2 downgradient	pH and Cl, others related to waste type. Levels in boreholes	On site determinations of pH, temperature, conductivity and dissolved oxygen.	WMP4, Appendix D NAWD8, section 3
	Six monthly	As monthly	As for 6 monthly surface waters (UK); list 1 and 2 substance in Directive 80/68/EEC (EC) Levels in boreholes	As monthly	WMP4, Appendix D NAWD8, section 3 EC Prop, Annex IV

Table 7.2 Continued

Monitoring type	Frequency of measurements	Number/location of sampling points	Parameters to measure	Comments	Source of recommendation
Leachates	Daily	All discharges	Volume/flow		EC Prop. Annex IV, 2
	Monthly	Minimum number of boreholes for co-disposal sites: <5 ha = 5 No. 5–10 ha = one *per hectare* >10 ha = 10+ $\sqrt{\text{area, ha}}$ Minimum number not specified for non-codisposal sites.	Leachate levels, pH, Cl, NH_4-N, COD/BOD/TOC, Conductivity, others in relation to types of wastes deposited	On site determinations of pH, temperature, Conductivity, dissolved oxygen	EC Prop. Annex III, 6.2 Annex IV, 2. WMP4, Appendix D NAWDC8, section 3
Gas	Weekly	Number and spacing dependent on sub-surface conditions, gas flux and proximity to buildings	Methane and carbon dioxide concentrations	High frequency on fissured strata with adjacent buildings; otherwise 50 m as uniform, granular strata, 20 m on fissured strata	WMP27, Table 7.1 WMP4, Appendix D
	Monthly	Sample point distribution as weekly	Gas and barometric pressures. CH_4, CO_2, O_2, H_2S, H_2 and others related to waste composition	Comments as weekly	WMP4 Appendix D EC Prop. Annex IV.2
Irrigation of leachate to land					
Irrigated leachate	6 monthly	Point of irrigation to land	As Table 2 of DoE Code of Practice for Agricultural Use of Sewage Sludge	No specific regulations or directive on this subject, therefore assume closest analogy. Frequency may be decreased to 5 years if concentrations in Table 2 not exceeded.	DoE Sludge section 3.2
Site in irrigation area	20 years (max)	One sample per 5 ha of site; to 250 mm depth	Heavy metals etc as listed in Table 3, DoE Sludge	Survey required before irrigation commenced	DoE Sludge section 3.3

Table 7.3 Monitoring following completion of landfilling (Minimum period 30 years – EC Proposal Annex IV, 1)

Monitoring type	Frequency of measurements	Number/location of sampling points	Parameters to measure	Comments	Source of recommendation
Stablization of wastes	Yearly	Not specified	Settlement		EC Prop. Annex IV, 5
Meteorological	Monthly, on same day of month	Not specified	Volume and intensity of precipitation. Max and min temp Wind direction and speed Evaporation Humidity	On-site measurements may be replaced by 'effective' rainfall estimates provided by local meteorological network.	EC Prop. Annex IV, 1

Table 7.3 Continued

Monitoring type	Frequency of measurements	Number/location of sampling points	Parameters to measure	Comments	Source of recommendation
Water balance	Six monthly (April and October)	Not specified	As Table 2	Provides estimate of changes in volume of free leachate	EC Prop. Annex IV, 4
Surface waters	Six monthly	Upstream and downstream of each potential discharge. 10 litre bulk sample at each point	pH, Cl, NH_4-N, COD/BOD/TOC, Conductivity and others related to waste type. Flows	On-site determination of pH, temperature, conductivity, dissolved oxygen	EC Prop. Annex IV, 2
Groundwater	Six monthly	Minimum of 3 boreholes, 1 upgradient, 3 down-gradient	pH, Cl, NH_4-N, COD/BOD/TOC, conduc-tivityand others related to waste type. Levels in boreholes	On-site determinations of pH, temperature, conductivity, dissolved oxygen.	EC Prop. Annex IV, 3
Leachates	Six monthly	All discharges. Minimum number of boreholes, see Table 2	Six monthly sum of flows. pH, Cl, NH_4-N, COD/BOD/TOC, conductivity and others related to waste type. Leachate levels in wastes.	On-site determination of pH, temperature, conductivity, dissolved oxygen.	EC Prop. Annex IV, 2
Gas	Not greater than 6 months	Number and spacing dependent on subsurface conditions of proximity to buildings, but generally at 50 m centres around sites on homogenous soils, or 20 m centres on fissured strata	CH_4, CO_2, O_2, H_2S, H_2. Other gases if appropriate to waste type	WMP27 contains two independent sets of criteria to determine end-point for gas monitoring: a) CH4 <1% (v/v) and CO2 <1.5% (v/v) over 24 months inc. 2 surveys with barometric pressure <1000 mb., b) 0.4 m diameter boreholes at 22 m centres through-out wastes shows complete decomp-osition of wastes and lack of gas	WMP27, seciton 7.9 EC Prop. Annex IV, 2
Irrigation of leachate to land					
Irrigate leachate	6 monthly	Point of irrigation	As Table 2 of DoE Code of Practice	Frequency may be decreased to 5 yearly if concentrations in DoE Table 2 are not exceeded.	DoE Sludge
Soil in irrigation area	20 years	One sample per 5 ha, to 250 mm depth	Heavy metals etc. Table 3, DoE Code of Practice		DoE Sludge

Sources of recommendations:
Department of the Environment, 1986. Waste Management Paper No 4 (WMP 4)
Department of the Environment, 1991. Waste Management Paper No 7 (WMP 27)
Department of the Environment, 1989. Code of Practice for Agricultural Use of Sewage Sludge (DoE sludge)
National Association of Waste Disposal Contractors. Code of Practice for Landfill of Waste, No 8,
Guidelines for Monitoring Landfill Sites. (NAWDC 8)
Commission of the European Communities, 1991. Proposal for a Council Directive on the Landfill of Waste (EC Prop)

References

ARNOT L (1990) Liner life. *New Civil Engineer*, 20 September, p55.

ASPINWALL and CO LTD (1991) The Sitefile Digest. 1991 Edition. Aspinwall and Co Ltd, Baschurch, Shropshire, 491pp. 2 Appendices.

BAKER L (1989) The response of the waste disposal industry to the challenges of the 1990s. *Proceedings Harwell Symposium, Waste Management in the UK*. UKAEA, Harwell, Oxon, 12-20.

BARBER C, NAYLOR J A AND MARIS P J (1976) Techniques for investigating groundwater pollution at landfill sites. In: *Papers and Proceedings, Water Research Centre Conference Groundwater Quality – Measurement, Prediction and Protection*, edited by W B Wilkinson. The Centre, Medmenham, 207–220.

BARBER C, YOUNG C P, BLAKEY N C, ROSS C A M AND WILLIAMS G M (1981) Groundwater contamination by landfill leachate: distribution of contaminants and factors affecting pollution plume development at three sites, UK. In: *Quality of groundwater. Proc Int Symp Noordwijkerhout*, edited by W van Duijvenbooden, P Glasbergen and H van Lelyveld. Elsevier. *Studies in Environmental Sciences* 17, 239–244.

BARBER C AND MARIS P J (1984) Recirculaton of leachate as a landfill management option: benefits and operational problem. *Q J Eng Geol* 17, 19–29.

BELL J (1990) Plastics: waste not, want not. *New Scientist*. 1 December 44–47.

BHATTY J I AND REID K J (1989) Lightweight aggregates from incinerated sludge ash. *Waste Management and Research* 7(4), 363–376.

BIDDLE C A R (1988) Generation using gas turbines. In: *Landfill Gas and Anaerobic Digestion of Solid Wastes*, edited by Y R Alston and G E Richards. UKAEA, Harwell, Oxon, 206–224.

BLAKEY N C AND CRAFT D G (1986) Infiltraton and adsorption of water by domestic wastes in landfills – leachate volume changes with time. *Proc Harwell Landfill Water Management Symposium*, AERE, Harwell, Oxon, 5–18.

BLAKEY N C AND MARIS P J (1990) Methane recovery from the anaerobic digestion of landfill leachate. Department of Energy Contractor Report ETSU B 1223, 48pp, 16 figures.

BLAKEY N C AND TOWLER P A (1988) The effect of unsaturated/saturated zone properties upon the hydrogeochemical and microbiological processes involved in the migration and attenuation of landfill leachate components. *Wat Sci Tech* 20(3), 119–128.

BRYAN J (1990) Chemical Waste Treatment – The Way Forward. In: *Proc 1990 Harwell Waste Management Symposium*, AEA Environment and Energy, Harwell, Oxon. 113–118.

COLE J A (1974) (Ed) Groundwater Pollution in Europe. *Proc Water Research Association Conference*, Reading, England, 1972. Water Information Centre Inc, New York. 546pp.

COOMBS J AND ALSTON Y (1988) The potential for recovery of energy from solid wastes using fabricated digester systems. In: *Landfill Gas and Anaerobic Digestion of Solid Wastes*, edited by Y R Alston and G E Richards. UKAEA, Harwell, Oxon. 454–466.

COMMISSION OF THE EUROPEAN COMMUNITIES (1991) Proposal for a Council Directive on the landfill of waste (91/C190/01). Official Journal of the European Communities, 22 July 1991. C190/1–18.

COMMISSION OF THE EUROPEAN COMMUNITIES (1982) Groundwater Resources of the United Kingdom. Th Schäfer Druckerie, Hanover, 252pp.

CROFT B AND CAMPBELL D (1990) Characterisation of 100 UK Landfill Sites. In: *Proc Harwell Waste Management Symposium,* AEA Environment and Energy, Harwell, Oxon, 13–27.

DAY J B W (1986) Groundwater sources in the United Kingdom. In: *Groundwater: Occurrence, Development and Protection, 5–48. Water Practices Manual 5. Institution of Water Engineers – Scientists, London,* edited by T W Brandon.

DEPARTMENT OF THE ENVIRONMENT (1975) Press Notice No 386. 53 Waste Tips Named. 29 April 1975. 5pp, The Department, Marsham Street.

DEPARTMENT OF THE ENVIRONMENT (1978) Co-operative programme of research on the behaviour of hazardous wastes in landfill sites. Final report of the Policy Review Committees. 169pp. HMSO, London.

DEPARTMENT OF THE ENVIRONMENT (1980) Digest of Environmental Pollution and Water Statistics. No 3, 106 pp. HMSO, London.

DEPARTMENT OF THE ENVIRONMENT (1981) Waste Management Paper No 23. Special Wastes: A technical memorandum providing guidance on their definition. HMSO, London.

DEPARTMENT OF THE ENVIRONMENT (1984) Standing Technical Advisory Committee on Water Quality. Fourth Biennial Report, February 1981 – March 1983, 110pp. HMSO.

DEPARTMENT OF THE ENVIRONMENT (1985) Digest of Environmental Protection and Water Statistics. No 8, 51pp, HMSO.

DEPARTMENT OF THE ENVIRONMENT (1986) Waste Management Paper No 26 Landfilling Wastes: A technical memorandum for the disposal of waste on landfill sites. 206pp. HMSO, London.

DEPARTMENT OF THE ENVIRONMENT (1988a) The Hazardous Waste Inspectorate – Third Report. 122pp. HMSO, London.

DEPARTMENT OF THE ENVIRONMENT (1988b) An assessment of groundwater quality in England and Wales: Sir William Halcrow and Partners. HMSO, London.

DEPARTMENT OF THE ENVIRONMENT (1989) Digest of Environmental Protection and Water Statistics. No 12. HMSO, London.

DEPARTMENT OF THE ENVIRONMENT (1991) Waste Management Paper No 27. Landfill Gas of Technical Memorandum providing guidance on the monitoring and control of landfill gas. 82pp. HMSO London (see also HMIP 1989).

ENDS (1991) Landfill Directive to allow co-disposal, but waste acceptance procedures in dispute. ENDS Report 192, 37–38. January 1991.

ENDS (1989) Devastating Harwell Report puts Leigh's solidification plant in limbo. ENDS Report No 173, June, 8–9.

GRAY D A, MATHER J D AND HARRISON I B (1974) Review of groundwater pollution from waste sites in England and Wales, with provisional guidelines for future site selection. *Q J Engng Geol* 7(2), 181–196.

HARRIS R C AND LOWE D R (1984) Changes in the organic fraction of leachate from two domestic refuse sites on the Sherwood Sandstone, Nottinghamshire. *Q J Eng Geol* 117, 57–69.

HARRIS R C AND PARRY E L (1982) Investigations into domestic refuse leachate attenuation in the unsaturated zone of Triassic Sandstones. In: *Effects of waste disposal on groundwater and surface water,* Proc Symp 1st Sci General Assembly IAHS, Exeter, edited by R Perry. IAHS Publication No 139. 147–156.

HAWKINS R (1991) Duty of Care whips industry into line. In: *A Practitioners Guide to the Environment Protection Act Part II,* 2–7, Surveyor.

HAZARDOUS WASTE INSPECTORATE (1984) Register of facilities for the disposal of controlled wastes in England and Wales. pp501. Department of the Environment, London.

HER MAJESTY'S INSPECTORATE OF POLLUTION (1989) Waste Management Paper No 27. The Control of Landfill Gas. A technical memorandum on the monitoring and control of landfill gas. 56pp. HMSO, London (see also DoE, 1991).

HOLMES J R (1989) The role of non-landfill processes such as incineration. *Proc Harwell Symposium, Waste Management in the UK: Issues and Priorities for the l990s.* UKAEA, Harwell, Oxon. 41–53.

HOUSE OF COMMONS ENVIRONMENT COMMITTEE (1989) Second Report. Paper No 22–1. HMSO, London.

JOHNSON J (1990) Waste that no-one wants. *New Scientist,* 8 September 1990, 50–55.

KNOX K (1990) A review of codisposal. In: *Proc 1990 Harwell Waste Management Symposium.* AEA Environment and Energy, Harwell, Oxon. 54–76.

LEAN G AND GHAZI P (1990) Britains buried poison. Observer Magazine pp11–18 and Observer pp10–11. 4 February 1990.

MATHER J D AND PARKER A (1978) The disposal of industrial and domestic waste to a landfill overlying Lower Chalk. Publd Rep AERE–R 9097, UKAEA, Harwell, Oxon.

MINISTRY OF HOUSING AND LOCAL GOVERNMENT (1961) Pollution of Water by Tipped Refuse, 141pp. HMSO, London.

MINISTRY OF HOUSING AND LOCAL GOVERNMENT (1970) Disposal of Solid Toxic Wastes. 106pp. HMSO, London.

MINISTRY OF HOUSING AND LOCAL GOVERNMENT (1971) Refuse disposal: report of the working party on refuse disposal, ppl98, HMSO, London.

MOSS H (1990) Landfill technology – developments in recent years and future priorities. *Proc 1990 Harwell Waste Management Symposium.* AEA Environment and Energy, Harwell, Oxon. 93–96.

NATIONAL ASSOCIATION OF WASTE DISPOSAL CONTRACTORS (1989) NAWDC Landfill Committee Codes of Practice for Landfill. 57pp. NAWDC, London.

NATIONAL RIVERS AUTHORITY (1989) NRA North West Region. Earthworks on landfill sites. 21pp. NRA, Warrington.

NAYLOR J A, ROWLAND C D, YOUNG C P AND BARBER C (1978) The investigation of landfill sites. Water Research Centre Technical Report No TR91. October 1978. The Centre, Medmenham.

NEWELL J (1990) Recycling Britain. *New Scientist,* 8 September, 46–49.

PARSONS P J (1990) Landfill sites and groundwater quality. *Waste Manage Today (News J)* **3**(2), 24–25.

REEDS J (1990) No time to waste. *Surveyor,* 16 August, 12–13.

REINA P (1990) Cleaning up contamination. *Surveyor*, 21 June 1990, 12–14.

RICHARDS K M (1988) The UK Landfill Gas and MSW Industry, So Far, So Good? In: *Landfill Gas and Anaerobic Digestion of Solid Wastes,* edited by Y R Alston and G E Richards. Harwell Laboratory, Oxon. 12–47.

RIVETT M O, LERNER D N, LLOYD J W AND CLARK L (1990) Organic contamination of the Birmingham Aquifer, UK. *Jour Hydrology* **113**, 307–323.

ROBBINS J (1990) Heat process converts sewage to aggregrates. *New Civil Engineer*, 22 February, p12.

ROBBINS N S AND HARRISON I B (1986) Private groundwater use and consumption in Scotland. *Jour Inst Wat Engrs and Scientists* **40**(4), 362–368.

ROBINSON H D AND MARIS P J (1979) Leachate from domestic waste: generation, composition and treatment. A review. Water Research Centre, Technical Report No TR108. 38pp. The Centre, Medmenham.

ROBINSON H D AND LUCAS J L (1984) Leachate attenuation in the unsaturated zone beneath landfills: Instrumentation and monitoring of a site in Southern England. *Wat Sci Tech* **17**(4/5), 477–492.

ROBINSON H D AND DAVIES J (1985) Automatic answer to leachate treatment. *Surveyor* **165**, 14 March, 7–8 and 26.

ROBINSON H D (1987) Design and operation of leachate control measures: Compton Bassett landfill site, Wiltshire, UK. *Waste Management and Research,* **5**.

ROBINSON H D AND BLACKLEY S G (1987) Attenuation of contaminants: How reliable a philosophy? *Surveyor,* 5 February, 12–15.

ROBINSON H D AND GRANTHAM G (1988) The treatment of landfill leachates in on-site aerated lagoon plants: Experience in Britian and Ireland. *Water Research* **22**(15), 733–747.

STONE C AND WILSON G (1991) All questions, few answers on aftercare. In: *A Practitioners Guide to the Environmental Protection Act Part II.* Surveyor. 22–23.

WATER SERVICES ASSOCIATION (1989) Waterfacts '89. 37pp. WSA, London.

WILLIAMS G M AND AITKENHEAD N (1989) Gas explosion at Loscoe, Derbyshire. Symposium; Methane – facing the problems. 26–28 September 1989. East Midland Conference Centre, Nottingham.

YOUNG C P, MOSEY F E AND MARIS P J (1988) Leachate digestion in the UK. In: *Landfill Gas and Anaerobic Digestion of Solid Wastes,* edited by Y R Alston and G E Richards. UKAEA, Harwell, Oxon. 441–453.

The Impact of Contaminated Land on Freshwater Quality

Report No: CO 2731-M

July 1991

Authors: M Beckett*, A J Dobbs and D Gourlay

* Consultant

Contract Manager: A J Dobbs

Contract No: 8157

Any enquiries relating to this report should be referred to the authors at the following address:

WRc plc, Henley Road, Medmenham, PO Box 16, Marlow, Buckinghamshire SL7 2HD.
Telephone: Henley (0491) 571531

Summary

I   Objectives

To review past and present information on freshwater quality issues relating to contaminated land.

  To assess future changes, remedial measures and regulations which could reduce risks of water pollution from contaminated land.

II   Reasons

The Royal Commission on Environmental Pollution are reviewing freshwater quality and required information on the potential effect of contaminated land on freshwater quality.

III   Conclusions

There exist few documented case histories of acute freshwater pollution resulting from contaminated land. However, there is evidence that diffuse land contamination is having a significant effect on groundwater quality in industrialised urban areas. The question of how contaminated land should be defined has been an obstacle to the setting of standards and estimation of the extent of contamination in the UK. Furthermore, approaches to contaminated land in the UK have tended to regard contaminated land as a hindrance to redevelopment rather than a threat to the environment or to freshwater quality. Industrial sites used in the future can be expected to operate according to stricter controls with respect to impact on the environment than current or historic sites. If Integrated Pollution Control and other legislative developments work effectively, then the importance of future industrial sites as a source of contaminated land should be negligible. There is still, however, a considerable residue of contaminated land which requires clean-up.

IV   Resume of Contents

This report reviews the following subjects:

i   The nature, extent and origin of contaminated land in the UK;

ii   Legislation controlling contaminated land in the UK, including both domestic and EC legislation; and

iii   The significance of contaminated land as a source of water pollution;

iv   Future changes.

The final section of this report summarises the main findings of the report, and includes recommendations for measures to reduce the risk of water contamination resulting from contaminated land in the future.

Contents

1 Introduction

This short report was commissioned by the Royal Commission on Environmental Pollution (RCEP) in order to summarise the current state of knowledge regarding the significance of contaminated land as a possible cause of water pollution. The recent report of the House of Commons Environment Committee and the evidence submitted to it have been valuable sources of information, but other sources and additional more recent information directly related to water has also been collected and analysed.

It is interesting and perhaps revealing that 'contamination' is used as a term for what is in effect soil pollution, ie the presence of existing or potential damage, yet in other media, water and air, the term contamination implies no damage. Perhaps the use of the term soil pollution would have led to earlier recognition in the U K of the problems that exist. As things stand, the U K approach to the existence of contaminated or polluted land in regulations has been somewhat narrowly focused on the problems that may arise when such land is to be reclaimed, redeveloped, or otherwise re-used. The possibility of wider environmental damage (eg water pollution) seems not so far to have received much consideration. Despite the slightly anomalous terminology we will continue to use the phrase 'contaminated land' in this report even in circumstances where 'polluted land' would be more appropriate.

Most reports on contaminated land start with a consideration of the definition. Such a definition is difficult unless there is some previous consideration of the environmental quality objective for the land in question. Land that is suitable as park land may be too contaminated for agricultural use. If a quality objective is established a quality standard for a variety of contaminants may be determined which could serve as a bench mark against which the degree of contamination can be assessed.

Although there is a dearth of detailed and specific information about the impact of contaminated land on water pollution, we have attempted to synthesise what is available, to put this information into the practical and legislative context, and propose future improvements.

2 Major Issues

At the outset of this study the Commission provided several key questions that they wanted addressed. These questions and our answers are summarised below. The supporting detail is given in the following sections, and the final section lists our main conclusions.

Which industries contaminate land?

All industrial activities have the potential to contaminate land, unless they are carried out in ways which take the possibility into account. This involves taking steps to avoid contamination occurring, or at least to minimise it. Particular attention has been focused on landfill sites, industrial development (especially those using or processing chemicals, metals, oil-based products, or preservatives), mining and resource exploitation, and old gas works.

What are the principal types of contamination?

Contamination can take many forms (solid, liquid, gas). Substances with the potential to cause harm to anyone or anything as a result of their presence in or on land are very numerous, but it does not necessarily follow that their presence is always likely to give rise to harmful effects. The more frequently occurring contaminants include:

heavy metals;
acids/alkalis;
organic compounds especially halogenated solvents; and
methane.

What is the geographic distribution of contaminated land throughout the UK?

Contaminated land is found in all parts of the UK, but is most concentrated in and around urban areas. Only in remote rural areas (eg moorlands or mountains) is the probability of encountering man-made contamination significantly lower than elsewhere. Even in these remote areas there remains the possibility of contamination from natural sources, such as the presence of heavy metals as mineral deposits or ore bodies in the host rocks.

How much contaminated land is there in the UK?

Difficulties in agreeing a definition of contaminated land, and the lack of a national database means that no accurate figures exist for the amount of contaminated land in the UK. The Department of the Environment estimates (based on derelict land surveys) place the figure between 10,000 and 27,000 hectares. However, this excludes land which is both in use and contaminated, and land which has already been redeveloped. Furthermore, it is based solely on previous use of the site, and thus indicates only potential, not actual contamination.

What forms of land contamination might current industrial processes create in future?

Current industrial processes have the potential to give rise to the same types of land contamination as have historically occurred. However, improved working practices and modern design have reduced the risk of this occurring. The requirement to apply BATNEEC in scheduled processes should act as a further control. However, industrial operations may exist which lie outside the scheduled works provisions, but which none the less have a high potential for contaminating land if poor working practices exist.

How can contaminated land lead to aquatic pollution before redevelopment?

Aquatic pollution of either ground or surface waters can occur as a result of leaching or entrainment of contaminated fine particulate matter in drainage water.

Describe with examples threats to groundwater and surface water

Leaching and entrainment of contaminants extends the contamination from the land into ground and surface waters. Specific case histories are few, but examples of chlorinated solvent contamination of groundwaters, and heavy metal contamination in streams and rivers, have resulted from previous land contamination.

Which is the most serious?

Groundwater contamination is potentially more serious than surface water contamination, as groundwater may remain affected for decades, or even centuries. Also, remedial measures for groundwater contamination are likely to be more difficult than those for surface water contamination.

What are the problems of pollution caused by the redevelopment of contaminated land?

Redevelopment can cause increased risks of water contamination due to the following factors:

Increased leaching of contaminants by rainfall, due to exposure of the site and disturbance of contaminated soil;

Penetration of impermeable layers below the site during construction work (particularly piling operations) allowing contaminants greater access to underlying aquifers.

Have there been any examples of contaminated land giving rise to groundwater or surface water pollution after redevelopment?

There have been instances of site works leading to the exposure of contaminated wastes (eg tarry oil/waste in gas works sumps). Unless the contractor anticipates such occurrences a danger of water pollution exists if water resources are located nearby. However, few incidents of any significance appear to occur, and documented case histories of such incidents are not available.

How does legislation protect the aquatic environment from pollution from contaminated land?

Protection of the aquatic environment and the range of problems associated with contaminated land have hitherto been seen as discrete objectives for the purposes of UK legislation. Within the past 20 years the inter-relationship of these different objectives has begun to be better understood. However, there is still no legislation which aims to reconcile all the various interests in either sector.

Are there particular problems legislation cannot or does not cover?

It follows automatically from the previous answer that present legislation does not cover all these problems. Examples of incomplete coverage include:

- control over land use changes and development controls operate largely independently of environmental protection legislation;

- even the most recent legislation on environmental protection does not encompass all industrial activities with the potential to contaminate land.

What remedial measures might be considered to reduce risks of water pollution from contaminated land?

The NRA should be statutory consultees on any planning applications for the redevelopment of contaminated land. A list of sites with high potential to contaminate water should be drawn up by the NRA. There is also a need for more research into appropriate remedial measures for the rehabilitation of contaminated land.

What measures might be considered to reduce the risk of water pollution arising from industrial land which is abandoned in the future?

There is a need for more consistent advice and regulation to discourage soakaways or spillage onto land being regarded as suitable disposal methods. Storage tanks with bunded walls and underground storage should incorporate special precautions to prevent leakage. Consideration should be given to extending the Scheduled Works definition to cover those activities most likely to lead to contaminated land.

3 Extent, nature and origin of contaminated land in the U K

3.1 Extent

No reliable estimate of the amount of contaminated land in the UK is available at present. Furthermore, until there is wider agreement than at present on how contaminated land should be defined, the likelihood of obtaining a precise estimate is small.

The fundamental reason for the lack of quantitative information on contaminated land is that the significance of contamination varies according to the land use, because the actual (or proposed) use of land determines which, if any, of the possible targets of contamination are in fact at risk.

The above point may be illustrated by reference to a frequently cited definition of contaminated land: 'any land which is shown to contain sufficient quantities or concentrations of a (harmful) substance or substances such as to pose a direct or indirect hazard to a specified target or targets' (IEHO 1989).

The problem with this type of definition is that the substances which may cause harm, the concentrations at which they may do so, and the targets which may be affected are not defined – and are indefinable because they differ from site to site even if only one type of land use is considered. In fact there are several possible land uses, and the importance of the contamination present depends upon which particular use is selected. Land contaminated by heavy metals in high concentrations, for example, would not be suitable for land uses which involve growing of crop plants, or for residential areas where young children may come into contact with the soil. But the same land containing the same contaminants in the same concentrations would not preclude safe and successful development for uses such as office buildings, warehouses and industrial premises. The significance of the contaminants depends upon the targets at risk, which in turn depend upon the land use.

What this means in practice is that the form of definition quoted above is inherently unsuitable for quantitative application. Nor can it readily be modified for quantitative use by specifying the substances deemed to be 'harmful'. Even if this were done, there would still be the problem of identifying land where the specified contaminating substances were present in concentrations likely to actually cause the harmful effects. This means that without an intensive programme of sampling and analysis, which would be very demanding of finance and resources, it is virtually impossible to use conventional definitions to obtain quantitative estimates of the extent of contaminated land in the UK.

Mainly for this reason, such official estimates as exist of the amount of contaminated land in the UK have been compiled from other sources. These are mainly of two types:

Estimates based on related land categories for which official estimates do exist, eg derelict land; and

Estimates based on surrogates for contamination, eg records or registers of previous land use.

Periodic estimates of the amount of derelict land in the UK are published by the Department of the Environment. These are compiled from returns prepared by local authorities, based on specified categories of dereliction such as colliery spoil heaps, excavations and pits, derelict railway land and general industrial dereliction. By selecting those categories considered most likely to comprise contaminated sites an estimate of contaminated land can be obtained by a process of summation.

This method was the basis of the estimate put forward by DoE in its evidence submitted to the recent Commons Select Committee Inquiry on Contaminated Land, viz approximately 27,000 hectares in England. Further details are given in Section 3.4.

The main objections to such a method of estimating contaminated land are as follows:

Being based on derelict land, it may underestimate the amount of contaminated land in local authority areas where there is little or no land which is derelict according to the official definition of that category.

Some 5% of local authorities failed in any case to submit the required returns in the most recent DoE survey, though it was considered unlikely that these missing returns would have greatly increased the totals for individual categories.

More importantly, the fact that a site is derelict according to the official definition is no guarantee that it is also contaminated. Land can be derelict without being contaminated, and vice-versa.

Thus the accuracy of estimates prepared by this process is unknown. Much depends on the reliability and thoroughness of the derelict land returns prepared by the local authorities and there have been no rigorous checks on this by DoE.

The principle that contaminated land might be quantified by methods not involving direct collection of soil samples for analysis is, however, worthy of further consideration. On such a basis, methods best described by the generic term 'prospective surveys' have been developed and applied. The best known of these is that commissioned by the Welsh Office in an attempt to estimate the amount of contaminated land in Wales. First prepared in 1982 and subsequently up-dated, this yielded an estimate of around 3,500 ha for the Principality as a whole. However, there were important exclusions from the survey which must cast doubt on the validity of this estimate of the total area of contaminated land in Wales. Sites individually less than 0.5 ha were excluded, as was industrial land currently in use (some of which may well have been contaminated) and sites which had already been redeveloped (ie former waste disposal sites since built on for whatever purpose would not appear in the above estimate). The most significant feature of the Welsh Office survey was that it demonstrated the validity of identifying from archival sources previous uses of land which had the potential to cause contamination, and to use this as the basis of a methodology for compiling estimates and registers of sites over a wide geographical area.

In 1986/87 the DoE, with the co-operation of Cheshire County Council, carried out as a research project a more comprehensive prospective survey of three complete local authority districts in the County of Cheshire. The exclusions made in the Welsh Office survey were not repeated in Cheshire, thus the results may be considered valid as a record of a very high proportion (probably greater than 90%) of all the potentially contaminated land in these three districts. In total some 1,500 individual sites were recorded, though no attempt was made to obtain an estimate of the area of land thus represented.

The DoE has since published the report of this research project so that other local authorities may study and if necessary adapt the Cheshire survey methodology to their own needs. The intention is to make available a common and workable means of identifying, recording and registering potentially contaminated land. This is needed for the purposes of complying with the forthcoming requirement, incorporated in the Environmental Protection Act 1990 (Part 8, S.143), by which local authorities will be under a statutory obligation to prepare such registers for their areas. There may be minor amendments to the scope, title and accessibility of these registers, but the basic methodology is unlikely to change in important respects from that used in the Cheshire survey.

Once such registers have been compiled for all local authority districts, a reliable information base for quantifying potentially contaminated land (more properly termed 'previously used land' in this case) will exist. Even then, however, it will be important to remember that the presence of contaminants will not have been proved by sampling and analysis. The estimates derived from such registers will represent land where the presence of contaminants may be inferred from knowledge of the site history. For the main purpose for which the registers are intended, namely applications by local authorities in the context of land use and development control, this limitation is not important. Contamination which is suspected or inferred from knowledge of past use is the first stage of obtaining actual proof of its existence. Subsequent stages of confirmation, assessment and rectification are not exclusively the responsibility of local authorities, nor of central government. Thus the inferential basis of these estimates is adequate for present purposes. To arrive at an estimate on a different basis, eg on proven contamination, would be so demanding in terms of cost and resources as to be too expensive to prepare.

3.2 Nature

For the purposes of this section contaminated land may be considered to include all sites which contain contaminants which give rise to the specified hazards listed in Table 3.1. It should be noted that the actual presence of these contaminants may not have been confirmed at the time when a particular site first comes to the attention of an interested party.

Table 3.1 groups the different types of contaminants on the basis of the hazards (whether potential or real) which they give rise to. Again it must be remembered that not all of these possible hazards will actually exist on a given site, nor are all potential targets equally at risk from the hazards. Table 3.2 lists the main possible land uses where the hazard-target link may occur. This is valid because it is the land use which determines what targets are, or are not, at risk in any given circumstances.

3.3 Origins

Although not exclusively so, contamination of land is usually the result of some man-made use or activity carried out on the land. The hazards listed in Tables 3.1 and 3.2 are predominantly associated with such uses or activities of man. These uses or activities may have occurred in the past and have since ceased; they may still be occurring, or they may occur in the future as a result of the continuing sequence of land use changes.

Landfills and other waste disposal sites are the most widely used method of waste disposal in the UK. They are controlled by the Control of Pollution Act, 1974. The main cause of pollution arises from landfill gas and leachate production. This leachate is often toxic and highly polluting to water resources.

Gasworks, and coal carbonisation plants, produce a range of gaseous and liquid products by heating coal in an oxygen free atmosphere. The major contaminants found on such sites include coal tars, phenols and spent oxide, which was used as a purifying agent for coal gas and contains free and complex cyanides, elemental sulphur, sulphates and sulphides.

Table 3.1   Contaminant/hazard links

Main contaminants	Hazards
Heavy metals (plant uptake) Heavy metals (grazing animals) Organics (PCB etc.)	Ingestion
Asbestos Metal dusts Toxic gases	Inhalation
Acids and alkalies Organics, eg phenols Some metal salts, eg chromates	Skin contact
Zn/Cu/Ni Sulphates Landfill gas	Phytotoxicity
Sulphate/sulphide Organics, eg oils, tars, phenols Acidity	Building material degradation
Carbonaceous matter Sulphur wastes (spent oxide) Gases	Fires
Landfill gas	Asphyxiation Explosion
Biological organisms Chemical warfare agents Biocides	Other (health)
Smell/odour/taint	Other (nuisance)
Biodegradation Fires	Instability

Table 3.2 Land use/hazard links

Proposed use	Principal hazards which may pose a threat
Residential with gardens	All
Residential without gardens (ie flats etc.)	All except phytotoxicity or ingestion
Allotments/market gardens	Phytotoxicity Skin contact
Agriculture – arable	Phytotoxicity – grazing Phytotoxicity and ingestion
POS/amenity/recreational	Phytotoxicity Skin contact
Commercial, e.g. offices, retail	Building material degradation Fire, explosion
Light industry (e.g. warehouses, factory units)	Building material degradation Fires, explosion
Heavy industry	Building material degradation Fires

Scrap yards are sites used for breaking up redundant or obsolete manufacturing items, such as vehicles, electrical equipment, machinery etc. The nature and degree of contamination therefore depends on the activities carried out on site. The heavy metals lead, zinc, copper, cadmium and nickel may originate from the types of items broken up. PCBs, other organic pollutants, cyanides, sulphates and acids and alkalis are also commonly found.

Metal mines are found in the major areas of metalliferous ore bodies. They are normally polluted by the very metal that they were exploited for. Most common contaminants therefore include lead, zinc, copper and tin. Some metals occur as guests within the main deposit, for example arsenic normally occurs with tin, cadmium with lead and zinc, and so these metals also occur as contaminants.

Industries which used the metals derived from these primary sources include steelworks, smelters, foundries, anodising and other metal finishing plants. These too will be primarily contaminated by metallic elements though other substances used in the various processes and activities carried out will also be present. As for other categories of sites the range of sizes is wide and can be up to hundreds of hectares.

Steel works often have associated works including their own energy producing plants with by-products reuse through chemical works. Steel works produced large quantities of blast furnace slag – often more than steel – which contains elevated concentrations of manganese, boron, chromium, lead, zinc and cadmium. The metals are normally fused within the slag and so have low impact.

Sewage works and farms often include effluent and sludge disposal areas and farmland and therefore may cover many hectares. Common contaminants normally include lead, zinc, copper, cadmium and nickel whilst almost any metal including arsenic, mercury, boron, and manganese can occur less frequently at lower concentrations. Other possible contaminants depend upon the local activities carried out in the particular area served by the treatment plant. There is also the possibility of biological contamination. This can occur on sewage farms, and on tanneries. Bacteria and viruses may be present originating from the former site use. It is not usual for these organisms to represent a major problem, but their existence needs to be considered and potential hazards assessed accordingly.

Much railway land, such as trackbeds of closed lines, is not contaminated but some has been constructed of waste ash and clinker from local industrial sources and may therefore contain contaminants. Again heavy metals predominate including iron, lead, zinc, copper, cadmium, nickel, and manganese. Less commonly chromium and arsenic are found. Other railway land was used for marshalling yards, maintenance depots, construction of locomotives and rolling stock etc. Such land is more likely to be contaminated to a significant degree because the nature of these activities resembles general industrial use both in range and intensity.

The above examples illustrate the range of types of contamination and the various routes by which the contamination has occurred. It should be readily apparent from these descriptions that the individual sites where such activities were carried out are, in general, readily identifiable from maps, plans and other archival sources. This supports the supposition stated in earlier sections, namely, that knowledge of the potential for contamination may be used as a reliable surrogate for positive confirmation by sampling and analysis for a wide range of the most important types of contaminated land. What cannot be inferred from such knowledge is the actual degree and distribution of contamination on an individual site. These still remain to be established by direct investigation, which is normally carried out in the context of land use changes requested by the relevant planning legislation. This, together with other areas of legislation applicable to the subject of contaminated land, is dealt with in a later section.

3.4   Extracts from DoE Memorandum (May 1989) to Environment Select Committee

3.4.1   Size of the problem

'Contamination is best regarded as a general concept, rather than as something capable of exact definition and measurement. For these reasons, there is no easy method to estimate total of contaminated land. From a sample of cases dealt with by ICRCL the Department estimated in 1986 that there were at least 10,000 hectares of contaminated land in England. But, if all contaminated land was required for the most sensitive use, ie housing, the significance of contamination (and hence the area of such land) would be greater.'

'The most likely category within the derelict land survey to contain a majority of sites which might also be described as "contaminated" is that of "general industrial dereliction". For example major industries such as refineries, power stations and shipbuilding have left a legacy of enormous derelict structures: iron and steel, chemical plants and gas works have left not only structures but serious problems of contamination as have sections of general manufacturing industry associated with metal working. The provisional total in 1988 for such land is 7,950 hectares.'

'Other relevant categories of dereliction where contamination is likely to arise, although not on every such site, are:

Metalliferous spoil heaps	3,700 ha	(Contaminants include heavy metals, sulphate etc)
Excavations and pits	6,200 ha	(Contaminated wastes, landfill gas)
Military dereliction	2,600 ha	(Chemical munitions, explosives)
Derelict railway land combustible materials, ashes	6,700 ha	(Coal, oil, clinker etc)

On this basis, a possible maximum total of 27,000 ha of derelict land might also be classified as potentially contaminated which would be 65% of all derelict land.'

3.4.2 Limitations

The main limitations on the data sources used to derive the above figures are:

i   The figures ignore development already carried out on contaminated land;

ii   The figures are derived purely from previous use: they may exaggerate/underestimate problem;

iii   The area of contamination on any particular site may be very localised;

iv   Above data only measures 'derelict' land. Many contaminated sites are still in use, and will thus not be recorded in a Derelict Land Survey. The above 'possible maximum' estimate of contamination is therefore likely to under-estimate the full extent of contamination.

4 Legislation controlling contaminated land in the UK

Although there is no legislation which deals exclusively with contaminated land, a wide range of legislation in related subjects does exist. The principal areas covered by related legislation are:

Planning for land use change and development control;
Building regulations;
Public health;
Environmental protection and regulation of pollution; and
Miscellaneous responsibilities of landowners, purchasers and vendors of land, and of users and occupiers in relation to health and safety matters.

The extent to which legislation in the above fields is relevant to the specific subject of this report, ie pollution of water by contaminated land, is limited. Where the various responsibilities and powers are relevant to this context, this is incidental rather than by design. The specific subject of contaminated land has not, so far, been the focus of any single statutory legislation. Even in the more closely related fields, such as development control, to date only a small number of departmental Circulars (which are not in themselves legislation) exist which address directly the subject of contaminated land. One of these Circulars does relate to a specific form of contamination, namely landfill gas, and it may be that in due course other more specifically directed official advice of a similar nature will be produced. Whether in time this will lead to specifically designed legislation on the subject to hand cannot be addressed at present.

Such legislation as does exist which is relevant in one way or another to contaminated land is listed in Table 4.1. The most apparently relevant requirements of the legislation are as follows:

Control of Pollution Act 1974 (Part I – Waste on Land) has been replaced by the Environmental Protection Act 1990, though until the latter is implemented the powers and the means by which they are exercised will remain as for the earlier legislation. This part of the 1974 Act dealt with the regulation of current waste disposal sites, and the disposal of controlled waste generally, with the objective of preventing or at least minimising adverse effects to the environment including water resources.

The Environmental Protection Act 1990 (Section 61) states:

'Where on inspection by a waste regulation authority of any land under this section, it appears to the authority that the condition of the land is, by reason of the relevant factors affecting the land, such that pollution of the environment or harm to human health is likely to be caused it shall be the duty of the authority to do such works and take such other steps (whether on the land affected or on adjacent land) as appear to the authority to be reasonable to avoid such pollution or harm.' (EPA, S61.)

This should impose on waste regulation authorities the responsibility for any environmental pollution caused by landfill sites which contain controlled wastes. It also imposes a duty to address problems arising from leachates from old landfill sites. The same section obliges the waste regulation authorities to inspect land within its area in order to locate what is commonly referred to as 'contaminated land". The authorities will be entitled to recover the cost of any reasonable actions taken to avoid pollution from such sites from the owner of the land.

Control of Pollution Act 1974 (Part II – Water Pollution) is now incorporated in the Water Act 1989. Under Section 31 of the 1974 Act a person is guilty of an offence if he causes or knowingly permits any poisonous, noxious or polluting matter to enter any stream or controlled waters of any specified underground waste, unless he is authorised to make such an entry, or it is caused or permitted in an emergency to avoid danger to the public.

Section 46 empowered a water authority to take steps to prevent the pollution of water or to clean-up existing pollution. Under the Water Act 1989 the NRA now takes this responsibility. The Water Act Section 54 makes it a criminal offence to supply water unfit for human consumption.

The Commons Select Committee Inquiry on contaminated land recommended that the NRA should be a statutory consultee on planning applications in relation to contaminated land. In its response the Government indicated that this recommendation will be discussed with the NRA.

4.1 Public Health Act 1936

Section 54 of this Act deals with ground filled with offensive matter, and empowers local authorities to reject applications under the Building Regulations if faecal or offensive animal or vegetable matter is present, unless it has

Table 4.1 Legislation affecting contaminated land

Area of legislation	Principal concerns
1. Town and Country Planning Act 1971	Control of new development Forward planning
2. Hazardous Substance Control Regs 1989	Control of hazardous substance storage
3. Housing and Planning Act 1986	Proper maintenance of privately owned land
4. Local Authorities (Land) Act 1963	Improvement of land
5. Building Regulations 1985	Protection of buildings from toxic substances
6. Public Health Acts 1936	Control of public nuisance
7. Building Act 1984	
8. Housing Act 1957	
9. Control of Pollution Act 1974*	Waste disposal licensing
10. Control of Pollution (Special Waste) Regs 1980*	Water pollution control
11. Water Act 1989	
12. Health and Safety at Work etc Act 1974	Safety of workers on site Safety of public in vicinity
13. COSHH Regs 1988	Protection of workers health
14. CIMAH Regs 1984 and NIHHS Regs 1982	Control of major hazard storage and use reporting of major spills
15. Occupiers Liability Act 1957	Safety of visitors to a site

* Will be replaced by similar powers under Environmental Protection Act 1990 when the latter is implemented

been rendered innocuous. It has therefore only been applied to landfill sites, especially those where methane generation may be a problem or infected animal matter has been deposited. It is evident that many authorities find the section too vague, and are therefore unwilling to apply it to contaminated sites other than landfill sites. This is particularly true for other hazardous materials, such as toxic chemicals or heavy metals, since only after a detailed chemical site investigation can the nature, intensity and distribution of contamination be determined. The section also omits to specify who should do this work and who must pay.

Section 92 read in conjunction with the Public Health (Recurring Nuisances) Act 1969 supplements the common law of public and private nuisance (nuisance being an interference of reasonable enjoyment of neighbouring property), by introducing the concept of a 'statutory nuisance'. The definition relates to:

i any premises (including vacant land) in such a state as to be prejudicial to health or a nuisance;

ii any accumulation or deposit which is prejudicial to health or a nuisance; or

iii any dust or effluvia caused by a trade, business, manufacture or process being prejudicial to health, and injurious or likely to cause injury to public health or a nuisance [as amended by Section 26 of the Local Government (Miscellaneous Provisions) Act 1982].

Every local public health authority has a duty to inspect its area for nuisance. If an authority is satisfied of the existence of a 'statutory nuisance', then it can serve an abatement notice, provided that there is proof of injury to health or a nuisance. The notice can specify any necessary action to prevent the nuisance. Under the 'recurrence of nuisance' provisions in the 1969 Act, when a local authority is satisfied that a statutory nuisance has occurred on any premises or is likely to recur on the same premises, they may serve a 'prohibition notice' which can specify the work necessary to remove it. Although contamination may fall within the definition of a statutory nuisance, there are a number of difficulties in applying these provisions. No nuisances can exist until the operations at the premises have given rise to them. They cannot therefore be used to prevent the unwise development of a contaminated site (eg new housing development on a gasworks site). They can only be used to ameliorate a problem once the development has been completed. Moreover, it may be many years before the health of occupants of buildings on contaminated sites is adversely affected, and a detailed site investigation would be required to establish the exact cause of any such effect.

The Environmental Protection Act 1990 empowers local authorities to take anticipatory action to deal with nuisances before they occur, similar to powers already applicable to noise. The Act also consolidates existing statutory nuisances into one list. Removing these provisions from the earlier public health legislation into a statute dealing with environmental protection may help to overcome the previously restricted applicability of powers in relation to nuisances.

4.2 Water Act 1989

Under Section 110 the Secretary of State for the Environment has a general power to make Regulations specifying appropriate precautions to be taken by persons having custody or control of polluting material, in order to prevent pollution of controlled waters. This power might be applicable to contaminating substances present on or in land, though this would have to be confirmed by judicial rulings. Regulations to control pollution from specified agricultural sources, eg silage, slurry and fuel oil, are to be developed.

The 1989 Act also provides for the designation of Water Protection Zones where the prevention or control of polluting matter in controlled waters is considered necessary.

4.3 Environmental Protection (prescribed processes and substances) Regulations 1991

This Statutory Instrument comes into force in England and Wales on 1 April 1991, and in Scotland on 1 April 1992. This lists the scheduled processes for the purpose of IPC. The list now includes processes involving the manufacture of asbestos or asbestos products, stripping of asbestos from railway carriages, and waste incineration or the production of fuel from waste.

The Statutory Instrument also lists prescribed substances for release into water (similar to the 'Red List' chemicals), and prescribed substances for release to land (Tables 4.2 and 4.3). The latter list now includes organic solvents.

4.4 Action in tort

A person suffering damage from anything which escapes from contaminated land may bring an action in tort, under the rule established in the famous case of Rylands v Fletcher (1886). The law provides that a person who for his own purposes brings on his land, collects and keeps there anything likely to do mischief if it escapes must keep it in at his peril. If he does not do so he is answerable for the damage without proof of negligence or lack of care if it escapes. This strict liability lies only against those persons who are responsible for the toxic materials coming on to the land and for their accumulation. It applies only to abnormal uses of land.

An action in the tort of negligence may lie against a person whose act in relation to the contaminated land causes damage to those living nearby. In such an action the plaintiff must prove three things:

i   that the defendant owed him a duty of care in respect of the act complained of;

ii   that there was a breach of that duty; and

iii that the damage was thereby caused.

4.5 EC Directives

EC Directive 80/68 (Protection of Groundwater against Pollution by Certain Dangerous Substances) was published in 1980. For the purposes of the Directive, the dangerous substances are grouped into two lists. List I includes substances and families of substances with definite potential for harmful effects, for example organohalogen and organophosphorus compounds, mineral oils and hydrocarbons. The substances in List II are considered less harmful; they include various metals and their compounds, certain biocides, and ammonia.

The Directive requires that discharges of List I substances are to be prevented, including those which introduce substances to groundwater by percolation through the ground or sub-soil. This does appear to include leaching of harmful liquids containing the specified substances from landfill sites, and possibly from other types of contaminated sites though the specific applicability of the provision to such sites is difficult to establish.

Similarly, all direct discharges of List II substances require prior investigation before any authorisation of discharges is given.

Table 4.2   Release into water: prescribed substances

Mercury and its compounds
Cadmium and its compounds
All isomers of hexachlorocyclohexane
All isomers of DDT
Pentachlorophenol and its compounds
Hexachlorobenzene
Hexachlorobutadiene
Aldrin
Dieldrin
Endrin
Polychlorinated biphenyls
Dichlorvos
1, 2-Dichloroethane
Trichlorobenzene
Atrazine
Simazine
Tributyltin compounds
Triphenyltin compounds
Trifluralin
Fenitrothion
Azinphos-methyl
Malathion
Endosulfan

Table 4.3   Release to land: prescribed substances

Organic solvents
Azides
Halogens and their covalent compounds
Metal carbonyls
Organo-metallic compounds
Oxidising agents
Polychlorinated dibenzofuran and any congener thereof
Polychlorinated dibenzo-p-dioxin and any congener thereof
Polyhalogenated biphenyls, terphenyls and naphthalenes
Phosphorus

Pesticides, that is to say, any chemical substance or preparation for destroying any organism harmful to plants or to wood or other plant products, any undesired plant or any harmful creature.

Alkali and alkaline earth metals and their oxides.

The Directive does not apply to discharges where the quantities of substances in either List I or List II are so small as to avoid future risk of deterioration in the quality of the receiving water. This proviso would require careful interpretation in the context of discharges, whether direct or indirect by percolation, from contaminated sites.

DoE Circular 20/90 provided further guidance on the classification and application of the EC Groundwater Directive in the UK. The main effect was to incorporate the creation of the National Rivers Authority and the introduction of the Water Act 1989. The NRA has to be consulted in relation to landfill sites used for the disposal of wastes containing List I substances, and all deposits of such wastes should be prohibited where the amounts concerned are likely to lead to discharge of these substances to groundwater. Some NRA regional offices have augmented the legislation by formulating their own policies for the protection of aquifers in sensitive areas. In the main these protection policies take account of currently active or recently operated sites used for disposal of waste to land: 'historic' contamination such as that likely to be present on industrial sites now abandoned has yet to be addressed by most NRA offices.

The EC is known to be preparing a new directive on landfills. In the most recent draft all landfills, both existing and new, must take steps to prevent pollution of the soil and groundwater. Many aspects have yet to be specified, and the scope and application of this draft directive are far from being agreed by member states at present. However, proposed European Community legislation would, if adopted, require that 'all water or leachate in or emanating from the landfill shall be collected' (Anon 1990).

5 Current industrial and other operations which may lead to contaminated land

Contamination of land can result from numerous industrial activities and land uses. The degree to which these sites are contaminated varies, as do the targets at risk. The hazards are therefore site specific. However, the following problems are fairly common, and likely to affect a number of districts within the U K:

a. Methane and other gases from existing and closed landfill sites;

b. Asbestos fibres resulting from the demolition of industrial premises, buildings and power stations. Asbestos contamination may also result from poorly operated waste disposal sites or from illegal and indiscriminate dumping;

c. High concentrations of cadmium, lead and other heavy metals which are a hazard to health;

d. Phenols, tars, benzenes and other organic compounds from old gas works, which in addition to being a health hazard can cause subsequent construction difficulties;

e. Phytotoxic elements which may not be a hazard to health but which can prevent the revegetation of the site;

f. Acidic sites which make redevelopment by building difficult.

g. Organic and chlorinated organic solvent contamination resulting in the longer term in groundwater pollution.

There are difficulties in identifying which industrial sites are likely to give rise to contaminated land, due to the large number of firms within the relevant industries, and the substantial differences in the operating practices within those firms. This leads to significant differences in the risk of contamination even within similar types of firms. However, there are a number of uses which may frequently give rise to contaminated land, the most common being:

waste disposal sites;
gas works, other coal carbonising plants, and ancillary by-products works;
oil refineries and petrol stations;
power stations;
iron and steel works;
petroleum refineries;
metal products fabrication and metal finishing;
chemical works;
textile plants;
leather tanning works;
industries making or using wood preservatives;
non-ferrous metals processing sites;
manufacture of integrated circuits and semi-conductors;
sewage works;
asbestos works;
docks and railway land, especially large sidings and depots;
paper and printing works;
heavy engineering installations;
installations processing radioactive materials;
tank cleaner companies;
munitions production and testing sites;
scrapyards.

One limitation of considering only specific industrial sites is that investigations are almost invariably restricted to within the site boundary, with insufficient attention being paid to the possible spread of contamination beyond the immediate site. However, severe problems can occur outwith these boundaries, due to the migration of tars, oils, and contaminated water into adjacent land. Hydrogeological factors, granular ground structure, and long term disturbance can result in significant levels of contamination spreading hundreds of metres from the original source. Parker and Mather (1979) described how both phenol and cyanide were being leached from a gasworks site in Fife which had been disused for 30 years. Although both were attenuated as they moved down the hydraulic gradient, phenol concentrations were still reported to be significant in the groundwater some 400 metres from the site.

Old gas works have been associated with a number of cases of land contamination. The wastes produced by the manufacture of gas include coal and oil tars, tar-oil-water emulsions, hydrocarbon sludges, ash, spent oxides and lime wastes, and sulphur products. Many of these wastes are potentially serious groundwater pollutants at trace concentrations, and a number of incidents have been recorded in the UK. Aspinwall (1974) describes the contamination of an industrial borehole in the Chalk of Essex. This was thought to have arisen from the disposal of water gas tar from a local gas works. Toft (1974) reviewed the pollution which had occurred through the deposition of gas works wastes in ponds formed in an old pit adjacent to the River Lee in Hertfordshire. Wastes, including tar acids, sludge from sulphate settlement ponds, and oil from gas holders, were deposited between 1905 and 1967 causing pollution of the river gravels over a wide area. Extensive remedial measures were necessary to prevent pollution of the River Lee.

Industrial and waste disposal sites are not the only types of land which can become contaminated. Agricultural land can also become contaminated, mainly through the deposition of waste (eg residues of pesticides, metal-rich sewage sludge, copper from pig slurry) but also from the over use or careless use of agrochemicals.

There are three main methods by which land contamination may occur. The first is that land can become contaminated during routine industrial operations due to accidental leaks and spills, possibly arising from bad work practices. This may occur over a long period of time, and can include aerial deposition around industrial premises and incinerators. The contamination of land may remain undetected for considerable periods. A small engineering works in the West Midlands, was cited by Clayton Bostock Hill and Rigby Ltd in evidence to the Environment Committee. In this case the improper use and disposal of chlorinated solvents used for metal cleaning, and the operation of a paint spray booth were implicated in the contamination of the sandy soil, and the underlying groundwater. The problem came to light when foundations for a building extension were found by the building control officer to be smelling strongly of solvents. An open skip containing paint residues was also present on the site, with contaminated water and residues spilling onto the ground. Plans to excavate the contaminated material were abandoned when it became clear that the contamination increased with depth. The foundations were subsequently sealed, without any attempt being made to deal with any resulting risk of groundwater pollution.

Secondly, the land may have become contaminated due to deliberate actions, such as past waste disposal practices, including illegal contamination by fly-tipping of wastes as well as 'controlled contamination' by landfilling.

Finally, contamination may occur as a result of a major incident, such as a fire. One notable example of this was the Chemstar fire. Chemstar Ltd carried on the business of solvent recovery at a site in Tameside from 1975. Drums of solvent were stored for reprocessing on site. On 6 December 1981 there were two explosions at the site, followed by the worst fire in Manchester for 20 years, with 37 appliances attending and 1,000 people evacuated. The water supply became contaminated and was declared unsafe, with the drums being the most likely source of the contamination. The site was massively contaminated with 400 chemicals. In the following months the Council became increasingly aware of the extent of contamination of the site, and work is still being undertaken to render the site safe. Chemicals were found to be flowing underground towards a nearby village, and amongst the recommendations made by consultants brought in by the Council was that a barrier should be constructed to prevent possible solvent migration from the site.

Proposed legislation on monitoring and control of landfill sites under waste legislation, and control over scheduled processes through Integrated Pollution Control requirements should help to improve controls on contamination. However, the contamination of land in industrial use is not merely a historical legacy but a continuing consequence of current industrial uses. Birmingham has recently been the subject of a study into prolonged urban pollution arising from industrialisation (Ford et al 1988; Rivett et al 1990). The Birmingham aquifer comprises of a Triassic Sandstone basin, with sandstone up to 200 metres thick. The main local industry is metal working, which generates both metal cleaning agent wastes and metallic wastes. Ford et al (1988) concluded that the pollution by inorganic species was not as bad as might have been expected. Correlation of water quality and land use indicated that metal industry boreholes had significantly higher water salinities than other boreholes; in particular chloride, sulphate and sodium concentrations were high. Nitrate concentrations were less well correlated with land use, indicating that the sources were more diffuse.

The survey of organic species (Rivett et al 1990) demonstrated that the aquifer was contaminated to high levels by trichloroethylene (TCE), and that other solvents such as 1,1,1,-trichloroethane (TCA) and perchloroethylene (PCE) were widespread at lower concentrations. The occurrence of solvents could be correlated with land use, and the majority of the contamination was linked to the widespread use of TCE in metal cleaning. The regional picture indicated numerous point sources, and it is expected that other UK aquifers underlying urban areas will show similar contamination.

Solvents appear in the groundwater because they are relatively mobile in the subsurface layers, are not easily broken down, and are used in large quantities by industry. With chlorinated solvents the presence of an immiscible phase which will progressively dissolve in the regional groundwater flow provides a reservoir of pollutant which is difficult to remove. Solvent pollution is highly correlated with the number of solvent users, including more modern industries like electronics. Contamination continues to occur due to careless handling and work practices. These include spillages, illegal discharges to sewers (many of which leak to pollute ground and groundwater), and dripping valves on storage tanks, and leaking containers.

Another factor leading to difficulties in identifying specific industrial activities causing land contamination is the principle of 'caveat emptor' in land transactions. When contaminated land is sold there is no general obligation on the vendor to reveal information to the purchaser about the state of the land. This encourages firms to play down any contamination, and to fail to disclose to prospective purchasers the nature and existence of such contamination. Unexpected problems of contamination are being encountered increasingly frequently by developers, as the ability to carry out soil sampling is extremely limited up to the point where a price is fixed.

6 Contaminated land as a source of water pollution

6.1 Contaminated land as a source of water pollution

The problems of pollution of groundwater arising from contaminated land have been recognised for a considerable period of time. In the mid-1800s, when many houses had their own wells, the Public Health Acts restricted house building close to burial grounds. The danger of contamination from tipped refuse was discussed by Woodward in 1906. Thus the problems for groundwater caused by contaminated land are not new, but are now more acute due to the subsequent growth of landfill sites, industrial development (particularly the engineering, nuclear, and chemical industries), mining and resource exploitation, and old gas works.

Contaminated sites can represent a threat to groundwater and surface water quality both in their undeveloped state, and as a result of disturbance due to redevelopment. The leaching of toxic substances from contaminated land provides a route for their transfer into other sectors of the environment through the medium of water. This can lead to the creation of risks and contamination remote from the original site. The pollutant may also be chemically different from the original contaminant, making identification of the source more difficult. The behaviour of leachates is difficult to predict, and will depend on the geological and hydrological characteristics of the area.

Gradual deterioration in local and regional groundwater quality can result through diffuse pollution from many sources. Only those sites which cause marked changes in groundwater quality abstracted from boreholes, or visible releases into surface waters are likely to be conclusively identified. Once the groundwater has become contaminated it will remain so for a prolonged period – possibly centuries – due to the very slow movement of water through the aquifer, and the residual impact of contaminant desorption. The pollution of groundwater is likely to be extremely long term, and practical solutions may be impossible to find. Once groundwater contamination occurs it may therefore be effectively permanent. In contrast, surface water pollution, although serious and undesirable, is more readily remedied. The emphasis must therefore be on the prevention of further deterioration of groundwater quality.

The contamination of land by industrial processes can create a risk of groundwater pollution from various sources. These include the disposal of wastes on site, leachate from ground, leakage from sewers and storage tanks, and accidental spillages. Pollution can arise from a point source or, in the case of heavily industrialised areas, from a multitude of point sources such that the whole of the aquifer is subject to contamination by diffuse pollution with the exact source being difficult to identify.

There is a danger that previously immobile pollutants in contaminated land may be remobilised if the hydrological conditions alter. Rises in the groundwater levels are currently occurring below London, Birmingham, Liverpool, and other cities. The construction of barrages in major estuaries is also likely to raise groundwater levels below adjacent cities and urban areas. Liverpool, Cardiff and Birmingham overlie a major aquifer, and groundwater levels in these areas have been rising due to less abstraction taking place. Around the Tame Valley area groundwater levels are now fairly near the surface. Solvent contamination is already widespread, and the risk of further pollutants leaching into the surface water systems is increasing as the rising groundwater comes into greater contact with contaminated land.

Leachates from contaminated land can also lead to pollution of ground and surface waters. The ability of leachates from landfill sites to cause pollution of groundwater is well documented. The main leachates arising fall into four categories (Department of the Environment 1986):

1. major elements or ions such as calcium, magnesium, iron, sodium, ammonia, carbonate, sulphate and chloride;

2. trace metals such as manganese, chromium, nickel, lead and cadmium;

3. a wide variety of organic compounds, which are usually measured as Total Organic Carbon (TOC) or Chemical Oxygen Demand (COD);

4. microbiological components.

Although the leachate from household waste is fairly consistent, the composition of leachate at sites receiving industrial waste is much more variable. A desk study of landfill sites in England and Wales by Gray *et al* (1974) indicated that there were 51 sites which represented a serious pollution risk to major or minor aquifers. Landfill sites can produce a highly polluting leachate, which can have a significant effect on groundwater supplies. However, some geological environments are effective in neutralising and cleansing leachates by geochemical processes, with carbonate aquifers being more effective in this regard than many sandstone aquifers (Edmunds *et al* 1987; Mather 1989).

The geological conditions found in the UK include a low water table and significant clay deposits. This has meant that we have in the past encountered fewer difficulties with the pollution of groundwater due to contaminated land than some other European countries such as the Netherlands. However, it has also led to less effort being made to protect such water resources in the UK than in some other countries, despite the fact that certain areas of the UK are heavily dependent on groundwater for their public supplies. Although only 30% of the total UK public supply is derived from abstraction from aquifers, some towns rely almost entirely on this source. In the Southern Water area 74% of supplies come from groundwater. In addition it is an important source of independent supplies for industry and agriculture.

Although urban areas are most commonly associated with contaminated land the mining of metals and minerals has left extensive spoil heaps in rural areas, containing various contaminants. Spoil from lead mining in Shropshire and Wales has led to elevated lead and cadmium levels in drainage water. In the Derbyshire Peak District the deposition of partially burnt limestone into waste tips has led to highly alkaline leachate contaminating the groundwater and surface waters. However, the principal mining activity contributing to groundwater pollution problems in the UK is coal mining. Many Nottinghamshire coal mines have deposited their spoil directly onto the exposed Triassic Sandstone and Manganese Limestone aquifers. As surface water penetrates through these spoil heaps the dissolved solids content rises significantly. Ranges of 1,300-3,000 mg/l chloride, 2,600-5,500 mg/l sulphate, 1,750-3,400 mg/l sodium, 0.1-5.3 mg/l iron and 0.1-2.7 mg/l manganese are quoted by Nicholls (1974) for a tip in Yorkshire.

The progressive long-term effect of pollution from colliery spoil has been documented at Markham Main Colliery near Doncaster. In this case an extensive spoil tip has been deposited over an outcrop of the Triassic Sandstone aquifer and into sand and gravel overlying the sandstone. When a borehole was constructed half a mile away in 1919 the chloride content of abstracted water was 12.9 mg/l. As the tip grew the chloride levels rose, reaching 337 mg/l in 1932 and 2925 mg/l in 1965. The borehole was abandoned for public supply in 1933 (Nicholls 1974). Confirmation that seepage from the tip was the source of the pollution was provided by a tritium study (Mather et al 1978). Elevated chloride levels from coal mining can arise not only as a consequence of spoil disposal, but also through the construction of slurry lagoons on exposed aquifers .

In Wales the most common sources of contamination of land are metalliferous mine waste, former industrial usage, or waste disposal. Aquatic ecosystems are being contaminated by drainage from old mines, leading to poor fish survival in some Welsh waters. Also, the mobilisation of mine wastes by wind-blow and by rain has had a marked effect on stream sediments and on nearby agricultural land with resultant risks to flora, fauna, and people. There are also numerous areas, particularly former industrial sites, which were used for the dumping of toxic substances prior to legislation to control the disposal of such waste. Many sites such as former quarries therefore contain drums of unidentified chemicals with the potential to contaminate the surrounding area, including the land, groundwaters and surface waters.

6.2 Redevelopment implications

Interest in the redevelopment of contaminated land has increased in recent years as land prices have risen and restrictions on the development of green belt has limited the availability of greenfield sites. This is particularly true in the South-East, where the available land resources are limited, so that land is often being redeveloped rather than developed for the first time.

Problems can arise when the contaminated site to be redeveloped overlies a water bearing formation, or aquifer, such as the chalk aquifers found in the Thames area. Developers frequently argue that as the contamination has already been present for many years the redevelopment of the site can cause no further harm. However, natural and man-made impermeable layers below the site can be disturbed by site investigation boreholes, site demolition and stripping, and the construction of foundations. This can result in the release of contaminants into the underlying aquifer. Also, the clearing of the site can lead to increased exposure to rainfall, and increased leaching of pollutants. If objections to foundation piling in contaminated sites are raised by the NRA to prevent penetration through the contaminanted zones and into the aquifer, then the developer may argue that such a restriction makes the site commercially non-viable. The final decision on the type of piling used is, according to Thames Region NRA, usually dictated by commercial interests rather than the risk to groundwater posed by the different methods.

These problems are exacerbated by a lack of the necessary expertise in planning departments to assess the impact of developments on water pollution. This combines with a lack of information on contaminated land within the area covered by the planning authority leading to the danger of water contamination being unrecognised by the planning department. Consequently consultations with the NRA may not take place, or else may occur only at an advanced stage in the planning of the development.

The NRA has expressed concern at a lack of integration between planning authorities and water authorities in relation to planning applications for contaminated land. In particular, the water authorities do not have the power to insist on particular treatments when a contaminated site is developed, and have instead to rely on the planning authorities imposing conditions on the granting of planning permission. In those cases where agreement is reached to impose conditions with a view to protecting groundwater the planning authorities are often reluctant to enforce them.

The difficulties encountered by the NRA were illustrated during the construction of the M42 near Bromsgrove, Worcester. The road passed through the middle of an old toxic waste site. The NRA were consulted by the agents of the Department of Transport, and certain conditions were agreed with the engineering consultants in order to protect water resources. However, when the contract was awarded for the building of the road the contractor appointed proved unwilling to transfer the waste to a licensed site for disposal, preferring instead to rebury it alongside the line of the road. The NRA were opposed to this proposal, as the area overlay an aquifer. The financial interests of the contractor were therefore over-riding environmental considerations, and the NRA were unable to enforce the original agreement. After long negotiations the contractor agreed to dig a new disposal site on clay for the purpose of disposing of the waste.

These deficiencies led the Environment Committee to recommend that the NRA be given statutory consultee status in relation to planning applications for the redevelopment of contaminated land. If implemented this would mean that NRA requirements would have to be incorporated into planning decisions. This would be a recognition of the implications for water resources of the redevelopment of contaminated land.

The nature of the problems for water resources created by redevelopment are not always immediate, due to the fact that they occur through the ground itself, often via the groundwater. This can lead to significant delays in the release of pollution manifesting itself. The nature of this route and the delays involved can increase the problems in identifying the source of the contamination, as well as preventing its rapid detection.

Although the ICRCL provides some guideline figures for contaminated land, known as 'trigger values', these relate to the impact on people or plants of direct contact with the soil or waste material, and do not indicate the danger to water resources. Indeed the lack of specific attention to the problems of water poulution from contaminated land is reflected in the statement of the ICRCL to the Environment Committee that 'advice formulated from other viewpoints such as the protection of health, ensuring plant growth, safeguarding buildings and site ancillary services etc, also provides adequate protection of ground and surface waters'. This view was refuted by the NRA, who emphasised that the critical factor for water contamination was leachability, which was ignored by the ICRCL guidance. There are many compounds which pose a threat to water quality but are not listed in the ICRCL guidelines, including a wide range of organic compounds. The guidelines are of little relevance as an indicator of the threat to water, as much of the contaminant is likely to be present in an insoluble form. Nearly all of the analytical data obtained from site investigations indicates the total level of contaminant present, not the water soluble component. In most cases such an analysis would require a different method of extraction. This could be a simple shake test with water, although if such a procedure were to be followed a uniform agreed aqueous leaching test would be required.

Further problems arise from the fact that sites are usually contaminated with a cocktail of different chemicals with little being known about the interactions between these substances, or between the pollutants and the components of the soil.

Many sites are being redeveloped by covering up the contamination with apparently minimal regard for the long term effectiveness of the solution, and frequently without any monitoring. The Environment Committee's investigations into contaminated land in 1990 led them to conclude 'We are not convinced that the remedial techniques currently employed in the UK represent the Best Practical Environmental Option.' In particular they were 'concerned at a tendency to ignore the impact on groundwater of *in situ* clean-ups'.

Covering over of contaminated land, either with topsoil or with hard surfacing such as tarmac leaves the contaminants *in situ*, where there may be a danger of them migrating, and continuing to constitute a threat to groundwater. The use of clean-up methods where the soil is actually cleaned is rare in the UK. The reliance on cover-up and off site disposal to landfill in the UK does not deal with the problem in the long term, and would seem to offer only a temporary relief. This situation has been encouraged by the comparatively low costs of landfill, together with a lack of attention to the long term environmental implications.

Excavation and off-site disposal in landfill sites is extensively used as a method of treating contaminated land in the UK. Conditions on the disposal of 'controlled wastes' as defined in the Control of Pollution Act, 1974, are not waived for contaminated soils. The same restrictions also apply to waste excavated from one part of a site and deliberately deposited at another part of the same site set aside for this purpose. Unless the site is already licensed under COPA, such a licence will have to be obtained, and this will involve obtaining a planning permission prior to licensing. However, although this is the legal position, it is not always observed in practice.

Another problem posed by excavation is that many of the sub-surface hazards may remain unidentified at the commencement of the site clearance, only to be revealed during the excavation works. These hazards can include underground tanks or pipes containing unidentified chemicals, drums of buried chemicals, or waste. Incidents have also been recorded of excavators accidentally breaking into underground tanks, full of substances such as coal tar, leading to a sudden release of large volumes of tar and causing further gross soil contamination.

Chemical treatment of contaminated soil may not actually return the soil to a condition which allows it to be used for the same purposes as before the contamination occurred. Furthermore, it may only 'lock-up' the pollutants in the soil so that they become less easily available to plant and animal life, or to leaching. In the longer term these contaminants may become mobilised again, thus becoming able to migrate through the ground and contaminate groundwaters.

There is a conflict between the developer's desire for rapid site development and the time taken to satisfy environmental needs. Also, the NRA have experienced difficulty in convincing developers of the reality of water pollution concerns. These concerns can necessitate lengthy and expensive site investigation. Once the developer realises the full cost and time implications of dealing with the contamination there is a tendency to refuse to recognise the existence of any threat.

Water quality, particularly of groundwater, can be affected by the way in which contaminated sites are investigated, stripped, prepared, and developed. It is therefore important that the implications for water pollution be considered at an early stage in the redevelopment of such land, as contamination of groundwater can occur even during site investigations unless appropriate precautions are taken.

Redevelopment proposals should include the precautions to be taken to prevent or avoid exacerbation of groundwater or surface water pollution. Drilling of boreholes should employ methods which minimise the risk of spreading contamination deeper into the ground. Temporary drilling casings should closely follow the base of the hole as it is drilled, and all perched water tables should be sealed out as effectively as possible. Wherever possible any clay layers below the site should be left intact. If it is necessary to penetrate an underlying aquifer special precautions may be necessary, as recommended in WRc Technical Report Number 91, 'The Investigation of Landfill Sites'. The need to include some permanent groundwater quality monitoring boreholes should be considered, and their location and construction carefully planned. These may be required to monitor the effect of the disturbance and redevelopment of the site on groundwater quality. Temporary boreholes should be adequately sealed up, normally using bentonite/cement grouts or plugs at appropriate levels, particularly against clay layers. Soil and water samples should be analysed for the chemical parameters appropriate to the previous use of the site, with due consideration given to testing for the water soluble component.

Dewatering of contaminated sites should not be carried out without consultations with the water authorities. A consent would normally be required for any discharge to soakaways or watercourses, under COPA II. Discharges to sewers would require a Trade Effluent Consent. Where discharges contain contaminants the only acceptable route is likely to be the sewer system, and then only after careful consideration of the amount and type of contaminants, to assess the likely effect on the receiving sewage treatment works.

One of the problems in assessing the effect of contaminated land on groundwater is that very few case histories are reported in the scientific literature. This may be because investigations were carried out on a commercial in-confidence basis, or because individuals within the water industry and their consultants do not have the opportunity to write up their work for publication in the open literature. However, it means that much valuable scientific data are lost, and the true extent of groundwater pollution from contaminated land is difficult to quantify.

6.3 Grants for clean up (England and Wales)

In England a number of grant schemes provide financial assistance for the reclamation of derelict land, although none is specifically targeted at contaminated land. The DoE operates four main mechanisms: Derelict Land Grant, City Grant, the Urban Programme and Urban Development Corporations. Estimates of expenditure and outputs for reclamation for the period 1982-83 to 1988-89 (all at 1989-90 prices) are given in Table 6.1.

The main source of funds for redevelopment of contaminated land in England is the Derelict Land Grant scheme (DLG). The aim of the DLG is to ensure that the subsequent use or development costs are no higher than they would have been if the development had taken place on a greenfield site. For bodies other than local authorities the grant is paid on the net cost of reclamation taking into account the increase in the value of the land due to reclamation. Local authorities are paid the gross costs of reclamation, but are required to repay some or all of the grant when the value of the reclaimed land is realised through sale, lease or appropriation. Ninety per cent of DLG resources are allocated to local authorities, and over 90 per cent of total DLG expenditure goes to the six most northerly regions.

One recent development in the Derelict Land Grant scheme was announced by Judith Denner of the Department of the Environment in February 1991. In line with the commitments made by the Government in the White Paper, the objectives of the DLG scheme have been reformulated to place greater emphasis on reclamation schemes that will improve the environment or deal with serious contamination, especially those that can demonstrate new clean-up methods. A total of £181m in DLG will be available over the next two financial years (1991–92 and 1992–93) to deal with derelict land reclaimed for a variety of soft and hard end uses.

In Wales, the Welsh Development Agency (WDA) can give 100 per cent grants to local authorities for derelict land reclamation to cover the costs of land acquisition, scheme design and implementation. The Agency maintains a rolling programme of such projects intended for completion up to four or five years ahead, according the highest priority to the removal of hazardous material where no-one else is under a statutory obligation by the private sector, providing 80 per cent of the net loss incurred in carrying out the work. The grant situation in Scotland and Northern Ireland is covered in the sections of this report on these regions.

Table 6.1   DoE expenditure on land reclamation. £million, 1989–90 prices (cash values)

Grant	1982–83	1983–84	1984–85	1985–86	1986–87	1987–88	1988–89
UDG[1]		6.00	12.51	17.90	19.72	15.73	10.16
		(4.41)	(9.64)	(14.56)	(16.56)	(13.90)	(9.63)
URG/City Grant							6.08
							(5.76)
UDC's[2]	19.23	47.78	31.00	24.71	21.21	19.81	40.63
	(13.50)	(35.10)	(23.90)	(20.10)	(17.80)	(17.50)	(38.51)
Urban Programme[3]	13.67	15.38	18.03	14.14	10.24	15.17	10.23
	(9.60)	(11.30)	(13.90)	(11.50)	(8.60)	(13.40)	(9.70)
DLG	87.02	92.82	90.60	92.40	97.82	91.29	82.41
	(61.10)	(68.19)	(69.85)	(75.15)	(82.11)	(80.65)	(78.11)
Total	**119.92**	**161.98**	**152.14**	**149.15**	**148.99**	**142.00**	**149.51**
	(84.20)	**(119.00)**	**(117.29)**	**(121.31)**	**(125.07)**	**(125.46)**	**(141.71)**

Source: Department of the Environment DPS Division, Dec 1989

Notes
[1]   Represents expenditure on all sites with land and/or buildings which were either derelict or abandoned
[2]   Assumes an even spend between 1982 and 1987 for the London Docklands Development Corporation
[3]   Includes expenditure on derelict land, vacant land, parks and recreational land

The Government has extended the scheme for funding environmental research, the Environmental Protection Technology Scheme, into *in situ* cleaning of contaminated soils.

7 Contaminated land in Scotland

7.1 Registers of contaminated land

The duty to compile registers of contaminated land, as introduced by the 1990 Environmental Protection Act, applies both north and south of the border. The intention to compile such registers is therefore the same in Scotland. However, there will be a separate consultation procedure carried out, which is due to begin later this year.

7.2 Existing information on contaminated land in Scotland

The existing information on contaminated land in Scotland broadly parallels the situation in England and Wales, in that studies carried out to date have surveyed 'vacant land', and 'waste disposal sites' rather than being specifically directed at assessing the nature or extent of contaminated land in Scotland.

A survey of vacant land in Scotland was carried out in 1988 by the Scottish Development Agency and Scottish Office Planners. Although this was not specifically about contaminated land it did contain a sub-section on this topic. This pilot study was by its nature neither comprehensive nor uniform; a more complete picture should emerge from a further more detailed study which has now been carried out, but the findings of this study are not yet available. The pilot study identified 7,392 ha of derelict land in Scotland and 5,060 ha of vacant land, giving a total of 12,452 ha. As illustrated in Table 7.1, vacant and derelict land was concentrated in Strathclyde and Lothian Regions, which accounted for 56% and 16% of the total respectively. It is expected that the more recent study will identify a significantly greater area of vacant or derelict land than the 1988 study.

Half of the total area (6,507 ha) had been vacant or derelict since before 1978. Only 3% land was known to be contaminated, 7% was suspected of being contaminated, 32% was not suspected, and the situation was unknown for 58% (see Table 7.2).

Table 7.1 Derelict and vacant land in Scotland by region and islands area

Area	Total derelict and vacant land			Derelict land			Vacant land		
	Hectares	(%)	No of sites	Hectares	(%)	No of sites	Hectares	(%)	No of sites
Strathclyde	6 993	(56.2%)	3 031	3 604	(48.8%)	1 262	3 389	(67.0%)	1 769
Lothian	2 040	(16.4%)	604	1 401	(19.0%)	310	639	(12.6%)	294
Central	793	(6.4%)	403	384	(5.2%)	109	409	(8.1%)	294
Grampian	644	(5.2%)	407	493	(6.7%)	232	151	(3.0%)	175
Fife	629	(5.1%)	222	454	(6.1%)	143	175	(3.5%)	79
Tayside	591	(4.7%)	188	456	(6.2%)	80	135	(2.7%)	108
Highland	398	(3.2%)	246	290	(3.9%)	120	108	(2.1%)	126
Dumfries and Galloway	249	(2.0%)	68	237	(3.2%)	43	12	(0.2%)	25
Borders	73	(0.6%)	47	47	(0.6%)	20	25	(0.5%)	27
Orkney	28	(0.2%)	35	21	(0.3%)	14	7	(0.1%)	20
Western Isles	15	(0.1%)	10	5	(0.1%)	2	10	(0.2%)	7
Total	**12 452**	**(100%)**	**5 261**	**7 392**	**(100%)**	**2 335**	**5 060**	**(100%)**	**2 924**

Table 7.2 Contamination of vacant and derelict land

	Hectares	(%)	No of sites
Known contamination	402	(3.2%)	48
Suspected contamination	834	(6.7%)	189
Not suspected	3 953	(31.8%)	2 488
Tested	14	(0.1%)	4
Unknown	7 247	(58.2%)	2 532
Total	**12 452**	**(100%)**	**5 261**

About three years ago a survey was carried out of waste disposal sites in Scotland with the potential to produce landfill gas. This covered those sites which had taken biodegradable waste in the period since 1960. A follow-up to this survey is currently being completed.

7.3 Grants for clean-up (Scotland)

There is no Derelict Land Grant Scheme in Scotland, as the structure of support for environmental schemes takes a different form. Grants for the redevelopment of contaminated sites can be awarded by Scottish Enterprise (successor to the Scottish Development Agency) or by Highlands and Islands Enterprise (successor to the Highlands and Islands Development Board). However, the remit of these organisations is to provide support for projects of benefit to the economy *and* the environment. The award of grants is therefore concentrated on those schemes which also have economic benefits, rather than simply removing contamination for environmental improvement reasons. There is no automatic right to the award of a grant, the decision on whether to make an award being the responsibility of the two Enterprise organisations. Most schemes receiving such grants involve reclamation relating to potential industrial or residential use.

Scottish Homes also have the power to award grants for redevelopment of contaminated land if the intended use is a housing project. However, in practice Scottish Homes tends to regard the award of grants for these projects as the responsibility of Scottish Enterprise.

During the year 1988/89 the SDA was involved in 145 projects, including the reclamation of contaminated land, enhancing tourist attraction and environmental improvements. Even though 300 hectares of vacant or derelict land have been reclaimed in the last 2 years, much remains to be done.

8 Northern Ireland

8.1 Registers of contaminated land

There is at present no duty to compile registers of contaminated land in Northern Ireland. This differs from the situation in the rest of the UK, where the 1990 Environmental Protection Act imposes this duty on waste regulation authorities. A recent House of Commons Select Committee on environmental issues in Northern Ireland recommended that a similar obligation to compile a register of contaminated land should be created in the province. This was accepted by the Government in its response to the Committee's report (published in March 1991).

8.2 Existing information on contaminated land in Northern Ireland

No information was found of any survey of vacant, derelict or contaminated land having been carried out in Northern Ireland. However, a number of contaminated sites are known to exist. Amongst the most serious of these there are nine sites contaminated with tarry wastes from acetylene production. Du Pont inherited the most serious of these, and has spent around £5 million on redeveloping the site. Other sites which are believed to have been contaminated include two former fibre production sites.

8.3 Regulation of contamination of land

A recent House of Commons Environment Committee report on environmental issues in Northern Ireland concluded that the province's environmental protection arrangements are much less highly developed than in Britain, with EC legislation often being implemented late and the statutory framework generally being some years behind the rest of the UK. The 1990 Environmental Protection Act applies only to Britain, not to Northern Ireland. However, the Government has promised to consult 'as soon as possible' on legislation to introduce integrated pollution control in the province by 1993. Legislation on the aftercare of landfills is also to be introduced in the province by 1993. These measures will be modelled on the Environmental Protection Act 1990.

The Select Committee on environmental issues in Northern Ireland also recommended that the Government take steps to prevent the contamination of land by industry in Northern Ireland by:

a. enacting provisions equivalent to those of the Environmental Protection Act 1990 relating to the aftercare of landfills and Integrated Pollution Control;

b. preparing a Code of Practice ensuring the contamination is addressed when land is sold;

c. ensuring that long-term environmental considerations are fully taken into account when financial inducements are given to incoming investors (Para 68).

A code of practice on contaminated land is now being prepared. However, the Government argue that well established arrangements already exist for consultations between the Industrial Development Board and the pollution control authorities before any decision is taken on grant aid.

8.4 Waste management

A recent review of waste disposal and regulation carried out for the DoE (NI) by consultants Aspinwall and Co recommended the transfer of waste regulation from district to regional level, and joint provision landfill facilities by the districts. The Environment Committee added that the DoE (NI) should itself take a hand in planning the provision of waste management facilities for 'special' waste. Regional disposal arrangements might also be better equipped to bear the costs of higher waste management standards.

8.5 Grants for clean-up (Northern Ireland)

The Select Committee also recommended that a clearly-defined system of grant aid should be introduced specifically directed at the clean-up of contaminated sites. The Government agreed to consider the question of financial assistance.

No Derelict Land Grant or equivalent scheme exists in Northern Ireland, nor any other national grant system aimed at contaminated land issues. However, EC funding has been obtained for the investigation of the nine sites contaminated with large quantities of tarry wastes from the production of acetylene.

In England and Wales the DoE has set aside £33 million for urgent remedial work carried out by local authorities on landfill sites leaking gas in quantities liable to present hazards of fire or explosion. No such funds are available to local authorities in Northern Ireland. However, even in England and Wales, the funds are only awarded if the council concerned has no sums left in any of its capital allocation which are not contractually committed. This means that in practice none of the funds available for 1989–90 were distributed.

9 Future changes

As indicated previously contaminated land has been treated as a special case of derelict land by Governments in the past and therefore the major public funding for contaminated land rehabilitation occurs as part of the Derelict Land Reclamation Programme. This programme has recently been announced for 1991/2. It involves the expenditure of £88m, a 23% increase on 90/1. Of this sum approximately £24m is earmarked for treatment at 'contaminated land' but once again we are drifting into problems of definition. This £24m is expected to reclaim approximately 230 hectares.

Contaminated land, and in particular its environmental implications, seem to have come much more into prominence recently. Both the Environment Committee report and statements from the NRA have outlined the actions they consider necessary. These statements are very relevant to the subject of this report.

The Environment Committee report (1990) on contaminated land made a number of recommendations for the development of standards and controls related to contaminated land, including the following statements:

'76. We recommend

i   that a range of quality objectives and standards be derived as appropriate for different classes of land use (residential, recreational, agricultural and industrial) and for designated sensitive areas, in particular where groundwater or other water systems are at risk from contamination;

ii   that the various statutory authorities with an interest in contaminated land (such as local planning authorities and the NRA) be placed under a legal duty to have regard to these standards in exercising relevant statutory functions; and

iii that the Secretary of State seek appropriate general powers with a view to implementation by subsequent regulation.

77.   We consider that until the establishment of an Environmental Protection Agency as suggested in our Report on Toxic Waste, the generation of standards on all aspects of soil quality can be best achieved within the Toxic Substances Division of the DoE and recommend that it be given this responsibility.'

(Sections 76 and 77, First Report of Environment Committee 1990)

The Environment Committee Report also addressed the problem of preventing the generation of contaminated land, and the role of the Environmental Protection Bill in increasing controls on potentially contamination processes:

"107. The Environmental Protection Bill will extend control over the generation of contaminated land in two ways: through Integrated Pollution Control [IPC] of scheduled processes by HMIP and by requiring after care of waste disposal sites. Integrated Pollution Control will for the first time give HMIP powers to control the generation of wastes to all media, including contamination of soil by leakages and spillages. However,it will apply only to a list of scheduled processes which, on present proposals, do not correspond exactly with those activities which the DoE has told us have the greatest potential to contaminate land. Polluting activities which the DoE apparently does not propose to schedule at present include waste disposal sites, the manufacture of integrated circuits and semi-conductors, installations processing radioactive materials, and asbestos works.

108. We welcome the tightening of control over discharges to all environmental media; but we feel that legislation should also place on industrialists a duty of care for the avoidance of polluting practices in future. We asked the minister about the imposition of such a duty and received a sympathetic reply. We recommend that the Environmental Protection Bill should impose on operators (whether subject to integrated pollution control or not) a duty to carry out their activities in a way which avoids soil pollution. We further recommend that the criteria for determining the processes to be scheduled for IPC should include consideration of their potential to contaminate land."

(Sections 107 and 108, First Report of the Environment Committee 1990)

NRA officials have recently stated that 'to maintain the momentum on the contaminated land problem the NRA will need to push forward on several fronts:

1. Identify those sites where leaching is causing significant contamination of the water environment;

2. Prioritise those sites on the basis of need for clean-up, and draw up action plans for implementation;

3. Investigate available leach tests and standardise on one, or a series;

4. Set guidelines (in conjunction with the DoE) for the standards we would wish to see imposed on the level of contamination which may remain on any site;

5. Continue to liaise with planning authorities, developers and consultants alike on the issues surrounding water pollution and contaminated land.

The time scale for the completion of these actions is uncertain at the present. Selected individual sites are already receiving attention, but looking at the problem as a whole, on a national scale, will take considerable extra resources.' (Harris 1991.)

As indicated earlier, IPC and BATNEEC should minimise soil contamination in future, at least from scheduled works. However, non-scheduled works may also lead to soil contamination and there is a continuing need for improved housekeeping at all industrial premises such that soakaways and spillages onto soil become recognised as unacceptable practices.

Remedial activities on contaminated sites have in the past generally consisted of burial or excavation and landfill disposal. Such practices will not usually be the best practicable environmental option, and *in situ* remediation will become increasingly important. The recent announcement of the initiation of a large research project at Warren Spring Laboratory into the technologies involved in such remediation is very welcome. However, it is important that the consequential environmental effects of such technology are also taken into account.

10 Summary and conclusions

The problem of how contaminated land should be defined is of the greatest importance. The issue of definition has a considerable influence on:

a. attitudes and policies towards contaminated land;

b. estimation of the extent of contaminated land in the UK. In this respect consideration should be given to introducing the term polluted land for some purposes.

As recommended by the Environment Committee, the introduction of soil quality objectives, and quality standards for specific contaminants, may provide a better framework for the development of policies related to contaminated land.

Legislation in the UK to date has been mainly concerned with the desirability, safety, and cost effectiveness of bringing contaminated land back into use, and to a much lesser extent with other issues such as environmental protection – including water pollution.

Legislation which gives effect to the above policy reflects this differing emphasis in that the main controls over contaminated land derive from Town and Country Planning Acts and related statutes, rather than from environmental protection legislation.

The reason for this difference in emphasis lies primarily in the 'time dynamic' of contaminated land. There is in fact a continuous sequence of such land:

a. Sites contaminated by industrial use before adequate environmental controls over their practices existed. Many former industrial sites were operated according to practices which, judged by modern standards of acceptability, would be regarded as unsatisfactory. Such sites ('historical contamination') comprise a large proportion of the total stock of contaminated land in the UK, but there is little or no prospect of bringing them within the present system of environmental controls. Moreover, they will only come within the scope of planning controls as and when changes of land use (eg redevelopment or reclamation) occur. The principle of retrospective legislation is uncommon in the UK;

b. Sites which are in active use but which are not operated according to best current practice, and are incapable of conforming with BATNEEC or other equally acceptable principles. These sites comprise most of the remaining stock of contaminated land, but probably do not represent a major source of increasing importance in the future;

c. Sites likely to be used by future industries, which can be expected to operate according to stricter controls with respect to impact on the environment than current or present sites. If Integrated Pollution Control and other legislative constraints work effectively, then the importance of future industrial sites as a source of contaminated land should be negligible.

There is little information on contaminated sites acting as point sources for water pollution. It must therefore be doubtful that such sites act as significant sources of acute pollution. Precise details of such sites as sources of diffuse pollution are also not readily available. However, evidence of ground and surface water pollution in urban areas indicates that contaminated sites almost certainly make a contribution.

The factors outlined in this report have led us to the following main conclusions in relation to water quality:

1. More information is required on the influence of remediation work on groundwater quality;

2. The NRA should become statutory consultees on planning proposals for the redevelopment of contaminated land;

3. There is a need for improved techniques for assessing water contamination from contaminated sites.

References

ANON (1990) Proposal for a Council Directive on the landfill of waste. Commission of the European Communities, Draft No 5 02/8/90. 28pp.

ASPINWALL R (1974) Phenolic pollution of chalk at Beckton, Essex. In: *Groundwater pollution in Europe* J A Cole (ed), 229-302.

DENNER J (1991) Contaminated Land - Policy Development in the U K. In: *Papers and Proceedings, IBC Technical Services conference, Contaminated Land - Policy Regulation and Technology London*, February 1991.

DEPARTMENT OF THE ENVIRONMENT (DoE) (1986) Landfilling Wastes. Waste Management Paper No 26, HMSO, London, 206pp.

EDMUNDS W M, COOK J M, DARLING W G, KINNIBURGH D G, MILES D L, BATH A H, MORGAN-JONES M and ANDREWS J N (1987) Baseline geochemical conditions in the Chalk aquifer, Berkshire, U K: a basis for groundwater quality management. *Applied Geochemistry* **2**, 251-74.

FEATES Dr F (1990) Integrated pollution regulation – The role of HMIP.

FORD M, TELLMAN J H, LLOYD J W, LERNER D N (1988) Inorganic groundwater pollution of the Birmingham aquifer. Pre-printed abstract, Royal Society of Chemistry. Water Chemistry Forum meeting on Groundwater Resource Protection and Exploitation, November 1988.

GRAY D A, MATHER J D and HARRISON I B (1974) Review of groundwater pollution from waste disposal sites in England and Wales, with provisional guidelines for future site selection. *Quarterly Journal of Engineering Geology* **7**, 181-196.

HARRIS R C and FLAVIN R (1990) Water pollution and contaminated land – an NRA perspective. In: *Papers and proceedings, Institution of Water and Environmental Management symposium, Redevelopment of Contaminated Land*, Solihull, 2 October 1990.

HARRIS R C (1991) Contaminated Land and the Water Environment. In: *Papers and Proceedings, IBC conference, Contaminated Land – Policy, Regulation and Technology*, London, February 1991.

HOUSE OF COMMONS ENVIRONMENT COMMITTEE (1990) First Report: Contaminated Land, Volumes 1-3, HMSO, London.

INSTITUTE OF ENVIRONMENTAL HEALTH OFFICERS (1989) Contaminated land – professional guidance, IEHO, London.

MATHER J D (1989) The attenuation of the organic component of landfill leachate in the unsaturated zone: a review. *Quarterly Journal of Engineering Geology* **22**, 241-246.

MATHER J D (1991) Groundwater pollution from contaminated land. In: *Papers and proceedings, IBC Technical Services Ltd conference, Contaminated Land: Policy Regulation and Technology* London Feb 1991.

MATHER J D, GRAY D A, SMITH D B and CLIPSHAM E W (1977) Environmental tritium as an indicator of potential groundwater pollution from landfills. In: *Papers and proceedings, Nater Research Centre Conference, Groundwater Quality - Measurement, Prediction and Protection*. Reading Sept 1976, 327-340.

NICHOLLS G D (1974) Pollution affecting wells in the Bunter Sandstone. In: *Groundwater pollution in Europe* Cole J A (ed), 116-125.

PARKER A and MATHER J D (1979) An investigation into pollution from a disused gasworks site near Ladybank, Fife. AERE Harwell Report No R9213, HMSO, London.

RIVETT M O, LERNER D N, LLOYD J W and CLARK L (1990) Organic contamination of the Birmingham aquifer. *Journal of Hydrology* **113**, 307-323.

TOFT H P (1974) Pollution of flood plain gravels by gas works waste. In: *Groundwater pollution in Europe* J A Cole (ed), 303-307.

WOODWARD H B (1906) The utilisation of old pits and quarries, and of cliffs, for the reception of rubbish. *Journal of the Royal Sanitary Institute* **27**, 476-469.

Pollution Impact of Cleaning Products

December 1991

Environmental Resources Limited

Acknowledgements:

ERL would like to thank the Staff and members of the Royal Commission on Environmental Pollution and the various regions and individuals of the National Rivers Authority and River Purification Boards for their help in carrying out this study. We also wish to thank the Trade Associations who helped us complete this Report.

Authors: S Clarke, J V Towner and
            S Yeoman

Contents

1 Introduction

1.1 Purpose of the Report

This report to the Royal Commission on Environmental Pollution assesses freshwater (including groundwater) pollution from UK cleaning products, (not including solvents). It reviews the scale of the problem in the UK, and addresses the issue of freshwater pollution on a regional basis.

The aquatic toxicological and biological effects of cleaning products are provided and highlighted by relevant case studies. The existing pollution control measures are reviewed, and areas of potential research interest are identified.

1.2 Sources of Information

The major sources of information used in the preparation of this report are detailed below.

- all regions of the National Rivers Authority (NRA) in England and Wales;

- all Scottish River Purification Boards (RPB);

- Water Services Association;

- Water Services plcs;

- British Effluents and Water Association;

- Her Majesty's Inspectorate of Pollution (HMIP);

- Scottish sewerage and water supply authorities;

- Water Research Centre (WRC);

- Soaps and Detergents Industry Association (SDIA);

- Fabric Care Research Council;

- published information; and,

- major UK producers of cleaning products.

1.3 Organisation of the Report

The report is organised as detailed below.

- *Section 2:* reviews the scale of the use and manufacture of UK cleaning products including the typical products of the industry and recent market trends.

- *Section 3:* evaluates the causes of the potential freshwater pollution and effects resulting from cleaning product use, and presents relevant case studies.

- *Section 4:* discusses in greater detail the key issue of eutrophication, in relation to phosphate enrichment in surface waters.

- *Section 5:* identifies methods of wastewater treatment.

- *Section 6:* details the existing pollution control measures, including legislation, and monitoring. Pollution is addressed on a regional basis, and areas of particular concern are identified.

- *Section 7:* identifies particular issues where insufficient information exists, and details areas of potential research.

- *Section 8:* summarises the key conclusions.

- *Section 9:* presents a bibliography of reference documents used in the preparation of this report.

2 Scale of the Industry and Detergent Use

2.1 Introduction

The UK cleaning products and detergents industry involves the manufacture of the following products:

- toiletry and hygiene products;

- household and industrial soaps; and

- washing products, surface cleaners and scourers (surface active agents).

This report is concerned mainly with surface active agents and household and industrial detergents as these constitute by far the greatest proportion of cleaning products consumed in the UK.

Furthermore, freshwater pollution from toiletry and hygiene products is being assessed in a separate report to the Royal Commission on Environmental Pollution by the Water Research Centre.

2.2 World Consumption

Worldwide soaps, detergents and other cleaning products manufacture represents a factor of considerable economic importance. Detergent consumption varies markedly from country to country as shown in *Table 2.2a*. An examination of changing patterns of use for detergents and cleansers over the last 20 years reveals a remarkable growth in overall consumption, with the absolute quantity rising from 10.8×10^6 t in 1960 to 31.5×10^6 t in 1984. This increase reflects greater use of automated machinery, such as washing machines, dishwashers and car wash facilities, as well as other factors including legislative changes, cost considerations and the development of new detergent constituents (Donahue, 1986).

According to Jakobi and Löhr, 1987, only a handful of companies are responsible for the production of most of the world's detergents and cleansing agents. The leader is Cincinnati-based Procter & Gamble, with Unilever of London second, Colgate-Palmolive in New York is third and Henkel in Düsseldorf, is fourth. Many small, local or regional companies also exist for example, the Association Internationale de la Savonnerie et de la Détergence (AIS), a trade association made up of European national detergent industry groups, which estimates that its members represent more than 700 individual firms.

2.3 UK Market

The UK has the seventh largest consumption of detergents in the world at 10.8 kg per capita, according to the latest figures available (1986). The industry employs about 15,000 people in Britain and had a turnover of £1,100 million in 1989 as compared to £1,000 million the previous year. Growth of the industry has been steady in recent years, with an overall increase in production terms, although the increase in prices in recent years has been slightly less than inflation (SDIA, (1990)).

Fabric washing powders represent the largest section of the UK cleaning products market, accounting for 34% of production and 31% of the UK consumption in 1988 (see Table 2.3a). Surface cleaning agents, dishwashing liquids and fabric rinsing liquids (18%,12% and 12% of the UK production, respectively) are the other major products of the industry.

2.3.1 Trends in Product Formulation

Cleaning products currently on the UK market can be classified into the following groups from a detergency standpoint:

- heavy-duty or all-purpose detergents which are made up of detergents, bleaching agents, and a variety of other ingredients;

- speciality detergents (eg anionic detergents which are the main constituents of household cleaners, non-ionic detergents which are chiefly used in industry, and cationic detergents which have germicidal properties and are mainly used for sanitary purposes);

- laundry aids, such as stain removers and whiteners; and

- after treatment aids eg fabric softeners.

Table 2.2a Worldwide consumption of detergents

Region	1960 1000t	Per capita kg	1970 1000t	Per capita kg	1980 1000t	Per capita kg	1984 1000t	Per capita kg
North America	2521	12.8	4574	20.2	7564	30.1	8200	31.3
Western Europe	3047	9.7	4767	13.8	7050	18.9	7800	20.7
Oceania	166	13.1	237	15.4	300	16.1	350	17.5
Eastern Europe	2034	6.5	2253	6.5	3268	8.6	3650	9.4
Central America	247	4.1	617	6.9	2757	7.8	3300	8.3
South America	652	4.6	887	4.7				
Africa	539	2.3	780	2.3	1494	3.2	1900	3.5
Asia	1594	1.0	2324	1.2	5241	2.1*	6250	2.3
World	10800	3.8	16439	4.6	27674	6.3 **	31450	6.6

* Excluding China: 2.5 kg. ** Excluding China: 7.7 kg

Source: Jakobi and Löhr, 1987

There has been a significant move towards liquid rather than powder formulations for cleaning products. This is a change which has been largely ascribed to customer preference for a more convenient product. This is illustrated by the fact that liquid formulations grew from 4% of the fabric detergents market in 1985 to 18% in 1987 and 33% in 1989 (Soaps and Detergents Industry Association (1990)). Powder formulations are reported to be becoming more concentrated: weight-size agreements for packaging in the industry as a whole have been changed three times in the last five years. 'Super-concentrated' powders have also been introduced and are said to occupy about 10% of the current market.

2.3.2 Recent Changes in Product Composition

An example of the typical composition of heavy duty detergents currently on sale in the UK is shown in Table 2.3b.

The amount of phosphate used in detergents in the UK as a whole is reported to have reduced recently. This is partly because of the increase in the use of liquid formulations, a major proportion of which do not contain phosphates, and partly due to the availability on the UK market of imported products which have to conform to more stringent standards in their country of origin.

Phosphate-free own-brand formulations were introduced in 1989 by several major supermarket chains. It has been reported to the consultants by Sainsbury that, for the 12 month period to October 1990, sales of their Environmentally Friendly products made up 17% of the total own label powder sales, and 30% of the total own label liquid cleaning product sales. Specialist companies have also recently been launched, and a campaign to ban 'environmentally unfriendly' ingredients in detergents in early 1989 resulted in the formulation of a bleach-free (and therefore perborate-free) detergent.

There is currently a certain amount of dispute over how 'green' or otherwise some detergent components are and the relative benefits of new products: a recent WRC report (1988) prepared for the Department of the Environment (DoE) states that recommended levels for boron in the environment are rarely if ever exceeded (see also Section 3.4.3).

At present there is no clear indication of product trends for the future, and this area of the industry is currently in a state of flux.

2.4 Detergent Additives

Detergents are formulated to satisfy the requirements of both the soiled substrate and the expected range of washing conditions. Common bar soap consists of essentially one ingredient (fatty acids); whilst hand dishwashing detergents contain a mixture of surfactants.

The range of reagents required to encompass the broad spectrum of detergent manufacture includes surfactants, inorganic salts, acids and bases, builders, organic additives and special purpose additives such as bleaching agents, fluorescent whitening agents, antimicrobial agents and blueing agents. These reagents are discussed in greater detail in the following sections.

Table 2.3a Annual Productions Statistics for Cleaning Product Manufacture in the UK 1988

Product Description	Production (tonnes)	Apparent Consumption (tonnes)	Consumption per capita in kg
Toilet Products			
Any kind of toilet soaps	120,500	73,000	1.259
Shampoos	13,000	13,000	0.229
Shaving products	4,300	4,300	0.074
Household and Industrial Soaps			
Special hand cleaners	16,200	16,200	0.279
Industrial Soaps	13,000	13,000	0.224
Fatty acid liquid soaps	5,200	5,200	0.090
Other hard soaps	3,800	3,800	0.066
Household hard soaps	3,300	2,000	0.034
Soft soaps	900	900	0.016
Washing Products, Surface Cleaners and Scourers (Surface Active Agents)			
Fabric washing powders	527,400	486,400	8.386
Synthetic liquid products	90,000	155,000	2.627
a) fabric washing	187,000	142,000	2.448
b) dishwashing	186,400	192,400	3.317
c) fabric rinsing	286,000	286,000	4.931
d) surface cleaning		57,600	0.993
Dishwashing powders	57,500	57,500	0.991
Scourers	36,000	36,000	0.620
Powdered surface cleaners	2,200	2,200	0.038
Auxiliary washing powders			
Total	**1,553,000**	**1,546,500**	**26.669**

Source: Soaps and Detergents Industry Association (1990).

2.4.1 Builders, inorganic salts, acids and bases

These substances do not contribute detergency but alternatively provide other functions such as regulation of density and assurance of crispness of powdered formulations. In particular, builders augment the detersive effects of surfactants. They have an important ability to remove hardness ions from the wash liquor and thus prevent them from interacting with the surfactant. A further function is the ability of builders to exert a suspending effect. This has the advantage of keeping detached soil suspended in the wash liquor.

Important builders include the following compounds.

Phosphates

Sodium tripolyphosphates (STPP) are the most commonly used builders in UK cleaning products. STPP, of which is pentasodium triphosphate ($Na_5P_3O_{10}$) is the most widely used builder in heavy-duty fabric washing. It is a strong sequestrant for calcium and magnesium, and provides excellent soil suspension.

Trisodium phosphate (Na_3PO_4) is an important constituent of hard-surface cleaners. Although Na_3PO_4 does not sequester to form soluble chelates, it precipitates many heavy-metal ions and acts as an alkali. Other examples are potassium phosphates (liquid detergents), tetrasodium pyrophosphate ($Na_4P_2O_7$), used to a lesser extent in heavy-duty laundry powders, and glassy phosphate. Recently, the use of phosphates as detergent builders has received much adverse attention. As a result, several alternatives have been introduced into the industry.

Sodium Carbonate

Sodium carbonate forms insoluble calcium carbonate ($CaCO_3$)with calcium ions in hard water. Unfortunately, the $CaCO_3$ can build up on machines and fabrics, and no suspending action is provided. Its primary use is as an alkali.

Table 2.3(b) The typical composition of heavy duty detergent products in Western Europe

Ingredients	Examples	Composition, %	
		with phosphate	without phosphate
Anionic surfactants	alkylbenzenesulphonates	5-10	5-10
	fatty alcohol sulphates	1-3	
	fatty alcohol ether sulphates		
	α-olefinsulphonates		
Nonionic surfactants	alkyl poly(ethylene glycol) ethers, nonylphenyl poly(ethylene glycol) ethers	3–11	3–6
Suds-controlling agents	soaps, silicon oils, paraffins	0.1–3.5	0.1–3.5
Foam boosters	fatty acid monoethanolamides	0–2	N/A
Chelating agents	sodium tripolyphosphate	20–40	
Ion exchanger	zeolite 4A, poly(acrylic acids)	2–20	20–30
Alkalis	sodium carbonate	0–15	5–10
Cobuilders	sodium nitrilotriacetate, sodium citrate	0–4	0–4
Bleaching agents	sodium perborate, sodium percarbonate	10–25	20–25
Bleach activators	tetraacetylethylenediamine	0–5	0–2
Bleach stabilizers	ethylenediaminetetraacetate, phosphonates	0.2–0.5	0.2–0.5
Fabric softeners	clays	N/A	N/A
Antiredeposition agents	cellulose ethers	0.5–1.5	0.5–1.5
Enzymes	proteases, amylases	0.3–0.8	0.3–0.8
Optical brighteners	stilbenedisulphonic acid, bis(styryl)biphenyl derivatives	0.1–0.3	0.1–0.3
Anticorrosion agents	sodium silicate	2–6	2–6
Fragrances		+	+
Dyes and blueing agents		+	+
Fillers and water	sodium sulphate, water	balance	balance

Source: Adapted from Jakobi and Löhr (1987). N/A – data not available.

Silicates

Silicates are used extensively as soap builders in laundering formulations, and are effective in sequestering magnesium. In addition to functioning as an alkali, silicates act as anticorrosive agents and prevent deterioration of metal parts in washing machines.

Zeolites

Zeolites are used in heavy-duty detergent formulations. Type A zeolite [$Na_2O.Al_2O_3.2SiO_4.4\frac{1}{2}H_2O$] has recently found application in replacing part of pentasodium triphosphate in those areas of Western Europe and USA where phosphate use is limited by law (see *Section 4*). However, it is not an effective builder for magnesium hardness and, therefore, is impractical for use as the sole builder in a nonphosphate detergent formulation.

Clays

Clays such as kaolin, the montmorillonites and bentonites, can have a marked detersive effect on ordinary soiled fabrics, particularly in soft water of low dissolved solids content.

Nitrilotriacetic Acid (NTA)

NTA is a powerful sequestrant builder, and is used as a phosphate replacement in some countries where phosphate is not permitted. It is less effective than Na_3PO_4 as a suspending agent and is not as easily processed in spray-dried laundry powders.

Alkalis

Sodium carbonate is the main alkali used as a builder. Its main effect is to maintain a high pH and saponify the acidic constituents of soil, thereby promoting cleaning.

EDTA

Ethylene-diamino-tetra-acetate is added to washing agents to prevent bleaching agents from becoming active prior to use. It also acts as a foam stabiliser and removes heavy metals from the wash water.

Neutral Soluble Salts

Sodium sulphate and sodium chloride are the principal neutral soluble salts used in manufacture. They enable the formulation of powders of a controlled density, and can reduce the concentration of detergent required for effective washing.

2.4.2 Other Additives

These additives are usually present in low percentages and have the following functions:

- to reduce the redeposition of soil from the detergent onto the substrate (eg sodium carboxymethylcellulose);

- to increase the whiteness or the appearance of cleanliness;

- to enhance cleaning effect on specific types of solids and stains (eg sodium perborate, $NaBO_4. 4H_2O$);

- to promote or inhibit foaming power and stability (eg amino oxides and alkanolamides);

- to increase the solubility of the detergent; and

- to sequester heavy metal ions.

2.5 Detergent Manufacture

2.5.1 Spray-Dried Powders

The first step in spray-dried powder manufacture is to slurry both solid and liquid components to form as homogeneous a mixture as practicable. This enables acids such as fatty acid and alkylbenzenesulphonic acid to be neutralised with sodium hydroxide to form soap and sodium alkylbenzenesulphonate. Homogeneity of the mixture is aided by the mixing vessel having heavy-duty agitators and heating provisions. A schematic diagram of the manufacturing process is given in *Figure 2.5a*.

After this initial preparation, the slurry is transported to an ageing vessel. Here, complete homogeneity is achieved by a neutralization process where sodium tripolyphosphate is hydrated, and by structural changes in the slurry itself. Following a residence time of 20 to 30 minutes, the slurry is pumped under high pressure to a spray-drying tower where it is forced through nozzles of 2½ to 3½ mm diameter arranged on a nozzle ring. The slurry emerges from the nozzle ring and is dried by hot air (250-350°C) which may be flowing co- or counter currently. Fines are collected by cyclones and transferred to scrubbing stations. Any scrubbing solution saturated with detergent fines is recycled to the water tank for slurry preparation.

Powder exiting the spray tower is transferred by belt conveyor and airlift to packaging machinery.

In general, this method can accommodate a relatively high content of surfactants. However, certain types such as alkanolamides and some nonionic surfactants should be added to the product after spray drying. This post addition not only protects the surfactant from the spray tower heat, but also prevents the formation of aerosols in the exit gas. In particular troublesome aerosols can be formed by unsulphonated matter from the manufacture of linear alkylbenzene sulphonate (LAS) and nonionic surfactants with short ethylene oxide chains.

2.5.2 Dry-Blended Powders

Advantages of this process are the lower capital outlay and the use of considerably less processing energy. Disadvantages are that the final product density depends on the density of the starting materials and that particle size and product densities are less consistent than in spray-dried powders.

2.5.3 Agglomerated Powders

For the agglomeration process, a spray of water or other liquid is aimed at dry powder under agitation. Best results are obtained by:

- maintaining a finely divided liquid;

- suspending both liquid and powder in space; and

- keeping the mixture in motion in order to constantly expose fresh material.

It is common to use sodium silicate as the usual agglomeration liquid.

Variations in equipment design include stationary mixers, rotating mixers with spray nozzles, and rotating blenders with liquid dispersion bars. Examples of products from the agglomeration process include automatic dishwashing detergents, special detergent powders and hydrated pentasodium triphosphate.

2.5.4 Liquid Products

The manufacture of liquid detergent products is fairly straightforward. Provisions need to be made for metered addition of individual ingredients, agitation, and in some cases heating.

Figure 2.5a Schematic Spray-drying flow Diagram for Detergents and Soaps

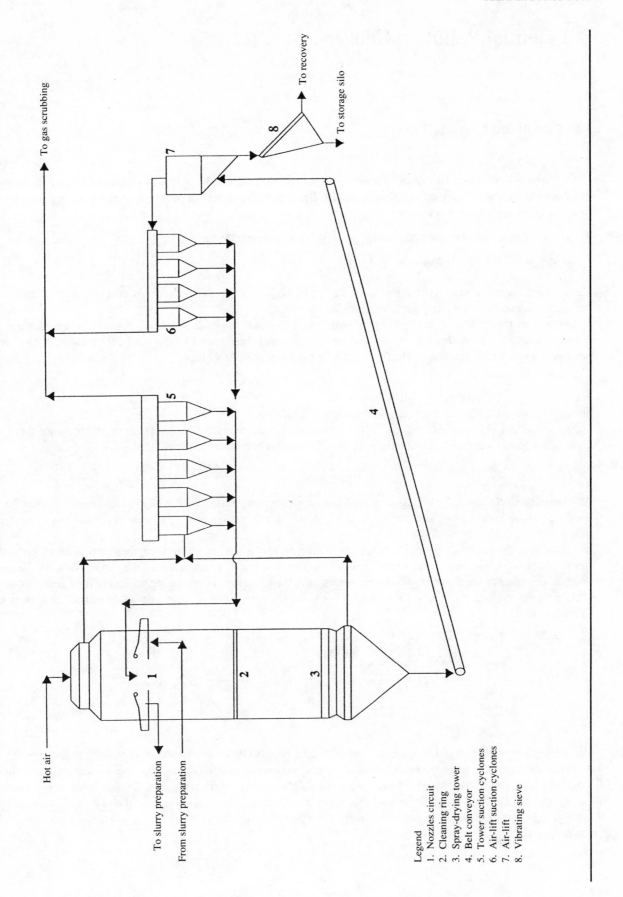

Legend
1. Nozzles circuit
2. Cleaning ring
3. Spray-drying tower
4. Belt conveyor
5. Tower suction cyclones
6. Air-lift suction cyclones
7. Air-lift
8. Vibrating sieve

3 Potential Pollution Causes and Effects

3.1 Constituent Characteristics

3.1.1 General

Detergents are substances that improve the cleaning properties of water. The ability of a cleaning product to remove dirt from the item to be cleaned (eg clothes, dishes etc) lies in the molecular structure of the detergent. The basic structure comprises two distinct parts:

- a 'polar' head, carrying an electric charge with hydrophilic properties; and

- a 'non-polar' tail with hydrophobic properties.

The detailed composition of a detergent molecule is variable, reflecting the commercial synthetic manufacture and the precise application of the specific detergent being produced.

Inherent in the ability of detergents to dissolve in water and improve its cleaning ability, are a number of potential sources of pollution arising from the treatment of and the disposal of the used detergent/water mix. The principal causes, mechanisms and effects are discussed in the following sections.

3.1.2 Surface Active Agents (Surfactants)

Surfactants are the main cleaning agents in detergent formulation.

The surfactant effect is imparted by the 'polar' head of a detergent molecule. There are three major types of surfactant, anionic, cationic and nonionic, reflecting the electric charge of the molecule.

Anionic Surfactants

Anionic (negatively charged) surfactants are the most common type of detergent. Soap is an anionic surfactant. It is a mixture of the salts of longchain carboxylic acids. A typical salt present in soap is sodium octadecanoate (sodium stearate) – $CH_3 (CH_2)_{16} COO^- Na^+$.

Soaps have the disadvantage that they form a scum with hard water, resulting from the reaction of the carboxyl functional group with calcium ions in hard water to form the insoluble calcium salt of the carboxylic acid. Anionic soapless detergents were therefore developed, which have the advantage of producing no scum. They are commonly alkyl benzene sulphonates. The early compounds produced consisted of sodium salts of branched alkyl benzene sulphonates, eg:

Other anionic synthetic detergents are of the sulphate ester type $(ROSO_3)^- Na^+$ (where R is an alkyl chain).

Many alkyl benzene sulphonates originally produced were largely nonbiodegradable due to their branched chain structures and are referred to as 'hard' detergents. Other 'hard' surfactants include non-ionic nonyl phenol ethoxylates (NPE). It was later discovered that the non-biodegradability was caused by the branched chains of the alkyl groups. Subsequently, straightchain compounds ('soft' detergents) were produced, which have a single chain structure and are biodegradable:

After soap, the most widely used surfactants are these Linear alkylbenzene sulphonates (LAS), which act as 'soft detergents'.

Cationic Surfactants

Cationic (positively charged) surfactants are mainly quaternary ammonium compounds of the type:

$(R\ Me_3\ N)^+\ Cl^-$

These compounds are usually strongly bacteriocidal, but are the least used of the three general detergent types.

Non-ionic Surfactants

Non-ionic (uncharged) surfactants are formed by reacting hydrophilic compounds containing carboxyl, hydroxyl, amido or amino groups with ethylene oxide. Typical non-ionic molecules are the ester type:

$$R - \overset{\displaystyle O}{\overset{\displaystyle \|}{C}} - O - (C_2H_4O)_xH$$

Production of non-ionic surfactants has increased over recent years as a result of decreasing manufacturing costs and increased appreciation of their merits, which make them appropriate for use as the main surfactants in hard surface and dishwashing products, particularly for institutional use (hospitals etc). The major industrial uses are in textile cleaning and metal working, including vehicle manufacture and other light engineering.

3.1.3 Builders

Builders are substances which do not contribute detergency but provide product functions such as:

- regulation of density and assurance of crispness of powdered formulations;

- augmentation of the detersive effects of surfactants;

- removal of hardness (mainly calcium and magnesium) from the wash liquor to prevent interaction with the surfactant; and

- a suspending effect which keeps detached soil particles suspended in the wash liquor.

Builders are vital components of clothes washing detergents. In practice, the higher the efficiency of the builder, the better the wash and the smaller the quantity of detergent needed.

The most commonly used builder is sodium tripolyphosphate (STPP). Although an effective builder, there is concern over its use due to its subsequent hydrolysis to orthophosphate and potential for eutrophication that this may cause in receiving waters (see *Section 4*). Consequently, alternative types of builder have been developed which do not contain phosphate. The three major alternatives are detailed below:

- Nitrilotriacetic acid (NTA), is an aminocarboxylic acid, and a water soluble organic chelating agent. Due primarily to its potential toxicity, carcinogenicity and strong heavy metal complexing capacity, NTA is unlikely to become a widespread replacement for STPP in the UK (see *Section 3.2.3*).

- Polycarboxylic acids (PCAs) are proposed for use as co-builders, although there is currently a lack of information on their biodegradability, toxicological effects and heavy metal complexation (Dwyer *et al* (1990)).

- Zeolites are water insoluble inorganic aluminosilicates. They are considered to be most useful as a co-builder, and are thus unlikely to fully replace STPP.

3.1.4 Other Additives

Bleaching Agents

The main bleaching agent used in detergents in the UK is perborate, which acts as a source of 'active oxygen'.

145

However, this can give rise to elevated levels of boron in receiving waters (see *Section 3.3.3*). Chlorine based bleaches find greater use in the USA, where cold water washes are used more frequently. However, there is no likelihood of the introduction of such bleaches in the UK.

As an alternative to perborate, percarbonate has been considered, but the instability of the compound during its storage has prevented its widespread use.

Optical Brighteners

Optical brighteners (or fluorescent whitening agents) are designed to counteract the yellowing of fabrics which occurs after repeated washing. They are conjugated aromatic molecules which absorb ultra-violet light and emit the absorbed energy as visible light at the blue end of the spectrum. They are used in relatively small amounts in domestic detergents and studies have shown that they are removed to a very large extent by sewage treatment. They are not considered to represent a significant impact on water quality (Jakobi and Löhr (1987)), but are deemed unnecessary by environmentalists.

3.2   Environmental Fate

3.2.1   General

Cleaning products may enter receiving waters in the natural environment by one of the following pathways:

- Direct discharge of wastewaters that may contain detergents from industrial use.

- Wastewater containing used detergent may pass to a sewage treatment works and the treated effluent will be discharged to a surface watercourse or to the sea.

- Sludge from a sewage treatment works may contain adsorbed detergent residue and be applied to land. Residues of cleaning product use may subsequently enter groundwater through downward percolation of water, or may enter surface waters as run-off.

The passage of detergents through a sewage treatment works and in the receiving waters and the ultimate fate of the individual constituents in the environment is dependent on their chemistry, and other factors such as rates of microbial degradation. An overview on the environmental fate of the main detergent constituents is given below in Sections 3.2.2 and 3.2.3.

3.2.2   Surfactants

Surfactants with low biodegradability create problems in the aquatic environment due to foaming and effects on gas exchange processes across water surfaces. Considerable concern over this effect has been expressed in recent years. As a result, surfactants are tested for biodegradability prior to product sale.

Two biological test methods are mandated for establishing biodegradability of UK detergents and/or anionic and non-ionic surfactants:

- the OECD Screening Test; and

- the OECD Confirmatory Test.

Detergents and/or anionic and non-ionic surfactants are considered biodegradable if they pass the 80% degradation level in the screening test. A confirmatory test is required when this level of biodegradation is doubted, and the results of this test are definitive. The experimental conditions of the confirmatory test are analogous to the biodegradation which may be expected at a sewage treatment works. Typical values for the degree of biodegradation of the major groups of surfactants are shown in Table 3.2a; note that the biodegradability of tetrapropylene benzene sulphonate (TPS) and ethoxylate/phenoxylate (EO/PO) block polymers falls below the required 80% degradation level. According to Jakobi and Löhr, (1987), years of systematic monitoring of sewage treatment plants and rivers has shown that, in general, the residual concentration of surfactants in the freshwater environment is small and has shown a consistent decrease in recent years despite the increasing use of surfactants.

Anionic Surfactants in Wastewater Treatment

Removal of linear alkylbenzene sulphonates (LAS) during sewage treatment is reported to be high (Berna *et al*, (1990)). In a typical activated sludge plant, the degree of removal from the water phase can be of the order of 97-99%. This removal is due to the combination of two parallel effects; biodegradation and adsorption/precipitation.

Table 3.2a Surfactant biodegradation in sewage treatment plant models

Surfactants	Primary biodegradation, OECD Confirmatory Test, % removal
Anionic surfactants	
LAS	90–95
TPS (Tetra propylene benzene sulphonate)	36
C_{12} Fatty alcohol sulfate	99
C_{13-18} *sec* Alkanesulfonates	99
C_{16-18} Sulfo fatty acid methyl esters	99
Nonionic surfactants	
C_{16-18} Fatty alcohols 10 EO	98
C_{12-14} Fatty alcohols 30 EO	98
C_{11-15} *sec* Alcohols 9 EO	86
C_{13-15} Oxo alcohols 12 EO	96
Isononylphenol 9 EO	97
C_{8-10} *n* - Alkylphenols 9 EO	96
EO/PO Block polymers	7
Cationic surfactants	
Cetyltrimethylammonium bromide (CTAB)	98
Dodecylbenzyldimethylammonium chloride (DBDMAC)	96
Distearyldimethylammonium chloride (DSDMAC)	94

Source: Jakobi and Löhr, 1987. EO stands for ethoxylate

Precipitation takes place in the primary stage of treatment, settlement. The percentage removal is directly related to water hardness. This is due to the precipitation of calcium and magnesium LAS salts. Thus, the average removal of 10-20%, can be increased to 30-35% where the water has a high hardness.

Biodegradation takes place in the secondary, biological treatment stage (activated sludge or percolating filters) and subsequently in the environment; Table 3.2b shows the removal efficiencies of various processes of sewage treatment. Biodegradation is an effective mechanism for removal of LAS and in some circumstances can completely mineralise LAS to carbon dioxide, water and sulphates.

Table 3.2b Removal of LAS in sewage treatment

Process	Percentage Removal
Sewage Treatment	50
Sewers	40
Sludge Drying	9
Land Application	1

Source: Berna *et al* (1990)

For effective removal in the sewage treatment works, treatment should include two stages of anaerobic sludge digestion, treating sludge from primary and secondary settling. The LAS which accumulates in the sludge is only partially degraded during anaerobic sludge treatment, since rates of biodegradation are slow by anoxic microbial processes. As a result, concentrations in the range of approximately 4 gkg^{-1} may occur in digested sludge (Brunner *et al* (1988)). The load of LAS in sludge applied to land is high (McEvoy and Giger, (1986)), and the latter authors have expressed concern about the potential phyto-toxicity resulting from large-scale application of these otherwise relatively low toxicity compounds. The loss of sea-dumping as a sludge disposal route may lead to a small increase in sludge application to land. However, a large proportion of currently seadumped sludge is likely to be incinerated in the future (probably 80–90%), and thus the degree of sludge disposal to land is not expected to increase to any significant degree; any increase would be expected to be from about 70 to 75% of the total sludge disposed in the UK.

Studies have shown a reduction in concentrations of LAS in wastewater following treatment as shown in Table 3.2b. Typical concentrations of LAS in a variety of environmental media are shown in Table 3.2c.

When applied to land as sludge, degradation of LAS is largely controlled by adsorption to soil particles and microbial activity. It has been shown that adsorption is significantly influenced by the pH and concentrations of organic matter and iron oxide substrates, present in soils (Litz *et al* (1986)); the influence of pH relates to the degree of ionisation of the LAS, the 'double-layer' charge on soil particle surfaces and behaviour of binding groups on the substrate surfaces. The strongest sorption is found in ferrous and humus-rich soils (Litz *et al* (1986)). The half life (the time required to achieve 50% removal of the compound) of LAS in various environments is shown in Table 3.2d. The half life provides an index of the persistence of LAS in any of the particular components of the environment.

Table 3.2c LAS concentrations in various environmental media

Media	Typical concentrations of LAS
Treated Sludge	3 – 7 g/kg dry matter
Surface Soils	2 – 200 mg/g
River Sediments	1 – 25 mg/kg
Untreated Wastewater	$4 - 24 mgl^{-1}$
Groundwater	$5 - 10$ mgl^{-1}
Treated Effluent	$0.05 - 0.9$ mgl^{-1}
River Water	$0.01 - 0.1$ mgl^{-1}

Source: Berna *et al* (1990)

Table 3.2d Half Lives of LAS in Range of Environments

Environment	Half Life
Sewage Sludge Treatment	10–50 Days
Sludge Amended Soils	10–30 Days
Subsurface Soils	4–20 Days
Laboratory Soil Tests	3–20 Days
Laboratory Ecosystem	13–16 Days
Groundwater	5–15 Days
Surface Soils	1–5 Days
River Water	1–2 Days
River Water + Sediment	0.5–1 Day
Sewers	10–15 Hours
Sewage Treatment Plants (Water Stream)	1–2 Hours

Source: Litz *et al* (1986)

The effectiveness of microbial activity in the breakdown of LAS is influenced by temperature, water content, and the availability of oxygen; the rates of biodegradation being slow under anoxic conditions.

Due to the persistence of LAS in the environment, it is recommended that the fate of LAS in the soil system is investigated to determine any subsequent impacts on plants, or groundwater resources, where recent data (Berna *et al* (1990)) from Switzerland indicate potentially high concentrations of LAS in groundwaters underlying areas where sludge disposal has been carried out.

Cationic surfactants

Information regarding the environmental fate of cationic surfactants is scarce, since quaternary ammonium compounds are the least used surfactants, and have relatively low toxicity and bioaccumulation potential (see *Section 3.3.1*). The measured residual concentrations of cationic surfactants in surface waters are reported to fall within the range $5 - 30$ µgl^{-1} (Jakobi and Löhr (1987)).

Nonionic surfactants

A study by Maki *et al* (1979) at Reynoldsburg Sewage Treatment Works (USA) investigated the effects of additions of the nonionic surfactant, Neodol 45–7, to the influent. Neodol 45–7 is an alkyl ethoxylate and a common constituent of cleaning products.

The aim of the study was to provide environmental data on both the degree of removal of Neodol 45–7 during treatment, and also the toxicity of the substance to aquatic biota.

The predose background total concentrations of nonionic surfactants at the influent averaged 6.7 mgl^{-1} when measured by the CTAS (non-specific cobalt thiocyanate substance) procedure. Neodol 45–7 was introduced to the plant influent in increments ranging from 5.0 mgl^{-1} to 14 mgl^{-1} above the normal influent concentration; ie at levels well above the normal concentration of any one particular nonionic surfactant.

The concentration of nonionic surfactants was measured in the effluent and the receiving water upstream and downstream of the effluent discharge. Additionally, the non-ionic surfactant content of water in an aquarium, which had been fed with 100% secondary effluent and supported aquatic organisms for toxicity testing, was monitored.

The background concentrations of nonionic surfactants in the plant effluent and the receiving water investigation (Maki *et al* (1979)) indicated that a very high proportion (>95%) of the introduced non-ionic surfactant was removed during treatment. Furthermore the measured CTAS level in the aquarium, which was originally fed with 100% secondary effluent from an influent dose of 30mgl^{-1}, was as low as 0.57 mgl^{-1} after 8 days (Maki *et al* (1979)).

From the results of these investigations it would appear that alkylethoxylate nonionic surfactants such as Neodol 45–7, are likely to have minimal impacts on the aquatic environment. Furthermore, unlike nonylphenol ethoxylates which undergo deethoxylation to form 'toxic' nonylphenol, the biodegradation products of Neodol 45–7 have been shown to be harmless to the aquatic organisms tested (Maki *et al* (1979)) (See *Section 3.3*).

By contrast, nonylphenol and partially degraded nonylphenolethoxylates have been reported to be present in sewage treatment works effluents (Giger *et al*, (1981)). High concentrations of nonylphenol have been found in anaerobically digested sewage sludge (Giger *et al*, (1984)); typical levels reported were a mean of 1.4 gkg^{-1} (range 0.4 – 2.6 gkg^{-1}) nonylphenol in anaerobic sludge, which compare with a mean of 0.28 gkg^{-1} (range 0 – 0.6 gkg^{-1}) in aerobically stablised sludge.

It has been suggested that nonylphenol ethoxylates are shortened to mono-, di- and tri-ethoxylated chains during aerobic treatment, and that these decomposition products being less water soluble become associated with sludge flow. These shortened chain ethoxylates are then further degraded to nonylphenol during anaerobic digestion, and accumulate in the sludge (Giger *et al*, (1984)).

3.2.3 Phosphates and Phosphate Alternatives in Wastewater Treatment

Phosphates

The concentrations of different forms of phosphorus in wastewater are dependent on the location of the treatment works and the origin of influent components. The typical distribution of phosphorus between various species in sewage is soluble orthophosphate 51%, insoluble orthophosphate 11%, polyphosphate 29% and organic phosphates 9%; it should be noted that during wastewater treatment hydrolysis to orthophosphate does occur. The reported concentrations of total phosphorus in different wastewaters vary greatly, ranging between 7.5 mgl^{-1} (Pitman *et al*, (1983)) and 34.5 mgl^{-1} (Gerber and Winter, (1985)). Variations occur on an hourly basis due to the 'wash-day' phenomenon where influent polyphosphate concentrations can increase to three or four times the mean influent value (Rossin *et al*, (1982)). Seasonal variations of phosphate species in wastewater can also occur, with higher orthophosphate concentrations being found during the summer months.

In situations where phosphate availability is unlimited, eutrophication, defined as an increase in nutrient concentrations leading to an uncontrolled growth of phytoplankton and/or macrophytes, may result (Marchetti, (1987)). The causes and effects of eutrophication are further discussed in Section 4.

In order to try to alleviate the problem of eutrophication, certain authorities have implemented bans on the use of phosphorus in detergents (Jones and Hubbard, (1986)). Currently, countries including Canada, Germany, Switzerland and Holland and parts of the United States all operate limits on the use of phosphorus in laundry detergents (DePinto *et al* (1986)). However, some reports have contended that the effectiveness of such bans in controlling eutrophication is debatable (Lund & Moss, (1990)).

It has been reported that the influent phosphorus loading to two sewage treatment plants in Milwaukee, Wisconsin decreased by over 1500 kg d^{-1} after the use of phosphorus in detergents was restricted. This scale of load reduction is reported to have caused a decrease in the quantity of chemicals required for phosphorus precipitation by up to 60% at treatment plants in Maryland (De Pinto *et al* (1986)). Alternative views have suggested that the bans have produced no significant reduction in phosphorus concentrations entering wastewater treatment plants elsewhere (Dwyer, *et al* (1990)).

Despite controversy over the contribution of STPP to eutrophication, potential inorganic and organic replacements have been developed. Inorganic compounds include sodium salts of carbonate, silicate, borate and sulphate plus the alumino silicate, zeolite type A (Berth, (1978)). The organic compounds include, nitrilotriacetic acid (NTA) and more recently polycarboxylic acids (PCAs) (Zini, (1987)). Undoubtedly the powerful chelating agent NTA has received the most widespread attention as the principal alternative (Anderson *et al* (1985)).

According to Lund and Moss (1990), the degree of STPP substitution in the UK market is probably insufficient at present to affect significantly the general pattern of nuisance algal growth. It is pointed out, however, that 'hypothetically, in some remote mountain regions the formulation of detergents might minimise a eutrophication problem caused by septic tank discharge from isolated hamlets'. The use of STPP substitutes in the UK is now thought to have reduced STPP use by about 20% (CES, 1991), which amounts to a total STPP reduction of 25–35,000 tonnes per annum (CES, 1991).

On the grounds of effectiveness, functionality, safety and competitive cost, no completely satisfactory replacement for STPP has been found, and despite the associated problems, STPP is still used extensively in the UK (Dwyer *et al* (1990)).

Aminocarboxylic Builders: NTA and EDTA

During sewage treatment, aerobic biological processes are critical for the effective removal of NTA, with enzyme acclimatization being an essential factor. The acclimatization period is long, of the order of 36–90 days, with the result that short term increases in NTA entering a sewage works are not readily accommodated and result in a period of reduced removal efficiency (Dwyer, *et al* (1990)). NTA can also lead to a decrease in heavy metals removal during activated sludge treatment, and thus higher heavy metal concentrations in the effluent may result; albeit that this leads to a reduction of metal levels in the sludge. NTA induced carry over of zinc through wastewater treatment and discharge in effluents has been noted by Giger (1990) in Switzerland, where NTA is used in domestic laundry detergents. This is a result of NTA forming strong complexes with heavy metals which prevents their adsorption by sludge particles. Increases of NTA levels in groundwater have also been noted (Giger, 1990).

The following features of interaction between heavy metals and NTA are generally accepted to occur at sewage treatment works (Dwyer *et al* (1990)):

- large scale use of NTA will decrease the adsorption of nickel on sewage sludges (to the extent that it would not be retained at all in a treatment plant);

- any metal – NTA chelate passing through a treatment plant will be stable for a longer time in soft than in hard receiving water; (this is due to lessened competition for NTA binding sites by calcium and magnesium in soft waters);

- naturally occurring humic substances cannot effectively compete with NTA for the complexation of metals such as copper and nickel.

Although very stable chemically, the biodegradation rates of most NTA – metal complexes are variable (Dwyer *et al* (1990)). In general, complexes of mercury, cadmium and copper are reported to be degraded more slowly than those of nickel, iron and zinc.

It has also been observed that rates of degradation of NTA and its metal complexes are greatly reduced under anaerobic conditions. In relation to groundwater, this means that NTA infiltrating through saturated soils shows very little degradation during its passage, with the majority of NTA entering groundwater unaltered (Dunlap *et al* (1972)). Further, NTA entering the groundwater may transfer metals such as iron, zinc, lead, cadmium and mercury from the soils into the groundwaters. Thus the greatest environmental risks associated with NTA substitution for STPP would seem to relate to increased concentrations of NTA in drinking water abstracted as groundwater, coupled with toxic effects and potential carcinogenicity of the NTA-metal complexes.

When discharged to rivers, low water temperatures have been found to reduce NTA biodegradation (Dwyer, *et al* (1989)). It is thus possible for water containing NTA to be abstracted and enter potable supplies. This is a particular potential problem in the UK where there is a heavy reuse of water. This factor coupled with its toxicology (see *Section 3.4.2*), make it unlikely that NTA will become widely used as a replacement builder for STPP.

EDTA is an excellent sequestrant of calcium and magnesium, but has not been used widely as a builder in detergents for this purpose because it is expensive, not readily biodegradable and would be difficult to include in powders in high concentrations (Woollat (1985)). However, EDTA is used at low concentrations (0.2%) as a stabiliser for perborate bleaches in the UK. EDTA finds greater use in Switzerland than elsewhere in Europe. Work on EDTA biodegradation in Swiss sewage treatment works, has indicated that EDTA degradation cannot be expected even under nitrifying conditions (Alder *et al* (1990)). High EDTA concentrations (up to 10 μgl^{-1}) in Swiss groundwaters are also considered to be a matter of concern (Houriet, 1990). The production of EDTA has been the cause of some environmental concern. EDTA is manufactured from ethylene diamine, formaldehyde (a known carcinogen) and hydrogen cyanide (a toxic gas). The use of EDTA has also led to problems of heavy metal mobilisation due to strong chelate complexation, and EDTA is reported to be even less biodegradable than NTA.

Polycarboxylic Acid Builders (PCAs)

PCAs perform the chief function of anti-redeposition and recent interest has been directed towards their use as co-builders. The behaviour of PCAs is poorly understood, but it is known that they have a high resistance to biodegradation (Hunter *et al*, (1988)).

It has been estimated that 90% of PCA (at 3% level in detergents) would be removed to the sludge during waste water treatment, which would result in effluent concentrations of 30 μgl^{-1} entering receiving waters (Kanowski (1986)). Opgenorth (1987) found polycarboxylates were completely eliminated from wastewater and did not reach surface waters in any appreciable quantities. However, the degree of removal is presumably dependent upon the polymeric builder involved and the known variation in population laundry habits, which lead to great variations in mean influent concentrations of builders at a treatment works during 'wash-day' phenomena (Hunter, (1988)).

The degradation behaviour of PCAs involves a decrease in molecular weight with a concomitant loss of free polymer properties (Grassie, (1966)). The resistance of synthetic polymers with a carbon backbone to biodegradation is well known, and studies have found poor biodegradation of PCA compounds during waste water treatment (Dwyer *et al* (1990)). Polyacrylic acid (PAA) has been the most widely investigated polymer with builder properties because of its failure to biodegrade (Hunter *et al* (1988)).

Berth *et al* (1977) found only 2–7% reduction of PHAA (poly-αhydroxyacrylic acid) in biological degradation tests (as BOD$_{30}$), compared with 3–74% for NTA in tests carried out without prior acclimatisation of the test inocula. The large range in NTA biodegradation reflects its dependence on a variety of different processes and pathways. However, with adequate acclimatisation times activated sludge systems can achieve near complete NTA breakdown (Dwyer *et al* (1990)); typical acclimatisation times required are of the order of 4 to 20 days (Dwyer *et al* (1990)).

The most comprehensive study of PCA biodegradation, has been undertaken by Abe *et al* (1986). In these studies a variety of PCA builders, with differing molecular weights, were examined for biodegradation in relation to their builder efficiency. However, the majority of PCA compounds rarely matched STPP for sequestration or dispersion capacity. Also, biodegradabilities were found to be variable and rarely exceeded 20%.

Further research into many aspects of PCAs is needed before they are widely introduced as alternatives to STPP.

Aluminosilicate Builders: Zeolite A

During sewage treatment, removal of zeolite can be of the order of 55–60% during primary sedimentation, and greater than 80% when secondary biological treatment is provided (Dwyer, *et al* (1989)). It is generally accepted that the presence of zeolite causes heavy metal adsorption, during sewage treatment. This presents the (probably marginal) potential risk of metal remobilisation in the environment when the Al-Si zeolite complex degrades. Thus removal of zeolite during sewage treatment is favourable.

In a study carried out by Hopping (1978), Zeolite A removal during the activated sludge process varied between 80 and 90% but was not influenced directly by precise influent concentration. Roland and Schmidt (1978) found that Zeolite A did not affect the dewaterability of sewage sludges at high or low influent concentrations.

Carrondo *et al* (1980) investigated the effects of treatment parameters on Zeolite A in the activated sludge process. Pilot plant experiments were carried out with influent Zeolite A concentrations of 15 and 30 mgl^{-1}. Calcium was exchanged for sodium in the Zeolite A to produce two levels of calcium substitution, as follows: Zeolite A with 25% of the exchange capacity occupied by calcium was used in the experiments to simulate the amount of calcium exchange that would occur during the wash process; Zeolite A with 75% of the exchange capacity occupied by calcium, which was thought to represent the degree of calcium exchange that might be expected once the zeolite arrives at the sewage treatment works. It was found that activated sludge settleability was improved in the presence of Zeolite A, as was sludge dewaterability. Zeolite A in the final effluent varied between 2 and 4 mgl^{-1}. No significant difference in removal efficiency was observed in relation to Zeolite A influent concentration.

Whilst Zeolite A improves sludge settleability without affecting wet volume, the total mass of solids at sewage treatment plants would increase if Zeolite A were substituted for STPP at a 20% of formulation level (CES, 1991). This could affect sludge incineration, which may be the disposal route for up to 25% of sludge in the near future. This may adversely affect the economics and logistics of incineration and incinerator ash disposal, due to decreased calorific content per unit sludge volume and increased ash content.

Other Compounds used as Builders

Sodium citrate finds use as a builder in built liquid detergents at a concentration of about 1%. Citrate is found at high concentrations in sewage regardless of the detergent inputs, since it is a constituent of human urine. Biodegradation occurs effectively under aerobic and anaerobic conditions, although if citrate concentration as a builder were increased to 25% of total formulation the influent BOD load of domestic wastewater could be increased by 5–10% (CES, 1991). Typical citrate concentrations in river waters are between 0.025 and 0.145 mgl^{-1}, although concentrations of up to 8.7 mgl^{-1} have been reported (CES, 1991).

Soaps (sodium salts of fatty acids) are used in many detergent products, and comprise up to 17% of the content of phosphate free, liquid formulations. In general, soap is readily diodegraded at sewage treatment works and causes no particular problems in plant performance.

Sodium carbonate and sodium silicate are used as builders. Neither is a cause for particular environmental concern, and both substances are abundant in natural waters. Natural carbonate concentrations depend on water hardness, which is dependent on catchment geology. Silicate concentrations are typically in the range of 0.5 to 3 mgl^{-1}, with peak levels up to 25 mgl^{-1}. The use of sodium carbonate and silicate builders at formulation levels as high as 25% would have no significant effect on environmental concentrations.

Carboxymethyltartrate (CMT) and carboxymethylsuccinate (CMOS) have both been proposed as potential STPP builder substitutes. However, neither compound is used in any detergents in the UK or Europe at present. There is little evidence that CMT or CMOS will find any future widespread use in detergent formulations in the UK (CES, 1991).

3.2.4 Other Additives

Bleaching Agents

The main bleaching agent currently used in UK cleaning products is sodium perborate. European laundry detergents generally contain up to 25% sodium perborate as a bleaching agent. Biological sewage treatment is generally unaffected by its presence (Speece (1987)), but a possible cause for concern is the resulting sodium borate, and with it the potential increase in environmental boron concentrations (see *Section 3.3.3*).

In practice boron is not known to be a cause of water pollution in the UK at present, with annual mean concentrations being in the range of 0.046 and 0.822 mgl^{-1} in the UK (Butterwick *et al* (1989)).

Nevertheless, boron levels as low as 1–2 mgl^{-1} possess a specific phytotoxicity with respect to certain agricultural plants, such as citrus fruit trees, tomatoes, and vineyard stock. Therefore, it is not advisable to recycle boron containing wastewater for irrigation purposes (Butterwick *et al* (1989)), although this is a greater potential problem in arid climates such as those of the Eastern Mediterranean (eg Cyprus, Israel).

Fluorescent Whitening Agents

Fluorescent whitening agents are additives used in fabric washing powders to enhance the appearance of the washed fabric. Although they are adsorbed by fabrics during the laundering process, they are also introduced to some extent into the wastewater in the course of repeated washing. Simple laboratory screening tests show fluorescent whitening agents to be biodegraded only to a very limited degree. Analysis conducted under conditions more closely resembling those found in a two-stage sewage treatment plant, however, reveal elimination values of up to 96%. These results are best explained on the basis of adsorption onto the sludge. Total elimination has been demonstrated in a system involving tertiary treatment. From these results, one may conclude that sewage treatment essentially ensures the absence of whitening agents in discharges to the surface waters (Jakobi and Löhr (1987)).

Studies of such rivers as the Thames in London, the Rhône at Lyon, the Seine at Paris, and the Rhine both at Basel and at Düsseldorf have shown concentrations of fluorescent whiteners are low. There is no evidence of the presence of fluorescent whiteners at their limits of analytical detection (0.25μg/l) (Jakobi and Löhr (1987)).

Soil Antiredeposition Agents

These are primarily water-soluble, high molecular mass cellulose ethers. Their biodegradation proceeds as slowly as that of natural cellulose. However, such compounds are completely non-toxic to fish, and no significant ecological problems are known to be associated with their use (Jakobi and Löhr (1987)).

Foam Regulators

Soap is one of the most important foam inhibitors used in detergents. It is readily biodegradable and presents no water quality problems. Other foam regulators used in very small amounts include silicones, which are virtually insoluble in water and undergo little biodegradation. Present knowledge suggests that these regulators are largely eliminated by adsorption on to sludge particles in sewage treatment plants (Jakobi and Löhr (1987)).

Foaming at weirs on many UK rivers appears to have increased recently. In Switzerland and Holland, it has been suggested that a reduction in STPP content of detergents has necessitated increased LAS use, with consequent enhancement of foaming problems at the outfalls of sewage treatment plants. This is unlikely to be the cause in the UK, which is more probably related to the unusually low river flows experienced during the summers of 1989 and 1990.

Detergent Enzymes, Fragrances, and Dyes
Enzymes are high molecular mass proteins. These are quickly inactivated and biodegraded by sewage treatment facilities and in receiving waters. Thus, there are no grounds for concern about their effects with respect to maintaining water quality or their general environmental behaviour.

This also applies to the other ingredients found in trace amounts in cleaning products such as those designed to confer pleasing fragrance and appearance (perfumes, dyes, etc.). These materials are either decomposed or adsorptively eliminated in the course of sewage treatment. Trace residues, which might escape removal and thus appear in the environment, are generally thought to be ecologically insignificant (Jakobi and Löhr (1987)). However, some carryover of dyes from toilet blocks to treated sewage has been reported; this has apparently resulted in blue tinted sewage treatment works effluents.

Apparently, the recent trend towards the use of liquid detergents is causing changes in fragrance formulations, since the plastic bottles used allow the build up of malodorous compounds. To counter this volatile fragrance compounds are used in liquid formulations. In gas permeable cardboard packages that prevent build up of unpleasant odours, less volatile compounds can be employed. It is not thought that these changes will have major environmental consequences as fragrances should be volatilised or biodegraded during sewage treatment.

3.3   Toxicological and Biological Effects

3.3.1   Introduction
The ecotoxicology of a chemical is based on a sequence of interactions and effects controlled by its physical, chemical and biological properties.

As a chemical is discharged into the environment it is subject to physical dispersal and may be chemically modified and degraded by abiotic processes.

Organisms may, therefore, be exposed to the original chemical and also its derivatives. The response of organisms will vary from negligible and sublethal reactions, to behavioural effects or ultimately death.

The bioaccumulation by organisms of chemicals controls the concentrations of contaminants within organisms and therefore the deleterious effects on biota. Organisms take up chemicals from two principal sources – directly from the ambient environment and/or from food. Food inputs would originally have been contaminated from the ambient environment lower down the food chain.

3.3.2   Internal Pathways of Toxins in Aquatic Organisms
The rate of accumulation of a toxin by an organism is not a simple function of exposure and total body concentration. A toxin becomes distributed at different rates and concentrations within the different tissue types of an organism. The toxic effect of a given substance also varies within the different tissues of an organism. Toxic impacts are not always fatal, with organisms displaying highly variable sub-lethal responses.

Accumulation of toxins within an organism can occur through three common pathways:

- bioaccumulation – accumulation via food; and direct uptake from the environment, therefore a function of time and exposure;

- bioconcentration – concentration of toxins within organisms due to the direct uptake from the environment, without the influence of food; and

- biomagnification – accumulation and concentration via the food chain.

Following the uptake of a contaminant the distribution of the chemical and its possible biotransformation within an organism is again highly variable.

Biotransformation of toxic substances by organisms is the metabolic reaction to foreign compounds in tissues. In higher organisms biotransformation occurs mainly within the liver, kidneys and to a lesser extent within the gills.

The assimilation of chemicals by organisms may induce a range of biological effects from the sublethal to the lethal.

Environmental toxicology is principally concerned with the investigation of lethal effects of environmental contaminants. This approach aims to establish the relationship between percentage lethality and toxicant concentration through exposure under controlled, laboratory conditions. The concentration at 50 percent mortality is described as the LC_{50}.

Although such data may give an indication as to the potential toxicity of a given chemical, data derived under experimental conditions needs to be treated with caution. The laboratory conditions and test animals may not be representative of those in the natural environment.

3.3.3 Effects of Cleaning Products on Organisms

The main constituents of modern cleaning products can be regarded as toxicologically well characterized with regards to mammalian effects and at the levels of exposure predicted they are certainly safe for the consumer (Jakobi and Löhr (1987)).

The usual commercial cleaning products display only minimal acute toxicity to humans. LD_{50} values normally fall within the range of several hundred to several thousand mg kg^{-1} body weight. Oral ingestion leads usually to vomiting, and this may be accompanied by irritation of the mucous membranes of the gastrointestinal tract and diarrhoea. Low toxicity and the fact that vomiting is virtually unpreventable after ingestion of large quantities of detergent essentially exclude any serious threat of poisoning through product misuse (Jakobi and Löhr (1987)).

However, the aquatic toxicological effects may be more pronounced due to the continuous exposure of aquatic organisms to pollutant levels in their surrounding medium. Furthermore it has been shown that near-lethal concentrations of detergents are attractive to fish and the avoidance behaviour associated with most pollutants is not adhered to (Hellawell (1986)). Typical data for the acute toxicity of the major groups of surfactants are provided in Table 3.3a.

The data in Table 3.3a indicate that it is safe to assume that the highly biodegradable anionic and nonionic surfactants permitted by law are of only marginal toxicity to aquatic organisms. This does not, however, dismiss the possibility that acute toxicity effects may occur during detergent spillages in the proximity of a watercourse.

A sub-lethal effect of some detergents is changed feeding behaviour. For example, apparently permanent changes were induced in catfish (*Ictalurus natalis*) by branched alkyl benzene sulphonates (ABS) when erosion of the taste-buds occurred and feeding stopped (Bardach *et al* (1965)). Normal feeding behaviour was suppressed in flatfish (*Jordanella floridae*) by ABS; food was taken but then rejected, presumably because the taste receptors were affected (Foster *et al* (1966)). These types of detergent are no longer in use due to their low biodegradability.

Anionic Surfactants

A study of LAS toxicity (Anderson *et al* (1990)) using two tubificid species showed that the presence of sediment modified LAS toxicity. This effect was not clearly seen in acute exposure. Results from tests of chronic exposure were less conclusive, and it was recommended that further investigation into the adsorption capacity of sediment and the amount of LAS irreversibly absorbed and accumulated was necessary.

Ventullo *et al* (1989) carried out lake enclosure studies to ascertain the effects of LAS on heterotrophic microbial communities. Acute exposure to LAS had an adverse effect on heterotrophy at concentrations greater than 0.5 mgl^{-1}. However, chronic exposure of lake microbial communities to LAS resulted in a biodegradation adaptive response, which resulted in the development of a more tolerant community and recovery of heterotrophy. At the 5 mgl^{-1} dose level, a substantial increase in biodegradation and number of degraders occurred relative to the control.

Another study examined the influence of sodium dodecyl sulphate (SDS) on the uptake of heavy metals by aquatic plants, using water hyacinth. The results showed a reduction in metal uptake in the presence of SDS (Anderson *et al* (1990)).

Cationic Surfactants

Cationic surfactants elicit acute toxic effects in aquatic organisms by disrupting the structure and function of gill tissues, which may result in the suffocation of the organism (Knezovich *et al* (1988)). In a study with the cationic surfactant, hexadecylpyridinium bromide (HPB), clams, minnows and tadpoles were used as test organisms to examine the relative availability of HPB to organisms that occupy distinct ecological niches. The results showed very low whole-body bioaccumulation in comparison with many other organic compounds such as polychlorinated biphenyls (pcbs) and polycyclic aromatic hydrocarbons (PAHs). The relative distribution of HPB within the organisms was measured as an important indication of the tissues which are at greatest risk. In each organism tested by Knezovich *et al* (1988), gill tissues accumulated the highest concentrations of HPB.

In a study by Ventullo *et al* (1989) the effects of dodecyltrimethyl-ammonium chloride (TMAC) were investigated. It was found to have no acute or chronic effect on microbial communities in a lotic (stream) environment, and biodegradation of TMAC was observed in the sediment and water column.

Measured residual concentrations of cationic surfactants in surface waters are reported to fall in the range of 5–30 μgl^{-1}. The corresponding safety factor in terms of acute LC$_{50}$ values for aquatic organisms is at least 60 (see *Table 3.3a*) and under normal circumstances it is unlikely that cationic surfactants are the cause of significant biological impacts. Furthermore, bioaccumulation of cationic surfactants in fish is reported to be very low (Jakobi and Löhr (1987)).

Non-ionic Surfactants

A study by Maki and Rubin (1979) on non-ionic surfactant toxicity indicated the following:

- the 96 hr static LC$_{50}$ for fathead minnows exposed to non-ionic surfactant ranges from 1.2 to 2.48 mgl^{-1};

- the acute toxicity of the surfactant tested was completely eliminated by secondary wastewater treatment, and was also lost in the receiving water, although at a slightly slower rate; and

- the degradation products of the surfactant are apparently non-toxic, as indicated by 96 hr acute exposures of fathead minnows at concentrations as high as 30 mgl^{-1}.

The non-ionic surfactant tested in the study by Maki and Rubin (1979) was Neodol 45–7, a primary alcohol ethoxylate which is known to be widely used in finished detergent formulations.

The effects of Neodol 45–7, a non-ionic surfactant, on microbial activity have also been studied in a lake environment (Ventullo *et al* (1989)). The results showed a reduction in turnover of glucose during acute exposure and an adaptive response and increased biodegradation of the surfactant during chronic exposure. Thus, despite a significant acute toxicity at high concentrations, there were no long-term adverse effects of Neodol 45–7.

3.3.4 Phosphate Substitutes

The toxicological and biological effects of phosphates in the freshwater environment are discussed in Section 4.

The toxicological and biological effects of the main non-phosphate detergent builders are discussed below.

Amino Carboxylic Builders: NTA and EDTA

Public health concern regarding the amino carboxylic builder NTA has been articulated largely in relation to toxicological, carcinogenic, mutagenic and teratogenic effects of NTA or NTA-metal complexes (Anderson *et al* (1985)). Overall, acute mammalian toxicity is low (NYSDEC, 1984). Mutagenic activity has been observed in pregnant mice when NTA was combined with cadmium and mercury (Venier *et al* (1985)).

NTA has been shown to be carcinogenic, to have a weak chromosome – breaking effect, to cause cytogenicity, mutagenicity and co-carcinogenicity through irritation of the urinary epithelium, and to be toxic to aquatic and terrestrial organisms.

More recently, it has also been shown that NTA can cause an increase in the toxicity of a surfactant. It has also been shown that NTA enhances the direct mutagenicity of several Cr(VI) compounds through rendering them soluble. NTA is not considered to be teratogenic or empryotoxic either alone or as a metal complex (Andersom, *et al* (1985)).

EDTA is not phytotoxic, but can act to reduce the toxicity of trace metals through complexation. For example, addition of EDTA to culture medium has been found to enhance survival of the shrimp (*Penaeus monodon*) and carp (*Cyprinus carpo*) (CES, 1990). LC$_{50}$(96 hr) concentrations of 41 mgl^{-1}, 159 mgl^{-1} and 532 mgl^{-1} to *Penaeus monodon* have been reported for EDTA in very soft, medium hard and very hard waters, respectively (CES, 1991). These concentrations are far higher than those expected in natural waters, even if EDTA were to be substituted for STPP as a detergent builder in the future (CES, 1991). EDTA is only moderately toxic to mammals, and there is no evidence of EDTA acting as a mutagen, carcinogen or teratogen.

Polycarboxylic Acids

There has been limited research into the toxicological effects of PCAs. Experiments have been undertaken on fish and rodents to determine the LC$_{50}$ (concentration of PCA required to cause mortality in 50% of a given population in a given time period). The data is presented in Table 3.3b. The results show evidence of antigenicity, mutagenicity and anti-tumour properties, and the toxicity varied between polymers.

Similar effects on humans are possible, although it is anticipated that exceptionally high doses of PCA would be required. The environmental fate of the PCAs is proving difficult to study due to the lack of an accurate, quantitative detection method especially in complex matrices (Dwyer *et al* (1989)). No information exists on the toxicological properties of polycarboxylic acid – heavy metal complexes which could be formed.

Aluminosilicate builders: Zeolite A

Studies on the toxicity of the aluminosilicate builder Zeolite A have shown that at the estimated concentrations in receiving waters it is non-toxic to marine and freshwater species (Dwyer *et al* (1990)).

Zeolite A has also been shown to be non-toxic to humans when ingested or inhaled and it does not cause irritation to the skin or eyes (Dwyer *et al* (1990)).

The only real concerns over the use of zeolite are its potential ability to adsorb organics and heavy metals during sewage treatment, and thus their potential for remobilisation in receiving waters.

However, there also remains the slight possibility of aluminium mobilisation from zeolites in acid waters. Given the evidence that surface waters in poorly buffered catchments have become acidified in the past several decades (Merilehto *et al* (1989)) it remains a matter for potential concern that elevated aluminium concentrations may occur as a result of the increased use of zeolites. In Norway, in particular, the incidence of Alzheimer's disease has been correlated with the aluminium content of surface and groundwaters. The unfortunate incident at Camelford (UK) in 1988 where aluminium sulphate was accidentally introduced into the public water supply is still causing controversy in terms of perceived health effects.

Table 3.3a Acute Toxicity of Surfactants

Surfactants	LC_{50} (fishes), mgl^{-1}	LC_{50} (*Daphnia*), mgl^{-1}	NOEC* (algae, growth inhibition), mg^{-1}
$C_{11,6}$ LAS	3–10	8–20	30–300
C_{14-18} αOlefinsulfonates	2–20	5–50	10–100
Fatty alcohol sulfates	3–20	5–70	60
Alcohol ether sulfates	1.4–20	1–50	65
Alkanesulfonates			
C_{13-15} up to $C_{16,3}$	2–10	4–250	N/A
C_{15-18} and C_{18}	1–2	0.7–6	N/A
Soaps			
O°d	6.7	N/A	N/A
5°d	20–150	N/A	10–50
Fatty alcohol poly(ethylene glycol) ethers			
C_{9-11} to C_{14-1}^5			
2–10 EO	0.25–4	2–10	4–50
10 EO	1–40	4–20	N/A
C_{16-18}			
2–4 EO	100	20–100	N/A
5–7 EO	3–30	5–200	N/A
10–14 EO	1.7–3	4–60	N/A
Nonylphenol poly(ethylene glycol) ethers			
2–11 EO	2–11	4–50	20–50
20–30 EO	50–100	N/A	N/A
EO/PO Block polymers	100	100	N/A
Fatty alcohol EO/PO products (>80% biodegradable)	0.5–1	0.3–1	N/A
Distearyldimethylammonium chloride	1.5–40	4–100	N/A

* NOEC = No observed effect concentration; N/A = no data available
Source: Jakobi and Löhr, 1987

Other Builders

Sodium carbonate and sodium silicate are of low toxicity, and environmental concentrations, even with high builder formulation contents, would not be significantly affected by likely detergent derived effluents. Silicate is thought to be a limiting nutrient to diatoms in certain natural waters. However, it is unlikely that significant diatom blooms would occur due to the increased use of silicate in detergents.

Table 3.3b Toxicological effects of selected polymeric polycarboxylic acids

Substance	Fish Toxicity LC$_{50}$ (mgl^{-1})	Acute Rodent Toxicity LD$_{50}$ (mgKg^{-1})	Other Effects
PAA	>250	39+	antiulcer and
PHAA	>250	2500*	antitumour activity
P(AA–AAL)	>250		
P(AA–MA)	>250	10,000*	
P(AA–MAn)			antitumour activity
		110+ +	
		800+	

Note: *oral, + intraperitoneal, ++ intra venous, – no information available
Source: Hunter *et al* (1988)

Sodium citrate is of low toxicity to aquatic organisms, the lowest median effect concentration (EC$_{50}$) is reported to be 560 mgl^{-1} and a no observed effect concentration of 320 mgl^{-1} has been determined for the water flea (*Daphnia magna*) (CES, 1991). There is no evidence that citrate acts as a mutagen, teratogen or carcinogen.

Bleaching Agents

The main bleaching agent currently used in UK cleaning products is sodium perborate (see *Section 3.2.4*).

The effects of boron in the aquatic environment are well documented.

Most laboratory toxicity studies are based on reconstituted water as the experimental medium (Butterwick *et al* (1989)). However, recent work by Procter & Gamble (unpublished) has found that when trout embryo-larval stages were exposed to boron in natural watercourses, it was found to be substantially less toxic.

Birge *et al* (1984) have recorded Lowest Observable Effect Concentration (LOEC) under natural water exposes of 1.0 mg B l^{-1} (boron amendment to natural waters) and found that 0.750 mg B l^{-1} (natural background boron) did not affect rainbow trout early life stages. Another more recent early life stage rainbow trout study by Procter & Gamble (90 days starting with green eggs) conducted in natural water indicated no impairment to rainbow trout early life stages at 17.0 mg B l^{-1}, the highest test concentration used.

Studies have found amphibians to respond to boron at concentrations similar to those for fish, requiring 9.6 mg B l^{-1} for detectable effects. In the case of the toad (*Bufo fowleri*) no effects occurred on its embryos until a boron concentration of 53 mg B l^{-1} was applied (Birge and Black (1977)).

In tests with the invertebrate *Daphnia magna* investigations have included assessing effects resulting from both acute and chronic exposure to boron. No observable effect concentration (NOEC) and LOEC values for this species are about 6 and 13 mg B l^{-1}. McKee and Wolf (1963) have presented additional data indicating a higher effect for boron in the form of sodium perborate. However, the formulation of boron should not significantly influence its aquatic effects at naturally occurring pH levels, as the predominant boron species under these conditions is undissociated boric acid.

Stanley (1974) has shown that a concentration of 40.3 mg B l^{-1} added as a tetraborate salt leads to a 50% inhibition of root growth in the freshwater plant *Myriophyllum spicatum* after 32 days of treatment.

There is no evidence that any aquatic organisms bioaccumulate boron.

A number of broad systematic studies have been carried out on the boron concentrations in rivers and drinking water. The concentrations found for the Federal Republic of Germany are very low (Jakobi and Löhr (1987)). Boron levels in drinking water are so low as to be negligible from a toxicological standpoint (0.25 mg B l^{-1}), although some mineral waters, for example, exhibit values ranging from a few mgl^{-1} to much higher concentrations. Similarly, boron concentrations in German streams are also
very low (Rhine: 0.1 – 0.25 mgl^{-1}; Neckar, Main, and Rühr: 0.2 – 0.5 mgl^{-1}; polluted rivers such as the Nette, Nidda, and Niers: 0.5 –1 mgl^{-1}; and those classed highly polluted, such as the Emscher:1–2 mgl^{-1}). In certain other countries, geological conditions are such that much higher natural boron concentrations are measured. In a survey of boron concentrations in UK fresh waters, WRC (unpubl) found levels to be in the range 0.046 – 0.822 mgl^{-1}, while boron concentrations in the range 0.25 – 0.62 mgl^{-1} were reported for rivers in the Anglian region during 1986.

A recent report to the DoE (WRC (1988)) recommended the following Environmental Quality Standards for Boron in the UK aquatic environment:

* 2.0 mg B l^{-1} for the protection of freshwater fish; and

* 5.0 mg B l^{-1} for the protection of other freshwater life and associated non-aquatic organisms.

157

Fluorescent Whitening Agents

Extensive toxicological investigations have been carried out to assess the effects of fluorescent whitening agents on algae, mussels and fish. These investigations have shown that fluorescent whitening agents are of very low toxicity (LC_{50} values > 100 mgl^{-1}), indicating a biological safety factor in rivers of $10^6 - 10^8$ (Jakobi and Löhr (1987)) (see *Section 3.2.4*).

Soil Antiredeposition Agents

These are primarily water-soluble, high molecular mass cellulose ethers. Their biodegradation proceeds as slowly as that of natural cellulose. However, such compounds are completely non-toxic to fish, and no significant ecological problems are known to be associated with their use (Jakobi and Löhr (1987)).

3.4 Case Studies

The following case studies highlight incidents of freshwater pollution which have been attributed to pollutants from cleaning products. Case studies particularly relating to eutrophication are presented separately in Section 4.3.

3.4.1 Fate of NTA in Canadian Surface Waters

One of the few field studies on the fate of NTA in rivers was reported by Shannon *et al* (1974) where NTA concentrations were monitored downstream of a sewage effluent discharge for a period of one year. Under summer conditions (> 10°C), mean NTA concentrations were reported to be 0.01 mgl^{-1}. This compares with mean winter (0.5 to 3.0°C) NTA concentrations of 0.106 mgl^{-1}. These results demonstrate the importance of temperature in determining the rate of NTA degradation. Woodiwiss *et al* (1979) studied NTA concentrations in receiving streams in Canada, upstream and downstream from effluent discharges. *Table 3.5a* indicates how differing concentrations of NTA in detergents affect concentrations of NTA in receiving water. These results confirm that generalised introduction of NTA in detergents would result in the persistence of variable concentrations of NTA in receiving streams (Perry *et al* (1984)), with subsequent effects on the biota (see *Section 3.3.4(ii)*).

Table 3.4a Mean NTA concentration upstream and downstream of effluent discharge points (EDPs) in Canada

% NTA in Detergent Composition	Mean NTA Concentration Upstream of EDPs (mgl^{-1})	Mean NTA Concentration Downstream of EDPs (mgl^{-1})
6	0.002 – 0.0021	0.002 – 0.045
15	<0.001 – 0.028	<0.001 – 0.667

Source: Dwyer *et al* (1990)

3.4.2 Repeated Foaming of an Un-named Tributary in the Thames Region

In April, 1989, a member of the public reported accumulated foam on a small ditch in the Thames catchment. The foam was reported to have been present for several days.

Inspection of the site and upstream premises confirmed that no discharge was occurring. It was, however, thought by the NRA pollution staff that a cosmetics company were rinsing shampoo blenders into a foul sewer which drained to a septic tank near to the site of the pollution incident.

No fish mortalities were reported, and the formal tripartite sampling procedure was not carried out. However, the cosmetics company were informed that alternative arrangements for drainage must be made.

In July, 1989, a repeat of the incident occurred. A tripartite sample was handed to the cosmetics company, the others taken away for chemical analysis. The owner of the site (not the cosmetics company), made arrangements for the offending pipe to be blocked off to prevent a further discharge.

The incident was very localised due to the stream above and below the inspection point being dry. Therefore, no further action was taken by the NRA, Thames Region.

In October of the same year, a further pollution incident was prevented by NRA action. A spillage of shampoo and conditioner mix (approximately 90,000 litres) had entered a recently dry waterhole. The detergent mix was removed by tanker as there was a danger of the waterhole overflowing into the nearby brook.

No subsequent pollution incidents have been recorded, although the situation is being carefully monitored by the NRA, Thames Region.

3.4.3 Fire and Detergent Spill, South East Wales

A pollution incident occurred in November 1989, when a large quantity of shampoo and other chemicals were washed into the River Rhumney, following a fire at a chemical plant. The discharge affected over 20 km of the river, killing over 19,000 fish, consisting mainly of brown trout, but also including grayling, salmon, sea trout, eels, and coarse fish. The discharge also resulted in the closure of abstraction intakes, and formal samples being served on the company involved.

3.4.4 Detergent Spill, South East Wales

A pollution incident occurred in October 1990, when a spillage of detergent occurred from a bulk storage tank at a premises on the Western Industrial Estate, Caerphilly. The chemicals discharged entered a feeder stream killing over 90,000 coarse fish. Formal samples were served at the premises concerned, although the discharge was said to have been caused by an act of vandalism.

4 Phosphates and Eutrophication

4.1 Introduction

Phosphorus is an essential life supporting nutrient. However, in excess concentrations in the freshwater environment phosphate may have detrimental effects on water quality, aquatic ecology and the aesthetic value of a waterbody.

4.1.1 Sources of Phosphorus

The majority of phosphorus enters watercourses and lakes either:

- as effluents from sewage treatment works;

- as a constituent of industrial discharges;

- from livestock manure; or

- from diffuse sources such as sediments and agriculture.

Table 4.1a gives data for the balance of different sources of phosphorus for four European countries, each with a contrasting dominant phosphorus source. In the UK domestic sewage is the greatest contributor to phosphate loadings, in Ireland diffuse agricultural and stock units are predominant, phosphorus loadings in Denmark are dominated by contributions from stock units, whilst in Norway natural diffuse sources are dominant. Clearly then, the variety of sources of phosphorus depends on the balance of land use, population size and climatic conditions.

Table 4.1a Estimated Percentage Contributions to the Total Load of Phosphorus for Selected Countries in Europe

	Point sources %			Diffuse sources %		Weight Total P load (thousands of tonnes yr^{-1})
	Domestic	Industrial	Stock Units	Agriculture	Natural	
U.K.	53	5	20	16	7	68
Denmark	21	2	58	13	6	15.6
Ireland	20	2	36	30	12	17.0
Norway	33	3	10	10	44	7.5
Mean for Europe*	37	4	30	17	14	28.1

Source: Lund and Moss *et al*, (1990)   * Mean for Europe is average of 27 countries examined.

The UK is reported to have a considerably greater load of total phosphorus per annum than elsewhere in Europe (Lund and Moss (1990)). Natural diffuse sources of phosphorus in the UK are only 7% compared to a mean of 14% of the total P load for Europe as a whole. As may be seen from Table 4.1a the main contributor to the total P load of the UK is domestic waste water; domestic point sources (sewage) constitute 53% of the total P load per annum. Based on estimates of detergent use in the UK (Table 2.3a) and detergent composition (Table 2.3b), it is estimated that 45–55% of the UK's domestic phosphorus loading to the aquatic environment is derived from detergent use; the balance is of mainly dietary origin. Note that 50% reduction in sewage phosphate loads due to sewage treatment is assumed (Matthews, (1985)).

Lund and Moss (1990) have suggested that several inputs of phosphorus may have increased during the 1980s. These include slurry, intensive arablisation, inland fish farms, and expansion of first time rural sewage systems. Phosphorus associated with the use of cleaning products has been stable at about 2.08 – 2.27 kg per capita per annum between 1984 and 1990 (CES, 1990). This indicates a total phosphorus load of about 30,000 tonnes per annum from STPP use (which is reduced by 50% during sewage treatment). This compares with the estimate of 68,000 tonnes total phosphorus load to the aquatic environment made by Lund and Moss (1990). Nevertheless, this indicates that cleaning products contribute 22% of the total phosphorus reaching the aquatic environment, and are the largest single contributor.

4.2 Impact of Phosphorus on Surface Waters

4.2.1 Introduction

The primary concern in relation to increased phosphorus concentrations in freshwaters relates to eutrophication, particularly algal blooms. In the following sections, we discuss eutrophication, its relationship to lake circulation, nutrient cycling and subsequent effects on algal growth.

4.2.2 Eutrophication

Since the limiting nutrient in most freshwater lakes, reservoirs and rivers is generally phosphorus (Vollenweider, (1968;1985)), the process of eutrophication in the freshwater environment can best be described as the enrichment of this element into receiving waters. Eutrophication is more prevalent in enclosed water bodies, eg lakes, and is less common in rivers where the residence time is normally low. In slow flowing lowland rivers, the effects of eutrophication may, however, be significant. The major problem has been the input of anthropogenic sources of phosphorus (probably about 25% of the anthropogenic load is derived from cleaning products). This accelerates the process of eutrophication which may proceed slowly in the natural ageing of a water body. As eutrophication advances the aquatic environment is characterised by:

- an abundance of algae, often 'blooms' of 'blue green' algae (*Cyanobacteria*);

- elimination of dissolved oxygen in the hypolimnion; and

- a further increase in the concentration of nutrients and other organic compounds.

The depletion of dissolved oxygen can be great enough to cause the death of fish or a decrease in the variety of species able to survive. Some 'blue green' algae which may develop also produce toxic compounds such as alkaloids and peptides (Codd *et al* (1985)) that have been implicated in the poisoning of fish (Davies (1980)) and possibly even livestock (Reynolds (1981)). Excessive growth of algae can also affect the treatment of water for potable supply by blocking filters or passing through and causing a bad odour and taste due to the secretion of various organic compounds (Collingwood (1977)). This in turn can make chlorination more costly, or produce astringent-tasting chlorinated phenolic substances in the domestic water supply (Walker (1983)).

Increased algal growth may also cause amenity problems in terms of loss of water clarity in surface waters. Algae may produce substances which are toxic to mammals and may support clogging communities of nematode worms, sponges, hydrozoans and insects in water distribution pipes.

Such problems associated with eutrophication have generated concern amongst several countries and in the UK, Lough Neagh (Gray (1985)) the River Ant and Barton Broad (Phillips (1984)) have particular problems.

4.2.3 Lake Circulation and Nutrient Cycling

In a temperate zone the majority of solar radiation impinging on a lake surface is absorbed directly by the water. The low thermal conductivity of water leads to the heating of the surface layers of a lake during periods of increased duration and intensity of solar radiation. This increase in temperature of the surface layers is generally more rapid than heat distributed by internal mixing within the lake, particularly during periods of decreased wind induced turbulence. As the warmer surface layers of water become less dense the relative thermal resistance to mixing increases. Under these conditions a lake may exhibit thermal stratification – the formation of thermal zones within the lake, (the epilimnion, metalimnion and hypolimnion). Within temperate regions lake stratification may be very stable, lasting from the spring through to the autumn. A drop in temperatures during the autumn combined with an increase in wind action on a lake may then cause the lake to 'turnover', the mixing of the stratified layers to give a uniform temperature distribution within the lake. Conversely very cold surface layers of water during winter may result in inverse stratification due to water having its lowest density at 4°C.

The establishment of temperature stratification within a lake is of significance for nutrient cycling. The formation of thermoclines (the zones of different temperature) also affects other chemical and physical parameters. The oxygen contents of the hypolimnion under eutrophic conditions, is depleted rapidly by oxidative degradation of organic detritus settling through the water column. This results in an anaerobic hypolimnion. In highly eutrophic lakes the hypolimnetic oxygen content is often depleted within a few weeks of summer stratification, and remains anoxic throughout the period of stratification.

Lake Circulation in the UK

The season of complete top to bottom mixing in UK lakes may last from one period of direct summer stratification to the next such period, a condition known as monomixis (single mixing). During cold winters, however, the maximum density of water at around 4°C leads to a period of inverse stratification during winter with the warmest and densest water usually at 4°C at the bottom (though it may be cooler) and with an upward gradient of colder and less dense water to the surface, where ice forms at 0°C (Moss (1988)).

The stratification of lakes often has large effects on the chemistry of the water. It may result in a large proportion of the lake (in the lower layer or hypolimnion) being almost completely isolated from the upper layer or epilimnion, from the atmosphere and from the inflow water. Under inverse stratification the deeper layers will be similarly isolated. These processes have significant consequences for lake water chemistry (Moss (1988)). The hypolimnion may become severely oxygen depleted, due to the lack of reaeration of the bottom water and consumption of existing oxygen reserves.

Biogeochemical Processes

A continual rain of phytoplankton cells, detritus, zooplankton and fish faeces and corpses and associated bacteria falls through the middle layer or metalimnion to the hypolimnion. The greater the epilimnetic production, the greater the supply of organic matter to the hypolimnion and the greater the demand of the irreplaceable (until overturn) oxygen reserves there.

As particles fall through the hypolimnion, they are decomposed by the aerobic bacteria which have colonised them and the hypolimnion, provided some oxygen remains, may become enriched in ammonium, nitrate, phosphate, silicate and other ions. These substances may be returned to the surface waters at overturn. In a temperate lake the overturn usually occurs at a time when production is becoming limited by light and when the increased winter flow from the catchment area is restocking the lake with nutrients (Moss (1988)).

Effects of Lake Circulation on Nutrient Availability

A large proportion of phosphorus in freshwaters is bound to inorganic colloids and particulate matter such as clays, carbonates and hydroxides. Concentrations of total and soluble phosphorus, in lakes of low nutrient status (oligotrophic), show little variation with depth. However, where lakes exhibit a high level of eutrophication and strong dissolved oxygen gradients form, a marked increase in the phosphorus content in the hypolimnion bottom layer commonly occurs.

This hypolimnetic increase comes mostly from the release of soluble phosphorus from near the sediment-water interface. Whilst the hypolimnion remains oxygenated, phosphorus is prevented from diffusing upward into the water column, partly by adsorption by settling particles of sediment. As the hypolimnion becomes anoxic, phosphate is released into the water column.

Soluble phosphorus can accumulate in high concentrations in an anaerobic hypolimnion. With the autumn 'turnover' of a lake, the phosphate precipitates out mainly by adsorption to iron oxyhydroxides. Bacterial action within a lake's sediments converts organic phosphorus into phosphate which is released into the water. In addition, phosphate is released from iron oxyhydroxides as iron (III) is reduced to iron (II).

In shallow lakes where water mixes constantly to the bottom, diffusion of phosphate ions (Holdren *et al* (1980)) from sediment surfaces occurs. In Lough Ennell in Ireland, Lennox (1984) found that as much as 17% of the total phosphorus load could come from the aerobic marginal sediments. This phosphate is largely derived from aerobic decay of the organic phosphorous component. Drake and Heaney (1987) found that at high pH (>10) significant amounts of phosphorus were released from the aerobic marginal sediments of a lake. In already eutrophicated lakes, the foraging of carp (*Cyprinus carpio*) for animals in the sediment may also mobilize large amounts of phosphorus (Lamarra (1975)). This appears to be consequential as the size of fish involved presupposes an already high productivity (Hellawell (1986)).

Phosphorus supplies from the hypolimnion may mix sufficiently into the epilimnion in mid-summer to be significant in maintenance of the summer algal crops (Cooke *et al* (1977)). The greatest problems seem to occur when the lake is well mixed and the sediment surface becomes anaerobic. In a shallow lake, wind circulation of water to the bottom is likely to be very efficient and oxygenated water must be expected always to be in contact with the sediment surface. Yet it is clear that phosphate release does occur to a substantial degree.

It is apparent that the supply of organic matter settling from the plankton to the sediment is substantial and highly labile, not having had time to decay in the short water column. This supports a degree of bacterial activity which cannot be sustained by diffusion of oxygen from the water to the sediment. Thus, despite overlying aerobic water, the sediment surface becomes anaerobic and the oxidized microzone breaks down. This allows both Fe^{2+} and PO_4^{3-} ions to escape. In the overlying aerobic water they should reprecipitate so that little net supply of phosphate should occur. However, in intensely reducing sediments with reduction of sulphate to sulphide by anaerobic bacteria, much

162

of the iron is reprecipitated as sulphide, leaving phosphate to accumulate unhindered in the water; phosphate concentrations in pore waters are controlled by formation of vivianite (iron (II) phosphate).

The phosphate can then help sustain a large summer algal community (usually limited for a time by nitrogen, so abundant is the released phosphate) which continues the supply of labile organic matter to the sediment and may maintain a self sustaining system (Moss *et al* (1986)).

4.2.4 Algal Growth

Algae are simple plants that lack true stems, roots and leaves, but possess chlorophyll and other pigments and so are capable of photosynthesis. Algae exhibit diverse life forms ranging from simple unicellular forms to complex colonial and filamentous forms. There are several groups of algal type.

In the aquatic freshwater environment the most frequently encountered algae are members of the green algae or *Chlorophyta*, Red algae (*Rhodophyta*) and brown algae (*Phaeophyta*) are more common in saline water, as seaweeds. Common species of freshwater green algae include *Cladophora* (blanket weed), a filamentous form which, as the name suggests, grows in profusion along the bed of a river or shallow lake receiving large inputs of nutrients. *Spirogyra* is another common form which tends to float in sheltered margins of a waterbody. Diatoms (algae rich in silica) are also common. Neither *Chlorophyta* nor diatoms secrete toxins.

During the early part of the growing season, an abundance of nutrients in surface waters combined with an increase in water temperature allows algae to rapidly multiply until the nutrients (usually phosphorus in the freshwater environment) become limiting. The phase of rapid growth is replaced by a massive and sudden mortality of algae. Decomposing algae consume large quantities of oxygen dissolved in the water, and may lead to anaerobic conditions. The waters gradually undergo a self – cleansing process as oxygen levels are re-established, although it is possible for a second bloom to occur under favourable autumn conditions.

4.2.5 Blue-Green Algae

Blue-Green Algae (*Cyanobacteria*) are a particular division of algae which are characterised by very simple species which resemble photosynthetic bacteria in their internal organisation (Isaacs, *et al* (1984)).

Blue-green algae are unicellular, but may become joined in colonies or filaments by a sheath of mucilage.

Blue-green algae have been shown to have the potential to produce toxins (Hunt, (1984)). To date, nine genera of freshwater *Cyanobacteria* have been shown to contain toxic species. The toxins reported so far have a wide range of structures including peptides, alkaloids, lipopolysaccharides and pteridines.

Common species of blue-green algae in the UK aquatic environment include the following (NRA (1990)).

- *Microcystis;*

- *Aphanizomenon;*

- *Anabaena;*

- *Oscillatoria;* and

- *Lynbya.*

Microcystis aeruginosa is the species to which toxic algal blooms are most frequently attributed in the UK (Hunt (1984)).

4.2.6 Toxic Algal Blooms

Toxic algal blooms are a world wide phenomenon. Reports of the deaths of livestock and human illness associated with contaminated water bodies prompted a nationwide survey of the problem in 1989/1990 (see *Section 4.4.3*).

Many species of blue-green algae are at a competitive advantage over other algae because they possess the ability to 'fix' gaseous nitrogen dissolved in water. One other distinctive characteristic is the possession, by some species, of specialised intracellular gas – vesicles. The effect is to lower the density of the organism, potentially below that of the surrounding water, such that it becomes buoyant (NRA, (1990)). This enables blue-green algae to flourish in situations where other algal forms could not exist, and the blue-green algal 'bloom' phenomenon arises (see Section 4.1.1).

It must be emphasised that there is nothing either new or unnatural about the occurrence of bloom-forming populations of blue-green algae, or their tendency to accumulate in surface 'scums'.

A twenty year study carried out by the Danish Institute of Water Quality (VKI) in Denmark has examined the relationships between nutrient status, particularly phosphorus, and algal community composition in about 150 lakes. This data has been summarised by VKI in the form of the relationship shown in *Figure 4.2a*, which indicates that a summer concentration of 0.5 mg Pl⁻¹ is the most likely to produce 'blue-green' algal blooms. This concentration is exceptionally high and in the freshwater environment such an occurrence is likely to be infrequent.

However, in certain enclosed waterbodies, which receive large amounts of phosphorus input from sewage treatment works, agriculture or other sources, such problems are more commonplace (see Section 4.4.3).

Figure 4.2a   Phytoplankton Growth Associated with Different Phosphate Concentrations

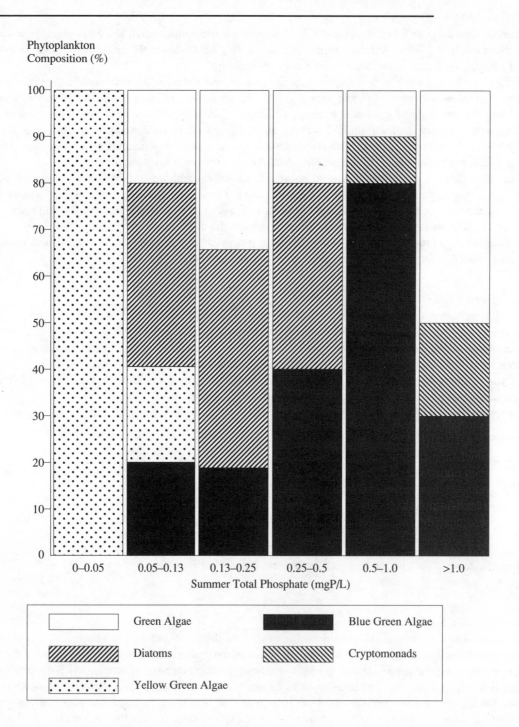

Acknowlegement: Danish Water Quality Institute, VKI

For most situations in Europe, the maximum level of phosphate in the freshwater environment is within the range 0.05 – 0.25 mgl^{-1}; according to Wetzel (1983) a eutrophic environment may have a total phosphorus, concentration of only 30–100 µgl^{-1}. In riverine situations, flushing will generally result in much lower concentrations of phosphorus. It is, therefore, apparent from *Figure 4.2a* that algal communities generally consist of green algae, diatoms, yellow-green algae, and blue-green algae in the freshwater environment.

4.3 Summary of Areas of Concern

4.3.1 General
The incentive to incorporate other builders (chelators) than sodium tripolyphosphate (STPP) was provided in the 1970s by the increased amount of evidence that phosphorus was a primary limiting factor for nuisance algal growth in surface waters. STPP had proved a cheap, effective and non-toxic water-softener having the advantage in environmental terms in that it broke down soon after its release, and thus its chelating capability was not transferred to freshwater ecosystems. Its breakdown product however, is orthophosphate, and in phosphorus-limited ecosystems the addition of phosphate produces larger algal crops. Controversy therefore exists over its acceptability on environmental grounds. However, there is increasing evidence that the effectiveness of a phosphate ban is questionable, particularly due to nutrient cycling within affected water bodies (see *Section 4.2*).

No equally efficient yet safe alternative to STPP has yet been developed, and STPP is still widely used in the UK (at high concentrations in some of the ultra-concentrated detergent formulations and in the majority of powder detergents).

4.3.2 Eutrophication
In itself, phosphate is not harmful, indeed, it is an essential nutrient for plants, animals, and humans. Normally, the phosphate concentration in surface waters is so low that it is a limiting factor for biological growth. Consequently, when additional phosphate is released into surface waters, it no longer becomes a limiting factor, and causes increased algal growth (see Section 4.2). Biodegradation of the algae in stagnant surface waters leads to oxygen depletion in the lower water layers, which in turn causes a general reduction of overall water quality. The result may damage fishing interests and, in some cases, loss of potable water supply may occur. For this reason, the use of sodium tripolyphosphate (STPP) in detergents has come under increasing scrutiny.

Phosphates from detergent builders remain an important source of concern for freshwater pollution in the UK, particularly since the sunny, dry summers in 1989 and 1990 have produced large, and often toxic, blue-green algal blooms. However it is important to note that whilst adequate phosphorus concentrations for algal growth are a necessary condition for algal blooms, they are not necessarily a sufficient precondition, since blooms generally require correct meteorological and hydrographic conditions. Even with a detergent phosphate ban, it is likely that the amount of phosphate from dietary origin and agricultural sources, together with sedimentary phosphorus, would still be sufficient to cause algal blooms, much as at present. The time period required before 'self-purification' of a water body with regard to phosphorus is achieved will depend on a variety of factors, including water body resistance time, release rates of nutrients from sediments and a variety of other biogeochemical factors. In general, it is considered that reductions of anthropogenic phosphorus loadings by 90-95% are required to manage eutrophication; this is greater than the 25% reductions that can be achieved with a phosphate ban in detergents (Lund and Moss (1990,) Doemel and Brooks, (1975)).

For example, experimental investigations by Doemel and Brooks (1975) were conducted using sewage effluents, from Crawfordsville, Indiana, to look at the effects on growth of algae from a number of Indiana lakes. No significant reduction in algal growth was observed when a 57% reduction in reactive sewage phosphorus was achieved by the use of non-phosphorus cleaning products. However, significant reduction in algal growth (a factor of 6-fold reduction in total biomass) was observed when advanced treatment was used to reduce phosphorus levels by 92%.

Further, recycling of phosphate already present in sediments could frustrate attempts to control phosphorus by bans on detergent use alone. Furthermore, no efficient, commercially acceptable alternative to STPP has yet been identified which is without inherent impacts to the aquatic environment.

4.4 Case Studies Concerning Eutrophication
The following case studies highlight situations where eutrophication of the freshwater environment has occurred, and discusses the presence of cleaning products as a possible contributory factor.

4.4.1 Algal Blooms, Lough Neagh, Northern Ireland
Algal blooms are reported to have caused difficulties in Northern Ireland's Lough Neagh, since 1960. The species *Anabaena* and *Aphanziomenon* were in greatest abundance. A study was commissioned by the Northern Ireland

165

Department of Agriculture and a Freshwater Biological Investigation Unit was set up.

Very early in the studies, it became apparent that the prime cause of excessive algal growth and fish kills, following the release of algal toxins on decomposition of the bloom, was due to the availability of large quantities of phosphates, and that the principal source of this was sewage treatment works.

Further studies of the lough showed that increasing urbanisation and detergent use had almost doubled the lough's maximum phosphate concentrations to nearly 80 µg Pl^{-1} between 1969–72 and 1978–81 with a consequent rise in peak algal concentrations from around 55 µg chlorophyll a l^{-1} to nearly 90 µg chlorophyll a l^{-1} over the same period. The typical reduction in species diversity associated with eutrophication was also observed (Gibson et al, (1988)).

In 1981, phosphorus removal was gradually introduced, and according to The Surveyor (1990), the volume of blue green algae (Cyanobacteria) fell from peaks of 20mm^{3}l^{-1} (1979–1981) to about 13mm^{3}l^{-1} by 1982–84. The recovery appears to have been sustained and even in hot summers (eg 1989), major problems were not reported. Long term improvements in the diversity of flora and fauna have yet to be evaluated.

4.4.2 The Norfolk Broadland

The Norfolk Broadland is the best-known lake district of southern England because of its use for boating holidays. It has a lengthy history of human involvement; the Broads are ancient man-made lakes formed by peat cutting between the ninth and fourteenth centuries.

The formerly clear water of the Norfolk Broads is now turbid with algae, due to eutrophication. It is reported that the lakes now contain ten times their former concentration of both phosphorus and nitrogen (Moss, 1987). The main sources of nutrients are sewage, which is rich in phosphate and agricultural run-off draining from East Anglian farmland, which is rich in nitrate.

The swards of submerged plants of the Broads, which earned much of the waterway the status of Nature Reserve have now largely disappeared, and the fish and insect larvae have declined in numbers due to habitat loss. Predation on the algal communities has, therefore, reduced.

At Cockshoot Broad, the Broads Authority have isolated the lake from the River Bure by dams. The amount of nutrient input to the lake is controlled by allowing only swamp water to enter. The swamp acts as a filter, the growth of plants reducing the amount of phosphorus and nitrogen by active uptake. Sediment was also removed, in order to increase water depth, and remove a further potential source of phosphorus, which could diffuse from the sediments. Many aquatic plants are now recolonising Cockshoot Broad.

At Alderfen Broad, the Norfolk Naturalists Trust and the World Wildlife Fund, diverted water around a system of channels in the surrounding fens. The sediment was untouched. For four years the water cleared and the plants returned in abundance. However, the plants created conditions at the surface of the sediment that released phosphate into the water column (Moss, (1987)). The isolation of the Broad meant that the phosphate could not be flushed out. In 1985 and 1986, dense blooms of blue-green algae occurred, and the submerged plants have now disappeared once more.

A further approach now put forward in an attempt to restore Alderfen Broad, and others which are unable to be isolated due to navigation rights, is biomanipulation. This is the process whereby the ecosystem is altered by the encouragement of a different community structure.

It has been suggested that refuges may be provided for aquatic species which graze on algae, eg water flea (*Daphnia magna*). Bundles of alder twigs bound together around a pole have been recommended (Moss, (1987)).

The programme has the support of the Broads Authority, the Soap and Detergent Industry Association and the Nature Conservancy Council who were involved in tests of suitable refuge materials.

4.4.3 NRA Monitoring of Toxic Blooms

The issue of phosphate enrichment became a matter of increased debate in 1989 and 1990 and a full scale survey concerning the development of blue green algae was carried out by the NRA. Toxic blooms of blue-green algae were recorded in 53 UK water bodies in 1989, (NRA 1990) and phosphorus control was given high priority by the NRA as a remedial measure because 'this approach has been widely used and, in some cases, has been shown to be effective'. (NRA 1990 p69 9.42).

Completed questionnaires were received from all the NRA regions, nine Water Services Companies and similar Scottish authorities. Regional results of the survey are presented in Table 4.5a.

Table 4.5a indicates the natural regional variation in occurrence of toxic algal blooms. It is apparent from the results of the NRA survey that the regions with most 'problem' waters are Anglian, North West, Thames and Yorkshire. These are also regions which have a higher incidence of eutrophication due to either a high lowland input of nutrients (mainly from agriculture and domestic sources), or historic pollution problems due to the discharge of domestic and industrial effluents. However, it should be noted that phosphate enrichment is not necessarily the cause

Table 4.5a The incidence of blue-green algal 'problems' in the UK, 1989.

Region	No of waters considered to have blue-green algal 'problems' (% of waters tested exhibiting 'problems')
Anglian	37 (70%)
Northumbrian	0 (Unknown)
North West	50 (100%)
Severn Trent	18 (40%)
Southern	1 (12.5%)
South West	27 (11%)
Thames	21 (84%)
Welsh	1 (8%)
Wessex	13 (40%)
Yorkshire	63 (91%)
Tay RPB	1 (100%)
Forth	1 (30%)
Highland	3 (Unknown)
Clyde	2 (Unknown)
Solway	2 (20%)
Tweed	0 (Unknown)

Adapted from NRA Survey Results (1990)

of algal blooms, Specific weather conditions, such as those which occurred during the hot, dry summers of 1989/90 may increase the incidence of 'problem' algal bloom occurrence (NRA (1990)).

It should be noted that the surveys carried out by the Scottish River Purification Boards on the occurrence of toxic blue-green algae, were not as extensive as those conducted in England and Wales. However, algal problems seemn to be very limited in Scotland; most upland waters are oligotrophic (low nutrient status).

4.4.4 Eutrophication of Lake Trummen, Sweden

After 30 years of discharge of sewage effluent into the Swedish Lake Trummen, it had become highly eutrophicated by 1951 (Begtsson *et al* (1975)). It was accumulating 8 mm year^{-1} of black, sulphurous mud and during ice cover in the winter its water column (2 m) became deoxygenated with consequent fish kills. The sewage effluent and some industrial discharges were diverted in 1958, but by 1968 the lake was still suffering high algal crops, low transparency, deoxygenation and fish kills. Much of the algal crop was being supported by phosphate released from the sediment. There was an internal load of 177 kg P per year compared with the external one which had been reduced to 3 kg P per year.

In 1970 and 1972 a slurry of surface sediment and water was removed from the lake. The sediment was settled in a lagoon and later disposed of as fertilizer whilst the water, after treatment with aluminium salts, was returned to the lake. Following sediment removal the water cleared, and winter deoxygenation no longer occurs.

4.4.5 Protection of the Trossachs Lochs, Scotland

The Trossachs Lochs include all of the large lochs at the heads of the Forth and Teith river systems. The Lochs are well known for their clear, high quality waters and their excellent fauna and flora. However, in 1989 a report by the Forth River Purification Board indicated that over the past 20 years, a combination of agricultural, forestry and tourist development had increased the potential nutrient load. In order to slow down what the Board referred to as 'the unnatural process of cultural eutrophication', a number of policies have been adopted by the Forth River Purification Board in respect of nutrient discharges to the Lochs in order to protect their current status.

The Board agreed to control phosphorus inputs by:

• using their statutory powers to restrict the quantity in new discharges to safe levels; and

• reviewing existing discharge consents where necessary and imposing new, lower limits.

The Board also agreed to reduce phosphorus inputs further in order of priority by:

• influencing long term plans on the type and scope of future developments;

• liaising with planners to enforce where possible land use guidelines to ensure least loss of phosphorus to waters;

- asking foresters and farmers to minimise loss of fertilisers to water by careful and sympathetic application;

- asking Strathclyde Water to use their powers in controlled supply catchments to limit nutrient inputs; and

- asking everyone in the catchments to help by using phosphate free detergents.

Concern was also expressed over the potential for adverse effects of eutrophication associated with large scale housing developments, and it was recommended that these should be prevented unless tertiary sewage treatment schemes to remove phosphorus were included as part of the development.

The effectiveness of such measures has yet to be evaluated. It is interesting to note, however, that the least importance was placed on the encouragement of the use of phosphate free detergents within the catchment areas.

4.4.6 Nutrient Enrichment of Other Water Bodies

Loch Leven

Although current concern over Scottish freshwaters has concentrated on the effects of acidification, the disappearance of Arctic Char (*Salvelinius alpinus L.*) from Loch Leven, and Vendace (*Coregonus albula*) from Castle Loch, Dumfrieshire is reported to be almost certainly due to nutrient enrichment (Bailey-Watts (1990)).

River Great Stour

Discharge of sewage effects has adversely affected this lowland chalk river. In particular, growth of the filamentous algae *Cladophora* has been of continuing concern since the early 1950s (Lund and Moss, (1990)). This has resulted in adverse effects on the fisheries of the river, particularly at Ashford. Apparently the scale of the problem, and the general condition of the river has improved. Whilst phosphate stripping at Ashford sewage treatment works has been proposed, there is apparently no shortage of available phosphorus to limit *Cladophora* and a decrease in phosphorus loadings may not affect standing crops significantly.

The Shropshire – Cheshire Meres

These lakes were formed by the melting of buried ice blocks in deposits left by retreating glaciers about 13.5 million years ago (Lund and Moss, (1990)). Because of the relatively high natural supply of phosphorus to the lakes, the phytoplankton has generally been nitrogen limited (Lund and Moss, (1990)). However, in at least one lake (Ellesmere) it is suspected that high phosphorus concentrations, ($>1\text{mgl}^{-1}$) are possibly caused by sewage effluents.

5 Wastewater Treatment Technology

5.1 Introduction

Detergents enter the water system with both municipal and industrial effluents. As already described in *Section 2.3*, the main constituents are surfactants and building agents such as:

- polyphosphates, carbonates, silicates;
- sequestering and complex-forming agents;
- reinforcing agents to improve the action of the active constituents; and
- additives.

The most significant wastewater components are the detergent builders. In particular, the builder sodium tripolyphosphate (STPP) tends to exacerbate the problem of eutrophication in lowland water bodies (see *Section 4*). As a result, recent investigation has led to the use of three major alternatives, namely:

- nitrilotriacetic acid (NTA);
- polycarboxylic acids (PCAs); and
- zeolite type A.

Wastewater treatment methodology is dependent upon the constituents of the detergent. Where phosphorus levels are high, phosphorus removal can be attained through precipitation/flocculation with iron salts. Generally however, standard treatment by coagulation/flocculation, clarification and filtration tends to remove little or no detergent from the water. Similarly, the addition of a pre-chlorination stage does not break down the detergents. For satisfactory destruction of detergent compounds, foaming, ozone or activated carbon must be used.

5.2 Localised Detergent Wastewater Treatment

5.2.1 Foaming

Foaming may be used when the detergent content of an effluent is high and needs to be brought below the foam threshold. The method consists of blowing large volumes of air into water at a point just below the surface. The resultant concentrated foam can be removed by either evaporation or the addition of activated carbon. In some cases it may be necessary to reduce the phosphate content of the treated water (see previous section).

5.2.2 Ozone

Ozone may be used to decompose those detergent constituents that are not biodegradable.

Initially, the quantity of ozone to be used varies logarithmically with the drop in detergent content. The rate of this removal varies according to the nature of the detergent and other trace compounds which are present in the water. As a rough indication, to reduce the quantity of non-biodegradable anionic detergents by 50% a dose in the range of 1.5g to 3g O_3m^{-3} of water is required.

Ozone does not completely destroy detergents. There is normally a residual content of between 5 and 30% of the original mass. The addition of chlorine as a pretreatment step is ineffective in reducing the amount of ozone required.

5.2.3 Activated Carbon

Activated carbon is a useful substance for absorbing branched anionic synthetic (hard) detergents. For example, it retains detergents to a greater degree (2 to 5 times) than phenol at the same final concentration in equilibrium.

The usual method is to inject powdered activated carbon at the clarification stage. Reduction in detergent content is generally expected to be of the order of 50% with carbon doses between 12.5 to 25gm⁻³ water. Final removal efficiency will depend on the nature of the detergent and the type of clarifier employed (ie static settling tanks or clarifiers with carbon-rich sludge blankets).

Powdered activated carbon is unsuitable for cases where the detergent content is high. Here, granulated activated carbon must be used.

5.2.4 Combined Action of Ozone and Activated Carbon

A combination of powdered activated carbon and ozone may prove useful during occasional surges of high detergent content. In addition, it may be necessary to combine the reagents when a very low residual content is required (ie near the detection threshold of approximately 0.01 mgl⁻¹).

This method is, however, only appropriate for short periods of time. For long periods, it is more economical to use granulated activated carbon solely.

In practice, activated carbon and ozone treatments are not combined when the wastewater contains detergents only. However, when other pollutants and micropollutants such as pesticides, hydrocarbons and phenol compounds are present, the combination is cost effective.

5.3 General Wastewater Treatment

Detergents in municipal effluents are treated at sewage works.

One of the most important processes in wastewater engineering is precipitation/flocculation with salts. This process not only removes phosphorus, but under certain conditions can remove other substances such as colloids and suspended solids, some of which are hazardous or water-pollutants. Further secondary effects include:

- retention of heavy metals in the sewage sludge;

- reduction of sludge volume index and odour;

- greater COD elimination;

- increased stability of the overall sewage treatment process; and

- elimination of hydrogen sulphide from the digester gas.

Generally aluminium sulphate (alum) is considered the best precipitant choice, followed by iron III, iron II salts and finally calcium.

Studies on nitrification/denitrification have indicated the impairment of nitrification when using iron sulphate at about 10% (Dwyer *et al* (1990)).

Since calcium salts are less efficient at phosphorus precipitation, coupled with operational problems from scaling, plugging and corrosion their use has declined leaving alum and ferric chloride the two main phosphorus precipitants employed today.

Aluminium sulphate (alum) undergoes the following reaction with phosphorus:

$$Al_2(SO_4)_3 \cdot 14H_2O + 2PO_4^{3-} \rightarrow 2AlPO_4 + 3SO_4^{2-} + 14H_2O$$

The dose of aluminium depends upon the concentration of soluble phosphate and colloidal particles, first reacting with the orthophosphate and only destabilising the organic-colloidal material after most of the phosphate is precipitated. Aluminium phosphate is formed because the precipitation is thermodynamically and kinetically favoured over aluminium hydroxide formation. At low phosphate concentrations (<10 mg P litre⁻¹), there is competition from the formation of hydroxides which prevents the occurrence of a metal to phosphate ratio necessary for metal phosphate precipitation (Dwyer *et al* (1990)).

For effective removal, the alkalinity must be high enough to buffer the acidic aluminium sulphate; with acidic wastewaters the alkalinity has to be adjusted to maintain the optimum pH 6 for aluminium phosphate precipitation.

The effectiveness of the various phosphate precipitation methods is shown in Table 5.3a for various countries.

Control methods for diffuse nutrient sources are much less well developed than those for point sources. Biological methods, eg the use of wetland buffers, such as reed beds are thought to offer more promise than chemical methods (Lund and Moss (1990)). The common reed (*Phragmites*) and the water hyacinth are species which have proved to be particularly efficient at active nutrient uptake. However, the nutrient absorbing capacities of wetlands requires further investigation if the conservation value of such habitats is not be impaired.

A Dutch paper on phosphate control using pellet reactors (Dijk and Eggers, DHV Consulting Engineers) has been examined. Whilst the technique appears to offer considerable removal efficiencies for phosphate, the method appears to be highly complex and may require a high degree of operator skill. This is due to the need for: balancing the calcium phosphate stoichiometry; correcting the pH for phosphate crystallisation and effluent; correct hydraulic adjustment to ensure initial mixing and plug flow conditions in the reactor. Further, post-filtration may be required to prevent carry over of fine calcium phosphate particles. The presence of various organic compounds in the sewage effluent may also detrimentally affect calcium phosphate crystal growth.

5.4 Septic Tank Wastewater Treatment

The DoE and the National Water Council (1981) have estimated that 5% of the UK population is served by septic tanks and cesspits, although no distinction between the two processes was made.

Septic tanks provide an anaerobic environment and microbial populations that remove/partially digest solids from household wastewaters. The effects of detergents on septic tanks can be summarised as follows.

Nitrogen Load

Nitrogen loads of septic tanks are important due to their potential to reach and pollute groundwater, principally as NO_3^- and to a lesser extent as NH_4^+. Generally carbonate – built detergents tend to reduce the wastewater nitrogen load to a greater extent than phosphate – built detergents, as carbonates are normally the limiting nutrient in household waste (Fresenius *et al* (1989)). Nitrogen and phosphorus particularly are required in considerable quantities for efficient septic tank operation. In relation to the BOD_5 value, a demand of 3 to 5 kg N and 0.5 to 1 kg P per 100 kg BOD_5 is calculated in practical plant operation. The relation in pretreated domestic waste water is roughly 100 kg BOD_5 : 21.3 kg N: 6.8 kg P (Fresenius *et al* (1989)).

Table 5.3a Phosphate precipitation methods and chemicals used in different countries

Stage of Treatment	Country	No. of Plants	Chemicals Used	P mg. litre^{-1}		
				Influent	Effluent	% Removal
Pre-Precipitation	Norway	1	Alum	7.9	0.5	94
	Canada	1	Lime	10.7	0.8	92
	Sweden	3	Alum	6.0	0.3	95
	USA	2	Ferric salts	8.1	0.8	90
Co-Precipitation	Norway	1	Ferrous salts	7.5	0.6	92
	Norway	1	Alum	5.8	0.7	88
	Finland	30	Ferrous salts	7.3	1.8	75
	Germany	1	Alum	9.0	2.6	71
	Sweden	1	Alum	5.1	1.1	78
	Switzerland	10	Ferrous salts	6.5	0.9	86
	USA	1	Ferric salts	10.00	0.4	96
Post-Precipitation	Canada	1	Lime	10.00	1.6	84
	Germany	1	Alum	11.00	1.8	84
	Sweden	20	Alum	6.5	0.4	94
	Sweden	8	Lime	4.8	0.8	83
	USA	1	Alum	10.00	0.5	95

Source: Environmental directorate: OECD, 1974, Paris

Bacteria Counts

Bacteria counts in wastewater are generally higher in tanks containing carbonate – built detergents than in those containing phosphate – built detergents (see above). The increased bacterial growth improves both the treatment and the degradation of organic matter.

Chemical and Physical Wastewater Constituents

Systems receiving phosphate – built detergents tend to have higher values of the following in the effluent:

- electrical conductivity ie dissolved salts;
- alkalinity;
- filtered and unfiltered total solids, volatile solids, total suspended solids, and volatile suspended solids;
- temperature;
- sodium absorption ratio; and
- BOD.

Detergent Residue:

Detergent residue can be measured by the methylene-blue test. Residues are degraded in septic tanks, regardless of the detergent formulation used, although problems with the biodegradability of certain constituents do occur (see below). It is apparent from the above that a lower nutrient load occurs in the effluent from a septic tank receiving carbonate – built detergents than a similar facility receiving phosphate – built detergents. However non-phosphate builders have inherent problems.

An investigation into NTA removal over a 9 month period by pilot scale septic tanks was undertaken by Klein (1974). The tanks had a capacity of 127.21 and received wastewater 6 times daily to simulate normal intermittent operation, with a nominal detention time of 2 d. Mean NTA removals of 26.5, 25.7 and 26.6% were achieved for influent NTA concentrations of 22, 33, and 55 mgl^{-1} respectively during the first 18 weeks of operation. Klein (1974) did not elucidate the mechanisms of removal.

Stephenson *et al* (1987) assessed the removal of NTA by full-scale septic tanks operating in the field by measuring over a 75 week period the removal of NTA dosed to two full scale tanks, each connected to a single dwelling. Concentrations of NTA in the effluent at both sites were always >10 mgl^{-1}. Mean 5 weekly estimates of NTA removal during the last 50 weeks of the study ranged from 33 to 52%. As no acclimatisation period or overall increase in removal during the length of the experiment was apparent, it was inferred that adsorption onto solids was taking place. Thus, the results of this study agreed in principle with the earlier work of Klein (1974), in that NTA removal in septic tanks is poor to moderate over a long period with no evidence of biodegradation taking place (Stephenson *et al* (1987)).

6 Pollution Control Legislation

6.1 Existing Legislation

The existing legislation regarding detergents and cleaning products and relating to freshwater pollution in the UK consists of the following:

- the Water Act, 1989;

- the Control of Pollution Act, 1974;

- Rivers (Prevention of Pollution) Scotland Act, 1951;

- the Water Resources Act, 1963;

- Salmon and Freshwater Fisheries Act, 1975;

- Salmon and Freshwater Fisheries (Protection) (Scotland Act, 1951);

- the Council Directive 78/659/EEC on the quality of fresh waters needing protection or improvement in order to support fish life;

- the Council Directive 86/80/EEC on limit values and quality objectives for discharges of certain dangerous substances included in List I of the Annex to Directive 76/464/EEC;

- the Council Directive 80/68/EEC on the protection of groundwater against pollution caused by certain dangerous substances;

- the Council Directive 75/440/EEC concerning the quality required of surface water intended for the abstraction of drinking water in the member states; and

- Council Directives 73/404 & 405/EEC on the approximation of the laws of the Member States relating to standard methods for testing the biodegradability of detergents, amended by Council Directive 82/242/EEC, and Council Directive 86/094/EEC.

6.1.1 The Water Act 1989 and Water Resources Act 1991

In England and Wales, the control of water pollution is now largely regulated by the Water Resources Act 1991. In Scotland, regulation is provided by equivalent provisions in the amended Control of Pollution Act 1974.

The Water Act was enforced on 6 July 1989. Prior to enactment of the Water Resources Act 1991, the Water Act provided the basis of pollution regulation in England and Wales. In general terms it had four main effects:

- it restructured the Water Authorities into new water and sewerage companies;

- it provided for the regulation of these and any other water service companies under the Act;

- it established new institutions to regulate the companies and the water environment;

- it amended the law relating to water supply, sewerage and the pollution and abstraction of water.

The formation of the National Rivers Authority (NRA) is a key element of the Water Act.

The Water Resources Act 1991 defines the NRA, in terms of its role, duties and functions. The Act is organised in nine parts. Relevant Parts are: Part I, which deals with the definition of the NRA, its functions and duties; Part II deals with Water Resources Management, including rights of abstraction; Part III deals with water pollution control; subsequent parts deal with flood defence, fisheries, financial provisions and various other aspects.

Part III of the Water Resources Act is arranged in four chapters.

Chapter I deals with Statutory Quality Objectives in terms of classification of waters, water quality objectives and NRA's duties to achieve and maintain these objectives.

Part III, Chapter II provides the basis for pollution control in England and Wales. This Chapter (Sections 85-87) establishes pollution offences for controlled waters (defined in Chapter IV Section 104), and provides uniform protection to surface and ground waters. Consents to discharge are made under Section 88(1) of the Act, and Schedule 10 of the Act provides the framework for consent applications, their determination, their revocation, alteration or impositions of conditions, and restriction on variation and revocation. Appeals in respect of consents

173

under Section 88(1) can be made under Section 91. Section 88(1) lays out defences in relation to authorised discharges. In particular, amongst other defences, discharges to waters may be made in accordance with:

- a consent made under Part II of the Control of Water Pollution Act 1974;

- an authorisation for a prescribed process under Part I of the Environmental Protection Act 1990;

- a waste management or disposal licence.

Section 89 outlines defences against prosecution, including 89(1) which deals with emergency discharges.

Sections of Part III Chapter III of the Act deal with water protection zones (93), nitrate sensitive zones (94–95) and consents made in these zones (96). Part III, Chapter III, Section 102 provides powers for the Secretary of State to incorporate EC legislation or other international agreements into UK Water Pollution Law.

6.1.2 Control of Pollution Act (COPA) 1974

Superseded in England and Wales by the Water Resources Act, 1991, Part II of COPA re-enacted and extended earlier water pollution controls mainly contained in the Rivers (Prevention of Pollution) Acts 1951-1961 and the Water Resources Act 1963.

Section 31 of COPA applies to the control of river pollution in Scotland, and provides discharges to be controlled by a disposal licence or a consent given by the Secretary of State or a River Purification Board. Section 31 also empowers a River Purification Board to make byelaws to prohibit or regulate the washing or cleaning of specified articles.

6.1.3 Rivers (Prevention of Pollution) Scotland Act, 1951

Section 1 of the 1951 Rivers in Scotland Act, makes it the duty of the Secretary of State to promote cleanliness of the rivers and other inland waters of Scotland. The Secretary of State acts through the Scottish Development Department.

River Purification Boards (as established under Section 135 of the Local Government (Scotland) Act 1973) also have the responsibilities for promoting the cleanliness of rivers and other inland waters and for conserving the water resources of their areas (Section 17). To fulfil these functions they have powers conferred by this Act and also the Control of Pollution Act 1974 (see *Section 6.1.2*).

The powers of the Scottish River Purification Boards (RPB) are similar to those of the statutory water undertakings in England and Wales, with one notable exception. That is, that an RPB has no powers to control abstraction of water. It is understood that the Scottish Development Department is giving further consideration to this, but it is considered likely that any amendments to existing legislation would apply only to abstractions of irrigation water.

6.1.4 Water Resources Act 1963

Section 79 of the 1963 Water Resources Act gives effect to Section 18 of the Water Act 1945 (see *Section 6.1.8*) to enable byelaws to be made under that Section by river authorities (as opposed to statutory water undertakers).

6.1.5 Salmon and Freshwater Fisheries Act, 1975

This Act imposes a statutory duty on the NRA to maintain, improve and develop fisheries for salmon, trout, freshwater fish and eels.

Section 4 of the 1975 Salmon and Freshwater Fisheries Act makes it an offence to cause or permit any liquid or solid matter to enter watercourses containing fish, that renders the water poisonous or injurious to fish or the spawning grounds, spawn or food of fish.

It is the duty of the water authority (NRA) to administer this Act, but they do not have exclusive powers, and a prosecution could be instituted by anyone.

6.1.6 Salmon and Freshwater Fisheries (Protection) (Scotland) Act, 1951

Section 4 of the 1951 Scottish Salmon and Freshwater Fisheries Act makes it an offence to put any poison or noxious substance in or near any waters with intent to take or destroy fish.

6.1.7 EC Directive for Protection of Freshwater Fish

Directive 78/659/EEC 'on the quality of fresh waters needing protection or improvement in order to support fish life', applies to those fresh waters designated by the Member States as needing protection or improvement to support fish life. Two categories of waters must be designated:

- salmonid waters for salmon, trout and whitefish;
- cyprinid waters for cyprinids and other species (pike, eel etc.)

Imperative and Guide values are specified for 14 physical and chemical parameters for both categories of water. The limit values for total phosphorus, expressed as PO_4 are 0.2 mgl^{-1} and 0.4 mgl^{-1}, for salmonid and cyprinid waters respectively. For lakes of depth between 18 and 300 m, a phosphorus loading formula is used. The phosphorus standards are designed to control eutrophication. It is of note that there are plans to build barrages on a number of estuaries, and that due to changes in the physical character of impoundments controls of phosphorus loadings may be required.

6.1.8 EC Directive on Dangerous Substances
Directive 76/464/EEC 'on pollution caused by certain dangerous substances discharged into the aquatic environment of the community', is a 'framework' directive which provides for the elimination or reduction of pollution of inland, coastal and territorial waters by particularly dangerous substances by means of 'daughter directives'. Member States are to take appropriate steps to eliminate pollution by substances defined as List I (eg organophosphorus and persistent synthetic substances and to reduce substances defined as List II. (eg inorganic and elemental phosphorus). The 'Daughter' Directive 86/80/EEC states limit values and quality objectives. Whilst phosphorus standards have not yet been proposed under this Directive, the Urban Municipal Wastewaters Directive does specify phosphorus emission standards for 'sensitive' waters.

6.1.9 EC Directive on Groundwater Quality
Directive 80/68/EEC 'on the protection of groundwater against pollution caused by certain dangerous substances' is designed to prevent or limit the direct or indirect introduction to groundwater of the families or groups of dangerous substances contained on List I (eg organophosphorus and persistent synthetic substances) and List II (eg inorganic and elemental phosphorus).

6.1.10 EC Directives on Drinking Water
Directive 75/440/EEC 'concerning the quality required of surface water intended for the abstraction of drinking water in the Member States' has two purposes:

- to ensure that surface water abstracted for use as drinking water meets certain standards and is treated adequately before being introduced to the public supply;
- to improve the quality of rivers and other surface waters used as sources of drinking water.

Member States must classify sources of surface water for the abstraction of drinking water by their existing quality into three categories, Al, A2 and A3. For each category, mandatory and guide values are given for 46 determinands, including taste and odour, surfactants, boron (guide value, 1000 mgl^{-1}), aluminium (mandatory value, 0.2 mgl^{-1}) iron (mandatory value, 0.2 mgl^{-1}) and phosphorus (mandatory P_2O_5 value, 400 mgl^{-1}); the latter value is high, and would represent grossly eutrophic conditions in natural waters.

Directive 79/869/EEC 'concerning methods of measurement and frequencies of sampling and analysis of surface water intended for the abstraction of drinking water in the Member States' supplements Directive 75/440 by recommending methods of measuring the determinands for surface water quality and setting frequencies for such measurements.

Directive 80/778/EEC 'relating to the quality of water intended for human consumption' sets standards for the quality of drinking water both directly and after treatment. It does not apply to natural mineral waters or medicinal water. Maximum admissible concentration (MAC) levels and guide levels (GL) for 62 determinands and minimum required concentrations (MRC) for four determinands are set.

6.1.11 Laws of Member States Relating to Detergents
The Council Directive (73/404/EEC) with amendments 82/242/EEC and 86/94/EEC relate to methods of testing the biodegradability of non-ionic surfactants and detergents. Standard methods for testing biodegradability of non-ionic surfactants are recommended (based on OECD guidelines (1976)).

The method in use in the UK is called the 'Porous Pot Test', as described in Technical Report No. 70/1978 of the Water Research Centre.

The Directive states that if the level of biodegradability of the non-ionic surfactants contained within a detergent is less than 80% when tested, 'the placing of the product on the market and (its) use ...' is prohibited.

For the purpose of this Directive, detergent may be defined as any product ... 'the composition of which has been specially studied with a view to developing its detergent properties, and which is made up of essential constituents (surfactants) and, in general, additional constituents (adjuvants, intensifying agents, fillers, additives and other auxiliary constituents).

6.2 Role of NRA, RPBs and HMIP

The National Rivers Authority (NRA), formed in 1989, has responsibilities pertaining to both surface waters and groundwater resources in England and Wales. These include:

- water quality monitoring;

- the setting of limits and consents for effluent discharges;

- the control and licensing of water abstractions;

- the protection of water quality for surface and groundwater users; and

- enhancement of conservation and recreation in the aquatic environment.

The Scottish RPBs have similar responsibilities to the NRA regarding surface water quality, although no controls over surface and groundwater abstraction formally exist in Scotland.

HMIP has the responsibility for the monitoring of industrial discharges from proscribed processes, and in particular for the levels of List I substances of the Annex to Directive 76/464JEEC (see *Section 6.1.8*). HMIP also has powers under the recently enacted Environmental Protection Act (see *Section 6.4*).

6.3 Regional Compliance with Existing Legislation

To assess the regional compliance of UK consents (*Appendix 1* shows typical consent conditions) associated with manufacture of detergents and cleaning products, all regions of the NRA and all Scottish River Purification Boards were consulted; it is of note that none of these refer to phosphorus limits, although Anglian Region and North-West Region have adopted phosphorus emission standards for sewage works on the Norfolk Broads and Lake Windermere, respectively. The responses to a detailed questionnaire are presented in Tables 6.3a and b.

The following details are apparent.

- The majority of effluents from UK cleaning products are discharged to foul sewer. Only 1 consented discharge to groundwater exists, and this is for surface water contaminated with trade effluent from a detergent manufacturing plant. The number of consented discharges to surface waters (excluding Thames Region) is 26. Most discharges occur in the Severn Trent and Thames Regions. In regions where eutrophication has historically been a problem eg Anglian Region (see *Section 4.4*) no discharges to surface waters associated with detergents and cleaning products are consented by the NRA.

- The number of licensed surface and groundwater abstractions varies considerably from one region to another. Most abstraction for industrial use in the detergents manufacturing industry occurs in the NRA, Welsh Region with limited abstraction occurring in the Yorkshire and North West Regions, and in Scotland. Elsewhere, water consumption is directly from the mains supply. Consultation with the Water Services Association and Water Service plcs indicates that the amount of mains water consumption by the industry is not sufficient to cause water quality impacts from over abstraction. In times of water shortage due to drought conditions, domestic water users are encouraged to conserve water, and industrial supplies are generally unaffected.

- The number of pollution incidents associated with discharges of detergents and cleaning products in the past 5 years has varied considerably between regions. The greatest number of incidents appears to have occurred in the River Clyde catchment and in the North-West, Severn Trent and Thames Regions. Most incidents have been of a minor nature. No groundwater pollution incidents have been recorded, although it may be several years before pollution of the aquifer is apparent even if it has occurred.

- The greatest number of prosecutions associated with discharges of detergents and cleaning products has occurred in the North-West region. However, the 20 incidents recorded include prosecutions for trade effluent discharge to sewer, prior to the formation of the NRA.

Three prosecutions are currently under consideration, suggesting that the NRA is adopting a more stringent approach to pollution monitoring than its predecessor.

- In general there has been a slight decrease in the number of pollution incidents associated with detergents and cleaning products, although in the Welsh Region, an increase in the recorded number of pollution incidents has occurred in some areas, and the number of prosecutions remains high.

6.4 Recent Legislation

The Environmental Protection Act is a further attempt to strengthen areas of pollution control not covered by existing legislation.

A system of Integrated Pollution Control (IPC) is now enacted, which involves HMIP regulating all polluting emissions and discharges from significant industrial processes.

The manufacturers of detergents are likely to be brought under IPC on 1st May 1994 with inorganic chemical industries. The IPC individual guidance notes would probably be issued for consultation in May 1993.

The Urban Wastewater Treatment Directive (91/271/EEC) specifies requirements for treatment levels for municipal waste water treatment plants discharging to areas 'sensitive' to eutrophication. These specify that total phosphorus concentrations in the effluent discharge do not exceed a maximum, average concentration of 1 mgl^{-1} and/or that the treatment of effluent should reduce influent phosphorus concentrations to the treatment plant by a minimum of 80%. It further specifies that more stringent requirements may be required to ensure that receiving waters satisfy any other relevant directive(s) (eg EC Directive 78/659/EEC 'on the quality of fresh waters needing protection or improvement in order to support fish life').

Table 6.3a Freshwater discharges from Production of UK Detergents and Cleaning Products

UK Region	No of consented discharges to surface freshwaters	No of consented discharges to groundwaters	No of licensed surface water abstractions	No of licensed groundwater abstractions
NRA Anglian Region	0	0	0	0
NRA Northumbrian Region	0	0	0	0
NRA North-West Region	4	0	0	4
NRA Sevem-Trent Region	14	U/A	U/A	U/A
NRA Southem Region	0	0	0	0
NRA South-West Region	0	0	0	0
NRA Thames Region	Some	U/A	U/A	U/A
NRA Welsh Region	4	0	13	7
NRA Wessex Region	0	0	0	0
NRA Yorkshire Region	3	0	4	2
Clyde RPB	0	0	N/A	N/A
Forth RPB	1	1	N/A	N/A
Highland RPB	0	0	N/A	N/A
North-East RPB	0	0	2(no licences required)	N/A
Solway RPB	0	0	N/A	N/A
Tay RPB	0	0	N/A	N/A
Tweed RPB	0	0	N/A	N/A
Total	**Some**	**1**	**19**	**13**

Source: Adapted from data supplied by NRA/RPBs

U/A = data unavailable
N/A = not applicable, as water abstraction does not require a licence under the requirements of Scottish law.

Table 6.3b Freshwater Pollution from Manufacture or Storage of UK Detergents and Cleaning Products

	No of pollution incidents in the past 5 years	No of prosecutions associated with the industry in the past 5 years	Increase or decrease in the frequency of pollution incidents in recent years
NRA Anglian Region	0	0	N/A
NRA Northumbrian Region	0	0	N/A
NRA North-West Region	Some	20 (including prosecutions for trade waste to sewer)	Neither
NRA Sevem-Trent Region	Some, mainly spillages not associated with consents	0	Neither
NRA Southern Region	0	0	N/A
NRA South-West Region	2	0	N/A
NRA Thames Region	Some	0 (two under consideration)	Neither
NRA Welsh Region	3	9	Both (dependent on area)
NRA Wessex Region	1	N/A	N/A
RA Yorkshire Region	1	2	decrease
Clyde RPB	Some	0	decrease
Forth RPB	2	0 (1 prosecution by sewerage authority	decrease
Highland RPB	0	0	N/A
North-East RPB	2	0	decrease
Solway RPB	0	0	N/A
Tay RPB	0	0	N/A
Tweed RPB	0	0	N/A
Total	**Several**	**32 (including prosecutions for trade waste to sewer)**	**Both, dependent on region, but mainly decrease**

Source: Adapted from data supplied by NRA/RPBs
  N/A – not applicable

7 Potential areas for further research

7.1 Introduction

Sections 7.2 and 7.3 highlight areas where existing information is limited, and where further research may promote greater understanding of pollution causes, effects and control, and may reduce the amount of freshwater pollution associated with cleaning products and detergents in the UK.

7.2 Freshwater Pollution

The potential areas for further research into freshwater pollution causes and effects are detailed below:

- ecotoxicological research to identify the environmental effects associated with detergents constituents eg LAS, since most current data relates to human health hazards;

- a comprehensive impact review of all currently used and proposed cleaners;

- research into more accurate methods of detection of detergent constituents, particularly PCAs;

- toxicological studies of breakdown products (eg nonylphenols);

- detailed research into the concentrations of anionic and nonionic synthetic detergents which cause persistent foaming in surface freshwater (a nationwide research programme is currently being conducted by NRA/SDIA);

- research into the potential pollution problems associated with the use of detergent based fire-fighting foams;

- assessment of the efficiency of anti-foaming agents; and

- research into methods by which wastewater phosphorus may be recycled and utilised.

Areas of research, particularly associated with the problems of eutrophication are detailed below:

- Biomanipulation offers possibilities for restoration of the many lakes where nutrient control alone may prove inadequate. It needs greater investment both in actual management measures and in the fundamental investigation of fish-zooplankton-algae relationships. The role of ephiphytes and their grazers also requires further investigation in situations where aquatic plant restoration is needed. The present biomanipulation research the Norfolk Broads is at the forefront of world research in this topic.

- Control methods for diffuse nutrient sources are much less well developed than those for points sources. Biological methods, eg the use of wetland buffers and corridors, probably offer more promise than chemical ones, but the nutrient absorbing capacities of wetlands need further investigation if the conservation value of such habitats is not to be impaired by such use.

- Recent work by the Aquatic Weeds Research Unit (Welch *et al* (1990)) has shown that the deployment of bales of barley straw may be effective in control of algae. However, the precise mode of action is presently unclear. Further research on this aspect is warranted.

7.3 Technological Advancement

Recent technological advancements in phosphate removal from wastewater have focused on biological methods. Biological phosphorus removal is a relatively difficult procedure in terms of process engineering. To date, investigations have been performed by both university facilities and some sewage works in Germany, but a number of major obstacles have emerged:

- operation of the processes cannot yet be mastered by routine staff, as special qualifications are required; and

- achieving consistently low residual phosphorus concentrations in the process effluent is extremely difficult, although occasional values below a residual phosphorus content of $2 \, \text{mgl}^{-1}$ are possible without additional chemical phosphate removal techniques.

A small number of European sewage treatment works are conducting experiments with biological phosphorus removal, although most feel that the process will be of secondary importance in the implementation of phosphorus removal programmes in both the short and medium terms. Recent effort to introduce precipitation/flocculation for phosphorus removal in existing sewage plants is, however, not impeding the possible introduction of biological phosphorus elimination at a later date. This is due to the following:

- conversion of plant operations from one process to the other is relatively simple; and,

- the use of precipitants and flocculants is unlikely to be completely eliminated. This is primarily due to their role in process stability.

8 Conclusions

8.1 Phosphates

The principal concern arising from freshwater pollution from UK cleaning products and detergents is eutrophication.

According to Lund and Moss (1990), eutrophication of water refers to its enrichment with plant nutrients. As commonly used today, the word includes both the processes which cause enrichment and the problems resulting there from. In the media, eutrophication is used to refer to 'an undesirable change in water quality produced by man's activities' (Lund and Moss (1990)).

8.1.1 Sources of Phosphates

The major sources of phosphates are domestic, agricultural, industrial and natural. The importance of each source varies between different countries, depending on geology, population density, agricultural practice and industry. In the UK, domestic sources provide 53% of the total phosphorus, of which at least 50% is derived from detergent use. This is a substantial contribution, and probably makes up the largest single anthropogenic phosphorus source (about one quarter of the total). Introduction of liquid and compact detergents (some of which have lower phosphorus contents) will probably result in a lower contribution from detergents to overall phosphorus loadings. This may further be accelerated by consumer preference for 'green detergent products' with low phosphorus contents.

8.1.2 Eutrophication and Phosphorus

Whilst a reduction in the phosphate content of detergents may be welcomed by certain members of the UK public the importance of other phosphorus sources such as agriculture dietary phosphorus, and sediment nutrients, indicate that the removal of phosphorus from detergents would not alone eliminate the problems of eutrophication.

These problems may include:

- excessive algal growth, which may result in the release of toxic compounds (*Cyanobacteria*);

- a reduction in oxygen levels following algal decomposition;

- subsequent impacts to aquatic fauna (eg fish mortality);

- under mild eutrophic conditions, excessive growth of macrophytes which may impede drainage/navigation; and

- increased competition by phytoplankton for available light, which may result in loss of other aquatic flora.

Phosphate removal by tertiary treatment of sewage effluent at sewage treatment is the most effective means of phosphate reduction in the UK freshwater environment. The proposed Municipal Wastewater Directive will reinforce this approach by stipulating discharge limits (1 mg Pl^{-1}) and/or treatment standards for sewage effluent discharges to waters sensitive to eutrophication.

8.1.3 Implications for Phosphate Bans in Detergent Manufacture

The processes described in Section 4.2 suggest that the removal of phosphorus from detergents would not eliminate the problem of eutrophication in lake water. In some remote areas, however, removal of detergent phosphorus might obviate the need to install a stripping process at all for a considerable time; and because reduction of phosphorus concentrations in lakes is proving difficult, any reduction must be deemed to be ultimately sensible (Moss (1988)).

There is little doubt that detergent derived phosphates contribute a significant proportion of the domestic input of phosphorus to freshwater ecosystems (Jakobi and Löhr (1987)). In much of lowland Britain, however, the dietary contribution is in itself sufficient to cause nuisance algal blooms, so that the most effective means of phosphate reduction remains tertiary treatment of sewage effluent at sewage treatment works (Lund and Moss, 1990).

However, whilst phosphate stripping by tertiary treatment is the most effective means of achieving reduced phosphate levels, there remains a problem relating to the disposal of the phosphate enriched sludge. This might be disposed to land, where it could leak back to water bodies. Therefore reducing the phosphate load requiring treatment would reduce the potential for secondary phosphate release from land disposed sludge. This argument would tend to militate towards reducing phosphate loadings to sewage works, which would be most readily achieved by reducing the phosphorus content of detergents; reducing dietary phosphate would seem a lost cause. In addition, reducing phosphate loads through reduction of STPP in detergents to sewage works could reduce the quantities of chemicals used in phosphate stripping. However, it must be reemphasised that a phosphate ban on detergents alone will not eliminate eutrophication problems.

8.1.4 Implications of Alternatives to Phosphate

Concern has been expressed by members of both water pollution control authorities and water suppliers of the UK over the use of alternatives to STPP as detergent builders, without adequate evidence regarding their environmental safety. The environmental fate and effects of substances such as PCAs is of some concern due to the difficulty in the accurate measurement and monitoring of environmental levels of PCAs. Other compounds such as NTA and EDTA are unlikely to be environmentally acceptable STPP substitutes. Zeolites do not give rise to major environmental concerns, but may affect sewage treatment.

8.2 Other Components of Cleaning Products

Concern regarding the effects of cleaning products on the UK freshwater environment has been expressed over:

- the lack of sufficient ecotoxicological research to identify the environmental hazards associated with detergents;

- the lack of sufficient information regarding the biodegradability of all currently used and proposed cleaning agents;

- foaming and the efficiency of anti-foaming agents currently used; and

- information regarding product effectiveness and efficiency.

Nevertheless, in terms of constituents of detergents other than builders, it is apparent that:

- major components such as LAS are largely removed during sewerage treatment, although problems have been reported in Switzerland in relation to sludge disposal;

- enzymes, fragrances, dyes and other minor additives are readily broken down during sewage treatment;

- bleaching agents, such as perborate, are not considered to be of major environmental concern in the UK;

- fluorescent whitening agents are apparently of little environmental concern, but are probably unnecessary in formulations;

- cellulose ester used as anti redeposition agents are non-toxic and of minor concern.

8.3 Product Formulation

This report highlights the attention currently directed towards product formulation and application. This concern has come to play a significant role alongside more traditional motives related to production and efficacy. Much valuable experience has already been gained through the successful implementation of laws and controls governing the use of such primary detergent components as anionic and nonionic surfactants and phosphates. It is, therefore, reasonable to anticipate that benefit/risk analyses will play an ever increasing role in the selection of raw materials and active ingredients in the future.

The UK cleaning products and detergents manufacturing industry is currently in a state of flux with regard to changes in market trends and product development. Research in the above areas is now recommended to further clarify the impact to the freshwater environment, and to enable recommendations for cleaning product formulations accordingly. A detailed independent review of existing formulations would be invaluable in providing advice on the potential environmental impacts of specific detergent use to the prospective retailer/purchaser, and in the development of future legislature.

A more immediate recommendation is that all cleaning products should be clearly labelled with details of their chemical composition, rather than unsupported statements of 'Environmental Friendliness'. At present, this is an option adopted by relatively few UK producers of cleaning products.

9 Bibliography

ABE Y *et al* (1986), **Yukagaku, 35**,167–175.

ALDER A C, HANSRUEDI S, GUIGER W, and GIGER W, (1990) **Behaviour of NTA and EDTA in biological wastewater treatment**, water research **24**, 733–742.

Anon (1990) **Ambio Vol XIX**, No. 3 Special Issue, Marine Eutrophication.

ANDERSON D J, DAY M J, RUSSEL N J, WHITE G F, (1990) Die Away Kinetic Analysis of the Capacity of Epilithic and Planktonic Bacteria from Clean and Polluted River Water to Biodegrade Sodium Dodecyl Sulfate. **Applied and Environmental Microbiology**, Mar. 1990: 758–763

ANDERSON R L, BISHOP W E and CAMPBELL R L (1985) **CRC Crit. Rev. Toxicol., 15**, 1–102.

BAILEY WATTS A E (1990) Eutrophication: assessment, research and management with special reference to Scottish fresh waters **Journal of IWEM** Vol 4: 285–294.

BARDACH J E, FUJIYA, M and HOLL A (1965). **Detergents: effects on the chemical senses of the fish Ictalurus natalis**, Science **148**:1605–1607.

BEGTSSON L, FLEISHER S, LINDMARK G, and RIPL W (1975) Lake Trummen restoration project I. Water and Sediment Chemistry. **Ver. int. Verein.l theor. angew. Limnol., 19**,1080–7.

BERNA J L, MORENO A & FERRER J (1990) **The Behaviour of L.A.S. in the Environment**, presented at Recent Advances in the Detergent Industry, University of Cambridge, U.K., March 1990.

BERTH P *et al* (1977) **Tenside Detergents, 14**;1–3.

BERTH P *et al* (1978) **J. Am. Oil. Chem. Soc., 55**. 52–57.

BIRGE W J (1984) **Toxicity of Boron to Embryonic and Larval Stages for Rainbow Trout** *(Salmo gairdneri)*. Completion report prepared for Procter and Gamble.

BIRGE W J and BLACK J A (1977). **Sensitivity of Vertebrate Embryos to Boron Compounds.** Report No. EPA – 506/1–76–008. Environmental Protection Agency Office of Toxic Substances, Washington D.C.

BROWN D *et al* (1987) **Removal of Nonionics in Sewage Treatment Plants II**. Tenside Detergents **24**:14–19.

BRUNNER P H, *et al* (1988) **Occurrence and Behaviour of Linear Alkylbenzenesulphonates, Nonylphenol nanutphenol mono – and nanylphenol diethoxylates in sewage and sewage sludge treatment**. Wat. Res. Vol 22, No. 12:1465–1472.

BUTTERWICK L, DE OUDE N and RAYMOND K. (1989) Safety Assessment of Boron in Aquatic and Terrestrial Environments. **Ecotoxicology and Environmental Safety 17**, 339–371.

CES (1991) **Pollutants in Cleaning Products**. Report to Department of Environment 82p + Refs and Appendices. Consultants in Environmental Sciences Ltd March 1991.

CARRONDO M J *et al* (1980) **J. Water Pollut. Control Fed., 52,11**, 2796–2806.

CODD G A, TECH B and BELL S G (1985) **J. Water Pollut. Control Fed., 84**, (2), 225–232.

COLLINGWOOD R W (1977) **Water Research Centre Technical Report** – TR40, 1977.

COOKE G D, McCOMAS M R, WALLER D W and KENNEDY R H (1977) **The occurrence of internal phosphorus loading in two small eutrophic glacial lakes in north eastern Ohio**. Hydrobiologia, **56**,129–35.

DAVIDSOHN A S *et al* (1987) **Synthetic Detergents**, 7th, Ed., Bath Press, UK.

DAVIES A W (1980) Dept. of the Environment; Central Directorate on Environmental Pollution Report, 8, 63–70.

DE PINTO, J V YOUNG, T C and McILROY L M (1986) **Environ. Sci. Technol, 20**, (8), 752–759.

DEPARTMENT OF THE ENVIRONMENT AND NATIONAL WATER COUNCIL (1981) **Standing Technical Committee Report** *20*, National Water Council, London UK.

DOEMEL W N and BROOKS A E (1975) **Detergent Phosphorus and Algal Growth**. Water. Res Vol 9.: 713–719.

DONAHUE (1986) **Soap. Cosm. Chem**. 81 Spec. **62**, 26–46.

DRAKE J C and HEANEY S J, (1987) **Occurrence of phosphorus and its potential remobilization in the Littoral sediments of a productive English Lake**. Freshwat. Biol. **13**, 545–60.

DUNLAP W J. *et al* (1972) **Ground Water 10**, 107–117.

DURYER M, YEOMAN S, LESTER J N & PERRY R, (1990) **A Review of Proposed Non-Phosphate Detergent Builders, Utilisation and Environmental Assessment Environmental Technology, Vol. II**: 263–294.

FOSTER N R, SCHEIER A and CAIRNS J (1966) Effects of ABS on feeding behaviour of flagfish *Jordanella floridae*. Trans. Am. Fish. Soc. **95**: 109–110.

FRESENIUS W, SCHNEIDER W, BOHNKE B and POPPINGHAUS K (Ed) (1989) **Waste Water Technology Origin, Collection, Treatment and Analysis of Waste Water**. Springer-Verlag.

GERBER A and WINTNER C T (1985) **Water Sci. Technol.**, **17**, (2/3), 81–92.

GERIKE P *et al* (1976) **Der Einfluss von Bor auf die aerobe biologische Abwasserreinigung**. Tenside Deterg. **13**,149–251.

GIBSON C E, SMITH R V and STEWART D A (1988) **A long term study of the phosphorus cycle in Lough Neath, Northern Ireland**. Int. Rev. gesmten. Hydrobiol., 73,3.

GIGER W (1990). **Beurteilung der Umweltvertraglichkeit von Detergentienchemikalien**. EAWAG CH–8600 Dubendorf, Switzerland.

GIGER W, STEPHANON E and SCHAFFNER. (1981). **Persistent organic chemicals in sewage effluents** Chemosphere **10**, 1253–1263.

GIGER W, BRUNNER P H and SCHAFFNER C (1984). **4-nonylphenol in sewage sludge: accumulation of toxic metabolites from non-ionic surfactants**. Science, 225, 623 – 625.

GRASSIE N (1966) **Degradation, In Encyclopaedia of Polymer Science and Technology**, **4**, Interscience Publishers, New York.

GRAY A V (1985) **J. Inst. Water Eng. Sci.**, **39**, (2),137–154.

HELLAWELL J M (1986) **Biological Indicators of Freshwater Pollution and Environmental Management**.

HMSO (1980) **Twentieth and Final Report on the Standing Technical Committee on Synthetic Detergents**. HMSO. London.

HOLDREN G C JR and ARMSTRONG D E (1980) **Factors affecting phosphorus release from intact lake sediment cores**. Envir. Sci. Technol., **14**, 79–87.

HOPPING W D (1978) **J. Water Pollut. Control Fed**. 50, 433-441.

HOURIET J P (1990). **Umweltschutz in der Schweitz. Bulletin des Bundesamtes fur Umwelt, Waldand Landschaft (BUWAL)**. 3003 Bern. Switzerland.

HUNT S M. (1984) **Algal Toxins – A Position Document**.

HUNTER M *et al* (1988) **Env. Technol. Lett**, 9;1–22.

ISAACS A *et al* (1984) **Concise Science Dictionary**. Oxford University Press.

JAKOBI G and LÖHR A, (1987) **Detergents and Textile Washing; Principles and Practice**. VDH. Publishers.

JONES E R and HUBBARD S D (1986) **J. Water Pollut. Control Fed**., 58, (8), 816–822.

JONES G *et al* (1990) **Collins Reference dictionary on Environmental Science**. Collins.

KING J E *et al* (1980) **Treatability of Type A Zeolite in Wastewater Part I**. Journal Water Pollution Control Federation, 52, 2875–2886.

KLEIN S A (1974) **J. Water. Pollut**. Control. Fed., 46, 78–88.

KNEZOVICH J P, LAWTON M P & INOUYE L S (1988), **Bioaccumulation and Tissue Distribution of a Quaternary Ammonium Surfactant in Three Aquatic Species**. Bull. Environ. Contam. Toxicol. 42: 87–93.

LAMARRA V (1975) **Digestive activities of carp as a major contributor to the nutrient loading of lakes**. Verh. Int. Verein. theoret. angew. Limnol., 19, 2461–8.

LARSON R J and GAMES L M (1981) **Biodegradation of Linear Alcohol Ethosylates in Natural Waters**. Environmental Science and Technology, 15, 1488–1493.

LENNOX L J (1984) **Lough Ennell: laboratory studies on sediment phosphorus release under varying mixing, aerobic and anaerobic conditions**. Freshwat. Biol., 14, 183–7.

LITZ N, DOERING H W, THIELE M and BLUME H P, (1986), **The behaviour of Linear Alkylbenzenesulphonate in Different Soils: A Comparison between Field and Laboratory Studies**, Ecotoxicology and Environmental Safety, 14, 103–116 (1987).

LUND J W E and MOSS B (1990) **Eutrophication in the United Kingdom – Trends in the 1980s**. The Soap and Detergent Industry Association.

MAKI A W and MACEK K J (1978) **Aquatic Environmental Safety Assessment for a Nonphosphate Detergent Builder**. Environmental Science and Technology, 12, 573–580.

MATTHEWS P J (1985). **Phosphate in water – is it really a problem? An English water authority over-view. In Perry R and Schmidke N. Management Strategies for Phosphorus in the Environment**. pp 446–53 Selper, London 1985.

MAKI A W and RUBIN A J (1979) **Reduction of nonionic surfactant toxicity following secondary treatment Journal W.P.C.F, 51**, No. 9: 2301–2313.

MCEVOY J and GIGER W (1986) **Determination of linear alkybenzene sulphonates in sewage sludge by high resolution gas chromatography/mas spectrometry**. Envir. Sci. Technol. 20, 367–383.

MCKEE J E and WOLF H W (1963) **Water Quality Criteria**. The Resource Agency of California, 2nd ed. State Water Control Board, Publ. No. 3A.

MERILETHTO K, KENTTAMIES K. and KAMARI J (1989) **Surface Water Acidification in the ECE Region**. Miljorapport 1988:14.

MOLMAN W F and HOPPING W D (1980) **Treatability of Type A Zeolite in Wastewater. Part II.** Journal Water Pollution Control Federation, **52**, 2887–2905.

MOSS B *et al* (1985) **Management of the consequences of eutrophication in lowland lakes in England – Engineering and Biological solutions. Management strategies for Phosphorus in the Environment** (Ed. by J.N. Lester and P. W. Kirk), Selper.

MOSS B (1987) *The art of lake restoration.* New Sci., 1550, 41–5.

MOSS B (1988) **Ecology and Freshwaters; Man and Medium**. Second Edition. Blackwell Scientific Publications.

MOSS B, BALLS H and IRVINE K (1985) **Proc. Int. Conf. Management Strategies for Phosphorus in the Environment. Selper Publications UK;** 180–185.

MOSS B, BASS H, IRVINE K and STANSFIELD J (1986) **Restorations of two lowland lakes by isolation from nutrient rich water sources with and without removal of sediment.** J. Appl. Ecol., **23**, 391–414.

NYSDEC (1984). **New York State District Environment Committee**.

OPGENORTH H G, (1987) **Tenside Detergents,** 24(6) 366–369.

NATIONAL RIVERS AUTHORITY (1990) **Water Quality Series No. 2**. Toxic Blue-Green Algae.

PHILLIPS G L (1984) **Water Pollut. Control., 83**, 400408.

PITMAN A R, VENTER S L V and NICHOLLS H A (1983) **Water Sci. Technol., 15**, (3/4), 223–259.

REYNOLDS C S (1981) **J. Inst. Water Eng. Sci., 35**, 74–76.

ROLAND W A and SCHMIDT R D (1978) **Vom Wasser, 50**,177–190.

ROSSIN A C, LESTER J N and PERRY R. (1982) **Environ. Pollut., b, 4**, 315–330.

SDIA (1990) **Pers. comm**.

SDIA (1990) **Statistical summary for 1988** (unpublished)

SPEECE R E (1987). **Boron Toxicity Levels in Anaerobic Digestion**. Unpublished report to Procter and Gamble.

STANLEY R A (1974) **Toxicity of heavy metals and salts to Eurasian watermill** (*Myriophyllum Spicatuma*) Arch. Environ. Contam. Toxicol., **2**, 331–341

STEPHENSON T, LESTER J N and PERRY R (1987) **Water Air Soil Pollut., 33**, 349357.

VARIOUS (1989), **International Seminar Alkylbenzene Sulphonates (LAS) in the Environment.** Tenside Detergents, **26**.

VENIER P *et al* (1985) Mut. Res., **156**, 219–228.

VENTULLO R M, LEWIS M A & LARSON R J (1989) **Response of Aquatic Microbial Communities to Surfactants, In Aquatic Toxicology and Environmental Fate: Eleventh Volume, ASTM STP 1007**, G W Suter II and M A Lewis, Eds. 1989, 41–58.

VOLLENWEIDER R A (1968) **Technical Report DAS/SCI/68,27**. OECD, Paris France.

VOLLENWEIDER R A (1985) **Proc. Int. Conf. Management Strategies for Phosphorus in the Environment**, Selper Publications, UK, 1–10.

WALKER W W (1983) **J. Am. Water Works Assoc., 75,** (1), 38–42.

WELCH I M, PRF BARRETT, GIBSON M and RIDGE I (1990) **Barley straw as an inhibitor of algal growth I:** studies in Chesterfield Canal. J Appl. Phycol. **2,** 231–239.

WETZEL R G, **Limnology** 2nd. Ed. Saunders College Publishing.

WOODIWISS C R, WALKER R D and BROWNRIDGE F A (1979) **Water Res., 13,** 599–612.

WOOLLAT E (Ed) (1985) **The Manufacture of Soaps, other detergents and Glycerine,** Ellis Horwood, UK.

ZINI P (1987) **Seifen-ole-Fette-Wachse, 113,** 45–48,187–189.

Appendix 1 Typical Regional Consent Limit Conditions for Cleaning Products and Detergents

	BOD	SS	pH (Units)	Anionic dets	Nonionic dets	Temp (°C)	PV	COD	Oils
NRA Anglian Region	N/A	N/A	N/A	N/A	N/A	N/A	N/A	N/A	N/A
NRA Northumbrian Region	N/A	N/A	N/A	N/A	N/A	N/A	N/A	N/A	N/A
NRA North-West Region	10 to 70	30 to 70	5 to 9	–	–	30	10	150	–
NRA Sevem-Trent Region	40	N/A	5 to 9	N/A	N/A	N/A	N/A	N/A	None visible
NRA Southem Region	N/A	N/A	N/A	N/A	N/A	N/A	N/A	N/A	N/A
NRA South-West Region	N/A	N/A	N/A	N/A	N/A	N/A	N/A	N/A	N/A
NRA Thames Region	50	N/A	5 to 9	N/A	N/A	30 to 35	N/A	N/A	No trace
NRA Welsh Region	–	–	5 to 9	–	–	26.0	–	–	None visible
NRA Wessex Region	N/A	N/A	N/A	N/A	N/A	N/A	N/A	N/A	N/A
NRA Yorkshire Region	40	20	–	–	–	2° C above ambient	–	–	None visible
Clyde RPB	N/A	N/A	N/A	N/A	N/A	N/A	N/A	N/A	N/A
Forth RPB	20	30	5 to 9	1.5 to	0.5	–	–	–	–
Highland RPB	N/A	N/A	N/A	N/A	N/A	N/A	N/A	N/A	N/A
North East RPB	N/A	N/A	N/A	N/A	N/A	N/A	N/A	N/A	N/A
Solway RPB	N/A	N/A	N/A	N/A	N/A	N/A	N/A	N/A	N/A
Tay RPB	N/A	N/A	N/A	N/A	N/A	N/A	N/A	N/A	N/A
Tweed RPB	N/A	N/A	N/A	N/A	N/A	N/A	N/A	N/A	N/A

Note:

All units are in mgl^{-1} unless otherwise stated.

No other discharge constituents are limited other than the nine shown.

– = No limit value indicated.

N/A = Not applicable due to no notified consents to discharge associated with cleaning products and detergents.

Source: Adapted from data supplied by NRA/RPBs from the Public Register

Glossary of terms

Biodegradation	The biological decomposition of a material (usually to nontoxic compounds).
BOD	Biochemical Oxygen Demand, the amount of oxygen required during microbial breakdown of organic material present, over a given time period.
	BOD_5 refers to the oxygen consumed by organic decay over a 5 day period at a standard temperature of 20°C, while BOD_{30} refers to the oxygen consumption due to organic decay over 30 days at 20°C.
Builder	A constituent of cleaning products which has no detersivity but enhances the effectiveness of the product by other means.
Carcinogen	Any substance capable of causing cancers in animal tissues.
Cyanobacteria	Blue Green Algae
Detergent	Any product with detersive properties, which is made up of surfactants and, additional constituents (adjuvants, intensifying agents, fillers additives and other auxiliary constituents).
Detersive	Ability of a substance to remove unwanted deposits from a surface when as an applied cleaning solution.
EDTA	EthyleneDiamineTetraAcetic acid, a sequestrant.
Epilimnion	Upper Water layer of a stratified lake.
EQS	Environmental Quality Standard
Eutrophication	An increase in nutrient concentrations leading to an uncontrolled growth of phytoplankton (algae) and/or macrophytes in the aquatic environment.
Heterotrophy	The utilisation of organic material from the environment as food, in order to generate their own organic constituents.
Hypolimnion	The lower, colder layer of water in a stratified lake.
IPC	Integrated pollution control.
LAS	Linear Alkylbenzene Sulphonate
LC_{50}	Lethal Concentration, a calculated dose which has caused the death of 50% of a defined experimental population, within a given time period.
LOEC	Lowest observable effect concentration
Macrophyte	Plants other than algae.
Metalimnion	Zone of rapid temperature change between the hypo and epilimnion.
Monomixis	Term used to describe lake circulation characterised by single mixing.
Mutagenicity	The ability to in some way alter the base sequence of the genetic code (DNA).

NOEC	No observable effect concentration.
NRA	National Rivers Authority
NTA	Nitrilo Triacetic acid, an organic detergent builder with strong chelating ability.
PCA	Polycarboxylic Acids, detergent builders or co-builders with anti-redeposition and dispersion properties.
SDIA	Soaps and Detergents Industry Association.
STPP	Sodium Tripolyphosphate, the most commonly used detergent builder in the UK.
Stratification	Process by which layers of lake water are isolated due to thermal effects on density.
Surfactant	A surface-active substance eg detergents
Teratogenic	Producing anatomical or biochemical adverse effects on the developing foetus.
Thermocline	Temperature zone within a water body due to thermal stratification.
Toxicology	The study of the effects of pollutants or toxins on biological processes.
Wash-day Phenomena	The variation in population laundry habits which lead to great variations in mean influent concentrations of detergent constituents at a sewage treatment works.
Xenobiotic	A man made (Synthetic) substance.
Zeolite A	A crystalline aluminosilicate with a uniform pore size and an internal surface area many times larger than the external surface area. It is a sequestrant of Ca^{2+} and Mg^{2+} by ion exchange.

Pollution Impact of Textiles and Woollens

December 1991

Environmental Resources Limited

Acknowledgements:

ERL would like to thank the Staff and members of the Royal Commission on Environmental Pollution and the various regions and individuals of the National Rivers Authority and River Purification Boards for their help in carrying out this study. We also wish to thank the Trade Associations who helped us complete this Report.

Textiles: T. Apted, S Clarke and
             J V Towner

Contents

1 Introduction

1.1 Purpose of the Report

This report to the Royal Commission on Environmental Pollution assesses freshwater (including groundwater) pollution from the UK textiles and woollens industry, based on the information received to date. It reviews the scale of the industry in the UK, and addresses the issue of freshwater pollution on a regional basis.

The toxicological and biological effects of the industrial emissions are provided and highlighted by relevant case studies. The existing pollution control measures are reviewed, and areas of potential research interest are identified.

1.2 Sources of Information

The major sources of information used in the preparation of this report are detailed below:

- all regions of the National Rivers Authority (NRA) in England and Wales;
- all Scottish River Purification Boards (RPB);
- Water Services Association;
- Water Services plcs;
- British Effluents and Water Association;
- Her Majesty's Inspectorate of Pollution (HMIP);
- Scottish sewerage and water supply authorities;
- Water Research Centre (WRC);
- Textile Institute;
- Textile Research Council;

- Textile Services Association (TSA);
- Textile Finisher's Association (TFA);
- International Wool Secretariat (IWS);
- Published information;
- Major UK producers of textiles and woollens.

1.3 Organisation of the Report

The report is organised as detailed below.

- *Section 2*: reviews the scale of the UK textiles and woollen industry, including the geographical distribution of industrial plants, and the typical products of the industry.

- *Section 3*: evaluates the potential freshwater pollution causes and effects, and presents relevant case studies.

- *Section 4*: discusses the existing pollution control measures, including legislation, monitoring and wastewater treatment. Pollution is addressed on a regional basis, and areas of particular concern are identified.

- *Section 5:* identifies particular issues where insufficient information exists, and details areas of potential research.

- *Section 6:* summarises the key conclusions and recommendations.

2 Scale of the Industry

2.1 Introduction

The UK textiles and woollens industry involves the manufacture of the following products:

- wool and synthetic yarns;

- cloth and clothing;

- carpets and rugs; and

- household textiles.

Public demand is for products of a high quality. Market research has identified recent UK trends for bright colours, and special finishes including:

- water resistancy and flame proofing;

- stain guard; and

- mothproofing.

2.1.1 UK consumption

In 1987, the industrial consumption of textile fibres worldwide was 35.24 billion tonnes, of which chemical fibres accounted for 16.21 billion tonnes, cotton fibres 17.38 billion tonnes and wool fibres 1.66 billion tonnes (according to Textile Organon, 1989). The UK was the fourth largest Western European, industrial consumer of textiles with 581,000 tonnes consumed in total in 1987.

Consumption of fibres was in the following proportions:

- 444,200 t chemical fibres;

- 49,900 t cotton fibres; and

- 86,900 t wool fibres.

2.1.2 Economics

The UK top ten textiles companies are detailed in Table 2.1a, together with approximate rates of annual turnover in 1986, the most recent year for which this data is available.

Table 2.1a   The Annual Turnover of the Top UK Textiles Companies in 1986

COMPANY	TURNOVER (£ million)
Coats Viyella	1741
Courtaulds	991
Tootal	433
Dawson Intl	354
John Crowther Group	141
Readicut Intl	138
Corah (N)	100
BBA Group	99
Illingworth Morris	93
Readson	88
Lamont Hldg (UK)	64
Total	**4242**

Source: Chemiefasern Textilindustrie, 1988

In 1986, the UK textiles and woollen industry had 20,000 employees throughout Britain, and the total annual turnover was £13.2 billion.

Between 1980 and 1988, pre-tax profits from the British cloth and clothing industry are reported to have grown an average of 25% per annum. The growth in profits was partially due to retrenchment of the industry and partially due to the economy.

In 1988, the British textile and woollen industry continued to grow. The carpet market, for example, rose 32% between 1983 and 1988.

However, in recent years, due to high interest rates and a reduction in consumer spending the productivity of the UK textiles and woollen industry is reported to have fallen. The Confederation of British Wool Textiles Limited (CBWT) announced, in December 1989, the following changes compared with the previous year:

- the consumption of all textile fibres fell by 19%;

- the production of tops [1] and wool yarns fell by 19% and 16% respectively; and

- the number of production personnel in the industry reduced nationally by approximately 6%.

2.2 Geographical Distribution

The distribution of the textiles and woollens industry in the UK is concentrated in the North, in areas where raw materials are readily available, and labour is less costly than in the south east.

The approximate regional distribution of registered companies in the industry is provided in Table 2.2a.

The industries are concentrated in the north west (mainly textiles) and in Yorkshire (mainly woollens) with only a small percentage of industrial plants occurring elsewhere in the UK.

Table 2.2a The Distribution of the UK Textiles and Woollen Industry

Region (based on area boundaries of the UK Water Industry)	Estimated % of the Industry
Anglian	< 1
Northumbrian	< 2
North West	38
Severn Trent	< 1
Southern	< 1
South West	< 1
Thames	< 2
Welsh	< 1
Wessex	< 1
Yorkshire	44
Clyde	6
Forth	< 2
Highland	< 1
North East	< 1
Solway	< 1
Tay	< 1
Tweed	5

Source: Adapted from data supplied by Textiles Finishers Association (TFA), CBWT and British Textiles Institute (BTI)

2.3 Major Processes Involved

2.3.1 Introduction

The enormous diversity of textile production techniques is a result of three basic features:

- the fibres treated (natural, artificial or synthetic);

- the dyeing processes (full-width, padder, screens, roller printer etc.); and,

- the products used, in particular the range of dyeing chemical.

The first stage of manufacture is primarily mechanical activity which results in only slight pollution. This activity is largely confined to spinning and weaving. Chemical treatment at the later process stages, namely textile finishing, bleaching, dyeing, printing and finishing, generally gives rise to substantial pollution, and it is in this area where recent pollution control studies are focused.

The chemicals used in textile manufacture can be summarised as follows:

- dyes which are discharged both in solution and solid forms: variations include acid, basic, mordant, reactive, disperse, sulphur and pigment dyes;

- organic and inorganic acids;

- alkalis;

- oxidants from bleaching, including hypochlorite solution, chlorite or perborate;

- reducing agents, including sodium hydrosulphite and sulphite;

- adjuvants;

- mercerizing and finishing products (starch, alginates, enzymes, carbomethyl, cellulose);

- emulsifiers.

In addition, carbamate pesticides are used in the wool industry, primarily to protect products such as carpets. These are finding increasing precedence over organo-chlorine and organo-phosphorus pesticides due to their enhanced biodegradability and reduced mammalian toxicity.

2.3.2 General Textile Manufacture

The Extrusion Process

Man-made fibres are formed by extrusion processes known as melt, dry, or wet spinning.

In melt spinning, molten polymer is pressure forced through a spinneret. The fluid jets emerge from many tiny holes and solidify in a cooling zone to form filaments which are wound onto containers. The diameter of the filament can be varied by altering the rate of extrusion and take-up. Although melt spinning is the most economical filament extrusion process, it does require polymers that are thermally stable under melt conditions. For this reason, only nylon, polyester and olefin filaments are produced using this method.

In dry spinning, the polymer is dissolved in a suitable solvent before being forced through the spinneret. The emerging fluid jet enters a heated zone where the solvent evaporates, leaving a solid filament. This method is used to produce acetate, triacetate and acrylics.

Conversely, in wet spinning the dissolved polymer solution is extruded into a liquid bath. Here, the filament is formed by a combination of precipitation, coagulation, and regeneration mechanisms. Material formed by this method includes rayon, spandex and some acrylics.

Drawing

The spinning or extrusion of filaments is normally followed by drawing, where the newly formed filaments are irreversibly extended and stabilised by either setting or crystallisation. In general, the structure of both man-made and natural fibres is that of a regular molecular organisation with considerable structural anisotropy. This is reflected in the large differences that can be found between the axial and transverse physical properties of fibres. The stabilisation process acts to develop this molecular organisation and gives the resultant product a high degree of orientation and crystallinity.

A recent advance in synthetic polymer manufacture is high speed spinning. The extrusion and drawing steps are combined into a single operation which induces a high degree of orientation and crystallinity. Favourable economics suggests that this method will become increasingly dominant over the two step spin-and-draw process, particularly for polyester fibres.

Cleaning

Naturally occurring fibres, with the exception of silk, generally require several cleaning and purification steps prior to yarn and fabric processing. Man-made fibres, on the other hand, require no cleaning and can be processed directly.

Fabric Manufacture

There are three methods for the manufacture of textile fabrics, each of which has been developed to accommodate the geometric and physical properties of the fibres:

- the cotton system;
- the wool system; and
- the worsted system.

The differences between these systems are primarily the length and texture of the fibre used in the yarn. For example, wool and worsted differ in that worsted yarns are manufactured from longer wool fibres that have been drawn parallel.

The typical operations to which fibres are subjected during yarn manufacture are detailed below:

- *In Carding*, the bundles are opened and impurities such as seeds and hulls are removed. The result of the operation is yarns irregular in diameter and strength, and with short and long fibres mixed together.
- *Combing* is an optional process which separates long fibres from short fibres, of which the short are discarded. The operation results in yarn that has regular strength, more regular diameter, smooth appearance and increased value.
- *Drawing* reduces the diameter of the yarn and draws it down to the required fineness and evenness under tension.
- In *Spinning*, the yarn is further drawn out, twisted and wound.

After the fabric-formation process, textiles are subjected to a variety of mechanical or chemical processes, including dyeing or printing, and finishing.

Dyeing

Dyeing is performed by immersing the textile material in an aqueous solution of dye. Normally, the dye liquor consists of dye, water and an auxiliary, and the process involves a partition or distribution of the dye from the aqueous phase to the solid fibre phase. This is mostly due to:

- forces of repulsion developed between the dye molecule and water; and,
- forces of attraction developed between the dye molecules and fibres.

In addition, some dyes are chemically reactive and bond covalently to the fibre polymer.

Dyes can be classified into three categories:

- *Anionic* dyes are substances in which the colour is contained in the negatively charged part of the dye molecule;
- *Cationic* dyes are substances in which the colour is contained in the positively charged part of the dye molecule; and
- *Disperse* dyes are substances in which the colour is contained throughout the whole molecule.

These categories of dyes can be further split into a number of classes, depending on the individual affinity for certain fibre types. Examples of these classes include: direct, azoic, basic, morda, vat, solvent, disperse, reactive, premetalised and sulphur dyes.

Water is an important component of dyeing, as it dissolves the dye and acts as a transfer medium for dye molecules to attach to the fibre. Unfortunately, this attraction of dye molecule polar groups to water molecules means there is some resistance for the dye molecules to leave the water and enter the fibre. For this reason, heat is necessary both to encourage the dye to enter the fibre, and to ensure adequate penetration of the polymer system. Temperatures can range from the 100°C used in commercial dyeing, to those of approximately 130°C that are required for polyester fibres.

Finally, multicolour patterns and designs can be achieved by printing, where insoluble pigments are utilised in the place of dyes. This process is much more rapid and considerably less energy intensive.

Finishing

Finishing treatment can employ mechanical or chemical procedures. The former, mechanical finishing, is primarily designed to produce special surface effects and can involve napping, shearing, embossing and calendering.

Chemical finishing operations involve:

- the addition of chemicals; or
- chemical modification of some or all of the fibres comprising the fabric.

200

Chemical finishing is principally performed on those fabrics that are composed either entirely or in part of cellulosic fibres (eg, cotton and rayon). For example, reactions with difunctional reagents capable of chemically crosslinking cellulose chains can improve fibre resilience, and therefore enhance wrinkle resistance and recovery. The same reactions can impart wash-andwear and durable press characteristics. Other benefits from chemical finishing treatments include:

- control of felt shrinkage when wet wool fabrics are subjected to mechanical agitation at elevated temperatures;

- ability to impart wash-and-wear and durable-press properties to wool fabrics;

- ability to heat-seal synthetic polymer fibres into desired configurations;

- soiling resistance;

- water repellency; and

- flame retardance.

2.3.3 Cotton and Wool Processing

The processing of cotton and wool fibres, from the natural fibre to the yarn stage, is similar to the general textile manufacturing process described in *Section 2.3.2* above. It should be noted however, that an important step in most cotton manufacture involves mercerization, whereby the cotton is treated under tension to reduce shrinkage and increase strength. The yarn or woven fabric is treated with a 20% solution of sodium hydroxide, which causes the fibres to swell. Whilst in this swollen state, the material is stretched and attains a tensile strength increase of between 15 to 20%. The resulting product offers a smoother surface for light reflection and is more lustrous than ordinary cotton.

Mercerization is a large contributor to water pollution due to both the amounts of water consumed and the products emitted (ie, starch alginate, enzymes and carboxymethylcellulose).

2.3.4 Rayon Manufacture

Rayon is made from cellulose, of which the major source is wood pulp. Here, the initial process of spinning is different to the process outlined in *Section 2.3.2*. This is depicted schematically in *Figure 2.3*a.

Treatment of the wood pulp with sodium hydroxide causes the pulp fibres to swell and form a substance called alkali cellulose. This substance is treated with carbon disulphide to form cellulose xanthate. The cellulose xanthate is dissolved in diluted caustic soda solution, form;ng a thick molasses-like xanthate substance which is filtered to remove any solid matter that could clog the spinnerets. The solution emerging from the tiny spinneret holes enters an acid coagulating bath, from where it passes over a series of reels, dries, and is wound on a bobbin.

2.3.5 Nylon Manufacture

Organic acid (ie adipic acid) and organic base (ie hexamethyl diamine) are chemically combined to form nylon salt. The salt is polymerised at high temperature in the absence of air, and water is removed continuously. The resultant polymer is forced out as a ribbon and cut into small chips. Flakes or pellets are blended and remelted before being pumped through the spinnerets. As with rayon, the filaments solidify as they cool on exposure to air. They are then gathered together to form a yarn, and during the twisting operation sizing or oils may be applied. *Figure 2.3b* illustrates the process.

2.3.6 Acrylic Manufacture

Acrylic fibres are formed by dry spinning. Acrylonitrile and small amounts of other monomers are polymerised and dissolved in dimethyl formantide. The solution is filtered, extruded through spinnerets, and enters a heated spinning container where the solvent is evaporated. This process is illustrated in *Figure 2.3c*. Molecular orientation and fibre fineness is achieved by stretching the hot fibre before drying.

2.3.7 Acetate Manufacture

Similarly to rayon, acetate derives its cellulose from wood pulp. The pulp is dissolved by progressive additions of acetic acid and acetic anhydride. Water is then added to a precipation tank which results in the formation of solid flakes of acetate. Acetate fibres are produced by dissolving the solid, washed cellulose acetate particles in acetone. The fibres are then filtered, pumped through spinnerets, and stripped of acetone by evaporation. Dry filaments from each spinneret are twisted together and wound onto a bobbin.

Figure 2.3a Schematic Illustration of Rayon Manufacture

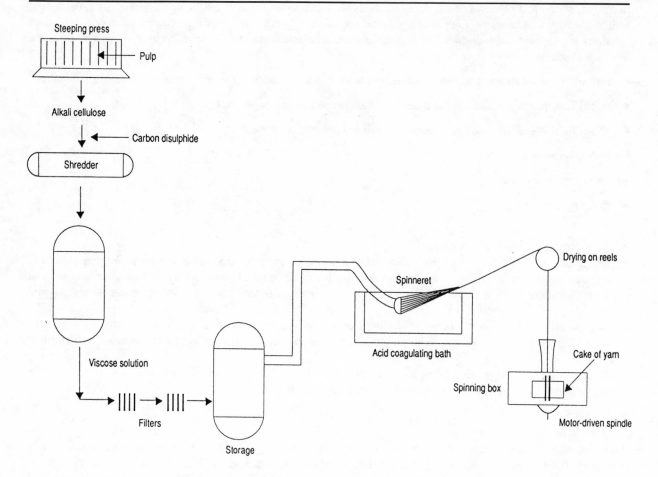

Figure 2.3b   Schematic Illustration of Nylon Manufacturers

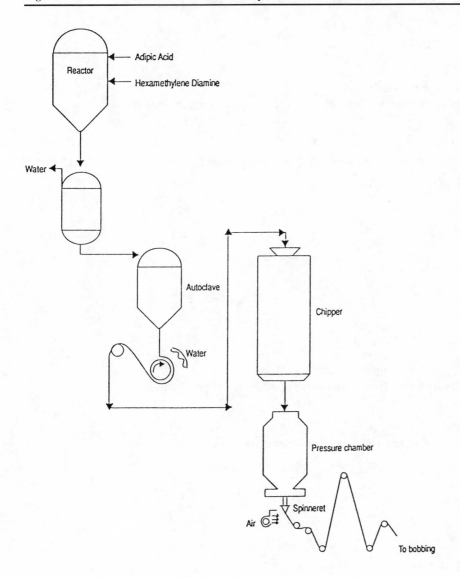

Figure 2.3c Schematic Illustration of Acrylic Manufacture

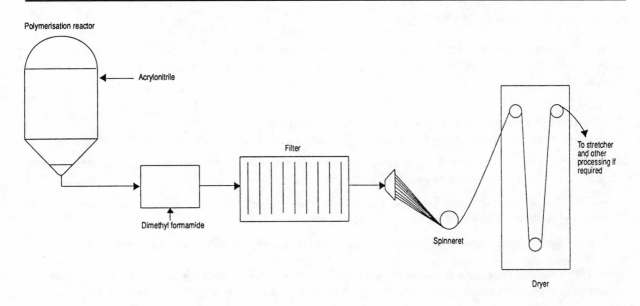

3 Potential Water Pollution Causes and Effects

3.1 Nature and Composition of Emissions

The major pollutants arising from waste water effluents of the UK textiles and woollens industry are detailed below.

3.1.1 Processing Plant Effluents

Processing plant effluents may contain high concentrations of the following contaminants:

- biochemical oxygen demand (BOD);
- oils;
- alkalis;
- ammonia;
- organic nitrogen;
- chloride;
- suspended solids; and
- detergents.

These originate from the raw materials themselves, and subsequent washing and processing.

3.1.2 Finishing Plant Effluents

Finishing Plant effluents may be contaminated with high concentrations of:

- BOD;
- hexavalent chromium;
- acids;
- suspended solids;
- organic moth proofing agents (eg pentachlorophenol and permethrin);
- dye constituents;
- phenols; and
- zinc and copper (from rayon manufacture).

These contaminants originate from the various finishing techniques employed.

Various 'cocktails' of the above pollutants may be found in the freshwater environment downstream of a textiles plant discharge.

3.2 Sources of Pollution and Environmental Concentrations

Pollutants from the UK textiles and woollens industry may enter the aquatic environment in the following ways.

- Direct discharges of contaminated wastewater to surface waters and groundwater may occur from either processing and finishing plants, or due to accidental chemical spillages.

- Indirect discharges may occur following treatment of trade effluents at a sewage treatment works or at an industrial waste water treatment facility.

- Indirect water pollution may occur from air emissions and the subsequent deposition of pollutants.

In the UK, most contaminated wastewater from the textiles and woollens industry is discharged to the foul sewer. Treatment at a sewage treatment works considerably reduces the loadings of most pollutants in the final effluent.

However, certain substances, particularly organic pollutants such as insecticides or dyes, are persistent and cannot be readily biodegraded at a sewage treatment works. The watercourses downstream of a sewage outfall may, therefore, contain elevated levels of dye colour, mothproofing agents, and other contaminants.

Table 3.2a presents water quality data, reported by the NRA, for a monitoring location approximately 3km downstream of a discharge from a sewage treatment works. The sewage treatment works treats industrial and domestic sewage from a catchment area where the textiles and woollens industry is historically successful.

Direct discharges of untreated contaminated waste water and accidental spillages associated with the UK textiles and woollens industry are extremely infrequent; these aspects are discussed in greater detail in *Section 4*.

Any atmospheric emissions associated with the UK textiles and woollens industry are unlikely to cause significant contamination of the air. Chemicals which are a possible source of atmospheric pollution are likely to be removed from emissions, or reduced to acceptable levels by control measures introduced under the Health and Safety at Work Act (1974). Freshwater pollution from atmospheric deposition is, therefore, unlikely to be significantly exacerbated by emissions from the UK textiles and woollen industry.

Table 3.2a 1989/1990 Typical Concentration of Contaminants in River Water Downstream of a Yorkshire Sewage Treatment Works Treating Textile Industry Wastewater

Determinand	Mean	Max	Min
ammonia (unionised) (mgl^{-1})	0.019	0.07	<0.001
chloride (mgl^{-1})	72.47	160	19.6
pentachlorophenol (μgl^{-1})	0.196	0.36	0.05
phenol (μgl^{-1})	40.2	<50	29
zinc(dissolved) (mgl^{-1})	0.17	0.04	<0.01
copper (dissolved) (mgl^{-1})	0.008	0.014	0.004
dieldrin (μgl^{-1})	0.004	0.008	<0.001
anionic detergents (mgl^{-1})	0.22	0.59	0.06
nonionic detergents (mgl^{-1})	0.098	<0.5	0.03

Source: NRA (Yorkshire Region)

The typical concentrations of mothproofing agents in the main surface freshwaters in Yorkshire and the North West region are presented in Table 3.2b. It is notable that maximum reported concentrations of all compounds exceed relevant Environmental Quality Standards of 2 μgl^{-1} for pentachlorophenol (PCP), 30 ngl^{-1} for dieldrin, and 10 ngl^{-1} for the pyrethroids. In the case of the pyrethroids maximum levels may exceed acute toxicity levels for certain species (see Table 3.4c).

Table 3.2b Range of Background Concentrations of Mothproofing Agents in Main Rivers of Yorkshire and the North West

Substance μgl^{-1}	Range	Estimated Mean
PCP	<0.1 to 40	<0.2
Dieldrin	<0.001 to 9.34	0.002
Permethrin	<0.02 to 0.8	<0.2
Cypermethrin	<0.02 to <0.4	<0.05

Source: NRA, Yorkshire and Northwest Regions

3.3 The Environmental Fates of Textile Wastes

3.3.1 Environmental Chemistry

The organic micropollutants used in the UK textiles and woollens industry comprise a wide range of compounds, many of which are now ubiquitous in the environment due to extensive use. A number of natural processes may lead to the removal of organic micropollutants from the water column. These include evaporation, adsorption by suspended sediments (particularly the organic fraction) and degradation. However, there is evidence that dissolved organic matter can bind to and enhance the solubilities of a range of organic micropollutants and may affect uptake and toxicity to organisms (McCarthy *et al* 1985).

The organic micropollutants found in freshwater have varying degrees of affinity for adsorption onto particles, particularly organically enriched particles. The adsorption affinity of organic pollutants onto particles is largely dependent on their lipophilicity (affinity for lipids), which is often described by an octanol partition coefficient; this is an experimentally derived coefficient which expresses the distribution of a substance within an octanol water test system. In general, a linear relationship between logarithms of the octanol-water and sediment organic matter-water partition coefficients is observed (Mackay & Powers, 1987). Measured water-sediment coefficients show a strong dependence on solids concentration, which becomes stronger with increasing octanol-water partition coefficient (Lodge & Cook, 1989). Further for substances such as phenolics or chlorophenolics, which have lower lipophilicities and are influenced by acid base characteristics, the partioning towards sediments is influenced by pH (Xie *et al* 1986), with sediment binding affinity increasing with greater chlorine substitution and decreased hydroxy substitution.

As with trace metals, organic micropollutants are subject to speciation effects such that compounds show varying affinities for natural or anthropogenic or different size class fraction of sediments (Brownawell and Farrington 1986, Readman *et al* 1982). Unlike trace metals, some organic compounds show a preference for coarse textured sediments rather than fine sediments, although such particle preferences depend on individual compound behaviour.

Accumulation of organic compounds by organisms has been shown to be related to octanol-water partition coefficient (McElroy *et al* 1989). Thus, for example, individual PCB compounds with greater octanol-water partition coefficients tend to be bioaccumulated to a marginally greater extent.

The organochlorine pesticides associated with the UK textiles and woollens industry are substances which tend to have low water solubilities and accumulate in sediments and biota. They include dieldrin, aldrin, lindane and pyrethroids amongst others. These compounds have found widespread past use in the textiles and woollens industry.

The adsorption of most chlorinated compounds is strongly related to the organic matter content of sediments, and sorption affinity increases with increasing octanol-water partition coefficients for individual compounds; octanol-water partition coefficients generally increase with increasing degree of chlorination within homologous series of compounds such as the chlorophenols (Hansch, 1979). During early diagenesis[1], there is evidence, that organochlorine compounds are associated with both sedimentary organic matter and dissolved and colloidal organic matter in the pore waters, the remainder being truly dissolved. The equilibria between these three phases is critical in terms of desorption and remobilisation of organic compounds to the water column from sediments, and bioavailability to organisms. An important consequence of these three phase equilibria is that the less soluble, highly chlorinated organic compounds tend to be enriched in the pore waters relative to the more soluble, less chlorinated organic compounds due to the former compounds association with pore water organic matter. The octanol-water partition coefficients for constituents of textile waste waters are presented in Table 3.3a. The order of the octanol-water partition coefficents indicate that the order of affinity to sediments is dieldrin > pentachlorophenol > phenol; conversely the reverse order indicates the trend in terms of compound water solubility.

3.3.2 Biodegradation

Organochlorine compounds

Organochlorine compounds, such as pentachlorophenol, in sediments are subject to slow processes of microbial and chemical degradation. The nature of these degradation reactions varies depending on whether they occur in the 'oxic', 'sulphide' or 'methanic' zones of the sediments. Under oxidised conditions, susceptibility to and rates of degradation depend on the number and substitution of chlorine atoms. For example, pentachlorophenol is not readily microbially degraded (Bailey *et al* 1983), while less substituted chlorophenols biodegrade readily. Under reducing conditions, it has been suggested that degradation of organochlorine compounds proceeds by reductive dehalogenation There is dispute as to whether these reactions are chemical, involving Fe (11) compounds as catalysts, or microbial (Brown *et al* 1984), possibly involving methanogenic bacteria (Sulfita *et al* 1983).

---

[1] Diagenesis refers to the sequence of biogeochemical processes that affect sediments following deposition.

Under reducing conditions, the ease of reduction appears to increase with increasing degree of chlorine substitution. Nevertheless, despite these processes many organochlorine compounds have considerable persistence in the environment.

Bioturbation of sediments may play an important role in the diagenesis of organochlorine compounds by two mechanisms; firstly, by increasing pore water exchange and fluxes of compounds to overlying waters; secondly, by changing the nature of degradation reactions by introducing oxygen into the lower anoxic zones of sediments. Accumulation of organo-chlorine compounds by organisms tends to correlate with octanol-water partition coefficients and storage occurs in lipid fractions (McElroy *et al* 1989). The octanol-water partition coefficients and degradation rates for constituents of textile waste waters are presented in Table 3.3a. These data show that the highly chlorine substituted pentachlorophenol and dieldrin are degraded at rates at least an order of magnitude lower than that for phenol. Similarly the order of the octanol/water partitioning coefficients indicates the increasing of order of biaccumulation (vis phenol < pentachlorophenol < dieldrin).

In situations where microorganisms are able to break down organochlorines, the process is complex (see *Figure 3.3a*) and, therefore very slow. Compounds such as the pyrethroids (allethrin, bioresmethrin, permethrin, cypermethrin etc) are more readily degraded in the environment, particularly due to the presence of photolytically unstable groups in the molecule. This is readily cleaved, and leads to the decomposition of the compounds. Nevertheless, there is evidence that the most persistent compound permethrin is bioaccumulated (Hellawell, 1985), other less persistent pyrethroids are not significantly bioaccumulated (Hellawell, 1985).

Table 3.3a   Octanol-water Partition Coefficients for the Major Contaminants of Textile Waste Waters

Substance	Degradation Rate in Sediments (per day)	Absorbed/Dissolved Partition Coefficient, K_{oc}
Pentachlorophenol	0.0007	12300
Phenol	0.008	138
Dieldrin	0.0007	63900

Source: US Department of the Interior, 1987

Figure 3.3a   The Degradation Pathway of Pentachlorophenol

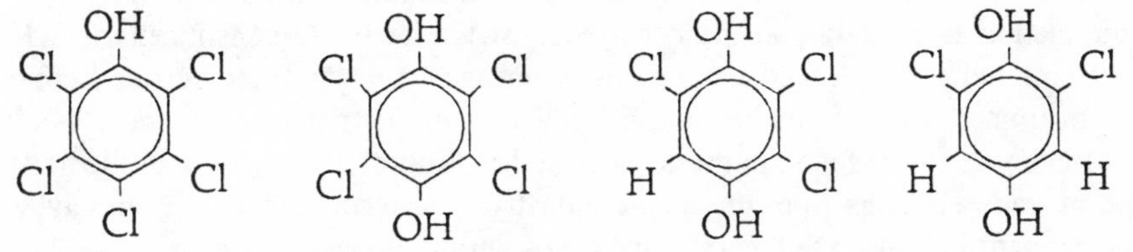

The above figure (3.3a) shows a cleavage pathway of pentachlorophenol, yielding compounds which microbes can then utilise.

Other Constituents

The biological process involved in the microbial breakdown of textile wastes is complex and sensitive to pH, temperature, loading, and the mix of chemicals. Aerobic biodegradation of organic materials may be summarised by the following equation.

$$\text{Biomass Organics} + O_2 + \text{Nutrients} \rightarrow \overset{\text{Biomass}}{\text{New Biomass}} + CO_2 + \text{Non-reactive Ingredients}$$

The accumulation of new biomass will depend on the degradability of the organic material, and the retention time employed.

In the treatment of textile's wastewaters, degradation may involve breaking only one bond in a compound, or total conversion of a compound to CO_2. The oxygen consumption rate, therefore, varies considerably during treatment.

Bio-degradable compounds may be arbitrarily defined as being those which consume over 10% of their weight of oxygen over a 5 day period (BOD = 100,000 mgl^{-1} in 5 days). Those using less oxygen are considered to resist biodegradation.

The BOD$_{30}$/COD[1] ratio provides a further indication of biodegradability of a waste. The higher the ratio is, the more biodegradable the waste. If the ratio is 1, this indicates that after a period of 30 days, degradation is complete. The BOD$_{30}$/COD ratios for several commercial textile dye chemicals were investigated by Porter and Snider (1976) and a summary is provided in Table 3.3c.

It is apparent from the data provided in Table 3.3c that many textile dye chemicals degrade only slowly during wastewater treatment. However, adsorption by suspended particulate matter may present an important removal route for these compounds.

Table 3.3c Biodegradability of Textile Chemicals

Textile Chemical	BOD$_{30}$/COD x 100 (100% = totally biodegradable)
butyl benzoate	73.0%
kerosene	1.1%
dye disperse red 68	14.0%
dye disperse blue 139	5.7%
dye disperse yellow 144	25.8%
dye reactive blue 21	1.7%
dye vat violet	9.3%
dye vat black	11.6%
resin finish	0.48%
nonionic polyethylene emulsion	10.0%
polyvinyl alcohol	60.0%

Source: Porter and Snyder, 1976

3.3.3 Fate in Sewage Treatment

When inert compounds are present in a waste stream, they may be removed by adsorption on mixed liquor suspended solids if the concentration is high, and the retention time is sufficiently long to allow for adsorption. If the retention time is short or the chemicals are particularly persistent (eg pentachlorophenol), biodegradation will not be complete, and residual levels of the contaminant may remain in the final effluent and sludge.

Little published information is available on the occurrence of textile waste constituents in UK sewage sludges. Woodhead (1983) determined permethrin concentrations in sewage effluents, filter slurries and pressed sludge cake in a single sewage treatment works following the introduction of permethrin into local woollen trade process effluents. Levels of 163 mgkg^{-1} were found in the sewage sludge. Approximately 60% of the trade effluent entering the works consisted of trade effluents from the textile industry. The results, therefore, are atypical. However, the data do indicate that permethrin is absorbed onto sludge solids during sewage treatment.

In 1989, the occurrence of *cis* and *trans* permethrin in twelve UK sewage sludges of varying catchment was investigated (Rogers *et al* 1989). The concentration data for the permethrin isomers is shown in Table 3.3d, together with details of the catchment served by each sewage treatment works. The results indicate that permethrins can be expected to occur frequently at concentrations in sewage sludge in a range of up to 50ppm.

Although the literature review has revealed no information on concentrations of other textile waste constituents in sewage sludge, it is likely that chemicals which are reported to be more persistent than permethrins (eg pentachlorophenol and dye constituents) would occur in concentrations greater than measured levels of permethrin in sewage sludge.

Organic contaminants in sewage sludge could cause environmental effects when sludge is applied to agricultural land. The level of chlorinated substances which could be regarded as having the potential for impact on soil-plant systems has been suggested to be 100 mgkg^{-1} by Rogers *et al* 1989; this general statement is in relation to compounds without specific phytotoxic action, based on an average of several compounds or agricultural pesticides. Present indications are that the expected concentration ranges for permethrin in sewage sludges are unlikely to cause immediate concern.

---

[1] BOD$_{30}$ (Biochemical Oxygen Demand) is the amount of oxygen taken up by microorganisms to decompose any organic waste matter present over a 30 day period. COD = Chemical Oxygen Demand

However, it should be noted that the estimation of a 'safe' level was based on agricultural pesticide application rates, and no account has been taken of the differences in the availability and chemical nature of organic contaminants in sewage sludges applied to agricultural land (Rogers *et al* 1989).

Table 3.3d The Concentrations of Permethrin in Twelve UK Sewage Sludges

Sludge No.	Treatment	Solids (%)	Disposal Route	Catchment Details	Concentrations of Permethrin (mgkg⁻¹ dry weight)	
					Cis	*Trans*
1	Digested	3.3	Incineration and landfill	Domestic and heavy industrial	2.46	4.72
2	Raw	5.1	Incineration	Domestic and heavy industrial	0.16	0.52
3	Raw	3.0	Agriculture	Domestic and shoe manufacture	1.35	4.23
4	Digested	3.2	Sea	Domestic and textile and chemical industy	5.67	3.42
5	Digested	3.3	Agriculture	Domestic and light industrial	4.47	11.0
6	Raw	7.6	Sea and landfill	Domestic and textile industry	2.15	4.13
7	Raw	3.6	Sea	Domestic and mixed industrial	<0.15	1.00
8	Digested	6.9	Sea	Domestic and heavy industrial	<0.15	<0.15
9	Digested	1.9	Agriculture	Domestic and light industrial	8.35	20.90
10	Digested	1.9	Agriculture	Domcstic	15.6	40.8
11	Raw	4.8	Agriculture and landfill	Domestic and chemical industry	<0.15	<0.15
12	Digested	19	Sea	Domestic and mixed industrial	1.43	1.01
Mean					3.51	7.67
Median					1.79	3.78

Source: Adapted from Rogers *et al*, 1989

3.4 Toxicological and Biological Effects

Toxicity data for the major pollutants associated with the textiles and woollens industry are detailed in Tables 3.4a, b and c.

Table 3.4a Aquatic Toxicity Data for Specific Pollutants from the Textiles and Woollens Industry

Substances	96hr EC$_{50}$* (ppb)		96hr LC$_{50}$ (ppb)			Threshold concentration for acute effects (ppb)
	Phyloplankton	Zooplankton	Fish	Benthic Inverts	Larvae of Fish/Inverts	
Ammonia	420,900	18,420	131,500	434,100	14,470	81.78
Chlorine	383	228	120	395	13.2	0.07
Pentachloro-phenol	895	883	165	621	18.1	10.25
Phenol	21,430	11,940	6,696	37,310	737	4.16
Zinc	669	9249	2,803	9,249	3,083	1.74
Copper	374.5	8.75	117	1323	12.8	0.04
Dieldrin	51	7.22	2.23	355	25 4	0.001

Note: 96hr EC$_{50}$ is the concentration dose at which, over a 96 hour period of exposure, 50% of the population will show a response.

96hr LC$_{50}$, is the concentration dose at which, over a 96 hour period of exposure, 50% of the population exhibit mortality.

The threshold concentration for an acute response is the minimum concentration of the substance which is predicted to have an effect.

Source: US Department of the Interior, 1987

3.4.1 Mothproofing Agents

The significance of mothproofing agents in the environment is threefold.

- They are pesticide compounds which have been selected for their biocidal properties and are applied in order to kill or control certain organisms (moths). Few are absolutely specific to their target organisms and other related species (in this case invertebrates) are often at risk.

- Sublethal concentrations of mothproofing agents may impact a significant change in the physiology, reproduction or behaviour of non-target groups (eg fish) which ultimately impairs their ability to survive in the affected habitat.

- Certain mothproofing agents or their immediate degradation products are persistent in the aquatic environment. The low water solubility and high lipid solubility causes bioaccumulation in fat tissues of organisms. This may result in 'bioaccumulation' of mothproofing agents. Many studies have shown that concentrations of organochlorine residues found in different species and in different tissues of the same species correlate well with their lipid contents (Hellawell, 1986).

As may be seen from Table 3.4a, mothproofing chemicals such as dieldrin and pentachlorophenol can potentially have significant acute toxic effects at relatively low concentrations on the aquatic biota of a watercourse, with fish and larvae being particularly susceptible. Further data on the toxicological properties of mothproofing agents are provided in Tables 3.4b and 3.4c.

The use of all chemicals listed in Table 3.4b, together with dieldrin, has been banned for more than ten years. The ban was brought about mainly due to the persistence of these organic chemicals in the environment (see *Section 3.3*). Pentachlorophenol is also persistent in the environment, and an Environmental Quality Standard (EQS) value

210

imposed by HMIP has resulted in a much lower usage of the chemical by UK cloth manufacturers. The chemicals (eg pyrethroids) currently used are less persistent and are thought to be safer to human health, although they are considerably more toxic to aquatic organisms. Due to its persistence in the environment, pentachlorophenol has an Environment Quality Standard (EQS) value of $2\mu gl^{-1}$ (annual mean). Furthermore, it is one of 26 'Red-list' substances whose concentrations are monitored and consented by HMIP. These substances have been identified by the UK Government, from the 129 List I chemicals, as substances requiring further detailed environmental assessment and priority action.

Table 3.4b Acute Toxicity of Mothproofing Agents to Fish

Substance	Species	Temperature (°C)	96 hr LC$_{50}$ (μg litre^{-1})
Eulan WA New (chlorphenylid)	Rainbow trout (*Salmo gairdneri*)	4	5400
		14	1500
		15	500–1000
Mitin FF (Sulcofenuron)	Brown trout (*Salmo trutta*)	13	3900
	Zebra fish (*Brachydanio rerio*)	23	1200
Mitin N (flucofenuron)	Rainbow trout (fry)	15	68
	Rainbow trout (fry)	15	800
	Rainbow trout (yearlings)	15	130
	Rainbow trout (yearlings)	14	11200
	Brown trout	13	1700-6800
	Zebra fish	23	4000

Source: Adapted from Hellawell, 1986

Mothproofing agents increasingly used as alternatives to pentachlorophenol and dieldrin include Pyrethrins. The natural insecticide pyrethrum is extracted mainly from the flowers of *Chrysanthemum cinerariaefolium*. Since the 1970's there is reported to have been a considerable shortfall in the world supply of pyrethrum extract (Evins, 1981) and pyrethroids, synthetic analogues of pyrethrum, have been developed. These are generally accepted as being relatively safe for mammalian and avian species (Coats *et al* 1989).

Aquatic species are, however, much more sensitive to pyrethroids (see Tables 3.4a to c). Permethrin has been found to have an LD$_{50}$ of 14 mg/kg to rainbow trout (Glickman *et al* (1987)). Cypermethrin has been found to have

Table 3.4c Acute Toxicity of Synthetic Pyrethroids to Invertebrates and Fish

Substance	Species	Test	Value (μg litre^{-1})
Cypermethrin	*Salmo gairdneri*	96 hr LC$_{50}$	0.5
	Salmo trutta	96 hr LC$_{50}$	1.2
	Cyprinus carpio	96 hr LC$_{50}$	0.9
	Scardinius erythrophthalmus	96 hr LC$_{50}$	0.4
	Cloeon dipterum	24 hr LC$_{50}$	0.6
	Gammarus pulex	24 hr LC$_{50}$	0.1
	Asellus aquaticus	24 hr LC$_{50}$	0.2
	Daphnia magna	24 hr LC$_{50}$	2.0
Permethrin	*Ictalurus punctatus*	96 hr LC$_{50}$	1.10
	Micropterus salmoides	96 hr LC$_{50}$	8.50
	Gambusia affinis	96 hr LC$_{50}$	15.00
	Procambarus clarkii (juv)	96 hr LC$_{50}$	0.62

Source: Adapted from Hellawell, 1986

LC$_{50}$ values of 1.2, 0.9 and 0.5 mgl^{-1} in brown trout, carp and rainbow trout respectively (Stephenson, 1982). Pyrethroids are also extremely toxic to aquatic insects and crustaceans, with most LC$_{50}$ values being well below 1 mgl^{-1} (Coats *et al* 1989).

In addition to acute toxicity, many pyrethroids may have potentially deleterious effects at sublethal levels. At concentrations below 1 mgl^{-1} changes in behaviour, feeding pattern, growth and survivability have been observed (Anderson, 1982) in early lifestages both of aquatic insects and fish. The effects are similar to those resulting from exposure to the pesticide endrin (Keilty *et al* 1989).

3.4.2 Colourants

There are many different substances used as commercial colourants in the textiles and woollen industry, and innovation of water soluble or water dispersable dyes to meet market demand is an area of major activity. The Ecological and Toxicological Association of Dyestuff Manufacturers (ETAD) members provide certain basic information on products (Anliker and Clarke, 1982).

- Information is provided on the likely degree of bioelimination when the dyestuff is subjected to aerobic biological treatment. The stability of dyes means that aerobic biodegradation is negligible, and bioelimination occurs by sorption onto sludges during sewage treatment (Brown, 1987).

- Information on the acute toxicity of dye chemicals to fish is provided using test procedures similar to those specified for their determination in the OECD Test Guideline 203 (1981) or by the EEC (1984). In a survey of 3000 dyes tested by ETAD, only 2% were found to be toxic at a level of less than 1 mgl^{-1} (Brown, 1987).

- The registration inhibition test (OECD, 1984) measures bacterial toxicity using activated sewage sludge as a bacterial source. No inhibition has been found at a dye limit dose of l00 mgl^{-1} and according to Brown, (1987) no adverse effects on river or soil bacteria should occur at the levels likely to be present.

The levels of colorants in UK freshwaters which would be tolerated in terms of visual impact are thought to be lower than those levels at which acute toxic effects to aquatic species are anticipated (Brown, 1987). The toxicological effects of colorants in the freshwater environment are, therefore, likely to be much less severe than for mothproofing agents. However, it should be noted that carcinogenicity has been attributed to certain aromatic dye compounds, especially azo dyes (Sax, 1979).

3.4.3 The 'Cocktail Effect'

The sensitivity of aquatic species to toxic chemicals may be altered by a variety of environmental conditions including temperature, the presence of suspended or dissolved solids, and stress caused by the presence of other pollutants or lack of food. Pyrethroid insecticides are unusual in that they exhibit a negative temperature coefficient; ie they are more toxic to aquatic organisms at lower temperatures (Coates *et al*, 1979).

The toxicity effects of untreated textile wastewaters in Egypt have been investigated using Nile water fish (Sohair *et al* 1988). The physico-chemical characteristics of the wastewater are provided in Table 3.4d. The combination of alkaline pH, high Chemical Oxygen Demand (COD), low dissolved oxygen concentrations, and high levels of unionised ammonia, together with unmonitored organic chemicals present, resulted in 'necrosis' which slowly deepened until a critical point when no response was obtained when fish were disturbed. Complete mortality was observed within a few hours at high concentrations of raw wastes 56%, by volume (Sohair *et al* 1988). Further dilution of wastewater to 32% and 18% caused mortality after 48 hours exposure.

No similar toxicity tests of combined textile effluent constituents are known to have taken place in the UK.

Table 3.4d The Physico-chemical Characteristics of Textile Wastewaters

Determinand	Mean Concentration
pH	8.7
Chemical oxygen demand mgl^{-1}	909
Biological oxygen demand mgl^{-1}	224
Ammonia mgl^{-1}	29.4
Total phosphate mgl^{-1}	6
Total residue at l05 mgl^{-1}	1831
Total dissolved solids at 105° mgl^{-1}	1593

Source: Sohair *et al* 1988

3.5 Case Studies
The following case studies highlight freshwater pollution from the textiles and woollens industry.

3.5.1 Dieldrin Pollution in the River Holme Catchment, Yorkshire
The protection of wool by chemical means has been practised for the last 60 years and is particularly well established for floor coverings and furnishings as their expected life is normally longer than in the case of clothing. Problems have arisen with the use of mothproofing agents, many of which are specialised insecticides targeted to kill wool-consuming pests, but which can affect fish or aquatic life when discharged with the processing liquor discharge; these effects may occur directly or via a municipal waste water treatment plant (see *Section 3.3*). Serious problems of this nature were encountered with the widely used and persistent insecticide, dieldrin, and eventually its use had to be discontinued. Typical effects of the chemical, which still persists in UK surface water systems, are provided in the following case study.

The River Holme is characterised by soft water due to thick peat deposits in the upland tributaries. Soft water is ideal for a successful textile industry and many mills and dyeworks operate along the river valley.

In 1977 a survey of the River Holme was carried out by Brown and Bellinger, to assess the effect of persistent textile chemicals and in particular dieldrin in treated sewage effluent discharges.

Only one site, out of 20 sampled, was found not to be polluted by dieldrin. This was situated upstream of textile industry operations. A positive correlation was also observed between textile industry activity and sediment concentrations of dieldrin. The concentrations of dieldrin found in river water ranged from less than 1 ngl^{-1} to 4,900 ngl^{-1}, the latter occurring in the downstream tributaries of the River Holme. Abnormally high concentrations of other textile contaminants were present, and it was inferred that fish reproduction may have been affected. On occasions where sustained concentrations of in excess of 1000 ngl^{-1} of dieldrin were observed, it was concluded that the levels may have contributed to fish and insect mortalities (Brown and Bellinger, 1979).

3.5.2 The Impact of Permethrin-based Mothproofing Agents in the River Clyde Catchment
A rapid switch from the use of traditional mothproofing agents to pyrethroids recently occurred in the UK. This change was mainly due to the emergence of the brown house moth (*Hofmannophila pseudospretalia*) as a serious pest; a species for which pyrethroids provide more effective control than other insecticides.

Within the River Clyde catchment, three companies using permethrin-based mothproofing agents discharged to the main sewer; this sewer in turn discharges to sea. However, under high flow conditions, sewage is discharged to the surface freshwaters in the area via a storm water overflow. According to the Clyde RPB, the River Annick and the River Irvine are polluted by mothproofing agents (permethrin), at levels in excess of those known to be toxic to freshwater life (see *Section 3.3*). A major fish-kill reported for the River Annick, in 1982, was attributed to the discharge of scour waste and dye residues from a textiles factory. A decrease in the diversity of the benthic invertebrate fauna in the River Irvine is also reported to have occurred between 1982 and 1985, and although not conclusively proven, permethrin based mothproofing agents are thought to have contributed to the impacts.

3.5.3 The Effect of Mothproofing Agents on The River Tweed
In 1986, concern was expressed by the Scottish angling community regarding the apparent absence of fly life in the River Tweed and declining trout catches generally. A detailed biological and chemical investigation was conducted by the Tweed RPB and strong circumstantial evidence was found linking the reduction in insect numbers to a discharge from the sewage treatment works at Galashiels. Mothproofing agents were suspected of being the cause of pollution. Increased biological monitoring was instituted to maintain a close watch on this stretch of the river. The following year, 1987, after some initial recovery in the diversity of invertebrates in the watercourse, a signiflcant invertebrate kill occurred, which extended over a distance of approximately 10 miles. Despite exhaustive analysis by Tweed RPBs Laboratory and staff of the Borders Regional Council's Water and Drainage department, no particular pollutant could be directly attributed to the invertebrate kill. No damage to fish was reported. The probable cause was thought to be associated with discharge of industrial biocide (moth proofer).

In 1989 the Regional Council's Water and Drainage department installed an additional filter at the treatment works affected, and at times when routine monitoring now indicates high levels of the moth proofing agent (Cyfluthrin) in the inflow to the works, the sewage is treated with activated carbon. The levels of mothproofing agents in the River Tweed are now within the Environmental Quality Standard 1 ngl^{-1} as 95% tile concentration, (see *Section 4.3*), and according to the Tweed RPB, the river fauna are exhibiting recovery. More recently in 1989 a potential discharge of a Cyfluthrin spill via Galashiels treatment works was successfully averted by implementation of emergency procedures developed to specifically deal with such an eventuality.

A total of 1.5 million gallons of biocide contaminated sewage was contained with no discharge to the river for 17 hours, and then treated with activated carbon to remove Cyfluthrin. A slight reduction in invertebrate numbers was noted downstream of the works, which was probably due to some discharge of contaminated treated sewage prior to containment. Nevertheless, overall it was considered to have been a highly successful operation, since the potential effect on the main mass of invertebrates was averted.

3.5.4 Organochlorine Pesticides in Yorkshire Rivers 1985–1990

Organochlorine pesticides (OCs) occur in the Rivers Aire and Calder in West Yorkshire largely because of emissions from sewage treatment works, which accept effluents from the wool textile industry. There are two sources of OCs within the industry. The first is in effluents from the scouring of raw wool from sheep which may have been treated with OCs to protect them from external parasites; the second is from past use of dieldrin as a mothproofing agent for wool (used primarily in the carpet industry). Dieldrin is very persistent and traces probably still remain in industrial plant and in the sewerage system despite the fact that mothproofing with dieldrin ceased more than 10 years ago.

OCs have also entered the UK environment from the leather industry, from timber preservative treatments and possibly from other sources. The relative contributions of the wool, leather and timber industries to OC levels in the Aire and Calder are unknown.

Since the UK wool textiles industry was made aware in 1987 of the downstream environmental consequences of the presence of pesticides in wool, steps have been taken to reduce the incidence of OCs in raw wools. Bans on the use of this class of pesticide for the treatment of sheep were introduced, and the effectiveness of existing bans was ensured by the NRA and HMIP (see *Section 4*).

A recent IWS Report (Sept, 1990) reviews water quality data for the Rivers Aire and Calder from the NRA Public Register (1985 – 1990). According to the report, no dieldrin concentrations in samples from the Aire between 1985 and 1990 have exceeded the present Environmental Quality Standard (EQS) of 30 ngl^{-1} and only one sample exceeded the EQS of 10 ngl^{-1} which will become operative in 1994. Similarly, concentrations of lindane (mainly gamma-HCH) in the River Calder have been reduced from levels of over 300 ngl^{-1} in 1985 to less than the EQS of 100 ngl^{-1} in 1988 and 1989.

In the River Calder, dieldrin levels were relatively high at the beginning of the period, but even so, the EQS of 30 ng^{-1} was only rarely exceeded. Since 1985, there has been a steady improvement in dieldrin concentrations, and presently the EQS value to be applied from 1994 is seldom exceeded (IWS, 1990).

The improvements observed since 1985 can be ascribed to:

- a virtual cessation of the use of gamma-HCH as a sheep-dip in the countries supplying most of the wool which is scoured in the UK; and,

- the gradual removal from the waste water treatment systems of dieldrin used historically as a mothproofing agent for wool.

According to IWS, in terms of organochlorine pesticides, the objective agreed by the North Sea Conference of reducing inputs of harmful substances to the North Sea to half of their 1985 values, has already been surpassed for these rivers.

4 Potential Water Pollution Causes and Effects

4.1 Existing Legislation

The existing legislation regarding water pollution and the UK textiles industry consists of the following:

- the Water Resources Act, 1991;

- the Environmental Protection Act 1990;

- the Control of Pollution Act (COPA), 1974;

- Rivers (Prevention of Pollution) Scotland Act, 1951;

- the Council Directive 78/659/EEC on the quality of fresh waters needing protection or improvement in order to support fish life;

- the Council Directive 86/80/EEC on limit values and quality objectives for discharges of certain dangerous substances included in List I of the Annex to Directive 76/464/EEC;

- the Council Directive 80/68/EEC on the protection of groundwater against pollution caused by certain dangerous substances;

- the Council Directive 75/440/EEC concerning the quality required of surface water intended for the abstraction of drinking water in the member states.

EEC legislation governing the discharge of organochlorine pesticides to the environment is contained in Directives issued as follows:

- hexachlorocyclohexane (HCH) (84/491/EEC) in 1984;

- DDT and pentachlorophenol (PCP) (86/280/EEC) in 1986; and

- 'drins' (Aldrin, dieldrin, endrin and isodrin) in 1988 (86/280/EEC and 88/347/EEC).

As required by this legislation, UK Water Authorities began to monitor the concentration of certain organochlorine compounds in surface waters in 1985. This is now the responsibility of the National Rivers Authority and HMIP.

4.1.1 The Water Act 1989 and Water Resources Act, 1991

In England and Wales, the control of water pollution was until recently regulated by the Water Act 1989. In Scotland, regulation is provided by equivalent provisions in the amended Control of Pollution Act 1974.

The Water Act was enforced on 6 July 1989. In general terms it had four main effects:

- it restructured the Water Authorities into new water and sewerage companies;

- it provided for the regulation of these and any other water service companies under the Act;

- it established new institutions to regulate the companies and the water environment;

- it amended the law relating to water supply, sewerage and the pollution and abstraction of water.

The Water Resources Act 1991 defines the NRA, in terms of its role, duties and functions. The Act is organised in nine parts. Relevant Parts are: Part I, which deals with the definition of the NRA, its functions and duties; Part II deals with Water Resources Management, including rights of abstraction; Part III deals with water pollution control; subsequent parts deal with flood defence, fisheries, financial provisions and variou.s other aspects.

Part III of the Water Resources Act is arranged in four chapters.

Chapter I deals with Statutory Quality Objectives in terms of classification of waters, water quality objectives and NRAs duties to achieve and maintain these objectives.

Part III, Chapter II provides the basis for pollution control in England and Wales. This Chapter (Sections 85–87) establishes pollution offences for controlled waters (defined in Chapter IV Section 104), and provides uniform protection to surface and ground waters. Consents to discharge are made under Section 88(1) of the Act, and

Schedule 10 of the Act provides the framework for consent applications, their determination, their revocation, alteration or impositions of conditions, and restriction on variation and revocation. Appeals in respect of consents under Section 88(1) can be made under Section 91 of the Act. Section 88(1) lays out defences in relation to authorised discharges. In particular, amongst other defences, discharges to waters may be made in accordance with:

- a consent made under Part 11 of the Control of Water Pollution Act 1974;

- an authorisation for a prescribed process under Part I of the Environmental Protection Act 1990;

- a waste management or disposal licence.

Section 89 outlines defences against prosecution, including 89(1) which deals with emergency discharges.

Sections of Part 111 Chapter 111 of the Act deal with water protection zones (93), nitrate sensitive zones (94–95) and consents made in these zones (96). Part III, Chapter 111, Section 102 provides powers for the Secretary of State to incorporate EC legislation or other international agreements into UK Water Pollution Law.

Section 87(1) of the Water Resources Act deals with discharges from and into public sewers. Section 87(2) provides defences for water companies if contravention of a consent can be shown to have been caused by others or a discharge could not be reasonably prevented from entering a public sewer or works.

Part III, Chapter IV, Section 103 deals with discharges by Water Companies which under the Water Act 1989 were determined by the Secretary of State. Section 103 transfers power of determination to the NRA, where the Secretary of State refers the matter to NRA for determination. In particular paragraphs 2 and 4 of Schedule 13 exempts discharges consented under Section 32 of the Control of Pollution Act Part 11,1974 and Section 113 of the Water Act 1989 from prosecution under Section 85 of the Water Resources Act 1991.

4.1.2 The Environmental Protection Act, 1990

The Environmental Protection Act, 1990 is a further attempt to strengthen areas of pollution control not covered by existing legislation. The issues which will have relevance to freshwater pollution from the UK textiles and woollens industry are detailed below.

A system of Integrated Pollution Control (IPC) has been enacted, which involves HMIP regulating all polluting emissions and discharges from significant industrial process. Discharges to whatever medium from Prescribed Processes now require authorization by HMIP, and the principle of BATNEEC (Best Available Technology Not Entailing Excessive Cost) will apply. This concerns the UK textile industry in that the Prescribed Processes include those used for the treatment or finishing of textiles with a potential to discharge into the water substances which appear on the red list, which includes PCP.

The list of Processes is derived from those which are already controlled by HMIP, and could be extended to include Sewage Treatment Works in line with the draft Waste Water Treatment Directive. Public pressure and environmental legislation of this type will force sewerage undertakings to improve the quality of their discharges and this in turn will force undertakings to control the discharges of trade effluent to sewers more tightly, which implies more pre-treatment or the avoidance of polluting effluent. The speed and the extent to which the pressures and constraints will affect the UK textiles and woollens industry are detailed below.

- As from 1 April 1991, regulations prescribe the industrial processes to fall within IPC and require all new installations and substantially changed existing installations to be subject to authorization, unless approved under an existing statutory system.

- From 1 April 1991, all large combustion plant (those over 50 MW) became subject to IPC. Operators were required within two months to submit an application for IPC authorization.

- IPC will be progressively extended to other existing installations from April 1992 with the target of completion by April 1996.

- Fibres industries IPC individual guidance notes will be introduced in May 1992, and IPC implementation for the industries will be completed by March 1993.

From an environmental standpoint, prevention is normally better than cure. For operators, it is more cost effective and less disruptive to design effective controls and operating procedures into a plant, rather than to face later remedial action and reactive adaptation. It is also better to minimise the creation of waste at source and to encourage recycling whenever practicable and to dispose of the remaining wastes in the most environmentally acceptable way. This thinking lies behind HMIP's approach to its regulatory responsibilities. It is also reflected in the objective outlined in Part 1 of the Environmental Protection Act and which HMIP must have regard to in issuing IPC authorizations. These include the following.

- A general duty on the operator to use best available techniques not entailing excessive cost (BATNEEC). To prevent or minimise releases of prescribed substances, and to render harmless substances which are released.

- Application of the best practicable environmental option (BPEO) to minimise pollution to the environment as a whole.

- Compliance with limits, plans, quality standards and objectives set by the Secretary of State for the Environment.

4.1.3 Control of Pollution Act (COPA), 1974

Consents made under COPA for the textile and woollens industry are now covered by the relevant Section (88) of the Water Resources Act 1991, which supersedes Part II of COPA. This latter re-enacted and extended earlier water pollution controls mainly contained in the Rivers (Prevention of Pollution) Acts 1951–1961 and the Water Resources Act 1963. COPA afforded uniform protection to all surface and underground waters, covered all sources of pollution (regular discharges, isolated acts and accidental contamination), and opened the regulatory system to public involvement.

Section 31 of COPA applies to the control of river pollution in Scotland. An offence is committed by any person who causes or knowingly permits any poisonous, noxious or polluting matter to enter controlled waters. An offence is not made if such an event is authorised by a disposal licence or a consent given by the Secretary of State or a River Purification Board. Section 31 also empowers a River Purification Board to make by-laws to prohibit or regulate the washing or cleaning of specified articles.

4.1.4 Rivers (Prevention of Pollution) Scotland Act, 1951

Section 1 of the 1951 Rivers in Scotland Act, makes it the duty of the Secretary of State to promote cleanliness of the rivers and other inland waters of Scotland. The Secretary of State acts through the Scottish Development Department.

River Purification Boards (as established under Section 135 of the Local Government (Scotland) Act 1973) also have the responsibilities for promoting the cleanliness of rivers and other inland waters and for conserving the water resources of their areas (Section 17). To fulfil these functions they have powers conferred by this Act and also the Control of Pollution Act 1974 (see *Section 4.1.3*).

The powers of the Scottish River Purification Boards (RPB) are similar to those of the statutory water undertakings in England and Wales, with one notable exception. That is, that an RPB has no powers to control abstraction of water. It is understood that the Scottish Development Department is giving further consideration to this, but it is considered likely that any amendments to existing legislation would apply only to abstractions of irrigation water.

4.1.5 EC Directive for Proctection of Freshwater Fish

Directive 78/659/EEC 'on the quality of fresh waters needing protection or improvement in order to support fish life', applies to those fresh waters designated by the Member States as needing protection or improvement to support fish life. Two categories of waters must be designated:

- salmonid waters for salmon, trout and whitefish;

- cyprinid waters for cyprinids and other species (pike, eel etc.)

Imperative and Guide values are specified for 14 physical and chemical parameters for both categories of water; a mandatory value for phenolic compounds is specified, as a concentration that will not adversely affect fish flavour. The Directive also specifies EQS's for zinc and copper, which are both frequently discharged from textile industries.

4.1.6 EC Directive on Dangerous Substances

Directive 76/464/EEC 'on pollution caused by certain dangerous substances discharged into the aquatic environment of the community', is a 'framework' directive which provides for the elimination or reduction of pollution of inland, coastal and territorial waters by particularly dangerous substances by means of 'daughter directives'. Member States are to take appropriate steps to eliminate pollution by substances defined as List I (eg persistent synthetic substances) and to reduce substances defined as List II (eg biocides). The 'Daughter' Directive 86/80/EEC states limit values and quality objectives; particular substances relevant to the textiles industry include lindane, PCP and dieldrin. Subsequent 'daughter' Directives 84/491/EEC (Hexachlorocyclohexane), 86/280/EEC (Pentachlorophenol) and 88/347/EEC and 86/280/EEC (dieldrin) have been introduced to provide controls on these compounds.

4.1.7 EC Directive on Groundwater Quality

Directive 80/68/EEC 'on the protection of groundwater against pollution caused by certain dangerous substances' is designed to prevent or limit the direct or indirect introduction to groundwater of the families or groups of dangerous substances contained on List I (eg persistent synthetic substances) and List II (eg biocides). List I includes lindane, PCP and dieldrin.

4.1.8 EC Directives on Drinking Water

Directive 75/440/EEC 'concerning the quality required of surface water intended for the abstraction of drinking water in the Member states' has two purposes:

- to ensure that surface water abstracted for use as drinking water meets certain standards and is treated adequately before being introduced to the public supply;

- to improve the quality of rivers and other surface waters used as sources of drinking water.

Member States must classify sources of surface water for the abstraction of drinking water by their existing quality into three categories, A1, A2 and A3. For each category, mandatory and guide values are given for 46 determinands, including taste and odour for phenols (maximum admissible concentrations (MAC) $0.5mgl^{-1}$)

Directive 79/869/EEC 'concerning methods of measurement and frequencies of sampling and analysis of surface water intended for the abstraction of drinking water in the Member States' supplements Directive 75/440 by recommending methods of measuring the determinands for surface water quality and setting frequencies for such measurements.

Directive 80/778/EEC 'relating to the quality of water intended for human consumption' sets standards for the quality of drinking water both directly and after treatment. It does not apply to natural mineral waters or medicinal water. Maximum admissible concentration (MAC) levels and guide levels (GL) for 62 determinands and minimum required concentrations (MRC) for four determinands are set.

4.2 Role of the National Rivers Authority, River Purification Boards and HMIP

The National Rivers Authority (NRA), formed in 1989, has responsibilities pertaining to both surface waters and groundwater resources in England and Wales. These include:

- water quality monitoring;

- the setting of lirnits and consents for effluent discharges;

- the control and licensing of water abstractions;

- the protection of water quality for surface and groundwater users;

- enhancement of conservation and recreation in the aquatic environment.

The Scottish River Purification Boards (RPB's) have similar responsibilities to the NRA regarding surface water quality, although no controls over surface and groundwater abstraction formally exist in Scotland.

HMIP currently has the responsibility for monitoring and consenting of all 'red-list' discharges. These are discharges which contain any of the 26 substances identified by the UK Government (1988), from the 129 substances in List 1 (76/464/EEC), for priority action (eg 'drins' and pentachlorophenol).

4.3 Regional Compliance with Existing Legislation

To assess the regional compliance of the UK textiles and woollen industry all regions of the NRA and all Scottish RPBs were consulted. The responses to a detailed ERL questionnaire are presented in Table 4.3a and 4.3b and discussed below.

4.3.1 Effluent Discharge Consents

The majority of effluents from the UK textiles and woollen industry are discharged to foul sewer. No consented discharges to groundwater exist, and consented discharges to surface waters throughout the UK amount to only a small proportion of total emissions.

The number of licensed surface and groundwater abstractions vary considerably from one region to another. Most water abstraction for industrial use in the textiles and woollen industry occurs in the North West and Yorkshire Regions. Elsewhere water consumption is directly from the mains supply. Consultation with the Water Services Association and Water Service plc's indicates that the amount of mains water consumption by the industry is not sufficient to cause indirect water quality impacts; ie where demand exceeds supply. In times of water shortage due to drought conditions, domestic water users are encouraged to conserve water, and industrial supplies are generally unaffected.

Table 4.3a Freshwater Discharges from the UK Textiles and Woollens Industry

UK Region	No. of consented discharges to surface freshwater	No. of consented discharges to groundwaters	No. of licensed surface water abstractions	No. of licensed groundwater abstractions
NRA Anglian Region	0	0	0	0
NRA Northumbrian Region	0	0	0	0
NRA North West	12	0	152	70
NRA Severn-Trent Region	31	0	U/A	U/A
NRA Southern Region	0	0	0	0
NRA South-West Region	2	0	0	0
NRA Thames Region	0	0	0	0
NRA Welsh Region	1	0	2	3
NRA Wessex Region	0	0	3	3
NRA Yorkshire Region	1	0	62	49
Clyde RPB	1	0	N/A	N/A
Forth RPB	1	0	N/A	N/A
Highland RPB	0	0	N/A	N/A
North-East RPB	0	0	N/A	N/A
Solway RPB	0	0	N/A	N/A
Tay RPB	1	0	N/A	N/A
Tweed RPB	0	0	N/A	N/A
Total	**50**	**0**	**219**	**125**

Note: U/A = Data unavailable
N/A = Not applicable due to Scottish Legislation
Sources: Adapted from information supplied by NRA/RPB

4.3.2 Pollution Incidents

The number of pollution incidents associated with discharges from the textiles and woollen industry varies considerably from one region to another. In the North-West Region and in Yorkshire, where the industry is most concentrated, several pollution incidents have occurred during the past 5 years. Elsewhere incidents have been relatively infrequent, and mainly associated with spillages.

In general, there has been a reported decrease in the number of pollution incidents associated with the UK textiles and woollens industry, although in the North-West region, improvements by industry and an increase in the number of pollution incidents notified to the NRA by the public has led to a similar level of pollution incidents being recorded as in previous years.

The number of prosecutions concerning water pollution from the UK textiles and woollen industry have been relatively few during the past 5 years. The greatest number of prosecutions over this period occurred in the Yorkshire and North–West regions (5 to 10, and 5 respectively) with 1 prosecution in the Forth catchment area and 2 in the Severn Trent region.

4.3.3 Other Issues

In addition to consultations with the NRA and RPB's, HMIP and Water Service plc's have been consulted. Particular concern has been expressed over discharges of pentachlorophenol (PCP) to foul sewer.

Discharges of PCP to watercourses have been limited according to the EC Directive 86/280/EEC. In the UK the

Table 4.3b Freshwater Pollution from the UK Textiles and Woollen Industry

UK Region	No. of pollution incidents in the past 5 years	No. of prosecutions associated with the industry in the past 5 years	Increase or decrease in the no. of pollution incidents in recent years
NRA Anglian Region	0	0	N/A
NRA Northumbrian Region	0	0	N/A
NRA North West	Many	5	Neither (improvements by industry but increase in public awareness and reporting of incidents).
NRA Severn-Trent Region	Some, mainly associated with PCP and colour	2	Neither (for direct discharge although the level of colour in sewage treatment works effluent has increased)
NRA Southern Region	0	0	N/A
NRA South-West Region	1	0	Decrease
NRA Thames Region	3 all minor	0	N/A
NRA Welsh Region	0	0	N/A
NRA Wessex Region	0	0	N/A
NRA Yorkshire Region	Many	Between 5 and 10	Decrease
Clyde RPB	1	0	N/A
Forth RPB	3	1	Decrease
Highland RPB	0	0	N/A
North-East RPB	0	0	N/A
Solway RPB	0	0	N/A
Tay RPB	1	0	Increase
Tweed RPB	Some	N/A	Decrease since 1986
Total	**Several**	**Between 13 and 18**	**Decrease**

Note: N/A = Not applicable due to no pollution incidents having recently occurred

Sources: Adapted from information supplied by NRA/RPB

Environmental Quality Standard (EQS) approach has been adopted. The EQS for any watercourse is $2\,\mu gl^{-1}$ of pentachlorophenol. In areas where the industry is concentrated (eg North West and Yorkshire Regions), the watercourses may have background concentrations of $2\,\mu gl^{-1}$ or more (see *Section 3.3*). In such instances pentachlorophenol is no longer permitted in trade effluent discharges to sewer, as it is persistent and not readily biodegraded in the traditional sewage treatment processes. Following discharge, residual levels in the sewage effluent could elevate the levels of PCP in the freshwater environment.

The trade industry associations are pressing for relaxed consent limits, as the technology for waste water treatment to remove PCP is claimed not to be currently available. Furthermore much of the PCP originates from imported grey cloth, from Africa and the Indian sub-continent and the problem is then inherited by UK finishers. The situation is aggravated by the fact that elsewhere in Europe, a uniform emission standard is set for each discharge, with a maximum permissable concentration of PCP (2 mgl^{-1}) in any discharge which effectively results in a relaxed standard relative to the EQS used.

The Water Research Centre has also proposed EQSs (as 95%-iles) of 10 ngl^{-1} permethrin and 1 ngl^{-1} Cyfluthrin for the protection of freshwater life, even though these levels are not detectable by existing methods (Seager and Oakley, 1986).

5 Wastewater Treatment Technology

5.1 Introduction

The batch-wise nature of many textile processes is such that the flow of waste waters is intermittent and variable and only occurs during the working week. The majority of this wastewater is derived from the bleaching, dyeing, printing and finishing-treatments, and the resultant pollution is characterised by two salient features.

- The pollution is often highly diluted due to the massive quantities of rinse water. This makes removal more difficult.

- The water can have intense coloration, the extent of which depends on the dye used and its application technique.

5.2 Use of Chemicals

A wide range of chemicals are used in textiles processing, most of which can be found in the wastewater to various extents. These include:

- dyes discharged in solution, which include the acid, basic, mordant and reactive types;

- dyes discharged in solution, which include the vat, oxidation, disperse, naphthol (soluble at certain pH values) pigment and sulphur types;

- organic acids (usually biodegradable) and inorganic acids;

- alkalis (caustic soda, carbonate);

- oxidants from bleaching (oxygenated water, hypochlorite solution, chlorite or perborate);

- oxidants from dichromates used as developers for certain dyes;

- reducing agents such as sodium hydrosulphite and sulphite;

- adjuvants (wetting agents and detergents);

- mercerizing and finishing products such as starch, alginate, enzymes, and carboxymethyl cellulose; and,

- emulsifiers such as alginates and white spirits which are used in the preparation of printing pastes.

5.3 Combined Effluents

An approximate indication of the pollution load in UK textile mill wastewater is illustrated in Table 5.3a. Generally, the waste is of sewage strength or stronger (based on BOD) and tends to contain a large proportion of nonbiodegradable matter, some of which may be organic matter originating from the raw fibre and dyes. In addition, it is common for the effluent to contain hexavalent chromium (up to 2–3 mgl^{-1}) and this is a major consideration when using biological treatment.

5.4 Wastewater Treatment

The current cost-benefit ratios for advanced water treatments, in plant, are relatively low. As a result, closed cycle treatment systems are being investigated with increasing interest. Recycle treatment systems provide for recovery and reuse of water previously discarded into streams, and enable the reduction of overall effluent quantities. However, it must be recognised that the concept of recycling has limits. It is suitable for lightly contaminated final rinse waters from mercerizing, bleaching and dyeing operations but cannot be applied to heavily contaminated scouring liquors. As a result, this section will discuss both recycling methods, and treatment methods prior to discharge.

5.4.1 Treatment of Mixed Waste Waters before Discharge

Initial treatment will usually comprise fine bar screening (for down and fibres), possible oil, grit and grease, removal stages, and a homogenisation tank Thereafter, a choice must be made as to the process adopted.

Table 5.3a Example Analysis of Mixed Wastewaters from Textile Mills

Nature of the Wastewater	pH	Suspended Solids (mgl⁻¹)	BOD (mgl⁻¹)	COD (mgl⁻¹)
Wool processing (includes grease at 300–2000 (mgl⁻¹)	6–10	20,000	600 – 1,500	N/A
Dyeing and scouring woollen piece goods (includes anionic detergents at 100–200 mgl⁻¹)	4–5	120	360	1,920
Cotton processing	4–12	30–300	100–1,800	N/A
Manufacture and dyeing of Terylene goods	N/A	N/A	3,100	5,300
Dyeing and finishing of piecegoods	6–10.5	90–130	250–300	600–800
Knitting and dyeing a wide range of fibres	N/A	N/A	800	3,500
Weaving, Scouring, dyeing and finishing of synthetic -polymer fibres	10–12	70–80	380	800

Note: N/A = Not available
Adapted from various sources

Physicochemical Treatment

This treatment involves coagulation, flocculation and settling. Chemical coagulants useful in colour removal include lime, aluminium sulphate (alum), ferrous and ferric sulphate, ferric chloride, and polyelectrolytes. Of these, alum is widely used, in particular for disperse, vat and sulphur dyes.

Flocculation provides good odour removal. In addition, COD is lowered, although results are variable. As an example, doses in the range 50 to 150 mgl⁻¹ alum have removed approximately 30 to 50% of the COD in some installations. Addition of a small amount of polyelectrolyte, after treatment with an inorganic coagulant, can produce a smaller volume of settled sludge that can be more easily dewatered.

Separation of the solids may be by settlement or flotation. The resultant sludge is usually unmarketable, of a hydrophillic nature and in need of dewatering (eg by filter press or by centrifugation).

Physicochemical treatment is essential whenever greases or toxic products such as chromium (VI) and sulphides are present. Here, although the presence of Cr (VI) increases the required coagulant dosage for decolouring, it can be almost completely eliminated from the waste water. Flocculants such as iron sulphate reduce Cr (VI) to Cr (III), and permit subsequent alkaline precipitation of $Cr(OH)_3$. This is removed with the sludge.

Generally coagulation is used in conjunction with further treatment at most works. A common practice is the use of biochemical oxidation by activated sludge plant or biological filters. This is discussed below.

Biological Treatment

The most suitable biological treatment techniques for textile wastewaters are activated sludge plants and aerated lagooning. Pretreatment by a physicochemical process is usually necessary, otherwise biologically inert material is absorbed by bacterial solids and the rate of biochemical oxidation is reduced. However, if absorption of coloured materials from wastewaters is not inhibitory to bacteria, biological treatment may be used as a first treatment stage. Degradation rates for BOD can be in the range of 80 to 98% for a sludge loading not exceeding 0.5 kg BOD/kg sludge. In addition, COD demand can be reduced to 80 – 90%.

Biological treatment rarely removes sufficient colour to comply with discharge regulations, as few dyes are biodegradable. If a combination of physicochemical and biological treatment is used, it is usually possible to obtain an effluent from which over 85% of the colour has been removed, and where residual BOD is less than 40 mgl^{-1}. If necessary, this can be further lowered by filter treatment with expanded minerals such as biotite. These substances fix aerobic bacteria in the infrastructures of their surface, and rapidly promote biological action.

Where biological oxidation is used as a primary treatment, removal of coloured material is usually achieved economically by a chemical polishing treatment, as discussed below.

Absorption on Activated Carbon

Activated carbon can effectively remove most soluble dyes. However, its prohibitive capital and regeneration costs usually limit its use to a polishing stage of treatment. Where this treatment is used as a tertiary phase, after physicochemical and biological treatment, an effluent from which all colour has been removed can be obtained.

In some cases, activated carbon is used immediately following flocculation and settling. As illustrated by the Hoechst plant in Griesheim, Germany, some effluents released from the production process (such as benzene derivatives, chlorinated and ester compounds), do not degrade easily and may even be toxic to bacteria. Initial treatment involves mixing powdered activated carbon with the effluent. This is followed by further carbon treatment in a column arrangement. Due to removal rates as high as 80% to 90%, carbon absorption is rapidly achieving recognition as 'the best available technology' for effluents like those found at Griesheim. In particular, its use in eliminating wastes such as phenol derives from its close affinity for compounds containing the benzene carbon ring. Of particular relevance to the UK is the ability of activated carbon to absorb pesticides, including some mothproofing agents.

Problems of interference with the efficiency of carbon adsorption may occur when oils and greases are present, as is the case in the woollens industry.

Chemical Oxidation

A number of powerful oxidising agents are available to destroy the colour of many organic materials. Chlorine is the cheapest, but compounds resulting from chlorination of organic matter are often non-biodegradable, and in some cases are more stable than the initial substance. For this reason, it is advisable to avoid the use of high concentrations of chlorine for reduction of the colour of wastewaters.

Alternative oxidising agents include hydrogen peroxide and ozone, of which ozone is the most frequently used material. Studies have shown that ozone is highly effective in removing colour. Disadvantages are that COD reduction is poor and that the ozone plant is expensive to install and operate. Ozonation may find application as a pretreatment stage prior to biological treatment, or as a sterilisation step after carbon absorption for particularly difficult wastes. Although some pesticides are little affected by ozone (eg dieldrin and HCH), other organo-chlorinated formulations (eg Aldrin) can be destroyed. In addition, ozone administered under the correct conditions of pH and concentration can destroy phenol and phenolic compounds.

Membrane Filtration

Membrane filters are rarely used for wastewater treatment in the UK textiles and woollens industry, due to their prohibitive costs. To date, applications of this technology have limited themselves to those where the material of value can be recovered as a concentrate. Further research is required to reduce costs and improve rates of separation. If these aims are achieved, it may be possible to use membrane filtration as a primary effluent treatment, or as the sole treatment for recycle water.

5.4.2 Recycling of Mixed Waters Before Discharge to Sewer

Four different recycling methods are available:

- evaporation;

- microfiltration;

- ultrafiltration; and

- reverse osmosis.

Evaporation

Evaporation is a process whereby waste water is boiled, enabling pure water to be condensed for recycling as hot water. Although process materials are not always recovered, solids in the wastewater are concentrated, reducing the volume and enabling easier handling. For textile wastewater treatment, the energy cost of evaporation is only justified when the concentrate is reusable. In addition, scale formation may present a major obstacle to the efficient operation of the evaporator.

Microfiltration

Microfiltration is a physical separation process which removes suspended solids from waste systems. The process is used when:

- suspended solids are undesirable in the recovery and reuse of waste water;
- suspended solids interfere with the operation of other advanced waste water treatment processes;
- the effluent is unsuitable for disposal in a receiving stream; or
- the suspended solids are valuable and recoverable for use.

Microfiltration is applicable only for clarification of slightly polluted water.

Ultrafiltration

Ultrafiltration (UF) is a pressure-driven separation process whereby waste systems are filtered by microporous membranes. These membranes remove macromolecules, colloids and suspended solids. The result of ultrafiltration is that the feed stream is separated into two streams, one proportion purified water or permeate, and the other a concentrate containing a high concentration of separated impurities. To date, the main application for UF has been where valuable components of the waste stream can be recovered. For example, UF has been used in textile wet processing to concentrate and recover polyvinyl alcohol sizing material from the desize waste system.

Reverse Osmosis

Reverse osmosis is a process whereby a feed system under pressure is passed across the surface of a membrane. A proportion of the permeate is forced through the membrane and leaves behind most of the solute. In addition, all suspended materials remain, and with the solute, form a concentrated stream. An application of this process in the textile industry has been the recovery of caustic soda from the mercerizing process.

6 Potential Areas for Further Research

6.1 Introduction

Sections 6.2 and *6.3* highlight areas where existing information is limited, and where further research may reduce the amount of freshwater pollution from the UK textiles and woollens industry.

6.2 Freshwater Pollution

The areas of potential research into freshwater pollution causes and effects are listed below:

- detailed research into the effects of mothproofing agents on sewage treatment processes;

- research into the effectiveness of alternative mothproofing agents to those which currently exist;

- an assessment of whether the import of cloth contaminated by controlled substances could be prevented in the UK or EC, and an indication of suitable methods.

6.3 Technological Advancement

The areas of potential research concerning new technologies in the UK textiles and woollens industries are detailed below:

- colour removal from textile wastewater;

- advanced treatment processes for the removal of mothproofing agents from textile effluents; and

- the development of alternative methods of applying mothproofing agents to textiles which would result in a reduction of impact on the aquatic environment.

Disposal options currently available for an effluent that cannot be legally discharged to a waterway, or that is too contaminated/expensive to send to local sewage works are decreasing. In-house biological treatment is becoming an increasingly competitive option for toxic effluents due to:

- moves by the EEC to limit the disposal of liquids to landfill;

- the high transportation and operational costs of incineration; and

- North Sea dumping bans by 1993.

A recent approach patented in the UK by the University of Kent is to develop a stable mixed microbial culture, which is able to degrade all the components in a speciflc effluent stream. The basis of these 'microbial custom blends' has been derived from detailed studies of enzyme action and metabolic routes. The resultant understanding has paved the way for the development of processes to degrade previously untreated compounds.

The stages in designing a custom blend are detailed below.

- Laboratory identification of the main components of the effluent is necessary, followed by isolation of the particular microbes which are capable of degrading or transforming them. The isolates are then combined to give an inoculum for continuous culture.

- The culture is grown in a synthetic substrate of readily biodegradable components. Gradual introduction of more toxic components enables the culture to adapt until it can biodegrade all components of the waste. In addition, exposure of the system to higher-than-normal concentrations of toxic compounds allows the culture to withstand variations in effluent compositions.

- The stable effluent is transferred to a bench-scale bioreactor prior to pilot scale trials on actual effluent. These trials demonstrate the effectiveness of the microbes in the process and provide data for full-scale plant design.

The custom blend process has been shown to biodegrade both phenol and pentachlorophenol, both of which can be toxic constituents of textile effluent.

Two further innovations in multi-component waste water treatment involve liquid-liquid separation and incineration. These are discussed below.

6.3.1 Liquid-liquid Separation

This method is being developed to remove coloured dyes from waste effluents. It incorporates micellar aggregation and ultrafiltration, and has the benefit of reusing detergents used in dyeing and scouring.

The process is successful in removing ionic dyes from textile effluents when the dyes are incorporated into the micellar structure. Entrapment of coloured particles in ionic micelles permits enlargement of the molecular size of the compound to be removed, and results in an inability for the substance to pass through the membrane. Optimisation of the process occurs when dye and surfactant ions bear charges of opposite sign.

Where adsorption of the surfactant onto the membrane surface occurs, the use of a membrane of higher cut-off than the mean micellar molecular weight may be considered.

6.3.2 Incineration

Incineration may be required as pretreatment for wastewater streams which are heavily loaded with organics, ie, over 50 g COD l^{-1}. The aim is usually to reduce the feed stream to less than 2.5 mg COD l^{-1} before biological processing.

In practice, incineration completely destroys the organics to carbon dioxide and water. This is a form of complete treatment, and as with most processes of this type, incineration has inherent problems. In particular, high transportation and energy costs can make incineration prohibitive.

7 Conclusions

The most significant area of recognised concern over freshwater pollution from the UK textiles and woollens industry relates to the toxicity of organic mothproofing agents to aquatic fauna.

Concerns over other possible pollutants, including chromium, dye constituents, and bleaching agents, have received much less attention recently, due to the following factors.

- The treatability of these other wastewater contaminants arising from the UK textiles and woollens industry is generally good.

- The ecotoxicities of other wastewater contaminants arising from the UK textiles and woollens industry are generally lower than those for organic mothproofing agents.

- The adoption of an Environmental Quality Standard (EQS) approach for the concentrations of organic mothproofing agents in the UK has created problems for the UK textiles industry. This is due to the difficulty in meeting limits which would effectively preclude the discharge of such substances, because of their presence in the water from diffuse sources, and their presence in sediments contaminated by historical discharges.

- Concerns over the inherent problems of pollutants (eg PCP) in imported grey cloth.

It is not yet clear whether the import of cloth contaminated by controlled substances can be prevented in the UK or EC. As far as we have been able to ascertain, other than a declaration by the receiving industry that to their knowledge the cloth is free of contamination, no enforcement controls on contaminated cloth entering the UK presently exist.

A further concern is that any sampling of imported cloth for analysis of the concentration of mothproofing agents present may not be representative. A total ban on the import of cloth from countries suspected of supplying contaminated material is a potential means by which subsequent impacts to the freshwater environment may be reduced. However, this could have far reaching effects on the UK industry and on the economy of the supplying nations, many of which are in a poor economic state. Furthermore, it is not clear how much contaminated cloth would be present within the UK already if a ban on imports was now enforced. It would, therefore, be difficult to set a period of time for relaxation of the controls, to allow for stocks to be utilised, whilst showing commitment to effective controls.

Little freshwater pollution from direct discharges to watercourses has been associated with the UK textiles and woollens industry over the past five years, as most discharges are made to foul sewer. In areas where the industry is concentrated (Yorkshire and the North-West) elevated levels of contaminants in the river water downstream of sewage treatment works have led to strict limits on the quantity of mothproofing agents in trade effluent discharged to sewer. According to the trade industry association of the UK textiles and woollens industry, the treatment technology is not as advanced as would be required to comply with the existing legislation. As a result of the technical problems of compliance with discharge consents (eg due to use of EQS approach and import of grey cloth), the Textile Finishers Association is advising members to appeal to the Secretary of State for relaxed consent conditions.

It is suspected, although it would be extremely difficult to establish, that the illicit use of certain banned pesticides (eg dieldrin) may have occurred in the past. Due to the persistence of such compounds in the environment, the levels in some UK freshwaters are still considerably elevated even though widespread use has been discontinued for several years. Due to this persistence, it would be wrong to conclude that such pesticides have been used recently.

The fashion for textiles has until recently been dominated by coloured materials with special finishes, for convenience. Most consumers take for granted the fact that items purchased are durable and protected from moth-damage.

However, recent trends appear to be towards natural materials, such as cotton or wool. Whether these products become future market leaders is dependent on a number of factors eg:

- cost of the product;

- whether the product is washable, or requires special treatment;

- whether the product is as durable as current alternatives.

Media concern in relation to environmental issues is high and it is quite possible that in the future, consumer pressure and preference may encourage the production of more 'environmentally friendly' textiles than those which are readily available at present.

The future of controls on freshwater pollution in the UK should be seen in the context of the longer term aims of the European Community, whereby similar standards of water quality are expected throughout the Member States, and similar enforcement procedures will be applied. When harmonisation of standards and procedures have been adopted, pollution control measures will be consistent throughout the Member States. Such harmonised pollution control may be more acceptable to those industries concerned.

Research in the following areas is recommended to focus on certain aspects relating to freshwater pollution from the UK textiles and woollens industry:

- research into better analytical methods of detection of small quantities of mothproofing agents;

- detailed research into the effects and fate of mothproofing agents in sewage treatment processes;

- advanced treatment processes (eg custom blends of bacteria) for the removal of mothproofing agents from textile effluents should be examined;

- the development of alternative methods of applying mothproofing agents to textiles, which would result in a reduction of impact to the aquatic environment;

- research into technical means for the removal of colour from textile wastewater; and,

- a rigorous programme of testing (eg toxicity, persistence, biodegradability) of all new mothproofing agents before commercial release.

The priority research should be directed towards reducing the actual emission rates of organic mothproofing agents to the aquatic environment.

Bibliography

ALLANACH D (1990) **The Insect Resist Treatment of Carpet Yarns using Low Volume Zero Pollution Technology**. In Proc. 8th. Int. Wool Text. Res. Conf. **IV**: 568–577

ANDERSON R L (1982) **Toxicity of fenvalerate and permethrin to several non-target Aquatic Invertebrates** Envir. Entomol **9**: 436–439.

BAILEY R E, GONSLOR S J and RHINEHART W L (1983) **Biodegradation of Monochlorobiphenyls and Biphenyls in river water.** Environ. Sci. Technol. **17**: 617–621.

BROWN D. (1987) **Effects of Colorants in the Aquatic Environment**. Ecotoxicology and Environmental Safety **13**: 139–147.

BROWN J F, WAGNER R E, BEDARD D L, BRENNAM M J, CARNAHAM J C, MAY R J and TOFFLEMINE T J (1989) **PCB transfonnation in Hudson sediments**. Northeast. Environ. Sci. **3**: 167–179.

BROWN L and BELLINGER Eg (1979) **Dieldrin Pollution in the River Holme Catchment, Yorkshire**. Environ Pollution **18**: 203–211.

BROWNAWELL B J and FARRINGTON J W (1986) **Biogeochemistry of PCBs in interstitial waters of a coastal marine sediment.** Geochem. Cosmochim. Acta **50**: 157–169.

CHEMIEFASERN TEXTILINDUSTRIE (1988) *UK:* **Top ten textiles companies** Vol: February: **89**.

CHEMIEFASERN TEXTILINDUSTRIE (1989) **Industrilever-branch (mill consumption) von Textilefasern 1987** Vol: April: **326**

CHERNIEFASERN TEXTILINDUSTRIE (1989) **Textilindustrie 1988**. Vol: Sept: **896**.

COATS J R *et al* (1989) **Toxicology of Synthetic Pyrethroids in Aquatic Organisms: An overview**. Environmental Toxicology and Chemistry, Vol. **8**: 671–679.

DUFFIELD P A *et al* (1990) **Wool Dyeing with Environmentally Acceptable Levels of Chromium in Effluent**. In Proc. 8th Int. Wool Text. Res. Conf. Vol **IV**: 97–106.

DUFOUR A P and CABELLI V J (1976) **Characteristics of Klebsiella from textile finishing plant effluents**. Journal WPCF **Vol. 48, No. 5**: 872–879.

ECONOMIST (1988) **After the recovery**. October 21st: 83–84.

EEC, (1984) **Council Directive 84/491/EEC, on limit values and quality objectives for discharges of hexachlorohexane** (9 October 1984).

EEC (1986) **Council Directive 86/280/EEC, on limit values and quality objectives for discharges of certain substances included in List I of the Annex to Directive 76/464/EEC, II. Specific provisions relating to DDT; III. Specific provisions relating to pentachlorophenol** (12 June 1986).

EEC, (1988) **Council Directive 88/347/EEC, amending Annex II to Directive 86/280/EEC on limit values and quality objectives for discharges of certain substances included in List I of the Annex to Directive 76/464/EEC, IV. Specific provisions relating to aldrin, dieldrin, endrin and isodrin** (16 June 1988).

EVINS C (1981) **A new substance for controlling animals in mains**. Water Services **85**: 280–289.

FAZULLINA P *et al* (1989) **Removal of Chromium compounds in the process of coagulation treatment of wool industry dyeing-finishing plant waste water**. Soviet Journal of Water Chemistry and Technology: 85–88.

GARDINER D K and BORNIE B J (1978) **Textile Waste Waters: Treatment and Environmental Effects**. JSDC August: 339–348.

GLICKMAN A H *et al* (1981) **Elimination and metabolism of permethrin isomers in rainbow trout**. Toxicol. Appl. Pharmacol. **57**: 88–98.

GOHE E P G and VILENSKY L C (1980) **Textile Science. An explanation of Fibre Properties**. Longman, Cheshire Pty Ltd.

GUPTA P K and DURVE V S (1986) **A study of the temperature dependence of the Acute toxicity of pentachlorophenol to a freshwater pond snail,** *Viviparus bengalensis l.* Revista de Biologia, **13**:103–112.

HANSCH C (1979) **Substituent constants for correlation analysis in chemistry and biology.** Wiley Interscience, New York.

HELLAWELL J M (1986) **Biological Indicators of Freshwater Pollution and Environmental Management**. Elsevier Applied Science Publishers.

HER MAJESTY'S INSPECTORATE OF POLLUTION (1990) pers. com.

HOLME I (1990) **Are Textiles Finishing the Environment?** International Dyer and Textile Printer, April: 17–24.

INTERNATIONAL WOOL SECRETARIAT (1989) Wool Facts 1989.

INTERNATIONAL WOOL SECRETARIAT (1990) **Organochlorine pesticides in Yorkshire rivers** 1985–1990. TIL/ET–5.

JAKOBI G and LÖHR A (1987) **Detergents and Textile Washing, Principles and Practice**. VCH Publishers.

KAWAMOTO K and URANE K (1989) **Parameters for predicting hte of organochlorine pesticides in the environment (I) Octanol-Water and AirWater partition coefficients**. Chemosphere, Vol. **18**, Nos. 9/10:1987–1996.

KEATING M I (1980) **Gas Liquid Chromatographic Determination of Dioxathion and Quintiofos in Organophosphorus Dip Washes**. J. Assoc. Off. Anal. Chem. Vol **63**, No. 1; 33–36.

KEILTY T J *et al* (1988) **Sublethal responses to endrin in sediment by Limnodrilus hoffmeistei; (Tubificidae), and in mixed culture with Stylodrilus heringianus (Lumbriculidae)**. Aquatic Toxicology **13**, No. 3: 227–249.

KRAMRISE B (1990) **Mothprooflng – the way forward** International Dyer and Textile Printer: **8**.

LEMORDANT D *et al* (1988) **Colour removal from textile effluents.** Textile month, Nov: 41–44.

LODGE K B and COOK P M (1989) **Partitioning studies of dioxin between sediment and water: the measurement of K$_{oc}$ for Lake Ontario sediment.** *Chemosphere* **19**: 439–444.

LYLE D 5 (1982) **Modern Textiles**. 2nd Edn. John Wiley and Sons.

MACKAY D and POWERS B (1987) **Sorption of hydrophobic chemicals from water: a hypothesis for the mechanism of the particle concentration effect.** *Chemosphere* **16**: 667–679.

MARKET LETTER (1990) **The UK's Top 10, Vol: Jan: 22**.

MARTINDALE R R and LANE G. (1989) **Trade Effluent Control: Prospects for the 1990s** J. IWEM, **3**: 387–396.

MASON Y *et al* (1990) **Carbamate Insecticides: Removal from Water by chlorination and ozonation**. Wat. Res. Vol **24 No. 1**: 11–21.

MCELROY A E, FARRINGTON, J W and TEAL J M (1989) **Bioavailability of polycyclic aromatic hydrocarbons in the aquatic environment.** In: Metabolism of PAH in the aquatic environment pp 1–39.

MIKESELL M D and BOYD S A (1985) **Reductive dechlorination of the pesticides 2, 3–D, 2, 4, 5–T and Pentachlorophenol in Anaerobic sludges.** *J. Environ.Qual.*, **Vol. 14, No. 3**: 337–340.

OECD (1981) **Test Guideline 203 for measurement of fish toxicity.**

OECD (1984) **The registration inhibition test for measurement of bacterial toxicity.**

OPIE R (1990) **Industrial Wastewater processing at its toughest.** World Water, April: 4244.

OTHMER K (1981) **Encylopaedia of Chemical Technology. Vol. 22.**

POLLUTION RESEARCH GROUP, Dept, of Chemical Engr. Univ. Of Natal, Durban, S. Africa (1988) **Closed Loop Recycling of Textile Sizing/Desizing Effluents.** American Dyestuff Reporter. October **88**: 26–53.

PORTER J J and SNIDER E H (1976) **Long-term biodegradability of textile chemicals.** Journal WPCF **Vol 48,** No. 9: 2198–2210.

RAWLINGS G C and SAMFIELD M (1979) **Textile plant wastewater toxicity.** Environmental Science and Technology **13**, No. 2: 160–164.

READMAN J W, MANTOURA R F C, RHEAD M M and BROWN L (1982) **Aquatic distribution and heterotrophic degradation of PAH in the Tamar Estuary.** Estuar. Coast Shelf Sci. **14**: 369–389.

RIVETT D E *et al* (1990) **New Initiatives in Mothproofing.** In Proc. 8th. Int. Wool Text. Res. Conf. **IV**: 548–557.

ROGERS H R *et al* (1989) **The Occurrence of Chlorobenzenes and Permethrins in Twelve UK Sewage Sludges.** Wat. Res. **Vol. 23**, No. 7: 913921.

ROTH G, OELLERMANN R A and ODHAV B (1989) **Bacteria in the aerobic biodegradation of wool scouring effluent.** Water S.A. **Vol. 15**, No. 4: 209–220.

RUSSELL I M (1990) **Cycloprothrin, an Environmentally safer pyrethroid for industrial insect resist treatment of wool?** In Proc. 8th, Int. Wool. Text. Res. Conf. **IV**: 606–615.

SAX N 1(1979) **Dangerous Properties of Industrial Materials** Van Nostrand Rheinhold, New York 1118p.

SHAW T (1990) **Environmental Issues in the Wool Textile Industry.** In Proc. 8th. Int. Wool Text. Res. Conf. **IV**: 533–547.

SHAW T (1990) **Environmental Issues in the UK wool Textile Industry.** Unpublished report presented at the Textile Institute Floor coverings Group serninar, October 1990.

SHAW T and ALLANACH D (1990) **Mothproofing and the Environment.** Unpublished.

SHUTTLEWORTH Dr A J (1990) **Trade Effluent Control and the textile industry.** Unpublished.

SMITH B F and BLOCK I (1982) **Textiles in Perspective.** Prentice-Hall Inc.

SOHAIR I A and WAHAAB R Sh. A (1988) **Fish Toxicity Bioassays of textile Wastewaters using Nile Bulti.** Environmental Technology Letters, Vol 9: 1147–1152.

STEHLY G R and HAYTON W L (1989) **Disposition of pentachlorophenol is rainbow trout** (*Salmo gairdneri*): effect of inhibition of metabolism. Aquatic Toxicology, **14**: 131–147.

STEPHENSON R R (1982) **Aquatic toxicology of cypermethrin. I. Acute toxicity to some freshwater fish and invertebrates in laboratory tests.** Aquat. Toxicol. **2**:175–185.

SULFITA J M ROBINSON J A and TIEDJE J M (1983) **Kinetics of microbial dehalogenation of haloaromatic substrates in methanogenic environments.** Appl. Envir. Microbiol. **45**:1466–1473.

TAYLOR D S (1986) **Wool technologies – present and future** Textile Month, June: 37–42.

Textiles Organon, (1989) Pers. Comm.
THE CONFEDERATION OF BRITISH WOOL TEXTILES LIMITED **(1989) Wool Industry Bureau of Statistics**, Monthly Bulletin 482.

THE TEXTILE FINISHERS ASSOCIATION (1990) **July Newsletter**.

THE TIMES (1988) **Textiles Year of Expansion**. April 25:25

TORTORA P G (1987) **Understanding Textiles**. 3rd Edn. Collier Macmillian Publishers.

US DEPARTMENT OF THE INTERIOR (1987) **Measuring damages to Coastal and Marine Natural Resources.** Volume II.

WATERS B D (1979) **Treatment of Dyewaste**. Wat. Pollut. Control: 12–26.

WIMBUSH J M (1990) **Pentachlorophenol in Wool Carpets – Investigating the source of contamination.** In Proc. 8th. Int. Wool. Text. Res. Conf. Vol **IV**:

XIE T M, ABRAHAMSSON K, FOGELQUIST E and JOSEFSSON B (1986) **Distribution of chlorophenslics in a marine environment.** Environ. Sci. Technol. **20**: 457–63.

Regional Consent Limit Conditions for Discharges to Freshwater

Table 1a   Typical Range of Regional Consent Limit Conditions for Discharges to Freshwater from the UK Textiles and Woollens Industry

	SS at 105°C	BOD	Cr (sol)	Zn (tot)	NH₃	Tot P	Hydro-carbons	Temp °C
NRA Anglian Region	N/A	N/A	N/A	N/A	N/A	N/A	N/A	N/A
NRA Northumbrian Region	N/A	N/A	N/A	N/A	N/A	N/A	N/A	N/A
NRA North-West	45 to 100	10 to 70	–	–	–	–	–	26 to 30
NRA Sevem-Trent Region	49 to 75	10 to 44	–	–	–	–	–	26
NRA Southern Region	N/A	N/A	N/A	N/A	N/A	N/A	N/A	N/A
NRA South-West Region	35	25	–	–	5	–	–	21.5
NRA Thames Region	N/A	N/A	N/A	N/A	N/A	N/A	N/A	N/A
NRA Welsh Region	100	4500	–	–	5	–	–	–
NRA Wessex Region	N/A	N/A	N/A	N/A	N/A	N/A	N/A	N/A
NRA Yorkshire Region	30	20	–	–	–	–	–	–
Clyde RPB Region	N/A	N/A	N/A	N/A	N/A	N/A	N/A	N/A
Forth RPB	30 to 45	20 to 30	0.4	0.5 to 1.0	5.0 to 12.0	3.0	None visible	–
Highland RPB	N/A	N/A	N/A	N/A	N/A	N/A	N/A	N/A
North-East RPB	N/A	N/A	N/A	N/A	N/A	N/A	N/A	N/A
Solway RPB	N/A	N/A	N/A	N/A	N/A	N/A	N/A	N/A
Tay RPB	100	100	1.0	3.0	–	–	–	25
Tweed RPB	N/A	N/A	N/A	N/A	N/A	N/A	N/A	N/A

Note: SS = Suspended Solids   Zn = Zinc
         BOD = Biochemical Oxygen Demand   NH₃ = Ammonia
         Cr = Chromium   Tot P = Total phosphorus

All units are in mgl⁻¹ unless otherwise stated.
–   = No limit value indicated
N/A = Not applicable due to no notified consents
Source: Adapted from information supplied by NRA/RPBS

Table 1b Typical Range of Regional Consent Limit Conditions for Discharges to Freshwaters from the UK Textiles and Woollens Industry: other parameters

	pH	Chlor	PV	Oil	COD	Abs	Anionic and Nonionic detergents	Phenols
NRA Anglian Region	N/A	N/A	N/A	N/A	N/A	N/A	N/A	N/A
NRA Northumbrian Region	N/A	N/A	N/A	N/A	N/A	N/A	N/A	N/A
NRA North-West	<5 to >9	1.6	110 to 80	5	–	–	–	–
NRA Sevem-Trent Region	<5 to >9	0.2	–	–	–	–	–	–
NRA Southern Region	N/A	N/A	N/A	N/A	N/A	N/A	N/A	N/A
NRA South-West Region	<6 to >9	0.5	–	–	–	0.1	15	0.5
NRA Thames Region	N/A	N/A	N/A	N/A	N/A	N/A	N/A	N/A
NRA Welsh Region	<4 to >9	–	–	–	9000	–	–	–
NRA Wessex Region	N/A	N/A	N/A	N/A	N/A	N/A	N/A	N/A
NRA Yorkshire Region	<6 to >8	–	–	–	–	–	–	–
Clyde RPB	N/A	N/A	N/A	N/A	N/A	N/A	N/A	N/A
Forth RPB	N/A	N/A	N/A	N/A	N/A	N/A	N/A	N/A
Highland RPB	N/A	N/A	N/A	N/A	N/A	N/A	N/A	N/A
North-East Region	N/A	N/A	N/A	N/A	N/A	N/A	N/A	N/A
Solway RPB	N/A	N/A	N/A	N/A	N/A	N/A	N/A	N/A
Tay RPB	<5 to >9	1.0	–	No visible trace	–	–	10.0	
Tweed RPB	N/A	N/A	N/A	N/A	N/A	N/A	N/A	N/A

Source: Adapted from information supplied by NRA/RPBS

Note: Chlor = Chloride
      COD = Chemical Oxygen Demand
      Abs = Absorbance
      PV = Permanganate value

All units are in mgl^{-1} unless otherwise stated.
– = No limit value indicated
N/A = Not applicable due to no notified consents

235

Pollution Impact of Transport

December 1991

Environmental Resources Limited

Acknowledgements:

ERL would like to thank the Staff and
members of the Royal Commission on
Environmental Pollution and the various
regions and individuals of the National
Rivers Authority and River Purification
Boards for their help in carrying out this
study. We also wish to thank the Trade
Associations who helped us complete this
Report.

Authors: S J Longhurst and J V Towner

Contents

1 Introduction

1.1 Background

Environmental Resources Ltd (ERL) has been contracted by the Royal Commission on Environmental Pollution to carry out an assessment, and prepare a report of its findings, into freshwater pollution from transport (road, rail, aviation and inland waterways).

1.2 Objectives

The overall objective of this study was to support the Royal Commission in carrying out its current study on freshwater pollution, of which transport is one aspect. Within this objective, there were the following tasks:

- to review background information on pollution sources;

- to define, on a regional and national basis, the composition and quantities of emissions discharged to the aquatic environment;

- to carry out an aquatic impact, pathway and facts review for each of the major pollutants;

- to provide an account of the mechanisms and processes that give rise to transport pollution;

- to carry out a generic regulatory review to identify the relevant statutory and legislative controls on water pollution;

- to draw conclusions as to whether transport pollution in the UK is increasing or decreasing, and to suggest possible technical, legislative or policy measures to reduce freshwater pollution from transport.

1.3 Sources of Information

The major sources of information used in carrying out this study are discussed below.

- *National Rivers Authority (NRA);* all ten regions of the NRA in England and Wales were consulted via a questionnaire survey.

- *River Purification Boards (RPB);* all seven RPB's in Scotland were consulted with the same questionnaire as the NRA.

- *Department of Transport (DTp);* many publications from DTp were useful source documents on transport in the UK, and several scientific reports from their research laboratory (TRRL) were useful references on road pollution.

- *Highway Authorities;* several highway authorities were consulted for local information.

- *Fire Services;* several Fire Services were consulted for information relating to accidents.

- *British Waterways Board (BWB);* several publications of BWB were useful source documents in relation to water pollution from boats.

- *Department of the Environment (DoE);* the Drinking Water Department of the DoE provided useful information on potable water quality.

- *Scientific Literature;* a thorough search of the scientific literature was carried out, using library services of the British Library, U K universities, the Water Research Centre, and the Transport and Road Research Laboratory.

1.4 Organisation of the Report

There is a considerable body of published literature on transport pollution, but with a large bias towards roads. Much of the research has been carried out in the USA, the UK and West Germany. Where possible, we have made most use of the U K publications in this report, since the differences in vehicle types, fuel, drainage systems and pollution legislation between countries reduce the relevance of many other publications.

This report contains five further sections, organised as follows.

- *Section 2* reviews the UK transport infrastructure (road, rail, air and inland water) including regional distribution; size; use; future changes; and accident statistics.

- *Section 3* discusses transport pollution in terms of its sources; the types of pollutant; the quantities emitted; their fate in the aquatic environment; their aquatic toxicology; and presents some case studies to highlight the preceding discussion.

- *Section 4* discusses the existing pollution control measures, including legislation; regulatory authorities; a review of regional pollution control enforcement and compliance; and identifies areas of particular concern.

- *Section 5* presents particular aspects of transport pollution where there are significant gaps in available information and where further research could therefore be helpful.

- *Section 6* summarises the key conclusions and recommendations of this study.

2 The Transport Infrastructure and its use

2.1 Introduction

2.1.1 General

The four main modes of travel in the U K are road, rail, air and inland waterways, providing both public and private means of transport, and the movement of freight. Much of the basic infrastructure has been in place for many years, but its expansion and modification is continually developing. These works include both privately and publicly funded schemes, such as the Channel Tunnel and its rail link to London; new motorways, trunk and minor roads; widening of, and extensions to, existing motorways; expansion of airport capacity; new electric 'trams' in large towns; improvements to navigable waterways; and new underground rail facilities.

The basic philosophy underlying these changes are the fundamental aims of the Government's transport policy: 'to promote economic growth and higher national prosperity and to ensure a reasonable level of personal mobility, while improving safety, conserving and enhancing the environment, and using energy economically' (Foreign & Commonwealth Office, 1991). It is of particular note however that, in the Department of Transport's standard on environmental assessment of trunk road schemes (Department of Transport, 1989), the Department states that 'Individual highway schemes do not have a significant effect on climatic factors and, in most cases, are unlikely to have significant effects on soil or water.' This is a statement which differs substantially from the tone of the EC Directive, which requires the following roads to have an EA, and by inference to have potentially significant effects on the environment: new motorways, 'Special Roads', trunk roads over 10 km in length, certain other trunk roads and certain other road improvements. The Department's statement is also one which reflects the traditional view of transport pollution, but is one which is rapidly becoming replaced with considerable concern over certain aspects of environmental impact from transport schemes, including the aquatic impact of road, rail and airport runoff. However, following the Department's attitude, little importance is placed on protection of the water environment during new road planning and construction.

2.1.2 Use and Economics

It is generally considered, that between 1978 and 1989, passenger travel in Great Britain increased by 30% (Foreign & Commonwealth Office, 1991). About 95% of transport is provided by the private sector. This proportion has increased with the privatisation of the Government's shareholdings in a number of publicly owned transport undertakings, including road haulage, airline services, airports and bus operations. It is estimated that in Britain in 1988, users' expenditure (including taxation) on transport totalled £86,600 million, of which £71,500 million represented expenditure on road transport (including buses).

2.2 Roads

2.2.1 Road Length and Use

In 1989, the road network in Britain totalled about 380,400km (236,400 miles). Of this length, about 16,000km (9,940 miles) were trunk roads[1], including about 3,000km (1,860 miles) of trunk motorways. A breakdown of these figures by region, is given in Table 2.2a.

The total road mileage in 1989 increased by 6% to a total of about 390,000 million vehicle–km. Although motorways and trunk roads account for less than 5% of road mileage, they carry about 30% of road traffic, including more than 50% of heavy goods vehicle traffic. Traffic on these roads has been growing at a much higher rate than on other roads.

2.2.2 Vehicle Ownership

At the end of 1989 there was a total of 24.2 million vehicles licensed for British roads, of which more than 80% were cars (see Table 2.2b).

Car ownership has risen substantially, with 66% of households having the regular use of one or more cars, and 18%, having the use of two or more cars.

---

[1] Trunk roads are those which come under the responsibility of the Secretary of State.

Table 2.2a Road Length (km) in Britain (as at April 1989)

Region	Total, public roads	Trunk roads, including motorways	Trunk motorways
England	271 615	10 380	2 536
Scotland	51 466	3 165	234
Wales	33 216	1 699	120
Northern Ireland	24 081	256	112
Total in Britain	**380 378**	**15 950**	**3 002**

Source: Foreign and Commonwealth Office (1991)

Table 2.2b Number of Vehicles Licensed for use on British Roads (at the end of 1989)

Type of Vehicle	Number
Cars	19.7 million (including more than 2 million 'company' cars
Light Goods Vehicles	2 million
Other Good Vehicles	644 000
Motor cycles, scooters and mopeds	875 000
Public transport vehicles (including taxis)	122 000
Total	**24.2 million**

Source: Foreign and Commonwealth Office (1991)

2.2.3 Passenger Travel

Car and taxi travel in Britain account for 84% of the total passenger mileage, whilst buses and coaches account for only 7%.

Between 1978 and 1989, travel by car and taxi increased by 43%; travel by motorcycle has been declining, and travel by bus, coach and pedal cycle has changed little.

2.2.4 Freight

Road haulage is the principal means of freight transport in Britain, representing about 82% of total tonnage carried, and almost 60% of tonne-km.

In 1989, there was an increase of 4% from 1988, in road haulage traffic by heavy vehicles, to a total of 129,800 million tonne-km.

In 1989, 1,704 million tonnes of goods were carried in the UK, by 478 thousand heavy goods vehicles (both rigid and articulated). Of these vehicles, 15,900 were liquid tankers (Department of Transport, 1990).

In 1989, the main commodities carried by road were crude minerals (399 million tonnes), food, drink and tobacco (289 million tonnes) and building materials (190 million tonnes). In addition, 65 million tonnes of petrol and petroleum products, and 55 million tonnes of chemicals were moved (Department of Transport, 1990).

2.2.5 Road Traffic Accidents

National statistics on road accidents focus mainly on human casualties, and do not identify the severity of the accident in terms of environmental damage caused by spillage of load. An indication of the frequency of such events can, however, be gained from the available statistics.

In 1989 there was a total of 459,172 vehicles involved in road accidents, indicating a rate of 113 vehicles involved in an accident for every 100 million vehicle km. Of this total, 43,687 (almost 10%) of the vehicles were classified as Goods vehicles (Department of Transport, 1990). Thus, on a purely statistical basis, it can be inferred that in 1989, about 1,300 liquid tankers were involved in an accident.

In 1984 it was reported (Bickmore & Dutton, 1984b) that there are on average, about 120 chemical incidents a year on the roads in Greater London, of which the majority are minor petrol spillages. More recently, personal communication with the Oxfordshire Fire Services revealed that in 1989 in Oxfordshire, there were 165 incidents, and in 1988, 137 incidents involving road accidents which required the fire brigade to wash down spillages, mainly of petrol and oil. The Chemical Industries Association estimate that there are 2–300 road spillages of chemicals annually in the UK (Bickmore & Dutton, 1984b).

Relative to the number of liquid tankers on the roads and the mileage travelled, it can be said that road tankers carrying liquids rarely overturn. However, when they do they can be ruptured easily and leak. Although most tankers are compartmental, and thus just one compartment may be ruptured, a fire resulting from the spillage can frequently lead to rupture of other compartments (Bickmore & Dutton, 1984a).

2.2.6 Future Developments
The UK Government has a programme to improve motorways and other trunk roads and private sector investment is being keenly encouraged.

In mid-1990, 59 national trunk road and motorway schemes were under construction in England (costing nearly £1,400 million), while over 500 schemes were in preparation, many of which are bypasses and relief roads. During 1990–91 the Department of Transport is supporting 344 major local authority road schemes. Major privately financed schemes include; a new bridge across the River Thames between Dartford and Thurrock, which should be completed during 1991; a second bridge across the River Severn estuary, which should be completed during 1995; a relief road to the north of Birmingham; and a new route between Birmingham and Manchester.

In Scotland, the Government's programme includes extensions to the M74, M8 and M80 motorways; the improvement of strategic routes beyond central Scotland to areas such as the north-east and some of the west-coast routes; the construction of more bypasses; and a bridge to the Isle of Skye.

In Wales, road communications are expected to benefit from the second Severn Bridge and improvements to the M4 motorway. Other priorities include improvements to the coast road in north Wales, including construction of the first immersed tube road tunnel in Britain, beneath the Conway estuary, and upgrading of roads which are important for industrial development.

In Northern Ireland, improvements are to be made to arterial routes and roads in the Belfast area, new bypasses are to be provided and a new cross-harbour link is planned for the mid 1990's.

2.3 Railways

2.3.1 Rail Length and Use
The total length of rail track in Britain has changed little over the last five years. During 1989–1990, the total length open for traffic was about 17,500km. Approximately, 95% of this rail system is operated by the British Railways Board. A breakdown of this figure in terms of operator and use is given in Table 2.3a.

About 27% of route-mileage is electrified, the remainder carrying diesel trains.

Table 2.3a Length of Rail Track in Britain (1989–1990)

Operator	Total Length (km)	Status
British Railways Board	16,588	Overground
Northern Ireland Railways Company Ltd	320	Overground
London Underground Ltd	239	Overground
London Underground Ltd	169	Underground
Docklands Light Railway	12	Overground
Glasgow Underground	–	Underground
Tyne & Wear Metro	56	Overground
70 other, private	–	Overground, mainly for tourism

Source: Foreign & Commonwealth Office (1991)

2.3.2 Passenger Travel

Rail travel represents approximately 7% of the total passenger mileage in Britain. Over the last five years, the number of passengers and distance travelled has changed little, with a total in 1989–1990, of 746 million passenger journeys over a distance of 33,323 million km.

2.3.3 Freight

The total rail freight traffic in 1989–1990 was 143 million tonnes (a 5% decrease on 1988–1989, but similar to the previous year). More than 90% of rail freight traffic is of bulk commodities, with the most important being coal, coke, iron and steel, building materials and petroleum.

2.3.4 Rail Accidents

During 1989, there was an 8% increase in rail accidents in the UK, with a total of 1,434 accidents (Department of Transport, 1990).

2.3.5 Future Developments

Three major new rail links to airports are planned; a new link under construction between Stansted airport and Paddington; and a link to connect Manchester airport to the Manchester to Wilmslow (Cheshire) line.

The Channel Tunnel, with terminals at Cheriton (near Folkestone) and Coquelles (near Calais) is due to be completed in 1993, and will provide passenger and freight services. To meet the forecast growth in demand for through rail services from London to Paris, a new high-speed rail link will be provided from London to Cheriton.

On the London Underground, major investment is planned, including an extension of the Jubilee Line to Stratford (east London), and the Government is also considering options which would provide a new line in central London.

The Docklands Light Railway is being upgraded, including extensions westward to the City of London and eastward to Beckton, which are already under construction.

A light rapid transit system in Manchester is under construction, The first stage will start operating from 1991–1992. In the West Midlands and in Croydon, work is also planned on major light rail projects and light rapid transit systems are also being considered in other areas including Bristol, Edinburgh, Glasgow, Sheffield and Southampton.

Other future developments include; completion of the electrification scheme for the east–coast main line between London and Edinburgh; new rolling stock and infrastructure improvements in Network South East; and investment in new diesel multiple-unit trains in the Provincial sector.

2.4 Inland Waterways

2.4.1 Length of Waterways and Use

A survey of river quality in England and Wales in 1985 (Department of the Environment, 1985) recorded a total length of about 38,900km of rivers and 2,500km of canals. The majority of the canals, and some part of rivers too, come under the responsibility of the publicly owned British Waterways Board (a total length of 3,200km). The majority of these waterways are maintained primarily for leisure use, but about 620km are maintained as commercial waterways for private sector traffic. Britain's inland waterways are popular for recreation, including boating (motor boats, barges, dinghies, yachts etc), angling and other water sports.

2.4.2 Freight

Over the last ten years, freight moved on inland waterways has shown a slight, but steady increase from 63 million tonnes in 1979 to 68 million tonnes in 1989. (It should be noted that these figures also include freight moved in estuaries). This amounts to 2,400 million tonne-km, representing about 1.5% of freight traffic. About 50% of this freight was carried in the south–east, mainly on the River Thames (see *Table 2.4a*).

2.4.3 Accidents

There are no national statistics for accidents involving boats on inland waterways.

2.4.4 Future Developments

British Waterways Board will continue to operate more commercially in order to be more responsive to market needs. In addition, substantial Government grants are available towards the construction of, or improvements to, inland waterways for the purpose of transferring freight from unsuitable roads to waterways.

Table 2.4a Freight Movement on Inland Waterways in 1989 (Provisional Figures)

Waterways	Goods carried (thousand tonnes)
River Thames	26 495
River Humber	9 600
River Forth	8 215
Manchester Ship Canal	6 764
River Mersey	6 594
River Orwell	5 035
River Trent	4 604
River Ouse	3 260
River Medway	2 928
Aire and Calder Navigation	2 462
River Clyde	1 753
River Severn[1]	631
All waterways[2]	68 384

Notes
[1] Includes Gloucester and Sharpness Canal
[2] Includes other waterways but the total is less than the sum since the same consignment is counted on more than one waterway

Source: Department of Transport (1990)

2.5 Aviation

2.5.1 Capacity and Use

There are 141 licensed civil aerodromes in Britain, of which the following 12 may be considered major. These are Heathrow, Gatwick, Manchester, Aberdeen, Glasgow, Birmingham, Edinburgh, Luton, Belfast, East Midlands, Stansted and Newcastle.

The size of the UK airline fleet continued to increase in 1989 to a new maximum of 787 aircraft, an increase of 17.8%.

In 1989, the number of air transport movements at UK airports increased by 6.9% to a total of 1,078 thousand movements (compared to 7.8% in 1988).

Over the last ten years there has been a steady increase in aircraft kilometres flown by UK airlines, from 612 million km in 1979 to 830 million km in 1989.

The total capacity offered on all services on British airlines amounted to 18,923 million available tonne–km in 1989.

2.5.2 Passenger Travel

Travel by air represents less than 1% of the total passenger mileage in Britain (Foreign & Commonwealth Office, 1991).

In 1989, a total of 75.4 million passengers travelled by air to or from Britain, an increase of 5% from 1988. Heathrow airport handled more international passengers than any other airport in the world, with Gatwick coming second.

The number of terminal passengers at UK airports was 87.1 million, an increase of 5.8%.

A breakdown of these totals by airport is given in *Table 2.5a*.

2.5.3 Freight

Air freight is important for the carriage of goods with a high value-to-weight ratio, especially where speed of movement is essential. Major categories of cargo include precious stones, live animals, medicinal and pharmaceutical products, clothing, leather and skins, and scientific instruments.

In 1989, cargo handled at UK airports totalled 1,101 thousand tonnes, representing a smaller increase than in the previous three years. A breakdown of this traffic by airport is given in Table 2.5b.

2.5.4 Aviation Accidents

Available statistics on aviation accidents are not considered relevant to this study, since they focus on accidents in the air, and do not indicate spillages of cargo, fuel or other material that may lead to water pollution.

Table 2.5a Number of aircraft movements and passengers at UK airports in 1989

Airport	Airport transport movements (landing or take-offs) (Thousands)	Terminal passengers (arrivals or departures) (Thousands)
Heathrow	347	39.6
Gatwick	191	21.1
Manchester	121	10.1
Aberdeen	76	1.7
Glasgow	67	3.9
Birmingham	61	3.3
Edinburgh	47	2.4
Luton	38	2.8
Belfast	36	2.2
East Midlands	30	1.5
Stanstead	26	1.3
Newcastle	25	1.5
TOTAL	**1 078**	**87.1**

Source: Department of Transport (1990)

2.5.5 Future Developments

In March 1991 a new terminal is scheduled to open at Stansted, with a capacity on completion of the first phase of the project of 8 million passengers a year. Outline planning permission has been granted for further expansion to cater for 15 million passengers a year.

Under major expansion plans at Manchester, the first phase of a second terminal is under construction and is expected to open in 1993, increasing capacity by 50% to 18 million passengers a year. A second terminal is also under construction at Birmingham, for completion in 1991, increasing capacity to 6 million passengers a year. Construction of a new airport at Sheffield is planned to start in 1992. Facilities at several other regional airports are also being improved.

Table 2.5b Cargo handled at U K airports in 1989

Airport	Cargo handled (thousand tonnes)
Heathrow	686.2
Gatwick	208.7
Manchester	64.9
Glasgow	16.3
Birmingham	14.4
Luton	19.3
Belfast	23.9
East Midlands	15.2
Stansted	29.3

Source: Department of Transport (1990)

3 Potential Pollution Causes and Effects

3.1 Nature of Transport Pollution

3.1.1 Introduction

Transport derived pollutants may enter and contaminate freshwater (surface water and groundwater) in the following ways.

- Insoluble particulates may be entrained in surface runoff and drain to nearby water either directly or via an engineered drainage system.

- Gaseous exhaust emissions may enter the hydrological cycle as contaminants in rainfall or may be deposited as particulate matter. In both cases the contaminants may then enter the surface runoff.

- Soluble contaminants will be removed as surface runoff.

- Liquids or solids either leaking or spilling from vehicles may enter watercourses directly or via surface drainage.

Thus the principal cause of water pollution from transport, is contaminated drainage.

In the UK, drainage from road, rail and airports is treated similarly. The principal approaches to drainage disposal are:

- direct discharge to a surface watercourse;

- discharge to sewer (either surface water sewer or foul sewer), with subsequent discharge to surface water or groundwater;

- direct discharge to groundwater via a soakaway.

Discharge direct to a watercourse or groundwater requires a consent (under the Water Resources Act 1991 or Control of Pollution Act, Part II, 1974 in Scotland) to be issued by the National Rivers Authority (NRA). In this consent, conditions may be set as to the quality that the discharge must attain.

Discharge of surface water drainage to sewer does not require a consent, although discharge of trade effluent does.

To meet the conditions of the discharge consents, treatment facilities may be incorporated into the drainage systems. In the UK, these are most likely to include *'gullypots'* and oil interceptors. The drainage system itself, may also assist pollutant removal through provision of facilities such as balancing ponds (retention lagoons), soakaways or french drains (see Section 4.4).

3.1.2 Sources of Pollution

The principal sources of transport derived contaminants which may enter surface runoff (and thence surface water or groundwater) or directly enter surface water, are:

- contaminated drainage from construction works;

- leakage of liquids, including fuel, lubricants and deicants, from road vehicles, trains and aircraft;

- accidental spillage of a vehicle load;

- deicants (road salt, glycols, urea etc.);

- gaseous or particulate exhaust emissions;

- engine emissions from boats;

- paint, anti-foulant or other chemicals applied to the outer surfaces of boats;

- wear and corrosion of tyres, vehicle components and bodywork;

- breakdown of the road/runway/rail surface;

- erosion of overhead power cables on electric train systems;

- herbicides, pesticides, fertilisers and nutrients derived from run-off from embankments, cuttings, verges or landscaped areas;

- deposited contaminants from industrial and urban sources other than transport derived.

3.1.3 Types of Pollution

The many different pollution sources give rise to a wide range of contaminants, many of which are common to more than one type of transport.

Oxygen Consuming Organic Substances

Many individual contaminants, including suspended solids, sewage, vegetative litter, oil, petrol, rubber and other hydrocarbons have an organic component which in water gives rise to a biochemical oxygen demand (BOD). This is a measure indicative of the reduction in oxygen that will occur as a result of the pollutant, and is thus a good general indicator of polluting potential.

Suspended Solids

Suspended solids are particles of insoluble matter of variable composition; they may be inert, toxic, organic, inorganic, metallic, and many other types. They may include particles of soil and cement (eg during road construction); metal corrosion products from road vehicles or trains; deicing grit; street dust; or small particles bound together by oil. A principal effect of suspended solids is their 'blanketing effect' on river beds, when they settle. Suspended solids may also give rise to the release of toxic compounds, or adsorb them from the aqueous phase.

pH

Many plants and organisms can exist only within a certain pH range. pH is a major influencing factor in the chemical speciation of many contaminants, particularly metals which affects their toxicity. It is also important in determining the degree of adsorption of many contaminants by suspended solids. Certain transport derived pollutants, such as chloride (from deicing salts) can alter the pH of water in receiving steams.

Metals

Metals and their products can be derived from vehicle bodies and parts, exhaust emissions (eg lead), rubber tyres (eg zinc), rail tracks (eg iron) and overhead transmission lines (eg copper), from road surfaces and from deicing salts. Many such metals are potentially toxic to aquatic biota.

Herbicides

Herbicides used for weed control along roads, rail, waterside pathways or at airports can enter the aquatic environment and cause ecological damage or may represent a risk to public health.

Hydrocarbons

Fuel such as petrol, diesel, or aviation fuel, and other oils for uses such as lubrication, can enter the aquatic environment through leakage of storage tanks, vehicle breakdown and routine exhaust emissions, from the 'first flush' of drainage from gullypots and ineffective oil interceptors installed in roads which may be particularly contaminated by oil. An important source of potentially toxic and carcinogenic hydrocarbons such as PAHs, is emissions from the internal combustion engine.

Freight Spillages

Freight (whether liquid or solid) may be spilled from road vehicles, trains, boats or (less commonly) aircraft, and enter the aquatic environment. The scale of water quality impacts will depend on the composition of the spillage.

Sewage

Sewage (which has a high organic, suspended solids and BOD content) can be discharged from trains onto the track; from railway stations into the sewage system; from boats into water or the sewage system; and from other facilities.

Deicants
Salt, urea, glycol or other chemicals are used for de- (or anti-) icing of roads, rail, runways and vehicles. One of the principal polluting effects of deicants such as urea and glycols is their very high BOD.

3.2 Suspended Solids

3.2.1 Introduction
Freshwater pollution from suspended solids occurs principally from road runoff into surface water, with the most serious (but less frequent) instances, arising from road construction. Where road runoff passes to groundwater, the level of suspended solids is considerably reduced by the filtering action of the ground strata or engineered soakaway/french drain. Similarly on railways, the majority of suspended solids are filtered by the track ballast. Runoff from airports frequently passes through balancing ponds, which effect some solids removal. Emissions of solids from boats, barges and other waterborne craft, are rarely significant, although solids re-suspension caused by outboard motors creating hydraulic disturbance, can be significant (this is not considered a relevant source of pollution in the context of this study).

As a result of the above, the following discussion focuses on suspended solids contamination from roads, for which there is most available information.

3.2.2 Suspended Solids in Road Drainage
The composition of suspended solids is highly variable including rubber, bitumen, corroded metal, soil, grit, salt, vegetative litter and manmade litter. In addition, hydrocarbons and heavy metals become associated with the particulates. The specific effects of these associated pollutants are discussed in individual Sections that follow.

The total concentration of suspended solids in road runoff varies greatly, depending on the particle deposition rate, the accumulation time, the volume and intensity of rainfall and the surface runoff rate; in general the higher the flowrate, the greater is the capacity of the run-off for suspended solids.

Studies have shown a wide range of suspended solids concentrations in road runoff. In the UK maximum values of 1,386 – 2,045 mg/l have been reported on urban roads, and 5,500 mg/l on motorways (Rose, 1985). A much more conservative estimate of an average suspended solids content in motorways runoff, suggests a concentration of 100mg/l (Bickmore and Dutton, 1984a) while a specific study on the M1 (Colwill, 1984) reported a mean winter concentration of 169 mg/l, and a mean summer concentration of 230 mg/l. A recent study in Germany (Stotz, 1990), found levels of between 140mg/l and 270 mg/l. For the M1 (Colwill, 1984), a total annual yield of suspended solids has been estimated to be 1,500 kg/km.

During road construction, levels of suspended solids in surface runoff may be greatly elevated, due to considerable disturbance of soil from various earthworks, and higher rates of surface runoff that result from topsoil and vegetation removal and soil compaction by heavy vehicles. A study (Extence, 1978) on a tributary of the River Roding during construction of the M11 motorway, reported a mean concentration of suspended solids of 86 mg/l within a range of 22–336mg/l downstream of the construction works, which compared with a mean level of 32mg/l (range 4–130mg/l) upstream of the works. The majority of the solids content was found to consist of soil particles.

In addition to providing a means of rapid removal of surface water from road surfaces, most road drainage systems also effect removal of suspended solids and thus of many associated pollutants.

- Retention basins can, assuming good hydraulic design, effect a high removal of suspended solids. In practice however, removal of between 45% and 85% can be expected (Stotz, 1990). Retention basins are used little in the UK, but, they have been shown to be capable of removing 40–50% of suspended solids if designed with a 2–3 hour retention time (Ellis, 1989a).

- French drains are highly efficient at solids removal, with annual average efficiencies of 60-85% (Ellis, 1989a).

- Gullypots are less effective, with suspended solids removal rates typically of the order of 20-25%. In addition, the first flush of stormwater through a gullypot can cause elevated levels of solids in the outflow water. It has been estimated that a reduction of up to 22% of the solids in water in urban sewers could result from removal of 50% of the road drainage gullypots (Ellis, 1989a).

3.3 Biochemical Oxygen Demand (BOD)

3.3.1 Introduction
Biochemical oxygen demand (BOD) is a measure of the dissolved oxygen in water used by aerobic micro-organisms as they metabolise the complex, biodegradable organic compounds present in water over a standard time period and

at a standardised temperature; this is normally measured on the basis of a 5 day period at 20°C. A high value of BOD (eg > 5mg/l) can be taken as indicative of a polluted water, and will result in a reduction in dissolved oxygen concentrations in the water body.

Sources of BOD from roads include soils, vegetative matter and and general organic detritus. Railway runoff can frequently have a high BOD load due to discharge of sewage to the track (and oil), and similarly boats can release sewage and fuel directly to the watercourse. Sewage from aircraft and airports, railway stations and other road, waterway and transport related premises is usually discharged to public foul sewer or to a private sewage treatment works. The BOD load in airport runoff can be very high, and is associated with deicing and anti-icing chemicals such as glycol.

3.3.2   BOD in Road Runoff

The BOD in road runoff is mainly made up of organic matter associated with soils, vegetative litter and other organic detritus. It has been found that 25 of the suspended solids load in motorway runoff may be organic (Rose, 1985).

The BOD content of urban road runoff is highly variable, and from a study of world literature has been reported in a range from 18 to 7,700 mg/l (Rose, 1985). Studies in the UK have reported maximum BOD levels of 100 to 350mg/l in urban road run-off. Levels of BOD from motorways are generally lower, with a reported maximum of l00mg/l and a mean value of 32 mg/l (Rose, 1985).

During road construction, despite the high input of sediment (see Section 3.2.2), the BOD concentration is not generally found to increase, and in some cases may decrease (Extence, 1978) due to the large proportion of inert, organic matter poor particles.

3.3.3   BOD in Airport Runoff

BOD in airport runoff may be derived from many of the same sources as road runoff, but additional sources include in particular, high concentrations of glycols (and/or urea) used for deicing (see Section 3.9.3); strong detergent solutions used for cleaning hard standing areas; and synthetic fire fighting foam (used routinely in fire training). Since glycol degrades slowly, it is usual to express its BOD on a 20 day (BOD_{20}) rather than a 5 day basis. The BOD of ethylene glycol is high, at 1,330 g/l. Although we have found no reliable estimates of the BOD load in airport runoff, it is clear that it can be considerably higher than in road runoff, and can represent a significant problem. The resultant BOD in effluent discharged to the aquatic environment is, to a certain extent, also dependent on the degree of treatment which takes place on-site. Further, the impact on oxygen concentrations will be dependent on environmental conditions, such as temperature and residence time of the water body.

Data obtained from Thames NRA for glycol concentrations in the outflow of a lake, which receives airport runoff from Heathrow, indicate a mean concentration of about 5mg/l with a maximum of 37mg/l, during the period August 1985 to June 1988. These glycol concentrations translate into a mean BOD_{20} concentration of approximately 6mg BOD_{20}/l with a maximum of about 44mg BOD_{20}/l, which indicate a significant potential for oxygen depletion in the lake.

3.3.4   BOD from Boats

Boats using freshwater can introduce significant quantities of BOD through discharge of sanitary waste. In most cases there are local byelaws (see Section 4.1.9) prohibiting such activities, but there are many cases of illegal releases.

3.4   Oil

3.4.1   Introduction

Oil pollution is a problem associated with road, rail, air and water transport. However, because of the relatively greater number of roads, road vehicles, garages, car parks, depots and other related facilities, oil pollution is generally considered to be mainly a problem of road traffic.

A large number of drainage systems are provided with facilities such as oil interceptors or 'gullypots' to remove and contain oil. Their efficiency, however, depends in part, on adequate capacity and maintenance (including emptying). Frequent cases of oil pollution occur as a result of ineffective oil interceptors or the 'first flush' from a gullypot at the beginning of heavy rainfall (Rose, 1985).

3.4.2   Oil from Road Runoff

Oil, fuel and lubrication fluids routinely leak in small quantities from motor vehicles and from their exhausts; particularly in urban areas and petrol stations where vehicle maintenance occurs. These emissions can be significant (although difficult to quantify) and most drainage systems are provided with oil interceptors/traps to reduce concentrations in runoff.

Recent research in West Germany (Stotz, 1990) reported levels of 1.68-6.82 mg/l of motor fuel and 1.81- 7.02 mg/l of mineral oil in runoff entering road drainage basins. Removal rates of these substances in the drainage basins were found to vary enormously, from 16% to 80% of inflowing concentrations. Another study (Colwill, 1984), on the M1, found rather higher concentrations of oil in runoff ranging from 6-40 mg/l, equivalent to a total annual yield of 126 kg/km.

Gullypots often show a film of oil or petrol on the water surface, which may be partly degraded to produce concentrations of soluble organic compounds amounting to a concentration of about 200mg/l over a period of a few days (Rose, 1985).

Accidental spillages of oil are discussed in *Section 3.11*.

3.4.3   Oil from Airport Runoff

Oil can routinely enter airport runoff from several sources as follows:

- aircraft washing;

- small spillages during refuelling;

- aircraft maintenance; and

- stand cleaning.

To counter the effect of oil entering receiving waters, the drainage systems at airports are normally fitted with oil interceptors. Their regular cleaning and maintenance is essential to ensure efficient operation. However, a particular risk of oil being washed out of the interceptors exists from the use of strong alkaline detergent solutions often used to clean the aircraft parking areas. We have seen no reliable estimates of quantities of oil pollutant in airport runoff. A further problem is that glycols used as deicants can increase the solubility of oils, and thus reduce the effectiveness of oil interceptors.

3.5   Polycyclic Aromatic Hydrocarbons (PAH)

3.5.1   Introduction

The 'polycyclic aromatic hydrocarbons' (PAHs) are a class of organic substances which exhibit a range of toxic, mutagenic and carcinogenic effects. PAHs occur naturally in crude oil and are thus present in fuel oil, petroleum and materials such as asphalt and bitumen. PAHs are emitted in exhaust fumes from petrol and diesel engines, and can also be formed from the decomposition of material such as rubber and bitumen.

3.5.2   PAHs from Road Traffic

The PAH content in fuel is highly variable; the content in diesel is different from that in petrol, and within those categories differences occur depending on the source oil. In general, the lower molecular weight PAH compounds such as naphthalene and alkyl naphthalene are usually present at higher concentrations than the higher molecular weight compounds. One of the higher molecular weight compounds, Benzo (a) pyrene (BaP) is the best understood PAH compound. Typical concentrations of BaP in different materials have been reported in the United States of America as shown in Table 3.5.2a (Neff, 1979).

Table 3.5.2a   Typical Concentrations of BaP Reported in the United States of America

Substance	Concentration (mg/kg)
Diesel Oil	0.029
Regular gasoline	0.212
Premium gasoline	0.480
Unused motor oil	0.28
Motor oil used for 220 km	6.4
Petroleum bitumen	3 to 5
Asphalt	0.1 to 27

Emission of PAH in exhaust fumes results primarily from the incomplete combustion of fuel at high temperatures. Most such PAH is associated with the particulate fraction of soot produced during combustion. Soot can be thought of as an agglomerate of pericondensed PAH, based on $C_{150}H_{30}$ or $C_{216}H_{36}$ molecules, which are essentially inert. The PAH compounds of environmental concern, are primarily adsorbed onto the surface of the soot through hydrogen bonding. Research has shown that as the ratio of fuel to air increases in the combustion mixture, the mixture becomes richer and the concentrations of the lower weight PAH's increase, whilst the concentrations of the higher molecular weight PAH's decrease.

The emission of PAH compounds depends on numerous factors such as type of fuel, use of emission control catalysts, engine capacity, vehicle maintenance and driving mode. There is also a large number of different PAH compounds emitted, and many studies have reported on different compounds. These factors all make the estimation of PAH emission rates from vehicles problematic and subject to considerable uncertainty.

Emission rates from four studies are given in Table 3.5a. Hewitt and Rashed applied the rates of Westerholm et al (1988) and Hagemann et al (1981) to their study of the M6 motorway (Hewitt and Rashed, 1990), and estimated a total daily emission rate of 5,808 µg/m/d for a daily average vehicle flow of 32,000 petrol vehicles and 5,600 diesel vehicles.

Low molecular weight PAH compounds such as phenanthrene and anthracene are emitted mainly in gas form and are thus mainly dispersed in the atmosphere. Less than 2% may be deposited on or near the road. Intermediate compounds such as fluoranthene and pyrene are emitted both in the gas-phase and particulate forms, and a larger fraction (of the order 8%) is deposited on or near the road. For the higher molecular weight compounds which are entirely emitted in the particulate form, a higher percentage is deposited on or near the road, for example, 30.8% benzo(a) anthracene/chrysene and 23.3% benzo(a) pyrene (Hewitt, 1990).

In their M6 motorway study, Hewitt and Rashed (Hewitt, 1990) found an average annual PAH concentration in motorway drainage of 1.79 µg/l, approximating to a removal rate of 196 µg/m/d.

In another motorway study on the M1, Colwill et al (Colwill, 1984) measured Total PAH concentrations ranging from 0.15 µg/l in runoff, with concentrations of PAH in the runoff sediment including 9.3 µg/g of fluoranthene and 5.4 µg/g of BaP. There was a marked peak in PAH concentrations in the 'first flush' of the storm. The study concluded that from this part of the M1, which has a very high traffic flow, including a high proportion of HGV's, the total annual yield of PAH was 18 g/km. This figure is about 2 orders of magnitude lower than that of Hewitt and Rashed (1990), who estimated a total annual yield equivalent to 2.12 kg/km.

Table 3.5a Emission Rates for some PAH Compounds

Compound	Gasoline µg/km	Diesel µg/km
Phenanthrene	01.0[+]/0.30[▲]	–
Anthracene	28.0[+]	–
Fluoranthene	20.5[+]/1.47[▲]	36.4*
Pyrene	21/6[+]	16.3*
Benzanthracene/Chrysene	4.3[+]/0.3*/2.10[▲]	10.2*
Benzo(b) fluoranthene	–	–
Benzo(a) pyrene	0.7*/4.2°/12.5°/0.07[▲]	2.4*/1.5°
Benzo(ghi) perylene	1.2*	<2.5*
Total PAH	5.77[▲]	–

Notes

+   After Westerholm *et al* (1988) (Hewitt and Rashed, 1990)

*   After Hagemann *et al* (1981) (Hewitt and Rashed, 1990)

°   Data from USA prior to emission controls. Emissions have now been reduced by mor than 90% (Neff, 1979).

▲   Calculated from analysis of road runoff water in Japan. Emissions are for gasoline and diesel vehicles combined (Bickmore and Dutton, 1984c).

3.6 Lead

3.6.1 Introduction

Lead (Pb) is a heavy metal which can have serious chronic health effects in humans and toxic effects in aquatic plants and organisms.

The principal source of transport derived lead is petrol exhaust emissions. Attention has mainly focused on car exhausts, but there have also been studies into lead pollution from motor boat exhausts.

3.6.2   Lead from Road Transport

Emissions
Lead is added to petrol in the form of tetra-alkyl lead compounds, predominantly tetramethyl and tetraethyl lead. In the UK, the quantity added has been considerably reduced over the last 15 years as a result of legislation, from 0.55 g/l in 1976 to 0.15 g/l in 1986. It is now also possible to buy unleaded fuel, and it is reported (Williams, 1990) that in July 1989, unleaded fuel represented 22.9% of the total petrol consumption in the UK.

The percentage of input lead emitted in the exhaust is critically dependent on engine speed and driving mode, and may vary from less than 5% during city-type driving to almost 2,000% during rapid acceleration, when lead particles deposited in the exhaust system are resuspended. Over a complete driving cycle, substantially less than 100% of the input lead is emitted. Estimates by the Department of Transport (1990) based on average lead content for petrol and assuming 70% lead emission, show a substantial reduction in lead emission from 7.3 thousand tonnes in 1979 to 3.1 thousand tonnes in 1988. The most notable decrease occurred in 1986 after the introduction of the 0.15g/l maximum lead content in petrol. The more recent effect of increased sales of unleaded petrol has not yet been fully assessed. A study by Hewitt and Rashed (1990) on a rural section of the M6 motorway, found a lead emission rate of 288 mg/m/d derived from a daily average traffic flow of 32,000 petrol vehicles and 5,600 diesel vehicles.

Lead is mainly emitted as particulate inorganic compounds, mainly in the form of lead halides ($PbClBr$ and $PbCl_2.PbClBr$) and lead oxyhalides ($PbO.PbBr_2$, $PbO.PbClBr$ and $2PbO.PbClBr$) with lesser amounts of lead phosphates, sulphates and lead-ammonium halides. Most of these compounds have a fairly high water solubility, but are converted to less soluble compounds either in the atmosphere or in the soil.

The deposition of emitted lead is determined to a large extent by the particle size. The lead appears to be emitted in one of two distinct particle size ranges; these are small particles < 1µm and larger particles between 5 and 50 µm (Laxen, 1977). An indication of the magnitude of lead deposition on the road itself is provided by the work of Shaheen (1975) who measured seasonal average deposition rates of 4.1-11.0 mg(Pb)/axle-km in Washington, and by Ter Haar et al (1972) who found levels of 8.8 mg (Pb)/axle-km (Laxen, 1977). Hewitt and Rashed (1990) found a lead deposition rate on the M6 motorway carriageway of about 23 mg/m/d, which is approximately equivalent to a rate of 0.36 mg/axle km and is an order of magnitude less than the levels found by Shaheen(1975) and Ter Haar et al (1972).

It has been estimated that of the total vehicular lead emissions, 40-50% form a stable airborne aerosol, whilst the remaining 50-60% are deposited on, or within 15m of, the road surface (Bickmore and Dutton, 1984a). Another study by Hewitt and Rashed (1990), found that 86% of emitted lead was subject to long - range atmospheric dispersal, whilst 6% was deposited within 50m of the motorway, and 8% on the road itself. It is generally accepted that a relatively small proportion of lead (and other metals) deposited on the road surface is removed with run-off. Other processes responsible for the removal of deposited metal are resuspension and road sweeping. A study by Hamilton et al (1987) in a small UK catchment found that 11.4% of deposited lead was removed in the runoff. Hewitt and Rashed (1990) found that from a rural section of the M6 motorway, 8% of emitted lead was removed in road drainage. This is equivalent to a daily deposition rate of 22.3 mg/m/d inorganic lead and 0.06 mg/m/d organic lead (excluding background atmospheric deposition), for a daily average vehicle flow of 32,000 petrol vehicles.

Concentrations In Run-off
Studies of the lead content in highway runoff show a wide range of concentrations (see Table 3.6a). The variation is dependent on many factors, of which the following are particularly pertinent.

- Runoff from urban roads is highly variable in composition due to the range of surfaces and pollution sources in an urban area. The heavy metal content (including lead) is generally low, due in part to the lower emission rates during city-type driving, although lead levels of up to 3.7mg/l have been recorded (Rose, 1985).

- The quantity of deposited lead available to enter the run-off is heavily dependent on the lead content of the petrol (which varies between countries depending on legislation controls etc).

- The quantity of rainfall varies regionally and temporarily, and thus considerably affects the baseline quality of surface runoff.

Allowing for a large amount of variability, typical figures for lead in road runoff in the UK have been considered to be 2.4mg/l in motorway runoff, with a negligible amount in urban road runoff (Rose, 1985). However, it should be noted that other reliable sources report concentrations of lead in motorway runoff at an order of magnitude lower - 0.20 mg/l (Hewitt, 1990) and 0.59 mg/l (Colwill, 1984). In the light of recent and future reductions in lead emissions, these lower figures are considered to be more appropriate indications of the order of lead content of motorway runoff. On the basis of the 0.59 mg/l value, a total annual yield of lead has been calculated as 4 kg/km (Colwill, 1984).

Speciation

Deposited lead is largely insoluble. Its physicochemical form is a matter of some discussion; it may be largely adsorbed onto other particles; it may exist mainly as lead sulphate; it may exist as a precipitate in the presence of sodium, the lead solubility being lower with soil present probably due to partial adsorption; or precipitated lead phosphates may also be important (Laxen, 1977). Soluble lead is a varying proportion of total lead in road drainage, and is probably present largely as the inorganic complexes $Pb(CO_3)^\circ$ and $Pb(HCO_3)^+$ (Laxen, 1977). Estimates of the proportion vary from 5–50% (Laxen, 1977 and Yousef, 1990) and are probably towards the lower end of this range.

The quantity and chemical speciation of lead (and other metals) in road drainage that enters a surface watercourse may be significantly altered by passage through road drainage systems. Much of the lead is associated with particulate matter, and its removal is, in part, therefore effected by solids removal and sedimentation.

In a recent study (Stotz, 1990) it has been shown that in a road drainage detention basin effecting 85% removal of suspended solids, the corresponding lead removal was 79%, with a subsequent concentration of the removed lead in the basin sludge.

In a similar way, drainage systems employing gullypots (as is commonly the case in the UK) tend to concentrate metals in the sediment sludge. A study by Harrop et al (1983) showed that the concentration of lead (and most other metals) in gullypot sediments is considerably greater than in the road sediments. This can be explained by the preferential removal of small particles (which due to their greater unit surface area, have a higher metal content) from the road surface into the gullypot, leaving the larger particles with a lower metal content on the road surface. During low flow storm events, gullypots are able to retain the solids, but during either high intensity or high volume storms, these sediments are readily washed into the gullypot outflow, leading to high levels of lead (and other metals) in the receiving waters.

During dry conditions, the dissolved metals in gullypot liquor and gullypot interstitial waters have been shown to be mainly in the strongly bound form (Ellis, 1989 and Morrison, 1988). At the beginning of a storm event, the pH of the liquor in a gullypot remains close to neutral due to the initial buffering of acidic rainfall by road dust. As the storm progresses, the pH decreases, resulting in an increase in soluble metal content. This effect is later countered by a pH/surface area dependent effect which generally produces an increase in concentration of suspended sediment in the gullypot liquor. Lead (and also copper) becomes predominantly associated with the exchangeable fraction of the sediments in the gullypot indicating the relatively weak surface association of this metal in the gullypot environment. Between storm events, bacterial activity and acid dissolution processes produce increases in total metal concentrations in gullypot liquor. The soluble metal leaving the gullypot is predominantly in bioavailable forms (the toxicological implications of this are discussed in Annex A (Section A2.10).

Table 3.6a Concentrations of Lead in Road Run-off

Source	Total Lead (mg/l) Mean	Range	Reference
Snow from road surface	5.5	3.6–8.5	Newton *et al* (1974)
Snow from highway	102	86–113	Oliver *et al* (1974)
Snow dumps	9.8	–	Van Loon (1972)
Highway run-off	–	2–8	Sylvester & De Walle (1972)
Highway run-off	–	1–14	Siccama and Porter (1972)
Highway run-off	6.2	–	Pitt and Amy (1973)
Highway run-off	2.1	0.25–12	Hedley & Lockley (1975)
Highway run-off	–	1–4	Shaheen (1975)
Highway run-off	2.4	–	Rose (1985)
Urban Roads	–	3.7 (max)	Rose (1985)
Highway run-off	0.19	–	Stotz (1990)
Highway run-off	0.59	0.1–8.0	Colwill *et al* (1984)

Table 3.6a continued

Source	Total Lead (mg/l)		Reference
	Mean	Range	
Highway run-off	0.028	0.25–26	Hamilton (1987)
Highway run-off	0.203	–	Hewitt and Rashed (1990)
	Soluble Lead (μ/l)		
	Mean	Range	
Highway run-off	100	50–2000	Van Loon (1972)
Highway run-off	60	–	
Highway run-off	100	10–1800	Oliver *et al* (1974) Shaheen (1975)

3.6.3 Lead from Motor Boats

In an analogous manner to lead pollution from road vehicles, it has been postulated that rivers, canals and lakes may also become contaminated with lead from motor boat exhausts. A study has therefore been carried out (Oates, 1976) to determine the lead levels in tissues of selected fish species from freshwater lakes in Nebraska, USA, which are used heavily for recreational motor boating. The fish examined, included largemouth bass (*Macropterus salmoides*), bluegill (*Lepomis macrochirus*) and black crappie (*Pomoxis nigromaculatus*). The highest mean concentrations of lead in one species was 0.77 ppm, in black crappie, and the lowest, was 0.18 ppm in bluegill. Statistical analysis indicated that concentrations of lead in black crappie were significantly higher in lakes where motor boating was heavy, than in the control lakes, although a similar test for bluegill showed the reverse to be true. The conclusion drawn was that lead levels in fish were not significantly affected by motor boating.

3.7 Zinc

Zinc is a constituent of the rubber used for vehicle tyres. Wear of the tyres, thus leads to deposition of zinc on the roads, which may then enter surface runoff and a surface watercourse. Other sources of zinc also include vehicle components and deicing salts.

Zinc has a lower environmental toxicity than lead (see Section 3.13) and has thus received less attention.

The concentration of zinc in road runoff has, like lead, been found to be highly variable, with higher levels found in runoff from major highways than from urban roads. In the UK, an average concentration of zinc in motorway runoff can be taken to be 3.5mg/l with lower levels in urban road runoff showing a maximum of 1.6 mg/l (Rose, 1985). Another study (Colwill, 1984), on the M1, found zinc concentrations ranging from 116 μg/l to 8,015 μg/l, with a mean concentration of 1.2 mg/l, equivalent to a total annual yield of 8 kg/km. A recent study near Watford, U K (Hamilton, 1987) recorded low levels of all metals, including a zinc concentration in runoff of 0.017mg/l. It is also of interest that a recent study in Germany (Stotz, 1990) found much lower zinc levels (and also lower levels of lead (see Table 3.6a), of 0.42 mg/l.

The concentration of zinc in the runoff may be considerably altered as it passes through the drainage system. Much of the zinc (50-70%) according to (Yousef, 1990) is associated with particulate matter, and its removal is in part, therefore effected by solids removal and sedimentation. It has been shown that in a road drainage detention basin effecting 85% removal of suspended solids, the corresponding zinc removal was 50% (Stotz, 1990). Much of the removed zinc is concentrated in the sediment of the detention basin sludge.

In a similar way, drainage systems employing gullypots, tend to concentrate metals in the sediment sludge. During high intensity storms, their solids can be readily washed into the gullypot outflow, leading to high levels of zinc (and other metals) in the receiving waters. In the gullypot, zinc becomes associated with the carbonate fractions, and bacterial activity and acid dissolution processes can increase the zinc (and other metal) content of the gullypot liquor (Morrison, 1988).

3.8 Other Trace Metals

3.8.1 Introduction

A number of other trace metals can be introduced to the aquatic environment particularly as a result of road drainage, from sources including deicing salt, and from railways, particularly from the track and overhead power lines.

257

3.8.2 Trace Metals from Road Transport

The following trace metals, in addition to lead and zinc, are commonly found in road drainage.

Copper

Copper is largely derived from vehicle brakes, and deicing salts. Published literature shows a wide range of copper emission rates and concentrations in road runoff, and little agreement between studies. For example, copper deposited on the road from brake systems has been estimated at 0.045 mg/vehicle/km (Malmqvist, 1983).

The concentration of copper in tyres has been measured at 5.5-29.3 µg/g (Hewitt and Rashed, 1990), which produces an emission rate of 0.03-0.13 mg/rn/d.

However, several studies (Hewitt and Rashed, 1990 and Harrison, 1985) have found that the actual quantities of copper deposited on the roadway and removed in road runoff are significantly higher than those estimated from the emission rates. For example, on the M6 motorway, Hewitt and Rashed (1990) found a deposition rate which was 180% of the estimated emission rate. The removal rate in road drainage was 393%.

The concentrations of copper in urban road runoff have been determined to be in the range 6.5-1,410 µg/l (Hamilton, 1987). Copper concentrations in motorway runoff are reported to be at the lower end of this range; 7-30 µg/l on the M1 (Colwill *et al*, 1984) and 68 µg/l on the M6 motorway (Hewitt and Rashed, 1990), which approximates to an average total daily quantity in motorway runoff of 7.2 mg/m/d (for a daily average vehicle flow of 37,300).

Chromium

Chromium is largely derived from deicing salts and has been found in road runoff at concentrations of 5-85 µg/l (Stotz, 1990, Bickmore and Dutton, 1984a and Colwill *et al*, 1984).

Cadmium

Cadmium is derived mainly from road vehicle tyres. However, there are few published data on quantities emitted, and they show considerable variation in results. Using experimentally derived values for the cadmium content of tyre rubber (0.28-4.96 µg/g), an average tyre wear rate of 30 mg/kg and a daily average vehicle flow of 37,300, the cadmium emission rate can be calculated as 0.001–0.023 mg/m/d (Hewitt and Rashed, 1990). However, the quantity deposited on or within 50m of the M6 motorway has been measured as nearly 600% of the estimated emission, and the quantity removed in road drainage has been estimated as 1087% of that deposited. Thus the cadmium emission rate based tyre wear rates and vehicle flows appears to be severely underestimated. This may be due either to an underestimation of the cadmium concentration in tyres or in the tyre wear rate, or a further unidentified vehicular source of cadmium.

The quantities of cadmium measured in road runoff have been reported to be in the range 0.8-102 µg/l (Hamilton, 1987, Bickmore and Dutton, 1984(c), Hewitt and Rashed, 1990 and Colwill, 1984). The value of 3 mg/l in M6 runoff (Hewitt and Rashed, 1990) approximates to an average total daily quantity in motorway runoff of 0.25 mg/m/d (for a daily average vehicle flow of 37,300)

Nickel

Nickel is largely derived from deicing salts, but concentrations of this metal in road runoff have not received extensive attention.

Iron

Iron and ferrous metal derivatives are major contaminants in rock salt. However, the peak concentration of iron in runoff tends to occur several weeks after salt application, suggesting a large contribution from vehicle corrosion. A maximum concentration of 440 mg/l in runoff has been recorded (Ellis, 1989).

As discussed in Sections 3.6.2 and 3.7.2 in relation to lead and zinc, passage of road drainage through a drainage system can significantly affect the concentrations of metals. Passage through a detention basin with a high efficiency of suspended solids removal (85%) can effect a high degree of metal removal; copper, 73%; chromium, 66%; cadmium, 63%; and iron, 74% (Stotz, 1990). In a similar way, passage through an efficient gullypot can initially remove a substantial proportion of suspended solids and thus particulate associated metals. However, retention in the gullypot, leads to dissolution of many metals which are subsequently released in gullypot outflow due to rapid depression of pH, during a heavy rainfall. Thus the total dissolved metal content of gullypot outflow can be significantly increased, and altered to a more bioavailable form, than was the case in the initial road run-off. It has been suggested (Ellis, 1989) that the total metal content of urban drainage could be reduced by up to 38% by the removal of 50% of the gullypots.

3.8.3 Trace Metals from Railway

Iron particles are emitted when a train brakes. The majority of emissions therefore occur at stations. However, an emission rate for a 'standard train kilometre' has been determined by the NV Nederlandse Spoorwegen (NVNS) (Dutch Railways Ltd) to be 7g (Fe)/standard train km (Ministry of Health and Environment, 1980). However, it should be noted that many trains now have brake blocks and disc pads made of metals other than iron. The majority of iron (or other metal) is likely to remain in particulate form.

Electric power cables for trains (including the new generation of urban rapid light railway systems) are generally made of copper. These cables are subject to erosion as a result of arcing between the wire and the collector pole. The emission rate estimated by NVNS (Ministry of Health and Env., 1980) is 0.15g (Cu)/standard train km. The copper is emitted to the atmosphere, and only a small proportion will fall to the ground and enter the surface runoff (probably less than 10% of the total). The majority of the copper will remain in particulate from, and will become coated in copper hydroxy carbonate (malachite) or copper hydroxide (tenorite), depending on the pH of the rainfall and runoff.

Other metals may be emitted from trains as corrosion products. The quantities emitted are likely to be relatively small compared to emissions from road vehicles, although no published data exist for these other metals.

3.9 Deicing Chemicals

For safety reasons, it is necessary to apply anti-icing or deicing chemicals to roads, airport runways, electric conductor rails, railway station platforms, car parks and other surfaces.

3.9.1 Introduction

The majority of information available relates to roads and to a limited extent, airports.

3.9.2 Road Deicing

During 1988/1989, there was a total expenditure in England and Wales of £57.6 million on winter road maintenance (Department of Transport, 1990). This total includes deicing, snow clearance and snow fences. In the UK, the majority of deicing is carried out using salt or grit, but in places (eg the Severn, Wye and Avon bridges) the more expensive alternative of urea application is used to minimise the risk of chemical corrosion. Research has also been carried out into the use of glycols, magnesium and calcium chlorides and under-road electrical heating, but none of these alternatives have yet indicated sufficient advantages over salt or grit to offset their much higher costs. This discussion here will therefore concentrate on salt and grit application.

The application of any salt will melt any snow and ice which is present on the road, and therefore generates road runoff. Salt that is used for road deicing is supplied at a consistent quality of particle size and chemical content, controlled by a British Standard. Particle sizes range to a maximum of 10mm diameter and are chosen to spread the melting action over a prolonged period; the fine particles act instantly and the larger particles dissolve more slowly. As an anti-caking agent sodium ferrocyanide is added to the salt, usually at a concentration of 50ppm (Bickmore & Dutton, 1984c).

The amount of salt required to melt ice and snow is related to the temperature; the lower the temperature, the more salt is required. In the UK the temperature of snow and ice is generally not lower than -1°C, and so the salt application rates should be low. In 1960, the British Standard for salt spreaders specified a salt application rate of 34–136g/m². In 1978, the Standard was revised, to 10-40g/m².

Actual application rates in the UK show considerable variation from year to year, and also between regions. For 1976, the salt application rate on motorways has been quoted as 35g/m² (Driver, 1989), and from 1969-1977, to range from 0.16 to 25.87 tonnes/lane km, with an average rate of about 9 tonnes/lane km (Thompson et al 1989). A comparison with application rates in West Germany and the USA shows a high degree of similarity, despite the more severe winters in these other countries (Thompson et al 1989).

It should be noted, however, that since the introduction of the 1978 British Standard (see above) application rates in the UK are likely to have reduced. A recent example of salt application rates comes from Devon County Council, where the average annual salt application rate over the last five years, has been 16,000 tonnes per annum, and during 1989/90, 4,122 tonnes of salt were applied to motorways and trunk roads, and 5,804 tonnes to County roads. This reduction may, however, partly reflect the mild winter.

Road runoff after salt application contains, in addition to the contaminants found in routine runoff, high concentrations of chloride ions and to a lesser extent, sodium ions, bromide ions, cyanide complexes, iron and trace metals including lead, zinc, copper and chromium. The corrosive effect of salt can also lead to corrosion of vehicular metal bodywork and damage to road surfaces.

Chloride in motorway runoff has been found to have an annual average concentration of 2,170 mg/l, with a peak chloride level of 65,000 mg/l and an average for the month of December of 24,000 mg/l (Ellis, 1989).

Although once more common than salt for road deicing, the use of grit is now considerably less popular. In 1960, the British Standard for grit and salt spraying specified an applied rate of 68-408g/m². In the revised 1978 Standard, no reference was made to grit. The deicing effect of grit is to make ice and snow less slippery. It does not melt ice or snow, or prevent its formation. Although cheaper than salt, the overall cost of its use can be up to four times that of using salt due to the need for repeated applications and its subsequent clearance (Driver, 1984).

Grit can cause deleterious effects on road drainage through causing blockage of gutters and drains and by causing abrasion of metal on vehicles leading to corrosion.

3.9.3 Airport Deicing

In order to allow continued operations at an airport during conditions of snow or ice, anti-icing is favoured over deicing. The chemicals commonly used are based on glycol formulations or urea. An example of the quantities used at an international UK airport, is 90,000 litres of glycol and 115 tonnes of urea during 3 months of the 1986/87 winter (Gay, 1987).

Deicing of aircraft is also necessary, and most commonly takes place by spraying the ice sensitive surfaces with a solution of about 25% propylene glycol. On average, 200 gallons of solution are used per aircraft. As an example, at the airport mentioned above, 320,000 litres of product (equivalent to 160,000 litres of pure glycol) were used during the same 3 month period (Gay, 1987).

Routine levels of glycol in airport drainage have not been reported in the literature, but occasional levels of several thousand mg/l have been measured (Gay, 1987). Due to the high BOD of glycols (and of urea) (see Section 3.3.3) discharges of this nature may lead to a significant impact on water quality and freshwater life.

In a survey of the National Rivers Authority (NRA) and River Purification Boards (RPB) carried out by ERL as part of this study (see Section 4.4), several of the authorities showed considerable concern over levels of deicing agents in drainage from airports, and also indicated a lack of information regarding their use. In particular, the North West and Welsh regions of the NRA and the North East RPB reported low oxygen levels in watercourses receiving airport runoff. From the information supplied to us, no specific limit on the glycol/urea content of airport drainage was specified in any consents, although several authorities attach general statements specifying that application of deicants should be approved by the NRA and that the effluent should not be injurious to aquatic life.

3.10 Herbicides

Maintenance of roadside embankments, cuttings, verges and central reservations, of railways, of airport runways and of waterway paths etc. frequently involves application of pesticides (principally herbicides) and other chemicals for vegetation management.

Many herbicides have appreciable water solubility and persistence in water and soil, and can therefore enter the surface or groundwater drainage system and subsequently, potable water. The actual quantity reaching water bodies will depend in many factors (in addition to chemical properties), including quantity of chemical applied, the degree of plant uptake, the time between application and rainfall events, and the rain intensity. The worst-case situation that can arise, is that of heavy rainfall following a prolonged dry period after an application of a herbicide.

We are not aware of any authoritive studies specifically concerned with pesticide (herbicide) pollution from transport, although a study, commissioned by the Department of Environment, assessing the non-agricultural uses of pesticides in the UK has recently been published. There has also been a recent (1989) national survey of pesticides in water supplies, by the Drinking Water Division of the UK Department of the Environment (DoE).

The principle pesticides used for transport maintenance (and other non-agricultural uses) are sodium chlorate, and the triazines, Atrazine and Simazine. Several hundred tonnes of each active ingredient per year are used in England and Wales. More detailed estimates have been given as follows: a total use of 550 tonnes in 1990 (Daily Telegraph, 4 January 1991); 9,000 litres during 1990 summer, in Devon (Devon County Council pers. comm.); and an average application rate by British Rail of 9 kg/km (pers. comm.). The main characteristics of these herbicides are given in Table 3.10a. Each is appreciably water soluble, fairly persistent and may reach natural waters.

Results of the DoE survey found that in nearly 60% of water samples, (estimated as 10% of drinking water) the levels of either Atrazine or Simazine exceeded the legal standard of 0.1 µg/l specified in the Water Supply (Water Quality) Regulations 1989. However, in each of these cases the samples were covered by legal Undertakings and are therefore not considered unwholesome for the purposes of the Regulations. Under Section 20 of the Water Act 1989, the Secretary of State may accept Undertakings from water companies to postpone the implementation of the standards for certain water quality parameters whilst they take steps to improve water quality. These Undertakings can give water companies up to ten years to achieve compliance with the standard, but only where there is no risk to public health.

It is understood that discussions between the Government's Drinking Water Inspectorate and the NRA are ongoing, regarding the possibility of imposing water protection zones, in which the use of specified herbicides would be restricted or banned, and that the Government's advisory committee on pesticides is considering a total ban on the use of Atrazine and Simazine (both of which are already specified as Government 'Red List' substances (see *Section 4.1.6*)).

Table 3.10a Characteristics of Herbicides

Herbicide	Solubility in water (mg/l)	Persistence		Comments	Drinking Water Standard mg/1[1]	Advisory Value mg/1[2]
		Water	Soil			
Atrazine	33 (at 20°C)	Fairly persistent	Fairly persistent. Some leaching into water	Likely to reach water – has been detected on many occasions	0.1	2
Simazine	5 (at 20°C)	Fairly persistent	Fairly persistent. Little leaching.	Likely to reach water – has been detected on many occasions	0.1	10
Sodium Chlorate	790 x 10³ (at 0°C)	No information. Probably persistent	Fairly persistent. No information on leaching.	May reach water	0.1	–

[1] Standard specified for drinking water in the Water Supply (Water Quality) Regulations 1989

[2] Value recommended as a maximum by the DoE, based on the World Health Organisation (WHO) Guidelines. No advisory value is specified for Sodium Chlorate due to an absence of appropriate data.

In a survey of the National Rivers Authority (NRA) and River Purification Boards (RPB) carried out by ERL as part of this study (see Section 4.4), several of the authorities showed considerable concern over the use of pesticides, and also indicated a lack of information regarding their use and polluting effects. In particular, Yorkshire region commented on high levels of triazine herbicide in the River Ouse. In an attempt to prevent contamination, Tweed RPB have an agreement with the highway authority, that only those herbicides which are approved for use in the aquatic environment will be used on the highway. Along with Yorkshire region, Severn Trent region recognised the need for further research into the use of triazine herbicides.

3.11 Accidental Spillages
This type of pollution tends to be local and infrequent. When it occurs it can cause substantial environmental damage, but the long term or more widespread consequences are difficult to assess.

3.12 Environmental Fate and Toxicity of Transport Derived Pollutants
A detailed Technical Annex (Annex A) is provided, which discusses the environmental behaviour and toxicity of typical contaminants present in transport derived run-off and effluents.

3.13 Case Studies

3.13.1 Introduction
In the following Sections, we summarise details of a selection of pollution incidents resulting from transport. The information has been collated from pollution records kept by the NRA, and articles from newspapers and journals. There is thus a bias towards accidental spillages, rather than routine, cumulative pollution. Where possible, UK examples are discussed, but some overseas incidents are also presented.

3.13.2 Routine Road run-off into a Freshwater Pond
A study of the influence of road, urban and agricultural runoff on the macroinvertebrate fauna of ponds and streams in north London provides a clear demonstration of the aquatic impact of routine road drainage (Shutes, 1988).

One of the ponds, known as Cat Hill Pond, is adjacent to a roundabout carrying a high density of urban traffic.

261

Survey data in 1985-86 showed a relatively low species richness and macroinvertebrate diversity. Of all the ponds surveyed, the highest levels of heavy metals, including lead and zinc were found in invertebrates in Cat Hill Pond. For example, 148 µg/g of copper and 692 µg/g of zinc were found in *Asellus aquaticus*, reflecting its detritivorous feeding behaviour and indicating its relative tolerance to metals.

High concentrations in *Gammarus pulex* (copper 238 µg/g; lead 227 µg/g; zinc 1,049 µg/g) reflect its capacity for bioavailable metal uptake.

3.13.3 Road Spillage of Insecticide into River Roding, Essex

On 2nd April 1985, a heavy goods vehicle carrying eighty 200 litre drums of insecticide (Dursban 4E) was involved in a road accident on the M11 motorway. Twenty-one drums were damaged on impact and an estimated 2,570 litres of product were lost. Although the majority of spilled material remained on the road surface and earth embankment, approximately 500 litres were discharged through the road drainage system into Brookhouse Brook, 3km from the confluence with the River Roding. Within 30–40 hours, the Dursban had polluted more than 20km of the Roding. The water quality and ecological effects of this were serious and long lasting, and have been studied in some detail. The initial 'catastrophic' phase of the spillage lasted for 2–3 days, during which time, the active ingredient, chlorpyrifos, reached a peak concentration of about 2.5µg/l, which is at least 10 times the lethal dose for aquatic arthropods; they were eliminated, resulting in a serious impact upstream. Ninety percent of the fish population was also killed. Further downstream, the more resistant molluscs and annelids dominated and the impact was less significant. The impact on aquatic bacteria, algae, macrophytes, breeding river-birds and water voles, was considered negligible other than in the extreme short-term. Within eleven weeks, the concentration of chlorpyrifos had reduced to less than 1 µg/l, but sediment within 5km of the spillage site remained highly contaminated for considerably longer. Of ten arthropod taxa previously common, Chironomid (midge) larvae were first to recolonise, 13 weeks after the spill. Other recovery rates were variable, mainly reflecting downstream carriage from tributary streams. Within 18 months, arthropod recolonization was well advanced. Following a full restocking of the fishery, the Roding ecosystem was almost completely restored, after 2 years.

The polluters were prosecuted by the predecessors of NRA (then Thames Water Authority).

3.13.4 Road Spillage of Beer into River Colne

On 26 September 1989, a road tanker carrying 25,310 litres of beer (bitter) overturned at the A41/M1 junction. The tank broke away from the lorry chassis and remained on its roof, leaking. Before the emergency services reached the site of the incident, much of the beer had already run down nearby gullies. The Fire brigade sought permission to hose the road down, and the NRA (Thames Region) assented. The beer entered the River Colne via a storm water sewer outfall just downstream of the A41 road bridge. Over the next few days, the NRA took a number of water samples to monitor the movement of the beer. The main problems were noticed 2 days later, with fish in distress due to low oxygen levels in the water, caused by the high BOD (biochemical oxygen demand) of beer. In response to this, the NRA carried out some re-oxygenation of the river, and only a few small fish were killed.

Thames NRA prosecuted the polluter and charged them £1,610 costs, incurred through personnel time and chemical sampling.

3.13.5 Road Spillages of Oil into River Itchen System

In January 1989, a major road traffic accident on the M27 motorway resulted in an oil spillage and pollution of the River Itchen, necessitating closure of the Portsmouth Water Company intake.

Another oil pollution incident on the River Itchen system was caused by an ineffective oil interceptor at a road haulage depot, allowing oil to leak into the Barton River (a tributary of the Itchen). The oil was observed to cover 80% of the water surface. The potential damage of this incident, on a high quality chalk stream, was largely offset by the fortunate coincidence of NRA officers in the locality observing the incident early, which allowed the NRA to take rapid action to contain and remove the oil, using oil booms and absorbent pads.

The polluters were prosecuted by the NRA (Southern Region), fined £750 and ordered to pay £250 costs.

3.13.6 Road Spillage of Petrol in a Birmingham Stream

On 23 September 1976 an articulated road tanker carrying 25m³ of petrol overturned at a roundabout of Birmingham's outer ring road (A4040) and the A38 in Erdington town centre.

The fire brigade arrived at the scene of the incident nine minutes later. They found petrol leaking from the front compartment of the tanker (which had been perforated by collision with a telephone junction box) and also from a valve on top of the fourth tank compartment. The leaked petrol entered a very large drainage system, which includes a culverted stream, under the main Erdington shopping centre. Due to the hazard of petrol, power supplies were cut off locally as a precaution. Tests after the incident showed that 20% of the culverted stream was contaminated with petrol, and explosive atmospheres were registered up to 1km from the incident.

3.13.7 Pollution of River Roding due to Motorway Construction

During the period October 1974 to November 1975 a study was carried out into the effects on the River Roding of constructing the M11 motorway. Important findings of this study were that levels of suspended solids (particularly inert solids) and iron were considerably elevated, but levels of BOD, orthophosphate and nitrate nitrogen were not worsened by construction activities. The effects on stream biology were thus principally those related to stream bed blanketing, such as changes in type of substratum, predation pressure and food availability. The population of leeches was found to be severely diminished, probably as result of the absence of suitably sized particles for leech attachment and cocoon laying. Substratum changes also accounted for the loss of the river limpet (*Ancylus fluviatilis*) and a reduction in the numbers of *Asellus aquaticus*. The mayfly *Caenis moesta* which is known to be tolerant of silted conditions, showed a continued presence, but in reduced population numbers. The instability of the river bed was probably the cause of a lower density of tubificid worms and other burrowers.

3.13.8 Groundwater Contamination from Road Spillage of Chicken Offal

On 31 January 1989, an articulated lorry carrying chicken offal overturned on the main A43 Oxford/Northampton Road. Approximately 2 tonnes of offal were spilled, and the fire brigade used about 4,000 gallons of water to hose the roads clean. The resultant slurry entered the road drains and a dry roadside ditch, and the majority soaked into the ground. Due to the close proximity of private water supply boreholes at a nearby farm and an estate, the land owners were informed of the nature of the incident.

The polluters were prosecuted by the NRA (Thames region) and ordered to pay costs of £105.

3.13.9 Groundwater Contamination from Kerosene

Anglian region of the NRA have reported substantial pollution of groundwater resulting from spillage of kerosene on the A180.

3.13.10 Herbicide pollution from Road and Rail Maintenance

There is national concern over the incidence of groundwater and surface water contamination with herbicides (particularly the triazines, atrazine and simazine) and the subsequent contamination of drinking water. These herbicides are used widely by local authorities, road builders and British Rail, for weedkilling on roadside verges and railways. Incidents of this nature are thought to be a particular problem in the Midlands and East Anglia, and have also been reported specifically by the Yorkshire and Severn Trent regions of the NRA.

3.13.11 Petrol Spillage into Reservoir from Train Derailment

On 30 November 1988, a train carrying gas, oil and kerosene was derailed. Three of the cars leaked petroleum into a reservoir in Walthamstow, London. No further details have been reported.

3.13.12 Chemical Spillage into a Canadian river from a Train Derailment

On 3 March 1982, a train derailment in Canada resulted in the spillage of 790 tonnes of ethylene dichloride (EDC) into the Thompson River. No further details have been reported.

3.13.13 Aviation Fuel Spillage to River Medway from a Train Derailment

On 28 November 1990, a train derailment led to the spillage of 240 tonnes of aviation fuel into the Medway estuary.

3.13.14 Fuel oil spillage into River Rhine from a waterway tanker

On 3 April 1989, an inland waterway tanker carrying 1,200 tonnes of fuel oil hit a stone embankment and grounded. The vessel was damaged and her cargo of oil spilled. The Rhine was closed for 24 hours.

3.13.15 Gasoline spillage into a Kentucky river from two barges

On 19 February 1989, seven barges carrying gasoline broke away from a tug after striking bridge piling. Two of the barges were ruptured, spilling 40,000 gallons of fuel into the Ohio River.

3.13.16 Sewage discharges from boats on Lake Windermere

During the summer of 1990, Lake Windemere were reported to be heavily contaminated with sanitary waste discharged from boats. This contributed to the formation of blooms of blue–green algae which forced the cancellation of several events and many swimmers reported stomach upsets, ear infections and rashes.

3.13.17 Spillages of Aviation Fuel from Military Airport

On 12 May 1989, 57,000 litres of Avtur (aviation fuel) were spilled from the RAF station, Brize Norton. Some of the spillage was contained in a bunded area, whilst the remainder spilled onto a grassed area where it had soaked into the ground. The NRA Thames region's Area Groundwater Protection Officer was advised of the incident and took appropriate action regarding potential contamination of groundwater resources. Arrangements were made to dig trenches for the oil to accumulate in and for contaminated soil to be removed to an approved site for disposal. Tankers were arranged to remove oil from the excavations and also oil interceptors should any of the aviation fuel gain access to the land drainage system.

A similar problem has been reported by the NRA Yorkshire region, from loss of aviation fuel to underground strata, from the Leeds/Bradford Airport.

3.13.18 Pollution of a stream from Deicing Agents at Manchester Airport

The North West region of the NRA has reported a lowering of water quality in a stream receiving runoff from Manchester Airport. This problem is inferred to be associated with deicers used at the airport.

Similar problems have been reported by the NRA Welsh region, from RAF St. Athan, and by the North East River Purification Board.

4 Pollution Control

4.1 Existing Legislation

4.1.1 General

Legislation relevant to transport pollution can be considered in two categories: that regarding the responsibilities of various authorities to provide and maintain the transport infrastructure and its drainage systems; and that regarding the protection of water quality in freshwaters and groundwater.

There are also, additional advisory notes and Codes of Practice issued by Government bodies and industry that provide recommendations and advise on specific aspects of transport and the control of water pollution.

In the following Sections, a summary of the major pieces of legislation is provided.

4.1.2 Highways Act 1980

The 1980 Highways Act, together with the 1936 Public Health Act (see Section 4.1.3) vest dual responsibilities for highway drainage to be shared between the highway authority and the statutory water undertakers. Either type of authority may provide and operate drains to carry, in part, flows for which the other type of authority has responsibility, although highway authorities are not required to contribute to renewals or replacements arising from improvements, diversions etc, and which result in increased intake of highway water.

4.1.3 Public Health Act, 1936, 1937 and 1961

Together with the 1980 Highways Act, the 1936 Public Health Act vests dual responsibilities for highway drainage to be shared between the highway authority and the statutory water undertakers (see *Section 4.1.2*).

Section 259 of the 1936 Public Health Act extends the statutory nuisance procedure enforceable by local authorities to cases connected with watercourses, ditches and ponds etc.

Discharge of trade effluents into sewers are controlled by the Water Service Companies (created by the 1989 Water Act) by a system of Licences issued under the Public Health (Drainage of Trade Premises) Act 1937 and the Public Health Act 1961, and strengthened by COPA, 1974 and the Water Act 1989.

4.1.4 Road Traffic Act 1972

Under the 1972 Road Traffic Act, the Secretary of State for Transport has powers to make Regulations on vehicle emissions. A whole series of such Regulations has been made to implement various EC Directives on air quality.

4.1.5 Water Act 1989 and Water Resources Act 1991

In England and Wales, the control of water pollution is now largely regulated by the Water Act 1989. (In Scotland, regulation is provided by equivalent provisions in the amended Control of Pollution Act 1974).

The Water Act was enforced on 6 July 1989. In general terms it had four main effects:

- it restructured the Water Authorities into new water and sewerage companies;

- it provided for the regulation of these and any other water service companies under the Act;

- it established new institutions to regulate the companies and the water environment;

- it amended the law relating to water supply, sewerage and the pollution and abstraction of water.

Many of the previous Acts relating to water pollution still apply under the Water Act.

The Water Resources Act 1991 defines the NRA, in terms of its role, duties and functions. The Act is organised in nine parts. Relevant Parts are: Part I, which deals with the definition of the NRA, its functions and duties; Part II deals with Water Resources Management, including rights of abstraction; Part III deals with water pollution control; subsequent parts deal with flood defence, fisheries, financial provisions and various other aspects.

Part III of the Water Resources Act is arranged in four chapters.

Chapter I deals with Statutory Quality Objectives in terms of classification of waters, water quality objectives and NRAs duties to achieve and maintain these objectives.

Part III, Chapter II provides the basis for pollution control in England and Wales. This Chapter (Sections 85-87) establishes pollution offences for controlled waters (defined in Chapter IV Section 104), and provides uniform protection to surface and ground waters. Consents to discharge are made under Section 88(1) of the Act, and Schedule 10 of the Act provides the framework for consent applications, their determination, their revocation, alteration or impositions of conditions, and restriction on variation and revocation. Appeals in respect of consents under Section 88(1) can be made under Section 91 of the Act. Section 88(1) lays out defences in relation to authorised discharges. In particular, amongst other defences, discharges to waters may be made in accordance with:

- a consent made under Part 11 of the Control of Water Pollution Act 1974;

- an authorisation for a prescribed process under Part I of the Environmental Protection Act 1990;

- a waste management or disposal licence.

Section 89 outlines defences against prosecution, including 89(1) which deals with emergency discharges.

Sections of Part III Chapter III of the Act deal with water protection zones (93), nitrate sensitive zones (94-95) and consents made in these zones (96). Part III, Chapter III, Section 102 provides powers for the Secretary of State to incorporate EC legislation or other international agreements into U K Water Pollution Law.

Section 89(5) of the Water Resources Act 1991 protects Highway authorities or other persons entitled to keep open a drain by virtue of Section 100 of the Highways Act 1980 from prosecution under Section 85 of the Water Resources Act 1991, except where the discharge is made in contravention of Section 86 of the 1991 Act; Section 86 provides for prohibition of certain discharges by notice or regulations. Section 89(2) provides defences from prosecution under Section 85 of the Water Resources Act 1991 for discharges of trade or sewage effluent from vessels (ships etc).

4.1.6 Environmental Protection Act, 1990

The Environmental Protection Act is an attempt to strengthen areas of pollution control not covered adequately by other legislation.

A system of Integrated Pollution Control (IPC) has been created which involves Her Majesty's Inspectorate of Pollution (HMIP) regulating all polluting emissions and discharges including 'Red List' substances. This list includes dangerous substances which are persistent, toxic and liable to accumulate in living tissues. Substances already on the list, which can be derived from, or are related to transport, include cadmium and its compounds, and the Triazine herbicides, Atrazine and Simazine.

4.1.7 Control of Pollution Act (COPA), 1974

Water Pollution

Part II of COPA re-enacted and extended earlier water pollution controls mainly contained in the Rivers (Prevention of Pollution) Acts 1951–1961 and the Water Resources Act 1963. The relevant Sections have now been replaced by the Water Resources Act. Certain sections of COPA apply only to Scotland, but their content is essentially the same as for England and Wales.

COPA affords uniform protection to all surface and underground waters, covers all sources of pollution (regular discharges, isolated acts and accidental contamination) and opens the regulatory system to public involvement.

Under COPA (Section 32), discharges of the following effluents to inland waters and specified groundwaters, require discharge consents: trade or sewage effluent; discharge from a drain or sewer serving buildings or yards attached to buildings and discharge from a highway drain which is the subject of a notice served by the water authority under Section 32(1). This is a prohibition notice which prohibits the discharge of road drainage unless it is consented. Thus at the discretion of the licensing authority (being the NRA in England and Wales, and either the Secretary of State or the River Purification Boards, in Scotland). Prior to enforcement of COPA, discharge of road drainage did not require a discharge consent under any circumstances.

An offence is committed by any person who causes or knowingly permits any poisonous, noxious or polluting matter to enter controlled waters. An offence is not made if such an event is authorised by a disposal licence or a consent. Following a spillage of a substance, causing pollution of a watercourse, it is a defence under Section 31 of COPA, if the substance was discharged to a watercourse in an emergency, to prevent danger to the public. This defence is now contained within Section 89(1) of the Water Resources Act 1991, for England and Wales.

Under Section 75 of COPA, the Secretary of State for Transport has powers to control the composition of motor fuel for the purpose of limiting or reducing air pollution (with the dual effect of also reducing water pollution). For example, five Statutory Instruments (1976, no.1866; 1979 no. 1;1981, no.1523; 1985 no. 1728) have been created in order to implement EC Directive 78/611/EEC, on the lead content of petrol.

4.1.8 Water Act 1945

Section 18 of the 1945 Water Act empowers the statutory water undertakers to make byelaws, restricting activities that may lead to pollution of surface or groundwaters which they have a licence to abstract. However, the water undertakers are not empowered to make any byelaw which would restrict the rights of a navigation authority.

Section 21 of the Act makes it an offence to cause pollution of water which is likely to be used for human consumption, domestic or manufacturing purposes. Provision is made however, that this Section does not prohibit or restrict the reasonable use of oil or tar on any highway maintainable at the public expense, so long the highway authority takes all reasonable steps for preventing the oil or tar or any liquid or matter resulting from their use form causing any such water pollution.

4.1.9 Rivers (Prevention of Pollution) Scotland Act, 1951

Section 1 of the 1951 Rivers in Scotland Act, makes it the duty of the Secretary of State to promote cleanliness of the rivers and other inland waters of Scotland. The Secretary of State acts through the Scottish Development Department.

River Purification Boards (as established under Section 135 of the Local Government (Scotland) Act 1973) also have the responsibilities for promoting the cleanliness of river and other inland waters and for conserving the water resources of their areas (Section 17). To fulfil these functions they have powers conferred by this Act and also the Control of Pollution Act 1974 (see *Section 4.1 .7*).

The powers of the Scottish River Purification Boards (RPB) are similar to those of the statutory water undertakings in England and Wales, with one notable exception. That is, that an RPB has no powers to control abstraction of water. It is understood that the Scottish Development Department is giving further consideration to this, but it is considered likely that any amendments to existing legislation would apply only to abstractions of irrigation water.

4.1.10 Countryside (Scotland) Act 1967

Section 63 of the 1967 Scottish Countryside Act empowers a water authority to designate waterways for public recreation and provide facilities for their use.

Conversely, a water authority may make byelaws prohibiting recreational (including boating) use of a waterway.

4.1.11 Countryside Act 1968

Regarding recreational facilities at water undertaker's reservoirs and other waters, Section 22 of the 1968 Countryside Act empowers statutory water undertakers to make byelaws relating to any waterway and adjacent land owned or managed by them, to prevent any sewage or other offensive or injurious matter from entering the water.

4.1.12 Salmon and Freshwater Fisheries Act, 1975

This Act imposes a statutory duty on the NRA to maintain, improve and develop fisheries for salmon, trout, freshwater fish and eels.

Section 4 of the 1975 Salmon and Freshwater Fisheries Act makes it an offence to cause or permit any liquid or solid matter to enter watercourses containing fish, that renders the water poisonous or injurious to fish or the spawning grounds, spawn or food of fish.

It is the duty of the water authority (NRA) to administer this Act, but they do not have exclusive powers, and a prosecution could be instituted by anyone.

4.1.13 Salmon and Freshwater Fisheries (Protection)(Scotland) Act, 1951

Section 4 of the 1951 Scottish Salmon and Freshwater Fisheries Act makes it an offence to put any poison or noxious substance in or near any waters with intent to take or destroy fish.

4.1.14 Water (Scotland) Act 1980

Section 71 of the 1980 Scottish Water Act contains provisions relating to byelaws for preventing pollution of water that are substantially identical to those of Section 18 of the Water Act 1945.

Section 75, relating to the offence of causing water pollution, is similar to Section 21 of the 1945 Water Act (see *Section 4.1.8*).

4.1.15 EC Directive for Protection of Freshwater Fish

Directive 78/659/EEC 'on the quality of fresh waters needing protection or improvement in order to support fish life, applies to those fresh waters designated by the Member States as needing protection or improvement to support fish life. Two categories of waters must be designated:

- salmonid waters for salmon, trout and whitefish;

- cyprinid waters for cyprinids and other species (pike, eel etc)

Imperative and Guide values are specified for 14 physical and chemical parameters for both categories of water.

4.1.16 EC Directive on Groundwater Quality
Directive 80/68 EEC 'on the protection of groundwater against pollution caused by certain dangerous substances' is designed to prevent or limit the direct or indirect introduction to groundwater of the families or groups of dangerous substances contained on List I (eg mineral oils and hydrocarbons) and List II (eg lead, zinc, copper).

4.1.17 EC Directive on Dangerous Substances
Directive 76/464/EEC 'on pollution caused by certain dangerous substances discharged into the aquatic environment of the community', is a 'framework directive which provides for the elimination or reduction of pollution of inland, coastal and territorial waters by particularly dangerous substances by means of 'daughter directive'. 'Member States are to take appropriate steps to eliminate pollution by substances defined as List I (eg persistent mineral oil and hydrocarbons of petroleum origin) and to reduce substances defined as List II. (eg metals including zinc, lead and copper; and biocides not classified as List I). The 'Daughter' Directive 83/513/EEC has converted cadmium to a List I substance.

4.1.18 EC Directives on Drinking Water
Directive 75/440/EEC 'concerning the quality required of surface water intended for the abstraction of drinking water in the Member states' has two purposes:

- to ensure that surface water abstracted for use as drinking water meets certain standards and is treated adequately before being introduced to the public supply;

- to improve the quality of rivers and other surface waters used as sources of drinking water.

Member States must classify sources of surface water for the abstraction of drinking water by their existing quality into three categories, Al, A2 and A3. For each category, mandatory and guide values are given for 46 determinands.

Directive 79/869/EEC 'concerning methods of measurement and frequencies of sampling and analysis of surface water intended for the abstraction of drinking water in the Member States' supplements Directive 75/440 by recommending methods of measuring the determinands for surface water quality and setting frequencies for such measurements.

Directive 80/778/EEC 'relating to the quality of water intended for human consumption' sets standards for the quality of drinking water both directly and after treatment. It does not apply to natural mineral waters or medicinal water. Maximum admissible concentration (MAC) levels and guide levels (GL) for 62 determinands and minimum required concentrations (MRC) for four determinands are set.

4.1.19 EC Directive on Bathing Water
Directive 76/160/EEC 'concerning the quality of bathing water' sets 19 physical, chemical and microbiological determinands for the quality of bathing water, the most important of which are coliform counts. The Directive defines 'bathing water' as fresh or sea water in which bathing is explicitly authorised by the Member State, or is not prohibited and is traditionally practised by a large number of bathers.

4.2 Advisory Documents

4.2.1 General
In addition to the legislation discussed in *Section 4.1* there are other relevant documents which provide advice on interpretation of the law, codes of practice, regulations and other relevant advice and information. Some of the more pertinent are discussed in the following Sections.

4.2.2 Control of Pollution Act 1974
There are two Government Circulars (DOE Circ 17/84 and WO Circ 35/84) which provide an explanation of implementation of Part II of COPA. They are aimed at local authorities, water authorities and water companies. The

Circulars describe the statutory and administrative provisions of Part II of the Act, relates them to other provisions of the Act and explains their function in relation to water pollution control in England and Wales.

4.2.3 Use of Herbicides

There is a Ministry of Agriculture, Fisheries and Food (MAFF) publication (Booklet 2078) which provides guidelines for the use of herbicides on weeds in or near watercourses and lakes. The guidelines advise on the correct use of herbicides which have been cleared under the Pesticides Safety Precautions Scheme for safe use in or near water. They advise on the precaution that should be taken, especially where water may be abstracted for public supply. The guidelines include treatment of water bodies, drainage channels and also banks and areas adjacent to water bodies.

4.2.4 Water Act, 1989

There are three Government Circulars (DOE Circ 20/89, MAFF Circ 1/89 and WO Circ 47/89) providing an interpretation of the Water Act 1989.

4.2.5 Transport of Dangerous Goods

The United Nations Committee of Experts on the Transport of Dangerous Goods has published a document known as the 'Orange Book'. This document contains recommendations intended to be used as a basis for national regulations in order to achieve a level of international uniformity regarding the safe transport of hazardous wastes and other dangerous substances.

Regarding the safe transport of dangerous goods by air, there are Technical Instructions, designed by the Specialised Agency International Civil Aviation Organisation (ICAO).

Transport of goods by rail has been regulated since 1890 by an International Convention (C I M). Annex I to this Convention contains international regulations for the carriage of dangerous goods by rail known as RID. These are revised regularly by the Central Office for International Rail Transport (OCTI) and the European Commission (EC).

For carriage of dangerous goods by road, there is a European Agreement known as ADR. These recommendations are developed jointly with, and are thus in line with, RID.

For the transport of dangerous goods by inland waterway, there are similar regulations to ADR and RID, known as ADN.

4.3 Regulatory and Other Responsible Authorities

4.3.1 General

In the following Section, a brief discussion is given as to the authorities responsible for transport in the UK and for enforcing the relevant legislation.

4.3.2 Administration of Roads

Responsibility for trunk road motorways and other trunk roads in Great Britain rests with the Secretary of State for Transport; in Scotland with the Secretary of State for Scotland; and in Wales with the Secretary of State for Wales. The cost of construction, improvement and maintenance are paid for by central government.

The highway authorities for non-trunk roads in England are the county councils, the metropolitan district councils, the London borough councils and the Common council of the City of London. In Wales the authorities are the county councils, and in Scotland, the regional or island councils. In Northern Ireland the Northern Ireland Department of the Environment is responsible for the construction, improvement and maintenance of public roads.

Research into road construction, traffic engineering and safety, and into problems associated with transport, is carried out by the Transport and Road Research Laboratory, the research body of the Department of Transport.

4.3.3 Organisation of Railways

The British Railways Board was set up in 1962 to manage the railway affairs and subsidiary activities of the majority of railways in England and Wales. The Board has five business sectors; InterCity, Network SouthEast and Provincial, are responsible for passenger services; and Railfreight and Parcels, are responsible for freight. Other subsidiary businesses are British Rail Maintenance and light repair of British Rail stock, and Transmark, which provides consultancy services overseas on railway and associated operations. In Northern Ireland, the Northern Ireland Railways Company Ltd operates the railway service.

Other railway companies include London Underground Ltd, responsible for the Underground system in London, and several other organisations in other large towns and cities responsible for other urban railways.

4.3.4 Management of Inland Waterways

British Waterways Board is a publicly owned organisation, responsible mainly for canals.

The National Rivers Authority (see *Section 4.3.7*) is responsible for the quality of inland waters in England and Wales, and in Scotland, responsibility lies with the River Purification Boards (see *Section 4.3.8*).

4.3.5 Administration of Aviation

The Secretary of State for Transport is responsible for most aspects of national and international civil aviation.

The Civil Aviation Authority (CAA) is an independent statutory body, responsible for the economic and safety regulations of the industry, and jointly with the Ministry of Defence, for the provision of air navigation services. Members of the CAA board are appointed by the Secretary of State for Transport.

4.3.6 United Kingdom Government

The Department of Transport is responsible for land, sea and air transport, including:

- sponsorship of the nationalised London Transport and British Rail;

- domestic and international civil aviation;

- oversight of road transport in Great Britain;

- motorways and trunk roads;

- oversight of local authority transport in England;

- road safety.

The Welsh Office is responsible for many aspects of Welsh affairs, including roads and environmental protection.

Scotland has its own system of law and wide administrative autonomy. The Secretary of State for Scotland, a Cabinet minister, has responsibility in Scotland for formulating and carrying out policy relating to many issues including roads, certain aspects of transport services and environmental protection. These issues are the responsibility of the Scottish Development Department.

The Secretary of State for Northern Ireland is the Cabinet minister responsible for Northern Ireland. Responsibility for construction and maintenance of roads, transport and traffic management and environmental protection comes under the responsibility of the Department of the Environment for Northern Ireland.

The British Government's transport policy has been stated as resting 'on the fundamental aims of promoting economic growth and higher national prosperity, and ensuring a reasonable level of personal mobility, whilst improving safety, conserving and enhancing the environment, and using energy economically' (F&CO, 1991). Britain is also taking an active part in the European Community's development of a common transport policy, in the context of the completion of the single European market by 1992.

4.3.7 National Rivers Authority

The National Rivers Authority (NRA) is a publicly owned organisation, created by the Water Act 1989. Its principal responsibilities include water pollution control, water resource management and maintenance, improvement of fisheries, and licensing of water abstractions and effluent discharges. The NRA is organised into ten regions throughout England and Wales.

4.3.8 River Purification Boards

In Scotland, responsibility for freshwater pollution control and resource management is primarily the responsibility of the seven River Purification Boards, created by the Local Government (Scotland) Act 1973.

4.4 Drainage Management

4.4.1 Introduction

In addition to pollution control legislation and enforcement, a second, equally important aspect of control of pollution from transport systems is drainage management. This includes the type of drainage system, and administration of its maintenance.

The main types of surface water drainage system include gullypots, french drains, oil interceptors and sedimentation ditches, lagoons and balancing ponds. Each of these effects some removal of pollutants, but in most cases, this is not the underlying reason for their design or provision. Road, other transport, and urban drainage in the UK has principally been provided for the rapid removal of surface drainage, for reasons both of safety and of convenience for the public. The simultaneous removal of pollutants, has traditionally been, and to a certain extent still is, an added bonus, and certainly a secondary issue. However, there is a growing appreciation of the significance of transport pollution (particularly from roads), reflected in a substantial body of research literature and the exercise of pollution control powers by certain responsible authorities (notably the West German Government and increasingly, some of the UK NRA regions).

In the following Sections, we review and discuss some of the major issues relating to the effectiveness of different pollution control management and strategies.

4.4.2 Combined and Separate Sewerage Systems

In urban areas, two types of sewerage systems can exist; combined and separate.

- **Combined systems** collect and transfer surface water runoff (including road drainage) and foul sewage to a sewage treatment works. The combined flow is then treated, and the effluent discharged to a watercourse. To prevent flooding during times of heavy rainfall, combined systems are provided with storm sewer overflows (SSO's) which discharge directly to a watercourse without treatment.

- **Separate systems** are, as the name suggests, drainage systems dedicated solely to either surface water runoff or foul sewage. A surface water sewer discharges directly to a watercourse, whilst a foul sewer passes to a sewage treatment works. Surface water sewers are provided with stormwater sewer outfalls (SWO's) whereas foul sewers have overflow capacity provided at the sewage treatment works.
There are advantages and disadvantages to each type of system.

- **Combined systems** may cost between 50% and 100% less than separate systems and are therefore often favoured. However, overflows from SSO's, although less frequent than from SWO's, are far more polluting. It has been reported that SSO's may contribute up to 33% of the total annual pollution load discharged to a watercourse, with concentrations of suspended solids in the range 176–647 mg/l (mean 425 mg/l) and BOD 4 225 mg/l (mean 90 mg/l) (Ellis, 1989). The concentrations of all pollutants in an SSO are greater (in many cases by an order of magnitude) than from an SWO. It has also been reported that 30–40% of SSO's in the UK operate unsatisfactorily, and cause increased pollution.

- **Separate systems** are considerably more expensive (by 50–100%) than combined systems, since two systems are needed in parallel. Nevertheless, in many cases this cost is outweighed by the overriding advantage of preventing untreated sewage from entering a watercourse. Thus, by the mid 1970's about 24% of the UK population was served by separate systems (Ellis, 1989). Another major disadvantage of separate systems is the risk of cross-connections from foul sewers to surface water sewers, with the consequent potential for pollution, particularly in industrial areas. Although less polluting than overflows from SSO's, polluting overflows from SWO's are far more common. Average concentrations of pollutants in an SWO overflow may be 21–582 mg/l (mean 190 mg/l) suspended solids, and 7–22 mg/l (mean 11 mg/l) BOD.

In general, both SWO's and SSO's typically operate only 2–5% of the time (Ellis, 1989).

In urban areas, road drains may be connected to either combined sewerage systems or separate surface water systems. In rural areas and adjacent to major highways, road drainage usually discharges directly to a watercourse. The water quality impact of three types of discharge needs therefore to be addressed.

Treated Effluent (Sewage and Road Drainage)

The quality of treated effluent from a sewage treatment works depends largely on the treatment processes employed and their efficiency. The effluent quality from different works may therefore vary considerably. In general however, a standard effluent may be expected to have a concentration of suspended solids of the order of 30mg/l and a BOD of about 20 mg/l. Concentrations of metals, oil and other organic compounds in the influent wastewater will also be reduced, although many of the metals such as lead, zinc and copper, may be toxic to bacteria in the works and may thus inhibit treatment processes. In general however, loads of these substances are not likely to be significantly increased to critical levels by the combination of road runoff with foul sewage. In many cases, the dilution of foul sewage with surface runoff may produce an influent that is easier to treat, and thus a higher quality effluent. We consider that in general, an efficiently operating sewage works treating a combined flow would produce an effluent which would be less polluting than untreated road drainage. An inefficient works may produce an effluent of a lower quality (with respect to certain determinands) than untreated road drainage, but this situation is likely to occur regardless of the combination of road drainage and sewage.

Storm Sewer Overflows (SSO's) (Untreated Sewage and Road Drainage)
The low quality of storm sewer overflow (SSO) effluent is one of the major causes of river pollution in the UK. The predominant pollutants are generally considered to be sewage related (including suspended solids, BOD, COD and nutrients but also include all the transport derived contaminants, with no removal effected. Thus combining surface (and road) runoff with foul sewage can result in significant river water pollution.

Road Drainage
The quality of road drainage entering a watercourse directly, is dependent on the following major factors:

- whether the road is urban, rural or a major highway;

- the number of vehicles and the relative proportion of petrol fuelled and diesel fuelled vehicles;

- the type and efficiency of drainage system provided.

The quality of road drainage has been extensively reviewed in *Section 3* of this report. The quality of road drainage has been found to routinely contain contaminants at sufficiently high concentrations to cause a significant impact on water quality and aquatic ecosystems, and occasional accidental spillages may also cause significant impact. Distinct from drainage leaving the road surface, is the drainage which actually enters the receiving watercourse. The two may be markedly different in quality as a result of passage through the drainage system. This may either improve or worsen the quality, as will be discussed in the following Sections. A road drainage system with a high efficiency for pollutant removal can significantly reduce the polluting potential of road drainage, and is our most favoured drainage option of the three discussed, for reducing freshwater pollution.

4.4.3 Infiltration Systems
Infiltration systems collect surface runoff and allow it to percolate into the ground. This principle has been engineered into various designs including soakways, french drains and filter drains.

The basic form of infiltration system is a simple soakaway, comprising a pit or ditch filled with gravel or rubble. More sophisticated soakaways are constructed from manhole rings with openings in the side and base to allow water to percolate out. In their simple form soakaways are quick and cost effective to use and are therefore favoured by developers, particularly in urban areas. Some highway authorities however, from whom the developer seeks adoption of the drainage system, regard soakaways as a maintenance liability and therefore unacceptable. Their concerns lie in the blocking of the filter media with solids in the runoff, and the subsequent growth of bacteria, algae, moss and weeds, which will reduce the efficiency of the soakaway and may lead to flooding, the scatter of the soakaway filter media, and the need for media cleaning and replacement. Conversely, an efficient soakaway located in the wrong hydrogeological conditions may lead to a rising water table and again cause flooding. In this latter context, trench designs are more effective than pits. The flooding problem can also be reduced by provision of an interconnecting network of soakaways with an overflow to a watercourse or sewer. Soakaways in the UK are designed according to Digest 151 published by the Building Research Establishment in 1973.

'French drains' are so called, after their original French designer, M Tresaguet, in the eighteenth century. French drains are a linear version of soakaway and have since been developed into 'filter drains'. A recent survey (Bird, 1990) estimated that about 50% of road cuttings in the UK are drained by filter drains. The drain may be a single pipe, or two pipe, system. Single pipe systems have one drain for surface water, sub surface and groundwater. Two pipe systems separate the functions of storm water and sub surface water collection. This latter system is most effective, but is more expensive.

Drainage of railways is essentially by soakaway or filter drain, with the track ballast acting as the filter material. Where the geology allows it, the ballast material drains directly into the ground and in other situations collector drains are provided which transport the drainage to a suitable point of discharge.

A study by the UK Transport and Road Research Laboratory (Colwill *et al*, 1985) has reported that infiltration trenches draining highway runoff can achieve mean annual removal efficiencies for suspended solids, metals, PAH, oil and chemical oxygen demand of 60–85%.

4.4.4 Kerbs, Gullies and Gullypots
Kerbs, gullies and gullypots form the most common system of road drainage in the UK. Gullypots have also been the focus of a considerable amount of study regarding their effects on the quality of road drainage. British Standard 497:1976 specifies design guidelines for road gully gratings and their spacing, and in line with this standard, Hydraulics Research Limited have produced updated guidelines on spacing, incorporating new types of gully grating.

The gully system acts by collecting runoff at the edge of the carriageway and directing it via the gully grating to a gullypot and then the drain beneath the road. The gullypot itself, is a hopper which acts as a silt trap and a water seal. In addition to water quality problems which will be discussed later, there can be many other problems with gully systems (Pearson, 1990). These include:

- poor construction of the supporting brickwork can allow settlement of the grating;

- loose bricks or a break in the seal between the ironwork and surfacing can allow water into the pavement;

- where gratings cross the entire width of the highway, the ironwork can be loosened by traffic loading;

- vandals and scrap metal merchants have been known to remove the gully grates.

To reduce some of the above problems, there is an increasing trend to locate the gullies away from and lower than the road. This approach however, tends to result in higher maintenance costs, since additional sweeping or manual cleaning is required.

A development of the conventional gully system, is the Beany Block. This is a combination of kerb, gully and collector drain and has the additional benefit of introducing a solid edge restraint to the pavement structure. This system is widely used, and appears to be relatively successful, excepting cases where there is inadequate maintenance (often due to access problems) and thus blockage.

The principal purpose of a gullypot is to prevent the solids and oil in road drainage from causing unpleasant odours during anaerobic degradation in the drainage system. This is achieved by providing a water seal. A related effect of the gullypot is to remove and collect a large proportion of the solids and oil from the drainage. The effluent leaving a gullypot thus has a different composition to that entering. Further, the gullypots need frequent emptying and cleaning.

It has been shown that drainage entering a gullypot becomes rapidly anaerobic (within 24 hours, or a week during cold weather) and that complex chemical changes takes place (Fletcher, 1978) (see Figure 4.4a).

It is the quality of water leaving the gullypot and entering the drainage which is important, as this is what may enter a watercourse. At the beginning of a rainstorm, the drainage entering and flowing through, the gullypot flushes out the standing water already in the pot. This effluent is called the 'first flush' and has been shown to be highly polluting.

Figure 4.4a   Loss of Dissolved Oxygen in a Gully Pot

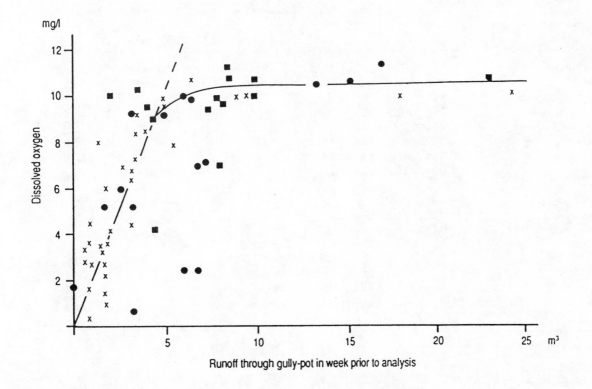

Source: Taken from Rose (1985)

Characteristic of a 'first flush' is a thick bacterial scum, removed from the surface of the gullypot liquor. This scum has been shown to have a concentration of up to 200 mg/l of soluble organic matter, formed from degradation of oil, petrol and other hydrocarbons, over a few days (Lysyj and Russell, 1974). Also characteristic of the first flush, are high concentrations of suspended solids, BOD, dissolved and total metals, and ammoniacal nitrogen. The concentrations of these and other material in a gullypot effluent in general show a characteristic rise to a peak (the time of this depending on hydrological conditions) and then a steady decrease once the contents of the gullypot have been washed out.

Between rain events standing water in a gullypot undergoes a series of complex chemical reactions under anaerobic conditions. The resultant compounds are then washed out of the gullypot in the first flush effluent. The following changes in drainage quality have been reported (Morrison et al, 1989).

- In road runoff, dissolved metals are mainly present as free metal ions and relatively weakly complexed metals (experimentally defined as the chelex removable fraction), principally as a result of acidic rainfall releasing metals from the road dusts.

- In road runoff, particle associated metals are mainly present as an exchangeable fraction (again delineated experimentally), in the form of surface bound metals on small particles with a high surface area.

- Between rain events, in the anaerobic conditions in the standing water of a gullypot the dissolved metals mainly become strongly bound, and the particle associated metals are mainly present as carbonate and hydrous metal oxides (also defined experimentally). Concentrations of nitrate-nitrogen are reduced, and concentrations or ammoniacal nitrogen are increased.

- As flow through the system increases, many metals are released from their particle associations, and the concentrations of dissolved metals increase.

- As flow further increases, the gullypot basal sediments are disturbed, and the concentrations of chelex removable metal released into the gullypot effluent is further increased.

The quality of effluent leaving a gullypot has been reported in a number of studies, and a summary is given in Table 4.4a. The maximum values can be taken to represent first flush flows. The different studies show a wide range of values, and demonstrate the generally accepted view that the quality of gullypot liquor is very difficult to predict, but is undoubtedly a significant source of water pollution (Harrop, 1983).

Table 4.4a Quality of Gullpot Liquor

Contaminant (mg/l)	1 Mean	1 Max	2 Mean	2 Max	3 Mean	3 Max	3 Min	4 Max	5 Max	6 Mean	6 Max
BOD			13.7	41.6	241.3	1500	2.3	350			
Suspended Solids	71	1032	35	252.8			0	4031	5427	160	305
Soluble Solids	282	5860	143.2	292.5					5360		
Total Solids	353	5964							8739		
Chloride	76	1829	18.2	36.0			6.4	31525			
Soluble Organic Carbon	29	255									
Ammonia N	0.7	4.5	1.39	4.62							
Nitrate N	0.08	0.34	9.6	28							
Nitrite N	0.8	3.0									
Phosphates					0.2	0.3					
Total copper	0.02	0.04									
Total manganese	0.2	0.62									
Total lead	0.17	0.6									
Total nitrogen					12.23	33.2	42.4	965			
COD			67.3	428.6	6589.2	37700					
Ca^{2+}			25.7	35.8					8.5		
pH			7.87	8.38							
Total Zinc	0.11	0.25	0.09	0.57							
Turbidiyy (NTU)									125		
Conductivity (umhos/cm)									9350		
Volatile suspended solids									385		

Notes:
1 Water Research Centre (1977)   2 Fletcher et al (1978)   4 Tucker (1975)   6 Waller (1972)
  & Mance and Harman (1987)   3 Sartor and Boyd (1972)   5 Harrop (1982)

Source: Urban Stormwater Pollution, Harrop (1983)

As has been discussed, a major cause of water pollution resulting from a gullypot is the first flush containing high concentrations of soluble metals, BOD, suspended solids and other material. Much of this polluting load results from chemical processes occurring in anaerobic conditions and from decomposition of organic matter, comprising leaves, oil, paper, animal faeces, soil etc. An effective way of reducing gullypot pollution is thus to ensure regular emptying, cleaning and maintenance. In the Local Authorities Association Highway Maintenance Code of Good Practice (Local Authorities, 1989), gully emptying is recommended, on average, between once and twice a year depending on local circumstances. It is widely accepted however, that the frequency of cleaning carried out is insufficient, due both to financial constraints (Harrop, 1990) and poor access. A study by Fletcher (1978) reports that in an area where gullypot cleaning was supposed to be once every four months, it was in fact carried out only once in 12 months. Following on from this, Ellis (1989) suggests that substantial improvements in the quality of the effluent from surface drainage stormwater sewer outfalls (SWO's) could result from reducing the provision of gullypots. He suggests that a 50% reduction of gullypots could reduce pollutant loads as follows:

- suspended solids by 22%;

- metals by 38%;

- oil by 45%.

Ellis also points out that since much of the first flush from SWO's can be attributed to the flushing of supernatant liquors and anoxic interstitial waters from gullypots, such a reduction in frequency would also serve to contain the acute slug impacts of toxic SWO discharges on receiving waters.

4.4.5 Permeable Paving

A drainage system which is receiving increasing interest for application in pedestrianised and car parking areas is the use of permeable paving. It is so far not generally used on roads due to financial considerations. The concept of permeable paving is relatively simple, and seeks to mimic the behaviour of undeveloped ground, whereby surface water infiltrates the ground, and produces relatively little surface runoff. At the same time, a considerable improvement in drainage quality results, from processes such as sedimentation, adsorption and chemical and biological degradation of contaminants.

Permeable paving typically comprises a porous macadam or open-textured concrete block wearing course and a geotextile layer, overlying a free draining road base or sub-base (see *Figure 4.4b*). The sub-base may be of various types of stone or crushed rock, and the road base is a similar material of smaller size if the wearing course is porous macadam, or gravel if it is concrete block paving. The sub-base provides a reservoir for temporary storage of water.

Drainage entering a permeable pavement may either percolate through the sub-base to groundwater, or be collected by sub-base drains for discharge to a sewer or watercourse.

The effects of permeable pavings on the quality of road drainage have been studied by Pratt et al (1989) and by Hogland (1990). Their results show in the following:

- Permeable pavements can be effective sedimentation devices, producing effluents with suspended solid concentrations generally of about 20 mg/l and less than 50 mg/l. However, the deposited materials may eventually lead to a decrease in water infiltration. To avoid this, the deposited material must be either flushed from the voids in the porous macadam, using vacuum cleaning combined with jet-spraying or the concrete blocks must be removed, clean gravel placed and the concrete blocks re-laid. The frequency with which this is necessary is highly variable, depending on a number of factors.

- Removal of pollutants, and particularly metals, from the road drainage varies with the construction materials used in the sub-base of the pavement, since this can affect the pH, hardness and alkalinity of the water. For example, lead concentrations in the effluent have been found to be lower using limestone as a sub-base material than using blast furnace slag. In all cases however, concentrations were one order of magnitude lower than that typically occurring in gullypot liquor.

- Clogging of the pavements is a particular risk during the construction phase, due to heavy vehicles use, erosion and corrosion of construction materials stored on site, stockpiled soil and sand, salting or gritting for deicing and other sources.

- An infiltration capacity of about 1mm/min is sufficient to infiltrate moderate/heavy rainfall, but to ensure better efficiency, an infiltration capacity of 50 mm/min is recommended. Newly constructed permeable pavements have an infiltration capacity of 500–700 mm/min.

- The permeability of the geotextile gradually decreases to near zero after one or two years use.

- The removal of pollutants is most effective for suspended solids, total solids, chromium and aluminium; it is moderately effective for copper, zinc and lead, but concentrations of nitrogen (in the form of nitrate, nitrite, ammonia and kjeldahl) and of chloride have been found to increase. This may be due to oxygen in the bottom layer of the construction or to contaminated drainage entering the construction from agricultural sources.

Other studies on permeable pavements have indicated that incorporation of additional geotextile layers or organic material such as peat or carbon granules in the pavement can increase pollutant removal (Hogland, 1987 and Gjessing, 1984).

Figure 4.4b   Typical cross-section of Permeable Paving

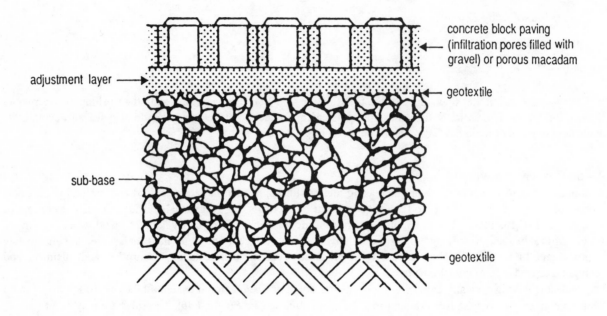

Apart from the relatively high cost of using a permeable pavement, other considerations include the following.

- The ground conditions should ideally be freely draining, in a similar way to the use of soakaways etc.

- Due to their relatively infrequent use, there are few reliable estimates as to the effective working life or maintenance demands of permeable pavements.

4.4.6 Storage Facilities

Storage facilities for drainage may be termed balancing ponds, retention lagoons or detention basins, but are all basically the same. Their principal purpose is to provide storage of road drainage to prevent flooding, but they can also be designed to reduce the pollutant loads in road and urban drainage. In the UK this latter function has received relatively little consideration, whereas in West Germany it has been studied more comprehensively.

In areas of West Germany designated as 'water resource conservation' areas, detention basins must be provided in conjunction with drainage systems. Historically, these basins were designed only to trap accidental spillages of pollutants, but present day basins are required to be of a design that also significantly reduces the concentrations of pollutants in highway runoff (Stotz, 1990). Since many transport related pollutants are particle associated, removal of solids can also effect removal of metals, PAH, BOD and other contaminants. The results of a study of pollutant removal efficiencies in three detention basins in West Germany are shown in Table 4.4b. The results show clearly that if properly dimensioned, a detention basin can effect 50–80% removal of most traffic related contaminants. Conversely, a hydraulically ineffective basin may remove very small percentages of pollutants and may increase the concentration of some pollutants, principally through remobilisation of metals, resuspension of solids and anaerobic conditions.

A UK study (Ellis, 1989) shows similar pollutant removal efficiencies as follows:

- suspended solids 40–50%;

- BOD 22–25%;

- metals 30–35%;

- ammoniacal nitrogen, cadmium and PAH, show an increase in concentrations.

Removal of pollutants by sedimentation results in a basal sludge in which the pollutants are accumulated. Maximum heavy metal contents of 2,800 mg/kg (Fe), 2,175 mg/kg (Zn), 840 mg/kg (Pb), 330 mg/kg (Cu), 45 mg/kg (Cr) and 19 mg/kg (Cd) have been reported (Stotz, 1990), with mineral oil contents in the range 1,600 – 3,500 mg/kg. Sludges of this composition are not suitable for agricultural application, and require either disposal or treatment.

4.4.7 Biofiltration Systems

Biofiltration systems rely on pollutant removal through biological activity on passage of the drainage through vegetation and soil. A biofiltration system can be arranged as filter strips or shallow wetlands, including grass and swale surfaces; or it can be incorporated into both wet and dry balancing ponds or other flood storage facilities.

When applied to the treatment of industrial, and sewage effluents, biofiltration systems have exhibited highly effective removal of metals and organics, of between 80 and 95% (Ellis, 1990). Removal mechanisms mainly include sedimentation, filtration, adsorption, bacterial decomposition, but also include precipitation, ion exchange and plant uptake. Although both heavy metals and hydrocarbons are generally toxic to plants, certain species with a high tolerance can be selected.

We are not aware of any detailed studies of the quality of road drainage after biofiltration treatment.

4.4.8 Geotextile Membranes

Geotextile membranes are receiving increasing interest and use to provide systems of positive underdrainage. They can be applied in situations such as permeable pavings, and in filter and fin drains. Some British Standard tests for geotextiles have now been published, and a complete range of European tests should be available by 1992. A specification of geotextiles is also in preparation by the Institution of Civil Engineers.

It is considered likely (Pearson, 1990) that there will be increasing use of geotextiles.

4.4.9 Oil Interceptors

Oil interceptors are generally provided in the drainage systems of car parks (nominally larger than 25 cars), depots, service stations and other facilities where spillage of fuel or oil may occur. The purpose of an oil interceptor is to separate oil from the surface drainage so that the effluent is suitable for discharge either to sewer or a watercourse. There are three designs of oil interceptor most commonly in use; these are the American Petroleum Institute (API), the tilting plate and the three chamber baffled flow designs. In all interceptors the technique employed is to slow down the rate of flow and hence to eliminate all turbulence so that the droplets of oil are allowed to rise to the surface. The minimum residence time for most oil interceptors is 9 minutes, although 5 minutes may be adequate for a tilted plate separator. Removal of the oil may be continuous, by a horizontal split pipe, or manually by hand pumps or hand held skimmers. Oil separators require cleaning at least once every six months and more frequently in certain circumstances.

Table 4.4b Polutant Removal Efficiencies in Four West German Detention Basins (%)

Pollutant	Ulm-West I	Ulm-West II	Pleidelsheim	Obereisesheim
Suspended solids	45	54	85	50
COD	18	39	63	26
Ammonia - N	10	-72	36	16
Total Phosphorus	3	12	32	9
Cadmium	14	60	63	28
Chromium	-60	7	66	33
Copper	-13	17	73	26
Lead	33	52	79	39
Zinc	24	29	50	37
Iron	24	29	50	37
Motor fuel	16	33	80	29
Mineral oil	17	33	80	29

Source: Stotz (1990)

The most common design used at small facilities such as petrol stations, is the three chamber separator (see *Figure 4.4c*). It is simple in design, but not highly efficient. Most of the oil is trapped in the first compartment, but small quantities may flow through the second or third.

The tilting plate separator (see *Figure 4.4c*) consists of a stack of parallel corrugated plates set at an angle of up to 45° to the water flow. As the oily water flows through the unit the droplets of oil agglomerate on the plates. The drawback with this design is that it is relatively easily blocked. Frequent cleaning is necessary.

API interceptors (see *Figure 4.4c*) are mainly used at sites where large flows will be generated. Their operation and efficiency depends on a large surface area, this also being their disadvantage.

4.5 Regional Compliance with Existing Legislation

4.5.1 Introduction
The major legal instrument for controlling pollution from transport is the issue of discharge consents (see *Section 4.1.7*), usually for routine drainage. Most other types of transport pollution that occur are accidental spillages and are thus more difficult to regulate.

In the following Section, we present a discussion of the results of a survey which ERL carried out to investigate the extent of transport related water pollution in the UK and the relative compliance with pollution legislation. In this survey, each of the ten regions of the NRA, and the seven Scottish River Purification Boards were consulted. The responses to our questionnaire are given in Tables 4.5a and b and are discussed in the following Sections.

4.5.2 Abstraction of Water for Transport Use
In Scotland, the River Purification Boards do not have powers to control abstraction of water (see *Section 4.1.10*) and our survey therefore does not show any details of water abstraction in Scotland.

Information on abstractions from the NRA was supplied by seven regions; in two there were no licensed abstractions; in three there were between one and five abstractions; and in Anglian and North West regions there were 10 and 23 abstractions respectively.

Figure 4.4c   Typical Oil Interceptors

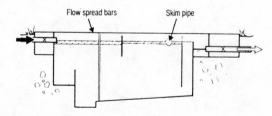

(i) Three chamber separator

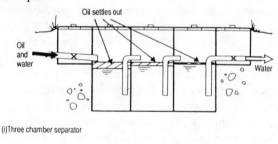

(ii) Tilted-plate oil separator

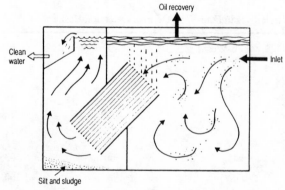

(iii) API separator

278

Table 4.5a Licensed Uses of Water for Transport, and Pollution Incidents in England & Wales (NRA)

NRA Region	Number of consented discharges to surface freshwaters	Number of consented discharges to groundwater	Number of licensed surface water abstractions	Number of licensed groundwater anstractions	Number of recorded pollution incidents	Number of prosecutions during last 5 years	Increase or decrease in pollution in recent years
Anglian	2	2	5	3	2+ many other small incidents	0	Increased
Northumbrian	1	0	0	0	Many small incidents	1	Increased
North-West	7	0	14	9	6+ many other small incidents	0	Constant
Severn-Trent	50	INA[1]	INA	INA	Many small incidents	2	INA
Southern	564[2]	0	–	–	30 (May 89 to Oct 90) + others	1	INA
South-West	0	0	0	0	Many small incidents	0	Constant
Thames	49+	8+	INA	INA	5 (Jan 89 to Sep 89) + Others	5	Increased
Welsh	266	0	0	1	Many small incidents	0	Increased
Wessex	0[3]	0	2	3	0	0	No problem
Yorkshire	106	0[4]	1+	4	7+ many other small incidents	2	Constant

[1] INA = Information not available
[2] 564 incidents made up of 471 road; 70 garages etc; 17 rail, 6 airports
[3] Discharges from MoD air stations have Crown Exemption from requiring a discharge consent
[4] British Waterways Board hold several licences to maintain water levels in the Sheffield and South Yorkshire Navigation.

Table 4.5b Licensed Uses of Water for Transport, and Pollution Incidents in Scotland (RPB)

River Purification Board	No. of consented discharges to surface freshwaters	No. of consented discharges to groundwater	No. of licensed surface water abstractions	No. of licensed groundwater abstractions	No. of recorded pollution abstractions	No. of prosecutions during last 5 years	Increase or decrease in pollution in recent years
Clyde	–	–	[1]	[1]	2 small incidents	0	–
Forth	1	0	[1]	[1]	2	1	Decreased
Highland	0	0	[1]	[1]	0	0	–
North-East	9	4	[1]	[1]	4+ many small incidents	0	Increased
Solway	0	0	[1]	[1]	Occasional small incidents	0	Probably increased
Tay	0[2]	0	[1]	[1]	Several small incidents inc. spillages at RAF base	0[3]	Remains high
Tweed	20	0	[1]	[1]	Occasional small incidents	0 RAF Base	Increased

Notes
[1] RPB's have no powers to control water abstraction
[2] One to tidal waters
[3] There is one prosecution pending, of an oil spillage to the Tay estuary.

These results show a uniformly small number of abstractions throughout England and Wales, reflecting the small requirement for water in transport activities. The two exceptions to this trend are in regions where the augrnenting of river/canal water levels is carried out by the British Waterways Board, by abstracting water from one watercourse and returning it at another location.

Since the water requirements for transport are similar throughout the whole of Britain, it can be assumed that the number of abstractions in Scotland is likely to be similarly small.

4.5.3 Discharge of Water

Information on licenced discharges of water was provided by all ten regions of the NRA and six RPB's.

The number of licenced discharges varied considerably between regions, ranging from zero in five regions, to 266 in Welsh region and 564 in Southern Region.

The main reason for this large range is that under existing legislation, licensing of road drainage discharged to freshwater, is not required, unless the N R A issues a Prohibition Notice (see *Section 4.1.7*). In the context of limited resources, many authorities regard transport pollution as a low priority relative to other sources of pollution and therefore do not generally issue discharge licences. Further, in regions where roads are mainly urban, discharge of drainage is to a public sewer, for which a discharge consent from the NRA is not required. It is also worth noting that facilities such as Ministry of Defence air stations and airports do not require a consent to discharge, as a result of Crown exemption. Finally, it should also be noted that several of the authorities indicated that the information supplied may be incomplete due to the way in which licensing details are recorded and stored. A summary of the details of the conditions of discharge consents is given in Tables 4.5c and d. The following comments can be made.

- Discharges from all modes of transport system are treated similarly, since many of the potential water contaminants are common.

- There is a general consensus between regions in relation to the quality required of consented effluent.

- The majority of transport related discharges are surface water drainage (eg road or runway runoff) and have either, no conditions attached to the Licence, or conditions relating only to oil and in some regions, a general statement (taken from the Salmon & Freshwater Fisheries Act, 1975) regarding the protection of fishlife.

- Consents for discharges of transport 'trade effluent' (eg from petrol stations, car washes, and railway stations etc) commonly have a limited set of conditions attached, usually specifying limits for oil, suspended solids, pH and less frequently, BOD and temperature.

- Consents for discharge to groundwater via soakaway are in general, less strict than for discharge to surface water, and in many cases unconditional.

- Only one region (Severn Trent) generally specifies a consent condition for chloride, although several other regions attach a general statement to the conditions specifying that application of deicants at airports should be approved by the NRA (Thames), and that nothing in the effluent should be injurious to fish life (Southern, Yorkshire, North East).

- No consent conditions are specified for herbicides, although one region (Tweed RPB) does have an agreement with the highway authority as to which herbicides may be used, and other regions specify protection of flora, fauna and fishlife in general clauses.

4.5.4 Pollution Incidents

Most of the authorities providing information on transport related pollution incidents found it difficult to give an accurate number of incidents. Most authorities reported large numbers of small, frequent pollution events, resulting mainly from road traffic accidents causing small spillages of oil or fuel, and from the contents of road gullypots being washed out in a 'first flush' at the beginning of a heavy rain storm. Where larger pollution incidents occurred, they were often due to major spillages of road tanker contents. Details of some of these are presented as case studies in *Section 3.13*.

4.5.5 Compliance with Discharge Consent

The opinions of the NRA on the general level of compliance of licence holders with the conditions of their licence were variable, ranging from poor to good.

Several comments were made as to the lack of water quality monitoring data available to adequately form an opinion on this issue, and also that many of the discharges have no conditions attached.

Of the River Purification Boards, only Tay and Tweed replied to this question, both indicating good compliance.

4.5.6 Pollution Trend

Four of the NRA regions and three of the RPBs indicated a general increase in transport derived water pollution over recent years. There was a general feeling that this was due to an increase in traffic. A further three NRA regions and the Tay RPB felt that traffic pollution had remained constant, and Wessex replied that there were no pollution effects anyway. The Forth RPB replied that traffic derived pollution had decreased, and Welsh region of the NRA replied that although there was a general increase in pollution, that from herbicide application had decreased in places.

Table 4.5c Typical Regional Consent Limit Conditions for Transport Discharges in England & Wales (NRA) [1,2]

NRA Region	Suspended Solids	Oil	pH	Temperature (°)	Chloride	BOD	No. of consents with conditions	No. of consents without conditions
Anglian	NO INFORMATION TO DATE							
Northumbria	(60)[3]	(NV)[4]					1	0
North-West	30–75[5]	10–20 (10)	5–11 (5–9)	(30)	–	(20)	7	0
Severn Trent	28–258 (50)	4–30 (5)	6.5–11.6 (6.7–8.1)	–	62–1288	5–88	18	32
Southern[5]	10–60 (30)	(5)	–	–	–	10–40 (40)	564	0
South-West	–	–	–	–	–	–	0	0
Thames[6,7]	5–200 (30)	(NV)[4]	(5–9)	–	–	–	45	12
Welsh	10–100 (50)	0–200 (5)	6–10 (6–8.5)	26–35 (26)	–	5–90 (20)	131	135
Wessex	–	–	–	–	–	–	0	0
Yorkshire[5]	(50)	20–40	(5–9)	–	–	(20)	106	0

[1]   All units in mg/1 unless stated otherwise.

[2]   Conditions have been quoted only where consents are conditional; many consents have no conditions attached.

[3]   Figures indicate ranges; number in parenthesis indicate the most common condition.

[4]   NV = No visible trace of oil or grease.

[5]   Southern and Yorkshire region frequently attach an additional condition stating that 'the effluent shall not contain matter in sufficient quantity to make the waters into which it is discharged, poisonous or injurious to fish or to the food or spawn of fish'. This is in line with the Salmon and Freshwater Fisheries Act, 1975.

[6]   Thames region have many more discharge consents than the 57 they have provided information for.

[7]   Stansted, Heathrow and Gatwick Airports fall within Thames region. To these consents, they attach a condition stating that 'No chemicals for the purpose of preventing the formation of or aiding the remove of ice or snow shall be applied to the runways, taxiways or other hardstandings, or any aircraft thereon, except in accordance with the Code of Practice for the time being in force and which is deposited with and approved by the NRA (Thames Region).'

4.5.7 Prosecutions

When considered together, the consensus that transport pollution in most regions is generally increasing, and the fact that the number of pollution incidents is high, it might be expected that the number of legal prosecutions would also be high. However, this was not found to be so. All of the authorities replied to the question on prosecutions, and only six had prosecuted, for a total of 12 pollution incidents over the past 5 years. The main reason for this situation is that it is only the relatively few major incidents for whom a culprit can be identified and thus prosecuted. It should also be noted however, that a major pollution incident from a road spillage may not be deemed an offence if the spilled material was deliberately allowed to enter a watercourse in an emergency, to avoid danger to the public. This can often be the case when the fire services are involved, and fire water, along with the spilled material plus any other chemicals, may be washed into a watercourse to remove the hazard from the road. However, it should be noted that in such instances permission from the NRA is still required.

The majority of road and rail pollution occurs as small, regular discharges from moving or stationary vehicles. The drainage may enter a watercourse as either a consented or unconsented discharge via a surface water stormwater outfall (SWO), combined with sewage as a storm sewer overflow (S S O), or as treated effluent. These discharges occur as episodic events, related to rainfall, which may cause either acute effects or lead to a long term build up of pollutants and cause a gradual deterioration of water quality and chronic stress.

The other major source of road and rail related pollution, is from periodic pollution incidents resulting from the 'first flush' of liquor from a gullypot or oil interceptor.

In these latter cases, prosecution is both difficult and not very appropriate.

A further source of pollution is at civil and military airports and airbases. Several incidents of pollution from deicing chemicals and spillages of oil and fuel have been reported. In many cases however, prosecution is not possible due to Crown Exemption.

Table 4.5d Typical Regional Consent Limit Conditions for Transport Discharge in Scotland (RPB)[1,2]

River Purification Board	Suspended Solids	Oil	pH	BOD	Iron	No. of consents with conditions	No. of consents without conditions
Clyde	–	–	–	–	–	–	–
Forth	–	(10)	–	–	(10)	1	0
Highland	–	–	–	–	–	0	0
North-East[5]	40–100[3] (60)	(NV)[4]	(5–9)	–	–	12	1
Solway	–	–	–	–	–	0	0
Tay	–	–	–	–	–	(0)[2]	0
Tweed[7]	–	–	–	–	–	0	20

[1] All units in mg/1 unless stated otherwise.

[2] Conditions have been quoted only where consents are conditional; many consents have no conditions attached.

[3] Figures indicate ranges; numbers in parenthesis indicate the most common condition.

[4] NV = No visible trace of oil or grease.

[5] NERPB generally attach a clause stating that 'the discharge shall not contain any substances .... to be harmful to flora and/or fauna ....

[6] One to tidal waters.

[7] Tweed RPB has an agreement with the Regional Council's Road & Transportation Department that only herbicides which are approved for use in aquatic environment will be used on the highway.

5 Suggested Areas for Further Research

5.1 Introduction

This study has included both a detailed Literature survey and a survey of water pollution control bodies, into the causes and effects of transport derived pollution. Both of these approaches have revealed aspects of the subject where further research would be beneficial to understanding the problems more fully and methods to reduce the incidence and significance of transport pollution.

5.2 Freshwater Pollution

The majority of the NRA regions and RPBs have, in the past, carried out no, or very little, research into transport pollution. The main exception to this is Severn Trent, which has carried out a study into the use of urea as a deicing agent on motorways. Anglian region has also carried out some general research into the herbicides simazine and atrazine. The RPB's showed very little interest in carrying out any future research in this field, but most of the regions of the NRA gave a strong indication of the necessity for many aspects of further research.

The main topics suggested were:

- assessment of sources, quantities and toxic effects of deicants used on roads and runways;

- assessment of usage of triazine herbicides and their effects;

- studies of the effects of trace metal and organic contamination;

- studies of the transport into, and fate of, fuels, oils and combustion products, in the freshwater aquatic environment; and,

- surveys of the biological quality of water bodies upstream and downstream of major road runoff discharges to enable assessment of impacts of discharge.

It should also be noted that the NRA has a national programme of research and development, of which one study concerns the effects of run-off from motorway and trunk roads.

From our study of the scientific literature, we also see a need for further research into the following issues. These include:

- a national survey of the current pollution loadings from motorways and urban roads, concentrating on the concentrations of lead, zinc, copper, other trace metals, PAHs, oil, other hydrocarbons, chloride and suspended solids in road run-off;

- a national survey of water pollution from railways, concentrating particularly on herbicides, oil and organics

- development of methods for using biological indicators to monitor impacts of episodic events of transport derived pollution;

- further work on examining the rates of discharge of transport derived pollutants to freshwater bodies in relation to runoff rate, in order to develop 'pollution hydrographs' of how such pollution episodes occur.

5.3 Pollution Control Measures

The NRA felt that further research is needed mainly into the two following aspects of engineered transport drainage:

- methods of containing the 'first flush' from gullypots;

- methods of preventing materials used in construction from entering watercourses.

We would further recommend the following:

- a study of the relative advantages of different road drainage systems and their feasibility in the UK;

- a study to determine optimum spacing, numbers and cleaning frequency of gullypots in terms of water quality;

- continued research into the advantages of and use of porous road surfaces and biofiltration techniques;

- a study into better control over types, quantities and application methods of deicants, particularly alternatives to glycol;

- investigation of treatment techniques to recover glycol economically after aircraft deicing.

6 Conclusions and Recommendations

6.1 Availability of Information

6.1.1 Roads

There is a considerable body of published material on the quality of road drainage, from many individual case studies. Most of the work has been carried out in the United States of America, the United Kingdom and West Germany. This research has focused both on urban roads (within towns) and on highways (including motorways). In general, information on contaminant concentrations from urban road studies shows highly variable results due to the wide range of variables and sources of pollution in towns, whilst results from highway/motorway studies show more clearly the impact of road transport on pollutant levels. However, the latter cannot be directly applied to an urban road situation due to factors including the differences of driving mode, which affects pollutant emission rates. The results of studies show agreement on the general types of pollutant of concern (suspended solids, BOD, oil, lead, PAH, trace metals etc), but show considerable discrepancies in terms in actual concentrations of pollutants in road run-off and their chemical speciation.

There is rather less information on the quality and composition of road drainage entering the aquatic environment after passage through the drainage system, but it is clear that drainage systems have a significant impact on the quality of road drainage. Thus the drainage effluent entering a receiving water may be substantially different in quality and composition from the original influent runoff entering the drainage system (eg gulleypots).

6.1.2 Rail, Air and Inland Waterways

The availability of information on aquatic pollution from railways and airports is markedly sparse by comparison with that on roads. This may be due to their lesser presence; the fact that many small airports are for national defence and therefore have tight security and, in the case of the UK, Crown Exemption from pollution legislation; that the construction of new railways and airports is relatively uncommon; or that public perception of rail and airport pollution (other than with regard to noise) is much lower than from roads.

Information on freshwater pollution from boats is particularly lacking, especially since marine pollution from vessels is well documented.

6.1.3 Toxicological and Biological Effects

Another noticeable gap in the published literature is case studies of the biological and toxicological effects of routine (consented) discharges of transport drainage into watercourses. It has been easier to find studies of the effects on aquatic biota of accidental spillages into watercourses. Apparently there has been apparently little systematic monitoring designed specifically to assess the impacts of episodic transport derived pollution on the biota of receiving waters.

6.1.4 NRA and RPBs

In our study we contacted each of the ten regions of the National Rivers Authority (NRA) in England and Wales and each of the seven River Purification Boards (RPBs) in Scotland, via a questionnaire and in some cases in person. A reply was received from each authority, varying in its detail and content. Some authorities were unable to provide some of the information requested, either due to it being not readily available, or because no relevant records exist.

In general however, sufficient information was provided to indicate the extent of transport pollution in the UK and atittudes of the regulatory authorities towards it.

6.2 Significance of Transport Pollution

6.2.1 Types of Pollution

Our study has clearly shown the high potential for aquatic pollution to result from each mode of transport studied-road, rail, air and inland waterways. The extent of resulting pollution is dependent not only on the contaminant sources and emissions, but also on the type and operating efficiency of the drainage system.

Many of the most important transport derived pollutants are common to more than one (or each) of the transport modes. Of particular significance are the following.

- During road, rail or airport construction, the suspended solids load in drainage can be very high, causing adverse effects on aquatic organisms, related to 'blanketing' effects.

- Suspended solids loads from routine road run-off, particularly from motorways, can be high.

- Oil, petrol and other fuel can be significant routine pollutants from roads and airports, and to a lesser extent from railways and boats. Particular problems arise from: the 'first flush' from gullypots at the beginning of heavy rainfall; undersized or badly maintained oil interceptors; and, release of oil from oil interceptors through the passage of detergents, particularly from airports, but also from carwashes and general urban drainage.

- Lead, zinc and other trace metals can be effectively removed from surface drainage when they are associated with solids, but soluble (bioavailable) forms frequently enter the aquatic environment, and can result in toxic effects on plants and organisms. Of particular concern, are the effects of gullypots which can increase the soluble metal content of drainage. It should be noted that the lead content of road drainage may be expected to decrease in the future as a result of the increased use of unleaded petrol.

- Deicants mainly including salt on roads and glycols and urea at airports, can lead to significant pulses of chloride or glycol entering watercourses, with significant biological and ecological effects.

- Herbicides (particularly atrazine and simazine), that are widely used in weed control along railways and roads have been found to cause significant pollution of surface water and groundwater, and can be transferred to potable water supplies.

- Accidental spillages of transported freight (liquid and solid) and of oil or fuel from transport depots, airports, garages etc, can cause serious pollution incidents. Road accidents and spillages are the most common cause.

In conclusion, on both a national and also on a vehicle/person/distance travelled basis, we consider roads to be the largest source of transport pollution, with the least polluting probably being the new generation of urban electric rapid light railway systems.

6.2.2 Emission Loadings

The majority of research into transport derived pollution has focused on determining the pollutant concentrations in road drainage. Some such studies have then related these values to the traffic flows to produce emission rates of various pollutants. For other pollutants, such as those emitted in exhaust fumes, emission factors can be directly measured, and estimates made of the proportion of airborne contaminants entering surface drainage. From such studies it is then possible to estimate a total pollutant load entering a watercourse. However, as a result of pollutant accumulation in road dusts between rain events, the relationship between pollutant emission rates and pollutant concentrations in runoff tends not to be constant, and in many situations, indicates loadings in excess of 100% of emitted pollutant in the runoff. For various reasons already discussed in this report (including vehicle related variables, climatic conditions, road structure, drainage systems and complex physico-chemical reactions), the emission rates, pollutant loads emitted, contaminant concentrations in surface runoff and in the receiving watercourses that have been derived from various studies differ widely.

It should also be understood that in general, total quantities (e.g. annual emissions) of contaminants emitted have little meaning in the context of their aquatic impact, since in reality the emissions entering a watercourse occur in episodic pulses, rather than as uniform emissions. In the case of most contaminants, it is the concentrations that occur during the duration of an individual event that are relevant, while the impact of the pollution episode depends on the location of its discharge. The total quantity of pollutant discharged to the aquatic environment averaged over longer time periods (e.g. greater than 1 day in all probability) does not take into account maximum concentrations of pollutants which may cause acute effects on water quality and organisms.

Allowing for the above considerations, an indication of quantities of pollutants emitted is given in Table 6.2a, in order to allow comparison with other sources of aquatic pollution in terms of total pollutant loads. As already discussed however, the value of this data is somewhat limited. In particular, the following should factors are important.

- The majority of the results are derived from road studies.

- Pollutant quantities vary widely between studies, but for consistency of relative concentrations between pollutants, we have shown results from two studies (Hewitt and Rashed, 1990 and Colwill et al, 1984). Thus the results shown are examples only, albeit of what we consider to be the most reliable data sets for the UK.

- The two main studies quoted (Hewitt and Rashed, 1990 and Colwill et al, 1984) refer to UK motorways – the M6 in the north-west and the M1 in the south. The results thus refer to situations of high traffic flows and high speed. The results are thus not representative of urban situations, where differences in driving mode affect emission rates of pollutants.

- The climatic and thus hydrological conditions that persisted during the two main studies were very different and these factors may have a significant effect on pollutant concentrations measured in runoff.

- There appear to be some inconsistencies and discrepancies between results of the two studies, for example, the total quantities of cadmium and of oil are of the same order of magnitude, and yet their emissions rates differ by more than 3 orders of magnitude.

6.2.3 Pollution Control

Legislation and Enforcement

Routine drainage from roads, rail or airports does not constitute trade effluent and therefore does not require a consent for discharge to inland waters or groundwater. In general therefore, no pollution control is legally enforced. However, the licensing authority (NRA in England and Wales, and RPB or Secretary of State in Scotland) does have the power (under the Water Resources Act, 1991 and previously COPA, 1974) to issue a Prohibition Notice on the drainage, requiring it to be consented.

Effluents from other transport related facilities including trade or sewage effluent and outfalls from drainage or sewers serving buildings or yards (including car parks, garages, stations etc), do require a consent to discharge to surface water or groundwater.

As part of a discharge consent, conditions may be set as to the quality and quantity of effluent permitted.

The result of this legislation is that the consenting of transport drainage (and in particular, roads) is dependent on the view of the relevant licensing authority as to the polluting potential of the transport drainage. Thus, different criteria may be applied regionally and the result is a highly variable distribution of consents throughout the UK. For example, the South West region of the NRA and the Highland RPB have issued no consents, whereas the Southern and Welsh regions of the NRA have issued several hundred. Our research suggests that the majority of outfalls are not consented, and that road drainage is not considered to be a particularly significant source of water pollution by some Authorities. This attitude is also apparently held by the Department of Transport which has stated that 'Individual highway schemes .... are unlikely to have significant effects on soil or water' (DTp, 1989). This apparent attitude cannot be supported by the evidence of this study.

Where discharge consents are issued it should be noted that many of them (particularly for road drainage) have no quality conditions attached. Thus despite issue of a consent, virtually no pollution control is being applied. Where consent conditions are set, relatively few constitutes of the drainage tend to be specified. This is a pragmatic approach, since limits are only set for those contaminants for which control is relatively straightforward; mainly suspended solids and oil. Contaminants of equal concern in the aquatic environment, such as chloride, PAH and trace metals, are rarely (if ever) limited to the consent and their concentrations are thus neither controlled nor routinely monitored. However, it is recognised that conventional chemical monitoring is highly problematic given the episodic nature of the pollutant discharges, thus biological monitoring and biomonitoring (chemical analysis of biota) may provide better means of monitoring discharges and their effects. Further, the pollutants for which conditions are set are likely to often exceed their consented limits due to 'first-flushes' from gullypots, or inadequate sizing and infrequent cleaning of oil interceptors and gullypots.

A further comment should be made regarding the high polluting potential of many Ministry of Defence, RAF and other airports which have Crown Exemption from discharge consents.

Drainage Management

A second and equally important aspect of pollution control is drainage management.

Road and urban drainage is provided firstly to facilitate removal of surface water for reasons of safety and aesthetics. Simultaneously, some removal of pollutant load occurs, depending on the type and design of the drainage system. Increasingly, pollutant removal is becoming a necessary design feature of drainage systems.

The most common drainage system in the UK employs gullies and gullypots. These systems require frequent cleaning and maintenance, which in practice is often not carried out sufficiently. There is considerable evidence that gullypots are a significant contributor to water pollution from surface water stormwater outfalls (SWO's) (see *Section 4.4.4*), and it has been suggested that a reduction in the number of gullypots could significantly reduce water pollution.

In other countries including West Germany, drainage retention facilities are widely used, and are increasingly being used in the UK. If designed to provide adequate flow characteristics and retention time, these structures can effect a high pollutant removal efficiency. The pollutants settle from the water and accumulate in a basal sludge, which requires periodic removal and disposal.

Table 6.2a Average Total Quantities of Pollutants Emitted from Transport in the UK

Pollutant	Emission Rate	Concentration in Runoff	Total Quantity in Runoff mass/km/year	mass/year	Reference	Section in report
Suspended Solids	–	169/230 mg/l	1 500 kg	570 550t[▲]	1	3.2.2
Biochemical oxygen demand (BOD)	–	32 mg/l	–	–	2	3.3.2
Oil	–	6–40 mg/l	126kg	47 950t[▲]	1	3.2.2
PAH from petrol	167 µg/l	1.79 µg/l	75kg*	28 150t[▲]	3	3.5.2
PAH from diesel	68 µg/l	1.79 µg/l	18g	7t[▲]	1	3.5.2
Lead	–	0.59 µg/l	4kg	1 500t[▲]	1	3.6.2
Zinc	–	1.2 mg/l	8kg	3 050t[▲]	1	3.7.2
Copper	7.2 mg.m.day	68 µg/l	2628kg*	1×16^6t[▲]	3	3.8.2
Copper from trains	0.15 kg/train/km	–	–	58t[+]	4	3.8.2
Chronium	–	5–85 µg/l	–	–	1,5,6	3..8.2
Cadmium	0.001–0.023 mg/m/day	3 µg/l	91kg	34 600t[▲]	3	3.8.2
Iron	–	440 mg/l (max)	–	–	7	3.8.2
Iron from trains	7g/train/km	–	–	2 750t[+]	4	3.8.2
Road salt	16 000 tonnes/ annum in Devon	–	1.1t[□]	418 500t[▲]	pers. comm.	3.9.3
Glycol at airports	90 000 litres/ 3months/airport	–	–	1M1[°]	8	3.9.3
Urea at airports	115 tonnes 3 months/airport	–	–	138t[°]	8	3.9.3
Herbicides	550 tonnes/year	–	–	550t	Daily Telegraph 4/1/91	3.10

[°] Calculated from emission rate
[▲] Based on a total road length in the UK of 380 378 km (see Table 2.2a)
[+] Based on a total of 393 million train km travelled in the UK 1989/90)
[□] Based on a total length in Devon 14,300 km calculated from an estimated 30% of roads in the South West Region being in Devon, and a total road length in the South West Reg 47 661 km
[°] Assuming 12 major airports in the UK (see Section 2.5.1.) and glycol application is during 3 months/year

References: 1 – Colwill *et al* (1984); 2 – Rose (1985); 3 – Hewitt and Rashed, 1990; 4 – MVNS (Ministry of Health and Environment, Netherlands, 1980); 5 – Bickmore and Dutton (1984a); 6 – Stotz, (1990; 7 – Ellis (1989); 8 – Gay (1987).

Infiltration systems such as soakaways and french drains can be effective pollutant removal systems, but are often unpopular due to the requirements for changing the filter media and the risk of water-logging of the ground and underground structures if located in inappropriate geology.

In drainage systems where oil and fuel spillage is considered likely, oil interceptors are provided. Their effectiveness depends not only on design, but also on maintenance and frequent emptying.

More recent technological developments which are not yet widely used, including permeable pavings and geotextiles. There is considerable scope for further use of these methods in specific applications.

Road drainage in the UK enters freshwater either via a separate surface water sewer (SWO), in a treated effluent from a sewage works or as an overflow of stormwater combined with untreated sewage (SSO). We consider that a separate sewered system, incorporating effective pollutant removal facilities to be the best option for reducing impacts of receiving freshwaters (see *Section 4.4.2*).

In summary, each type of drainage system can effect a substantial degree of pollutant removal if designed to do so. Equally importantly such systems require adequate maintenance and cleaning. More thoughtful selection of the drainage system, in relation to quality of influent drainage, manpower resources for maintenance, geology, and land use, and the quality of the receiving watercourse, could result in a considerable reduction in traffic related pollution, without further requirements for consenting of discharges or stricter conditions.

6.3 Recommendations

6.3.1 Further Research

Further research into both the extent and control of transport pollution could significantly reduce its occurrence and therefore significance. In particular, we consider the following areas of research to be important:

- Studies into the fate and toxicity of hydrocarbons, particularly PAH.

- Assessment of the usage and effects of the herbicides atrazine and simazine.

- Research into alternatives to glycol as a deicant and techniques for its reuse.

- Development of more effective road drainage systems to reduce road pollution.

- Further study of biological and ecotoxicological effects of road run-off, to include focussed biological studies in the vicinity of large road drainage outfalls.

6.3.2 Administrative Changes

In addition to further research, the following administrative changes could significantly reduce the impact of transport pollution.

- Tougher restrictions on the use of herbicides such as atrazine and simazine, and replacement with more environmentally sensitive alternatives.
- Restrictions on applications of road salt and airport deicants.
- More frequent cleaning and maintenance of gullypots and oil interceptors.
- More selective choice and better design of drainage control measures.
- Enforcement of stricter control over quality of discharged effluents.
- Placing a higher degree of environmental importance on location and type of new transport systems.

6.4 Summary

In this study of freshwater pollution from UK transport, ERL has carried out both a detailed literature review and also a questionnaire survey of the National Rivers Authority and River Purification Board (the regulatory bodies with main responsibility for water pollution).

The results of both of these aspects of study have shown clearly that water pollution from transport is a widespread problem.

Key conclusions are as follows.

- Many contaminants in transport pollution are common to road, rail, boat and aircraft.

- Road derived pollution is more significant than the other types of transport although occasional incidents, such as accidental spillages, can be equally significant from each type of transport.

- Further research is needed into the quantities and behaviour of transport derived pollutant (particularly PAH), their environmental toxicology, and methods of reducing and controlling aquatic pollution.

References

BALL I R (1967) **The toxicity of cadmium to rainbow trout** (*Salmo gairdnerii*) Wat Res l:X05-X06

BICKMORE C and DUTTON S, (1984a) **Environmental Effects of Motorway Runoff** Surveyor 10 May 1984

BICKMORE C and DUTTON S, (1984b) **Oil and Toxic Spillages in Motorway Runoff** Surveyor 24 May 1984

BICKMORE C and DUTTON S, (1984c) **Water Pollution in Motorway runoff** Surveyor 3 May 1984

BIRD R (1990) **Road Drainage Systems, Seminar on Road Drainage** Hydraulics Research Limited, Wallingford 13 Dec 1990

BROWN B E (1976) **Observations of the Tolerance of the Isopod** *Asellus Meridianus* **Rac. to copper and Lead**, Wat Res 10: 555-559

COLWILL D M, PETERS C J and PERRY R (1985) **Report 37**, Transport & Road Research Laboratory, Crouthorne, Berkshire

COLWILL D M, PETERS C J and PERRY R, (1984 **Water quality of Motorway Runoff,** TRRL Supplementary Report 823, Transport and Road Research Laboratory

Department of the Environment, Welsh Office **River Quality in England and Wales 1985** A Report of the 1985 Survey, HMSO, 1987

The Department of Transport, **Transport Statistics Great Britain, 1979–1989**, HMSO, 1990

Department of Transport (1989), **Highways and Traffic, Departmental Standards HD 18/88**, Environmental Assessment Under EC Directive 85/337

DRIVER F T, **Winter Maintenance: Practice and Policy**, Paper II

ELLIS K V, (1989) **Surface Water Pollution and its Control**, 1989 McMillan

ELLIS, J B, (1990a) **Bioengineering Design for Water quality Improvement in Urban Runoff, in Development in Storm Drainage; A Symposium on Infiltration and Storage of Stormwater in New Developments 3–4 January 1990**, Sheffield City Polytechnic, IWEM & CIRIA

ELLIS J B (l990b) **The Management and Control of Urban Runoff Quality**, J IWEM, 1989, 3, 116–124

ELLIS J B (1989), **The Development of Environmental Criteria for urban detention pond design in the UK, in, Current Practice and Design Criteria for Urban Runoff Water Quality Control** Amer. Soc. Civ. Eng., New York.

EXTENCE C A (1978), **The Effects of Motorway Construction on an Urban Stream**, Environ. Pollut. 17, 245–252

FEICK G, HORNE R A & YEAPLES D (1972), **Release of Mercury from Contaminated Freshwater Sediments by the Runoff of Road Deicing Salt**, Science Vol 175,1142–1143

FLETCHER I J, PRATT C J, and ELLIOTT G E P (1978) **An Assessment of the Importance of Roadside Gully-Pots in Determining the quality of Urban runoff**, in Urban storm Drainage, Pentech Press

Foreign & Commonwealth Office, Britain 1991 **An Official Handbook**, HMSO, 1991

FÖRSTNER U and WITTMAN G T W (1981) **Metal Pollution in the Aquatic Environment** Springer-Verlag, Berlin 1981, 485p 2nd Ed

FRASER J *et al* (1978), **Tolerance to lead in the freshwater isopod**, Asellus aquaticus, Wat Res, 12: 637-41

GARDINER J and MANCE G (1984) **United Kingdom Water Quality Standards Arising from European Community Directives**, Technical Report TR 204, Water Research Centre

GAY J, *et al* (1987) **Stormwater Contamination at Airports and Remedial Options, with Particular Reference to Stansted**, J IWEM, 1, 2, 253-262

GJESSING E, et al (1984), **Effects of highway runoff on lake water quality** Sci. Total Enviom. 33, 245-247

TER HAAR G L LENALLE DL HU N and BRANDT M (1972) **Composition, size and control of automotive exhaust particles**. Air Pollut. Control Ass. 22 39-46.

HAGEMANN R, VIRELIZER H, GAUDIN, DAVID PESNEAU, A (1981) **Polyclyclic aromatic hydrocarbons in exhuast particles emitted from gasoline and diesel automobile engines**. Presented at the Workshop on the Chemistry and Analysis of Hydrocarbon in the Environment Barcelone (1981)

HAMILTON R S, REVITT D M, WARREN R S and DUGGAN M J **Metal Mass Balance Studies within a small Highway Dominated Catchment**, The Science of the Total Environment, 59 (1987), 365 - 368

HARRISON R M *et al* (1985), **The budget of lead, copper and cadmium for a major highway**, Sci Total Environ 46,137-145

HARROP D O, ELLIS, J B & REVITT D M (1983) **Temporal Loadings of Sediment and Heavy metals to Roadside Gully Pots**, In: Heavy Metals in the Environment, eds, PERRY, R, MULLER G and FORSTNER, U

HARROP O (1983) **Urban Stormwater Pollution: Research Report 6: Stormwater Pollution from Highway Surfaces: A Review** Middlesex Polytechnic Research and Consultancy

HELLAWELL J M (1986), **Biological Indicators of Freshwater Pollution and Environmental Management**, Pollution Monitoring Series, Elsevier Applied Sciences Publishers

HEM J D and DURUM W H (1973) **Solubility and occurrence of Pb in Surface Water**, J.Am. Wat. Wks. Ass. 65(8), 562–568

HEWITT C N and RASHED M B, (1990), **An Integrated Budget for selected Pollutants for a Major Rural Highway**, the Silence of the Total Environment, 93: 375–384.

HILMER T and BATES G C, **Observations on the Effect of Outboard Motor Fuel Oil on Phytoplankton Cultures**, Environmental Pollution (Series A) 32 (1983), 307–316

HOGLAND W, NIEMSCZYNOWICZ J and WAHLMAN T (1987), **The unit superstructure during the construction period**. Sci Total Environ. 59, 411-424 37

HOGLAND W (1990), **Pervious Asphalt Constructions An overview of the situation in Sweden and the United States, in, Developments in Storm Drainage: A Symposium on Infiltration and Storage of stormwater in New Developments**, 3–4 Jan 1990, Sheffield City Polytechnic, IWEM & CIRIA

HOLCOMBE *et al* (1976), **Long term effects of lead exposure on three generations of brook trout** (*Salvelinus fortinalis*) J Fish Res Bd Can 33; 1731-41

JOHN E D, COOKE M and NICKLESS G, (1979) **Polycyclic Aromatic Hydrocarbon in sediments Taken from the Seven Estuary Drainage System** bull. Environm. Contam. Toxicol. 22, 653–659

JOHNSON B T and ROMANENKO V I A **Multiple Testing Approach for Hazard Evaluation of Complex Mixtures in the Aquatic Environment: The Use of Diesel Oil as a Model.** Environmental Pollution, 58 (1989) 221–235

LAXEN D P H and HARRISON R M, **The Highway as a Source of Water Pollution: An Appraisal with the Heavy Metal Lead**, Water Research, 11, 1–11, 1977

LEE G F (1975) **Role of hydrous metal oxides in the transport of Heavy Metals in the Environment** In, Heavy Metals in the Aquatic Environment, Edited by Krenkel P A pp 137–147, Pergamon Press

LEWIS D (1986) **Overturning Dangers**, Hazardous Cargo Bulletin, June 1986

LYSYj I and RUSSELL E C (1974) **Dissolution of Petroleum-derived Products** in Water Research, 8

Local Authorities Associations – **Highway Maintenance – A Code of Good Practice** Association of County Councils, London 1989

MODHUN Y A, FREED V H and YOUNG J L (1986) **Binding of ionic and neutral herbicides by soil humic acid soil** Sci Soc Am J, 50, 319-322

MALMQVIST P A (1983), **Urban storm water pollutant sources**, Chalmers University, Gothenberg

McCARTHY J F, JIMINEZ, B D and BARBEE T (1985) **Effect of Dissolved Humic Material on Accumulation of Polycyclic Aromatic Hydrocarbons: Structure - Activity relationship**, Aquatic Toxicology, 7, 15–24

MERLINI M and POZZI G (1977) **Lead and Freshwater fishes; Part I Lead accumulation and water pH** Environ Pollut 12: 167–72

Ministry of Health and Environmental Protection, Handbook of Emissions Factors, Part 1, Non Industrial Sources, government Publishing Office, The Hague, 1980

MORRISON G M *et al* (1988) **Transport Mechanisms and Processes for Metal Species in a Gullypot System,** Wat. Res. 22, (11), 1417–1427

MORRISON G M, REVITT D M and ELLIS J B (1989) **Sources and Storm Loading Variations of Metal Species in a Gullypot Catchment**, The Science of the Total Environment, 80, 267–278

NEFF J M (1979) **Polycyclic aromatic hydrocarbons in the Aquatic Environment – Sources, fates and Biological Effects** Applied Science, Barking

NRIAGU J O (1974) **Lead orthophosphates – IV Formation and Stability in the environment**, Geochim Cosmochim Acta 38, 887–898

OATES D (1976) **The Effects of Boating upon Lead Concentrations in Fish**, Trans Kan Acad Sci, 79 (3–4), 149–153

PEARSON D (1990) **Highway Drainage and its Problems** in Developments in Storm Drainage: A symposium on Infiltration and Storage of Stormwater in New Developments, 3 & 4 Jan 1990

PRATT C J, MANTLE J D G and SCHOFIELD P A (1989), **Urban Stormwater Reduction and Quality Improvement Through the Use of Permeable Pavements** Wat Sci Tech Vol 21, 769-778

ROSE P L **Pollution Aspects of Highway Drainage**, The Public Health Engineer, 13, 167–168, 1985

Royal Society of Chemistry, **The Agrochemicals Handbook**, Nottingham, 1987

SHUTES R B E (1988) **The influence of agricultural and urban runoff on the macroinvetebrate fauna of ponds and streams**, Ecological Bulletins, 39, 154–156

Shaheen D G (1975) **Contributions of urban roadway usage to water pollution**. Environ. Prot. Agency EPA 600/2-75-004 228pp Washington.

STOTZ G (1990), **Decontamination of Highway Surface Runoff in the FRG**, The Science of the Total Environment, 93, 507–514

STUMM W and MORGAN J J (1970) **Aquatic Chemistry**, 583 pp, Wiley Interscience, New York

THOMPSON J R, RUTTER A 1, RIDOUT P S and GLOVER M (1989) **The Implications of the Use of De-Icing Salt for Motorway Plantings in the UK**, Paper 13

WARNICK S L and BELL H L (1969) **The acute toxicity of some heavy metals to different species of aquatic insects** J Wat Pollut Control Fed 41 – 280–284

WARREN R S **PhD Thesis**, Middlesex Polytechnic, London (1987)

The Water Supply (Water Quality) Regulation 1989, **Statutory Instrument** No 1147, HMSO 1990

WESTERHOLM R N, ALSBER T E, FROMMELIN M E, STRANDELL M E, RANNUG U, WINQUIST L, GRIGORIADIS V and EGEBACK K E (1988) **Effects of fuel polycyclic aromatic hydrocarbon content on emissions of polycyclic aromatic hydrocarbons and other mutagenic substances from a gasoline-fuelled automobile**, Environ Sci Technol, 22, 925

WILLIAMS M L **The Role of Motor Vehicles in Air Pollution in the UK**, in The Science of the Total Environment, 93 (1990) 1–8, Elsevier

YOUSEF Y A, HVITVED-JACOBSEN T, HARPER H H and LIN L Y, (1990), **Heavy Metal Accumulation and Transport through Detention Ponds Receiving Highway Runoff**, The Science of the Total Environment, 93, 433–440

Environmental Fate and Toxicity of Transport Derived Pollutants

Al.l Introduction
On entering the aquatic environment, the impact of contaminants on water quality and aquatic life, depends on their physico-chemical behaviour in the freshwater environment. These properties of the contaminants determine their ultimate fate.

A1.2 Oil
The environmental fate of oil depends in part on the form in which it enters the watercourse, its properties such as composition and viscosity, and environmental factors such as temperature and wind.

If unconfined, most oils will rapidly spread to a thickness of about 1.0mm or less. Contaminated or dirty oil will spread more slowly and thick oils such as heavy fuel oils may form lumps in the water. If the oil enters water in an area of turbulence, a water-oil emulsion may form. Oil films will move with the current, but are more effectively influenced by the wind. Usually the oil film will move at between 3% and 4% of the wind velocity.

Evaporation of the oil can occur, particularly soon after it enters the watercourse, and during high winds.

Oil entering a watercourse from road drainage may already be associated with particles, and may thus rapidly settle. Oil in a slick may also become associated with suspended matter and settle. Once in the sediment the oil will be slowly degraded by aerobic and anaerobic processes. However in many cases, the inflow of oil may exceed degradation and the oil may be accumulated. Floating oil may also be removed from the water by coating algae or clinging to the feathers or fur of birds and animals.

If an oil-water emulsion is formed, degradation will occur through dissolution, chemical oxidation, photochemical oxidation and microbial degradation.

In many cases, where the quantity of oil in the watercourse is large, such as from a spillage, a clean-up processes will be carried out to remove the oil. The oil is usually contained using a floating boom, or on smaller watercourses, ditches, drains or channels, a temporary dam may be constructed. Removal of the oil then involves skimming to remove the bulk of the oil, followed by further cleaning usually using a sorbent material. The oil that has been removed must then be disposed of.

When oil is introduced to a watercourse, the total effect on water quality is, in addition to the physicochemical processes described above, related to it ecotoxicological effects. Thus, the changes that occur are as follows (Johnson, 1989):

- community respiration exceeds autotrophic (use of CO_2 etc) productivity;

- CO_2 rapidly increases;

- pH decreases;

- calcium is released from the sediments;

- alkalinity and conductivity of the water increase.

A1.3 Polyclyclic Aromatic Hydrocarbons (PAH)
The solubility of PAH compounds is generally low, and is inversely related to molecular weight. Thus the most soluble compounds are those of low molecular weight such as naphthalene, phenanthrene and anthracene, whilst the higher molecular weight compounds such as fluoranthene, pyrene and benzo(a) pyrene, have a lower solubility. PAH solubility also increases with increasing temperature, and organic matter (particularly humic and fulvic acids and other products of degradation) may also serve to solubilise PAH compounds.

Related to their solubility, is their affinity for particulate matter. Thus, the low molecular weight PAH, with their higher solubility, tend to be enriched in the water column relative to the sediments, whilst PAH with a higher molecular weight and a low solubility, demonstrate a high particle affinity and are enriched in the sediments. Unlike trace metals and some organic contaminants, PAH compounds do not show an adsorption affinity for fine grain-sized particles, but rather for coarse sand-sized particles. There is evidence that an exchange mechanism exists between adsorbed and soluble PAH.

Surveys of UK rivers have shown that rural rivers remote from human activity have very low concentrations of PAH, and that PAH content is heavily influenced by industrial mining and urban activity. Concentrations of total

PAH in water have been reported at between 20 and 2 350 ng/l (see *Table A1.3a*), and the same studies found the soluble PAH to represent only 2–16% of the concentration of particulate PAH.

Table A1.3a   Concentration of Dissolved PAH in River Water

River	Concentration (ng/l) Total PAH	BaP	Reference
Thames	800–2 350	170–280	Acheson et al 1976
Trent	25–3 790	5.3–504	Lewis, 1975
Seven	20–266	1.5–48	Lewis, 1975

Source: Neff (1979)

A study of the concentration of PAH in sediments in the river catchments of the Severn Estuary (John *et al*, 1979) found concentrations of individual PAH compounds ranging from 0.1–6.4 mg/kg (dry weight). Many of the highest concentrations were attributed to coal mining, but there were also noticeably high concentrations at one site just downstream of a road bridge carrying a high density of industrial traffic.

The presence of PAH in groundwater is due mainly to leaching from soils. Concentrations are generally of the order of a factor of ten lower than those reported in river water (Neff, 1979).

The cycle of PAH in the aquatic environment can be summarised as follows (Neff, 1979).

- PAH compounds are rapidly adsorbed onto organic and inorganic particulate matter, which are then deposited in the bottom sediments.

- Leaching or biological activity may return a small fraction of sediment PAH to the water column.

- PAH are readily accumulated by aquatic biota to levels higher than those in the ambient media.

- The relative concentrations of PAH in aquatic ecosystems are generally highest in the sediments, intermediate in aquatic biota and lowest in the water column.

- Removal of PAH from the aquatic environment can occur in several ways most of which take place in aerobic conditions. Thus in anoxic environments PAH compounds are generally stable. Removal can occur as follows:

    volatisation of PAH from the water surface (mainly of low molecular weight compounds);

    photooxidation;

    chemical oxidation;

    biological metabolism (particularly microbial decay of low molecular weight compounds).

A1.4   Metals

Transport

The two most important factors for the transport of trace metals within the freshwater environment are water discharge and biological activity, both of which exhibit strong temporal variations. The behaviour of a metal is also highly dependent on its chemical form, particularly whether it is dissolved or particulate. The general relationship between metal transport and water discharge is as follows.

- The concentration of dissolved metals decreases with increasing water discharge, as a result of dilution.

- The concentration of particulate metals increases with increasing water discharge, as a result of re-suspension of particles from the river bed and banks.

A strong seasonal variability has been observed in metal concentrations, related to changes in rates of organic decay, changes in metabolic activity of river biota and adsorption by planktonic material (Forstner and Wittman, 1981).

Association of metals with sediments

Many metals, particularly lead, have a low water solubility and become rapidly associated with particulate matter in a stream or river. To fully assess the extent of metal pollution, it is thus essential to carry out analysis of sediment in addition to water. Of particular importance in sediment analysis is the grain size. In general, there is an increase in metal concentration with decreasing particle size. Exceptions to this rule occur at either end of the size spectrum; with particles >63 μm there is an increase in metal concentration due to the presence of detrital minerals rich in heavy metals; with particles <2 μm, there is a decrease in metal concentration due to a reduced adsorption capacity of the partially less crystalline or amorphous substances (Förstner and Wittman, 1981).

There are several ways in which metals can be associated with sediments. The type of bonding that occurs is dependent on the depositional environment, characterised by the chemical composition, particularly important are the amount of dissolved iron and carbonate available for reactions, ionic strength, pH and redox conditions and by the hydrodynamic conditions. The general effects of these influential factors may be described as follows (Forstner and Wittman, 1981):

- **Detrital Minerals**. The presence of a large proportion of heavy minerals results in enrichment of trace elements, particularly in the silt and fine sand fractions of sediment.

- **Sorption**. A generalised sequence of the capacity of solids to sorb heavy metals is

  manganese oxide > humic acid > iron oxide > clay minerals.

  pH has a controlling effect on metal adsorption. The hydrogen ions compete with heavy metal cations for exchange sites, thereby releasing the latter. Adsorption also varies according to the solid and the metal. For example, the sequence of affinity of heavy metals to clay minerals is as follows:

  lead > nickel > copper > zinc.

- **Coprecipitation with Hydrous Fe/Mn Oxites ant Carbonates**. In an aquatic system under oxidising conditions, hydrous iron and manganese oxides constitute a highly effective sink for heavy metals.

- **Complexation and flocculation with organic matter**. In organic matter rich systems the reactive humic acids and organo-clays compete for metal ions more strongly than the Fe/In oxides.

- **Heavy metal precipitates**. Sediment can be formed from the direct precipitation of heavy metal hydroxides, phosphates carbonates and sulphides.

Release of Heavy Metals from Sediments

Despite being readily removed from solution into the solid phase, the adsorbed metals may be released back into the water column as a result of physico-chemical changes in the aquatic system. The tendency of a metal to remain in solution or to be adsorbed onto sediments can be described by its residence time in the aqueous phase. Metals which readily come out of solution have a short residence time, and conversely, those which tend to stay in solution, have long residence times. In general, equilibrium between solution and solid phases cannot normally be reached in rivers due to the short residence times caused by the flow of the river.

Characteristic differences exist for the behaviour of a number of elements in freshwater and sea water, which has important implications for freshwaters that are subject to contamination from winter road deicing salt. Metals including iron and lead, and to a lesser extent zinc, copper and chromium, tend to be increasingly removed from a solution with an increase in water salinity (Forstner and Wittman, 1981).

Heavy metals may be released from suspended material and sediments in the following ways:

- Elevated salt concentrations can lead to competition with the sorbed metals from other cations. In particular, it has been shown (Feick 1972) that road deicing salt entering a watercourse can lead to competition from Na^+ and Ca^{2+} ions with mercury (Hg^{2+}) in the sediments and its subsequent release into the water column. It is likely that the same phenomenon also exists with other heavy metals, such as cadmium and zinc, which tend to be relatively less tightly bound to sediments.

- Changes in redox conditions (for example in a gullypot) can lead to the dissolution of iron and manganese hydroxides and release of incorporated heavy metals. However, depending on sulphide levels in the gullypots the metals may be reprecipitated as metal sulphides.

- A lowering of pH can lead to a dissolution of carbonates and hydroxides, as well as to increase desorption of metal cations due to competition with hydrogen ions.

- Natural and synthetic complexing agents (for example in urban or domestic runoff) can form soluble metal complexes of high stability with heavy metals that would otherwise be adsorbed to solid particles.

- A further phenomenon affecting the removal and re-release of metals is planktonic and other biological activity. Dissolved metals may be transported into particulate matter by planktonic activity and subsequently released into the water on decomposition of sedimentary plankton.

A1.5 Herbicides

The herbicides atrazine and simazine have appreciable solubilities (33 mg/l and 5 mg/l respectively (Royal Soc. Chem., 1987)) and are also fairly persistent in the aquatic environment. They thus exist primarily in a dissolved form, but may also become associated with sediments and aquatic organisms. The degree of adsorption by sediments is influenced by the organic matter content of the sediments and water. High organic matter contents in sediments increase adsorption (Madhun *et al* 1986), while interactions with dissolved organic matter can stabilise higher concentrations of atrazine and simizine in the dissolved phase. The overall distribution of such herbicides is therefore decided by competitive partitioning between the organic matter in the two phases (Madhun *et al*, 1986).

A2   Toxicological and Biological Effects

A2.1   Classification of Water Quality

The principal concern with pollutants entering the aquatic environment is their biological and toxicological effects on organisms and plants in the receiving water, on animals and birds higher up the food chain, and on man, if the water is abstracted for potable supply.

The UK standard water classification system for freshwater (the NWC (National Water Council) system) is based on concentrations of selected chemical determinands (primarily organic), known to be detrimental to aquatic life or man. Accordingly, Water Quality Objectives are set by the NRA using this system, and their water quality monitoring measures those determinands. The determinands that are specified in detail are dissolved oxygen, BOD and ammonia, and there is an additional category stating that the water should be 'non-toxic to fish in EIFAC (European Inland Fisheries Advisory Commission) terms, or best estimates if EIFAC figures are not available'. To meet this criterion, the NRA sampling therefore also generally allows for analysis of a suite of trace metals and organics that may be toxic to freshwater aquatic life. Since the NWC recommendation of classification according to EIFAC limits, EC Directives on water quality for the protection of freshwater life and for water intended for human consumption (78/659/EEC; 75/440/EEC and 80/778/EEC), which also contain chemical water quality standards, have been implemented in the UK.

However, intermittent (and often infrequent) chemical sampling of waters may not be the most appropriate method of determining water quality. The quality of water varies considerably due to natural processes, and occasional samples (particularly if taken at regular intervals) will provide only an instantaneous and transient picture of water quality. It may also completely miss a pollution episode. Continuous recording methods offer some solution, but due to practical and economic considerations are not generally suitable. Analysis of substrate material (sediments, epilithic algae etc.) can also give a longer term picture of the stream quality.

An alternative method of water quality monitoring is to use biological methods. The main advantage of using biota, is that since they are continually exposed to the varying water quality conditions and demonstrate an integrated response, they can provide equivalent information to an extensive array of continuous chemical samplers. Biota can provide evidence of recent environmental history in two ways:

- by the differing sensitivities and recovery rates of components of plant and animal communities;

- by the concentration and storage of substances in their tissues.

However, it should be noted that the level of understanding of the aquatic toxicology of many pollutants is still relatively poor. More combined sampling (chemical and biological) programmes would be beneficial to furthering our understanding of the biological effects of water pollution.

Pulses of pollution are stressful to aquatic ecosystems and the relative importance of biological monitoring over chemical sampling can often be seen in streams receiving road drainage, where the chemical analysis indicates satisfactory water quality, despite a marked absence of species diversity and numbers. This represents the common case of an episodic pollution event resulting in biological damage; following the episode, water quality appears to recover far more rapidly than the biota.

Toxicity to aquatic organisms can be classified as either acute (usually when the effects occur rapidly) or chronic (when the effects build up slowly). Acute effects usually occur as a result of a high dose, and chronic effects from long term exposure to a low dose of contaminant. Consequently, toxicity tests on fish or other aquatic organisms, can be either short term or long-term. Short term tests are usually used to determine the median lethal concentration

(LC_{50}) which is the concentration of test material at which 50% of the test organisms are killed in a given time (usually 96 hours). Intermediate tests usually take place over 8–90 days, and provide further information as to the effects of the toxicant on the adult form of the species over a longer period of time. Long term tests provide information on the whole life cycle, such as survival of different life stages, behaviour modifications, bioaccumulation, and growth and success of spawning and hatching.

In the following discussions we present a review of the biological and toxicological effects of transport derived pollutants on aquatic life. The relevant water quality criteria for the protection of freshwater life and drinking water are given in Tables A2.1 a and A2.1 b.

Table A2.1a Water Quality Criteria for Protection of Freshwater Fish and Aquatic Life

Substance	Salmonid fish (EC)	Coarse fish (EC)	Other aquatic life (EC)	Fish (EIFAC)	Fish (EPA)	Other aquatic life (EPA)
Cadmium (Cd)	5[1]	5[1]	5[1]	0.6–1.5[4,15]	1.2[2]	12[2]
Chromium (Cr)	5–50[4]	150–250[4]	–	5–50[4]	0.4[3]	4[3]
Copper (Cu)	1–28[4,5]	1–28[4,5]	1–28[4]	5–112[4,15]	(c.10)[2]	
	5–112[4,6]	5–112[4,6]			(c.2)[3]	
Lead (Pb)	4–20[4]	50–250[4]	5–60[4]	–	(c.500)[2]	(NOTE 7)[2]
					(c.5)[3]	(NOTE 7)[3]
Mercury (Hg)	1[8]	1[8]	1[8]	–	0.05	0.05
Nickel (Ni)	50–200[4]	50–200[4]	8–100[4]	–	(c.25)[2]	(NOTE 7)[2]
Zinc (Zn)	10–125[4]	75–500[4]	100	30–5000[4,15]	(c.25)[2]	(NOTE 7)[2]
	30–500[9,4]	300–2000[9,4]		300–2000[4,16]	(c.3)[3]	
Cyanide (CN)	–	–	–	–	5	(NOTE 7)[3]
Dissolved or emulsified hydrocarbons	(NOTE 10)	(NOTE 10)	–	–	–	5
BOD (as O2)(mg/l)	3[11,12]	6[11,12]	–	–	–	–
pH	6–9[13,14]	6–9[13,14]	–	–	–	–
Suspended solids	25[13,11]	25[13,11]	–	25	–	–
Oil	–	–	–	–	(c.100)	(NOTE 7)

Notes

All concentrations are given in µg/l unless stated otherwise.

Standards are defined as an annual average unless stated otherwise.

All substances are measured as dissolved.

(100) Numbers in brackets indicate a value derived from application factors of the 96hr LC_{50}.

1   Total concentration ie dissolved plus particulate

2   Hard water

3   Soft water

4   Range, according to water hardness (<50mg/l CaCo₃ to >250mg/l CaCo₃).

5   A higher value may be acceptable where acclimation is expected or copper is present in organic complexes.

6   Guide value, defined as a 95 percentile

(NOTE7)   An application factor of the 96 hr LC_{50}

8   Total concentration (dissolved plus particulate) defined as an annual average

9   Mandatory value, referring to the total zinc concentration (dissolved plus particulate) defined as a 95 percentile.

(NOTE 10) Must not adversely affect fish flavour. Mandatory standard. Hydrocarbons must not form a film on the water surface or bed and must not produce harmful effects in fish.

11 Guide value

12 Applies to BOD test without indibition of nitrifcation.

13 May be waived in the event of expectional meteorological or geographical conditions

14 Mandatory value

15 Salmonids

16 Coarse fish

Source: Hellawell, J M (1986)

A2.2   Organic Contamination (BOD)

Effects

The main ecological effects of organic contamination are to cause a reduction in the dissolved oxygen content of the water, modifications of the substrate, and in some cases, addition of nutrients. The result is to cause a change in the biological community composition and the relative abundances of organisms.

Many of the biological effects of organic pollution are well understood and are largely associated with rapid oxygen reduction and subsequent recovery. Most studies on the effects of organic contamination have been related to sewage effluent or other effluents which contain far greater concentrations of organic matter than those derived from transport.

Many of these effects can be predicted as a series of successional changes in the composition of the biological community. All aquatic life can be adversely affected by organic contamination, including fish, macrophytes, algae and macroinvertebrates, although low oxygen tolerant opportunists (e.g. tubificid oligochaetes and some chironomids) are able to thrive due to lack of competition from less tolerant species.

Water Quality Standards

EIFAC does not specify standards for protection of freshwater quality in relation to BOD. The EC Guide values for BOD concentrations are 3 mg/l (as O_2) for the protection of waters for salmonoid fish and 6 mg/l (as O_2) for the protection of waters for the protection of waters for coarse fish.

There is no standard for BOD in drinking water, but the UK standard for BOD in water to be abstracted for potable use is a 90 percentile guide value of 3-7 mg/l (as O_2).

Table A2.1b UK Water Quality Criteria for Surface Water Intended for Abstraction for Drinking Water Supply

Substance	Drinking Water		Raw Water	
	G	MAC	G(90%)	I(95%)
Cadmium (Cd)	–	5	1	5
Chromium[1] (Cr)	–	50	–	50
Copper (Cu)	1003–3000[4]	3 000	20–1000	50[8]
Iron[2] (Fe)	50	200	100–1000	300–2000
Lead[2] (Pb)	–	50[5]	–	50
Mercury (Hg)	–	1	0.5	1
Nickel (Ni)	–	50	–	–
Zinc (Zn)	100[3]–5000[4]	5 000	500–1000	3000–5000
Cyanide (CN)	–	50	–	50
Dissolved or emulsified hydrocarbons	–	10	<500	50–1000
Pesticides	–	0.1[6]–0.5[7]	–	1–25
Polyclic aromatic hydrocarbons (PAH)	–	0.2	–	0.2
Chloride (Cl)	25	400	200	–
BOD(mg/l) (as O_2)	–	–	3–7	–
COD (mg/l) (as O_2)	–	–	<30	–
Dissolved oxygen (%)	–	–	>30–>70	–
pH	6.5–8.5	9.5[3]	5.5–9	–
Suspended solids (mg/l)	0	–	25	–
Turbidity (FTU)	1	4	–	–

Notes

All concentrations are given in µg/l unless stated otherwise

All substances measures as total ie dissolved plus particulate

G = Guide value to be observed if possible

MAC = Maximum admissible concentration

I = Indicative or Mandatory value

90% = standard defined as a 90 percentile

95% = standard defined as a 95 percentile

1   Defined as total chromium (ie Cr III plus Cr VI)

2   Defined as dissolved iron

3   In water leaving the treatment plant

4   In water at the consumer's tap

5   In running water

6   Individual

7   In total

8   May be waived under exceptional climatic or geographical conditions.

Source: The Water Supply Regulation, 1989 and Gardiner, 1984

A2.3 Suspended Solids

Effects

Suspended solids can have adverse effects on freshwater communities in the following ways:

- Increased turbidity may cause a reduction in light penetration and a consequent reduction in the photosynthetic rates of algae and submerged macrophytes.

- Direct mechanical effects may occur such as abrasion, clogging the respiratory surfaces of gills, and/or interference with feeding through collection on feeding appendages or nets of filter-feeding invertebrates.

- Most commonly, suspended solids modify the nature of the habitat by changing the character of the substratum when they settle. Many invertebrates, and some fish depend upon the permeability of the gravel for respiration or feeding, and may be affected by the fine material settling and filling the interstices of the gravel or silt on the stream bed.

- Deposition of inert mineral solids (as is frequently the case with road drainage) can alter the proportions of inert and organic components, with the result that the burrowing, filter-feeding or surface detritivores are overwhelmed by inedible material, and the habitat becomes sterile.

Suspended solids entering a river during motorway construction (see *Section 3.13.7*) have been observed to cover the river bed with sand of particle size < 1mm (Extence, 1978). The result was, that the populations of species such as the filter feeding caddis *Hydropsyche augustipennis,* the mollusc *Lymnaea peregra* and the leeches *Erpobdella octoculata* and *Glossiphonia complanata* were rapidly reduced. The freshwater limpet *Ancylus pluviatilis* completely disappeared. One species commonly tolerant of silty conditions, the mayfly *Caenis moesta* was less abundant in the affected area, whilst another tolerant organism, the bivalve mollusc *Pisidium,* was found in increased numbers, but relatively low densities, due to the high proportion of inert solids and thus the lack of a food source. Tubificid worms and chironomid fly larvae were almost unaffected, since both are burrowing or tube-building forms and are commonly associated with soft, depositing substrates. The filamentous alga *Cladophora* disappeared.

In summary, high suspended solids concentrations and deposition rates result in:

- a lowering of benthic community diversity;

- the colonisation of a replacement fauna consisting of burrowing forms;

- lower densities of fish.

Water Quality Standards

The EIFAC (1964) criteria for suspended solids have been adopted in the EC Directive on freshwater fish, where the guideline value for mean suspended solids concentrations is 25 mg/l for both salmonid and cyprinid waters. No standard is set for the protection of other freshwater life.

The UK drinking water standards specify a 90 percentile guide value of 25 mg/l in raw water and 0 mg/l in tap water.

A2.4 pH

Effect

The natural variation in pH in freshwater environments is wide, ranging from 3.5 or 4 in acid moorland streams, to 8 or so in chalk strams. The intense photosynthetic activity of algae and higher plants in bright weather may increase pH to 9 or 10 (Hellawell, 1986).

The direct effects of extreme pH are believed to be interference with normal physiological functions, especially those associated with respiration (Hellawell, 1986). It is thought that pH may also affect the permeability of membranes. In waters of low pH, fish show increased loss of sodium and other ions through gill membranes.

Studies on aquatic insects have shown that in general, the most tolerant species to low pH are caddis flies; stoneflies and dragonflies exhibit a moderate tolerance of low pH; and mayflies are quite sensitive to low pH (Hellawell, 1986).

It has been established that pH in the range of 5-9 is not directly lethal to fish, although since the toxicity of certain common pollutants is modified by changes in pH, it is quite possible that changes in pH within the range 5-9 can cause indirect toxic effects to aquatic biota.

Water Quality Standards

The EC standard for the protection of both salmonid and coarse fish is a pH range 6–9. No standard is set for other aquatic life.

A similar range is set for drinking water, being a 90 percentile guide value of pH 5.5–9 in raw water, a guide value of pH 6.5 – 8.5 in treated water, with a maximum admissable of pH of 9.5.

A2.5 Chloride and Glycol Deicants

Toxicity

Chloride is not very toxic per se, but it can significantly affect osmotic balance in organisms. With time, many organisms can adapt to a wide range of chloride concentrations, as is demonstrated in part by the seasonal migration of certain fish species from rivers to the sea and back again. However, pulse inputs of high concentrations of chloride, which can occur following snowmelt containing deicing salt, can result in a rapid destruction of plants and invertebrates; particularly those that are sessile. Table A2.5a summarises data on toxicity and sublethal effects of chloride on aquatic organisms.

Ethylene glycol is a water miscible liquid with a low toxicity to aquatic organisms; 96 hour LC_{50} to fathead minnow (*Pimephales promelas*) of >2g/1; 24 hour TLm50 of >32 g/l to mosquito fish (*Gambusia affinis*). A secondary, indirect effect of glycol is its high BOD (see *Section A2.2*).

Water Quality Standards

There are no standards for chloride or glycol for the protection of freshwater fish or other life.

For chloride, in drinking water, a 90 percentile guide value of 200 mg/l in raw water is set; a guide value of 25 mg/l in tap water and a maximum admissable concentration of 200 mg/l.

Table A2.5a Chloride Toxicity

Species	Test	Concentration (mg Cl/l)	Reference
Fathead minnow (*Pimephales promelas*)	96 hr LC_{50}	7650	Adelman *et al*, 1976
Goldfish (*Carassius auratus*)	96 hr LC_{50}	7341	Adelman *et al*, 1976
Mosquito fish (*Gambusia affinis*)	96 hr LC_{50} 48 hr LC_{50} 8 hr LC_{50}	15000 10000 10000	Al-Daham & Bhatti, 1977
Hydropsyche bettini, Cheumatopsyche analis, Gammarus pseudo limneaus	Drift patterns	800[1] 1000[2]	Crowther and Hynes (1977)

Notes
1   No effect
2   Drift became apparent

Source: Hellawell, J M (1986)

A2.6 Oil

Toxicity And Effect

The effect of oil in the aquatic environment varies with such factors as type and quantity of oil, wind velocity, ambient temperature, rate of stream flow, duration of spill and the techniques employed in any clean-up operations.

Oil spreading as a thin film on water has the effect of interfering with gas exchange and hence preventing, or severely reducing, the rate at which atmospheric oxygen can be absorbed into de-oxygenated water. Most oils, if unconfined, will rapidly spread to a thickness of about 1mm, but the thinnest film seen on water may be as little as 4 x 10^{-5}mm (0.04μm). It is considered unlikely that oil films thinner than 10-3mm (lμm) affect the rate of solution of atmospheric oxygen.

Most oils have an effective biochemical oxygen demand (BOD) content related to their mass concentration by a factor of between 0.4 and 0.7 (Ellis, 1989).

All aquatic organisms can be affected by oil. Algae can be coated with floating oil and will be destroyed. Fish and other invertebrates can be seriously affected, and larger animals such as swimming birds, voles, otters, can be affected by oil sticking to their fur or feathers, through the direct ingestion of oil, or through destruction of their food resources.

Many oils also exert a direct toxic effect on fish and other aquatic organisms, which varies with factors such as hardness, temperature, pH and the presence of other polluting materials. Studies on the effects of oil on algae have shown that toxicities of whole fuel oils are different from that of the water soluble faction (WSF). The WSF is important, as it is the water solubility of oil that facilitates transport into organisms. The WSF may be more or less toxic than the whole fuel oil.

Studies on the effects of oil on algae are generally in agreement that fuel oils are more toxic than crude oils. The principal effect of toxicity is a suppression of photosynthesis. The cause has been suggested as either, direct effects on the chlorophyll a molecule or, interference with the electron transport chain. A study (Hilmer, 1983) of the effects of light fuel oils as used on outboard motors of small boats found that the oil had a measurable effect on photosynthesis, with the green flagellate (*P. paradoxa*) and the diatom (*P. tricornutum*) being the most sensitive, and the flagellates *P. Iutheri* and *T. suecica* being the most resistant. Their study showed that different species have different sensititivities to different hydrocarbons, and therefore it cannot be said that certain algae are more sensitive than others.

Fresh clean oils in water are repelled to some extent by the slimy outer coating of fish and many water weeds. This provides them with some protection against fresh, light spillages. Waste oils, however, often contain components which enhance their dispersing and emulsifying properties and as a result are able to cling more readily to the surfaces of living organisms.

Oil tends to adhere to the gills of freshwater fish and as a result, interferes with respiration. To some extent fish are able to counter slight oil pollution by the production of a mucous film which repels the oil film, but any severe pollution will result in the accumulation of oil into the gills and eventual asphyxia. Oil can also enter the life cycle of fish by being ingested by food organisms or as the result of settling into the bottom sediment.

Much floating oil can be adsorbed onto suspended particles in the water and eventually deposited in the sediment. It will then be slowly degraded by aerobic and anaerobic processes, but may also cause deoxygenation of the lower water levels, release of toxic compounds or may be resuspended.

The sensitivity of fish to oil varies between species. Studies which demonstrate this well (Ellis, 1989) have been carried out using wastewater from an oil refinery. Based on acute toxicity tests, these studies showed that species sensitivity to oil toxicity, decreases in the order rainbow trout, bluegill sunfish, fathead minnows, goldfish, channel catfish, mosquito fish and the common guppy.

It can be useful to examine the effect of pollution on a total community rather than individual species. Taking this approach, Johnson and Romanenko (1989) simulated and studied, a diesel oil spillage into a freshwater pond. Diesel oil was dosed at a concentration of 1.0 mg/l, and its effects on water, sediment, plants and animals were studied over a seven day dosage period and a seven day recovery period. The results showed that daphnids and green algae were extremely sensitive to the diesel oil, causing 100% mortality of daphnids after 48 hours. At this concentration, the oil was found to be non-toxic to roach and midge larvae. Evidence of oil-induced changes in the metabolism of the community was observed, with respiration exceeding productivity. Both bacterial and heterotrophic activity were significantly increased, indicative of the rapidly deteriorating water quality. By the end of the recovery phase, and with the removal of the oil slick, the community had recovered considerably, but there were still some slight bioperturbations.

Water Quality Standards

Neither the European Commission (EC) nor the EIFAC (European Inland Fisheries Advisory Committee) specify an oil standard for the protection of aqutic life. The United States EPA (Environmental Protection Agency) specifies standards based on the 96 hour LC_{50} for freshwater fish, this approximates to l00μg/l (0.1 mg/l). In the U K, where oil is limited in a discharge consent, a concentration limit of between 5–20 mg/l in the effluent is often specified.

There is evidence that some people can taste or smell petrol in water at concentrations as low as 0.005 mg/l. Crude oil is detectable at between 0.2 and 1.0mg/l, and the more inert products such as lubricating oil at possibly 2.0-2.5mg/1. There are no standards in the UK for the concentration of oil in water abstracted for potable supply.

A2.7 Polycyclic Aromatic Hydrocarbons (PAH)

Toxicity

Many organisms are able to accumulate PAH present at low concentrations in the ambient medium, food or sediments. PAH are rapidly transferred from the aqueous phase into lipophilic compartments such as biological membranes, macromolecules and deposited lipid stores in organisms. Conversely, PAH may also be released into the water from organisms, either passively or actively, involving metabolic transformation. Some of the products of PAH metabolism may be retained in animal tissues longer than unmetabolised PAH.

PAH uptake can occur direct from water or from food. Species differ in their ability to absorb and assimilate PAH from food (Neff, 1979). In general, the following trends exist.

- Polychaete worms have a limited ability.

- In fish, adsorption from the gut is limited and variable depending on species, the PAH compound and the food matrix.

- Crustaceans readily assimilate PAH from their food.

Uptake of PAH direct from sediment has been studied little, but the evidence there is, suggests that sediment-adsorbed PAH have a limited bioavailability, and the uptake that does occur appears to be mainly due to uptake of PAH desorbed from the sediment particles into the interstitial water.

Toxic responses to PAH can occur in two ways.

- PAH may bind reversibly to lipophilic sites in the cell and thereby interfere with several cellular processes.

- PAH metabolites, which are more hydrophilic, reactive and electrophilic than the parent PAH, may bind covalently to many cellular structures causing long-term damage. Less is known about the toxicity of the metabolites, but it is likely that they may have a higher toxicity.

PAH compounds may exhibit both chronic and acute toxicity. In general, acute toxicity increases with molecular weight of the PAH compound. Species vary in their sensitivity, and in general, crustaceans are the most sensitive, with polychaete worms intermediate, and fish the most resistant. A selection of toxicity data are given in Table A2.7a.

Table A2.7a Polycyclic Aromatic Hydrocarbon (PAH) Toxicity

PAH Compound	Species	Test	Value mg/kg	Reference
Phenanthrene	Mosquito fish (*Gambusia affinis*)	96 hr LC_{50}	150	EPA, 1970
	Grass shrimp (*Palaemontes pugio*)	24 hr LC_{50}	0.37	Young, 1977
Fluoranthene	Marine polychaete (*Neanthes arenaceodentata*)	96 hr LC_{50}	0.5	Rossi & Neff, 1978
Benzo(a) anthracene	Bluegill (*Lepomis macrochirus*)	96 hr LC_{50} in 6 months	1.0	Brown *et al*, 1977
Chrysene	Marine polychaete (*Neanthes arenaceodentata*)	NAT	1.0	Rossi & Neff, 1978
Benzo(a) pyrene	Marine polychaete (*Neanthes arenaceodentata*)	NAT	1.0	Rossi & Neff, 1978

Notes
NAT = Not acutely toxic in 96 hr

Source: Neff, J M (1979)

Some PAH compounds exhibit chronic toxicity, primarily in the form of mutagenesis, carcinogenesis and teratogenesis. This behaviour is due to the covalent binding of certain electrophilic PAH metabolites to cellular macromolecules. Mutagenic (and by inference carcinogenic) metabolites have been observed in rainbow trout, and there are several reports of cancerous growths in aquatic organisms in the vicinity of oil spills (Neff, 1979). Secondly, chronic exposure to low concentrations of PAH compounds may produce sublethal responses which may be detrimental to the long term survival of the organism.

Environmental factors such as dissolved solids concentrations and temperature substantially modify the nature and magnitude of organisms' response to PAH. Slightly stressful conditions may significantly increase sensitivity to PAH.

It has also been demonstrated (McCarthy, 1985) that the presence of dissolved humic material reduces the rate of uptake and bioaccumulation of PAH compounds in *Daphnia magna*.

Water Quality Standards

There are no UK or European standards specifically for PAH compounds, but a standard for dissolved or emulsified hydrocarbons exists. This states that the concentration must not adversely affect the flavour of salmonid or coarse fish, and hydrocarbons must not form a film on the water surface or bed and must not produce harmful effects in fish. Standards exist for PAH levels in surface waters abstracted for use as drinking waters; these specify maximum concentrations of 0.2μg/1 for DW1 and DW2 water and 1μg/l for DW3 waters, the classification of the waters being related to degree of treatment.

A2.8 Cyanide

Toxicity

The complex cyanide used as an anti-caking agent in deicing salt is not toxic, but in solution in the presence of bright sunlight, it can form cyanide. At low pH, toxic hydrocyanic acid (HCN) is formed. This is sometimes referred to as 'free cyanide' and is regarded as the primary toxic component.

Poisoning by cyanide is essentially by inhibition of oxygen metabolism (respiration). Its acute toxicity is modified particularly by temperature and also by other factors including pH.

It has been stated however (Bickmore and Dutton, 1984a), that due to the very low concentrations of cyanide used in deicing salt, and the environmental conditions found in receiving waters, cyanide toxicity is of negligible concern.

Water Quality Standards

Neither the EC nor the EIFAC specify a standard for cyanide concentrations in waters for fish. The United States EPA specifies a concentration of 5 μg/l for the protection of freshwater fish and other aquatic life. The EC standard for the abstraction of surface waters for drinking water specifies that maximum cyanide concentrations should be below 50 μg/l.

A2.9 Herbicides

Toxicity

The herbicides atrazine and simazine (along with most other pesticides) are not exclusively toxic to the target plants. Thus, other organisms can also be adversely affected. Further, sub-lethal concentrations of herbicides may impart a significant change in the physiology, reproduction or behaviour of non-target groups which ultimately impairs their ability to survive in the affected habitat. A further problem with many pesticides (including atrazine and simazine) is that they may persist in the environment. This characteristic is facilitated by the low water solubility of many pesticides and the high solubility in lipid or fat tissues of organisms.

Atrazine is more soluble than simazine, their respective water solubilities being 33 μg/l and 5 μg/l (at 20°C). Both are fairly persistent in the aquatic environment. Atrazine has a higher toxicity to fish than simazine, as shown in Table A2.9a.

Both atrazine and simazine have been classified by the UK Government as 'Red List Substances', reflecting their environmental persistence and toxicology.

Water Quality Standards

Table A2.9a Herbicide Toxicity

Herbicide	Species	Test	Value mg/l
Atrazine	Rainbow trout (*Salmo gairdneri*)	96hr LC$_{50}$	4.5–8.8
	Crucian carp	96hr LC$_{50}$	76–100
	Bluegill (*Lepomis macrochirus*)	96hr LC$_{50}$	16.0
Simazine	Rainbow trout (*Salmo gairdneri*)	96hr LC$_{50}$	>100
	Crucian carp	96hr LC$_{50}$	>100
	Bluegill (*Lepomis macrochirus*)	95hr LC$_{50}$	90

Source: Royal Society of Chemistry, the Agrochemicals Handbook, Nottingham, 1987

There are no UK or European standards for the protection of freshwater life from the herbicides outlined above at the time of compiling this report.

The UK drinking water standards for pesticides are mandatory 95 percentiles of 1 and 25 µg/l in raw water (depending on treatment), and maximum admissable concentrations of 0.5 µg/l total and 0.1 µg/l individual pesticides in tap water.

A2.10 Metals

General

Metals in a watercourse may create either acute or chronic toxicity in fish and other organisms. It is usually the ionic forms which produce the acute toxic effects, whilst the complexed metal compounds tend to act by accumulation in the body tissue over a considerably longer time period.

The toxicity of metals to aquatic organisms differs widely, both with the metal and its speciation, and with the organism. It is therefore more difficult to generalise on toxicity effects than with organic pollutants (see Section A2.2). However, there is evidence that the effects of a low continuous dose of one metal are similar to the effects of larger, fluctuating inputs of several metals.

Metal toxicity also depends on the quality of the ambient water and the presence of other toxicants. For example, the presence of calcium is antagonistic to the effect of lead and zinc; and copper behaves synergistically with zinc, cadmium and mercury but antagonistically with cyanide. In general, metal toxicity tends to increase with decreasing dissolved oxygen and decreasing pH, and decreases with increasing hardness.

Macroinvertebrates

In studies of macroinvertebrate response to metal pollution, three stages have been observed:

- In the most heavily polluted reaches, the normal macroinvertebrate fauna (including the bivalve, *Pisidium*, gastropod *Physa*, isopod *Lirecus*; flatworm *Dugesia*, and crayfish *Orconectes*), excepting the tubificid worms and chironomid larvae, are virtually eliminated.

- Moderate metal pollution reduces the invertebrate fauna, but Trichoptera (caddis flies) remain, along with chironomids.

- Mild pollution is characterised by a fauna which also includes Ephemeroptera (mayflies).

Groups of macroinvertebrates considered to be resistant to metal pollution include many insect orders such as diptera and trichoptera; oligochaetes show an intermediate resistance; and molluscs and malacostracan crustacea show the highest sensitivity.

Plants

Studies of metal toxicity on freshwater algae have shown a reduction in number of species present in heavily polluted waters, and changes in the species composition of the community. Aquatic bryophytes have been observed to have a high tolerance to metal pollution. They also accumulate high levels and may be used as indicators of heavy metal contamination.

Higher, flowering plants seem less able to survive heavy metal pollution, although few studies of their responses have been reported (Hellawell, 1986).

Fish

Fish vary in their responses to metal contamination, and the only reasonable generalisation is that salmonids tend to be more sensitive than cyprinids.

A2.11 Lead

Toxicity

Most lead salts have a low solubility and are thus not readily bioavailable. Acute toxicity is therefore unlikely to be observed under natural conditions, the more significant effects of lead toxicity being sublethal; principally, lead uptake and tissue contamination, changes in haematological parameters and spinal curvatures.

The toxicity of lead is affected by water hardness. For example, in hard water, rainbow trout (*Salmo gairdneri*) and most other coarse fish are unaffected by dissolved lead concentrations of 20-30 µg Pb/l, whilst in soft water, the threshold is much lower, at about 5-10 µg Pb/l.

The toxicity of lead is also different for dissolved and total concentrations. For example, in softwater of hardness

44 mg/l as CaCO$_3$, the maximum acceptable toxicant concentration (MATC) for brook trout (*Salvelinus fontinalis*) was 58–119 µg/l total lead and 39-84 µg/l dissolved lead (Holcombe, 1976).

The toxicity of lead is also affected by pH. For example, it has been reported that at pH6, up to 3 times as much lead was accumulated by sunfish (*Lepomis gibbosus* L) than at pH 7.5 (Merlini, 1977).

Lead toxicity in other freshwater invertebrates has been the subject of many studies, and show a range of results (see Table A2.11a). There is also evidence that in some crustaceans, including *Asellus meridianus* and *A. aquaticus*,

Table A2.11a   Lead Toxicity

Species	Hardness (mg/1 CaCO$_3$)	Test	Concentration (mgPb/1)	Reference
Fathead minnow	20	96 hr LC$_{50}$	6.5	Pickering, 1966
(*Pimephales promelas*)	360	96 hr LC$_{50}$	482	Pickering, 1966
Bluegill	20	96 hr LC$_{50}$	23.8	Pickering, 1966
(*Lepomis macrochirus*)	360	96 hr LC$_{50}$	442	Pickering, 1966
Goldfish	20	96 hr LC$_{50}$	31.5	Pickering, 1966
(*Carassius auratus*)				Pickering, 1966
Guppy	20	96 hr LC$_{50}$	20.6	Pickering, 1966
(*Poecilia reticulatus*)				Pickering, 1966
Rainbow trout	28	96 hr LC$_{50}$	1.32	Pickering, 1966
(*Salmo gairdneri*)	50	96 hr LC$_{50}$	1	Pickering, 1966
	353	96 hr LC$_{50}$	471	Pickering, 1966
Mayfly	40–50	7 day LC$_{50}$	3.2	Warnick & Bell, 1969
(*Ephemerella*)				
Daphnia magna	45	3 wk LC$_{50}$	0.3	Boesinger & Christensen, 1972
Freshwater snail	139	20 wk LC$_{50}$	0.022	Borgmann *et al*, 1978
(*Lymnaea palustris*)				
Chironomus tentans	–	LD100	70	Rathore *et al*, 1979
(Larvae)				
Stonefly	44–48	28 days	0.565*	Spehar *et al*, 1978
(*Pteronarcys dorsata*)				
Caddis	44–48	28 days	0.565*	Spehar *et al*, 1978
(*Brachycentrus*)				
Snail	44–48	28 days	0.565*	Spehar *et al*, 1978
(*Physa integra*)				
Gammarus pseudolimnaeus	44–48	4 day LC50	0.124	Spehar *et al*, 1978
		28 day LC50	0.028	

Notes

Values given are total lead. In soft water, total and free lead may be considered to be the same.

* = concentration at which no effects were observed.

Source: Hellawell, J M, 1986

populations exposed to lead have acquired increased resistance through genetic adaptation (Brown, 1976 and Fraser, 1978).

Many organo-lead compounds (including those used as petrol additives) are highly toxic, although little is known as to their accumulation in fish. It is evident that these compounds exhibit enhanced toxicity, similar to that observed for organo-mercury compounds.

Water Quality Standards

The EIFAC sets no standards of lead concentrations for the protection of freshwater fish, and standards set by the EC and EPA vary widely, reflecting the complexity and lack of understanding of environmental lead chemistry and its toxicology. The EC standards for salmonid fish range from 4 to 20 µg/l depending on water hardness; for coarse fish, from 50 to 250 µg/l; and for other aquatic life, from 5-60µg/l. The EPA standards are related to the 96 hr LC$_{50}$ and for fish, approximate to 500 µg/l.

The UK standards for drinking water are a 95 percentile of 50 µg/l in raw water, and a maximum admissible concentration of 50 µg/l in tap water.

A2.12   Cadmium

Toxicity

Cadmium is toxic to many organisms at low concentrations (< 1 µg Cd/l). Cadmium accumulates in the tissues of organisms and is thought to damage ion-regulating mechanisms rather than respiratory or nervous functions. There is evidence that cadmium may be absorbed into tissues rapidly, but is lost slowly. Thus organisms may survive exposure for a short period to large doses, but may die subsequently. This may explain the apparent discrepancy between acutely lethal doses and chronic lethal toxicity. For example, for rainbow trout the 96 hr LC$_{50}$ is 2–3 mg Cd/l, whilst the 7 day LC$_{50}$ is 8–10 µg Cd/l (Ball, 1967).

In a similar way to lead, the toxicity of cadmium varies with water hardness, with sensitivity being greater in soft water. A selection of toxicity data demonstrating this phenomenon in fish, is given in Table A2.12a.

Some macroinvertebrates are particularly sensitive to cadmium whereas many insects show a high resistance (see Table A2.12a).

Water Quality Standards

Despite the high variability in cadmium toxicity, there is a good degree of consensus on the standards set for the protection of freshwater fish and other life, from cadmium. The EC sets a standard of 5 µg Cd/l (dissolved plus particulate) for each category of Salmonid fish, coarse fish and other freshwater life; the EIFAC sets a lower standard for salmonids, of 0.6–1.5 µgl (depending on water hardness), and a higher standard for coarse fish of 20–50 µg/l; and the EPA sets standards of 1.2 µg/l for fish and 12 µg/l for other freshwater life.

The UK standards for drinking water are in raw water, a mandatory 95 percentile concentration of 5 µg/l and a guide 90 percentile concentration of 1 µg/l, and in tap water, a maximum admissible concentration of 5 µ/l.

A2.13   Chromium

Chromium has two major oxidation states in natural waters; the most common naturally occurring state is the trivalent ion (Cr^{3+}), but hexavalent chromium is also important.

Fish are generally not very sensitive to chromium, but tend to show a higher sensitivity to the trivalent form (see Table A2.13a).

The toxicity of trivalent cadmium to mayfly (*Ephemeralla subvaria*) and caddisfly (*Hydropsyche betteni*) have been shown to be widely different (Warnick and Bell, 1969), with the mayfly exhibiting a far higher sensitivity (see Table A2.13a).

The algae (*Palmella, Oedognium, Hydrodictyon* and *Palmellococcus*) have been found to have a moderate sensitivity to chromium toxicity, while the floating macrophytes, *Lemna* and *Spirodela* were more tolerant. Growth of all of these plants was inhibited at chromium concentrations of 10 µg/l.

A2.14   Zinc

Toxicity

Zinc is unusual in that it has a low toxicity to man but a high toxicity to fish. As with other heavy metals, toxicity of zinc is modified by environmental factors including hardness, temperature, dissolved oxygen and suspended solids of which, hardness is probably the most important. In general, the relationship between water hardness and zinc toxicity is an inverse linear logarithmic correlation. A suggested explanation for this is that calcium ions in the water hardness provide some protection from zinc by competitively occupying sites on enzyme molecules which would otherwise be taken up by zinc.

In general, non-salmonid fish species are more resistant to zinc than salmonids. To aquatic insects, zinc has been found to have a lower toxicity than many other metals (Warnick and Bel, 1969).

A selection of toxicity data is given in Table A2.14a.

Table A2.12a   Cadmium Toxicity

Species	Hardness (mg/1 CaCO₃)	Test	Concentration (µg/1)	Reference
Rainbow trout (*Salmo Gairdneri*)	Soft 54 24*	50 day LC₅₀ 408 hr LC₅₀ 96 hr LC₅₀	10 5.2 1.0	DoE, 1972 Chapman & Stevens, 1978 Chapman, 1978
Coho salmon (*Oncorphynchus kisutch*)	22	215 hr LC₅₀	3.7	Chapman & Stevens, 1978
Chinook salmon (*O. tshawytscha*)	24*	96 hr LC₅₀	3.5	Stevens, 1978
Brook trout (*Salvelinus fontinalis*)	44	MATC	1.7–3.4	Benoit *et al*, 1976
Goldfish (*Carassius auratus*)	140 140 20 20	96 hr LC₅₀ 48 hr LC₅₀ 96 hr LC₅₀ 48 hr LC₅₀	46.8 46.9 2.13 2.76	McCarty *et al*, 1978
Fathead minnow (*Pimephales promelas*)	–	MATC	37–57	Pickering & Gast, 1972
Daphnia magna	41–50 41–50	48 hr LC₅₀ 3 wk LC₅₀	65 5	Biesinger & Christensen, 1972
Daphnia pulex	41–50	3 day LC₅₀ 4 day LC₅₀	62 47	Bertram & Hart, 1979
Stonefly (*Pteronarcella badia*)	Hard	96 hr LC₅₀	1,800	Chubb *et al*, 1975
Mayfly (*Ephermerella grandis*)	Hard –	96 hr LC₅₀ 28 day LC₅₀	2,800 <3	Chubb *et al*, 1975 Sephar *et al*, 1978
Chironomus larvae	Hard	48 hr LC₅₀	25000	Rao & Saxena, 1981
Tubifex tubifex	34.2 34.2 261 261	24 hr LC₅₀ 48 hr LC₅₀ 24 hr LC₅₀ 48 hr LC₅₀	63–77 31–45 1200 720	Brkovic - Popovic & Popovic (1977)
Physa integra		7 day LC₅₀ 28 day LC₅₀	114 10.4	Spehar et al (1978)

Notes
* = juveniles

Source: Hellawell, J M, 1986

Water Quality Standards

Standards for the protection of freshwater life from zinc, vary widely according to water hardness. The EIFAC standards have been adopted by the EC namely, 30–500 µg/l for salmonids, 300–2,000 µg/l for coarse fish, and 100 µg/l for other aquatic life. The EPA standards, based on the 96 hr LC₅₀ are rather lower, at 3–25 µg/l.

A2.15   Copper

Toxicity

The toxicological effects of copper are fairly well documented. Its toxicity is mainly attributable to the Cu^{2+} ion. However, there are difficulties in ascertaining the toxicity due to adsorption of copper onto particles and formation of complexes with organic matter.

Table A2.13a   Chromium Toxicity

Species	Hardness (mg/1 CaCO₃)	Test	Concentration Cr³⁺	Cr⁶⁺		Reference
Fathead minnow (*Pimephales promelas*)	20	96 hr LC₅₀	5.1	17.6		Pickering & Henderson, 1966, and Benoit, 1976
	360	96 hr LC₅₀	67.4		27.3	
Bluegill (*Lepomis macrochirus*)	20	96 hr LC₅₀	7.5	118		
	360	96 hr LC₅₀	71.9		133	
Goldfish (*Carassius auratus*)	20	96 hr LC₅₀	4.1	37.5		
Guppy (*Poecillia reticulata*)	20	96 hr LC₅₀	3.3	30		
Rainbow trout (*Salmo gairdneri*)	45	96 hr LC₅₀	–	69		
Brook trout (*Salvelinus fontinalis*)	45	96 hr LC₅₀	–	59		
Mayfly (*Ephemerella subvaria*)	44	96 hr LC₅₀	2	–		Warnick & Bell, 1969
Caddis fly (*Hydropsyche betteni*)	44	96 hr LC₅₀	64	–		Warnick & Bell, 1969
Tubifex tubifex	260	24 hr LC₅₀	86	–		Brkovic – Popovic & Popovic (1977)
	260	48 hr LC₅₀	4.6	–		
	34	24 hr LC₅₀	10–15	–		
	34	48 hr LC₅₀	1.4–1.5	–		

Source:
Hellawell, J M (1986)

Table A2.14a   Zinc Toxicity

Species	Hardness (mg/1 CaCO₃)	Test	Concentration (μg/1)	Reference
Brook trout (*Salvelinus fontinalis*)	45	95 hr LC₅₀	2.0	Holcombe *et al*, 1979
Rainbow trout (*Salmo gairdneri*)	26	96 hr LC₅₀	0.4	Sinley *et al*, 1974
			7.2	Sinley *et al*, 1974
	33	96 hr LC₅₀	0.9	Herbert & Shurben, 1964
			2.7	Herbert & Shurben, 1964
	44	48 hr LC₅₀		
	240	48 hr LC₅₀		
Fathead minnow (*Pimephales promelas*)	20	96 hr LC₅₀	0.8–1.0	Pickering (1966)
	360	96 hr LC₅₀	33.4	
Gudgeon (*Gobio gobio*)	320	7 day LC₅₀	8.4	Bell (1967)
Stonefly (*Acroneuria*)	44	14 day LC₅₀	32	Warnick & Bell, 1969
Mayfly (*Ephemerella*)	44	10 day LC₅₀	16	Warnick & Bell, 1969
Caddis (*Hydropsyche*)	44	11 day LC₅₀	32	Warnick & Bell, 1969
Tubifex tubifex	34	48 hr LC₅₀	3.0	Brkovic- Popovic and Popovic, 1977
	260	48 hr LC₅₀	60	

Source:
Hellawell, J M (1986)

Copper is quite acutely toxic to fish and other organisms, and is commonly used as a molluscicide and an algicide.

A selection of toxicity data is given in Table A2.15a.

The EIFAC standards for copper to protect salmonids have been adopted by the EC namely a range, depending on water hardness of 5–112 µg/l. The EIFAC considered the data on coarse fish inadequate even for tentative criteria, whereas the EC apply to same standard of 5–112 µg/l For other aquatic life, a lower range of 1–28 µg/l is set. The EPA standards, based on the 96 hr LC_{50} are of the same order of magnitude, being 2–10 µg/l.

The U K drinking water standards are: in raw water a 90 percentile guide value of 20–1,000 µg/l and a mandatory 95 percentile of 50 µg/l; in water leaving the treatment plant, a guide value of 100 µg/l; and in tap water (allowing for contamination from domestic pipes) a guide value of 3,000 µg/l

Table A2.15a   Copper Toxicity

Species	Hardness (mg/1 CaCO₃)	Test	Concentration (µg/1)	Reference
Brook trout (*Salvelinus fontinalis*)	45	96 hr LC_{50}	0.1	Alabaster & Lloyd, 1980 and, Chapman & Stevens, 1978
Atlantic salmon (*Salmo salar*) parr	10	96 hr LC_{50}	0.03	
Rainbow trout	250	96 hr LC_{50}	0.9	
	42	96 hr LC_{50}	0.06	
	250	8 day LC_{50}	0.5	
	12	7 day LC_{50}	0.03	
Pike (*Esox lucius*)	250	96 hr LC_{50}	3.0	
Eel (*Anguilla anguilla*)	53	96 hr LC_{50}	0.81	
	260	96 hr LC_{50}	4.0	
Gammarus	45	96 hr LC_{50}	0.02	Arthur & Leonard, 1970
Campeloma	45	96 hr LC_{50}	1.7	
Physa	45	96 hr LC_{50}	0.039	
Biomphalaria glabrata	100	96 hr LC_{50}	0.04	Bellavere & Gorbi, 1981
Daphnia magna	200	24 hr LC_{50}	0.05	
	100	24 hr LC_{50}	0.07	
Tubifex tubifex	34	24 hr LC_{50}	0.36	Brkovic – Popovic & Popovic, 1977
	261	24 hr LC_{50}	1.38	

Source:
Hellawell, J M (1986)

A2.16   Nickel

Toxicity

Nickel is generally not very toxic to fish or other aquatic life (see Table A2.16a). Nickel has however, been found to have a harmful effect on fish gill morphology. It is also highly phytotoxic to certain macrophytes (*Elodea* and *Lemna*) and can inhibit the growth of several species of green algae. Species of blue-green algae however, have a much higher tolerance, possibly due to the formation of nickel complexes with the extracelluar products. Concentrations of nickel in road runoff are also not as significant as those of lead, cadmium, copper and zinc.

Water Quality Standards

The EC water quality standards for nickel vary according to water hardness. For both salmonid and coarse fish, the range of values is 50-200 µg/l, and for other freshwater life, 8-100 µg/l. The EPA standards, based on 96 hr LC_{50} are similar, of the order of 100 µg/l for fish.

Table A2.16a   Nickel Toxicity

Species	Hardness (mg/1 CaCO₃)	Test	Concentration (μg/l)	Reference
Rainbow trout (*Salmo gairdneri*)	240	48 hr LC$_{50}$	32	Hughes et al, (1979)
Fathead minnow (*Pimephales promelas*)	20 360	96 hr LC$_{50}$ 96 hr LC$_{50}$	4.6–5.2 42–45	Pickering & Henderson, (1966)
Bluegills (*Lepomis macrochirus*)	20 360	96 hr LC$_{50}$ 96 hr LC$_{50}$	5.2–5.4 39.6	
Goldfish (*Carassius auratus*)	20	96 hr LC$_{50}$	9.8	
Guppy (*Poecilia reticulata*)	20	96 hr LC$_{50}$	4.5	

Source: Hellawell, J M (1986)

A2.17   Iron

Toxicity

The principal effects of iron in suspension is destruction of benthic organisms, (mainly as a result of their effects as suspended matter (see Section A2.3)), and subsequent indirect effects on fish. Ferric iron in suspension has been found to have little direct effects on fish.

Water Standards

The EQS for iron in freshwaters adopted in the UK (DOE Circular 7/89, WO Circular 16/89) is 1000 μg/l as dissolved iron for the protection of fish (*salmonids* and *cyprinids*) expressed as an annual average. The drinking water standards are 1,300 μg/l (95 percentile) for A1 water, and 2,000 μg/l (95 percentile) for A2 water; both are for dissolved iron.

Pollution from Pipelines

1 Introduction

1.1 Background

Environmental Resources Ltd. (ERL) has been requested by the Royal Commission on Environmental Pollution to supplemnent our Report on Transport Pollution with an addendum relating to pollution to freshwaters due to pipelines.

1.2 Objectives

The overall objective of this study was to support the Royal Comrnission in carrying out its current study on freshwater pollution, of which transport is one aspect. Within this objective, there were the following tasks:

- to review background information on pollution sources;

- to define, on a regional and national basis, the frequency of ernissions discharged to the aquatic environment;

- to provide an account of the mechanisms and processes that give rise to pollution from pipelines;

- to draw conclusions as to whether pipeline related pollution in the UK is increasing or decreasing, and to suggest possible technical, legislative or policy measures to reduce freshwater pollution from transport.

1.3 Sources of Information

The major sources of information used in carrying out this study were as follows.

- National Rivers Authority (NRA); all ten regions of the NRA in England and Wales were consulted via a questionnaire survey.

- River Purifications Board (RPB); all seven RPB's in Scotland were consulted with the same questionnaire as the NRA.

- The British Pipelines Agency.

- Relevant scientific literature.

1.4 Organisation of the Addendum

This Report contains the following sections:

- *Section 2* reviews potential water pollution arising from pipeline construction.

- *Section 3* examines the risk factors involved in pollution from pipelines during operation.

- *Section 4* summarises the information collected from the NRA's and RPB's in relation to actual spillages.

- *Section 5* gives our conclusions in relation to the potential impact of pipelines on freshwater pollution.

2 Water Pollution Arising From Pipeline Construction

2.1 Introduction

The construction of new pipelines is now subject to Environmental Assessment (EA) under the Statutory Instrument No. 442 the Electricity and Pipeline Works (Assessment of Environmental Effects) Regulations 1990. Under these regulations the National Rivers Authority (NRA) and River Purification Boards (RPBs) are Statutory Consultees, who are consulted by the British Pipelines Agency in relation to impacts of pipelines on the aquatic environment. In fact, the number of major pipeline applications is quite small (4–5) since the introduction of the Regulations. However, promoters of pipeline applications made prior to the Regulations often consulted with the NRA (and its predecessors) and RPBs during pipeline planning and promotion.

There is no relevant pollution control legislation that particularly deals with pipeline construction other than the relevant passages of the Water Resources Act 1991 and Control of Pollution Act Part Il (1974) for Scotland, which establish offences related to unconsented discharges to watercourses. Part VII, Sections 159-164 deal with pipelaying, particularly in relation to foul sewers and water mains. Other UK and EC legislation may apply depending on the substances discharged during pipeline commissioning.

2.2 Pipeline Planning

The general rationale of pipeline route selection has been to avoid centres of population, mainly on the basis of potential hazard. Similarly, there has, in the past, been a tendency to avoid high grade agricultural land areas (Ryder, 1987), although more recently the trend has been to also attempt to avoid areas of high nature conservation value or particular archaeological importance.

In general, pipeline routes are often chosen to avoid major river crossings, due to factors relating to engineering difficulty, economic liabilities or environmental risk. The nature of crossings required is often decided on engineering grounds, nevertheless different construction methods have a range of effects on freshwater bodies.

However, it is clear that avoidance of construction phase impacts on freshwater bodies can be achieved both by route planning and choice of appropriate construction method.

2.3 Pipelaying and Pollution of Water Courses

The principal issues of concern in relation to water pollution during pipelaying relate to:

- changes in river characteristics;

- disturbance of the river bed suspended solids release during pipelaying activities;

- accidental spillages of stored materials from construction worksites.

It is essential to note that all of these impacts may be obviated by carefull route selection, choice of pipelaying technique and good work practice. It is noticeable, though, from our communications with NRA and RPBs that the most frequent cause of pollution during pipelaying is related to the use of JCBs or other diggers causing high suspended solids loadings to be released to water bodies.

A brief summary of the key problems resulting to different types of water bodies from a variety of operations is given in Table 2.3a; adapted from Dawson (1989).

2.4 Commissioning

On the basis of replies from the various NRA Regions and RPBs contacted, we are unaware of any spillages or impacts to freshwaters resulting from the commissioning process. However, Tweed River Purification Board reported that chlorine escape occurred during the disinfection of a new water main prior to commissioning due to a leaking valve.

Pipeline commissioning is of greater concern in the marine environment, where pickling liquors may be left in laid pipes for up to 18 months. Typical constituents include amine corrosion inhibitors, quaternary ammonium salts or glutaraldehydes, biocides, bisulphite oxygen scavengers and dyes (rhodamine-based, in general). Concentrations are generally in the range of 100 to 200 mg l^{-1}.

The precise formulations are proprietary, and the Department of Energy has a three category toxicological classification scheme to control substances used. However, precise information on individual substances used is difficult (impossible) to obtain, beyond a definition of the toxicity band within which each proprietary product falls.

For marine discharges of commissioning solutions, marine disposal licences are required under the Food and Environmental Protection Act, 1985. Discharges are then licensed by MAFF, or DAFS in Scotland.

We are unaware of any applications ever having been made for the disposal of commissioning solution to freshwaters.

Table 2.3a   Impacts of Pipelaying on Aquatic Environment; adapted from Dawson (1989)

Site	Operation	Area of Environment Concern
Wetlands	Removal and storage of surface reed vegetation deep sheet-piled trench	Correct storage conditions water levels; effects of lowered water levels on adjacent plants.
Ditches	Dammed or blocked and pumped over	Effects on biota of static water.
Streams	Dry construction Installation of pipes sealed to channel sides excavated beneath	Effects of loss of small section of bed; removal of clay seals; new stream bed section.
Small River	Wet construction Installation of bridge open excavation of bed and river banks Water from pipeline trench excavation	Effects of suspended material; oxygen demand; loss of section of river bed; loss of debris, etc from bridge; suspended material; bank collapse.
Rivers	Wet construction Large open excavation of bed by drag-lines backfill with compatible material	As above, but in greater quantities; excavators working in unison; bank reinstatement.
Large river and estuaries	Lateral bore (expensive)	No impact.

2.5 Control of Pollution During Pipelaying

The following measures are of importance in minimising pollution during pipelaying.

- Direct access by mechanical plant to a watercourse should be kept to an absolute minimum. Where it is necessary for machinery to be used in a watercourse then it should be maintained to the highest standard in respect of fuel, lubrication and hydraulic systems to ensure no leakages.

- All diesel/petrol powered pumps utilised should be placed on impervious drip trays and positioned away from any watercourse or drain, and surrounded by an earth or sand bund. Any oil spilled onto the ground should be cleaned up and contaminated soil removed from site for proper disposal.

- Tracking across the river course with mechanical plant should be avoided except in exceptional circumstances.

- All fuel, oil or chemical storage on site shall only be located within designated areas complying with the following:

- all storage tanks should be located on an impervious base and surrounded by an impervious bund capable of retaining 110% of the volume of the largest tank within;

- all valves, vent pipes and couplings should be located within the bund and delivery hoses should be fitted with trigger-type spring handles and hung within the bund after use;

- no fuelling, washing or maintenance of plant or machinery should be carried out in, over or adjacent to a drain or watercourse.

- Disturbance of the watercourse should be completely avoided during the periods when fish spawning grounds are most at risk from pollution.

- Cement/cement grout is highly polluting and should be prevented from entering a watercourse. Concrete should not be placed into flowing water. Where it is necessary that concrete is placed into water, that water should be static for at least 24 hours following the placement and the resultant alkaline water should not be discharged directly to a watercourse but disposed of by other means. No concrete placement operation should be carried out over water without suspended sheeting deployed to catch cement spillages.

- Where blast cleaning and painting of steelwork is being carried out, suitable protection measures should be employed to prevent debris or effluent entering the watercourse.

- Excavation and construction within a watercourse should be carried out behind suitably constructed bunds and water from within the bund should not be discharged direct to a watercourse but via settlement or other treatment.

- Cleaning agents and any water from the hydraulic testing of pipework (Commissioning Fluids) should be disposed of in accordance with temporary Discharge Consents agreed by NRA or RPB's.

- A list of contractor's personnel, including telephone numbers that can be contacted outside of working hours, should be made to the NRA or RPB, so that any spillages can be rapidly notified to the appropriate authority and dealt with.

3 Pollution from Operational Pipelines

3.1 Introduction

The issue of pollution from operational pipelines is of particular concern due to a recent discharge of crude oil in 1989, when several hundred tonnes of crude oil was lost to the Mersey Estuary following rupture of a pipeline between Stanlow Oil Refinery and Tranmere Oil Terminal. A smaller spill from Llanwern Steel Works recently affected local drainage ditches (reens) and the Severn Estuary.

Whilst these spillages are of concern, it is clear that the issue is not necessarily related to the nature of the substances transported, but more to factors that might contribute to pipeline failure. The legislation on operational pipelines relates principally to Sections 159-164 of the Water Resources Act 1991; Section 162 deals with sewers and pollution control. Otherwise pollution from pipelines is subject to pollution offences established under Section 85 of the Water Resources Act 1991. Defences against prosecution are detailed in Section 89(1) of the Act.

3.2 Factors Affecting Pipeline Failure

The most significant factor contributing to the failure of a pipeline is damage to the line caused by the activities of people along the route of the line. Damage generally occurs during construction of other facilities which are associated with providing the services for commercial, industrial and human enterprises and dwellings. The prevalence and provision of services, such as water, gas and electricity supply, sewerage systems, drainage lines and ditches, buried power and communications cables, streets and roads etc, as population density becomes greater. Therefore, the possibility of damage to pipelines tends to increase with larger population density. Special conditions may also contribute to a pipeline failure and these include, long self supported spans, unstable ground, mechanical or sonic vibration, weight of special attachments, stresses caused by unusual temperature differences, over pressure due to operator errors, failure of metallurgy, and erosion by rivers. A comparison of failure rates is shown in Table 3.2a below. The data is given in terms of likely frequency of failures on the basis of time as well as length of pipeline.

These data confirm that European Oil and Gas pipelines are slightly more at risk than gas pipelines in the UK, reflecting lower design, construction, and maintenance standards. Also, gas pipelines in the United States are prone to a higher risk than UK Gas Lines or European Oil and Gas pipelines, design, construction and maintenance factors.

Table 3.1a   Comparison of Failure Rate Frequencies (per 1000km years) Data from Morgan (1989)

Failure Mode	US Gas Line Data 1970–1980 Raw Data	UK Gas 1969–1977 (HSE 1978)	European Oil & Gas Lines 1979–84
Defect	0.13	0.07	0.16
Corrosion	0.20	0.16	0.23
External Impact	0.31	0.16	0.22
Environmental	0.11	0.01	0.05
Operational/Other	0.04	0.17	0.03
Total	**0.79**	**0.57**	**0.69**

Pipeline failures in European pipelines may be distributed into the following categories: defects, corrosion, external impact, environmental factors and operational factors. Of the 0.69 failure rate frequency in European pipelines per 1000km years, 0.16 are associated with defects, 0.23 are associated with corrosion and 0.22 are associated with external impact. Environmental factors account for 0.05 and operational factors 0.03. In Britain though, operational factors are the single largest class of cause of failure of pipelines. However, there is a wide variation in the proportion of failures due to each cause between countries, and locations and factors such as pipeline diameter. External impacts can contribute up to 50% of all failures, with the contribution of external impacts to failures rising as pipeline diameter increases. No data is available for sleeved pipelines.

It should be pointed out that, frequently, pipelines in the United States are not buried, since it is considered that this allows ready inspection of the pipe for leaks etc. In the case of the trans-Alaskan pipeline, the potential for rupture of the pipe by frost-heave is a major factor militating against burial. Similar arguments apply in the UK, in upland areas as well as in wetland areas where frost-heave is a significant environmental factor. A further argument for non-burial of pipes in the USA is that buried pipes are more likely to cause pollution of groundwaters.

However, given the importance of external impacts in terms of pipe failures, it has been argued (and confirmed by risk assessment) that in many cases, burial of pipelines may well be preferable in terms of reducing pipeline failure risk. Important exceptions are cases where environmental factors may lead to preference for surface pipes. These include locations subject to:

- frost-heave;

- significant erosion (eg by rivers);

- landslip risk;

- earthquakes.

All of these factors could lead to significant pipe failures.

3.3 Pipework Failures and their Management

A number of studies (eg Bellamy et al, 1989) have demonstrated the importance of management in preventing pipeline failures. These analyses have shown that 90.4% of all pipework failures can potentially be prevented by one of the following mechanisms:

- hazards studies, such as HAZOPS (Hazard and Operability Study);

- Human Factors Review (failure to prevent those sources of unsafe conditions which resulted in human errors within the man-machine system or in the following of procedures):

- task checking, carrying out checking/testing after tasks have been completed, such as checking that a pipe has been purged before maintenance;

- routine checking (all routine activities which form part of a vigilance system for unsafe conditions in plant/processes, such as sampling for corrosion).

The very high percentage of failures which were judged as preventable highlights the significant role that management can play in improving safety, as well as their role as underlying causes of failure.

Human error itself is of importance, and an analysis of over 500 pipework failures in the UK has indicated that:

- operator error accounted for 30.9% of failures of known cause;

- dropped loads or vehicle impacts accounted for a further 5.6% of pipe failures;

- bad welding, incorrect installation or incorrect equipment accounted for a further 4.5% of known causes of failures.

After operator error, overpressure and corrosion were the next greatest contributions to failure.

It is widely recognised that management have a direct effect on human error rates through the provision of training, correct staff selection and supervision, as well as by more subtle influences such as placing priorities on production rather than safety. Therefore, the prevalence of operator error is a first and clear indicator of the role of management in safety.

In terms of management control of risk, key areas of action are the prevention of operator error and the avoidance of overpressure in the pipes. It is also of note that a large number of operator errors actually during maintenance.

Particular measures that should be adopted to prevent releases of transported materials from pipelines to freshwaters may include the following.

- The annulus of pipes should be monitored for contamination and pressure drops caused by leaks.

- Frequent external inspection of pipelines should be carried out, and supplemented by internal inspections using 'intelligent pigs'.

- Additional protection should be given to pipelines at points where impacts are more likely, and this may include marking of pipelines, concrete slabs or other armoury.

3.4 The Role of Environmental Hazard and Operability Assessment in Pipeline Planning

The previous two sections have discussed the causes of potential pollution due to pipeline failure. On the basis of this discussion, the following recommendations are made.

- Existing pipelines of a sufficient size to require an EA under SI442 of the Electricity and Pipeline Regulations 1990 should be subject to an Environmental Hazard and Operability Review, as distinct from a formal, human hazards and risk assessment. This would focus on areas where management can be strengthened to prevent environmental damage from spillages.

- New pipelines are subject to formal safety and HAZOP assessment during the planning application stage to the British Pipelines Agency. They are also now subject to Environmental Assessment (EA). It is suggested that EA should include a stage of Environmental Risk Assessment (including freshwaters). This would involve the following aspects:

- screening of route options for sensitive aquatic receptors, in order to avoid them;

- undertaking formal hazard and risk assessments of potential for spillage, and consequences for receptors other than man (to include formal toxicological assessment);

- examination of management procedures to reduce spillage risk.

4 Case Studies

4.1 Introduction

As part of this additional study a questionnaire was submitted to all the regions of the NRA and to Scottish River Purification Boards (RPBs). It is clear from replies that the greatest current concerns relate to pollution resulting from pipeline construction. However, it is clear from all the responses received that NRA Regions and RPBs are consulted over pipeline routeing and construction phase water pollution control. All reported that emergency and contingency planning with emergency services and agencies is carried out. It should be emphasised that only a single major pipeline spillage to freshwater would alter this perception. The degree of detail in responses is also highly variable.

4.2 Responses of National Rivers Authority

4.2.1 Anglian Region

The Anglian Region reported that a watercourse was impounded by contractors during the construction of a pipeline in 1990. This appeared to cause stress to fish, and the incident was reported by members of the public. Nevertheless, no fish were lost apparently. No other major surface freshwater pollution incidents were recorded between 1986 and 1991 due to pipelaying or commissioning. The Anglian region reported that 'Several minor' incidents caused by the fracture of fuel lines in industrial and domestic heating supplies had occurred. However, no major spillages to surface fresh waters or groundwaters were recorded.

It was reported by Anglian Region that routine monitoring surveys of surface freshwaters and ground waters was sufficient to monitor potential pollution from pipelines. Monitoring is carried out directly after hydrostatic pressure testing. The quality of the discharge is checked.

4.2.2 Northumbrian Region

Only operational spillages from pipelines have been recorded. Two have arisen from oil pipelines and one from a chemical pipeline. NRA (Northumbrian Region) have commented that particular problems are encountered when the pipe is buried and the spillage migrates through the ground to a watercourse. In one incident, the period between the commencement of the spill and its detection was considerable.

One incident resulting from an alkaline discharge during water mains relining was also reported, and apparently did cause a fish kill.

4.2.3 North West Region

NRA (North West Region) reported four minor construction phase incidents over the past five years due to pipelaying activities.

No discharges from operational pipelines to freshwaters have been recorded, although the Mersey Estuary spill was major and resulted in a substantial fine (£1 million) to the polluter.

4.2.4 Severn-Trent Region

NRA reported a single potential pollution incident during pipelaying. This occurred during the replacement of a length of pipeline. No pollution incident occurred since oil was successfully contained on-site. Two minor incidents of discharge to groundwaters were reported, both caused by valve blockage. Only very localised and minor pollution problems were caused.

Severn-Trent Region reported that the scale of the Region and the extensive total lengths of pipelines precluded policing of potential problems through monitoring. The most practical means proposed by Severn-Trent Region was based upon comprehensive emergency planning. This involves identification of sensitive sites and ensuring good communications and adequate emergency procedures between emergency services, NRA and the pipeline agency.

4.2.5 Southern Region

NRA (Southern region) reported that pollution incidents involving pipelines are of relatively minor importance, forming less than 1% of total recorded pollution incidents.

The incidents included:

- one pipework failure at a water works;

- three water mains failures;

- four sewer pollution incidents;

- two releases of contaminants from effluent pipelines;

- a discharge of 4,500 litres of heating oil from a pipeline.

In three case mechanical diggers were involved in the pipeline incidents.

4.2.6 South West Region

South West Region estimate that between 4–6 incidents of pollution of surface waters occur annually due to pipeline construction. These largely relate to water supply pipelines, and a recent prosecution involved failure of contractors to prevent excavation water run-off entering a watercourse similarly, commissioning discharges mainly arise form water mains commissioning.

An estimated 200 incidents in the last 5 years were reported by South West Region. These included almost weekly discharges from China Clay Works pipelines, sewage systems, water supply chlorinated systems and oil distribution pipelines.

Oil spillages resulting in contamination of private water supplies or subsequently to springs were reported. The possible frequency of these events was considered to be about 2 to 3 per annum.

Specific monitoring of pipelines is not undertaken, except in relation to rivers subject to accidental discharges from china clay works, which regularly lead to incidents. In these cases monitoring has been set up at high risk sites.

4.2.7 Thames Region

No specific instances of groundwater pollution were reported by NRA (Thames Region). Two pollution incidents related to pipelines were reported in the past five years.

- Spillage of 300,000 litres of aviation fuel was recorded, which seeped into the Kennet and Padworth streams. However, no fish kill occurred, and clean up and pollution prevention measures were successful.

- High pressure testing of a pipeline has caused a problem due to washing away of bitumen lining. This left a highly phenolic aqueous residue requiring disposal, although no major pollution incident resulted.

4.2.8 Yorkshire Region

One incident of an accidental discharge to a surface water was reported. This occurred in March 1990, and involved the fracturing of a pipeline carrying PFA slurry from Ferrybridge Power Station to the ash disposal site at Gale Common. Large amounts of thick slurry discharged from the fractured pipeline to an adjacent ditch system causing a screw pump to fail. The failed pump acted as an effective barrier to downstream movement of the slurry, but caused the threat of flooding of fields upstream. The company was in the process of laying a new pipeline alongside that which fractured and were quickly able to deploy contractors to repair the pipeline and excavate the slurry from the drain. In the meantime, a pump was installed to by-pass the failed screw pump and pump clean water from upstream of the spillage.

No incidents involving pipelines discharging to groundwaters were reported.

4.2.9 Welsh Region

The majority of the incidents reported by NRA (Welsh Region) related to either water mains or sewers. Of the total of 35 spillages (all small) over the last five years, 24 were due to sewer leakage, 7 were due to fractured water mains and 2 were the result of oil pipeline leaks. The others resulted from a coal washery, pipe leakage and a leak at a farm.

4.2.10 Wessex Region

Wessex Region has been involved in the planning of pipelines construction and monitoring.

They reported only a single incident where a contractor failed to dechlorinate the wash out water following disinfection of a new water main. Between 50 and 100 fish were killed, and the incident resulted in a prosecution.

4.3 River Purification Boards

The following River Purification Boards (RPBs) recorded no pollution incidents related to pipelines over the last five years:

- Forth River Purification Board;

- Highland River Puriflcation Board;

- North East River Puriflcation Board;

- Tay River Purification Board;

Clyde RPB reported a single incident caused by silt release to Darkhall Burn in 1990 during excavation for the laying of water supply pipelines. No other incidents were reported.

Tweed RPB reported two incidents of water discolouration during pipelaying; the first was due to excavator use and the second was due to pumping out of water from the pipeline trench. In addition, Tweed RPB reported one incident where chlorine release occurred from a leaking valve during disinfection of a new water main.

It should be pointed out, however, that all the RPBs, and particularly North East RPB, have extensive codes of practice on water pollution control during pipeline construction.

5 Conclusions

Pollution incidents resulting from pipelines can potentially occur during both construction and operation.

It is evident that construction phase pollution can be controlled by adequate work site management and sensitive choice of method for traversing watercourses during construction. In particular, use of thrust bore techniques is the preferred environmental option, albeit being the more expensive engineering option. Nevertheless, through good site practice, as outlined in Section 2, it is possible to control water pollution during pipelaying.

No incidents of pollution of surface freshwaters or groundwaters have been recorded due to comnussioning of major pipelines, although commissioning of water mains appears to have caused occasional incidents.

The frequency and occurrence of significant freshwater pollution incidents in the UK is apparently low. However, by their nature serious incidents are infrequent, but are likely to have an extensive impact if they occur. The emphasis in terms of control must, therefore, be on prevention through good management. Rapid response, emergency procedures are already in place with the NRA and RPBs to deal with incidents. The major emphasis in terms of prevention of incidents, beyond current safety related practice, should be:

- the introduction of screening of pipeline routes to prevent them crossing sensitive watercourses or aquifers;

- the introduction of formal environmental hazard and risk assessment, as distinct from human hazard and risk assessment, into the Environmental Assessment procedures for pipelines.

There is some debate as to whether prevention of pollution from pipeline failure is best achieved by pipeline burial. It would appear that unless particular environmental factors (landslip risk, river erosion or frost-heave) prevent burial, burial reduces the risks of pipeline rupture due to external impacts, which is a significant cause of pipeline failure. Against this factor, buried pipelines are more difficult to monitor externally for leaks.

6 References

BELLAMY L J, GEYER T A W and ASTLEY JA (1989) **Evaluation of Human Contribution to Pipework and In-line Equipment Failure Frequencies**. Contract Research Report No. 89/IS, published by HSE. ISBN 071760 3245.

DAWSON F H (1989) **Pipelines and the Aquatic Environment**. Pipes and Pipelines International, 3410–14.

MORGAN J (1989) **Risk Analysis – a Methodology for Assessing The Safety of Pipelines**. Presentation to the Pipelines Industries Guild by Technica Ltd.

RYDER A (1987) **Pipeline Routeing – experiences from Northern Scotland**. Pipes and Pipelines International, 32, 3–7.

Market Mechanisms and Fresh Water Quality

A Paper for the
Royal Commission on
Environmental Pollution

London Economics

April 1991

This paper was written by Dr Nicholas Owen drawing mainly from two previous studies carried out by London Economics: on Nitrates in the Water Supply, directed by Nick Morris, and on the Potential Role of Market Mechanisms in the Control of Acid Rain, carried out for the Department of the Environment, and published since by HMSO. The Department of the Environment's permission to draw from the latter study is gratefully acknowledged.

Contents

Executive Summary

Can market mechanisms offer cost-effective and workable solutions to water quality problems? This paper reviews the theory and practice of market mechanisms, noting the respective merits of charges and tradeable permits, and discusses how both could be applied either to pollution discharges or to the impact of these discharges on the environment.

The paper describes and draws from two pieces of modelling work carried out by London Economics – one dealing with water quality (nitrates in freshwater) and the other with permit markets. The nitrate study explains how nitrate concentrations in different parts of England and Wales are determined, by the interaction of climate, geology and farming. It also suggests how the UK could meet its likely obligations under the proposed European Directive on nitrates in the most cost-effective way, by a combination of water treatment and changes in farming practice. It also indicates, in broad terms, how an economically efficient nitrate charge might be structured.

The permit modelling study considers whether oligopolistic behaviour in permit markets would reduce their efficiency.

The paper concludes by noting that where market mechanisms have been applied in a wholehearted fashion, they have been effective (tradeable permits in the US in the air quality context, water pollution charges in the Netherlands). Conversely, where they have been introduced in a half-hearted fashion and with muddled objectives (effluent charges in Europe), or hedged about with inhibiting conditions (tradeable permits on the Fox River, Wisconsin), they have been ineffective.

It is also clear that substantial quantities of information and analysis would be required in order to set pollution charges at levels which would deliver approximately the desired improvements in environmental quality; but it is also the case that the knowledge and the techniques are available to handle this problem. What may be found wanting is a determination to solve environmental problems in a least-cost fashion.

Tradeable permits are the solution to the information requirements; they require little more than would need to be in place to administer any effective environmental policy. The limited nature of permit markets within river systems could restrict their efficiency. However, this would be a problem for polluters rather than for the pollution control authority, and simulations of such markets suggests that the anti-competitive effects are slight.

1 Market Mechanisms and their Applications[1]

The market mechanisms which are available to control water quality are broadly of two kinds: charges levied on the volume of pollutant discharged, and tradeable permits to discharge.

Both charges and permits could apply either to discharges, or to their environmental impacts. Because permits are assets they could in principle be transacted, like any asset, in a variety of ways: traded, banked, offset against other emissions by the same company, leased, or even traded in futures markets. And, because permits are akin to property rights, it is a matter of great interest to polluters whether they would be issued free, or auctioned.

Charges establish the price to be paid for polluting, and allow the market to determine the total quantity of pollution; permits ration the total quantity, and allow the market to determine the price. Which approach is to be preferred?

Starting from first principles, an early contribution to this discussion was made by Weitzman (1975) who observed that from a strictly theoretical point of view, there is really nothing to recommend the control of quantities over the control of prices, since there is a close connection between the two:

> 'Generally speaking it is neither easier or harder to name the right prices than to name the right quantities because in principle exactly the same information is needed to correctly specify either.'

Weitzman concluded that the answer turns on the relative sensitivity of costs and benefits to the variable one is seeking to control, and on the relative uncertainties surrounding them. These aspects are discussed below.

A significant factor weighing in favour of permits rather than charges is the political dimension; polluters will have a natural preference for permits, since (in the US) they are distributed without cost, and represent a valuable property right, which can confer competitive advantage. Environmentalists, on the other hand, are attracted to the principle that the polluter should pay a tax, in payment for the use of, and damage to, a common environmental asset, and feel uneasy about conferring explicit rights to damage the environment. We note, in passing, that there is no practical difference, in terms of the environmental damage which is allowed, between regulations which permit pollution and granting permits to pollute. Nonetheless, this is a factor to be reckoned with; in the assessment of Hahn and Hester (1989), a presentational concern to play down the property right aspect of permits has restricted the development of permit markets in the US.

Let us begin in the idealised situation in which a well-functioning permit market exists where no agent is able to influence the price of permits by his own actions, and where we are dealing with a uniformly-mixed pollutant. In that case it is desirable to minimise total control costs; this requires that marginal control costs are equalised across sources, for if they were not, total costs could be reduced by switching the burden of control from a high control-cost source to a lower-cost source.

Figure 1 shows the marginal cost (MC) of control (the rising curve) and the marginal benefit (MB) of control (the falling curve). Note that the marginal benefit of control is the same as the marginal cost of pollution damage. The figure is a simplification in that it supposes that the MC and MB curves are known, whereas in reality a key issue in environmental economics is the estimation of these costs and benefits.

The issue of charges versus permits (prices versus quantities) becomes critical when there is uncertainty about where the MC and MB curves lie. In figure 1(b) it is assumed that the position of the MB curve is known, but that the MC curve is unknown to the regulator. Two possible MC curves are shown. In figure 1(b) the MB schedule is relatively steep and MC curves are relatively shallow. A charge would be unpredictable in its effect on the amount of control because of the shallowness of the MC curve. But the steepness of the MB curve makes it important to establish approximately the right quantity. In these circumstances the quantity instrument (permits) would do better than charges in maximising the expected benefits of control. Figure 1(c) depicts the reverse case: shallow MB and steep MC. Fixing the quantity would make the cost of control very unpredictable, which is undesirable given the steepness of the MC curve. Here charges perform better than permits in maximising the expected benefits of control.

---

[1] Sections 1, 2, 3, and 5 of this paper include material which has been derived from a study by London Economics for the Department of the Environment: "The Potential Role of Market Mechanisms in the Control of Acid Rain", Department of the Environment Economics Research Series, HMSO, March 1992.

Figure 1   Pollution Control Policy under Uncertainty

Figure 1(a)

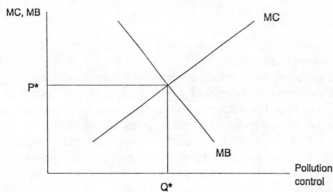

Figure 1(b)

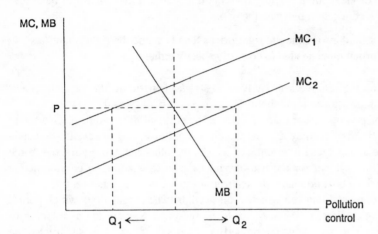

Figure 1(c)

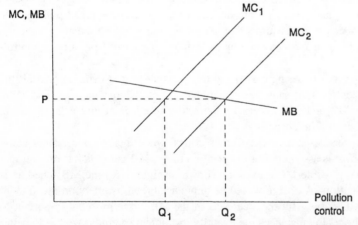

Figure 1 illustrates a general principle, explained by Tietenberg (1988, page 328):

When the marginal damage curve [i.e. the MB of control curve] is steeply sloped and the marginal cost curve is rather flat, certainty about emissions is more important than certainty over control costs. Smaller deviations of actual emissions from expected emissions can cause rather large deviations in damage costs, whereas control costs would be relatively insensitive to the degree of control. Permits would prevent large fluctuations in these damage costs and would, therefore, yield a lower cost of being wrong than charges.

Suppose, however, that the marginal cost curve was steeply sloped, but the marginal damage curve was flat. Small changes in the degree of control would have a large effect on control costs but would not affect damages very much. In this case it makes sense to rely on charges to give more precise control over control costs accepting the less dire consequences from possible fluctuations in damage costs.

These reservations suggest that the choice of permits or charges in the face of uncertainty depends on the circumstances. Theory alone is not strong enough to dictate a choice; empirical studies are necessary. It is worth noting that even though the control authorities may be highly uncertain about the marginal benefit relationship, in relation to water pollution, for example, this does not always dissuade them from adopting environmental criterion which are dogmatic about this relationship, eg the acceptance of precise national targets. In other words, the control authority may choose to behave as if the MB curve in Figure 1 is vertical, and precisely known, even when it is not.

While it is conceivable that the right level of charge could be found by trial and error, it must be doubtful whether this process would be politically acceptable, especially given the likely hostility to the introduction of charges. Moreover, varying the charge would tend to undermine its credibility and weaken responses to it.

By the same token, future permit prices may also be uncertain and be perceived to be subject to changes in government policy. There could be concern that the Government might issue more permits in future, for revenue purposes.

Table 1 summarises the theoretical merits and demerits of permits and charges.

Table 1   Comparison of charges and permits

Criterion	Charges	Permits
1. Certainty of effect	Poor, unless control authority is well informed about industry's costs and likely responses	High, provided monitoring
2. Information requirements	High; detailed modelling of source industries necessary	Slight
3. Cost to industry	High; needs to pay charges as well as control costs unless latter are subsidised by charges	Low, if permits issued free; similar to charges if auctioned (although possibly higher if there is imperfect competition in the permits market)
4. Vulnerability to market manipulation	Nil	Possibly high in water context
5. Adaptability to location-specific targets	Differential taxes by region could be applied	Ambient permits could be tailored exactly to environmental objectives
6. Administrative burden	No higher than for an effective administrative solution	High if authority wishes to intervene in the market, but much less so if spot checks and fines used in place of detailed regulation
7. Efficiency	High compared to administrative solution	High, even when market is subject to manipulation

Application to Water Quality

Two basic approaches have been followed in pollution control – emission standards and environmental quality standards. Thus, as regards water quality, there is an issue whether environmental standards should apply to discharges themselves, or to the quality of water in rivers, aquifers and estuaries. There has been a long-running dispute between the protagonists of these two approaches, which has featured in the dealings of the UK with the EC. Thus, for example, the Dangerous Substances Directive (76/464/EEC) and its 'daughter' directives allow control of 'List 1' substances either on the basis of uniform emission standards or on environmental quality standards. The Nitrates Directive, whose implications are discussed later in this paper, imposes water quality standards: at no time, should nitrates in groundwater and surface water supplies exceed 50 mg/litre.

If one takes the view that pollutants are of concern only in so far as they actually reach a sensitive target, such as a natural habitat, humans, or buildings, in quantities likely to inflict damage, then the approach based on environmental quality standards is to be preferred. According to this view, if no damage is done, there is no pollution; and that to eliminate pollution, it is not necessary to wholly restrict emissions[2].

If one focuses on environmental damage, it is obvious that uniform effluent charges cannot be cost-effective, because they take no account of the damage which each polluter causes to critical points in the river system. To illustrate the point, consider the effect of the oxygen demands imposed on a river by the discharge of biodegradable wastes on the level of dissolved oxygen (DO) – one measure of water quality. Some sections of the river could assimilate the discharges; at others the DO level may be critically low. An economically efficient charge structure would charge polluters in relation to their contributions to causing these critical lows (so-called ambient charges). These would depend on their upstream distance from these lows, and on the temperature and flow of the river. In short, location matters, in water and in air pollution, and environmental modelling is needed if an efficient charging structure is to be devised.

---

[2] Thus it could be asked why a country with the UK's natural environmental advantages – estuaries which are sluiced twice daily by powerful tides, and short, fast-running rivers – should comply with emission standards which were required by neighbouring countries without these advantages. Why, in short, should the UK not be allowed to exploit a comparative advantage in water-polluting industries!

2 Market Mechanisms: Other Countries' Experience

In general, Europe has preferred charges and the US has chosen to rely on permits. However, it needs to be added that European experience to date has little guidance to offer on the relative effectiveness of the two modes of control since the imposition of charges in Europe have, for the most part, been half-hearted affairs, designed more to raise revenues for investment in pollution control equipment than to meet demanding pollution standards.

European Experience

Several European countries have imposed water pollution charges, for the purpose of 'raising revenues' for pollution control. This concept is somewhat muddled. As we noted in Section 1, pollution control is not some worthy cause, for which one 'raises revenue'; it is an economic activity which has measurable costs and benefits. These need to be brought in to line with each other, at the margin, by setting a charge which encourages the optimum amount of investment in pollution control. The message from economic analysis is clear: if charges are set at a level which equates the marginal costs and benefits of pollution control, as in figure 1 above, the appropriate investment in pollution control will follow.

Several West European countries are reported by ERL (1990) as levying charges on effluent discharges – France, Germany, Norway and Netherlands. In addition, Sweden imposes a charge on nitrogen and phosphorous fertilizers. Most charging structures are designed only to raise limited amounts of revenue for financing water treatment investment and, for the most part, are too low to have an incentive effect. For example, the Swedish 5% tax on fertiliser sales has had no effect, according to ERL (op.cit. Annex 3, p.A3.23). The German Federal Wastewater Charging Act was introduced in 1976 in order to reinforce water standard regulations. The charges themselves were not introduced until 1981, by which time only 10% of dischargers complied with the minimum standards, according to an OECD survey (1989).

The German charges were set initially at a very low level, which was increased annually until 1986. If the discharger met the minimum standard, 50% of the charge was waived. ERL reported (op. cit. Annex 2, page A2.13.) that 'the charge is considered to be successful in reducing BOD/COD pollution, especially from local authorities. It had a large incentive impact immediately prior to its implementation but it is considered that the charge is too low to have much effect on industrial investment in pollution control'. This is not a surprising result, in view of the fact that the charge was well below the average cost of water treatment.

The European country whose experience of effluent charges appears to be of most value in this context is the Netherlands since, according to Bressers (1988), the Dutch effluent charges are both substantial (double the German levels), and longstanding (in operation since 1970). Bressers compares the contribution of incentives and directives to raising Dutch water quality. The charges were introduced by the Pollution of Surface Waters Act 1970, at a time when water quality was badly degraded. In common with some other European countries, the Dutch introduced the charges to raise revenue for water treatment, rather than to discourage discharges.

The charges were regionally differentiated, according to the cost of treatment. Bressers was able to provide a statistical explanation for inter-regional variations in the rate at which (oxygen-consuming) water pollution declined between 1975 and 1980, in terms of the industrial structures of each region and by the extent to which effluent charges increased in that period[3].

Bressers was less successful in explaining variations in heavy metal pollution, but this appears to have been due to the fact that charges were too low. Charges were more successful when they were increased.

Bressers' study also sheds light on the question whether charges were more effective than administrative controls (issuing permits and attaching conditions to them). Administrative action (measured as the weighted number of official reports on non-compliance) was found to have a statistically significant effect on improvements in water quality, but it could only explain 40% as much of the water quality improvements as increased charges.

The US Experience

The US has taken pollution control more seriously, and for this reason alone, their preference for and experience

---

[3] The decrease in oxygen-consuming pollution = 0.96 times the % decrease to be expected on the basis of regional industrial structures + 1.55 times the % increase in charges. The t ratios were 12 and 8 respectively, and the R^2 was 0.96.

with permits deserves to be given due weight. Since emissions trading has so far found substantial application only in the United States, it is natural to enquire whether this instrument is useful for other countries as well.

The greatest innovation in the use of market mechanisms has been evident in the US air quality policies. These policies are characterised by regulation on a detailed technical level and a precisely defined system of ambient air standards, whereas in Europe, except perhaps in Germany, requirements for installations are settled through negotiations, on the basis of much vaguer air quality standards. In this sense, emissions trading might be regarded unkindly as a way out of a problem of the United States' own making; having imposed a rigid and expensive system, it is perhaps no surprise that the market can offer less expensive solutions. On the other hand, as the air quality problem is perceived with increasing urgency in Europe, and the costs of achieving stringent air quality standards begin to be understood, the attractions of emissions trading may begin to be appreciated.

The United States' emissions trading policies need to be understood against the background of the regulations which were laid down in the Clean Air Act of 1969. National Ambient Air Quality Standards were set by the United States' EPA and implemented by states under State Implementation Plans (SIP). SIPs were developed for 247 Air Quality Control Areas. The SIPs determine emission levels for existing, modified or new sources, the last category being required to meet more stringent technology standards than existing sources, based on industry-by-industry New Science Performance Standards (NSPS). Under this regime, States are allowed to specify the technologies to be applied by individual firms in a detailed way, whether these are cost-effective or not.

SIP deadlines were rarely met; the States lacked the necessary detailed knowledge about emission sources, about relationships between emissions and ambient air quality and about control technologies and their costs. When it became clear that many States could not meet SIP deadlines, EPA began formulating its offset policy. Without an emissions trading programme, it was becoming difficult to see how any new industrial development could take place at all in areas which had failed to achieve EPA standards. New and modified sources were allowed in 'non-attainment areas' provided that any additional emissions were offset.

The US emissions trading has always been contentious. As the OECD report comments, despite the fact that Emission Reduction Credits (ERCs) conferred a 'right to pollute', emissions trading differs only in degree from direct regulation, which also provides a certain 'right' to pollute. A difficulty which emissions trading has encountered is that the modelling and emissions data which has been used to calculate the impact on ambient air quality brought about by emissions trading is not sufficiently robust to convince sceptics that trading can maintain or raise air quality standards. It was objected that if baseline emission levels were not correctly calculated, some of the reductions which are traded may be illusory, and hence could lead to increases in emissions ('paper credits'). Another point of debate concerned the validity of ERCs from shut-downs. When a plant is closed for economic reasons it was argued that resulting emission decreases should contribute to a better air quality and not be banked for later use. Some argue that banked credits should be 'discounted' so as to speed compliance with air quality standards.

There are four types of trade to which US firms can have recourse: offsets, bubbles, banking and netting.

- 'Offsets' require that emission sources which wish to establish themselves in a new area must purchase or acquire (through internal trades) emissions credits, such that their entry does not add to the total emissions in the area concerned.

- 'Bubbles' enable firms to treat an existing plant with multiple emissions as a single source, as if the plant were enclosed by a bubble with a single emissions vent.

- 'Banking' enables firms to hold ERCs as assets for later use or for sale.

- 'Netting' allows firms to increase emissions at one source, offsetting the increase sufficiently at another source such that the net increase is below a certain threshold for defining a major source.

Hahn (1989) reviewed the performance of market methods in three environmental areas: Wisconsin Fox river water permits, lead trading between gasoline refiners, and emissions trading under the US Clean Air Act. There has been only one trade in river water permits and few evident cost savings. Hahn blames the nature of the market (imperfect competition) and the restrictive rules for trading and grandfathering of allocations for this disappointing result. However, in the gasoline lead case, a reasonably active and well-functioning market developed, which was attributed by Hahn to the ease of monitoring and to political consensus.

The volume and variety of trading in the air quality permit market is by far the largest of these three cases and provides by far the most useful lessons for this study. The history of external offsets trades in air quality permits, and the estimated savings associated with them, is set out in Table 2, reproduced from Hahn and Hester. Banking of emission reduction credits has been negligible; netting apart, external transactions have also been negligible. The attractiveness of netting is attributed to the fact that the US regulatory system bears more stringently on new than on existing sources; netting allows firms to modify existing sources more easily, in preference to establishing new facilities. The relatively poor tradeability of ERCs appears to be due to two related factors. The first is uncertainty about the property rights embodied in them, associated with the issue of whether the regulators will recognise the baseline from which the emission reductions have been made. For example, banked credits are sometimes discounted. The second is the reported difficulty in finding trading partners, and judging prices of future permit prices. Hahn argues that restrictions, grandfathering, and high transactions costs have discouraged external trading and the attainment of the full benefits.

Hahn and Hester conclude that although the amount of emissions trading has generally fallen well short of the levels predicted by the theory, and that it has taken place in forms which were not expected, emissions trading is still estimated to have saved billions of dollars.

Tietenberg's (1990) summary of the US experience, set out in Table 3, cites ten empirical studies of air pollution control in the US, all but one of which conclude that the actual cost of achieving air quality standards exceeds the theoretical 'least cost'; in most cases by a significant ratio.

The US strategy for water quality depends almost entirely on direct regulation; discharge permits generally result in uniform (and hence inefficient) effluent limitations for particular classes of dischargers. In 1981 Wisconsin became the first state to adopt regulations that allow the use of transferable discharge permits for water pollution control. However, only one trade has occurred despite predictions of substantial savings of $7 millions annually in pollution abatement costs. Does this result indicate that tradeable permits markets are unlikely to work for water pollution?

An obvious reason why they might not is that the market size is limited to those dischargers affecting a single critical point on a river (the minimal dissolved oxygen 'sag points'), and that those dischargers could well be in competition in the same product market. The Lower Fox River happens to host the world's greatest concentration of pulp and paper mills. Moreover, they are grouped into three clusters, each of three or four companies, above each of three 'sag points.'

Table 2 History of External Offset Trades for the South Coast Air Quality Management District, from 1983 to 1985

External Offset Transactions for Volatile Organic Compounds 1983-1985				
Year	Number of Trades	Mean Size in Tons Per Year	Mean Price Per Ton	Price Range Per Ton
1983	3	16	NA	NA
1984	5	27	NA	NA
1985	42	51	$2,500	$850 to $3,250

NA = Not Available

External Offset Transactions for All Pollutants 1985					
Pollutant	Number of Trades	Total Volume Traded	% of Total Emissions	Mean Price[1]	Price Range[2]
Nitrogen Oxides	5	575	<0.5	$5000	$2000 to 5500
Carbon Monoxide	3	27	<0.1	$3000	$1250 to 2100
Sulphur Dioxide	2	310	<0.5	$3000	$2900 to 3000
Particulates	3	27	<0.5	$2000	$1250 to 2100
Volatile Organic Compounds	42	2142	<1.0	$2500	$ 850 to 3250

[1] Mean price for a transaction at the end of 1985 as estimated by a knowledgeable offset broker
[2] Price range for actual offset external transactions which took place during 1985

333

Table 3 Empirical Studies of Air Pollution Control

Study	Pollutants Covered	Geographic Area	CAC Benchmark	Ratio of CAC Cost to Least Cost
Atkinson & Lewis	Particulates	St Louis	SIP Regulations	6.00[a]
Roach *et al*	Sulphur dioxide	Four Comers in Utah	SIP regulations Colorado, Arizona and New Mexico	4.25
Hahn & Noll	Sulphates standards	LosAngeles	California emission	1.07
Krupnick	Nitrogen dioxide regulations	Baltimore	Proposed RACT	5.96[b]
Seskin *et al*	Nitrogen dioxide regulations	Chicago	Proposed RACT	14.40[b]
McGartland	Particulates	Baltimore	SIP regulations	4.18
Spofford	Sulphur Dioxide	Lower Delaware Valley	Uniform percentage regulations	1.78
	Particulates	Lower Delaware Valley	Uniform percentage regulations	22.00
Harrison	Airport noise	United States	Mandatory retrofit	1.72
Maloney & Yandle	Hydrocarbons	All domestic DuPont plants	Uniform percentage reduction	4.15[c]
Palmer *et al*	CFC emissions from non-aerosol applications	United States	Proposed emission standards	1.96

Notes:

CAC = command and control, the traditional regulatory approach

SIP = state implementation plan

RACT = reasonably available control technologies, a set of standards imposed on existing sources in non-attainment areas

[a] Based on a 40 $\mu g/m^3$ at worst receptor

[b] Based on a short-term, one-hour average of 250 $\mu g/m^3$

[c] Based on 85 per cent reduction of emissions from all sources.

Novotny's study (1986) suggests that these permit markets, imperfect as they are, were denied an opportunity to function. Buyers of permits had to demonstrate need; permits were defined in terms of discharges, not impacts, so that extensive modelling was required in order to establish that a trade would not reduce the level of dissolved oxygen at sag points – one reason why trading a permit would take at least 175 days. Trades that merely reduced operating expenses were prohibited. The greatest obstacle was that the status of the acquired property right was unclear, because of the provision that dischargers were required to waive all rights to the transferred allocation beyond the permit expiry date. It was not clear what was actually being traded: was it an asset, or just a lease?

Considering these reviews of the US experience together, it is difficult not to conclude that although the benefits from emissions trading are disappointing, the savings it has achieved are in many instances substantial. The unfulfilled potential of emissions trading is significant and under less discouraging regulatory regimes, this potential could be realised. The failure of the Lower Fox River experiment is particularly instructive: if cost-minimisation – the *raison d'etre* of permit trading – is excluded by administrators as a justification for permit trades, it can be no surprise that such a market fails to develop.

3 Design and Performance of Permit Markets

Ambient Permits

Having considered, in general terms, the respective merits of charges and permits, it is evident that permits offer the attractive advantages of offering certainty of effect coupled with zero information requirements on the part of the regulating authority. Consider first so-called ambient permits – those that permit pollution at a specific location.

The operation of ambient permits can be illustrated by considering the type of control problem for which they are suited – a problem in which the control authority wishes to achieve a water quality standard at a particular critical 'low' location on a river. The authority has information which enables it to attribute responsibility for the oxygen deficiency at that point to each of the dischargers of effluent which places biochemical oxygen demand (BOD) on the river. A simplified example is set out in Table 4, involving two sources, discharging 50,000 tonnes of BOD a day. Source 1 is situated further from the critical location than Source 2, and accounts for half as much dissolved oxygen, both absolutely and per tonne of BOD discharged, as Source 2 at that location.

Table 4 Trading Ambient Permits

		Source 1	Source 2	Total
Baseline Position	Discharges to river system (tonnes BOD/day)	50	50	100
	Impact at critical point (parts per million dissolved oxygen) consumed	2	4	6
Position after issuing ambient permits to consume only 50% of baseline dissolved oxygen levels	Discharges (tonnes BOD/day)	25	25	50
	Impact at critical point (parts per million dissolved oxygen)	1	2	3
	Control Costs* (£m/yr)	20	20	40
Position after trade in Permits	Discharges (tonnes BOD/day)	50	12.5	62.5
	Impact at critical point (parts per million dissolved oxygen)	2	1	3
(Source 1 buys permits to consume 1 part per million dissolved oxygen from Source 2)				
	Control Costs* (£m)	–	30	30

* Calculated on basis of £0.8m/tonnes BOD/day for both sources

Let us suppose that the control policy calls for a 50% reduction in the consumption of dissolved oxygen at the particular location and issues ambient permits to each source to give effect to that policy. Suppose also that the permits are distributed free, in proportion to the two sources' respective oxygen consumption, recognising the spatial difference between them. If both sources opt to use their permits to the full, they both reduce emissions by 50% each, at a cost of £20m/year.

There is a better solution for them, however. If Source 1 buys permits from Source 2 to consume 1 part per million of dissolved oxygen at the critical location, it can avoid £20m/yr in control costs. Source 2 will control more, but at an additional cost of only £10m/yr. There is no net increase in oxygen consumption at the critical location but because total reduction in BOD discharges is less (37.5 rather than 50 tonnes BOD/day), there is a saving of £10m/year. The price of the permit to add one part per million of dissolved oxygen at the critical point on the river would be negotiated by the two sources: it would lie somewhere between zero and the value of the saving in Source 1's unit control cost (£20m/yr).

Thus even when ambient permits are distributed in a way which takes into account location and the transfer relationships from pollution source to the environmental target, trade in ambient permits can reduce (the increase in) industry costs, without hazarding the desired water quality standard. In this sense, tradeable ambient permits provide a well-directed and efficient mechanism.

Imperfect Competition in Permit Markets

In a market for emission permits, if all pollution sources take the price of permits as given, they will have the appropriate incentives to find optimal control methods, and the marginal cost of control (equal to the permit price) will be equalised across sources. This will not happen if a single firm has market power in the permit market. If that firm is a net buyer of permits it will buy fewer permits than if it were a price-taker; if it is a net seller it will sell fewer than it would if it were a price-taker. A monopsony buyer does not wish to drive up the price against himself and so holds back purchases; a monopoly seller similarly holds back sales, so as not to 'spoil his market'.

A further consideration is that a dominant firm could also have a strategic motive in relation to its rivals. Fringe firms in the dominant firm's industry might have higher emission control costs (because they cannot exploit the economies of scale in control technology), and are for that reason likely to wish to buy permits rather than to control costs. By buying more permits than it would otherwise judge to be appropriate on cost-minimisation grounds, the dominant firm could increase the costs of these rivals by more than its own, and in this way, reduce the supply from its rivals and increase its own profits.

Now combine this with the effect discussed in the previous paragraph. When the dominant firm is a net buyer of permits, the strategic ('buy more') effect works in the opposite direction to the earlier 'buy less' effect, and is not necessarily damaging. But when the dominant firm is a net seller of permits, the strategic ('buy more' = 'sell fewer') effect works in the same direction as the earlier 'sell fewer' effect, and the inefficiency of a permit market is exacerbated. Market failure in the final product market – imperfect competition – can distort all input markets, and the permit market would be no exception. Moreover – and this is a key point – activity in the permit market can further distort competition in the final product market. These considerations cannot be ignored when considering the prospects for discharge permit trading. Their practical significance is discussed in Section 5.

Organising Permit Markets

The key choices as to the form of permit market are:

- should permits be issued or auctioned?

- what institutional arrangements are needed for an effective market?

- how should permits be denominated?

In making these choices, account would need to be taken of whether the arrangements are likely to:

- create or increase entry barriers

- add significantly to industrial costs

- be conducive to an efficient market.

To what extent would market efficiency matter to the control authority? From the authorities' point of view, pollution control would be achieved (provided always that emissions and permits are monitored effectively) irrespective of how the permit market behaves. The issue is whether the market would perform so badly that pollution control costs under permits turn out to be higher, and are distributed less acceptably, than under an administrative system.

Academic studies of this point conclude that although restraints on competition in the permit market reduce the savings in control costs which permits can achieve, control costs are still likely to be substantially lower than under the command-and-control alternative. Maloney and Yandle (1984) simulated the effects of cartelisation in the sulphur and hydrocarbons permit markets and concluded that even a high degree of cartelisation would not significantly erode the large savings to be achieved from permit markets. They concluded that when the cartel controls 90% of the emission credits, control costs would be some 40% higher than they would have been under competition. Nonetheless, the cost savings, relative to the command-and-control alternative, would still be significant. Tietenberg (1990) concluded that price manipulation would increase control costs by less than 1%. The figure is so slight because:

'the only control cost change is the net difference between the new larger control burden borne by the permit searcher and the correspondingly smaller burden borne by the sources having larger-than-normal allocations of permits. Only the costs of the marginal units are affected.' (Tietenberg, 1990, p.26).

An auction is to be preferred in principle to a free issue on economic efficiency grounds since it would be more likely to allocate permits to those who value them most, and for whom the permits would achieve the highest savings in control costs. A secondary market in freely-issued permits could in principle approach the same solution, but transactions costs, and possibly strategic behaviour as well, might impede this transfer mechanism. An auction would also avoid the bias against new investment, which is a feature of all environmental controls, and which impedes growth and competition.

Are dominant suppliers any less likely to manipulate the permit market if permits are auctioned, rather than issued free? We suggest that they will be less likely to do so, for two reasons. An auction market involving the entire stock of permits would be 'thicker' and would engage most of the players, whereas if permits were issued, the market would tend to be thin. Those that would wish to be net purchasers of permits under the free-issue arrangement (small sources, with their above-average control costs) would have a better chance of obtaining the permits they need in an auction for the entire stock. The 'buy less' effect would work in the right direction, in favour of smaller sources acquiring more-than-proportional quantities of permits and thereby controlling emissions less.

But more importantly, an auction provides an opportunity to the issuing authority to reduce opportunities or incentives to manipulate the market.

There are auction designs which discourage price manipulation. It would be advisable to adopt sealed bids, rather than open bidding. If the concern is that dominant buyers will buy too few permits (ie the imperfect competition effect dominates the strategic effect), the auction should be structured so as to encourage such bidders to reflect fully the value of permits to them in their bidding. An auction in which all successful bidders pay a price which is lower than their bid price offers a solution to this problem. This is known as a Groves mechanism. Under this arrangement, permits would be allocated to the highest bidders, as under a single-price auction, but with the difference that a bidder which secured X permits in the auction would be charged on the basis of the X highest rejected bids. Thus, a bidder's own bids would never directly affect his payments. It is argued that such an arrangement would weaken or even remove the link between bidding behaviour and the permit price. Bids are made instead on the basis of truthful estimates of each bidder's emission control costs.

This type of auction would involve lower permit costs, since the prices paid would be equal to the average of the X rejected bids, rather than the lowest accepted bid or the highest rejected bid – an attractive consideration to industry. Each bidder would pay different prices; the largest bidders would pay the lowest price because the average of a large number of the highest rejected bids would be lower that the average of a smaller number. And herein lies a weakness of this proposal. A system which discriminates in favour of larger bidders, in order to deal with a possible abuse of their monopoly power, hardly seems an improvement. It would shift the burden of emission control to those whose cost of emission control is relatively high.

A simpler variant, which avoids this problem, is that all successful bids are charged either the lowest successful or the highest unsuccessful price which is bid. There is no way in which collusion in auctions can be eliminated, but by weakening the link between price and quantity demanded, this type of auction would reduce incentives to manipulate prices. By encouraging truthful bidding, this form of auction would counter the 'buy-less' effect.

These observations suggest that:

(i)   imperfections in permit markets are not an overwhelming argument against their use; most markets are imperfect;

(ii)   to minimise the imperfections, permits should be auctioned; this would deny incumbents advantages over new entrants. It would reduce the likelihood that the existing incumbents would hoard permits;

(iii)   permits should be sold either at the lowest successful or at the highest unsuccessful price;

(iv)   the regulator of the industry concerned should act as the issuing authority.

4 Case Study of a Diverse Source Problem: Nitrates in the Water Supply

A study carried out jointly by London Economics and ICI Fertilisers investigated whether:

- the nitrate pollution process can be understood and modelled
- this modelling can suggest a cost-effective mix of policies for controlling nitrate pollution.

The purpose of this discussion is to examine the role which economic instruments could play in such a mix.

Background

The European Commission has proposed stringent standards for nitrate both in drinking water and raw water. The UK is in breach of the standards proposed in the draft EC Nitrate Directive ('concerning the protection of fresh, coastal and marine water against pollution caused by nitrates from diffuse sources', Com (88) 708), but is now committed to meeting agreed drinking water nitrate levels in most regions by 1992 and in the remainder by 1993-95. The proposed standard is 11.3 mg/l N. *Figure 2* shows the areas of the UK in which it is exceeded for groundwater.

Policy responses

The UK government has already taken some limited initiatives. These include 'set-aside', whereby farmers are compensated for voluntary land use changes away from high nitrogen releasing crops and, more recently, a framework for the designation of 'Nitrate Sensitive Areas (NSAs)'. The latter scheme is voluntary and experimental, and places prime emphasis on changes in farm practice and land use. Many of the changes would not attract compensation, but some of the more stringent – such as wholesale replacement of arable land, restrictions on stocking density and changes in crop mix – would do so.

Sources of Nitrate in Water

Nitrate occurs in drinking water for a variety of reasons. First, rainwater contains nitrate. Empirical evidence on how much, and why, is sparse, but there exists a body of opinion which holds that rainwater nitrate content is rising, possibly as a result of increased car exhaust emissions. Some nitrate is also deposited, in dry form, directly from the atmosphere.

Secondly, all plants, trees and animals contain nitrate. When they die, and decay, this nitrate re-enters the soil. Similarly, animal and human excreta also contains nitrate; slurry and effluent use and control are therefore important in the nitrogen cycle. All soil contains a 'pool' of nitrate, which is left over from organic crop residues from previous land use. Rain washes some of this into watercourses or aquifers; ploughing and other agricultural practices can help to destabilise the pool and accelerate this process.

Thirdly, arable crops and grassland release (or 'leach') nitrate. They require it for their growth either in inorganic form as manufactured N-fertilizer, or in organic form as animal manures, or direct from the soil 'pool' or rainfall. Different crops take up different amounts of nitrate during their growing process; the amount available to be 'leached' by subsequent rainfall varies widely. Modern seed varieties are designed to use particular amounts of nitrate, and substantial variations in this amount can have dramatic effects on yields. Livestock farming requires nitrate to grow the grass on which animals feed; lower application rates imply lower stocking densities.

Nitrate does not stay in water forever, and a process called denitrification occurs – faster at higher temperatures – when water is left to accumulate in reservoirs, ditches and in aquifers. This involves the decomposition of the nitrate ions to form their constituent elements, nitrogen and oxygen.

Surface waters

Surface waters are more responsive to measures to reduce nitrate. They are often fed directly by water which runs off fields and hills. Typically, nitrate concentrations take only 1-2 years to move from their source to the relevant abstraction point. These waters typically have lower nitrate concentrations than ground water (from which drinking water is abstracted through boreholes), although seasonal variations can make it difficult to comply with a year round maximum level.

The major problems with surface waters arise in areas where effluent discharges occur near to abstraction points, or where drainage conditions allow nitrate to run off into water courses.

Figure 2 Nitrate concentrations – groundwater

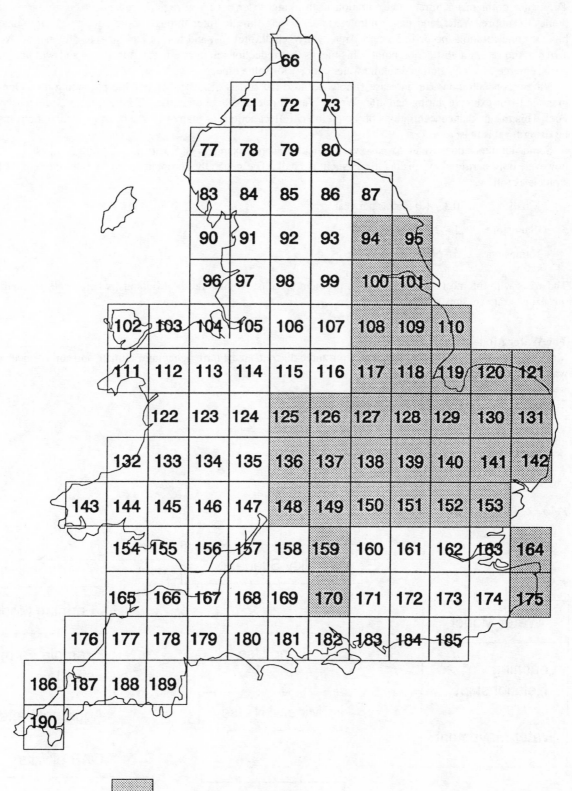

Over 11.3 mg/litre

Ground waters

The major problem for nitrate concentration in drinking water occurs in regions dependent on ground waters for domestic supply. Water, and hence nitrates, takes a long time to filter through some aquifers. Unfortunately the highest concentrations occur in Eastern Areas where chalk prevails, and here it can take 40-50 years for water to arrive at the relevant abstraction point. This means that reductions in nitrate leached from the soil will not, in some areas, emerge as a reduction in drinking water content for some time.

Nitrate concentrations can increase simply because the soil is disturbed. Hence the ploughing-up of long-term grassland (for example during and after World War II) releases large quantities of nitrate from a previously stable pool. This means that concentrations observed today reflect actions of many years ago, and concentrations may still be rising for this reason.

Some aquifers allow water to pass very quickly, as for example in fissure flow through limestone. Others, however, only permit slow 'piston' flow, such as chalk. The generally accepted speed of flow through each rock strata is as follows:

Chalk   0.3 – 1.0 metres per year

Sandstone   1 – 2 metres per year

Limestone   5 – 50 metres per year

The areas with the most substantial nitrate problem are East Anglia and the Midlands, where chalk or chalk-based mesozoic strata are important.

The Water Model

Modelling has brought together evidence from three discrete areas; farm behaviour, climate and soil science, and the water system as shown in Figure 3.

Figure 3   Conceptual Overview of Model

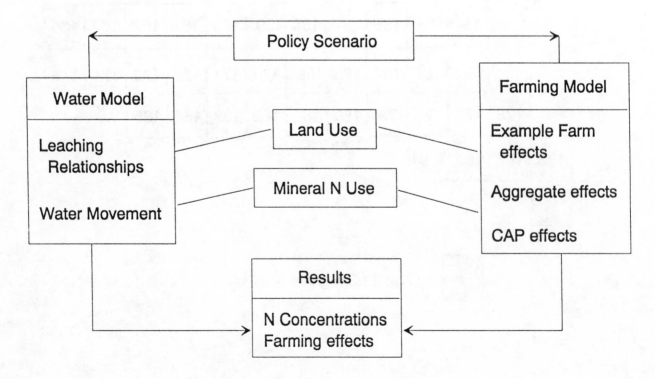

The water model explains the flows into, through, and out of each of the 114 40 x 40 kilometre squares into which England and Wales is divided for meteorological analysis, (known as MORECS squares). This modelling is illustrated in Figure 4.

Within each square, the model traces rainfall, either as surface flow or into the aquifer. It also contains data on the relative proportions of different pervious and impervious rock strata, on hydrological gradients and the mixing process which occurs in the saturated zone.

A complex mass-balance exercise ensures that all water is tracked throughout its progress to the sea. Validation of the model indicates a broad match between its predictions and observed outcomes both of water flow and of existing nitrate concentrations, notwithstanding the long time required for water to percolate through the aquifers. This validation has been pursued in some detail in the Anglia and Severn-Trent water regions.

Figure 4 Surface Water Flows

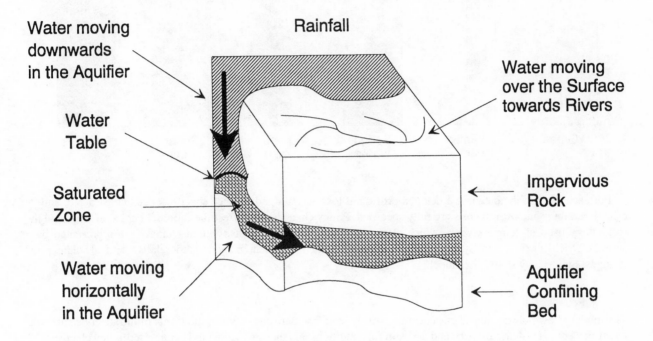

Leaching

The water and farm models are linked partly by common inputs, such as climate, and partly by results of farmers' behaviour. So land use changes and crop mixes, as well as any changes in the use of mineral-N fertilizers, are important in determining eventual nitrate concentrations.

A key feature which links farmers' decisions and nitrate concentrations is the extent to which crops release or 'leach' nitrate into the soil. This feature is represented by a set of 'leaching equations'. These characterise for each crop, soil type and rainfall, the amount of nitrate which can be expected, for a given application of fertilizer, to be leached through to the watercourse.

Figure 5 summarises the leaching properties of various crops. It compares, in the left hand column, a 'normal' application of N with the amount that is left, on average, to be leached through the soil. The difference is taken up by the crop. Grassland, unploughed, leaves little for leaching, although land left fallow and unfertilized can still leach considerable amounts.

Most crops take up the majority of the N applied, but spring-sown wheat, winter barley, oilseed rape, sugar beet and potatoes all leave considerable amounts of N to be leached.

The Farm Model

In order to understand and characterise the effects of each policy on farm incomes and crop production, a database of 567 farms was constructed, reflecting variations in farming practice by: region, type, size and ownership structure.

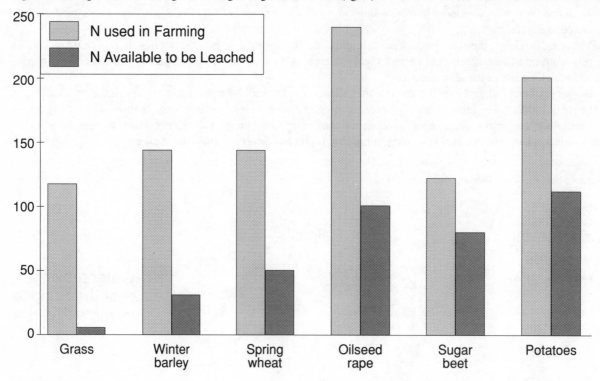

For each farm in the database a detailed profit and loss account and balance sheet has been constructed, and its crop mix, inputs and overall costs are fully specified. Policy changes then affect the farmers' choice of crop, and the technology used in complex ways, which affect costs, incomes and inputs. Output changes are represented by a series of yield curves, and by behavioural equations which represent responses to relative and absolute price changes. Figure 6 illustrates the model.

Summary
The model as a whole is capable of generating steady-state comparisons between the levels of nitrate concentrations under present agricultural practice and agricultural conditions and those which would occur after policy changes.

Figure 6   The Farm Model for England and Wales

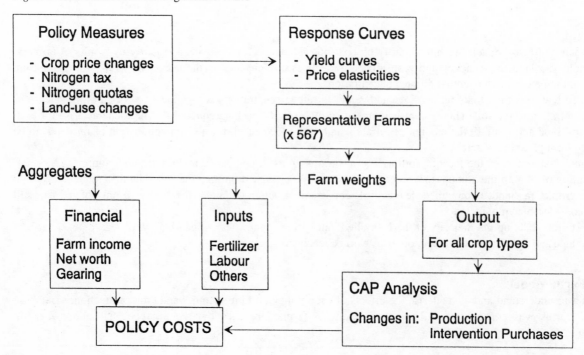

Policies to reduce nitrate concentrations

Curative: Water treatment and management

If the sole objective were the immediate reduction in nitrate concentrations in order to meet the European Commission's 1980 Directive which is aimed at protecting domestic suppliers, then the most straightforward solution would be to reduce directly the nitrate concentrations in water as it is abstracted and supplied. Water treatment and management[4] is the only solution which can yield results in a short time-frame in many areas; it is also the cheapest option in terms of overall cost to the UK economy.

Preliminary estimates of the costs of water treatment as the sole solution to the drinking water problem have been derived.

The model has identified the 34 MORECS squares in which the predicted combined groundwater and surface-water nitrate concentration exceeds 45 mg/l (to allow a small margin below the 50 mg/l limit as in other studies) in steady state. In each of these squares, the total abstraction of ground and surface water, and their mean base concentration, has been computed. Broad estimates of the costs of building and running sufficient plant to reduce these concentrations to below 45 mg/l have then been made, on a square-by-square basis.

The average excess concentration in the 34 squares was 23 mg/l NO_3. Some 18 million people are estimated to live in these squares. Of the total of 5,200 million cubic metres of water abstracted in England and Wales each year, one third is abstracted to supply them and industrial and commercial needs. The total treatment cost, on an annualized basis, required to bring the nitrate concentrations to 45 mg/l NO_3 is estimated to be £65 million at 1990 prices. This estimate includes the costs for pumping, subsequent treatment of water, chemicals and effluent disposal.

Preventative: Farming

Land use changes

We noted that crops vary in how much nitrate they leached into water sources. Grassland and woodland create less of a problem than arable land, and wheat and barley leach less nitrogen than, for example, oilseed rape, sugar beet or potatoes.

We have used the model to explore the magnitude of the changes which would be necessary in order to solve the problem by this route. In some regions, the required changes would be extensive, involving the forced removal of many traditional crops and a substantial reduction in the amount of land devoted to farming.

We have explored in some detail two possible options for East Anglia, the most problematic region:

1. The conversion of East Anglian arable land to grazing land. The model indicates that, on average, 50% of the land would need to be diverted in this way, although not all squares are 'solved' even by such a diversion. The effects on the market for sheepmeat would be substantial, with knock-on effects on hill farmers in other locations. In East Anglia alone, such a shift would reduce net farm surpluses by £170 million a year and reduce agricultural employment by 6,000.

2. The progressive removal of crops on a localised basis, assuming that they are replaced by woodland or some other low-leaching land use. Here we have "removed" the highest-leaching crops first and ascertained, on a square-by-square basis, the crops that would need to be replaced with either unfertilized grass or woodland. To solve the problem for East Anglia, all potatoes, sugar beet, oilseed rape, spring cereal, peas and beans would need to be replaced, as well as around 40% of winter wheat and barley. Under this option, which comes closer to solving the problem than conversion to grazing land, and which does not have the knock-on effect on hill farmers in other regions, net farm surplus is estimated to fall by £280 million a year, with substantial employment effects.

---

[4]   The water industry can reduce the nitrate concentration of drinking water by: (a) extended storage to permit natural denitrification; (b) mixing of water from low nitrate concentration sources; (c) treatment using a variety of techniques, of which ion exchange and biological removal are the two most developed. **Water Management** solutions – the flrst two options – can, in the right circumstances, remove the peak problem addressed by the European Commission Directive. However, if nitrate concentrations continue to rise (the evidence on whether they will is mixed, with groundwater concentrations increasing and surface water concentrations decreasing), the numbers of low-nitrate sources may be insufficient to make this a nationally viable option. With droughts and shortage of reservoir capacity, the scope of these methods to reduce average concentrations by extended storage is also limited. **Water Treatment** processes include the construction of additional reservoirs or tanks in which water is held while natural denitrification occurs over a period of months. This process can be accelerated in specially constructed plant with a continuous fluidised bed where methanol, ethanol or acetic acid is added to encourage bacterial growth. This 'biological denitrification' does, however, produce several poisonous and corrosive by-products which then have to be removed from the resulting water.

Both options highlight the damage to UK farming if the EC limit is to be attained by land use changes alone.

Fertilizer limitations

Reduction of inorganic fertilizer use could be achieved by:

1. Direct quotas on the application of N-fertilizer. These would be difficult to police – much more so, for example, than milk quotas – and might merely cause a shift to the use of organic manures. Crop-by-crop monitoring would be difficult, but an overall restriction on the amount each farmer could apply would be inefficient, given local variations in circumstances. The model indicates that even a 20% cut in N-fertilizer use would only reduce the average N concentration in England and Wales by about 0.5 mg/l N, and 'solve' the problem in 5 squares for each of surface and groundwater. It would, however, reduce cereal output by around 0.9 million tonnes, net farm surplus by £20 million and employment by 2,500.

2. A tax, or levy, on fertilizer. This would raise the post-tax price of fertilizer, and encourage farmers to use less. However, because yields are in many cases very sensitive to fertilizer application, and because in any case fertilizer forms a small part of overall farming costs, the empirical evidence is that price elasticities on fertilizer use are low. The accepted range is 0.2 to 0.4; for each 1% increase in the price of fertilizer, the volume of fertilizer used falls by between 0.2% and 0.4%. Hence, taxes have to be very high before they have a substantial impact on fertilizer use. The model indicates that, using an elasticity of 0.3, even a 40% tax would only 'solve' 3 squares, and reduce the average by around 0.3 mg/l N. Although tax revenues of £140 million would be raised, this is mostly a transfer from farmers to the Government and would contribute little to solving the problem.

'Best Farm Practice'

Recent experimental evidence suggests that there are numerous ways in which farming practice could be improved in order to reduce the nitrate leached from various crops, albeit at some cost and inconvenience to farmers. This evidence has resulted from research programmes at agricultural research centres.

A key ingredient to these changes is to minimise the disturbance which farmers make to soil equilibrium. The amount of nitrate already in the 'pool' in the soil far exceeds any which is added during normal agricultural applications. It is now, for example, well established that the ploughing-up of long-term grassland is one of the major contributors to the nitrate problem.

The methods which have been suggested, many of which have been shown to be extremely powerful in reducing leaching, are:

1. Minimise soil disturbance.

2. Change the timing of ploughing and seeding to reduce the nitrate which is washed out of the soil before the crop can begin to utilise it. Earlier sowing of winter wheats and barleys has been shown to be very valuable.

3. Slurry management.

4. Drainage systems, to minimise run-off and permit denitrification.

5. Changes to seed and fertilizer technology, for example through pelleting, to ensure the appropriate timing of release.

Experimental evidence also suggests that considerable reductions in lost nitrate can be achieved by early sowing of crops, and the progressive introduction of winter varieties. We have used the model to simulate the possible effects of such changes, through the leaching equations embodied in the model. Although changes such as those listed above will not solve all problems – and high surface water concentrations due to sewage discharges are one particular problem – they are shown to make a substantial contribution. In contrast to the more draconian changes explored above, their cost to UK farming is low.

An Overview of Model Results

Table 5 summarises the results simulated by the model for the policies described above. It shows:

Effectiveness   in terms of the number of problem squares where drinking water concentrations are reduced to below the 50 mg/l limit, and the effect on average concentrations *in the long-run steady state*.

344

Only major diversions of land use away from arable farming can make major inroads into the problem. The effect of NSAs, nitrogen taxes and quotas on average concentrations are shown to be limited. Best farm practice has a contribution to make, but cannot by itself solve the problem.

Direct cost   The large effects on farm incomes of comprehensive land changes, and of fertilizer taxes, are demonstrated.

Government revenue   This is principally the effect on the UK's contribution to the Common Agricultural Policy by the reduction of surpluses.

Land area affected   A comprehensive change in land use for the whole country would affect 5.8m hectares of the total 11.8m hectares devoted to agriculture in the UK.

The conclusions which emerge from this analysis are:

(i)   a mix of policies would be required in order to minimise the cost of complying with the Nitrate Directive; no one solution can solve the problem as cheaply as a mix of policies

(ii)   that this policy mix should vary by region, and preferably by MORECS square.

Lessons on the Use of Market Mechanisms for a Diverse Pollutant

The case illustrates the diverse source problem. The environmental damage caused by each farm depends upon its:

- location
- crop mix
- farming practices
- nitrogen applications.

We noted that a nitrogen tax would be an inefficient and unworkable solution. It would fail to discriminate in terms of environmental damage. The appropriate charging approach would be to tax each farm in relation to its contribution to a nitrate problem. This amounts to asking:

1.   to what extent does the farm leach nitrate into the soil?

2.   how damaging is this contribution, in terms of contributing to an *excess* nitrate concentration problem?

3.   what is the least cost alternative method of treating the problem?

These questions pose considerable requirements on information and analysis, but as this case study has demonstrated, this kind of analysis is feasible, and its findings could be translated into a charging structure, at some level of aggregation e.g. in terms of a limited number of crop types, and localities.

To devise the structure of a nitrate tax, one might classify farms in terms of high/medium/low leaching crop mixes, and by MORECS square. A nitrate tax could then be applied to turnover, according to crop mix and region. Variations in farming practice might be difficult to codify; they could perhaps be best handled by outlawing certain practices, such as ploughing up grasslands, in vulnerable regions.

The setting of the level of such a tax is not a problem, because the objective *would not be to reduce nitrate discharges by farmers by a predetermined amount*. Rather it would be to determine the proportion of the total nitrate problem it would be economically efficient to solve in this way. The tax which would be appropriate for this would be the least cost alternative method of treating the problem e.g. water treatment. It would not be necessary to predict the response of farmers to the tax, although this would be useful (and feasible) for planning water treatment investment.

Table 5

Impact of Measures to reduce Nitrate Concentrations

Policy	Effectiveness — Drinking Water: Numbers of squares solved	Effectiveness — Eutrophication: Average reduction mgl/N NO₃ — ground	Effectiveness — Eutrophication — surface	Direct Cost — Change in Net Farm surplus	Direct Cost — Capital and running	Government Revenue — EC Budget	Government Revenue — Tax Revenue	Farming Land Area Affected (hectares)
Comprehensive change in land use throughout England & Wales	34 (9 remain unsolved for surface water)	Not estimated	Not estimated	–£340m (Non compliant squares only)		Not estimated		5.8m
East Anglia: up to 80% switch from arable crops to extensive livestock	9 (4 remain unsolved for surface water)	6.6 (East Anglia only)	4.9	–£170m East Anglia only		Budgetary cost of compensation less EC budgetary effect: over £100m		1.5m
Nitrate Sensitive Areas 1. No potatoes 2. 10% switch from arable to rough grazing	0 0	0.2 1.1–3.7	0.2 0.6–2.6	Arable land change only NSA only: –£0.5m All non compliant squares: –£1m		Minimal		15,000
Best farm practice: 10% reduction in leaching of arable crops	1	0.6	0.4	Low		Minimal		All
Nitrogen Tax: 40% increase in price	0	0.5	0.3	–£130m		reduced by less than £2m	£140m	All
Nitrogen limit: fertilizer application restricted to 80% of current levels England and Wales	5	1.0	0.7	–£70m		reduced by £17m		All
Water Treatment	All	Minimal			max £110m			None

5 The Possible Distortion of Permit Markets

As part of its study on the use of market mechanisms to control acid rain, London Economics investigated the concern that permit markets would be distorted by dominant players, by means of a theoretical model of ambient permit markets. The model featured three players: two duopolists in one industry and a third from a different industry. The duopolists sell to a relatively price-insensitive market (e.g. as for electricity), whereas the third player sells to a price-sensitive market (e.g. as for manufacturing). The unit costs of controlling pollution for the duopolists is cheaper than for the manufacturer (because of the scale at which they would install pollution control).

The third player would wish to acquire permits because its emission control costs are likely to be relatively high. The issues are whether the structure of the oligopoly would frustrate trade in permits, and whether any reluctance on the part of the oligopolists to trade permits is likely to place the third player in a position of having to shoulder a higher share of the emissions reductions than would be predicted in a competitive market.

The model explained the difference between competitive behaviour in this oligopoly with the oligopolistic behaviour, modelled on the Cournot model of oligopoly in which each producer chooses a quantity such as to maximise profits in the light of the price-elasticity of the market demand curve and its own costs, disregarding the effects of its own decision on the behaviour of the others.

The third player was assumed to be a price-taker in its product market. All three producers were assigned realistic cost structures, pollution control relationships, and demand relationships.

In this model, all three producers cause pollution at three sensitive locations, which could for example be dissolved oxygen low points in a river system. They all choose how much pollution control investment to undertake to reduce the pollution; permits have to be purchased in order to cover the remaining pollution. A limited number of permits are available for each location. Permits are auctioned, in a market which establishes market-clearing prices.

The findings of these simulations were:

- If the duopolists behaved in an oligopolist fashion, they would trade fewer permits, but permit prices did not vary greatly according to the competitive scenario. They depended mainly on pollution control costs and the consequent demand for permits (which depended in turn on levels of output, discharges, transfer relationships) relative to the existing number of permits.

- The effect on the third player of oligopolistic behaviour in the permit market was negligible. He was not forced, by the hoarding of permits by oligopolists, to control significantly more of his discharges than he did under a competitive permit market scenario.

- The number of permits which were auctioned had a major effect on the level of pollution control but not on industrial output.

These (tentative) results suggest that if trade in permits between competing oligopolists is mutually advantageous, trade will occur, at a scale not much less than under perfect competition.

6 Conclusions

The conclusions which we would draw from this review are:

1. Where market mechanisms have been applied in a wholehearted fashion, they have been effective (tradeable permits in the US in the air quality context, water pollution charges in the Netherlands).

2. Conversely, where they have been introduced in a half-hearted fashion and with muddled objectives (effluent charges in Europe), or hedged about with inhibiting conditions (tradeable permits on the Fox River, Wisconsin), they have been ineffective.

3. Our own work on simulating possible uses of charges for the control of both water and air pollution confirms that substantial quantities of information and analysis are required in order to be able to determine levels of pollution charges which will deliver target improvements in environmental quality.

4. However, we would also submit that our work also demonstrates that the knowledge and the techniques are available to handle this problem. What may be found wanting is a determination to solve environmental problems in a least-cost fashion.

5. Tradeable permits are the solution to the information requirements problem; they require little more than would need to be in place to administer any effective environmental policy – accurate monitoring of each polluter's discharges and a model of the transfer mechanism between polluter and the environment.

6. Tradeable permits could be transacted in a variety of ways, like any other asset. They could be traded, leased, or banked. Their versatility also has advantages from the control authority's point of view; they could be denominated by year, in declining quantities, in line with environmental objectives. The control authority could buy them back, if it later decided that it had issued too many; the prospect of having to do so argues for selling, rather than issuing, permits in the first place.

7. A problem associated with permit markets is that their effectiveness could be reduced by market imperfections – collusion, or unwillingness to sell, or buy, on the part of the major players. This could pose a difficulty in the inherently limited permit markets which would exist within some river systems, where the market might be restricted to just a few polluters upstream of critical low points.

8. The available empirical evidence is not particularly helpful in resolving this issue; for example, the absence of permit trading in the Fox River probably owed more to the discouraging regime, which ruled out trading on cost grounds and which failed to define property rights. Simulation exercises, including our own, suggest that this problem is not a significant one.

9. Imperfections in permits markets may be no greater than those in many other markets: whether they are or not would be a problem for polluters, not for the pollution control authority.

10. Permit systems would present polluters with new uncertainties – such as whether they could acquire permits when they needed them, or whether they would expect to use them fully. But these same uncertainties are confronted routinely, in respect to other inputs such as land and buildings, and are handled by a variety of market mechanisms, including options, leases and futures, which could apply equally to permits.

References

BRESSERS, HANS, 'A Comparison of the Effectiveness of Incentives and Directives: the Case of Dutch Water Quality Policy', Policy Studies Review, Spring 1988, Vol.7, No.3, pp 500-518.

ENVIRONMENTAL RESOURCES LIMITED, Annexes to 'Market Mechanisms, Charging and Subsidies', January 1990.

HAHN, R. (1989), 'Economic prescription for environmental problems: how the patient followed the doctor's orders'.

HAHN, R. and G. HESTER (1989), 'Where did all the markets go?: An analysis of EPA's emission trading program', Yale Journal on Regulation, 6, 109-53.

MALONEY, M. T. and YANDLE B. (1984), 'Estimation of the Cost of Air Pollution Control Regulation', Journal of Environmental Economics and Management, 11, 244-63.

NOVOTNY, GERALD, 'Transferable Discharge Permits for Water Pollution Control in Wisconsin', private mimeo, 1986.

OECD, 'Economic Instruments For Environmental Protection', Paris, 1989.

TIETENBERG, T. H. (1980), 'Transferable Discharge Permits and the Control of Stationary Source Air Pollution: A Survey and Synthesis', Land Economics, Vol 56, No 4, November 1980.

TIETENBERG, T. H. (1988), Environmental and natural resource economics, 2nd ed, Scott Foresman & Co., esp. chs. 14 (Economics of Pollution Control: An Overview) and 16 (Regional and Global Air Pollutants).

TIETENBERG, T. H. (1990), 'Economic instruments for environmental regulation', Oxford Review of Economic Policy, 6(1).

WEITZMAN, M. L. (1975), 'Prices vs Quantities', Review of Economic Studies, 1975.

APPRAISAL OF THE POTENTIAL ROLE OF MARKET MECHANISMS IN WATER QUALITY ISSUES

Research Report to the
Royal Commission on Environmental Pollution

by

Nick Hanley, Stephen Hallett, Ian Moffatt
David Farley and Kim Taylor-Duncan

River Pollution Control Unit
Departments of Economics and Environmental Science
University of Stirling

and

John Pezzey

UK CEED Research Fellow
Department of Economics
University of Bristol

1991

Acknowledgement

Although this report was funded by the Royal Commission on Environmental Pollution (RCEP), the prior research at the University of Stirling on pollution in the Forth estuary, without which this report would not have been practicable, was made possible through the generous funding of the Economic and Social Research Council (ESRC). The Stirling team would also like to thank all those agencies, councils and firms who gave both their time, assistance and data as necessary. Particular thanks is given for the extreme generosity of the Forth River Purification Board (FRPB). John Pezzey would like to thank ICI plc., the Dulverton Trust and the Kleinwort Foundation for core support, through the UK Centre for Economic and Environmental Development (UK CEED), of his research at Bristol, and to thank IBM UK Ltd. for computing support.

Although the report as a whole is a joint product of all of the authors, it seems appropriate to give credit where due for individual contributions to particular tasks and chapters. Stephen Hallett produced all the water quality analysis described in Chapter 3, and the Environmental Information System work detailed in Chapter 5. He also wrote the first draft of Chapter 2. Nick Hanley was lead author on Chapters 4, 5, 6 and 7, second author on Chapter 8, and he also programmed the Economic Optimisation model. Ian Moffatt wrote and programmed the water quality model 'FEDS', and wrote Section 5.2 on the model. He also helped with Chapter 2. Kim Taylor-Duncan updated Chapter 2 and with Stephen Hallett, organised the draft version of this report. John Pezzey wrote Chapter 1, was second author of Chapters 6 and 7, and lead author of Chapter 8. He also wrote the Executive Summary and helped edit the report. David Farley and Stephen Hallett ran Ian Moffatt's 'FEDS' environmental water quality model, and produced the graphical model output.

Table of Contents

Appraisal of The Potential Role of Market Mechanisms in Water Quality Issues

Executive Summary

The report considers six policy mechanisms which could in principle be used to control discharges of effluent by a diverse collection of firms and sewage treatment works (STWs), in order to achieve a targeted improvement in water quality. 1–2 are regulatory mechanisms, and 3–6 are market mechanisms:

1. Uniform regulation (equal percentage cuts in effluent by all dischargers)

2. Flexible regulation (the regulator uses its judgment to impose different cuts on different dischargers to save costs)

3. Auctioned tradeable effluent permits

4. Granted tradeable effluent permits

5. Pure effluent charges (i.e. at an incentive, not cost-recovery, level)

6. Effluent charge-subsidies (i.e. a scheme to charge when effluent exceeds a certain baseline, and to subsidise when effluent falls below it)

Each mechanism imposes three different costs:

a. The 'resource cost' or true economic cost of installing and running equipment to reduce effluent discharges

b. The 'transfer payments' of auction prices or effluent charges, which are handed over by dischargers as revenue to the pollution control authority (PCA) in the case of mechanisms 3 and 5 only

c. The administration cost to the PCA

Economic theory predicts that market mechanisms, by inducing dischargers to control their effluent in ways that equalise marginal control costs across all discharges, minimise the resource costs of control, and so offer considerable savings compared to regulatory mechanisms. However, concern has been expressed that high transfer payments and/or administrative costs may outweigh these savings. This report estimates costs (a)-(c) for mechanisms 1–6 for the particular case of reducing discharges which exert a Biochemical Oxygen Demand (BOD) in the Forth estuary, a case which differs from the standard theory in a number of potentially important ways. The report does not try to place a value on the environmental benefits of lower discharges. [Chapter 1]

A detailed history of water quality legislation in the UK is presented. Control of water quality has up till now been achieved largely through flexible regulation, and since 1951 has been based on consents which take into account the condition of the local watercourse. The 1989 Water Act brought about major structural changes in water quality control in England and Wales, and formalised the concepts of Environmental Quality Objectives and Environmental Quality Standards. It also reflected a small but increasing influence of EEC water quality policies such as uniform emission standards. Further new legislation would be necessary to introduce any market mechanisms into the control system. [Chapter 2]

The main point sources of pollution in the Forth estuary, from both firms and STWs, are described, together with their effects on water quality. Only Dissolved Oxygen (DO) currently fails to meet the Environmental Quality Standard, which is why only discharges exerting a BOD are considered in this report. The failure happens particularly in the central part of the estuary during summertime, when natural flow is low and temperatures are high, giving rise to a 'sag' in DO. [Chapter 3]

Seven firms account for 84% of BOD discharges into the Forth estuary, with STWs contributing another 12%. (Rivers contribute only 4% and are ignored in cost-minimising calculations.) Information on effluent control costs has been obtained from six firms and all STWs by a survey which asked them how much 10%, 25% and 50% cuts in BOD discharges would cost in the short run (1 year) and long run (5 years). Capital costs are annualised using a 6% real discount rate, and added to running costs to give the overall annual cost. [Chapter 4]

The Economic Optimisation model, which uses the control cost information to calculate the least cost way for the BOD discharges to be reduced in order to meet given targets for minimum DO levels throughout the estuary, is described. Firms are assumed to be well-informed and to maximise profits. The model uses a step-wise linear programming framework to cope with the 'indivisibilities' or 'lumpiness' in BOD control technologies which the cost survey revealed. The Economic Optimisation model needs a matrix of transfer coefficients which estimate how much BOD discharged in one part of the estuary affects the DO level in another part. A second model, called the Environmental Water Quality model, is therefore needed to calculate these transfer coefficients. The one-dimensional Environmental Water Quality model under development at Stirling, called FEDS (for Forth Estuary Dynamic Simulation model), is described. FEDS is an improvement on existing steady state models of the Forth estuary, in that it models the dynamic effect of twenty point sources on dissolved oxygen, interfaces with a geographical information system, and estimates the transfer coefficients between point sources in any reach of the estuary and other reaches in the estuary. Unfortunately FEDS cannot yet produce transfer coefficients with acceptable accuracy, so all calculations using the Economic Optimisation model have had to use transfer coefficients set to unity, which is equivalent to assuming that the estuary is a single, well-mixed body of water. However, mixing is good in the lower part of the estuary, so this is not a bad approximation there. [Chapter 5]

Results are reported for the costs of achieving target reductions of 10%, 25% and 50% in total BOD discharges, using firstly uniform percentage cuts, both for the 'industry only' (excluding STWs) and 'full' (including STWs) versions of the model. The least cost solution is also calculated, although only one case of the full model is calculated as STWs have little effect on total costs. In some cases the exact targets cannot be hit because of the above indivisibilities in pollution control costs. In all cases the least cost solution saves about 70-90% of the control costs incurred under uniform percentage cuts. One potential of market mechanisms is thus demonstrated, since a system of **tradeable permits** for BOD discharges can in theory achieve the least cost solution, provided that permit markets are competitive.

However, competitive permit markets are unlikely on the Forth estuary if granted rather than auctioned tradeable permits are used, because no more than five interfirm trades are possible, and two of the firms would dominate the market. Also, some of the firms produce similar products and so may hoard permits instead of trading, for strategic reasons. Nevertheless, other studies have shown that, even though reduced permit market competition can greatly alter the money transfers between firms, it has little effect on the savings achieved in the total resource costs of effluent control. Recommendations are made as to how best to design a permit market.

One calculation is done of the least cost way of just eliminating the DO 'sag' in the central part of the estuary, and of the cost using a **flexible regulation** scheme suggested by the Forth River Purification Board (FRPB, the relevant PCA here). The savings of the least cost solution may be between 0-15% compared to flexible regulation. Given the drastically lower savings here, market mechanisms are hardly worthwhile in this case. More calculations with 'flexible regulation' for tougher environmental targets such as raising minimum DO levels in the estuary would be desirable, but this would not be easy owing to the lack of suitable data from the FRPB and the lack of a functioning Environmental Water Quality model.

The FRPB's estimate of the cost of administering a tradeable permit system is small, being less than one tenth of the smallest calculated saving in effluent control costs achieved by moving from uniform percentage cuts to tradeable permits. However, it may be a significant proportion of the savings in moving from flexible regulation to tradeable permits.

Choosing auctioned instead of granted tradeable permits would require discharges to make large transfer payments to the PCA to buy permits at auction. In the one case calculated, the auction payments would amount to more than three times the resource cost of BOD control. But because transfer payments are only one-third of the control costs saved by not using uniform percentage reductions, the total costs to the industry (control costs plus transfer payments) will be substantially less under auctioned permits than under uniform percentage reductions. A separate distributional issue is the way in which granted tradeable permits result in transfer payments between firms (as opposed to payments from the group of firms to the PCA). This may have equity advantages in comparison to flexible regulation. Provided existing discharge levels are regarded as fair in the sense that firms are entitled to them, then granted permits are likely to result in an equitable distribution of the costs of a reduction in total BOD, since they induce some firms to pay control costs and sell spare permits, while other firms buy spare permits. Under flexible regulation, only firms with low control costs end up paying for effluent control, while high-cost firms pay nothing. [Chapter 6]

The Economic Optimisation model is also used to calculate the resource costs and transfer payments from using pure effluent **charges** to achieve given reductions in total BOD, again using transfer coefficients set to unity, and this time giving results just for the 'industry only' model (i.e. excluding STWs). Because of indivisibilities in pollution control costs, small changes in the charge rate (an induced 'effluent price') cause large jumps in BOD discharges, so one cannot attain 10%, 25% and 50% reductions exactly. It is therefore hard to compare results for charging directly with results for tradeable permits. However, the indication is that charges can also save 70-90% of the control costs resulting from uniform percentage cuts. No problems of non-competitive permit markets are encountered here, but they are replaced by the problem of how the PCA would calculate the correct charge rate to achieve the intended effect. The transfer payments of a pure charging scheme amount to around three to six times the resource cost of pollution control, and two thirds of the value of savings. The extra administration costs of a charging scheme are again small in comparison to the potential savings in control costs.

Calculations were also done for the effect of **charge-subsidies** per unit reduction in BOD effluent, a scheme where a firm pays a charge for each unit by which its effluent exceeds a given baseline amount, or receives a subsidy for each unit by which its effluent is less than the baseline. As expected, using the same unit 'effluent prices' causes exactly the same reductions in total effluent and the same resource costs as occur with charging. However, the distributional consequences are very different: providing that the total of all baselines equals the total effluent the firms want to discharge at any given charge rate, there will be transfer payments between firms, but zero net transfer payments from the group of firms to the PCA. This may again have equity advantages in comparison to flexible regulation. If existing discharge levels are regarded as fair, then charge-subsidies probably result in a more equitable distribution of the costs of a reduction in total BOD, since they involve some firms paying control costs and getting subsidies, while other firms do not control but pay charges instead. [Chapter 7]

The main results of Chapters 6 and 7 are summarised in Tables 8.1, 8.2 and 8.3. The conclusions of the report are that, for the case of controlling BOD discharges on the Forth estuary:

1. Least cost solutions for reducing total BOD discharges into the Forth estuary clearly offer substantial (70-90%) savings in resource costs when compared to uniform percentage reductions in discharges.

2. Flexible regulation can approach and perhaps achieve the least cost solution, depending on how much the PCA knows about firms' and STWs' costs of control for a particular environmental objective. One can therefore immediately conclude that uniform percentage reductions in discharges are very inefficient in comparison to available alternatives such as flexible regulation or market mechanisms.

3. Market mechanisms have the potential, but are not guaranteed, to achieve a least cost solution. Charges and charge-subsidies cannot hit precise targets for total effluent reductions, because of indivisibilities in effluent control technologies; they also require charge rates to be calculated by the PCA. Tradeable permits suffer neither of these disadvantages, but hoarding and noncompetitive behaviour are likely to occur on permit markets, particularly if permits are granted. Moreover, hitting a precise target may not be a sensible objective in the first place, since the indivisibilities mean that the last units of BOD controlled may require a disproportionately high cost. The choice between permits and charges is therefore not clear-cut.

4. Choosing between flexible regulation and market mechanisms is not easy either. Market mechanisms offer no immediate cost advantage over flexible regulation as a means of eliminating the summertime DO sag in the estuary. However, little is known about what the comparison may look like for a tougher environmental goal such as raising DO levels throughout the estuary. Also, flexible regulation cannot match the ability of market mechanisms to create a continual incentive to discover better effluent treatment techniques. Nor can it offer such an equitable distribution of financial costs between different firms.

5. The transfer payments by firms which result from using auctioned permits instead of granted permits, or pure charges instead of charge-subsidies, are significant in relation to resource costs, and are very likely to reduce the political acceptability of auctioned permits and pure charges. One way round the transfer payment problem is distributive charging backed up by regulations, as used in Germany, although this may result in high administrative costs and a distortion of effluent control efforts in favour of capital-intensive investments.

6. In theory, market mechanisms perhaps need less information to be collected by the PCA, but FRPB considers that running a market mechanism would incur extra administrative costs. These are hard to judge accurately, but they certainly seem small in relation to the substantial savings made by a market mechanism compared to uniform cuts; however, they may be significant in relation to the savings made by a market mechanism compared to flexible regulation.

7. No calculations have been done of the costs of raising minimum DO levels in the estuary, because an accurate environmental water quality model is not yet available. However, it seems unlikely that the above general picture of cost savings would be changed much for this more complex objective. It is even harder to say how much our results will apply to other pollutants and locations, but many of the important qualitative results described above will remain. [Chapter 8].

1 Economic, Political and Practical Analysis of Market Mechanisms of Effluent Control

Table of Contents

List of Figures

List of Tables

1.1 The Cost-Saving Potential of Market Mechanisms

Since February 1989 the Departments of Economics and Environmental Science, through the River Pollution Control Unit at the University of Stirling have been carrying out research on the potential for using market mechanisms such as effluent charges, and tradeable effluent permits, to achieve more cost-effective control of water pollution in the Forth estuary[1]. This report, written in conjunction with John Pezzey of the Economics Department at the University of Bristol, sets out current results from the project. Before describing in Section 1.5 the history of British interest in market mechanisms (in particular the Royal Commission's own Third Report and the Rowley Report which followed on from that), and setting out in Sections 1.6-1.7 the overall scope of our project, some basic ideas about market mechanisms are outlined in Sections 1.1-1.4. This may seem rather lengthy at times, but it is important for understanding what follows.

A market mechanism somehow or other creates an artificial price on a unit of effluent. In theoretically ideal circumstances, an effluent price will achieve a given amount of total effluent reduction at the least cost to society, and this least-cost property is the prime attraction of market mechanisms. Using a price rather than standards to control effluent allows market flexibility: firms with low effluent control costs are allowed to control more than they would under standards, and firms with high control costs (perhaps because they are older, or produce a very different product) are allowed to control less than they would under standards. Such flexibility allows a pollution control authority (PCA[2]) to achieve the least overall cost of 'buying' a given total reduction in effluent control from a group of firms, just as the flexibility of being able to buy individual clothing items from the shops where such items are cheapest allows us to meet our overall clothing requirements at minimum cost. (However, as discussed at length in Section 1.3 below, a market mechanism which achieves the least real resource cost to society will not necessarily produce financial cost savings for firms, because of the transfer payments that some mechanisms require firms to make.)

It will prove useful to illustrate the cost saving potential of market mechanisms in diagrammatic form. Figure 1.1 plots cost per unit of effluent on the vertical axis, and 'group effluent', the level of total effluent discharged by a group of several firms, on the horizontal axis. The graph MCC_R shows the cost of controlling (i.e. reducing) group effluent by one more unit, if this is done by setting tighter regulatory standards for each firm. As shown, this 'marginal cost of group effluent control' starts from zero at the level of effluent E_U that the group would discharge in the absence of any control policy, and generally rises[3] as group effluent is reduced and opportunities for effluent control become technically more difficult. Using a market mechanism instead of standards leads to a lower total cost of group effluent control[4], and generally to a lower marginal cost as well[5]. This is illustrated in Figure 1.1 by a graph of marginal cost of group effluent control such as MCC_M. The area between the two marginal control cost curves shows savings in total group control costs; for example, the shaded area S measures the cost savings from using market mechanisms, instead of standards, to reduce group effluent from E_U down to some 'desirable' level E_D[6]. A prime purpose of the Forth project is to estimate how big an area such as S might be for a specific pollutant in a specific location.

---

[1] The terminology used for market mechanisms of pollution control is very variable and can be confusing. *Appendix 1.1* lists the variants for 'market mechanisms', 'tradeable permits', 'effluent', 'pollution', etc. However, the distinction between effluent and pollution is worth emphasising here, since much writing on market mechanisms uses these terms more or less interchangeably. In this report we try where possible to use 'effluent' to mean the physical quantity of waste matter discharged, and 'pollution' to mean the economic damage caused by the effluent.

[2] See *Appendix 1.2* for a complete collection of all acronyms used in this report.

[3] This may not happen if there are economies of scale in effluent control.

[4] A market mechanism induces all firms to control up to the point where their marginal control cost equals the 'effluent price' created by the mechanism, so that for firms A, B,... have $MCC_A = MCC_B = ...$ This equality of marginal control costs will minimise the total control costs, a result used in the economic model in Chapter 5. In contrast, because regulation implicitly creates different 'effluent prices' for each firm, it will not achieve the least cost solution.

[5] The exception is again if there are economies of scale in effluent control, in which case MCC_M may not be everywhere lower than MCC_R.

[6] Note that two complications have been omitted from Figure 1.1 because they would complicate an already lengthy analysis without affecting the substance of the argument:
1. In practice one rarely starts from the position of completely uncontrolled effluent E_u, because existing regulations will have already reduced effluent to some level below E_u
2. As pointed out in Pezzey (1988), unless the economic cost of effluent damage to the environment suddenly leaps at effluent level E_D, it will in general be socially desirable to aim for a lower total effluent level if one is using a more efficient, market mechanism of effluent control, rather than aiming for the same level E_D under both regulatory and market mechanisms, as Figure 1.1 implies. Since very little is known about the monetary valuation of environmental damage in the case studied, no quantitative study could be made of this point in any case.

To preview some of our most important findings and to set a theme that recurs throughout the later chapters in the report, we will find that the position of the regulatory curve MCC_R varies dramatically with the *type* of regulatory control. *Uniform regulation*, whereby every discharger has to cut back emissions by the same percentage, proves to be a very expensive way of reducing pollution, and the savings in control costs from moving to a market mechanism are substantial. *Flexible regulation*, whereby the PCA takes account of dischargers' control costs when setting effluent control targets, can be much less expensive, i.e. it has a lower MCC_R curve. In one special case that we study, the MCC_R ends up being very similar to the MCC_M curve, so that savings from moving to a market mechanism are much smaller.

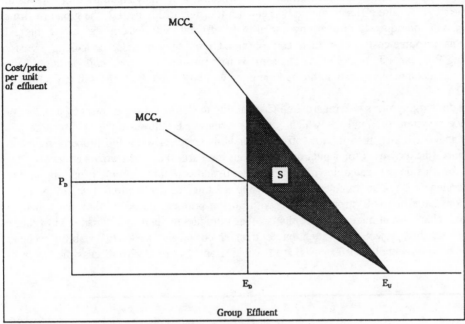

Figure 1.1   Cost saving potential of market mechanisms

1.2   Charges and Tradeable Permits: Control-by-Price Versus Control-by-Quantity

So far we have not distinguished between various types of market mechanism, because in theory they all give rise to the same curve MCC_M and the same cost saving. This and the following sub-section set out two differences in the way that the various mechanisms work that have enormous practical and political implications. The first difference is whether the market mechanism initially controls the price of effluent - 'control-by-price' - or the quantity of effluent - 'control-by-quantity'. Clearly, levying an effluent charge (or paying an effluent reduction subsidy) on each unit of effluent discharged is a method of control-by-price. In Figure 1.1, setting a charge (or subsidy) rate at the level of P_D per unit of effluent will in itself give sufficient incentive for the group to control effluent down to E_D.[7] By contrast, distributing tradeable effluent permits, where a unit permit allows the legal discharge of one unit of effluent, is a method of control-by-quantity[8]. Trade in permits between discharges then establishes a price per unit permit, and hence per unit of effluent. In Figure 1.1, distributing E_D tradeable effluent permits would (provided competitive trading takes place) establish a price of P_D per permit, and therefore per unit of effluent.

The difference between control-by-price and control-by-quantity is crucial in the real world, where a pollution control authority will be uncertain about both the marginal control cost, and the economic cost of the damage that an extra unit of effluent will do to the environment (marginal damage cost) at any level of effluent. If it is reasonably confident that marginal damage costs are more sensitive than marginal control costs to the level of effluent, then controlling effluent by quantity is preferable to controlling effluent by price. This result, first formally proved by

---

[7] Charges at this rate will on occasion be referred to as *incentive charges*, in order to distinguish them from *distributive charges* (charged at a rate much less than P_D, and aimed mainly at raising revenue for subsequent distribution as subsidies for effluent control equipment) and *cost-recovery charges* (charges which recover the PCA's costs of administering a control system, which even if they bear some relation to the amount of effluent discharged, are usually not formally tied to effluent amounts and are certainly not charged at the full incentive rate). Unless otherwise noted, in this report effluent charging always means charging at the full incentive rate.

[8] Although standards are also clearly a method of controlling effluent quantities, we reserve the phrase 'control-by-quantity' exclusively for a market mechanism which controls quantity, i.e. a tradeable permit.

Roberts and Spence (1976), is the basis of the 'common sense' view that effluent charges (control-by-price) will not give adequate protection to the environment. However, there is a lesser-known flip-side to this argument: if industry's control costs are more sensitive than environmental damage costs to the level of effluent, then control-by-price is superior, as it avoids the risk of unacceptably high control costs being imposed on industry. The Forth project measures only control costs, and so sheds light on only one side of this debate. This will be an important limitation to the conclusions about market mechanisms that can be drawn from this project.

1.3   Who Pays What: The Effect of Market Mechanisms on *De Facto* Effluent Rights

The second major difference among the various market mechanisms is whether or not they entail transfers of wealth from discharging firms to the PCA. A pure effluent charge will entail a transfer. In Figure 1.2, the group of firms paying an effluent charge P_D, and consequently discharging a total of E_D effluent, will not only be paying the real economic costs (also known as 'resource costs') of effluent control (area C), but they will also be making 'transfer payments' of charges totalling $P_D E_D$ (area T) to the PCA. The same is true for *auctioned tradeable permits*: if the PCA sells E_D effluent permits at a competitive auction, the auction price will be P_D and the firms will pay a total of $E_D P_D$ (area T again) to the PCA.

Pezzey (1988) argues that discharging firms will regard the PCA's ability to charge for the effluent E_D as a loss of *de facto* effluent rights, since a system of standards which currently achieves E_D allows them to discharge this amount free of charge, as if they have a right to it. Now effluent standards are clearly not full property rights: in British law, discharge 'consents' (the term used for standards for aqueous discharges) can be revoked after two years (see Section 2.1.3.2), many consents do get scaled down in the long term, and consents certainly cannot be sold to other dischargers. Pezzey's argument is not an argument for converting existing standards into full *de jure* property rights. It is more a prediction that firms will strongly resist, with all the political influence they have, market mechanisms such as incentive charges and auctioned permits, so that introducing such mechanisms will require more 'political will'. Therefore, this project pays attention to transfer costs, and seeks to establish whether alternative mechanisms, which do not entail transfer costs, are feasible. Hanley *et al* (1990) discuss the extent of such resistance in practice.

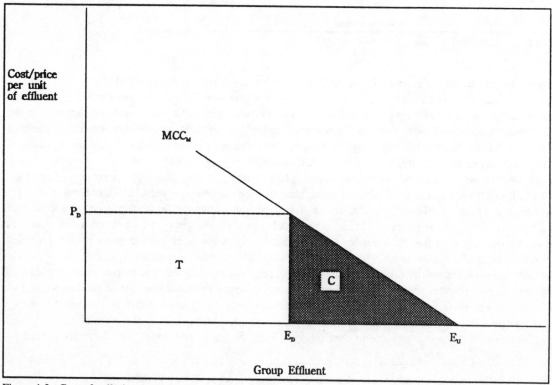

Figure 1.2   Cost of pollution control and transfer payments

One such alternative mechanism is for the PCA to give away E_D permits, which are then referred to as *free, granted or grandfathered tradeable permits*. The net costs to the group of firms are then just area C on Figure 1.2, although there may be transfers between individual firms, depending on how the PCA initially distributes the permits. A less obvious, untried alternative, discussed at length by Pezzey (1990), is for the PCA to implement a *charge-subsidy* at rate P_D, using a total baseline or benchmark effluent of E_D. Figure 1.3 shows how this works.

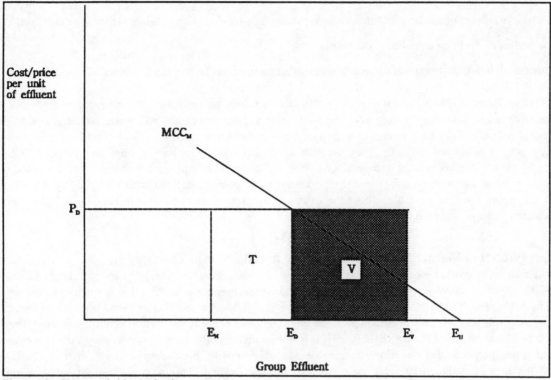

Figure 1.3   Charge-subsidy mechanism

If the group chose to discharge a total effluent of E_V it would pay the PCA a charge of $P_D(E_V-E_D)$ (area V). (How much each firm in the group pays depends on how the PCA distributes the total baseline E_D, just as with granted permits.) However, if it discharged E_N, it would receive a subsidy of $P_D(E_D-E_N)$ (area T) from the PCA. Given the group's marginal cost schedule MCC_M, it will choose effluent E_D, and no net charge or subsidy will actually be paid. The controversial element that is needed for the charge-subsidy scheme to achieve long-run efficiency, by rewarding existing firms that shut down and cease to pollute, and charging new firms that open up and start to pollute, is for the baseline subsidy E_D to be treated as a property right, so that closed-down firms would continue to receive subsidy payments. This sounds strange, but it is identical in economic principle (if not in administrative detail) to the idea that closed-down firms can lease out unused tradeable effluent permits.

Note that the choice of property rights to be embodied in a market mechanism is not restricted to zero or the desired effluent level E_D. Any preferred level E_L of group effluent rights can in principle be implemented in either tradeable permit or charge-subsidy form, simply by respectively distributing E_L granted permits or E_L baseline subsidy rights.

1.4   Practical Problems with Market Mechanisms
So far, the above analysis has mostly taken for granted the large number of simplifying assumptions that are needed to make the theory work. These now need to be made explicit, and briefly they are:

a.   Each firm's effluent is of the same type. This is not as restrictive as it sounds, since it can be used to define the group of firms under consideration; but it does require the 'size' of any firm's effluent to be measurable by a single number, and rules out cases where both the amount and concentration of the effluent are separately important.

b.   The receiving environment is well-mixed, so that one unit of effluent does the same environmental damage, irrespective of the geographical location of the firm discharging it; that is, marginal damage costs do not vary between sources. This could be the case either when all firms discharge to the same, well-mixed lake, river or estuary, or when they all discharge to the same sewage works.

c.   Each firm discharges effluent at a constant rate.

d.   There is no permanent accumulation of the effluent.

e.   Monitoring or administration costs are negligible.

f.   The marginal costs of effluent control increase smoothly as effluent is reduced; in particular, there are no increasing returns to scale in effluent control.

g. There is a large number of discharging firms in the group, with no one firm having a large share of total effluent.

h. There is perfect competition in all firms' output markets.

i. There are no legal or institutional barriers to adopting market mechanisms in the form that economic theory requires.

Pezzey (1988), Hahn (1989) and Hanley *et al* (1990) have all discussed at length the observation that market mechanisms have largely failed so far; they have been little used as policy tools, and when used have failed to fulfil their theoretical potential. Each author notes that most of the above assumptions do not hold in practice, and shows how these broken assumptions, together with the fundamental political problem of changing property rights described in Section 1.3, can be powerful reasons for failure. In Section 1.6 we give a brief preview of how good or bad each of the list of assumptions a–i is in the case of the Forth estuary, and we shall be returning to the list throughout the report; but first we look at how the British body politic has responded to economists' consistent recommendations that a price be put on pollution.

1.5 British Interest in Market Mechanisms, and the Broad Scope of This Study

The basic idea of using market mechanisms for environmental management is seventy years old, dating back to Pigou's 1920 analysis of incentive effluent charges (hence the term 'Pigouvian charge' that is often used for such charges). Tradeable permits are a more recent idea, but still over twenty years old (Dales 1968). No official interest in market mechanisms was apparent in Britain until the environmental crisis of the early seventies, when the Royal Commission produced its Third Report (RCEP, 1972). In a minority report within this, Sir Solly Zuckerman and Wilfrid Beckerman proposed that pollution charging be adopted forthwith, but the majority report recommended instead that the idea of pollution charging be researched thoroughly first. This recommendation led to a long programme of research into the possibility of effluent charging on the tidal stretches of the River Tees, culminating in the Rowley Report (Rowley *et al*, 1979).

The Rowley Report used a one-dimensional environmental water quality model to describe how the slow mixing process of tidal ebb and flow affects water quality in forty stretches of the tidal River Tees, and information on industrial effluent control costs. It combined these two data sources to calculate the charge rates for nine key pollutants in each stretch of the river that would bring about the least-cost allocation of new effluent treatment plant needed to clean up the river enough to allow the passage of migratory fish. Sewage treatment was found to be subject to economies of scale and so was excluded from the calculation. Thus immediately we see how Rowley *et al* took account of the failure of assumptions (a), (b) and (f) in Section 1.4.

However, by restricting their attention to charging alone, and by ignoring the likely costs of collecting 360 different charge rates (for 9 pollutants in 40 stretches), Rowley et al left out the tradeable permit options analysed above in 1.2, the property rights considerations of 1.3, and a key practical consideration of 1.4, that of monitoring and administration costs (see Pezzey, 1988 for further analysis). Our project for the Forth estuary takes forward the debate on market mechanisms by correcting all these deficiencies, albeit only for the one commonly adopted index of pollution (BOD, or biological oxygen demand) which does any significant environmental damage in the Forth. It thus takes over from where the solely economic quantifications of the Rowley Report, and the solely qualitative discussions in Pezzey (1988) and Hanley et al (1990) left off. The broad scope of our study can be very crudely summarised by:-

1. Table 1.1, which classifies the four main market mechanisms according to whether they control by price or quantity, and whether they effectively give effluent rights to the PCA (resulting in a revenue-raising scheme) or to the discharging firms (resulting in a revenue-neutral scheme):

Table 1.1 Fourfold classification of main market mechanisms

Classification		Parameter directly controlled by mechanism	
		Effluent Quantity	Effluent Price
Holder of *de facto* effluent right	Pollution Control Authority	**Auctioned tradeable effluent permits**	**Effluent charging** (at full incentive level)
	Discharging Firms	**Granted** (grandfathered) **tradeable effluent permits**	**Effluent charge-subsidies** with charge/subsidy baseline at total effluent amount

2. Figure 1.4, which pulls together the diagrammatic analysis of preceding sections:

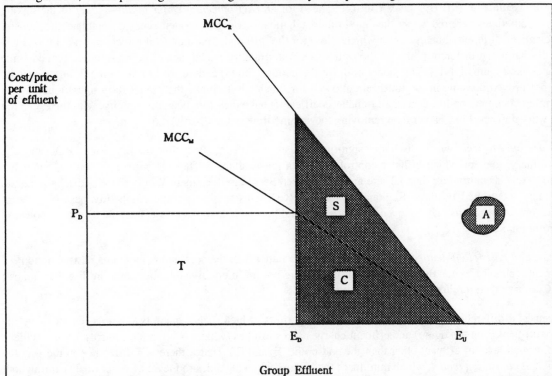

Figure 1.4 Control costs savings, transfer payments and administration costs

In the figure:

- E_D is the desired total effluent level

- P_D is the 'effluent price' needed to bring this effluent about

- Area $T = E_D P_D$ is the transfer payment made by firms under some mechanisms

- Area $C + S$ is the estimated effluent control cost under the present system of standards, and C is the estimated effluent control cost under a market mechanism, whence S is the saving in control costs from using market mechanisms rather than standards

- Area A (drawn free-floating because it is likely to be largely unrelated to effluent level) is an estimate of the *extra* monitoring and administration costs of running the market mechanism instead of standards.

If S is much larger than A, the market mechanism is a success in efficiency terms. It can be implemented with transfer payments equal to either zero by using charge-subsidies with a baseline equal to E_D or free (grandfathered) permits equal to E_D; or transfer payments can be T, by using pure charging or auctioned permits; or transfer payments can conceivably be anywhere between zero and T by using a baseline level of effluent somewhere between zero and E_D, which (the baseline) could be the baseline for a charge-subsidy scheme, as already discussed, or the effluent level for which free permits are issued, with the remainder (E_D minus the baseline) being auctioned. Remembering that baselines are *de facto* property rights in the environment, the choice of baselines and their resulting transfer payments is essentially a political one, although it may also be influenced by differences in administration costs A among the schemes corresponding to different baselines.

1.6 Practical features of the Forth Study

The main practicalities of the Forth study are now listed. The research reported on here refers to a case study in Central Scotland, and a detailed discussion of the estuary chosen, and reasons for that choice, can be found in Chapter 3. Most of them depart from the ideal assumptions laid out in Section 1.4 in a number of important ways.

1. *Only one determinand of pollution (biological oxygen demand or BOD) is studied.* This is both because there is no available index of the environmental damage done by all pollutants in the Forth estuary; and because other pollutants apart from BOD appear not to cause significant environmental damage, since none exceed their EQS levels (where these are set) on a regular basis. This means that assumption (a) of Section 1.4 is met, but the applicability of the results to other pollutants becomes an important issue.

2. *The receiving environment is an estuary,* with its own particular pattern of mixing, far from the ideal of perfect mixing in assumption (b). This gives rise to the need for an *environmental water quality model* of the mixing process, sometimes referred to as the 'environmental model'. Such a model aims to calculate the transfer coefficients or differential charge rates which allow for the different environmental effects of one unit of BOD when discharged at different points in the estuary. A water quality model cannot be represented on economic diagrams like Figures 1.1-1.4. The model built for this report (FEDS) is described in Section 5.2; unfortunately, it has not proved possible in the timescale allowed for this study to make the model fully operational. When performing economic optimisations, all transfer coefficients have therefore been set to unity, with the exception of the work described in Chapter 6 on removing the summertime sag in dissolved oxygen.

3. *There are only 6 firms* which discharge significant quantities of organic pollutants exerting a BOD into the Forth estuary, and for which effluent control cost data are available. (There is a seventh source, but it has refused to reveal control cost data.) There are also thirteen Sewerage Treatment Works (STWs) discharging into the estuary, controlled by three Regional Councils (RCs). This may affect the competitiveness of trade in permits: one or two firms may have a dominant share, and thus be able to wield considerable distorting power in the permit market.

4. *The marginal costs of effluent control are step functions* rather than the continuous functions of assumption (f). Treatment technologies for BOD exerting substances are not infinitely divisible, but come in discrete 'lumps'; the MCC curve therefore looks something like Figure 1.5.

This causes a difference between tradeable effluent permits (which, being quantity controls, can achieve the level of effluent E_1 on the figure) and effluent charges and subsidies (which, being price controls, cannot achieve any controlled level of effluent other than the end-points E_0 and E_2). Hence there is a difference in the way the *economic optimisation model,* which minimises the cost of achieving a desired level of water quality throughout the estuary, is formulated for tradeable permits and for charges (see Section 5.1). The economic model is sometimes referred to as the 'LP model' as it uses linear programming (LP) minimisation techniques.

5. *Monitoring and administration costs are significant* (as already envisaged in Section 1.5) and will be estimated, although it turns out to be impossible to do this accurately.

6. *The existing regulatory system of consents is not one of rigid uniform standards.* As already mentioned at the end of Section 1.1, existing effluent consents are already sensitive to effluent control costs to some extent, particularly in the way that consents given to new factories are generally stricter than existing consents. This system, referred to throughout the report as *flexible regulation,* means that the cost savings available from moving to a cost-minimising market mechanism are that much smaller than a comparison with a system of rigidly uniform emission standards would suggest (in Figure 1.1, the graph of MCC_R will be lower and the savings S will be smaller).

1.7 Outline of Report

Chapters 2-4 give the necessary build-up to the main calculations in the report. *Chapter 2* gives a detailed review of UK legislation and practice in the field of water pollution control, and in particular the evolution of the discharge consent system. This is important to know, both for estimating effluent control costs under the existing system, and for seeing how well any market mechanisms might fit into the system. *Chapter 3* sets out the sources and classifications of available water quality data (particularly those held in the FRPBs Tidal Waters Chemistry Database - TCHEM) for the Forth estuary. *Chapter 4* sets out the details of how the six firms' costs of reducing discharges of BOD-exerting substances have been collected by survey, and simplified into an effluent reduction step-function. This chapter also describes the collection and treatment of control cost data for STWs.

The technical heart of the report is *Chapter 5,* which explains the cost-minimising calculations performed by the economic optimisation model, and the BOD-mixing calculations performed by the environmental water quality model; as already noted in Section 1.6, the latter model is not fully operational, so it is effectively not used for most of the economic optimisations. As envisaged in Section 1.5, the results of the economic optimisations are estimates of likely control cost savings and revenue transfers of the various market mechanisms under study. These results are presented and discussed for tradeable permits (both granted and auctioned) in *Chapter 6,* and for charges and charge-subsidies in *Chapter 7. Chapter 8* then summarises the implications of these results for BOD control in the Forth estuary.

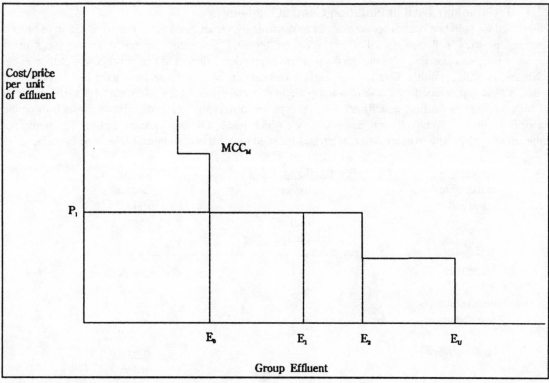

Figure 1.5   Lumpiness in effluent control costs

References

DALES, J. H. (1968). *Pollution. Property and Prices.* Toronto: University of Toronto Press.

HAHN, R. W. (1989). Economic Prescriptions for Environmental Problems: How the Patient Followed the Doctor's Orders. *Journal of Economic Perspectives,* Vol 3 No 2, 95-114.

HANLEY, N., HALLETT, S. AND MOFFATT, I. (1990). *Why is More Notice Not Taken of Economist's Prescriptions for the Control of Pollution?* Environment and Planning A, Vol 22, 1421-1439.

PEZZEY, J. C. V. (1990). Charge-Subsidies Versus Marketable Permits as Efficient and Acceptable Methods of Effluent Control: A Property Rights Analysis. University of Bristol: Department of Economics. Discussion Paper No. 90/271. Now published as Pezzey, J. C.V. (1992, forthcoming). The symmetry between controlling pollution by price and controlling it by quantity. *Canadian Journal of Economics*, Vol 25.

PEZZEY, J. C. V. (1988). Market Mechanisms of Pollution Control: 'Polluter Pays', Economic and Practical Aspects. In Turner, R. K., ed., *Sustainable Environmental Management - Principles and Practice.* London: Belhaven Press.

RCEP (1972). *Pollution in Some British Estuaries and Coastal Waters.* 3'rd Report, Royal Commission on Environmental Pollution. London: HMSO.

ROBERTS, M. AND SPENCE, M. (1976). Effluent Charges and Licenses Under Uncertainty. *Journal of Public Economics*, Vol 5.

ROWLEY, C., BEAVIS, B., WALKER, M. *et al* (1979). *A Study of Effluent Discharges to the River Tees.* DOE/DTp Research Report 31. London: HMSO. ['The Rowley Report']

ZUCKERMAN, SIR S. AND BECKERMAN, W. (1972). *Minority Report* in RCEP (1972).

Appendix 1.1 Terminology Used in Pollution Control Economics

The terminology used for pollution control economics can be confusingly varied. Sometimes one word can have several different meanings, as with 'pollution' (see Pezzey 1988, pp 200–201). Sometimes several different words mean essentially the same economic concept, even though the political or emotional flavour of that concept will change as the word used changes, as with 'permit', 'licence' and 'right'. Throughout this report we have tried to use consistent terminology that is most appropriate to the case of water pollution, as underlined in the following tables. The words in each column are equivalent to the first, underlined word (except for 'distributive' or 'redistributive', which mean the same but are different from 'incentive'; and 'cost-recovery', which has a different meaning again). The numerous possible combinations explain why so many different phrases get used for what is economically the same concept.

tradeable	effluent	permit
marketable	emission	licence
transferable	waste	right
	pollution	consent
	discharge	

incentive		charge
		tax
distributive		fee
redistributive		levy

cost-recovery		subsidy
		bribe
		payment
		compensation

Also note that the following three phrases, which are used in different places throughout the report, are identical concepts:

free tradeable permits
= granted tradeable permits
= grandfathered tradeable permits

Appendix 1.2 Acronyms Used in the Report

BATNEEC	=	Best Available Technology Not Entailing Excessive Cost
BOD	=	Biological oxygen demand
BPEO	=	Best Practicable Environmental Option
COPA	=	Control of Pollution Act (1974)
DCL	=	Distillers Company Ltd
DO	=	Dissolved oxygen
DOE	=	Department of the Environment
EEC	=	European Economic Community
EQO	=	Environmental Quality Objective
EQS	=	Environmental Quality Standard
ET	=	Emissions trading
FEDS	=	Forth Estuary Dynamic Simulation Model
FRPB	=	Forth River Purification Board
GIS	=	Geographical information system
HMIP	=	Her Majesty's Inspectorate of Pollution (England and Wales only)
HMIPI	=	Her Majesty's Industrial Pollution Inspectorate (Scotland only)
IPC	=	Integrated Pollution Control
IS	=	Information system
LP	=	Linear Programming
MCC	=	Marginal control costs
MDC	=	Marginal damage costs
NRA	=	National Rivers Authority (England and Wales pre-1979 only)

NWC	=	National Water Council
PCA	=	Pollution control authority
PPP	=	Polluter Pays Principle
RC	=	Regional Council
RCEP	=	Royal Commission on Environmental Pollution
RPB	=	River Purification Board (Scotland only)
RWA	=	Regional Water Authority (England and Wales only)
SDD	=	Scottish Development Department
SS	=	Suspended solids
STW	=	Sewage treatment works
TCHEM	=	Tidal Waters CHEMistry Data Set
TDP	=	Tradeable discharge permit
TDR	=	Tradeable discharge right
WQI	=	Water quality index
WRC	=	Water Research Centre

2 UK Water Pollution Control: Legislation and Practice

Table of Contents

List of Figures

List of Tables

2.1 Introduction

This chapter provides an overview of the legislation concerning water quality and water pollution control to-date. The main focus will be on the more recent legislation and upon proposed changes which will affect water quality in the U.K.. A four fold typology is presented (Table 2.1). The formative period (1876-1950) is identified as one in which water quality problems were correctly acknowledged as important by successive British Governments but where, unfortunately, the legislation alone was unable to produce effective control on the water quality. The second phase (1951-1972) witnessed the formation of the regional water authorities together with new legislation and the important consent system. This judicious mixture of appropriate institutional arrangements, new legislation and a means of implementing these changes resulted in a major improvement in water quality (Hammerton, 1983). The third period (1973-1988) introduced a European dimension into the legislation concerning water quality via the use of European Directives as well as the introduction of the Control of Pollution Act (1974) (COPA). The European and United Kingdom legislative acts taken together have the potential to improve water quality but again there has been a certain degree of resistance to actually implementing COPA to ensure that the quality of UK water does not deteriorate. The most recent phase (1989 onwards) is described in the light of the new Water Act although the impact of this piece of legislation has not yet had sufficient time to affect the quality of water in the UK. EEC legislation is also fundamental to the creation of current water quality controls in the UK, and this situation will become even more pronounced after 1992.

Table 2.1   A Typology of UK Water Quality Legislation 1876-1989.

Phase	Date	Description
I	1876–1950	The Formative Period
II	1951–1972	The Impact of the Consent System
III	1973–1988	The European Influence
IV	1989–........	The Water Act and Privatisation

2.2 A Review of Water Quality Legislation in The United Kingdom (1876–1989)

Water quality in the UK is addressed by both statutory legislation and Common Law. Statute Law is the legislation provided in the Parliamentary Statutory Acts and Common Law is the body of rules developed in case law and by precedent. In practice Common Law is largely unable to cope with modern incidents of pollution; but it is often the case that Statute Law will support the Common Law. Individuals wishing to initiate their own legal proceedings against dischargers may now do so under the 1974 Control of Pollution Act (COPA). Table 2.2 lists the major statutory legislation concerning water quality and pollution control in the UK, from 1876 to date. Legislation passed in the period during and immediately after the Second World War was primarily concerned with water quality solely in terms of public health (Walker, 1979). This attitude has been changing as water quality has become recognised more in its own right as an environmental and a recreational amenity. Today, legislation affects all the different aspects of water quality control in our inland and immediate coastal waters. This section provides a four fold typology of water quality legislation in the UK 1876 to 1989 highlighting the more important Acts.

Table 2.2   A Summary of Water Quality Legislation in the UK 1876-1989

Date	Statute
1876	Rivers Pollution Prevention Act
1893	Rivers Pollution Prevention Act
1923	The Salmon and Fresh Water Fisheries Act
1934	The Water Supplies (Exceptional Shortage Orders) Act
1936	The Public Health Act
1937	The Public Health (Drainage of Trade Premises)Act
1944	The Rural Supplies and Sewerage Act
1945	The Water Act
1946	The Water (Scotland) Act
1948	The River Boards Act
1948	The Water Act
1951	The Border Rivers (Prevention of Pollution) Act
1951	The Rivers (Prevention of Pollution) Act

Table 2.2 Continued

Date	Statute
1951	The Rivers (Prevention of Pollution)(Scotland) Act
1955	The Rating and Valuation (Miscellaneous Provisions) Act
1955	The Rural Supplies and Sewerage Act
1960	The Clean Rivers (Estuarine and Tidal Waters) Act
1960	The Tidal Waters Orders
1961	The Public Health Act
1961	The Rivers (Prevention of Pollution) Act
1963	The Water Resources Act
1965	The Rivers (Prevention of Pollution)(Scotland) Act
1967	The Water (Scotland) Act
1968	The Sewerage (Scotland) Act
1968	The Tidal Waters Orders
1968	The Water Resources Act
1970	The Rural Supplies and Sewerage (Scotland) Act
1971	The Rural Supplies and Sewerage Act
1971	The Water Resources Act
1972	The Clyde River Purification Board Act
1973	The Water Act
1974	The Control of Pollution Act (COPA)
1974	The Local Government (Scotland) Act
1975	The Reservoirs Act
1976	The Drought Act
1976	The Water Charges Act
1980	The Water (Scotland) Act
1981	The Water Act
1983	The Water Act
1985	The Food and Environmental Protection Act
1987	The Control of Pollution (Landed Ships Waste) Regulations
1987	The Control of Pollution (Anti-Fouling Paints and Treatments) Regulations
1987	The Control of Pollution (Exemption of Certain Discharges from control) (Variation) Order
1988	The Control of Pollution Act 1974 (Commencement No 19) Order
1988	The Control of Pollution (Special Waste)(Amendment) Regulation
1988	The Public Utility Transfers and Water Charges Act
1988	The Transfrontier Shipment of Hazardous Waste Regulations
1989	The Water Act
1990	The White Paper, This Common Inheritance

2.2.1 The Formative Period (1876-1950)

In 1868 the River Pollution Commission 'made a chemical analysis of water quality, recorded every source of pollution in the major rivers, detailed the processes and the waste products of every factory causing pollution and interviewed numerous witnesses from local government, industry, land-owners, medical officers of health and sanitary inspectors' (Hammerton, 1987, 333-334). The result of this intensive investigation into water pollution was to propose effluent standards as well as appointing inspectors and conservancy boards. These well-intentioned and sensible recommendations were not, however, incorporated in the 1876 River Pollution Prevention Act which provided the basis of all legislation for the control of river pollution for the following seventy-five years. Between 1898-1950 several pieces of legislation were introduced to try and improve river water quality, for example, the 1937 Public Health Act enabled local authorities to enter a premises and sample effluent. The resulting analysis could then provide the basis for legal proceedings against the discharger, the penalties for which were also laid down in the Act. Despite this activity and legislation, by 1951 many of the industrial rivers and estuaries 'were in a state little different from that described in the reports of the Rivers Pollution Commission some eighty years previously' (Hammerton, 1987); this can be attributed to a growth in overall pollution, due to an increase in both population and industry, combined with a lack of political will, the inability to enforce standards and the cumbersome procedure for taking legal action (Hammerton, 1987).

2.2.2   The Introduction And Impact Of Consents (1951-1972)

The Rivers (Prevention of Pollution) Acts of 1951 and 1961 and the Rivers (Prevention of Pollution, Scotland) Acts of 1951 and 1965 may be considered together, as the 1961/5 Acts were essentially designed to bring the former Acts up to date by ensuring the upkeep of cleanliness of rivers and other inland or coastal waters in England, Wales and Scotland. To do this the Acts were concerned with the issues of: (i) criminal offences for polluting rivers, and (ii) the licensing of outlets and discharges to streams. Within the Acts, provision was also made to lay before Parliament the annual reports of the river boards (Tearle, 1973).

The success of these Acts and of subsequent legislation can be attributed to the new powers given to relevant authorities to specify the conditions of discharge. This new method of pollution control, known as the consent system, meant that all effluent charges to non-tidal rivers were made subject to the issue of a consent while some tidal and estuarine waters were subject to similar controls by special order. Consents can be granted either unconditionally or conditionally, with respect to the siting of the outlet, its construction and use and to the nature, composition, temperature, volume and rate of discharge of the effluent. Also, dischargers assumed an obligation to allow the sampling of effluent by the relevant authorities. Whilst the 1951 Acts applied to new discharges only, the 1960 Acts extended control to existing sources as well. There have been criticisms of the consent system as a *de facto* right to pollute (Pezzey, 1989).

The 1963 Water Resources Act empowered the relevant authorities to demand any information deemed relevant concerning the operations of any party removing water from rivers, or adding effluents. The Water Resources Act laid the foundations for subsequent legislation concerning the control of pollution and the access to information regarding the activities of parties utilising rivers and estuaries. Much of the legislation included in the 1974 Control of Pollution Act (COPA), was derived from the Water Resources Act. The Rivers (Pollution Prevention)(Scotland) Act 1965 was extremely important, as it brought all dischargers under the control of the seven River Purification Boards (RPBs) whose brief is to monitor Scottish water quality. Within their watershed boundaries, their duties are to promote the cleanliness of rivers and other watercourses, and to conserve the water resources within the region. To do this, the RPBs grant consents to dischargers and monitor the compliance with conditions imposed. By using the consent system, the long standing local authority discharges to rivers were regulated. 'These included the vast majority of sewage and industrial effluents responsible for over 90% of the polluting load in Scottish rivers' (Hammerton, 1986, 914). There was, during this period, a widespread improvement in water quality throughout Britain and fish life was restored to many waters (Hammerton, 1987); the new consent system and legal powers to enforce the conditions of discharge made this possible.

2.2.3   The Influence Of European Legislation (1973-1988)

In 1973 the UK adopted the Community Action Programme on the Environment, which had the following three specific aims. First, to prevent or reduce pollution and nuisances; next, to husband natural resources and the balance of ecological systems; and finally, to improve the quality of life and working conditions. Improvements in water quality were given further potential impetus when the UK joined the EEC.

Legislation concerning water quality and pollution in the UK comes from two sources. Firstly there is the legislation created as a response to an issue in the UK. This would be passed by the Government as Statute Law. Secondly there is a large body of legislation passed by the European Community concerning both general and specific issues. Immediately enforceable in member states, EEC legislation must be made law by respective governments. This would then become Statutory Law when passed by the Government. EEC legislation is fundamental to the contents of UK statutes, which are often direct implementations of it.

2.2.3.1   Water Quality Legislation From The EEC

The EEC passes legislation concerning all aspects of the community by means of Directives, Regulations and Decisions. The Directive is the most commonly used mechanism in environmental matters, since whilst it is binding as to the results to be achieved, it allows flexibility in the methods of achieving these standards. A Directive requires immediately applicable legislation in all member states, or in the member states to which it was issued. Member states must submit to the Commission the national laws implemented to meet the specifications of the Directives. If these laws are considered unsatisfactory, the Commission may refer the case to the European Court of Justice.

The EEC has issued several Directives to its member states concerning water quality (See Appendix 2.1). These have become fundamental to water pollution control, water quality and water supply in the UK There are, however, differences over the level of pollutants allowed and in policy, between the EEC and the UK. EEC pollution control policy is based on the concept of 'Fixed Limits' which seeks to restrict discharges to a predetermined national level regardless of dilution. In the UK, by contrast, an 'Environmental Quality Objective (EQO) approach is preferred. The EQO system incorporates 'Environmental Quality Standards' (EQS). The EQO defines 'the uses for which a stretch of water is suitable' (SDD, 1988) and it may be described in qualitative terms. The EQO system, therefore, allows for regional variation in the levels and types of pollutants permitted with reference to the receiving capacity of waters and to the effects upon the potential use of the water after dilution (House of Commons Environment Committee, Session 1986-7: Pollution of Rivers and Estuaries, HC 183-I). There is no legal definition of dilution but an example of a typical definition, adopted by the Highland River Purification Board, is that dilution is believed to have taken place when all of the plume of a discharge of effluent has 'welled' to the surface (Meeting with HRPB, 8.8.89). The EQS is more specific and defines the concentration and emission standard of a substance in the receiving water, a standard which must not be exceeded if the EQO is to be met (SDD, 1988). It is a more flexible system than the 'Fixed Limits" approach, due to its selective application.

The EQO, and incorporated EQS, for a particular watercourse is often supplemented by an additional national requirement or 'Uniform Emission Standard' (UES) whereby the same limit is applied to all emissions of a particular contaminant. An example of this is the 20/30 ppm Biological Oxygen Demand/Suspended Solids Royal Commission standard. UES's are easier, and less costly, to implement and control but they only limit pollution at source thereby ignoring the effects of dilution and interaction.

Appendix 2.1 summarises EEC Water Quality Legislation, of which, arguably, the most important has been the Dangerous Substances Directive, 76/464/EEC. This was prepared by the Commission of the European Communities and adopted by the Council of Ministers on 4 May, 1976. This Directive is comprehensive and covers all aspects of aquatic pollution in rivers, estuaries, ground-waters and the sea. A number of substances considered to be toxic or dangerous to the aquatic environment, are named and classified into one of two lists. List I, or the 'Black List', includes substances which are particularly toxic, persistent or bioaccumulable, except where they are biologically harmless. Included are such pollutants as organohalogens, organophosphates, organotins, carcinogens, mercury and cadmium compounds, persistent petroleum originated mineral oils and hydrocarbons, and persistent synthetic substances, (Directive 76/464/EEC and CEC Second Report 1979). Persistence is an important factor where pollutants will accumulate, especially in estuarine environments where flushing rates may be slow.

List II, or the 'Grey List', consists mainly of those substances whose effects would be restricted to certain areas at a more local level. The intended water usage is therefore of great importance. The list groups together various dangerous metals and metalloids, and twenty families or groups of metals or metal compounds are detailed, including arsenic, lead, copper, silver and cobalt. Also included are substances affecting the taste or smell of the water, toxic or persistent compounds of silicon, inorganic compounds of phosphorous, non persistent petroleum based oils and hydrocarbons, cyanides and fluorides and substances affecting the oxygen balance of the water, (Directive 76/464/EEC and CEC Second Report 1979).

Directive 76/464/EEC also provides for a system of licensing by consent before discharge of listed substances occurs. The responsibility of member states to comply with these regulations is firm, the exact methodology used in achieving the standards is a matter for the states to decide themselves. The UK has adopted a 'Red List' (See Table 2.3) as an updated supplement to the EEC Black and Grey Lists of prescribed substances. It is intended that the UK Red List will reinforce the original EEC measures, and introduce a new system for controlling inputs of the most dangerous substances to water, with reference to Environmental Quality Objectives (EQOs) and Environmental Quality Standards (EQSs), as discussed above, (Scottish Development Department 1988).

The Government aims to reduce the inputs of these substances to the North Sea by 50% by 1995. Plans to make the agreed reductions have been drawn up and mercury inputs have been reduced by 20% between 1985-88 and cadmium inputs by 18%.

2.2.3.2 Water Quality Legislation From The U.K.

In the U.K, water supply was operated at a municipal level (Howard, 1989) until the 1973 Water Act. Municipal authorities were responsible for waste treatment, while local river boards were responsible for controlling the rivers. In 1973, the 29 river authorities, 187 water undertakings and 1395 sewerage and waste-water authorities in England and Wales were amalgamated to establish the nine regional water authorities (RWAs) and the Welsh Water Development Authority. These exist today as private companies, namely: Anglian Water, Northumbrian Water, North West Water, Severn Trent Water, Southern Water, South West Water, Thames Water, Welsh Water, Wessex Water and Yorkshire Water. Before privatisation of the industry, private water companies did supply water, in certain areas, acting as the agents for the former RWAs. In Scotland, river quality, was, and still is, the responsibility of seven independent river purification boards (RPBs) namely the Highland, North East, Tay, Clyde, Forth, Solway and Tweed river purification boards and the three island councils, namely the Shetland Islands Council, the Orkney Islands Council and the Western Isles Islands Council.

Maintenance of the sewerage system, except for sewage treatment works (STWs) themselves, was usually a function of the local authorities, or as in Scotland the regional and island councils. This was changed in the 1974 Local Government Act when responsibility for the management of STWs was also given to these regional councils, of which there are eleven in Scotland.

The 1974 Control of Pollution Act (COPA), was designed to bring together much of the legislation of previous

Table 2.3   Red List Substances

Mercury and its compounds
Cadmium and its compounds
Gamma-hexachlorocyclohexane
DDT
Pentachlorophenol and its compounds
Hexachlorobutadiene
Aldrin
Dieldrin
Endrin
Polychlorinated Biphenyls
Dichlorvos
1,2-Dichloroethane
Trichlorobenzene
Atrazine
Simazine
Tributyltin compounds
Triphenyltin compounds
Trifluralin
Fenitrothion
Azinphos-menthyl
Malathion
Endolsulfan

Source: Government Environmental Protection Green Paper, 1990

bills into one coherent approach (Royal Commission On Environmental Pollution, 1984). Given royal assent in July, 1974, COPA has been one of the most important recent legislative measures concerning water pollution and water quality in the UK, although now superseded by the 1989 Water Act. COPA covered many aspects of environmental pollution, water being only one part, and the control of water quality and pollution is covered by Part II of the Act. It empowered the granting of 'consents to discharge' by the water authority, excluding specific activities from the legislation. Walker notes that 'unlike the old legislation, there is no system of consents to outlets as such' (Walker, 1979, 33). Thus under pre-determined conditions, pollution may legally be discharged into watercourses. In order to determine the dilution required of the effluent discharge, consents take account of the relative flows of the effluent, the river flows in dry weather, and the quality of the water upstream. This is a very different approach to the method of 'Fixed Limits' as preferred by the EEC and adopted by all other member states. The UK system allows the degree of control over discharge water quality to vary with the background quality of the particular watercourse.

A decision regarding the granting of a consent had to be reached within a six week period by the then Water Authority. There are two exceptions to this, firstly when the Secretary of State issues an 'Exemption Certificate' for the activity, and secondly when the water authority considers the proposed discharge to have no appreciable effect on the environment. Once granted, consents cannot be revoked within a two year period without compensation to, or the agreement of, the discharger; in effect this gives the discharger a limited property right over the consent.

Because of the extensive range of pollution covered by COPA, and the costs of administration of the Act at all levels, small output discharges were deemed consented until the application was determined by the, then, relevant water authority. This, however, excluded discharges containing the pollutants highlighted in the EEC 'Dangerous Substances' Directive 76/464/EEC. At present, the NRA is preparing to implement a charges scheme to recover those costs associated with consent administration and pollution control, including standard charges for all consent applications whether successful or not; this is discussed below.

The 1983 Water Act brought the 1973 Water Act up to date and was the basic legislation for water supply and distribution in the UK till 1989. Under the 1983 Act, the water authorities were once more re-structured and given responsibility for water conservation, treatment, pollution control, land drainage, fisheries and recreation.

One of the consequences of the UK adopting a European perspective on pollution control is that more sophisticated analysis of natural waters is required. The stricter control over Grey, Black and, more recently, Red List substances will require detailed and costly monitoring of these pollutants in UK rivers and estuaries. Clearly, if the more stringent water quality standards, arising from adherence to the controls over Red List substances and the EQOs, are to be achieved, then funding for further research, equipment and staff training is required.

In Northern Ireland, the Department of the Environment (DOE Northern Ireland) assume the role of water authority and undertake to issue and monitor consents in the manner of the water companies of mainland Britain. The 1972 Water Act (N.I.) empowered the then Ministry of Development to promote 'the conservation of the water resources in Northern Ireland ..and.. the cleanliness of water in waterways' (The Water Act (N.I.), 1972). The 'waterways' defined by the Act, unlike those of its counterpart in Great Britain, extended to estuarine *and* marine waters. The 1973 Water and Sewerage Services Order made the Ministry of Development responsible for 'the provision and maintainance of facilities for draining and dealing with domestic sewage and trade effluents' (Water and Sewerage Services Order (N.I.), 1973).

In 1974, the DoE Northern Ireland assumed responsibility for the management of water quality and supply, and sewage treatment. Control is exercised through the use 'consents' issued to effluent discharges. The DoE Northern Ireland also have responsibility to pursue reported pollution incidents

2.2.4 Water Privatisation And Beyond (1989 Onwards)

In 1989 the Government privatised the water industry in England and Wales as part of a wider privatisation programme, whereby, since 1979, the size of the state sector has been reduced by nearly 40 percent. Under the 1989 Water Act, several changes were prescribed for the industry and the ten public regional water authorities have now become privately owned, limited water companies, each listed on the Stock Exchange. Prior to the Act many of the 29 smaller water bodies had already had their debt quoted on the Exchange, and were increasingly subject to investment by outside interests as financial controls were lifted. Several French water companies stepped into the market and invested heavily in these smaller companies, as did some of the former public sector water authorities. Lyonnaise des Eaux, in particular, is a substantial share holder in several UK water companies. The water industry as a whole was valued, by the Financial Times, at 5.3 billion pounds at the end of 1989.

The 1989 privatisation has not directly affected the Scottish River Purification Boards (RPBs) or the regional and Island councils, but there have been changes here too. The RPB's brief is to monitor water quality and, within their watershed boundaries, their duties are to promote the cleanliness of rivers and other watercourses and to conserve the water resources within the region. To do this, the RPBs grant consents and monitor the compliance with conditions imposed. During the Second Reading of the Water Bill on 7 December, 1988, the Secretary of State for the Environment announced that the Government intended to introduce a limited number of amendments relating to drinking water and the protection of the water environment in Scotland at the Report Stage. The changes to occur in Scotland were tabled in the form of amendments to the Bill on 15 March, 1989. These included a new clause which firstly makes minor changes to Part I of COPA, and secondly revises a large portion of Part II of COPA: the water quality section. This has in effect re-enacted most of the existing clauses of COPA Part II in Scotland, whilst including certain amendments consequent to consultations made in 1986, and 1988. The latter amendments are comparable with provisions already in the 1989 Water Act itself, but also include changes specific to the structure of the water industry in Scotland, such as the substitution of 'River Purification Board' for 'Water Authority', 'loch' for 'lake' and so on. The definition of 'controlled waters' has been re-defined for Scotland to include underground waters, lochs, rivers, estuaries and the sea within the three mile limit. The major changes affecting Scotland are: provision for RPBs to charge consent holders for expenditures incurred in monitoring and processing consents; and regulations enabling RPBs to enforce 'due care' standards for the storage of certain potentially polluting materials (currently regulations have been issued covering the storage of silage, slurry and fuel oil).

In England and Wales, privatisation has dramatically altered the balance of power in the water industry, and the water supply industry can assume a freedom from the controls of government. Water pollution, drainage and river management are monitored and controlled by the new 'watchdog'' organisation, the National Rivers Authority (NRA), set up by the new Water Act. The NRA was a late addition to the early design of the Water Bill, and was added when it was found that it would be breaking European law not to set up such a body. The NRA employs 6,500 staff and is responsible for the enforcement of government set water quality standards, but is not directly linked to the industry itself.

2.2.5 The National Rivers Authority

The NRA has wide ranging responsibilities for managing water resources and must balance the interests of all who use them. It has responsibility for controlling pollution in inland, estuarine and coastal waters. The 1989 Water Act requires the NRA to control pollution by issuing discharge consents, to monitor water quality and the achievement of national water quality standards, taking enforcement action where necessary. The Government has increased from £2,000 to £20,000 the maximum fine which magistrate's courts can impose for water pollution offences. The NRA also has responsibility to manage water resources and to protect their long-term future by controlling abstraction rates and by managing a wide range of related activities, for example, land-drainage and fisheries.

The NRA will advise the Government on Water Quality Objectives (WQOs) by maintaining water quality and by identifying where current water quality needs to be improved and will set the timetable for improvements. Specifically, during 1990, the NRA is to survey river and estuary quality and will also review its own monitoring practices.

In July 1990, the NRA published its first report 'Water Quality Series No 1'. In it two key changes are recommended. First, controls for discharge from industry and from STWs ought to be put on the same footing in order to make assessment of compliance or non-compliance clearer. Second, they recommend that preparations be made, over several years, to substitute Total Organic Carbon (TOC) for Biological Oxygen Demand (BOD) and Turbidity for Suspended Solids (SS), as the conventional sanitary determinands[9]. These changes are aimed at promoting a wider spread of automatic and continuous monitoring of discharges. Discharges are to be actively encouraged to provide full information, for example by the introduction of 'Action Warnings' as a formal, urgent signal with a strong preventative emphasis. The report also highlighted two crucial areas, namely sampling practice and the introduction of consent charges, which are discussed below.

2.2.5.1 Sampling Practice: Proposed Changes

In order to be used as evidence in court in England and Wales, samples of all discharges other than of sewage effluent, have to be taken on a tripartite basis, whereby one sample is retained by the discharger, one is tested and one is held in storage for reference. The samples may be evaluated using a well-established methodology of mass-balancing modelling, that is, patterns of discharge flow are determined and expressed in numerical terms. The variable natures of a discharge inevitably causes several numbers or values to be generated from the evaluation, giving a statistical distribution curve which illustrates the aggregate spread of concentrations (NRA, 1990). From the distribution curve, the percentage of a discharge within the required consent limit can be read. At present, a 95 percentile limit is required, that is at least 95% of the samples, over a specified time period, must not exceed the consented limit. The time-period is usually twelve months but not necessarily so; for certain discharges, a shorter period of six or even three months may be required (NRA, 1990).

Under percentile limits, the sampling regime is both time and resource consuming. As a result, some consents had percentile limits and some were enforceable only by tripartite sampling, but these two rules did not apply together to the same consents. The Water Act changed the status of Water Authorities to private companies, therefore, the NRA believes there is a case for giving them the protection of tripartite sampling. It was not, however, considered practical to end the application of percentile limits to STWs at the same time.

In Scotland, all consent limits are still expressed as absolutes, and references to percentile limits have no legal force. The NRA recommends that all numeric consents should include absolute limits for all relevant determinands. For some discharges going to sensitive receiving waters, the setting of new percentile limits could bring a greater degree of control of routine operating levels while absolute limits constrain peak discharges. The NRA, in its Water Quality Series Report, believes that there is a strong case for adopting the 80 percentile limit in preference to the current 95 percentile limit, the former bringing greater sensitivity to detect real deterioration in effluent quality from a limited number of samples of a discharge prone to variation; additional control over the level of effluent concentration; and more effective use of effluent quality data generally. Controls which highlight the long-term performance of a discharger ought to encourage good discharge-management on the basis of it being a regular operational commitment.

2.2.5.2 Consent Charges

The UK is a member of the Organisation for Economic Co-operation and Development (OECD) and member countries are committed to the 'Polluter Pays Principle' (PPP). Application of this principle may involve different policies, and economic instruments, for example charges and Tradeable Discharge Rights (TDRs), may be used as policy tools (OECD, 1989).

Charges for consents may take two forms entailing two different policies. First, charges may be set at an 'incentive level' whereby the polluter pays a charge, per unit of effluent, which is set high enough to act as a pressure to reduce effluent and thereby minimise costs (Pezzey, 1988). Alternatively, charges may be set at a level aimed at 'cost-recovery' in order to raise revenue which will be used to off-set the costs associated with pollution control (OECD, 1989).

The NRA proposes to introduce consent charges effective from April 1st, 1991 (NRA, Private Communication, December 1990), and are now considering the stages beyond that; they intend to introduce 'cost-recovery' charges progressively and expect to recover a substantial part of the cost of pollution control. The charges will be those permitted under the Environmental Protection Bill 1990 and the 1989 Water Act; the latter allows for:

a.   a single charge in respect of the whole period for which the consent is in force;

b.   separate charges in respect of different parts of that period;

c.   both such a single charge and such separate charges.

---

[9] This is allowed for in the draft EC Directive on Municipal Waste Water

Also, a charges scheme may:

a. make different provision for different cases, including provision in relation to different circumstances or localities;

b. contain supplemental, consequential and transitional provision for the purpose of the scheme.

The DoE and Welsh Offices' discussion paper 'Paying for Pollution Control' (Feb 1989), gives more details of the Government's proposals. The charges scheme is to recover that portion of the NRA's costs associated with water quality regulation and pollution control. The emphasis on cost-recovery differs from the recommendation of the House of Commons Environment Committee who favoured a charges scheme based on incentive-levels (HCEC, 1987). There will be, however, an incentive element for environmental improvement, for example lower charges for the conducting of water abstraction at night.

Any form of cost recovery should discourage discharger's pollution even if it doesn't encourage minimisation of it. Charges will apply to all consents, not just successful ones and existing consents will be brought into the scheme over time. Charges will reflect costs and there ought to be no undue preference or discrimination in fixing charges. Discharges have the protection that the scheme and any charges will be subject to approval by the Secretary of State.

The proposed cost-recovery scheme will have two main elements:

a. a National Scheme based on standard principals and method so that dischargers would pay the same in different locations, and

b. actual costs, which are variable in different locations may be incorporated into a separate charge.

The costs of follow-up work where compliance is being questioned may be recoverable costs, as will be costs relating to special circumstances, for example, pollution involving the 'Red List" substances. In general, the costs to be recovered are those relating to administration, staffing, initial surveys and investigation into discharge impacts and also those relating to the monitoring of river quality, sampling and modelling etc.

In deciding the methodology for cost-charging, the DoE (DoE, 1989a) outlines three criteria: charges must be reasonable; the scheme must be cost-effective and easily understood; and the scheme must be flexible to respond to a range of local and special circumstances. There are three possible bases for charging. Actual Costs may be used although the administrative burden of monitoring these may actually increase costs; Average Costs would be the simplest base to use but would not be equitable between large and small discharges. The recommended base is that of Formula Apportionment with reference to the volume and 'quality' of discharge. This method would produce a spread of charges more favourable to the small discharger while 'banding' of volume and quality would provide a matrix for determining charges with reference to the terms of consented discharge. It would also be possible to introduce, in future, an element of 'incentive' charging via this method as it measures the nature of the discharge not only the cost of monitoring it.

The NRA confirm that the charges to be introduced, will consist of a standard Application Charge of £350 per annum (or a £50 charge for insignificant discharges) plus an Annual Charge based on a National Formula and set according to the volume and nature of the discharge:

Figure 2.1 The NRA's formula for charges

Charge = R (V x C x RW)

Where: R = Financial factor (Annual unit charge of £270 per annum)
V = Banded weighting factor based on consented discharge volume
C = Banded weighting factor based on consented discharge content
RW = Banded weighting factor based on category of receiving water

On the broader issue of 'incentive charges' mentioned above, the NRA are fairly enthusiastic and are investigating the possibilities; such charges would be based on the volume and nature of the discharge with reference to the Marginal Damage Costs (MDC).

The privatisation of the water industry has brought about massive changes in the organisation of both water quality and pollution control in England and Wales, separating ownership of water companies from regulation of the services they provide, namely water supply and pollution control. An important element in these matters is the creation of the National Rivers Authority (NRA) as discussed above. Control of water quality has passed directly from the hands of the former water authorities to the NRA. In Scotland, RPBs will make their own national cost

Table 2.4   Summary of Weighting Factors. Source: NRA 'Scheme of charges in respect of applications and consents for discharges to controlled waters' 1991.

Category	Band		Factor
	0-5		0.4
	>5-20		0.7
	>20-100		1.0
	> 100-1,000		2.0
	> 1,000-10,000		3.0
	> 10,000-50,000		5.0
	>50,000-150,000		9.0
	> 150,000		14.0
Content	A	Complex Organic, Pesticides	15.0
	B	Potentially Toxic, Metals etc	5.0
	C	Organic Sewage, Trade Effluent	3.0
	D	General Trade Effluent	2.0
	E	Site Drainage	1.0
	F	Low Environmental Effect	0.5
	G	Mainly Cooling Waters	0.3
Receiving Water	Ground		0.5
	Coastal		0.8
	Surface		1.0
	Estuarial		1.5

recovery scheme public on June 24th, 1991. Whilst they will make the same £350/£50 application charge as the NRA, the scheme differs in that RPBs will base their annual charge on the cost of work *actually* carried out. This charge will have the following elements: a monitoring charge to recover sampling costs, an analysis charge with standard charges per unit of effluent type; and an attendance charge to cover the varying costs of sampling. The RPBs retain responsibility for water pollution control although there are moves to formalise consultations with Her Majesties Industrial Pollution Inspectorate (HMIPI) and waste disposal authorities (ie. the regional and Island councils) for certain specified pollutants and processes (eg. Red List substances and processes involving the creation of significant quantities of special waste). Similarly, the NRA must consult Her Majesties Inspectorate Pollution (HMIP) in England and Wales to gain authorisation to grant consents involving Red List substances. The NRA does not forecast changes in water quality management (NRA, private communication, December 1990), however, they do intend to move to watershed management whereby the whole 'picture' is taken into consideration, for example, they intend to clamp down on non-point sources of pollution. The possibility of a Nitrate Charge has been viewed favourably.

Whilst this change is underway, new systems for the control of water quality will also be brought in, using the 'Polluter Pays Principle' (PPP) again discussed above. The most important of these is the proposed usage of technology-based emission standards, which will be applied to significant discharges of Red List substances on a plant by plant basis. This will be achieved by scheduling relevant processes (SDD, 1988), and new processes must receive authorisation before start-up. Authorisation will be based on an analysis of the plant with reference to the 'Best Available Technology Not Entailing Excessive Cost' (BATNEEC). The establishment of this practice on a wider basis and the proposed granting of statutory status to the concept of BATNEEC will assist the introduction of 'Integrated Pollution Control', (IPC) as allowed for in the Environmental Protection Act.

The proposed EEC Directive on Municipal Waste (see Appendix 2.1) was expected to be adopted in January 1991; this would set minimum emission standards for certain STWs in the UK. This might necessitate the re-issuing of all STW consents and involve considerable cost.

Control of Water Quality in the UK has traditionally been addressed through the application of the 'Best Practicable Environmental Option' (BPEO) (Turner, unpublished) and Best Practical Means. To achieve this, EQOs, which incorporate EQSs, discussed above, have been used. In Clause 101 of the 1989 Water Act, the EQOs were given statutory status, following consultation with the relevant Water Authorities and River Purification Boards. In this way, control over the less harmful substances entering watercourses was strengthened, whilst offering a better basis than before for the allocation of resources and for informed debate and decision making. For substances more threatening to the environment, the EEC has issued various Directives, for example, the 76/464/EEC Dangerous Substances Directive (1976) and the associated Black and Grey Lists. This, as discussed, has been reinforced by the acceptance of the Red List in the UK.

2.3 Discussion and Conclusion

This chapter provides an overview of water quality legislation in the U.K from 1868 to 1989, and the development of the current water quality control system that has followed.

The early legislation, in the 'formative period', had little real effect upon water quality and the infrastructure provided, in terms of personnel and equipment, was inadequate. From 1951 onwards, consents were introduced and there was a marked improvement in the water quality of rivers and estuaries in the UK. Consents took into account local and unique conditions of the water courses they protected.

Prior to the 1989 Water Act, the 1974 Control of Pollution Act was undoubtedly the most important piece of water quality legislation. The introduction of COPA represented a real chance to make a major impact upon the quality of UK waters. COPA was, however, sufficient for dealing with routine, direct discharges but it offered inadequate control over diffuse discharges, for example, nitrate leaching. Arguably, it was also compromised in practice and influenced by the interests of dischargers (Royal Commission On Environmental Pollution, 1984 and Pearce, 1984). Part II of the Act (the water quality section) was only fully implemented, in a reduced form, some sixteen years later. The ineffectiveness of the implementation of COPA may now be used as a yardstick by which to judge the impact of the new 1989 Water Act.

The 1989 Water Act is the most recent Act in a continuing series of 'environmental' pieces of legislation. The Act has brought about major structural changes to the pollution control system of England and Wales. It is worth noting that there are many features of this new look attributable to EEC policies. There has been some conflict caused by the merger of two effectively different systems for the control of water quality. Certainly new legislation brought in will increasingly reflect the European perspective.

Under the Water Act, ownership of the water industry in England and Wales has been split away from the regulation of water quality and pollution control which is now the responsibility of the NRA. This has created a situation similar to that currently operated in Scotland, which is seen by many to be a model for the forthcoming changes; certainly it works well in practice, although independence of the two sides of the industry does cause certain problems of watershed management: the abstraction of drinking water by Regional Councils for instance. It is still too early to comment upon the effects and implications to water quality that the new Water Act and privatisation have brought, although this will undoubtedly be debated in future. Certainly, there is a new direction in pollution control and it is one that is strongly influenced by European policy and this trend is expected to continue.

Among the many new measures being brought in, the discussion of market mechanisms to institute quality control should be noted. The NRA intends to start charging for consents in 1991 although the exact design of the scheme and the methodology of charging is not yet clear. Within the new privatised industry, the current system of 'command and control' measures is being discussed with reference to improvement in water quality but it has still to be demonstrated that market mechanisms can achieve this aim. There are several ways of introducing market mechanisms, for example tradeable permits, into water pollution in order to enhance the quality of water in rivers and estuaries and the need is to develop a system that is rigorous in theory, applied efficiently and which is equitable in practice.

We note, however, that at present, legislation would not allow the introduction of a tradeable permit system in Scotland, whilst guidelines on charging schemes are currently aimed at cost recovery charging rather than incentive-level charges (DoE 1989a and SDD, 1988).

References

CEC, Commission of the European Communities (1979) *State of the Environment*, Second Report. CEC.

CEC, Commission of the European Communities (1989) Environmental Research Newsletter. No 4, December 1989, CEC.

DOE (1989) *The Water Bill. 1. Water Privatisation*. DOE & Welsh Office, London.

DOE (1989) *The Water Bill. 2. Drinking Water Quality*. DOE & Welsh Office, London.

DOE (1977) *Environmental Standards: A Description of United Kingdom Practice*. Pollution Paper No. 11. HMSO London.

DOE (1989a) *Paying for Water Pollution Control*. DOE & Welsh Office.

DOE (1989) *The Water Bill. 5. Price Regulation and the Director General*. DOE & Welsh Office, London.

DOE (1989) *The Water Bill. 3. Customer Standards and Consumer Rights*. DOE & Welsh Office, London.

DOE (1989) *The Water Bill. 4. A New Structure for Pollution Control: The National Rivers Authority*. DOE & Welsh Office, London.

European Review of Agricultural Economics, *Economics and Nitrate Pollution*, 17(2), 1990.

FRPB Interview undertaken on 29/5/89, between W. Halcrow, Director FRPB, D. Holloway, Chief Hydrologist and Pollution Control Officer FRPB and T. Leatherland, Chief Scientific Officer FRPB, and members of the Research Team from Stirling University

GOVERNMENT, *This Common Inheritance: White Paper,* 1990, HMSO, London.

GOVERNMENT, *The Water Act 1989,* HMSO, London

HAMMERTON, D. (1987) *The Impact of Environmental Legislation*. J. Water Pollution Control. Vol 86, 333-344

HAMMERTON, D. (1983) *The History of Environmental Water Quality Management in Scotland*. J.I.W.C.J. 336-346

HAMMERTON, D. (1986) *Cleaning the Clyde - a Century of Progress?* J. Opl. Res. Soc. Vol 37, No 9,1986, 911-921.

HIGHLAND RIVER PURIFICATION BOARD (HRPB) Meeting, 8.8.89

HOUSE OF COMMONS ENVIRONMENT COMMITTEE. Session 1986/87. *Pollution of Rivers and Estuaries*. HC 183-I

HOWARD, M. (1989) *Water Issues in the United Kingdom*. J. WPCF. Vol 61, No 1, January 1989, 27-31.

HOWE, G.M. (1972) *Man. Environment and Disease in Britain: A Medical Geography of Britain Through the Ages*. Barnes and Noble David and Charles.

INSTITUTE FOR ENVIRONMENTAL STUDIES (1987) *European Environmental Yearbook* 1987. IES, Milan.

JENKINS, S. (1989) Struggling in a nice stretch of water. *The Sunday Times*, 12 March 1989.

LUCAS, S. (1988) Maintaining and Improving Scotlands' Rivers. *The Water Bulletin*. No 321. 12 August 1988.

MACRORY, R. & ZABA, B. (1978) *The Control of Pollution Act Explained*. Friends of the Earth, London.

MᶜLUSKY, D.S., ELLIOT, M., AND WARNES, J. (1978) The Impact of Pollution on the Intertidal Fauna of the Estuarine Firth of Forth, in McLusky, D.S. and Berry, A.J. (Eds) *Proceedings of the 12th Europ. Mar. Biol. Symp.,* Pergammon Press, Oxford.

NATIONAL RIVERS AUTHORITY (1990) *Water Quality Series* No. 1, July 1990.

NATIONAL RIVERS AUTHORITY (1990) Briefing paper, 'Charging for discharging', unpublished.

NATIONAL RIVERS AUTHORITY (1991) 'Proposed Scheme of Charges in respect of discharges to controlled waters'.

NATIONAL RIVERS AUTHORITY (1991) 'Scheme of Charges in respect of applications and consents for discharges to controlled waters'.

ORGANISATION FOR ECONOMIC CO-OPERATION AND DEVELOPMENT (1989) *Economic Instruments for Environmental Protection,* OECD, Paris.

PEARCE, F. (1984) The Great Drain Robbery. *New Scientist.* 15 March 1984.10-16.

PEZZEY, J. (1988), 'Market mechanisms of pollution control: 'Polluter Pays', Economic and practical aspects'. In Turner, R.K (ed) *Sustainable Environmental Management,* Belhaven Press, Colorado, Press/ESRC, Colorado.

ROYAL COMMISSION ON ENVIRONMENTAL POLLUTION (1984) *Tackling Pollution – Experience and Prospects.* Tenth Report. HMSO. London.

SCOTTISH DEVELOPMENT DEPARTMENT (1989) *Consideration of Bill. Water Bill. as Amended. New Schedules. Control of Pollution in Scotland.* SDD, Edinburgh.

SCOTTISH DEVELOPMENT DEPARTMENT (1988) *Inputs of Dangerous Substances to Water. Proposals for a Unified System of Control: Control of Dangerous Substances to Water (the 'Red List').* December 1988, Edinburgh.

SCOTTISH DEVELOPMENT DEPARTMENT (1989) *Water Bill: Control of Pollution in Scotland. Explanatory Notes on Provisions to be Introduced by Amendments to the Bill at Commons Report Stage.* March 1989, Edinburgh.

SCOTTISH DEVELOPMENT DEPARTMENT (1989) *Pollution Control in Scotland: Proposals for Changes.* SDD, Edinburgh.

SILKE, E. (1988) Cash Caps Scots' Rising Standards. *The Surveyor.* 16 June 1988.

TEARLE, K (ed) (1973) *Industrial Pollution Control. the Practical Implications.* Business Books Ltd. London.

TURNER, R.K (unpublished) Assessment of Effectiveness of the BPEO via Case Studies. Department of Environmental Sciences, University of East Anglia.

Unattributed, 'Water Industry valued at £5.3bn', *Financial Times,* 12.11.89, p.26.

WALKER, A. (1979) *Law of Industrial Pollution Control.* George Godwin Ltd. London.

WATER SERVICES IN SCOTLAND (1987) *Scotlands' Water Services.* Geo. E. Findlay & Co Ltd. Dundee.

WILSON, J.G. & HALCROW, W. (1985). *Estuarine Management and Quality Assessment.* Plenum Press. New York.

Appendix 2.1

The Major EEC Directives Concerning Water Quality and Pollution Control to Date

DATE   DIRECTIVE

December 17, 1973   73/405/EEC
On the Approximation of the Laws of the Member States relating to methods of testing the Bio-degradability of anionic surfactants.

December 17, 1974   74/404/EEC
On the Approximation of the Laws of the Member States relating to Detergents.

June 16, 1975   75/440/EEC
On the Quality Required of Surface Water Intended for the Abstraction of Drinking Water in the Member States.

July 25, 1975   75/437/EEC
Council Decision concluding the convention for the prevention of marine pollution from land-based sources.

December 8, 1975   76/160/EEC
Concerning the Quality of Bathing Waters.

May 4, 1976   76/464/EEC
On Pollution Caused by Certain Dangerous Substances Discharged into the Aquatic Environment of the Community.

December 12, 1977   77/795/EEC
Establishing a Common Procedure for the Exchange of Information on the Quality of Surface Fresh Water in the Community.

February 25, 1978   78/176/EEC
On waste from the titanium dioxide industry.

June 26, 1978 Council Resolution for setting up an action programme of the European Communities on the control and reduction of pollution caused by hydrocarbons discharged at sea.

July 18, 1978   78/659/EEC
On the Quality of Fresh Waters Needing Protection or Improvement in Order to Support Fish Life.

October 9, 1979   79/869/EEC
Concerning the Methods of Measurement and Frequencies of Sampling Analysis of Surface Water Intended for the Abstraction of Drinking Water in the Member States.

October 30, 1979   79/923/EEC
On the Quality Required of Shellfish Waters.

December 17, 1979   80/68/EEC
On the Protection of Groundwater against Pollution caused by Certain Dangerous Substances.

June 25, 1980   80/836/EEC
Commission Decision setting up an Advisory Committee on the control and reduction of pollution caused by hydrocarbons discharged at sea.

July 15, 1980   80/778/EEC
Relating to the Quality of Water Intended for Human Consumption.

DATE   DIRECTIVE

December 10, 1981   81/971/EEC
Council Decision establishing a Community information system for the control and reduction of pollution caused by hydrocarbons discharged at sea.

March 22, 1982   82/176/EEC
On Limit Values and Quality Objectives for Mercury Discharges by the Chlor-Alkali Electrolysis Industry.

April 22, 1982   82/242/EEC
On the Approximation of the Laws of the Member States relating to methods for testing the Bio-degradability of non-ionic surfactants and amending Directive 73/404/EEC.

April 22, 1982   82/243/EEC
Amending Directive 82/243/EEC on the approximation of the laws of the member states relating to methods of testing the Bio-degradability of anionic surfactants.

December 31, 1982   82/883/EEC
On procedures for the surveillance and monitoring of environments concerned by waste from the titanium dioxide industry.

February 3, 1983   83/29/EEC
Amending Directive 78/176/EEC on Waste from the titanium dioxide industry.

February 7, 1983 Council Resolution concerning the combating of water pollution.

September 26, 1983   83/513/EEC
On Limit Values and Quality Objectives for Cadmium Discharges.

March 17, 1984   84/156/EEC
On Limit Values and Quality Objectives for Mercury Discharges by Sectors other than the Chlor-Alkali Electrolysis Industry.

July 16, 1984   84/358/EEC
Council Decision concerning the conclusion of the agreement for cooperation in dealing with pollution of the North Sea by oil and other harmful substances.

October 9, 1984   84/491/EEC
On Limit Values and Quality Objectives for Discharges of Hexachlorocyclohexane.

December 6, 1984   84/631/EEC
On the Supervision and Control Within the European Community of the Transfrontier Shipment of Hazardous Waste.

September 26, 1985 Proposal for a Council Directive on the Dumping of waste at sea.

December 31, 1985 Proposal for a Council Directive on Water Quality Objectives for Chromium

March 6, 1986   86/85/EEC
Commission Decision establishing a Community information system for the control and reduction of pollution caused by the spillage of Hydrocarbons and other harmful substances at sea.

December 31, 1986   85/613/EEC
Council Decision concerning the adoption, on behalf of the Community, of programmes and measures relating to mercury and cadmium discharges under the Convention for the prevention of marine pollution from land-based sources.

March 25, 1986   86/94/EEC
Amending for the second time Directive 73/404/EEC on the approximation of the laws of the Member States relating to detergents.

DATE   DIRECTIVE

June 12, 1986   86/280/EEC
On Limit Values and Quality Objectives for Discharges of Certain Dangerous Substances Included in List I of the Annex to Directive 76/464.

November 28, 1986   86/574/EEC
Amending Decision 77/795/EEC establishing a common procedure for the exchange of information on the quality of surface fresh water in the Community.

January 27, 1987   87/57/EEC
Council Decision concluding the Protocol amending the Convention for the prevention of marine pollution from land-based sources.

June, 25, 1988   88/347/EEC
Amending Annex II to Directive 86/280/EEC on Limit Values and Quality Objectives for Discharges of Certain Dangerous Substances Included in List I of the Annex to Directive 76/464/EEC (First Amendment)

88/432/EEC Com. Proposal for Second Amendment to Directive 86/280/EEC on Limit Values and Quality Objectives for 4 Substances, EDC (1-2 dichloroethane), TRI (trichloroethane), PER (tetrachloroethylene), TCB (trichlorobenzene).

July 14, 1989 Proposal concerning the procedure for harmonizing the programmes for the reduction and eventual elimination of pollution caused by waste from the titanium dioxide industry.

November 11, 1989 Proposal for a Council Directive on Treatment of Municipal Waste Waters. This will be adopted in January, 1991.

3 Case Study – The Forth Estuary

Table of Contents

List of Figures

List of Tables

3.1 Characteristics of Estuaries

An estuary represents one of the most dynamic settings upon which to base an environmental investigation. Estuaries are in a constant state of flux, never, or rarely, finding equilibrium between the inflow of saline marine waters and fresh river waters. Flow of the body of water in an estuary is often slow, or at least complicated due to these opposing forces of river and tide. As a consequence, the 'flushing' time for an estuary is often long; it takes water approximately 12 days to pass through the Forth for instance (McLusky, 1989). Levels of salinity will vary along the region of interface between salt and freshwater (the FSI freshwater saltwater interface) as mixing occurs due to tidal, freshwater and Coriolis effects. The characteristics of this mixing are distinct and allow classification. The Forth is an example of a temperate partially mixed estuary (Table 3.1).

Table 3.1   Classification of Estuaries

Classification:	Example
1. Highly Stratified	N. Esk (UK)
2. Fjord	West of Scotland Lochs (UK)
3. Partially Mixed	**Forth (UK)**
4. Homogenous	Solway Firth (UK)

Source: McLusky, 1989

The Royal Commission on Environmental Pollution, an important source of environmental legislative and policy direction in the UK, recommended in their 1974 report (RCEP, 1974) that estuarine waters should firstly support, on the mud bottom of the estuary, the fauna essential for sustaining sea-fisheries, and secondly allow the passage of migratory fish at all states of the tide. Furthermore, the Water Authorities Association have proposed that tidal waters should support 'healthy biological systems comparable with the physical characteristics of the waters' (Leatherland, 1987, 290). Such recommendations for the creation of 'Environmental Quality Objectives (EQOs) (see Chapter 2), are taken on by the National Rivers Authority or River Purification Board. Table 3.2 gives an extract from the FRPB Water Quality Objectives (1989), outlining the biological EQO used.

Table 3.2   Biological EQO Criteria as used by the Forth River Purification Board

The basic water quality objective for all tidal waters is that they should be fit for all reasonable uses to which they are physically suited. They must support healthy biological systems compatible with their physical characteristics, and must not be subject to aesthetic or chemical pollution.

Compliance with this broad objective is determined through a series of more detailed Environmental Quality Objectives (EQO), and numerical Environmental Quality Standards (EQS). Biological EQO are that:

a. The mud bottom must have the ability to support the biota necessary for sustaining indigenous fisheries.

b. Water quality must be sufficient to allow the passage of migratory fish at all states of the tide.

c. The levels of contaminants in the biota should be insignificant and should not impair their normal utilisation in the food cycle of predators, including man(sic).

Source: Extracted from FRPB, 1989b

The estuary is dynamic also in terms of the fauna and flora supported along its length. Conditions within the estuary are harsh, the ever changing saline/freshwater conditions exert a great strain upon the organisms present. This is compounded by the fact that an organism may, by the very nature of the tide, have to live a large proportion of its life out of the water. Organisms that live in estuaries have evolved many fascinating methods to protect themselves from these variations. Species richness within the estuary is characteristically high, as the few species that can eke out a living make good their advantage. Conversely, species diversity is characteristically low. Estuarine dwellers are often species that could equally be found either in marine (approximately 35% salinity) or freshwater (less than 3% salinity) environments; typically competition from other species drives them to this relative haven. Many other anadromous[1] and catadromous[2]

---

[1] Anadromous: those organisms that ascend into rivers, via estuaries to spawn.

[2] Catadromous: fishes descending periodically for spawning from the upper reaches of a river to the lower parts of the river (estuary), or to the sea.

species use the estuary as their habitat for at least some of their life. Best known are the eels and salmon, that spend a part of their life cycle in these waters. The estuary is also an overwintering area for shoals of sprat and herring (Leatherland & Halcrow, 1988). There are many other species that also use the estuary in a similar fashion, for instance the large populations of birds that use it as a staging post in their migrations (Bryant, 1987) and for their permanent habitat (eg. curlews).

The Forth exemplifies many of the problems typical to estuaries. There are many demands upon the estuary, including the requirements of large scale industry, amenity and leisure. In Britain estuaries are a focus of major concentrations of population and industry. Hence from an economic perspective estuaries are often regarded as sinks for water-borne emissions derived from these activities. Ecologically, an estuary is a delicate environment, and the environmental management strategies employed in it must reflect this.

3.2   The Forth River Purification Board

It is the brief of the Forth River Purification Board (FRPB) to monitor and manage water quality in the Forth watershed. The estuary itself is a fraction of the total area under their see. The FRPB list their 'Purpose, Objectives and Performance' in Appendix Three of their 1989 Annual Report (FRPB, 1989, 54). This is supplemented by the FRPB Annual Plan 1989/90, in which key objectives are highlighted. These are: to make further improvements in water quality; to ensure compliance of discharges within the consent conditions; to improve sampling and analytical programmes; and to develop the analytical capabilities needed to achieve these objectives.

3.2.1   Organisational and Operational Aspects of the FRPB

The FRPB 1989 Annual Report lists 71 full-time and 8 part-time staff. The internal structure is divided into Sections, each with a specific remit, including: Pollution Prevention (16 staff), Chemical (12 staff), Hydrological (9 staff), Biological (6 staff), Tidal Waters (11 staff), Data Processing (3 Staff), Administration (17 staff) and the Consents Registry (1 staff member).

In April 1990, the FRPB relocated their headquarters to the Heriot Watt Research Park, Edinburgh, situated in the campus of Heriot Watt University. They also retain regional offices in Alloa and Glenrothes.

The FRPB is empowered to grant and monitor consents to discharge; currently they monitor and process approximately 450-500 consents per annum. It should be noted that under current legislation, the FRPB could not set up a Tradeable Permit System, although they were prepared to entertain the idea as long as their position of intermediary, with control over trades of permits, was enforced.

In the event of a breach of consent the FRPB enter into a predefined series of communications with the offender that, at worst, may result in a case being put before the Procurator Fiscal. Breach of consent is a pollution incident outside the limit allowed. The FRPB recognise two 'levels' of pollution. First, if an event is slightly over the limit, it results in a series of letters of increasing severity to the offender. If re-sampling demonstrates no improvement, the issue is passed from the District Officer, via the Senior Officer, to the Management for further consideration. The second pollution event is that where a gross breach of consent is made, perhaps deliberately or by accident. In such Class 2 cases the FRPB act quickly to take witnessed samples, thus providing evidence for ensuing court cases. There were 24 cases involving Class 2 pollution incidents cited in the 1989 Annual Report. The maximum fine for a Class 2 discharge pollution has been increased from the previous sum of £2,000 to £20,000 (Water Act, 1989), although the FRPB would prefer some form of 'rolling fine' where a continuous breach was fined, for example, on a daily basis. In all cases, the immediate concern of the FRPB is to ascertain the nature and extent of the problem, deal with it and with any subsequent consequences.

The FRPB undertake to collect data for many aspects of environmental quality relating to the watershed of the estuary and the Firth of Forth; these surveys are given in Table 3.4. The FRPB operate 24 hour automatic samplers (not continuous but periodic), at many of the major discharge points along the estuary. In an interview they noted that vandalism was making this job increasingly difficult (FRPB, Personal Communication, 29.5.89)

3.2.1.1   The Future for the FRPB

Although water privatisation does not directly affect Scotland, there are many knock-on effects. For instance, the 1989 Water Act fully implemented the 1974 Control of Pollution Act as intended for Scotland. The new organisation of the water industry in England and Wales is similar to that currently operating in Scotland. The FRPB sees this convergence of approach as an advantage.

The FRPB recognise the ever increasing importance of EEC legislation; not only that now in place via EEC Directives, but also that imminent as European market integration progresses. The FRPB is responsible for implementing and monitoring compliance with a number of EEC Directives in its area. Those listed in the FRPB 1989 Annual Report (see Table 3.3) are those for which effluent discharge and environmental data were collected.

Table 3.3   EEC Directives pertinent to the management of the Forth estuary

76/160/EEC	On the Quality of Bathing Water
76/464/EEC	On Pollution Caused by Certain Dangerous Substances Discharged into the Aquatic Environment
77/795/EEC	On the Exchange of Information on the Quality of Surface Fresh Water
78/659/EEC	On the Quality of Freshwaters Needing Protection in Order to Support Fish Life
79/923/EEC	On the Quality of Shellfish Waters
84/156/EEC	On Limit Values and Quality Objectives for Mercury Discharges other than the Chlor-Alkali Electrolysis Industry
84/491/EEC	On Limit Values and Quality Objectives for Discharges of Hexachlorocyclohexane
85/513/EEC	On Limit Values and Quality Objectives for Cadmium Discharges
86/260/EEC	On Limit Values and Quality Objectives for Discharges of Certain Dangerous Substances Included in List I of the Annex to Directive 76/464/EEC
88/347/EEC	Amending Annex II to Directive 86/280/EEC

The progress toward EEC integration in 1992 is likely to bring increasingly stringent EEC water quality legislation. This will, therefore, become of increasing importance to the management of the FRPB's activities. Current differences between the European and UK viewpoints, will need to be resolved, for example, the issue of quality and 'intended use'. The recent North Sea Conference also set out the likely future of the management of water quality in Scotland and marked the start of a move away from the application of EQOs to the more uniform 'Fixed Limits' or 'Standard Emission Controls'.

The FRPB will continue to develop their computing and data storage facilities, and it is envisaged that the entire consent dataset will be fully computerised (see Section 3.2.1). Also, the FRPB are increasingly interested in the applications of environmental information systems. As part of this interest, they intend to evaluate, with a view to future purchase, a Geographical Information System (GIS) which will interface with the databases, described in Section 3.3.1. below, which are already in place.

Research interests will continue to be pursued by the FRPB, with Universities, Polytechnics and other research institutions. The 1989 Annual Report (FRPB, 1989, 29) outlines several of their collaborative interests.

3.2.2   Management of the Forth Estuary

In order to make informed management decisions, it is important to have a comprehensive view of the state of the estuary at all times. The manager should have the means to assess water quality along the whole estuary concurrently, and the effects of a discharge at one geographical point ought to be understood in terms of the entire water body. In the Forth estuary, this is facilitated firstly through the systematic use of a network of monitoring stations, maintained both in the estuary itself and along the many rivers and burns feeding into it, and secondly by the means of environmental water quality models running from data collected in the field. In the Forth estuary the monitoring stations and computer models are operated by the FRPB. Data is collected on many aspects of the environmental state of the estuary, including the biological and chemical water quality, an analysis of sediment and fauna, the levels of trace metals and rates of flow. At the present time, the FRPB has records from eighteen surveys that have been conducted over differing periods, the earliest of their surveys having commenced in 1957 (see Table 3.4).

In the Forth estuary, the FRPB has adopted a target EQS for monitoring purposes of a minimum estuarine dissolved oxygen (DO) level of 4 mg/l, which is implemented as a 95 percentile of 4.5 mg/l (FRPB, 1988, 44). When all EQOs and EQSs are met, the Forth estuarine waters would attain Class A in the current estuarine classification system.

In order to see if such EQO and EQS levels are being achieved it is essential to undertake detailed empirical investigations into the actual patterns of pollution in the estuary. Such a study forms a base-line upon which the various measures of water quality can be ascertained, and the impact of current pollution control practices on water quality be assessed. This chapter provides an empirical analysis of pollutants in the Forth estuary, in order to assess the effectiveness of current environmental standards, whilst also determining ways in which Water Quality Indices (WQIs) can be used for indicating change in the spatio-temporal pattern of pollutants in the estuary.

Section 3.3 describes the sources of the water quality data for the estuary, and the databases involved. Section 3.4 then describes the analyses undertaken upon them.

3.3   Data Sources

To facilitate the storage and retrieval of the information they collect, the FRPB uses a Relational Database Management System (RDBMS) which allows comparisons to be made, with ease and flexibility, between different datasets. The use of Structured Query Language (SQL), specifically Oracle SQL*Plus[3] run on a Digital Wax 11/780

---

[3] ORACLE SQL*Plus, Oracle Corporation, Belmont, California

Table 3.4   A summary of the surveys undertaken by the FRPB in the Forth estuary

Survey Name	Purpose of Survey	Begun	Frequency of Survey
1 Forth Estuary Water Quality	To assess the chemical status of the waters	1957	18 per annum
2 Firth of Forth Water Quality	Assess chemical status of the waters of the Firth	1977	Yearly
3 Firth Shellfish Waters	Check compliance with EEC directive of designated waters	1981	Quarterly
4 Bridges water column	Assess seasonal trends and export of materials	1987	Weekly
5 Water Quality Monitoring Stn	Provide continuous record of water quality near Alloa	1987	Servicing visits
6 Cadmium Directive Shore Sampling	Compliance with EEC directive	1985	4 per annum
7 Inner Firth of Forth Metals	Check compliance with DOE EQS for List 11 substances	1985	4 per annum
8 Lower Estuary Trace Metals	Monitoring compliance with EEC directives	1983	4 per annum
9 River Carron Surveys	Provide water quality data for predictive model	1986	4 during summer
10 Estuary Sediment Survey	Assess physico-chemical status	1979	Every two years
11 Seafield Sediment Survey	Assess physico-chemical status of sediments	1979	Every two years
13 Mussel Watch	Determine 'hot-spots', assess long term changes	1981	Yearly
14 Mercury in Indigenous Fish	Assess concentrations in flounder and eelpout	1981	Annual
15 Largo Bay: Directive Monitoring	EQS compliance for PCP Cd and Gamma-HCH	1987	4 per annum (ex-PCP)
16 Leven Valley Sewer PCP Survey	Assess area affected by L.V.S. discharge in terms of [PCP]	1988	Undecided
17 Inverkeithing Bay PCP	To check EQS compliance of PCP discharge from Caudwells PM	1988	12 per annum
18 Port Edgar Pier Survey	Long term plankton survey	1981	2 per week
19 Forth Estuary Shore Survey	Assess Chemical Status of Estuary waters	1957	Periodic

Source: TCHEM (see below)

under DCL VMS and a Hewlett Packard HP 9000/835 Central Server under HPUX Unix, allowing the researchers to try different extractive approaches as required.

3.3.1   Water Quality Databases Maintained by the Forth River Purification Board
The FRPB operates three principal relational databases concerning the estuary and catchment, namely 'TCHEM' the

Tidal waters CHEMistry dataset; 'STARRS' the freshwater dataset and 'ROCI' the Register of Consents Index. Other databases are held; for example, those concerning hydrogeological survey information.

TCHEM is of primary interest as it holds all the data gathered from the eighteen FRPB surveys of the estuary and Firth of Forth (see Table 3.4). This data can be used to analyse water quality at present and over differing time periods. It holds information on all aspects of the nature and purpose of each survey, the determinands used and the methodology of sampling. TCHEM also holds a range of related general information, for example, the units of measurement for each of the 102 determinands. It is possible to cross-reference the relationships between different aspects of the water quality quickly and easily. The Freshwater database, STARRS (standing for Sample Tracking and Results Recording System) is similar to TCHEM, but it covers the rivers, burns and brooks under the see of the FRPB as opposed to the tidal waters. The database was computerised and first used around September 1988, and now contains some 300,000 results, being considerably larger than TCHEM. The Register Of Consents Index (ROCI) holds summary information on the 4,674 consents dealt with by the FRPB, of which approximately 500 are 'active'. It is, in essence, an automated reference to the full and exact records stored on paper at FRPB headquarters in Edinburgh although there are plans to store more of the consent information on the database. The register consists of the details of the nature of the intended discharge, the status of the application, the National Grid Reference (NGR) and the Hydrological Code for the proposed discharge points. Storing a geographical location is important to the design of an automated information system whose purpose is to examine the status of the estuary.

In this report analyses of the data, accessed from TCHEM using SQL, yielded descriptive statistics for each of the selected determinands which were supplemented by graphical representations of the changing patterns of water quality through time at specific monitoring stations. These assisted in the design of a one-dimensional non-linear dynamic water quality model of the estuary. Section 3.4 reports on the results of this analysis.

3.3.2 Selection of Determinands

Initially, analysis was restricted to the 16 determinands in Table 3.5 in order to align the results of our research on the Forth to a former study of the Clyde, (Mackay, 1975). The determinands were grouped into a three-fold classification; namely those concerning the physical-biological condition of the water, secondly nutrients and lastly trace metals. Extraction of data from the TCHEM database was subsequently confined to the following determinands: salinity, temperature, pH, DO, BOD and Ammonical Nitrogen.

Table 3.5   Classification of the 16 parameters used in the Forth estuary study

Physical-Biological	Nutrients	Trace Metals
Salinity	Nitrate	Zinc
Temperature	Nitrite	Copper
Dissolved Oxygen	Ammonia	Nickel
Biological Oxygen Demand	Phosphate	Lead
Chlorophyll	Silicate	Cadmium
Suspended Solids	–	–

3.3.3 Uses of the Forth Estuary

The Forth estuary, like other estuaries in the UK, is subject to different and often conflicting needs and uses (see Table 3.6). Firstly, the water and shoreline/beaches are used for recreation, including swimming, fishing and sailing. The estuary is also a valuable ecological habitat, especially for birds (migratory and resident) residing on the mud-banks. Water is taken for use as a coolant and as a process input for manufacturing plants located along the Forth, and also for the power stations at Kincardine, Longannet, Cockenzie and Methil. The estuary is further used as a repository for sewage and industrial effluent discharges. The upper reaches of the estuary have been affected by organic effluent from industries located around Alloa, (although due to a newly opened treatment plant at one particular site this should constitute less of a future problem). This effect is exacerbated by climactic conditions and by the winding, narrow nature of the upper estuary and will be worst in high summer when flow is at its lowest and microbiological activity is at its highest. Water abstraction for both potable (in certain of the tributaries) and industrial usage further decreases dilution of pollutants in the water body. The lower reaches tend to be more affected by effluent from the petro-chemical works and oil refinery at Grangemouth. The estuary is also used extensively as a shipping canal for the civilian and Navy ports along its length.

Table 3.6   Some of the factors affecting, or placing a demand upon the water resource of a typical estuary

Industrial effluent discharge
Municipal effluent discharge – including sewage effluent
Power station cooling water discharge
Abstraction for potable supplies
Agricultural leachate run-off
Forestry run-off
Passing migratory fauna in estuary (ie. salmon, eels)
Needs as an ecological habitat for native fauna/flora (ie. Fish, benthic community)
Needs as a supporting ecological habitat for visiting fauna/flora (ie. migratory birds)
Needs of shell fisheries
Needs of commercial fishing
Needs of amenities (ie. recreational fishing, sailing, bathing and aesthetic appearance)
Needs as a shipping channel

These various uses of the Forth estuary produce different pollutants. In the upper estuary, the inputs of sewage and other organically rich discharges, combined with low flow and high temperatures in May-June, can result in severe oxygen depletion in the water column and increased organic enrichment in sediments and sediment load. This leads to decreased activity of estuarine fauna and ultimately even fish mortalities (Collett & Leatherland, 1985). The climate is a significant factor in oxygen depletion in the upper estuary. The pumping of cooling waters into the estuary may lead to thermal pollution of the water. Industrial effluent discharged into the estuary may also lead to pollution; industries along the estuary range from those concerned with paper making, yeast manufacture and aluminium sheet production to those of a petrochemical nature. Grangemouth, on the southern side of the estuary, has one of the largest petrochemical plants in Europe. Dredging activity for the shipping and submarine lanes can also disturb the ecology of the estuary, especially for the benthic mud dwellers; this occurs locally and in areas where silt resettles on the estuary bed.

Some of these activities can co-exist whilst others are potentially a source of conflict. It is part of the duty of the Forth River Purification Board to ensure that as far as is reasonably practicable these conflicting uses are accommodated within the limits of the Environmental Quality Objective (EQO). The FRPB sets consents within the EQOs and EQSs (see Hallett et al, 1989) to increase the health of the biological systems in the estuary. The state of the estuarine waters with respect to these levels reflects the potential or real problems at any time. In this study, 'water quality' is defined as the physical, biological and chemical characteristics of the water column in a reach of the river or estuary, all with respect to the ecological demands placed upon it as a habitat by its flora and fauna, and with demands placed directly and indirectly upon it by the population living around the estuary. In determining water quality it is important to recall the various, and often conflicting, uses of and demands upon the water-body which is to be protected. Other important factors to consider are the interactions between compounds in the water (both natural and unnatural) which may be additive or synergistically antagonistic. An example of an additive effect upon fish is that of the metals cadmium and zinc, where the combined effect is twice that of the individual metals alone (Open University, 1975). A synergism occurs when 'the sum effect of the whole is greater or lesser than the effect of the constituent parts' and it may be positive or negative. Environmental Quality Objectives set in the estuary must clearly reflect such interactions; the difficulty lies in the enormous complexities inherent between the many factors at play.

Modelling such combinations between all the physical, biological and chemical characteristics accurately is exceedingly difficult (Metcalfe, 1986; Moffatt *et al*, 1990a and 1990b). Nevertheless, as these interactions could result in a significant change to water quality in the Forth estuary, they must be accounted for. This is the principal argument in favour of Water Quality Indices, discussed in Section 3.4, as a measure of water quality.

3.3.4   Description of Major Discharges to the Estuary

In this report, data from the databases held by the FRPB have been supplemented by detailed information gathered regarding the major sources of discharge into the Forth estuary. These are the discharges selected by the economic and environmental water quality model. This is not, however, an exhaustive list of dischargers in the estuary, but in the case of the STWs and the selected industries, it represents the most significant inputs of BOD to the estuary.

3.3.4.1   The Sewage Treatment Works

The STWs discharging into the Forth estuary vary their level of treatment among: none at all, primary, secondary or tertiary level treatment. Primary treatment generally consists of settlement, screening and primary sedimentation; these achieve 50-60% purification of waste water. Secondary treatment is, however, necessary if the Royal

Commission standard of 20/30, i.e. discharged quality (in ppm) of BOD/Suspended Solids, is to be achieved. The secondary stage may consist of activated sludge treatment or aerobic digesters, and up to 95% purification may be achieved. Disposal of treated waste involves land dumps (Stirling and Falkirk districts); river or sea outfalls (Lothian region) or; incineration (Clackmannan). To clean waters beyond the 20/30 standard, a tertiary treatment is necessary and this may consist of micro-straining, land or chlorophyll treatment. None of the STWs discharging into the Forth estuary apply this level of processing and, indeed, by no means all achieve the 20/30 standard. Table 3.7 gives a breakdown of each STW's treatment level, current standard attained (if known) and location in terms of distance below Stirling (km).

Table 3.7   Sewage Treatment Works Discharging into the Forth Estuary

STW	Distance below Stirling Bridge (km)	Treatment Level
Stirling	5.35	2
Fallin	13.20	2
Cowie	18.85	2
Alloa (1)	21.55	1
Kincardine	28.36	1
Dalderse	31.31	1
Grangemouth West (2)	31.31	0
Kinneil Kerse (3)	34.83	1
Bo'Ness (4)	38.31	0
Bluthur Burn	38.66	0
Ironmill Bay Sewer	43.01	0
South Queensferry	50.41	1
Dunfermline	51.06	1

Notes on Table:
(1)   Alloa STW is being fully upgraded to secondary treatment level and will achieve the 20/30 standard in 1992.
(2)   Grangemouth West pumps directly into Dalderse STW
(3) & (4)   Bo'Ness and Kinneil Kerse are to be upgraded to secondary treatment level and should, therefore, attain the 20/30 standard. Details of the capital costs and running costs are held by the research team.

3.3.4.2 Industrial Inputs

The industries along the Forth vary widely in nature, and so also do the compounds discharged to the estuarine waters. Variations occur also according to the stages in the production cycle of the industries concerned. This is an exceedingly important point when considering the effectiveness of a monitoring and sampling regime. A 24 hour composite sample may well completely miss a discharge event of a particular compound due to the time of capture. The following table lists the seven industries most significantly contributing to a BOD in the estuarine waters.

Table 3.8   Selected Industries Discharging into the Forth Estuary

Industry Discharging a BOD into the Forth Estuary	Distance below Stirling, (km)
United Grain Distillers	15.70
Distillers Company Limited	21.83
Weir Paper Products Limited	26.58
ICI	31.81
BP Oil	33.78
BP Chemicals	34.13
GP Inveresk	51.66

United Grain Distillers have two consented outfalls. The first and most significant BOD source emanates from the process line in their Dark Grains Plant, being a single source from the dilution chamber for the process wastes. The second outfall comes from the coolers and the distillery sewer. This includes washing liquor from the CO_2 scrubbers which contributes a BOD.

Distillers Company Limited (DCL), part of Guinness plc., also have two outfalls. One is simply cooling water being returned to the River Devon. The second includes wastes from the yeast growing process, which is piped over 5 miles to the DCL outfall in the Forth near Alloa. The quality of the discharge has improved dramatically subsequent to the installation of a plant capable of retaining condensed mollasses solids, which are extracted and sold to the animal feedstuffs industry.

Weir Paper Products discharge the waste waters used in their paper making process to the Forth estuary via the Canal burn. Water is taken into the plant either from reservoirs, or from groundwater extraction; after use it is directed via a settlement machine to settling ponds from which water is partly purified and drained to the estuary. Solids are retained and currently go to consented landfill sites.

ICI operate one diffuser outfall located in midstream 2 km out from Skinflats. ICI Grangemouth make many hundreds of products, and operate many process lines. The effluent composition is therefore extremely complex, and will vary in time depending upon production stages. Effluents are collected across the plant and put through a Screening Plant comprising two sumps. The resultant effluent is pumped to the estuarine waters. ICI are currently planning substantial investment in their effluent treatment procedures.

BP Oil operate one outfall, located 1 km to the west of the River Avon. This is one of several outfalls operated by the BP group in the Forth estuary. The Oil Refinery effluent is put through a gravity separator and then discharged to the estuary. BP Oil plan to add secondary and tertiary plants to treat the refinery effluent in future.

BP Chemicals also operate an outfall to the west of the River Avon, and up until 12 years ago they discharged into the River Avon itself. Today, BP are planning to make significant investments in their treatment processes for the plant. Petrochemical pollutants give rise to a complex mixture of aqueous pollutants. These arise directly from the plant's process operation, and from contamination, by hydrocarbons, of surface waters run-off.

GP Inveresk operate two discharge outfalls. One merely discharges waters used for cooling purposes in the plant. The other outfall, however, discharges effluent from the paper mill plant, which is treated to consent conditions before being discharged direct to the estuary. The effluent contains fibres, clays and on occasion dyes and, again, the exact composition depends upon the current process in operation, for example upon which paper types or colour are being manufactured. No future investment in abatement equipment is currently planned by the company.

3.3.4.3 Rivers Discharging into the Estuary

The following table lists the seven main rivers considered as point sources of 'inflow' to the estuary. Note that Bonnywater is not included in this count, as it joins to the River Carron beyond the tidal limit and can thus be treated as having imposed any likely impact upon the waters of the Carron before they flow out.

Table 3.9   Rivers Discharging into the Forth Estuary

Rivers Discharging into the Forth Estuary	Distance below Stirling, (km)
Joining of the Rivers Forth and Teith	-5.60
The Allan Water	-3.10
Bannockburn	10.85
The River Devon	15.70
The River Black Devon	23.30
Bonnywater[1]	31.76
The River Carron	31.76
The River Avon	34.56

Notes: [1] - Flows upstream into the River Carron, considered in model as R.Carron

3.4   Analysis of Water Quality Data Held in TCHEM

From the TCHEM data, a graphical overview of water quality in the estuary and simple descriptive statistics were derived. The determinands chosen for direct analyses were: Biological Oxygen Demand, Dissolved Oxygen, Temperature, Salinity, pH and Ammoniacal Nitrogen. Table 3.5 shows the subset of the 16 determinands chosen as representing the six relevant determinands used in the environmental water quality model of the estuary constructed for the research (Moffatt et al, 1990c).

Overall, the levels of determinands shown below are largely acceptable and the estuary may largely be considered as unpolluted. From a national perspective the estuary is clean, and it should be remembered that the vast majority of Scotlands population and industry reside in the central valley and the Forth watershed. Recent reductions in overall levels of estuarine pollution have been effected by the installation of treatment processes by industries along the estuary. Some have ambitious plans for the next decade which will bring further reductions in estuarine pollution.

3.4.1 Graphical Description of Water Quality along the Forth estuary

Due to inconsistencies in the sampling regime of the FRPB, for example in depth and timing, it would be misleading to see the following series of graphs as wholly representative of the water column. Data are shown below throughout an entire year - 1988, chosen as the base year for the environmental model. Sources of effluent emissions to the estuary, according to distance below Stirling Bridge, are discussed above.

The following five graphs show values at different depths for the chosen determinands as measured throughout 1988. Depths taken were 0, 1, 2, 3, 4 and 5 metres respectively - single points alone indicate missing neighbouring data.

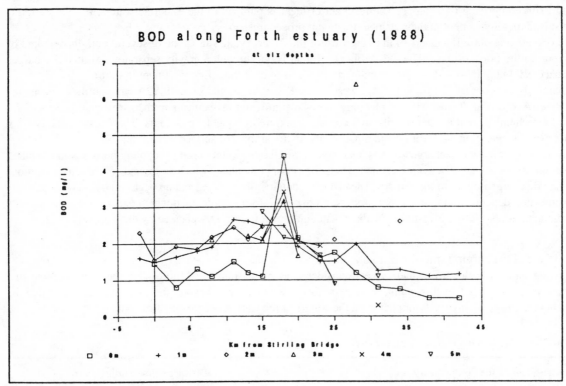

Figure 3.1 BOD values at depth in 1988

Figure 3.2 shows mean Dissolved Oxygen (DO) along the estuary. There is a clear sag downriver of Stirling Bridge. In part this is likely to be of natural origin due to the dense reed beds of the area, but it also corresponds to the site of a yeast factory discharge point. The estuary has a natural DO sag in its upper reaches due to the slow flushing of the water and the expansive flora along the shore. Further downstream, where flow is faster, and thus circulation and re-aeration, the natural DO levels are higher. Note that the EQS for DO is 4.5 mg/l. Figure 3.1 shows Biological Oxygen Demand (BOD) along the estuary. The peak matches the sag of DO in Figure 3.2.

Figure 3.3 shows that the mean temperature along the estuary remains constant at around 11 to 12 degrees celsius. There is some evidence of a rise at 15 to 16 kilometres from Stirling bridge. This corresponds to the site of Longannet power station, which pumps cooling waters to the estuary. It seems probable that this may be a cause of some degree of thermal change, but evidence from this graph is tenuous. A heightened BOD in the water is exacerbated by increased water temperatures. Tributary waters are themselves naturally warmer than the predominantly marine waters of the lower estuary.

Figure 3.4 measures Salinity and shows the characteristic transition from marine to fresh water conditions we would expect from a partially mixed estuary as the salt wedge intrudes up the water channel. The graph shows annual means at selected depths, but clearly, at given times of the year, tidal conditions cause the curve to appear

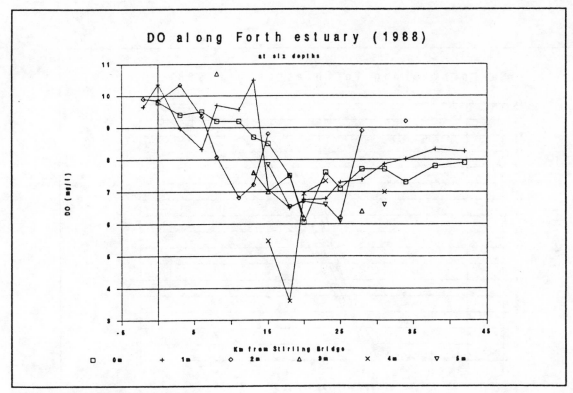

Figure 3.2 DO values at depth in 1988

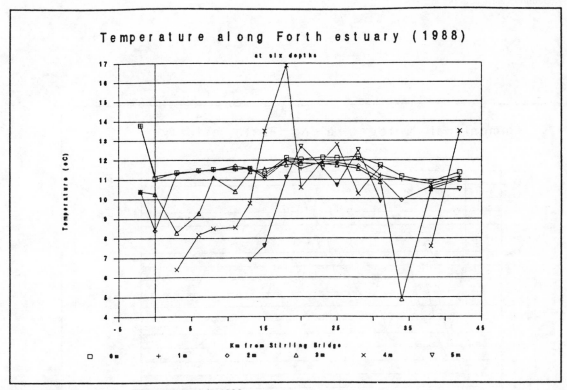

Figure 3.3 Temperature Values at depth in 1988

differently. This graph confirms the classification adopted by McLusky (see Table 3.1).

The following five graphs show values recorded at different times of the year for the chosen determinands throughout 1988. The months taken were February, May, August and November and, as mentioned, single points alone indicate missing neighbourhood data. Data is shown for an 'averaged' depth taken as a mean from data held for the selected depths as given above.

397

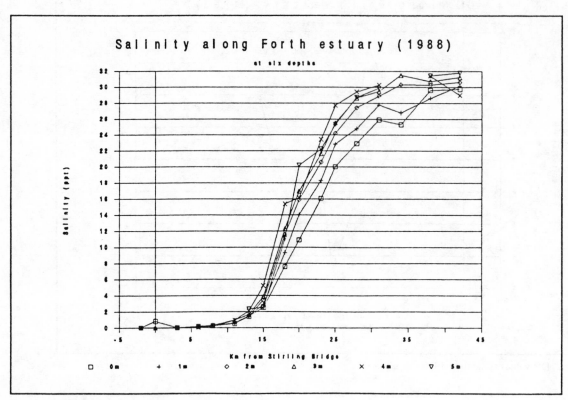

Figure 3.4 Salinity values at depth in 1988

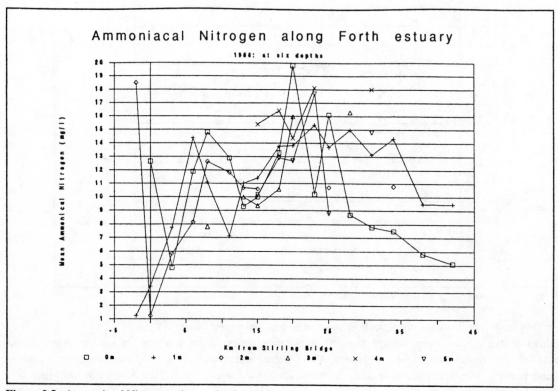

Figure 3.5 Ammoniacal Nitrogen values at depth in 1988

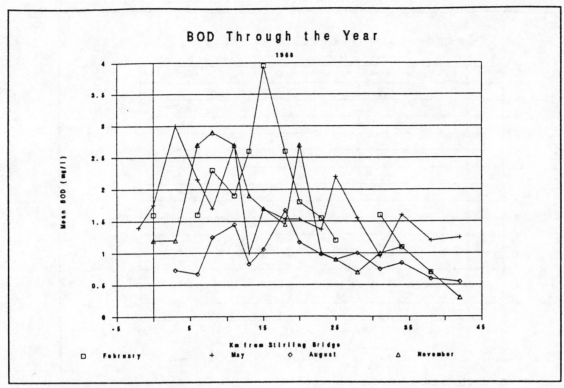

Figure 3.6 BOD values through 1988

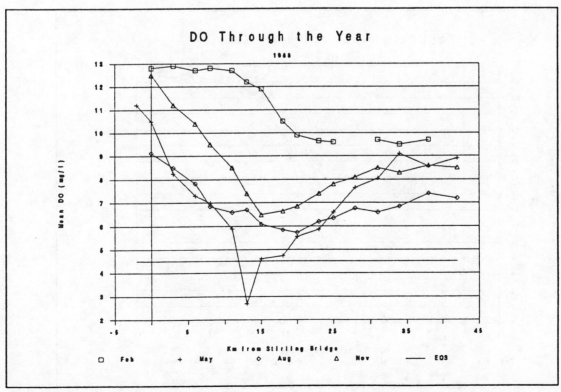

Figure 3.7 DO values through 1988

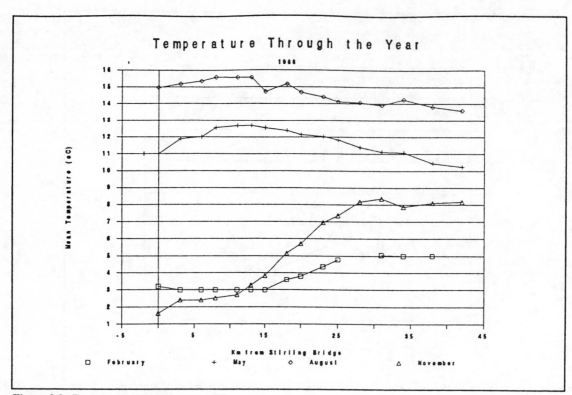

Figure 3.8 Temperature values through 1988

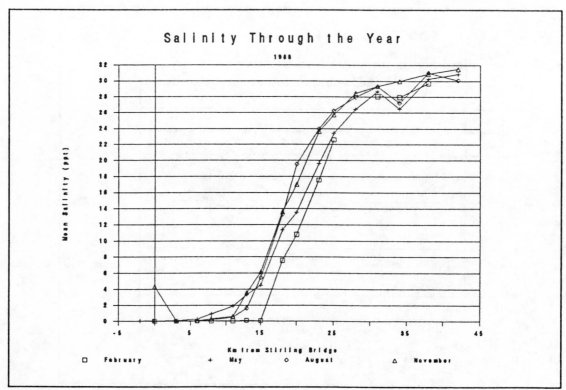

Figure 3.9 Salinity values through 1988

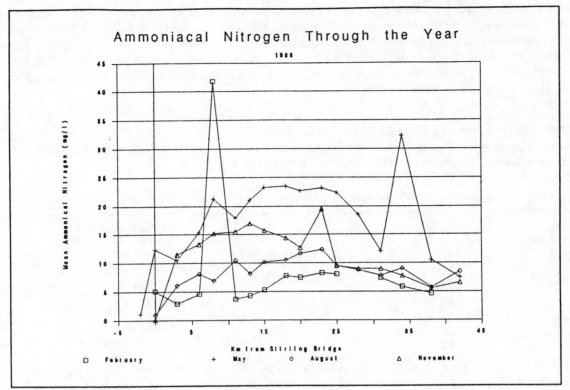

Figure 3.10 Ammoniacal Nitrogen values through 1988

Figures 3.6 to 3.10 above highlight changes found in water quality, still for 1988, but at different times of the year rather than at different depths in the estuary. In these graphs, the values are derived from an average of all the values found at the selected depths. From these graphs we can see clearly that management policies chosen must reflect these intra-year variations. Dissolved oxygen, as shown in Figure 3.7, is clearly lower in the summer months, and it can be seen that in May at least the EQS (marked on the graph - 4.5 mg/l) was breached. Temperature (Figure 3.8) shows the expected seasonal variation through the year. Salinity, Figure 3.9, shows little tendency to vary.

Figure 3.11 (below) shows changes over recent years in the values of DO and BOD for one specific sampling station, namely South Alloa (E20, typically a stretch of the estuary with summer BOD problems). The values were

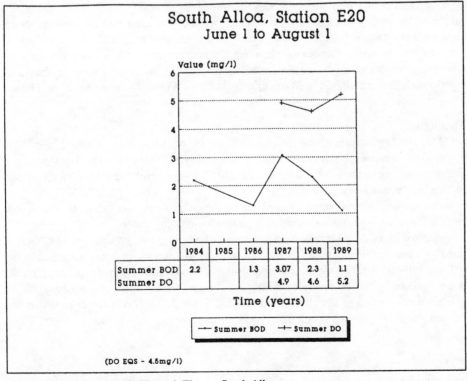

Figure 3.11 DO and BOD Through Time at South Alloa

read directly from the database TCHEM, and show the mean value during June and July (as opposed to previous graphs where data was given for the entire year), when the natural levels of stress are greatest upon the environment. Note that the database TCHEM has records for DO during these months from 1987 onwards. Specific interpretation is again difficult to make with such a short dataset, however, one can see that the last recorded DO value is greater than the first, and that the last BOD value recorded is less than its first. If this trend continues, it will represent an increase in the biological quality of the estuarine waters.

3.4.2 Statistical Description of TCHEM Water Quality Data

The mean and ranges were gathered for the 1988 Determinand Values for the Forth Estuary from TCHEM and, where appropriate, were compared to the EQS as adopted by the FRPB (Table 3.10).

Table 3.10 Comparison of Observed Data Values Against EQS Values

Determinand	Mean Value	Range of Values	FRPB Estuarine EQS
Salinity (ppt)	12.82	0.04–30.65	–
Temperature (°C)	11.34	10.55–12.67	–
pH	7.50	7.19– 7.93	6.0 - 8.5
DO (mg/l)	8.03	6.51– 10.23	Min 4.5 (95% ile)
BOD (mg/l)	1.78	1.08– 2.53	–
Ammoniacal Nitrogen (mg/l)	11.22	4.31– 16.15	1.5 uM

Note: Missing values in EQS column are for determinands without an EQS. Source of FRPB data: FRPB, 1989b

3.5 Water Quality Classifications and Indices

The previous section has described some of the patterns of water quality in the Forth estuary emerging from data held in the Forth River Purification Board's TCHEM database. Such patterns aid the understanding of the nature of the water body currently, historically and spatially. To aid operational management of the water body, a clear and comprehensive understanding of the complex dynamic interactions between the determinands in the estuary is required. Computer models of environmental water quality together with the data, offer one practical way to express these relationships, simulating these conditions within the waterbody (Moffatt *et al*, 1990b).

The aims and objectives of the water quality manager must be clearly defined[4] and are of crucial importance to interpretations and actions taken from the data. It is, therefore, essential for the manager to be able to classify water quality in a water body by chosen criteria and a number of classification systems exist. These vary not only in approach and aims, but also in ease of implementation and computerisation. There is increased interest in the more objective classification frameworks such as those offered by Water Quality Indices (WQIs) which are discussed below.

3.5.1 Fresh Water Classifications

Past systems, introduced in 1972 (by the Department of the Environment and the National Water Council) and 1975 (by the SDD), reflected river quality in terms of the physical, chemical and biological characteristics. The subjective nature of these methodologies, however, presented difficulties and the SDD subsequently developed their Water Quality Index (SDD, 1976), which we discuss further in 3.5.3.

In the case of UK rivers and estuaries, the currently adopted classification schemes are based on the above National Water Council proposals. There are separate classifications for fresh and saline waters.

The fresh water scheme, summarised in Table 3.11, sub-divides the water body into five groups, from 1A (Good) to 4 (Bad). Each class is defined by 'class limiting criteria' for each parameter, which must be achieved annually by 95 percent of the samples (House, 1980). Whilst this is undoubtedly useful for long or grossly polluted linear features like rivers it is still not necessarily the best way of portraying the rapidly changing quality of water in estuaries. Table 3.11A gives detailed description of the classification, while Table 3.11B shows the criteria that are used if Class Two is sub-divided. Table 3.11C gives a simple description of the classes.

---

[4] For instance the FRPB publish their 'Water Quality Objectives'

Table 3.11A The National Water Council Classification of Fresh Waters

River Class[1]	Class Limiting Criteria[2]	Current and Potential Uses
1A	DO Saturation > 80% BOD < = 3 mg/l Ammonia < = 0.4 mg/l	High quality water suitable for potable supply, abstractions and all other abstractions. Game or high class fisheries. High class amenity value.
1B	DO Saturation > 60% BOD < = 5 mg/l Ammonia < = 0.9 mg/l	Lower quality than Class 1A but useable for substantially the same purposes.
2	DO Saturation > 40% BOD < = 9 mg/l	Suitable for potable supplies after advanced treatment. Supporting reasonably good coarse Fisheries. Moderate amenity value.
3	DO Saturation > 10% BOD < = 17 mg/l Not Likely to be aerobic	Fish are absent or only sporadically present . May be used for low grade industrial abstraction. Considerable potential for further use if cleaned.
4	Inferior to Class 3 in terms of DO Saturation, and likely to be anaerobic at times	Grossly polluted and likely to cause nuisance.
X	DOS > 10%	Insignificant watercourses and ditches not useable; objective is simply to prevent nuisance developing

Source: Robinson, 1980

Notes on Table:

[1] Under extreme weather conditions (eg. flood, drought, freeze-up), or when dominated by plant growth or aquatic plant decay rivers usually in Classes 1,2, or 3 may have DO Saturation, BOD or Ammonia levels outside the stated values for those classes. When this occurs the cause should be stated along with analytical results.

[2] BOD determinations refer to 5 day carbonaceous BOD (ATU). Ammonia figures are expressed as NH_4. In most instances the chemical classification used above will be suitable. However the basis of the classification is restricted to a finite number of chemical determinands, and there may be a few cases where the presence of a chemical substance other than those used in the classification reduces markedly the quality of the water. In such cases, the quality classification of the water should be downgraded on the basis of the biota actually present, and the reasons stated.

Table 3.11B Criteria for the Sub-Division of NWC Class 2

River Class	Class Limiting Criteria	Current and Potential Uses
2A	DO Saturation > 50% BOD < = 7 mg/l	Waters suitable for potable supply requiring advanced treatment. Supporting good coarse fisheries and trout fisheries when artificial stocking takes place. Amenity value.
2B	DO Saturation > 40% BOD < = 9 mg/l	Waters suitable for potable supply after advanced treatment and the provision of adequate safeguards. Supporting reasonably good coarse fisheries. Moderate amenity value.

Source: Robinson, 1980

Table 3.11C A Simplification of the NWC Fresh Water Classes

Class	Description
1	Unpolluted, high quality. High class fisheries.
2	Doubtful, needing improvement. Undrinkable without treatment.
3	Poor, urgently needing improvement. Fish may be absent.
4	Grossly Polluted and likely to cause a nuisance.
X	Insignificant Watercourses and Ditches - not useable. .

Source: NWC, 1981; NRA, 1990

3.5.2 Classifying Water Quality in Estuaries

Estuarine waters are also classified into four corresponding categories (Portman & Wood, 1985). This classification was used by the National Water Council for the 1980 estuarine survey, when some 2,700 km of estuarine waters were examined. The classification accounts for several determinand parameters, including dissolved oxygen, biological quality and aesthetic quality. The classification was designed to:

a. enable a simple assessment to be made of the state of the nation's estuaries, and,

b. enable changes in the quality of estuarine waters to be recorded, particularly changes in water quality resulting from measures to reduce pollution.

Priority in the classification was to be afforded to the 'intended use' of the estuary, eg. passage of migratory fish, fishing, shell fisheries, wildlife, amenities such as sailing, bathing and appearance etc. and the needs of industry (Portman & Wood, 1985). Local factors were also to be considered in addition, such as the physical nature of the estuary, management objectives and the availability of funding.

The riverine survey classifications were considered by the DOE for use in the first estuarine surveys. However, a new system was devised due to the heavy dependency of the riverine system on chemical criteria for which good estuarine data was not widely available. Also the chosen riverine parameters were not always suitable or applicable to the marine situation, eg. suspended solids (Portman & Wood, 1985, 176). The estuarine classification quantified water quality in three distinct areas: namely chemical quality, biological quality and aesthetic quality. Separate surveys for these would be combined to give the final evaluation. In each case, points would be awarded for the state as found - the more points the 'better' the state. For instance, in terms of chemical quality, a DO value of 60% would receive 10 points, whilst a DO of < 10% would receive 0 points. Values between these extremes have corresponding points awarded, but only according to the specified scale (intermediate 'in-between' values are not interpolated for points, instead the nearest 'point' on the scale is selected). Finally the points are added up (with no bias towards any one group), and the classification made (see Table 3.12).

Table 3.12 The National Water Council Classification of Estuarine Waters

Classification	Number of Points	Description of Quality
Class A	30–24	Good
Class B	23–16	Fair
Class C	15–9	Poor
Class D	8–0	Bad

Source: Portman & Wood, 1985

The Forth estuary has not been given an NWC classification due to the lack of hard data needed to evaluate the biological and aesthetic qualities of the water. Chemical quality can, however, be measured from information held in the TCHEM database.

3.5.3 Water Quality Indices

The divisions of the above classifications are made on the basis of expert opinion, leading to cross-comparison difficulties, and the breadth of the classes may obscure essential information pertaining to actual change in water quality. A Water Quality Index (WQI) can be defined as 'a form of average derived by relating a group of variables to a common scale and combining them into a single number'. The advantages of a WQI over the NWC five-way classification are many. First, it is objective, as classifications are computed from concentrations of chosen determinands; the results are, therefore, comparable between separate water bodies which have been classified by different managers. The use, also, of continuous scales rather than restrictive classes offers exact scoring on a day-to-day basis and gives information as to immediate changes. If required, 'groupings' can be identified from a range of 'scores' thus serving all levels of management needs. The use of a water quality index (WQI) allows 'good' and 'bad' water quality to be quantified by reducing a large quantity of data on a range of physico-chemical and biological determinands to a single number in a simple, objective and reproducible manner (House & Newsome, 1988). The WQI furthermore has been demonstrated (Tyson & House, 1989) to:–

Table 3.13 Strengths of the Water Quality Index

– detect annual cycles and trends in surface water quality

– to highlight river reaches which have shown a change in quality over a specified period

– to reflect both clean and polluted rivers alike and allow rivers to be placed into ranked order thus indicating spatial variations in water quality

– differentiate between rivers within the same NWC Class and indicate where class thresholds have been approached or crossed

– adequately reflect potential water use thus providing information to operational managers in terms of EC Directives for specific water uses

– assist in the evaluation of benefits to accrue from investment in capital schemes

The determinands chosen for the WQI should contain 'the most significant parameters of the data set, so that the index can describe the overall position and reflect change in a representative manner' (SDD, 1976,1). The most 'significant' parameters as used in the SDD index were those ten considered by the SDD and participating River Boards to be the 'most relevant in the assessment of general water quality' (SDD, 1976, 4). The following table gives the chosen parameters for the SDD water quality index.

Table 3.14 The Ten Chosen Parameters of the SDD Water Quality Index

Parameter	Units
Dissolved Oxygen	DO, as % saturation
Biochemical Oxygen Demand	BOD, as mg/1
Free and Saline Ammonia	NH3, as mg/l(N)
pH	–
Total Oxidised Nitrogen	TON, as mg/l(N)
Phosphate	PO_4, as mg/l(P)
Suspended Solids	SS, as mg/l
Temperature	T, as °C
Conductivity	g, as umho/cm
Escherichia coli	E.coli, as coli/100 ml

Source: SDD, 1976, 4

Management objectives may vary, thus the criteria upon which a WQI classification is based may also be altered accordingly (House & Ellis, 1980). WQIs are designed to address major 'uses' or 'needs' of the water resource, for instance potability and public water supply, the ability to support fish and wildlife populations (ecological), irrigation needs and recreational uses (House, 1981).

Clearly, any attempt to derive either a classification or a water quality index depends ultimately on the quality or the quantity of the available data for the given water body. In the case of the Forth, the data available in TCHEM gives researchers information covering the location of the surveys as well as the number of determinands over time. Unlike the NWC classification, a WQI is also ideally suited for computerisation (House & Ellis, 1987), and thus databases maintained, such as TCHEM, can offer the water quality manager almost instant access to the 'latest' computed classification. This allows information to be made available on an immediate basis, rather than as an 'annual' classification.

3.6 Discussion

This chapter has examined the manner by which the FRPB TCHEM data has been selectively examined within chosen parameters such as 'determinand type' and 'date'. Graphical analysis gives a good overview of the data, both historically and spatially. Difficulties with the integrity and frequency of the data within TCHEM have precluded the furthering of this analysis via, for instance, time series analysis. The year 1988 was selected as that of primary interest due to considerations made for the environmental modelling of the estuary (Moffatt *et al*, 1990b and 1990c).

For the wider purposes of this report, BOD and DO have been selected as the principle determinands of interest in the Forth estuary. It is fully realised that to focus upon only these factors may bely the effects of other perhaps more 'significant' determinands. However, in the Forth estuary at least, which is a relatively unpolluted estuary by UK 'standards', BOD stands out as the one accepted measure of pollution where current levels exceed target EQS levels. BOD is also a widely used and accepted 'index of pollution', and until comparatively recently was often one of a limited number of factors considered (now biological, chemical and aesthetic factors are considered). Perhaps the most important and decisive reason for the selection of BOD/DO as the major item of interest was that several discharges affecting BOD are to be found along the estuary both in the private and public sector. This has important implications for the aims of our wider ESRC funded research project, of which this report is only a part. It is the intention of this report to investigate the role that market mechanisms have to play in estuarine water quality management (Hanley *et al*, 1989). To this end it was necessary to establish a pollutant (or determinand) for which there could be a 'market' in the case study area, that is, the Forth estuary.

Clearly there are limitations in concentrating on one measure of pollution; these are fully acknowledged. Using BOD alone precludes the consideration of many compounds that may exert a great impact on the aquatic environment, for instance the Red List substances (SDD, 1988). However, it must be remembered that BOD was chosen to explore the potential of Transferable Discharge Rights (TDR) markets. If the research indicates that this approach is promising, then other measures of pollution may be chosen, such as a Water Quality Index, with discharge rights being denominated in terms of unit impacts on such an index, weighted according to the physical location of the discharge.

3.7 Conclusion

This chapter has reported on the pattern of water quality in the Forth estuary, Scotland. By drawing on an extensive relational data-base provided by the FRPB the spatio-temporal pattern of pollutants in the Forth estuary has been described. Generally, the levels of most significant individual pollutants in the Forth estuary have declined over the last decade; the water body of the estuary may generally be considered to be unpolluted. Pollution incidents will, however, occur both by accident (or intention) at any time of the year, and during the summer months when the natural stresses upon the environment (for example, the climate and low natural flow are compounded by other factors such as high abstraction rates). Clearly a predictive capability is of crucial importance to the manager of water quality.

The combination of classification schemes with spatial and temporal databases comprised of water quality data, such as TCHEM, allows the environmental manager a useful means of quickly and automatically assessing 'change' in quality. The finer the scale of the classification, the greater the potential resolution of the noted change. The latter point is one favouring water quality indices, which may be used at many scales - from fine to broad 'groupings', dependant upon the requirements from the classification. Clearly the potential is great for the development of environmental management information systems comprising elements such as Geographical Information Systems (GISs), Computer Models and Expert Systems, acting as monitors of 'quality control'. This is an area towards which future research efforts should be orientated.

It has been argued that water quality classifications such as the NWC system are best employed at the Directorate level of river authorities and that water quality indices should be restricted to the operational management level (House, 1989). Whilst there may be some merit in this approach, it would appear that with the recent emphasis on alternative ways for paying for water pollution control (DoE, 1989), and the ever increasing concern with the state of our waters, that Water Quality Indices should be used at all levels in the National River Authority and the River Purification Boards. We note, however, that the FRPB does not consider that water quality indices to be applicable to estuaries (Webb, 1989).

References

BRYANT, D.M. (1987) Wading Birds and wildfowl of the estuary and Firth of Forth, Scotland. *Proceedings of the Royal Society of Edinburgh,* 93B, 509-520, 1987.

COLLETT, B.A. AND LEATHERLAND, T.M. (1985) The Management of Water Pollution Control in the Forth Estuary. In. *J. Wat. Pollut. Control,* Vol. 84, pp. 233-241.

DEPARTMENT OF THE ENVIRONMENT (DoE) (1989) *Paving for Water Pollution Control: The Governments Consultive Proposals for Charging by the National Rivers Authority for Consents to Discharge into Controlled Waters.* DoE & Welsh Office, London, February, 1989.

FORTH RIVER PURIFICATION BOARD (FRPB) (1988-1989a inclusive) *Annual Reports.* FRPB.

FORTH RIVER PURIFICATION BOARD (FRPB) (1989b) *Water Quality Objectives.* FRPB Report A3/89.

HALLETT, S., HANLEY, N. AND MOFFATT, I. (1989) Water Quality and Pollution Control in the UK. Working Paper Two. River Pollution Control Unit, Departments of Economics and Environmental Science, University of Stirling.

HANLEY, N., HALLETT, S. AND MOFFATT, I. (1989). Why is more notice not taken of economists prescriptions for the control of pollution? Working Paper Three. River Pollution Control Unit, Departments of Economics and Environmental Science, University of Stirling.

HOUSE, M.A. (1980) Urban Stormwater Pollution, Research Report 4: *Water Quality Indices: A Management Tool.* Middlesex Polytechnic, June 1980.

HOUSE, M.A. (1981) Urban Stormwater Pollution, Research Report 5: *The Selection of Determinants for Water Quality Classification.* Middlesex Polytechnic, April 1981.

HOUSE, M.A. (1989) Urban Stormwater Pollution, Research Report: *Water Quality Indices As Indicators Of Ecosystem Changes.* Middlesex Polytechnic, April 1989.

HOUSE, M. AND ELLIS, J.B. (1987) The Development of Water Quality Indices for Operational Management. In. *Wat. Sci. Tech.* Vol.19, pp.145-154.

HOUSE, M.A. & NEWSOME, D.H. (1988) Water Quality Indices for the Management of Surface Water Quality. In. *Wat. Sci. Tech.* Vol 21. pp. 1137-1148.

LEATHERLAND, T.M. (1987). *The estuary and Firth of Forth. Scotland: Uses and Aims.* In McClusky, D.S. (Ed.) *op cit.* pp. 285-297.

LEATHERLAND, T.M. & HALCROW, W. (1988) Water Quality Management in Scotland - the estuary and Firth of Forth. in. Newman, P.J & Agg, A.R. (Eds) (1988) *Environmental Protection of the North Sea.* Heinemann Professional Publishing, WRC. Oxford.

MCLUSKY, D.S. (1989). *The Estuarine Ecosystem.* Blackie, Glasgow.

MACKAY, D.W. (1975) Techniques for Pollution Control in Estuarine Waters. in. Helliwell, P.R. & Bossanyi, J. (Eds) *Pollution Criteria for Estuaries.* Pentech Press.

METCALFE, A.P. (1986) A 1-D Tidally Averaged Water-Quality Model for the Forth Estuary. FRPB Unpublished, Report. ES 3/86.

MOFFATT, I., HANLEY, N. AND HALLETT, S. (1990a) A Framework for Monitoring, Modelling and Managing Water Quality in the Forth Estuary, Scotland. Working Paper Four. Pollution Control Unit, Departments of Economics and Environmental Science, University of Stirling.

MOFFATT, I., HALLETT, S. AND HANLEY, N. (1990b) Modelling Estuarine Environments. Working Paper Six. River Pollution Control Unit, Departments of Economics and Environmental Science, University of Stirling.

MOFFATT, I., HALLETT, S. AND HANLEY, N. (1990c) A Dynamic Estuary Simulation Model. Working Paper Seven. River Pollution Control Unit, Departments of Economics and Environmental Science, University of Stirling.

NATIONAL RIVERS AUTHORITY (NRA) (1990) *Water Pollution and its Effects*. NRA Severn Trent Region.

NATIONAL WATER COUNCIL (NWC) (1981). *River Quality - the 1980 Survey and Future Outlook*. NWC, London.

OPEN UNIVERSITY (1975) *Clean and Dirty Water: Water Analysis Standards and Treatment*. Open University Press, Milton Keynes.

PORTMAN, J.E AND WOOD, P.C. (1985) The UK National Estuarine Classification System and its Application. In. *Estuarine Management and Quality Assessment*. ed Wilson, J.G and Halcrow, W., Plenum Press, New York.

ROBINSON, R. (1980) The Control of Pollution Act 1974: Implications for River Quality Management. *Journal of the Institute of Water Engineers*. March, 1980 vol. 34, No. 2.

THE ROYAL COMMISSION ON ENVIRONMENTAL POLLUTION (RCEP) (1974) Fourth Report: *Pollution Control: Progress and Problems*. HMSO, London.

THE ROYAL COMMISSION ON ENVIRONMENTAL POLLUTION (RCEP) (1984) Tenth Report: *Tackling Pollution - Experience and Prospects*. HMSO, London.

SCOTTISH DEVELOPMENT DEPARTMENT (SDD) (1976) *Development of a Water Quality Index*. Applied Research and Development, Report ARD3. Engineering Division. SDD, Edinburgh.

SCOTTISH DEVELOPMENT DEPARTMENT (SDD) (1988) *Inputs of Dangerous Substances to Water, Proposals for a Unified System of Control: Control of Dangerous Substances to Water (the 'Red List')*. December 1988, SDD, Edinburgh.

TYSON, J.M. AND HOUSE, M.A. (1989) The Application of a Water Quality Index to River Management. In. *Wat. Sci. Tech*. Vol 21, pp.1149-1159, 1989.

4 Estimation of Pollution Control Costs

Table of Contents

List of Tables

4.1 Methodology

Having identified Dissolved Oxygen levels (DO) as the principle pollution problem in the estuary amenable to a permit and/or charge system of control, we next set out to list all those sources in the estuary generating significant amounts of BOD. These sources are described in Chapter 3. A table of loadings by discharge type is given below. As can be seen, industrial sources account for 84% of all BOD loading in the estuary, and this domination will rise as planned improvements to STWs are carried out.

Table 4.1 1988 Discharges loadings of BOD: breakdown by discharge type.

In Reach	Input	BOD loading kg/day
	RIVERS	
2	Bannockburn	50.88
4	R. Devon	1013.80
7	R. Black Devon	67.45
10	R. Carron	283.18
14	R. Avon	367.94
16	Bluthur Burn	354.24
	SUB TOTAL	**604.86**
	STWs	
1	Stirling STW	460.00
3	Fallin STW	16.65
5	Cowie STW	16.01
6	Alloa STW	3088.00
9	Kincardine STW	159.27
10	Grangemouth W. STW	561.60
10	Dalderse STW #1	280.00
14	Kinneil Kerse STW	2750.00
15	Bo'Ness STW	1250.00
16	Bluthur Burn STW	354.24
17	Ironmill Bay Sewer	172.74
18	S Queensferry STW	820.92
19	Dunfermline STW	4034.88
	SUB TOTAL	**13964.31**
	INDUSTRY	
4	United Grain # 1	1650.00
4	United Grain #2	340.00
6	DCL	25000.00
8	Weir Paper	2000.00
11	ICI	20000.00
12	BP Oil	3000.00
13	BP Chemicals	10000.00
20	GP Inveresk	11374.00
	SUB TOTAL	**73364.00**
	TOTAL	**87933.17**

Rivers as percentage of total	**0.7%**
STWs as percentage of total	**15.9%**
Industry as percentage of total	**83.4%**

4.2 Industiral Sources

The gathering of data on BOD control costs for industrial sources was done in two stages, following on from discussions with people who had worked on the Tees estuary study. Stage One involved sending a 'Technology Questionnaire' to each firm. A covering letter sent with the questionnaire stressed the academic nature of the research project; the cost savings made in the USA under the ET programme; and the strict confidentiality in which the data would be held. The questionnaire (see Appendix 4.1) sought information, for each firm, on the following:

1. The number of processes and production lines that should be separately considered;

2. Inputs and pre-treatment of raw water to these processes;

3. Other raw materials used in the production process;

4. What products, and in what quantities, were being produced;

5. The nature, volume and variability of residuals from production; and

6. The treatment of these residuals (including the age and capacity of treatment plant, and labour requirements).

A follow-up interview was held with each firm to check on details revealed in the first questionnaire, to visually inspect treatment plant, and to discuss the second 'Abatement Cost' questionnaire (see Appendix 4.2). The Abatement Cost questionnaire presented respondents with three target reductions in their pollution output (a 10%, 25% and 50% cut) for two target dates: 12 months and 5 years hence. This second target reflects the average life cycle of production plant for firms on the estuary. For five of the industrial sources, these targets were in terms of BOD. For the two paper mills, they were in terms of SS, as their consents were specified with respect to this parameter. SS values were converted to BOD values using data from the FRPB. For each target/date combination, firms were asked to state how these reductions in BOD/SS were to be achieved. Not all firms were able to provide a breakdown of capital and variable abatement costs, therefore total cost figures are analysed for companies B, C and E.

4.3 Data Treament

For each target/date combination, for each firm, we first annualised capital expenditures necessary to meet the relevant targets, using a 6% real discount rate and assuming a lifespan of four years, in line with conventional accounting procedures. These annualised capital costs were then added to running costs, to give a total annual cost of meeting each target/date combination. Firms' *consented* 24 hour discharge levels were used to convert these figures into a unit cost per kilogramme of BOD discharge reduction per day. This gave, for each firm, three points on their short run (12 months) and long run (5 years) cost functions, corresponding to three 'steps' in each function (see Chapter 1).

4.4 Comments on the Cost Functions

The most interesting feature of the cost functions estimated (which cannot be revealed for reasons of confidentiality) is that, for several of the sources, per unit treatment costs fall as the total level of BOD reduction increases. This occurs, for source A, in both the short and long run scenarios, over all discharge levels for which we have information. For source C, unit treatment costs fall in moving from 25% removal efficiency to 50% removal in both short and long runs. Source B has constant unit costs over the 25% and 50% cuts, whilst unit costs fall slightly for source D in going from 25% to 50% removal in the long run.

For two sources, D and F, cuts in BOD greater than 10% are not possible within twelve months due to technical constraints, whilst source E would find it impossible to cut emissions by 50% within twelve months[1]. Where given reductions are possible in both the long and short runs, it can be noted that for most companies the long run abatement costs per Kg/day are either similar or, usually, lower than is the case in the short run. This is especially true for the 25% and 50% reduction bands. Notable exceptions are companies D and E, where heavy capital expenditure is envisaged in the long run.

Finally, we note that the contribution to total BOD discharges is very uneven across the six firms: this is shown more fully below:

---

[1] The fact that these forms *may* have ignored output restrictions as a way of cutting BOD emissions is discussed in Chapter 8.

Table 4.2   BOD Loading by Industrial Source

(DCL= 100)

Source	Loading
DCL	100
United Grain #1	6.6
United Grain #2	1.4
BP Chemicals	40
BP Oil	12
ICI	80
Weir Paper	8
GP Inveresk	45

Note: Calculated from consented discharge levels.

This table does not represent the relative impact of each Kg of BOD discharge from the six sources, as this depends, for each source, on its transfer coefficient.

We also note that the very fact that the marginal control costs currently vary so widely across dischargers indicates that the current location of control is inefficient. These differences can frequently be traced to past abatement investments in that sources who have improved discharges substantially in the past face higher marginal costs of further improvements, than sources who have made fewer previous improvements. This factor should not be seen as entirely explaining differences in marginal control costs, however, as these are also related to the nature of the process and products of each discharger.

4.5 Municipal Sources

As will be apparent from Table 4.2, STWs jointly account for 12% of BOD loadings discharged into the estuary. Improvement of the performance in STWs (in terms of reducing the BOD of their output) is principally achieved through works up-grading; from no treatment to primary stage, and from primary stage to secondary stage. Such up-grading is, in any time period, restricted by Scottish Office spending limits for capital projects imposed on Regional Councils; and on the amount within that budget that councils allocate to upgrading. Central Region Council's (CRC) water and drainage budget for 1989 was £5.2 million, of which £2.6 million was spent on sewage treatment. CRC estimate that an additional £10-£15 million (1990 prices) is necessary to meet current and forthcoming EC directives on water quality.

However, some improvement in STW performance may be possible without capital spending. In this section, we report our data collection process and results for improvements through both routes.

4.5.1 Improvements in STW performance without capital upgrading

We commissioned the WRc to appraise the potential for improving the performance of STWs on the estuary (or contributing to BOD loading in the estuary indirectly) without capital spending. What follows is a summary of their results: their results are spelled out in full in their report (WRc, 1991).

Decreasing the BOD in STW output without capital improvements is only feasible in works with secondary, activated sludge treatment. There are two such STWs located on the estuary (Stirling and Dalderse), and three discharging into tributary rivers (Denny, Bonnybridge and Polmonthill). The WRc, at our request, conducted detailed investigations at all these sites except Polmonthill. Activated sludge treatment lowers the BOD of settled sewage as it contains 'bugs' which digest organic matter. The activated sludge is mixed with settled sewage in activators, where oxygen is provided through injection or agitators. The resultant material is then settled out, the activated sludge returned to the process, and the remaining effluent discharged. This effluent usually has a BOD of around 10–12 mg/l, representing a 90% reduction in BOD concentration relative to the inflow concentration. BOD concentration can be reduced further by increasing the Mixed Liquor Suspended Solids (MLSS): a higher MLSS means more bugs working on the settled sewage. However, this route to BOD reduction is constrained by two factors:

1. The amount of aeration. More bugs need more oxygen, which must be introduced. This can be done by lowering the level of the activators. This increases power consumption.

2. The settlement capacity of the plant. As the MLSS is increased, there are more solids to be settled out. If insufficient settlement capacity is available, then the Suspended Solids (SS) level of the effluent will rise, pushing the BOD concentration back up. The settlement capacity is fixed by the physical size of the tanks; and by the 'settleability' of the input. This is usually measured as 'Stirred Sludge Volume Index' (SSVI).

Turning to the four STWs in question, the following was discovered:

Dalderse. Currently has a BOD output of 10 mg/l. This works serves a population of 50,000, and handles many trade effluents due to its location (close to Grangemouth). The MLSS was found to be currently 2700 mg/l (mean value), which could be raised at most to 3000 mg/l given constraints (1) and (2) above. This would reduce BOD by 5%. Due to the extra oxygen needed (about 3% extra), power costs rise by £1000 per annum. Increasing the MLSS above 3000 mg/l runs into a settlement problem.

Stirling. Stirling serves a population of around 50,000. It currently has a BOD output of 23 mg/l. This is due mainly to the poor settleability of solids due to the shallowness of the secondary settlement tanks. No further reduction in BOD is thus available by increasing MLSS, as the SS value would increase.

Bonnybridge. Serves a lower population (11,000) than either of the above two sites. The current BOD concentration of effluent output is around 12 mg/l, but settleability of the activated sludge is poor. Nevertheless, the WRC estimate that a 25% cut in BOD loading could be achieved by raising the MLSS. What is more, this improvement would involve no additional power costs as current aeration would not need to be increased. However, the poor settleability of the sludge may increase the SS level of the effluent. Bonnybridge STW discharges into the Bonny Water, a tributary of the River Carron, 7 km upstream of tidal waters.

Denny. Denny serves a population of 11,000 and currently has an effluent output BOD level of 11 mg/l. Clarification is good, and excess aeration exists at present. Given the low MLSS figure, this means that the BOD of effluent could be reduced by up to 25% for no increase in costs. Denny STW discharges into the River Carron 9 km upstream of tidal influence.

We summarise these results in the table below:

Table 4.3   Short run improvements in BOD at four STWs

Works	Current BOD Levels (Mg/1)	Current Loadings (Kgs/Day)	Possible Reduction in Loadings (Kgs/Day)	Annual Cost per KG/Day reduction in BOD
Stirling	23	620	0	Infinite
Dalderse	10	280	14	36
Bonnybridge	12	84	21	0
Denny	11	77	19	0

A problem in interpreting this data occurs in the case of the Denny and Bonnybridge works, since these do not discharge directly into the Estuary. Without a detailed model of the behaviour of organic pollutants in the River Carron, it is impossible to say precisely how changes in the BOD loadings from these two works will impact on DO level in the Estuary. In the water quality model, we incorporate the improvements by adjusting the loading coming down the River Carron into the estuary on a 1:1 basis, ie treating the works as if they were located at the tidal limit. This is obviously inaccurate, but is our only option at present. In the 'full' version of the economic model, this route is also followed: the two works are treated as sources on the estuary. However, given the very small size of their discharges, it is unlikely that this gives rise to significant inaccuracies.

Finally, we note that the reduction in BOD possible from Dalderse is very small, and well within the normal operating range of performance.

4.5.2 Improvements in STW performance when capital expenditure is permitted

In this section we report our efforts to gather STW cost data for the *long run* version of the full economic model. Our principle problems in gathering this data were that

1. Capital costs are very much site specific, and the Region thus only hold estimates for those sites where improvements are currently planned; and

2. The Region were, understandably, very cautious in their attitude to releasing detailed cost estimates to us.

We were able to gain data on the capital and running costs of improvements to three sites, which for confidentiality reasons we refer to in the table below as works A, B and C. Capital costs were annualised over fifteen years, in line with standard water industry practice at a real discount rate of 6%. This gave the following:

Table 4.4   Cost of long-run improvements in BOD at three STWs

STW	Annualised Capital Cost £/Year	Running Cost £/Year	Reduction in Loading Kg/Day	Cost per Kg/Day of BOD Reduced £/Kg
A	339,900	56,000	2576	153
B	133,900	30,000	1125	145
C	439,810	70,000	2708	188

These three sources of BOD reduction were incorporated into the long run version of the economic model, with appropriate right-hand-side capacity constraints.

Appendix 4.1

Technical Questionnaire

Efficiency, equity and uncertainty in the control of pollution: an economic analysis

Technology Questionnaire – please provide numbered answers on separate sheets

Section A

A1.   Name of firm, and name of contact person

A2.   How many processes/production lines do you operate on your current site that should be considered separately?

Section B: Water Requirements and Pre-treatment Processes
            (please make separate comments for *each* process/ production line

B1.   Where is the raw water used in the works initially obtained from?

B2.   Is any of the raw water pre-treated?   YES/NO

      If the answer to B2 is 'YES', please answer questions B3-B6. If the answer is 'NO', ~please go on to Section C.

B3.   Why does pretreatment occur?

B4.   What volume of water is pre-treated?

B5.   What residuals (if any) are produced by pre-treatment? In what quantities? What happens to them?

B6.   Is there a daily/seasonal variation in the quantity of pre-treatment necessary? If so, why and how much?

Section C: Individual production processes
            (please make comments for each process/production line)

C1.   What quantities and types of raw materials are used?

C2.   Is water used on an input? If so, in what quantities and from what sources?

C3.   Is water used as a coolant? If so, in what quantities and from what sources?

C4.   Are there any current *or* planned re-cycling facilities for water used at (C2) and (C3)?

C5.   *Flows from production processes*

      a.   *Products*

           What types of products are produced?

           What quantities are produced?

           Roughly how much of the water introduced into the process is included in them?

           For those products transferred to other processes, what quantity is transferred and to which process?

      b.   *Residuals*

           What types and in what quantities?

C6.   What is the daily capacity of the process?

C7.   Seasonal and daily variation of operations?

Section D: Residual Waste Treatment Processes

D1.   a.   For residuals from pretreatment processes:

           i.   Are they discharged without further treatment, if so where?

ii. If not then they must either be stored (which we will consider as just another treatment process) or they are treated in some other process. Where are these residuals treated?

b. Residuals from production processes:

i. Are they immediately discharged? If so where?

ii. Are they further treated? If so where?

D2. *For each treatment process*

a. Quantity and quality of residuals entering the process

b. Flows from treatment process

i. products – eg re-usable raw materials etc
   What quantity and where do they go to?

ii. residuals - what quantity and what quality?
   Are they immediately discharged? If so, where?
   Are they further treated? If so, where?

c. Seasonal and daily variation in the operation of the process and/or the release of residuals from the processes.

d. Capacity of capital equipment.

e. Age of capital equipment.

f. Proposed investments in treatment: what investments are planned at present?

g. The number and grades (including supervisory staff) of employees in treatment? If men are employed part-time please give the number of man hours per day.

h. What raw materials are used in the process?

i. Is water (other than that contained in the residual flow) introduced into this process. If so what quantities are used and what is its quality? Where does it come from?

j. Are there any recycling or reuse facilities for any of the water entering the process?

THANK YOU FOR COMPLETING THE QUESTIONNAIRE

Appendix 4.2

Abatement Cost Questionnaire

Forth Estuary Water Quality Management Research Programme Abatement Cost Questionnaire

1. Name of Firm:

2. Plant or process name/code number:

3. Please provide your best current estimates of the costs of meeting the following three hypothetical target improvements in the quality of discharge to the estuary/linked watercourse. For each target, we suggest two dates by which these aims should (again, hypothetically) be met. Here, we are only interested in BOD as a measure of polluting potential:

Estimated costs of reductions in BOD level of discharge from this plant/process (all values in £000s please).

Timescale – >	Within 12 Months	Within Five Years
Target One		
Target Two		
Target Three		

The targets are as follows:

Target One	Reduce BOD by 10% of current level
Target Two	Reduce BOD by 25% of current level
Target Three	Reduce BOD by 50% of current level

4. For each target/date combination, please provide information on how these targets would be achieved.
    For example, for target one within 12 months, your answer might look something like:

    'We would meet this objective by increasing the energy input to our treatment plant by x%. This, given current prices, would cost the sum given in the table.'

    For longer time periods, plant re-design (whether it would have occurred anyway or not) is clearly a 'treatment' option. Please provide your answers to Question Four on a following sheet. Please include any other information you think we should know about the assumptions you have had to make in arriving at your answers to both 3 and 4.

5. If your plant discharges Ammonium to the estuary and/or its tributaries, please provide estimates of the costs of meeting the following combinations of target reductions and dates.

Estimated costs of reductions in Ammonium level of discharge from this plant/process (all values in £000s please).

Timescale – >	Within 12 Months	Within Five Years
Target One		
Target Two		
Target Three		

The targets are as follows:

Target One	Reduce Ammonium by 10% of current level
Target Two	Reduce Ammonium by 25% of current level
Target Three	Reduce Ammonium by 50% of current level

6. For each target/date combination, please provide information on how these targets would be achieved. For example, for target one within 12 months, your answer might look something like:

'We would meet this objective by increasing the energy input to our treatment plant by x%. This, given current prices, would cost the sum given in the table.'

For longer time periods, plant re-design (whether it would have occurred anyway or not) is clearly a 'treatment' option. Please provide your answers to Question Six on a following sheet. Please include any other information you think we should know about the assumptions you have had to make in arriving at your answers to both 5 and 6.

THANK YOU VERY MUCH FOR YOUR CO-OPERATION

5 A Model for Predicting Water Pollution Control Policy Impacts

Table of Contents

List of Tables

List of Figures

5.1 The Economic Optimisation Model

The main purpose of the Economic Optimisation model is to allow theoretical predictions about the relative efficiency of policy options to be tested, using empirical data gathered for dischargers located on the Forth estuary. The principle policy options we are interested in are tradeable emission permits and emission charges. Both of these policy instruments are defined with respect to a water quality target specified in terms of Dissolved Oxygen (see Chapter 3). The model seeks to simulate the response of dischargers to these policy options, assuming that (a) firms know their own abatement costs; and (b) firms act to minimise costs. Local Authority discharges are currently handled separately, by predicting their demand for Dissolved Oxygen, and incorporating this demand in the Environmental Water Quality model.

The main characteristic of abatement cost curves in the estuary is that they are not smooth functions of the level of treatment, but rather are stepped functions. Figure 5.1 below shows this for a representative firm:

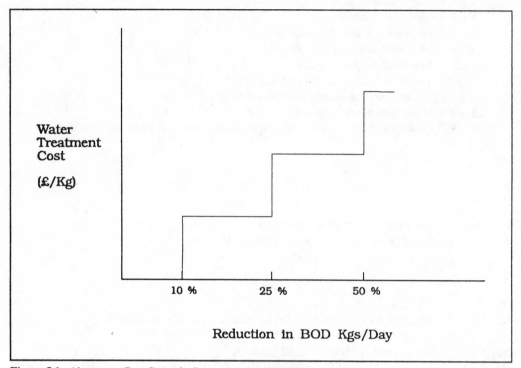

Figure 5.1 Abatement Cost Curve for Representative Company on Estuary

Follow-up interviews with dischargers confirmed that this pattern of discrete 'jumps' in the marginal control cost function were not mere artifacts of the way data was gathered. Investment in control equipment is indeed lumpy, whilst output reductions are not favoured by dischargers over the range of discharge reductions – over which we gathered data. Thus, meeting a 5% reduction in the BOD level of a discharge may require a firm to install an extra unit of treatment plant, as treatment plants may well be operating at or near their optimal design capacity.

Accordingly, a step-wise linear programming framework is adopted. The model seeks to minimise total abatement costs C_i, where:

$$C_i = \int (X_i)$$

for discharge reductions X from the i'th source. Each source is divided into n segments, where each segment represents a particular 'step' in the cost curve for that firm. Our abatement cost questionnaire (see Chapter 4) asked firms for information on the costs of meeting 3 target reductions in BOD: a 10% cut, a 25% cut, and a 50% cut. These form the steps in the LP model, where such a step was deemed possible by the discharger. If a particular cut was impossible in either the short run (12 months) or long run (5 years), then this step was not included in the objective function (Z) of the model.

5.1.1 The Constraint Matrix

Currently, we have data for six out of the seven relevant firms on the estuary. One firm has two separate plants discharging, giving a total of seven discharge sources. This means that, in 'industry only' mode, the objective function in the LP model contains 21 activities, where an activity is reducing BOD by 1 Kilogram (Kg)/day for each step/source combination. In the 'full' version of the model, activities are included for discharges from the four major sewage works on the estuary. Separate models are run for the short run and long run situations.

The constraint matrix for both LP problems is composed of 3 sub-matrices:

    i.   a step-wise tie-line sub-matrix (S_m)

    ii. a transfer co-efficient sub-matrix (H_m) and

    iii. a policy tie-line sub-matrix (P_m)

The S_m stepwise tie-line sub-matrix is necessary to prevent the programme allocating too much emission reduction to an activity. For instance, where marginal abatement costs are increasing, the programme would, if unconstrained, allocate all emission reduction for a source to the '10% cut' activity, which clearly has an upper limit. This produces a (i x n) size sub-matrix. It may also be necessary to introduce constraints to specify minimum abatement levels associated with individual activities where a discharger has decreasing marginal control costs: otherwise, small amounts of emission reduction would be allocated to a treatment process designed for large flows.

Step-wise tie-lines, together with the breaking up of discharges into a number of discrete levels of discharge quantity, also allows for economies of scale to be modelled, since firms are allowed to select large reductions in discharges (if this produces savings in control costs) rather than just marginal ones.

The transfer co-efficient matrix, H_m, controls for the spatial dimension in the model: in other words, it allows for the fact that a unit reduction of BOD from a given source will have different impacts on water quality at the J (J= 1,2,3...n) stretches of the estuary. These coefficients are derived from the water quality model run at low flow conditions, and form a (j x i) matrix H, where each h_{ij} value shows the impact on water quality on stretch j if source i increases or reduces emissions of BOD by one unit (1 Kg/24 hours). This translates into a (j x n) sub-matrix in the model.

The policy tie-line sub-matrix, P_m simply sets up, for any policy option, the constraints necessary to make the model work. For a permit market, we clearly need a constraint covering the buying and selling of permits, to match to a buying/selling activity in the objective function, Z. For the charge-policy, we need a similar set-up. The size of this submatrix depends on which policy is being simulated.

The step-wise LP problem, when the transfer co-efficients have been estimated, will thus constitute a [(j + i) * n] size constraint.

5.1.2 Introducing STWs into the Economic Optimisation Model

When emission reductions from Sewage Treatment Works (STWs) are brought into the model, then this increases the number of activities in the LP matrix. For works where capital improvements are necessary to reduce output loading, the short run version of the model is clearly inappropriate. We thus introduce one activity for each STW into the long-run version of the model. This only applies, however, to those STWs for which we have been able to get data on upgrading costs (see Chapter 4). Where loading reduction is possible without changing the capital stock, then such STWs can be included in the short run model. In all cases, a constraint row for each STW specifies an upper limit on BOD loading reduction through either the capital improvement and/or short-run improvement routes.

5.1.3 Model Output

The linear programming problems implicit in all model runs (see Chapters 6 & 7) are solved using the LINDO programming package. This uses the standard simplex algorithm to iterate towards the constrained minimum value for the objective function (the abatement cost function). The package, like most LP packages, produces three types of output, which are all essential to running the simulations. These are:

1. The optimal solution for a particular model run, giving the levels of all activities (amounts of emission reductions from each source), and the value of the objective function at the optimal solution. This is not necessarily the resource cost of each run, as it includes charge, subsidy or permit expenses which, as transfer payments, must be deducted from this objective function value to give a figure for resource costs. Also output are the values for all the constraint (right hand side) limits. This indicates whether a given constraint is binding in the optimal solution;

2. A sensitivity analysis showing, for each activity currently in the optimal solution, how much the value of this activity needs to change by before its level, or the levels of other variables, changes. Thus, for the activity 'charge BOD', the output shows by how much the charge rate needs to change to bring about a change in the least-cost solution. For those activities not currently in the optimal solution, the output shows by how much their value needs to change before they enter the least-cost solution. Thus, for example, if discharge Bx is excluded from the 25% reduction target optimum at a marginal abatement cost of £x per Kg BOD, the model shows by how much x must fall before Bx enters the solution;

3. A dual-value analysis. For all *binding* constraints, the model computes dual, or shadow, prices. This shows by how much the objective function value changes if the constraint is altered by one unit. They are computed from the dual of the LP problem (Chiang, 1967). Dual values do not exist for non-binding constraints, as if a constraint is non-binding ('slack'), it is in excess supply, and increasing this excess will not change the optimal solution. Dual values are thus equivalent to the Langrangean multipliers of classical constrained analysis, and may be interpreted as shadow prices. Frequently in LP studies they can be interpreted as the marginal value product of inputs.

5.1.4 Model Assumptions
As with any LP model, this model depends on three assumptions:

1. That there is no uncertainty over co-efficient values

2. That co-efficient values are stable

3. That all functions are linear

Assumption 1 may be relaxed by performing sensitivity analysis, or by generating coefficient values through a Monte Carlo process. Assumption 2 is saying that nothing in the simulation affects the co-efficient values, either exogenously or endogenously. There are clear parallels here with input-output analysis. However, if co-efficients (transfer co-efficients, for instance) are thought to change in some predictable way, then a dynamic programming approach could be used. This is, however, outsider the scope of the present model Assumption 3 holds in our model, since we model the stepped actual abatement cost functions by using a stepwise approach, as explained above. If, however, abatement cost functions were thought to be smooth, continuous convex functions of emission reduction levels, then quadratic programming offers a possible solution. This is clearly not an appropriate alternative in our case.

5.2 The Environmental Water Quality Model
One of the original aspects of the research was to develop a dynamic simulation model of water quality for the estuary. Unlike the steady state models of the estuary which are used by the Forth River Purification Board (FRPB) the new model known as the Forth Estuary Dynamic Simulation (FEDS) had to achieve four goals (Moffat *et al* 1990a, 1990b, 1990c). First, it had to mimic the actual value of water quality in the estuary using dissolved oxygen (DO) as the major state variable. Next, it had to address the input of effluent from the 20 point sources along the 56 km length of the estuary. Third, it had to produce results in such a way that it could interface with the geographical information system and the data base. Finally, and most importantly, it had to be able to estimate the transfer co-efficients ie, the impact of one point source in the estuary on other reaches of the estuary. These transfer coefficients were then used by an economic optimisation model in order to estimate if economic schemes were able to improve water quality in the Forth estuary.

5.2.1 Description of the FEDS model
The Forth Estuary Dynamic Simulation model (FEDS) is a one dimensional dynamic causal process model of water quality in the Forth estuary. The term one dimensional means that it explains the mean axial concentration of dissolved oxygen in mg/l along the 56 km length of the Forth estuary. It is dynamic, as distinct from a steady state model, in so far as it simulates the movement of water in the estuary over a 24 hour period which is approximately the duration of two tidal cycles. It is a causal process model, not a black box, as it includes several processes affecting water quality. The processes included are biodegradation, reaeration, diffusivity along the mean axial length of the estuary and suspended sediment inputs. It also includes tidal flushing, river input and the effluent discharges from the twenty point sources considered in this study. The model is by definition a simplification of the real estuarine system; in particular it does not address non-point source inputs to the estuary.

The materials balance approach forms the underlying framework for the FEDS model. This approach examines the quantity of materials involved in production, distribution, consumption and waste generation in an economy. In the case of the Forth estuary only the effluent discharged from the firms and sewerage works along the banks of the Forth will be examined.

Consider, then, the sketch map of a hypothetical estuary (Figure 5.2), which is divided into three reaches. Each reach being defined as the axial distance between one point source input and the next point source. The first input is river flow at the head of the estuary set arbitrarily at 450 units per hour. The value for the inflow of polluted water is say 25 units per hour and a second point source input is another 50 units of water added to the system. Hence, the total volume of water flowing to the sea is 525 units. If a measure of water quality is taken at the head of the estuary it can be ascertained that say a biodegradable effluent has a value of 2.4 units. Then by using the materials balance

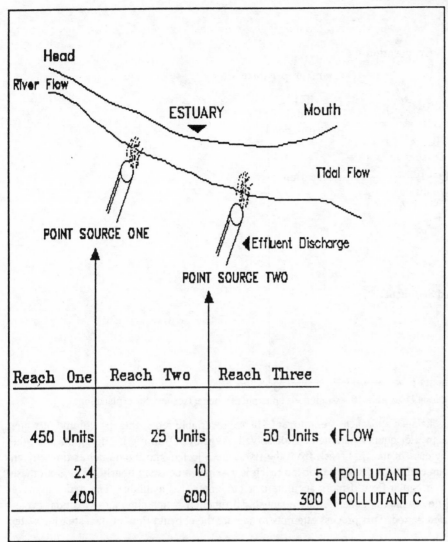

Figure 5.2 A Hypothetical Estuary With Two Polluted Reaches.

approach it is possible to calculate the impact of each point source of effluent discharged into the system when 2.8 and say 5.0 units of the same effluent are entered into the estuary. As the substances biodegrade then the value of the pollutants in each reach are 1.18 and 0.65 respectively. In this simple hypothetical example the transfer coefficients from one reach to another can also be calculated – although in a real estuary the twice daily tidal movement would cause a more complex pattern of pollution dispersion (Moffatt *et al*, 1990a). The way in which a more realistic pattern of pollution movement can be simulated in the Forth estuary based upon the materials balance concept is described below.

A convenient way of describing the causal processes in the FEDS model is by the use of a directed graph or digraph illustrated in Figure 5.3. First, for any reach the volume of water is calculated for the lowest river flow and tidal conditions in the twenty-four hour simulated period. In the model the main state variable is dissolved oxygen (DO) measured in mg/l although other biodegradable pollutants and conservative pollutants could be incorporated in the model. The input from any point source is represented as a mean hourly flow. The main feature of the causal diagram is the influence of the control feedback loop which links the actual water quality in any specific reach with the water quality objective used for pollution control. In the case of DO in the Forth estuary the environmental quality standard (EQS) is currently 4.5 mg/l. In the base run simulation should the predicted water quality in a specific reach fall below the EQS then the input into that reach is turned off in the model. In the real world, however, using the consent system the FRPB would endeavour to persuade the polluter to reduce their effluent input from this point source. Should this fail then legal action could be taken against the polluter. It could, of course, be argued that economic mechanisms, as distinct from the consent system of flexible regulation, could achieve this goal of improving water quality by use of economic incentives. In fact the FEDS model allows some estimates of the reduction in the physical amount of effluent discharged into the estuary from a specific point source to achieve a given environmental standard. The way in which this is captured in the model is described below.

As in other models of estuaries several processes are incorporated in the model and Figure 5.4 illustrates the flow chart for the FEDS model. These processes include hydrological and physical-chemical dynamics. With regard to

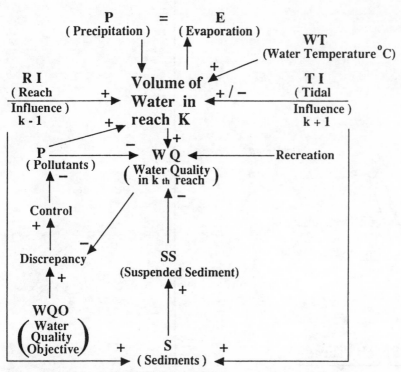

Figure 5.3 Water Quality Model: Causal Diagram   10 Assumptions underpin the model (see text for explanation).

the hydrological processes a mass balance approach is employed. The state variable represents the volume of water in one reach of the estuary and its water quality parameter is dissolved oxygen (DO) in mg/l. The inputs from the upstream adjacent reach or, in the case of the first reach from the river, are injected into the model as time driven functions. Similarly, the point source effluent discharge for the reach is given as a constant hourly flow. Both these inputs could be altered to capture irregular flow if more accurate discharge data was available. The major input of water into any reach is the tidal flow which is generated by a sinusoidal function which simulates two tidal cycles over the twenty four hour simulated period. This process attempts to capture the ebb and flow of the estuarine water during the simulation.

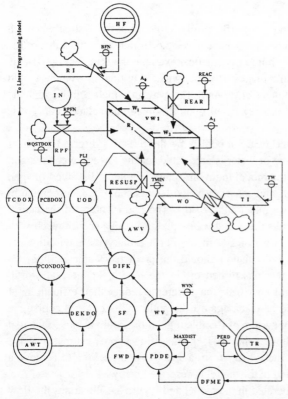

Figure 5.4 Flow chart for the Forth Estuary Dynamic (FED) Simulation Model (see text for explanation).

Several physical-chemical processes are also included in the model. The average water temperature in degrees Celsius is derived from the TCHEM database and fed into the model as time driven function. This parameter influences the rate of biodegradation. The most important process is diffusion along the axis of the estuary and this is governed by both the water velocity which alters during the tidal cycle and salinity which is derived within the model. Re-aeration in the atmosphere/water surface is included in the model as is the impact of suspended sediment from the bed of the estuary. Lastly, the water quality parameter is taken as dissolved oxygen measured in mg/l. In the model the concentration of decaying effluent is expressed in units of ultimate oxygen demand (UOD). As in earlier steady-state models of the Forth estuary it is assumed that there is a one-to-one relationship between the rate of decay of the effluent and the rate of decay of oxygen. As a first approximation the UOD is directly related to the five day biological oxygen demand (BOD5).

The FEDS model is written in a continuous simulation language (DYSMAP) and the set of simultaneous equations are solved using a finite difference method based on Eulers integration technique. The length of the simulated period is twenty-four hours and the solution interval is set at one hour. There are over three hundred active equations in the program which runs on IBM compatible 286 based micro-computers. The output is generated as tables and graphs on both enhanced graphic colour monitors or printers. Alternatively, the output can be transferred in ASCII code so that it can interface with the environmental information system (see section 5.3) including the geographical information system and the economic optimisation model.

5.2.2   Results of the FEDS model

The model was run to simulate the dissolved oxygen in the estuary for low flow conditions in May 1988. The empirical data used to calibrate and verify the FEDS model was extracted from the FRPB databases, TCHEM and STARRS, which collectively hold all the current and historical field data obtained from the FRPBs water quality surveys within the estuary (see Table 3.4). As the model requires hourly DO data for the entire estuary and this does not exist within the available databases - apart from the automatic recording buoy at Alloa - then some differences between the predicted and actual observations are to be expected.

In its present form, the FEDS model is able to capture the spatio-temporal pattern of dissolved oxygen in the Forth estuary reasonably well. The results of the latest run with the model are given in Figures 5.5 and 5.6. As can be observed the model tends to be within 2 mg/l of the observed measures of dissolved oxygen for most of the estuary. Two major discrepancies still exist, however, namely the oxygen sag and the tendency to over-predict the actual values of the dissolved oxygen for most of the estuary. The observed critical sag in the dissolved oxygen (DO) at a point approximately 20 km from Stirling Bridge, is not reproduced by the FEDS model simulation. However, the DO sag appears only as a major feature in summer months such as May 1988 (see Figure 3.7) - although studies of other estuaries have noted this sag effect. Several factors could explain the discrepancy between

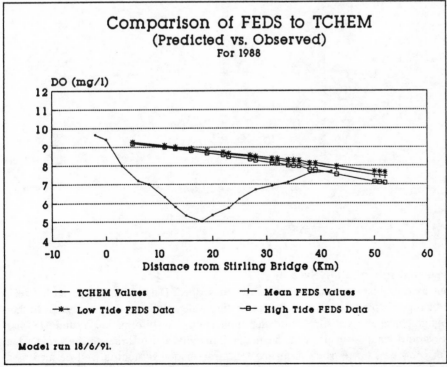

Figure 5.5 Dissolved Oxygen predicted by FEDS versus observed levels

the predicted and observed dissolved oxygen curve including the physical morphology and hence flow characteristics of the estuary at this location. These finer details cannot be satisfactorily addressed by one dimensional models and the data does not permit two or three dimensional models to be tested. Further research into incorporating other processes such as organic carbon, organic nitrogen and ammonia may improve the models performance. As such changes would require a new cycle of model building, sensitivity testing, calibration and testing these were not attempted here.

Unlike the steady state models of the estuary the Forth estuary dynamic simulation model (FEDS) is able to provide the transfer co-efficients along the estuary for any hour of the simulated run of the model. At a qualitative level the pattern of the impact of one reach on any other is given (see Table 5.1). As expected the matrices are not symmetrical. Obviously, each reach has an impact on itself but the pattern towards the mouth of the estuary is more complicated than that near the head of the estuary. Part of this pattern is due to the initial definitions of the reaches. If, for example the mid point between successive point sources had been used then a different pattern would emerge.

At a quantitative level it is possible to indicate the impact of each reach on others in the estuary over the 24 hour simulated period. Using the simulated data then the differential pattern of the impact of one reach on another is observed. Quantitative estimates of the transfer of dissolved oxygen contributions from one reach to others can be seen (Table 5.2). In particular reaches 9-20 show a complex pattern of interactions which may have important implications for applying economic based schemes in pollution control especially when it is recalled that these patterns are changing continuously.

Clearly, the geometry of the estuary and the way in which the point source reaches are defined do influence the pattern of the transfer coefficients. Again, more detailed investigations into the spatio-temporal patterning of water quality in the estuary would be required perhaps using three dimensional models before a more accurate picture of water quality in the Forth estuary could be given. Nevertheless, by setting the impact of the transfer coefficients to unity it is possible to use the linear programming model to ascertain the cost savings inherent in using market mechanisms to reduce pollution and hence improve water quality in the Forth estuary (see Chapters 6 to 8).

Table 5.1   The Matrix of Transfer Coefficients
Note: x : reach impacts itself (n)
             1 : reach impacts from (n)

0	1	2	3	4	5	6	7	8	9	10	11	12	13	14	15	16	17	18	19	20
1	X																			
2	1	X	1																	
3		1	X	1																
4			1	X	1															
5				1	X	1														
6					1	X	1													
7						1	X	1												
8							1	X	1											
9								1	X	1	1									
10									1	X	1	1	1	1						
11									1	1	X	1	1	1						
12											1	X	1	1						
13											1	1	X	1						
14											1	1	1	X						
15														1	X	1				
16														1	1	X	1			
17																1	X			
18																	1	X	1	1
19																	1	1	X	1
20																1	1	X	1	1

5.3   Construction of an Integrated Information System

In the above sections, the models used in this research are outlined and described. Data are interchanged between these models in order to allow a thorough exploration of the factors affecting water quality in the estuary. To further this analysis, use is made of both graphical and statistical computer applications. An Information System (IS) has been developed to interface the various component parts of the research activity and to bring to the project the advantages offered by the use of computers on research problems. The Information System is well defined as a 'system using formalised procedures to provide management at all levels in all functions with appropriate

Table 5.2   Quantitative Estimates of DO between Reaches

Reach Number	FEDS DO mg/1	Amount of mg/1 in reach n on other reaches
1	9.27	
2	9.09	
3	9.01	
4	8.93	
5	8.82	
6	8.73	
7	8.66	
8	8.55	
9	8.50	
10	8.39	
11	8.38	
12	8.30	
13	8.29	
14	8.28	
15	8.14	
16	8.13	
17	7.97	
18	7.96	
19	7.67	
20	7.65	

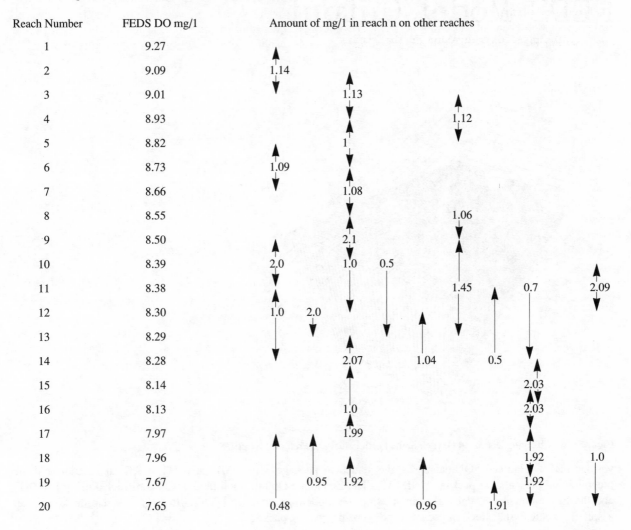

information, based on data from both internal and external sources, to enable .. timely and effective decisions for planning, directing and controlling the activities for which they are responsible' (Lucy, 1989).

The following section details how both economic and environmental computer models have been combined to offer a coherent way of assessing the fullest impacts of given policy measures upon the local industrial economy and the environment. The specific elements of the Information Technology referred to in this section include Geographical Information Systems (GIS), relational databases, mapping, modelling and statistical packages

The use of Information Technology in this project offers the researchers many benefits. The most important of these is the manner whereby a GIS allows the researchers to combine the inputs and outputs to/from the two models. In this study the Economic Optimisation model and the Environmental Water Quality model are linked so that the resultant raw data may be processed, stored and displayed graphically through the use of a Geographic Information System (GIS), thus allowing easy assimilation of relevant information by the manager. The latter point is important when considering the mechanisms by which the results of computer modelling are disseminated and presented for analysis. For example, a graphical description is excellent for demonstrating 'change' in environmental quality due to differing policy proposals, and in any case is easier for the reader to 'digest' than statistical tables. Figure 5.6 shows a three dimensional isometric plot of dissolved oxygen along the length of the Forth estuary, throughout the day, as predicted in an initial base run of the Environmental Water Quality model FEDS. Note that the Forth estuary unusually has four tides a day; the so-called 'Leaky' or 'Lackie' tides occur most significantly upstream of Grangemouth (Webb *et al*, 1987). Clearly the means by which information is represented is of enormous import when considering an Environmental Information System. This plot was achieved using the UNIMAP graphical mapping package on the University of Stirling mainframe.

5.3.1   Constituent Parts of the Information System
The Information System comprises the Economic Optimisation model, the Environmental Water Quality model, the

FEDS Model Output
Dissolved Oxygen Along Forth Estuary

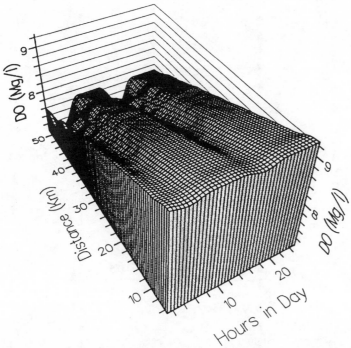

Figure 5. 6   Changing Dissolved Oxygen in the Forth Estuary as Predicted by FEDS

various FRPB relational SQL databases, the statistical package MINITAB[1], an AUTOCAD[2] application and the mapping and presentation package UNIMAP[3]. The Economic Optimisation model was constructed using LINDO[4], and the Environmental model was written using the modelling language DYSMAP-2[5]. Use is also made of other assorted graphical, statistical, spreadsheet and word-processing packages.

5.3.2 Integration of the Information System
It is only when these components are bought together that one may first explore the true environmental impacts of both policy and locational decisions relating to effluent discharges to the estuary. Figure 5.7 demonstrates some of the more pertinent flows of information in this system.

The Economic Optimisation and the FEDS Environmental Water Quality models interact in two important ways. Firstly the Economic Optimisation model produces new effluent discharges resultant from a proposed policy change for the control of estuarine pollution for the companies included in this study. These new values are input to the Environmental Water Quality model in order to permit the calculation of the resultant changes in estuarine environmental impacts. The GIS allows the generation of maps of 'change', both positive and negative, to these environmental impacts arising from proposed changes in management policy.

The second interaction between the models concerns the 'Transfer Co-efficients' from the water quality model, used to describe the migration of a pollutant both up and down the estuary from known point sources. These co-efficients are then used by the Economic Optimisation model to demonstrate the environmental impacts arising from the 'location' of a given industrial activity along the estuary. Therefore the spatial context of impacts may be more easily assessed when proposals regarding the siting of discharging activities to the estuary are made.

---

[1] MINITAB: The data analysis and statistical computer based package from Minitab Inc., PA, USA.

[2] AUTOCAD: IBM PC based CAD program from Autodesk Inc.

[3] UNIMAP: Part of the UNIRAS suite sold by UNIRAS A/S, Denmark.

[4] LINDO: Linus Schrage (1989) Scientific Press

[5] DYSMAP-2: the DYnamic Systems Modelling and Analysis Program, the product of the University of Salford Computing Services Section.

5.3.3 Observations on the use of the Information System as a Management Tool

It is clear that modern computer-based metholodogies offer many advantages over more traditional ways of collating, storing and interpreting data pertaining to natural resource management. A computer model is, however, by design a simplification of reality – allowing for the isolation of factors held to be most influential upon environmental impacts. As was discussed in Chapter 3, there are enormous complexities to a natural system, with synergisms and antagonisms of great subtlety. Accounting for these complexities in a thorough manner is a task of enormous proportion, but one of great importance when management decisions are based upon information resulting from this system.

One of the improvements that could be made to this IS, is its implementation on a microcomputer-based platform. The extensive use made of the mainframe resources in our IS puts it effectively beyond the reach of field-based application. Decreasing costs of powerful desktop computers and optical disk data storage media put this improvement within the foreseeable future.

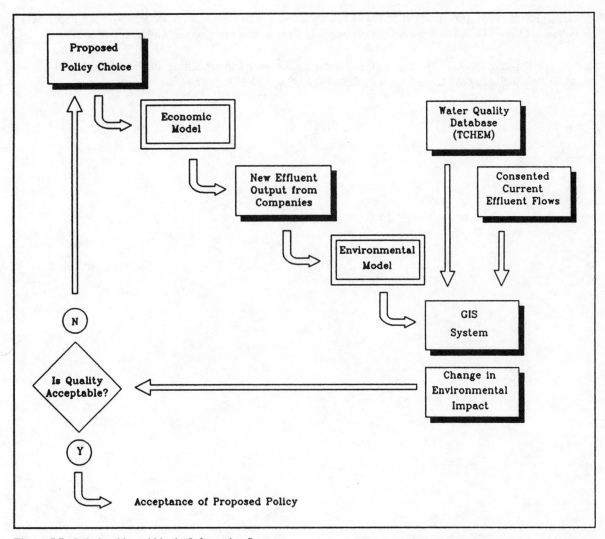

Figure 5.7 Relationships within the Information System

References

ANON. (1964). *Effects of Polluting Discharges on the Thames Estuary*. Water Pollution Research Technical Paper No. 11. Reports of the Thames Survey Committee and of the Water Pollution Research Laboratory. HMSO, London.

CHIANG, C. (1967) *Fundamental Methods of Mathematical Economics*, McGraw-Hill.

LUCY T. (1989). *Management Information Systems*. DP Publications Ltd. London.

METCALFE, A P. (1986). A One Dimensional Tidally Averaged Water Quality Model for the Forth Estuary. *Forth River Purification Board Report ES 3/86. FRPB*.

MOFFATT, I., HANLEY, N. AND HALLETT, S. (1990a) A Framework for Monitoring, Modelling and Managing Water Quality in the Forth Estuary, Scotland. Working Paper Four. Pollution Control Unit, Departments of Economics and Environmental Science, University of Stirling.

MOFFATT, I., HALLETT, S. AND HANLEY, N. (1990b) Modelling Estuarine Environments. Working Paper Six. River Pollution Control Unit, Departments of Economics and Environmental Science, University of Stirling.

MOFFATT, I., HALLETT, S. AND HANLEY, N. (1990c) A Dynamic Estuary Simulation Model. Working Paper Seven. River Pollution Control Unit, Departments of Economics and Environmental Science, University of Stirling.

WEBB, A J. & METCALFE, A.P. Physical aspects, water movements and modelling studies of the Forth estuary, Scotland. in *Proceedings of the Royal Society of Edinburgh*, 93B, 259-272, 1987.

6 A Tradeable Permit System for BOD Emissions in the Forth Estuary

Table of Contents

List of Tables

This Chapter reports the results attained from running the Economic Optimisation model under two scenarios: a policy of uniform emission reductions; and a competitive permit market which allows the least-cost pattern of emission reduction to be achieved. We also consider the case of emission reductions necessary to achieve the removal of the Dissolved Oxygen (DO) sag during low flow conditions (times of highest environmental stress) in the upper estuary. In all these cases, we have used Transfer Co-efficients set at unity. This is due to the current state of the Environmental Water Quality Model (FEDS), as described in Chapter 5. We comment on the effects of this simplification in Chapter 8. The ultimate goal of our work will be to specify targets in terms of DO levels directly, rather than indirectly as at present.

Whilst this chapter, and the following chapter on charges, concentrates on the direct efficiency properties of market mechanisms relative to uniform reductions, it is useful to recall here one other attribute of market mechanisms. This is that, by placing a marginal cost price on emissions, they create an incentive for dischargers to seek out the lowest cost way of managing innovation in pollution control. This property of market mechanisms is well known, and arises because firms make greater savings from switching to new, cleaner technology under a market mechanism than under regulation. These savings are made both in resource costs and in transfer payments.

6.1 Costs of Uniform Regulation Solutions

In this section, we report the costs of achieving a range of BOD loading reductions to the estuary from a policy of uniform reductions. This implies demanding that all dischargers reduce their BOD loadings by a given percentage (in the spirit of North Sea Conference undertakings), where this percentage equals the target reduction in total BOD loading. This figure, in turn, relates to desired improvements in DO levels.

We calculate these costs under two versions of the model:

    i.   the 'Industry Only' version

    ii. the 'Full' version

The 'Industry Only' version excludes Sewage Treatment Works (STWs): the 'Full' version includes them. We run the models for both long and short run situations and for *three* target total reductions in BOD loadings:

    i.   10% reduction

    ii. 25% reduction

    iii. 50% reduction.

6.1.1 The Industry Only Version, 10% Cut BOD Loadings, Uniform Reductions.

In the *short run*, all firms could achieve a 10% reduction in their BOD loading. A 10% reduction is equivalent to 6,199 kg BOD/day. This figure can be derived from the discharge levels reported in Table 4.1, excluding GP Inveresk's discharge (since we have no control data for this source it is excluded from the model). If all firms are forced to make this 10% cut, then the total cost is £1,076,060 per year. In the *long run*, all firms can make the 10% cut, with one source over-achieving due to indivisibilities. Here, the reduction increases to 6,499 kg BOD/day due to this over-achievement. The long run cost is £1,340,560 per year.

6.1.2 The Industry Only Version, 25% Cut BOD Loadings, Uniform Reductions.

In the short run, two sources cannot make the required reduction in the time span permitted. This means that a uniform 25% cut rule imposed on the remaining sources produces a BOD reduction of 14,247 kg BOD/day. The total resource cost is £3,546,550, or £248 per kg BOD reduced as the annual cost of making a one kg cut in daily BOD emissions.[1] In the *long run*, all sources can make the desired cut, which gives a total reduction in BOD loading of 15,497 kg. The total cost is £7,382,976 per year, which exceeds the short run figure again due to higher reductions. The costs per kg BOD reduced rises to £476 as, although sources which can achieve that cut in the short run face reduced costs in the long run, sources coming into the long run solution have very high abatement costs.

---

[1] Note the wording carefully. The '£ per kg BOD reduced' unit which occurs frequently from now on is a convenient shorthand for '£/year per kg BOD/day reduced'; 248 is simply 3,546,550/14,247, and the division makes no allowance for the different time units (year and day) involved.

6.1.3   The Industry Only Version, 50% Cut in BOD Loadings, Uniform Reductions.

In the *short run*, only three firms could achieve a 50% cut in BOD emissions. This gives a total reduction of 18,495 kg BOD/day, at an annualised (total) cost of £4,760,600 or £257 per kg BOD reduced. In the *long run*, all firms could make the cut, translating into a 30,970 kg BOD/day reduction, at a total cost of £15,059,050 or £486 per kg BOD reduced. Again, the long run/short run comparison is dominated by the high abatement costs of those sources coming into the long run picture. These more than offset reductions in costs for sources in both scenarios.

6.1.4   The Full Version

Here, we take the contribution to BOD loadings from Sewage Treatment Works into account along with the industrial sources.

The full model has two different versions, namely a short run and a long run version. In the short run, only adjustments in BOD that are achievable without changing the capital stock are permitted. As we reported in Chapter 4, such adjustments are limited to secondary stage STWs with sufficient settlement capacity – namely, in this instance, Dalderse, Denny and Bonnybridge. At most, a 25% reduction in loading is possible, at a zero cost, for Denny and Bonnybridge. Dalderse achieves at maximum a 5% reduction in loading.

In the *short run*, this new abatement produces the following results for the uniform reduction scenario:

Table 6.1   Cost of Uniform Reductions, Short Run, Full Version

Reduction in loading by each source	Total BOD reduction (kg BOD/day)	Total Cost/Year (£)
10%[a]	6,234 kg/day	1,177,060
25%	14,287 kg/day	3,546,550
50%[b]	18,495 kg/day	4,760,600

Notes: [a] includes Dalderse at 5%
         [b] no change over 'Industry Only' version

Comparing this with the 'Industry Only' version, we see that very little change has occurred in either the total BOD reduction or the annual cost. The largest change in BOD loading reductions is only 0.7% (10% reduction target), whilst the largest increase in total cost is a mere 0.09%. These very low figures are entirely due to the very small reductions in BOD which STWs are capable of making in the short run.

In the *long run*, much larger decreases in BOD are possible for STWs, through changing their plant. The current situation regarding such changes, together with cost estimates, was given in Chapter 4. For the uniform emission reduction scenario, combining industrial sources with STWs gives the following:

Table 6.2   Cost of Uniform Reductions, Long Run, Full Version

Reduction in loading by each source	Total BOD reduction (kg BOD/day)	Total Cost/Year (£)
10%[a]	6,499 kg/day	1,340,560
25%[a]	15,497 kg/day	7,382,976
50%	37,379 kg/day	16,128,660

Notes: [a] No change over 'Industry Only' version.

Here, as can be seen, the only change is to the '50% cut' version of events, since the capital improvements at each works which we have been able to cost produce at minimum a 50% reduction in BOD loading (for two out of three works, the reduction is much more than 50%). This is not to say that smaller reductions could not be achieved by smaller scale works, although the scope here is limited (an example is the deepening of secondary settlement tanks at Stirling STW aiding clarification of activated sludge-treated sewage). However, we have no data on such small scale improvements; and all works currently envisaged are concerned with large decreases in BOD concentrations by moving to the next stage of treatment.

For the 50% reduction scenario, the 'Full' version gives a 6,409 kg/day further reduction in BOD loading over the 'Industry Only' version, whilst total costs rise by £1.069 million *per annum*.

6.2 Cost of BOD Reduction in the Least Cost Solution

As is well known from economic theory (Montgomery, 1972), a tradeable permit market should, in competitive circumstances, result in the least cost solution to a pollution reduction target being attained. This, as was pointed out in Chapter 1, is because firms adjust emission levels and permit holdings until, at the margin, each firm equates its marginal control costs to the permit price. As there is only one permit price in equilibrium, then this is sufficient to ensure that marginal control costs are equated across all sources, a necessary condition for efficiency in pollution control. In an ambient permit market, prices are weighted by Transfer Coefficients meaning that, in equilibrium, the marginal cost of water quality improvement is equated across sources.

With this in mind, the first step in modelling a tradeable permit system is to calculate the least cost solution under the range of scenarios described above in Sections 6.1.1 to 6.1.4. This enables permit prices and least cost charge rates to be calculated by deriving dual values from the Linear Programming Model for the 'target reduction' constraint. These dual values are synonymous with the shadow price in each scenario and also with the lagrangean multipliers of classical constrained optimisation. We now proceed to a description of our results in this respect. In all cases, the target reduction in total BOD loadings is taken as that used (that is, the reduction possible) in the uniform emission reduction scenarios, described in Sections 6.1.1 to 6.1.4.. This is so that we can compare least cost and uniform reduction outcomes on an equivalent basis. Again, all Transfer Co-efficients are set to unity.

6.2.1 Industry Only Version, 10% Cut BOD Loadings, Least Cost Solution

In the *short run*, the necessary 6,199 kg day cut in loading is achieved in the least cost solution for a total of £255,552. The shadow price is £48 per kg BOD, which relates to the marginal cost of the next-cheapest source of discharge reduction not included in the current least-cost solution. Emission reduction is concentrated on three sources only: C, E and F, with source E achieving a large cut in emissions. For these sources, it would be cost effective to sell permits and reduce emission levels.

In the *long run*, the necessary 6,499 kg day cut in loading is almost all achieved by one (decreasing cost) source, with only one other source, F, entering the least cost solution. The resource cost of the loading reduction is £275,455 and the shadow price is £45 kg BOD/day.

6.2.2 Industry Only Version, 25% Cut BOD Loadings, Least Cost Solution

In the *short run*, the target reduction is 14,247 kg BOD/day. The least cost solution involves reductions in emissions by four sources (A,C,E,F) at a resource cost of £678,279 and with a shadow price of £57 kg BOD/day. However, this involves one source investing in capital equipment capable of effecting a 50% BOD cut, and utilising it at only one-third capacity. This is rather unrealistic, in that it seems unlikely that a firm would spend what in this case is a large sum on a machine and then run it at only a third of its operating capacity - unless, that is, expansion of the production process was planned for the near future. Nevertheless, the linear program does show this overcapacity to be the cheapest way for the firm to reach the desired effluent level. As a check, the model was re-run when adjusted to prevent this occurring. This resulted in an increase in resource cost to £738,984 and to a shadow price of £72 kg BOD/day. Abatement equipment is now used at a minimum 90% capacity in the solution.

In the *long run*, a total reduction of 15,497 kg BOD/day is required. The first attempt to calculate the least cost solution in this scenario gave a similar problem to that outlined above, namely, a very low rate (50%) of capacity utilisation at one source. This implied a resource cost of £687,856 with a shadow price of £48. Correcting for this gave a higher resource cost of £692,365 with a shadow price of £45 and a minimum capacity utilisation rate of 80%. Three sources were involved in the emission reductions.

6.2.3 Industry Only Version, 50% Cut BOD Loadings, Least Cost Solution

In the *short run*, the cut in loading necessary to make the least cost solution comparable to the uniform reduction calculations in Section 6.1.3 is 18,495 kg BOD/day. This is achieved in the least cost solution at a resource cost of £920,415, with a shadow price of £57 kg BOD/day. Four dischargers are involved in emission reductions, with source A, again, dominating.

In the *long run*, a much larger cut in BOD loadings was required, that is 30,970 kg BOD/day. This is met in the least cost solution at a resource cost of £4,209,965, with a shadow price of £381 and with almost all dischargers having to be 'switched in' due to the large cut in BOD required. Some of these dischargers, who do not come in to the 10% and 25% scenarios, have relatively very high marginal control costs.

6.2.4 Comparing Least Cost with Uniform Reduction Scenarios

The following tables draw together the information presented in this section, and in Section 6.1:

Table 6.3   Cost Comparisons, Short Run, Industry Only Version

Short Run	Actual Reduction in Emissions kg BOD/Day	Cost of Uniform Regulations £/Year	Least Cost Solution £/Year	Least Cost of % Regulations of Uniform Costs
10% BOD Cut	6,199	1,076,060	255,552	23.7
25% BOD Cut	14,247	3,546,550	678,279[a]	
			738,984	20.8[b]
50% BOD Cut	18,495	4,760,600	920,415	19.3

Notes on Table: [a] Unrealistic   [b] Takes higher figure for least cost

Table 6.4   Cost Comparisons, Long Run, Industry Only Version

Long Run	Actual Reduction in BOD kg BOD/Day	Cost of Uniform Regulations £/Year	Least Cost Solution £/Year	Least Cost Solution as % of Uniform Costs
10% BOD Cut	6,499	1,340,560	275,455	20.5
25% BOD Cut	15,497	7,382,976	687,856[a]	
			692,365	9.4[b]
50% BOD Cut	30,970	15,059,050	4,209,965	27.9

Notes on Table: [a] Unrealistic   [b] Takes higher figure for least cost

Taking the *short run* scenarios first, we see that in all cases, the least cost solution implies a resource cost of meeting the target which is at most 24% of the cost of meeting the same target via uniform regulations, a saving of at least 76%. As the total in BOD loading is made more severe, then the relative cost saving increases.

In the *long run* scenarios, flexibility in emission control again results in big savings over uniform reduction requirements, with, at worst, a reduction of 72% in total resource costs. The most impressive cost saving occurs for the 25% reduction target. Here, though, the relative cost saving falls as we move from a 25% to 50% reduction.

It should be recalled that all these results set all Transfer Co-efficients at unity. Solutions are, however, dominated by a large discharger with low marginal control costs and which is located at the most sensitive part of the estuary. This trend could only be reinforced by correct Transfer Co-efficients, yet the overall effect would be of a small degree as the discharge reductions from this source are, in almost all cases, set at maximum in the least cost solution.

6.2.5 Least Cost Scenarios in the 'Full' Version of the Economic Optimisation Model

In Section 6.1.4 above, we saw how little difference including STWs makes to the short run version of the model, due to the very limited capability of STW managers to reduce BOD concentration without altering the capital stock. We have thus omitted calculations of the least-cost outcome in the short run, and have concentrated on the long run situation. Also, since the minimum reduction in BOD loading involved in the capital works programme currently being planned/carried out is 50%, only the 50% reduction scenario was investigated. This involved adding extra activities and constraints to the Economic Optimisation model, as described in Chapter 5.

The STWs have marginal control costs significantly lower than some sources included in the least-cost solution to the 'Industry Only' solution. Including STWs reduces the resource cost of hitting the target to £3,075,989, whilst the shadow price on the emission reduction constraint falls to £357 (from £381 in the 'Industry Only' scenario). All STWs enter the least cost solution at the maximum level. Installing planned treatment improvements at the three STWs we consider is thus efficient in terms of a target of total BOD 'loading reduction' of 50% for the estuary.

6.3   Cost of Eliminating the DO SAG

As was shown in Chapter 3, the EQS for Dissolved Oxygen (DO) is violated in the estuary at low flow conditions in only a limited part of the estuary. This section, which corresponds to reaches 1 to 10 in the FEDS model/GIS representation, occurs in what the FRPB refer to as the 'upper estuary': that is, upstream of Kincardine Bridge. It is therefore relevant to consider what reductions in BOD emissions might be sufficient to remove this sag. Ideally, this desirable pattern of emission reduction could be verified using FEDS, but given the current state of the FEDS model, this is not possible. Instead, we questioned senior pollution prevention officials from the FRPB, to find out what emission reduction pattern they thought might be suitable. This pattern consists of:

1. Reducing the BOD loading of one firm from 75 to 30 tonnes per week, with maximum daily emission falling from 25 to 10 tonnes. This constitutes a maximum daily reduction of 15 tonnes.

2. Improving one STW's performance by installing secondary stage treatment. This would mean a reduction of 2.7 tonnes BOD in the daily effluent loading from that works (assuming no change in flows).

This constitutes a total reduction of 17.7 tonnes (17,700 kg) per day in BOD loading in the upper estuary. Current discharges are 41,462 kg day BOD in this stretch: we are thus looking for a 43% reduction. Interestingly, in the FRPB's view (meeting February 1st, 1991), this target could not be achieved by reductions in BOD loadings from sources downstream of Kincardine Bridge. Here, the main concentration of discharges is around Grangemouth (BP Oil, BP Chemicals, ICI, Grangemouth West and Grangemouth East STWs). However, these emissions are thought to have mainly local effects, that is, in that part of the estuary around Grangemouth or in reaches 12 to 18 in the FEDS model. This is because the natural decaying processes affecting organic effluents are 'dominating' pollution transport, compared with the movement of waters (the two incomings of the tide each day).

What the above means is that, to model the BOD loading reduction necessary to get rid of the DO sag around Alloa, we need to use a restricted form of the 'full version' of the economic model, which excludes all sources outside of reaches 1 to 10. This is equivalent to all sources within reaches 1-10 having a Transfer Co-efficient of one, with all those in reaches 11-22 having a Transfer Co-efficient of zero. This gives us 3 industrial sources (United Distillers, Weir Paper and DCL) and 2 major STWs (Stirling and Alloa). We calculated the long run cost of eliminating the sag by the FRPB's programme described above. This gives an annualised cost of £1,184,010. We then ran the restricted (long run) version of the economic model with a target BOD reduction of 16,800 kg day. This gave a comparable cost figure of £1,016,840, as other sources are bought into the least cost solution. The saving in resource cost is relatively small, however, at 14%. This is because the current plan comes very close to the least cost solution in terms of the pattern of abatement.

However, the least cost solution involves running an STW at only 56% effectiveness. This is obviously impractical. Forcing the improvement in each STW to be 'all or nothing' makes the least cost solution identical to the FRPB's current plan - which targets the two lowest marginal control cost dischargers, who also have significant impacts upon estuarine DO levels. Given the drastically lower savings here, market mechanisms are therefore hardly worthwhile in this case. More calculations with 'flexible regulation' for tougher environmental targets such as raising minimum DO levels in the estuary would be desirable.

6.4 Design and Operation of a Permit Market

The permit market we consider most suitable for the control of Dissolved Oxygen (DO) levels on the Forth estuary would have the following characteristics:

1. Permits would be specified in terms of kg of BOD per 24 hour period permitted to be discharged. Simplest of all would be that each permit allows a source to emit one kg of BOD per 24 hour period.

2. Permits would initially be distributed freely and pro-rata. This:-

    i. avoids the transfer payment problem associated with an auctioning of permits; and,

    ii. addresses the fairness issue, interpreted here as meaning that the initial (free) allocation should reflect current consented discharge levels (and thus current investment in abatement equipment). This is a working assumption only and does not necessarily constitute a recommendation for how a permit system on the Forth *should* be designed.

3. The total supply of permits would be such that, given the initial allocation, target DO levels are met at all points on the estuary. This would necessarily reflect the geographical location of dischargers. If current DO levels were viewed as acceptable, then each discharger would receive an initial allocation identical to either their *actual* or *consented* discharge, whichever was felt more practical and/or acceptable. Initial allocation based on consented discharge levels might result in a degradation of DO levels if current discharges are below consented levels, *and* if the switch to a permit system made dischargers want to increase discharges to the maximum level permitted. It is not immediately apparent why they should wish to make this change.

4. The permit system would be managed by the Forth River Purification Board.

5. Permits would be valid for a fixed period of time and it would seem desirable that this period should be determined by predicting the longest time period over which no upward revision in DO targets is planned or foreseen. This is due to the difficulties involved for the FRPB in reducing the total supply of permits, as compulsory purchase might arouse political objections whilst the buying up of permits on the open market might encounter financing difficulties. For example, the NRA has suggested to us that revenues from permit auctions or charges on permit allocations might well be removed by the Treasury from NRA/control agency budgets at the end of the financial year and thus would not be available for financing permit purchases.

   We recommend that this fixed period of time be no shorter than 12 months, and preferably stretching towards 36 months. Too short a time period would discourage capital investment in abatement equipment. Too long a time period would encourage hoarding.

6. In line with current cost-recovery proposals, a fee could be levied on all dischargers on a pro-rata basis when permits are initially issued. This fee would be set at a level Fi for each discharger:

$$Fi = (TCp \,/\, TD) \, x \, Di$$

Where:

TCp = total administration costs to the FRPB of setting up the permit system where these are incremental to existing administration costs.

TD = total discharges of BOD to the estuary measured in kg of BOD per 24 hours.

Di = source discharge (i) measured in kg of BOD per 24 hours.

TCp is estimated in Section 6.7; TD and Di are given in Table 5.2.1.

7. When a trade in permits between the two dischargers is proposed, the FRPB would apply the trading rule that: 'Trades are only permitted if they result in no violation of target DO levels at any receptor point in the estuary'. The FRPB would make this calculation by running the proposed re-allocation of discharges through a water quality model similar to FEDS i.e. disaggregated by discharge source. This is the 'pollution offset' rule, first introduced by Krupnick et al (1983). Total BOD loadings cannot rise above the total implied by the fixed supply of permits: no additional trading rule is thus necessary to control this. Alternatively, the 'modified pollution offset' rule of McGartland and Oates (1985) could be imposed, which states that trades are permitted so long as neither the pre-trade water quality level nor the ambient standard (in terms of DO mg/l), whichever is the most stringent, is exceeded in any stretch. This prevents one possible implication of the simple pollution offset rule occurring, namely that the simple pollution offset rule allows deterioration of water quality up to the EQS in any stretch. The FRPB would levy a charge on all transactions according to the administration costs incurred in enforcing the trading rule. These costs are estimated in Section 6.7.

   Where proposed trades lead to a violation of target DO levels, they cannot be allowed on a 1:1 ratio. In this case, buyer and seller could agree to the FRPB depreciating the value of permits to the buyer. For example, if United Distillers was proposing to buy 1,000 permits from BP Chemicals, this might lead to a decrease in DO levels below the target in the 'Alloa sag', due to United Distillers' location. Accordingly, the FRPB could depreciate these 1,000 permits whilst they remained in United Distillers possession by an appropriate factor, d, where $O < d < 1$. If $d = 0.5$, then United Distillers could increase emissions by 500 kg BOD/24 hours as a result of the trade. The value of d would depend on the ratio of Transfer Co-efficients for the two sources in the water quality model.

8. Once the lifetime of permits had expired, the current stock would be declared invalid. A new supply of permits would be issued in line with (revised) target DO levels. Again, the initial allocation would be pro-rata according to permit holdings on the expiry date of the previous tranche. Few sales would be expected near to the expiry date as firms might be unwilling to reduce their new, expected allocation.

9. All significant point sources of BOD would be subject to the permit system, that is, both industrial and municipal sources.

10. New firms proposing setting up on the estuary would need to bid for permits from existing sources. Alternatively, the FRPB could withhold a small pool of permits from the initial allocation for issuing to new entrants. This withholding would push up the equilibrium permit price and thus produce an increased level of abatement, relative to the 'no withholding' situation, until all withheld permits had been issued.

6.5 Impact of Market Size on Efficiency Properties

6.5.1 Theoretical Considerations

Most work on the impact of market size on the cost-saving properties of permit markets appears to have been done in auction, as opposed to grandfathering, systems. An overview of the literature is provided by Tietenberg (1984). Tietenberg sees the problem arising from one, or a few, large firms acting as price-setters, with a competitive fringe of dischargers accepting the market permit price, being too small to influence it individually.

The following factors are important in determining the degree to which sources will attempt to manipulate the market price:

1. The relative strength of demand for permits from the price-setting source compared with the demands of the competitive, price-taking fringe. If the price-setter's demand for permits, within the area of the cost-effective allocation, is only a small proportion of the total demand, then the source's manipulation of its demand will have little influence on permit price.

2. The shapes of the costs functions for both price-setting and price-taking sources are important as the slope of the price-setter's control function determines the degree to which it can gain from manipulating the price. Since the price-setting source causes price decreases by controlling more emissions (demanding fewer permits), the cost of this behaviour is determined by its marginal cost function. As Tietenberg has noted, 'The higher the marginal costs of control beyond the cost-effective allocation, the less the source is able to gain from a given reduction in demand because the costs of producing the compensating emission is so high' (Tietenberg, 1984). The cost function of the competitive fringe is also significant. For example, if their demand for permits was perfectly inelastic, then the price-setting firm could act as a monopolist, lowering permit price to zero while obtaining all the permits it needed.

    It is the *financial burden* of all sources which would be seriously affected by price manipulation and not the control costs themselves. The ability of any source to reduce its financial burden would be diminished when the demand for permits by the competitive fringe was reasonably price-sensitive. In this situation, any given price reduction would cause a larger increase in the demand for permits from the competitive fringe thereby causing a larger increase in the need for the price-setting source to control, that is reduce, its own emissions, which is an expensive requirement.

    It may be that on non-competitive behaviour grounds, auctioned TDRs are preferable to grandfathered TDRs, since the former results inevitably in more trades (if we include and classify initial bidding as 'trades', along with subsequent exchanges) than the latter. This means that permit markets are thicker in auction settings, thus reducing the likelihood of price-setting behaviour. Auction settings also allow the Pollution Control Authority (PCA) to minimise the possibility of strategic behaviour, by adopting 'Incentive Compatible Preference Revelation Mechanisms', such as the Groves second-price auction (London Economics, 1991).

6.5.2 The Mohawk River Study

The influence of market power on total control costs must be analysed with reference to the specific circumstances in which it operates; in this way some insight into the magnitude of its effects may be gained. There are few empirical studies which look into this. De Lucia's study of the Mohawk River (1974) concluded that the price-setting source does achieve a slightly lower financial burden than it would if no source acted as a price-setter. The effect of this on regional control costs was, however, negligible. In a hypothetical market with only two polluters (one a price-setter, one a price-taker and both with similar emissions, the permit price was found to be quite sensitive to the market structure, falling in the non-competitive market to less than half its competitive level (see Table 6.5).

From the above table, we note that the total control costs rise by only $3,090 in the noncompetitive market: an increase of less than 1%. The financial burden, that is control costs plus permit price, for both firms falls, however, in the non-competitive case. Price-taking firms show more benefit because the price-setting firms incur higher control costs in lowering the permit price. Obviously the higher control costs would need to be measured against the savings achieved, relative to the existing control system.

With respect to *grandfathered* systems, the potential for market power to be exercised depends on the initial (free) allocation, as this determines net demands and net supplies. (If the initial allocation corresponds to the least-cost solution, no net demand or supply will exist). If one source has either a large net demand or large net supply from the initial outcome, then they may be able to reduce their financial burden by using their market power to lower or raise the permit price. This will push the system away from the least-cost solution. So, if the EPA wanted to ensure that a permit market reproduced the least-cost solution, it would need to get the initial allocation exactly correct, for which it would need full information on all firms' MCC functions.

But how serious is this deviation from the least-cost solution if the initial allocation is not made on this basis?

Table 6.5   Non-competitive Function Markets and Financial Burden: The Mohawk River

The Mohawk River Study	Permits Purchased	Control Cost ($)	Permit Cost ($)	Total Financial Burden ($)	Permit Price ($)
Non-competitive Market					
Source 1: price setter	217	327,891	42,789	370,680	197.18
Source 2: price taker	283	142,446	55,804	198,250	197.18
Total	**500**	**470,337**	**98,593**	**568,930**	
Competitive Market					
Source 1: price setter	245.47	314,769	116,337	431,105	473.95
Source 2: price taker	254.53	152,478	120,635	273,112	473.95
Total	**500**	**467,247**	**236,972**	**704,217**	

Source: Tietenberg (1984) Discussion Paper D123. Adapted from de Lucia, R J *An Evaluation of Marketable Effluent Permit Systems*, Report EPA-600/5-74-030 to the US EPA (September 1974): Table 6-11, p.29.

Empirical evidence from Hahn (1984) is that unless a strong monopolist emerges, then control costs will vary little from the competitive level. Hahn and Noll (1982) found control costs varying very little when a strong monopoly power firm exerts partial control over the permit price. Finally, Maloney and Yandle (1984) looked at the formation of cartels in grandfathered permit markets. They found that the increase in control costs over the competitive market outcome varied as follows:

Table 6.6   Cartel Effects on the Permit Market: 85% Environmental Standard

Percentage Plants[a] owned by Cartel (%)	Percentage of Permits Cartelized (%)	Percentage Change in Costs[b] (%)	Percentage Change in Price[b] (%)
Monopoly			
90	91	41	697
80	81	30	292
20	67	26	271
10	44	3	47
Monopsony			
10	9	0.1	−0.5
20	19	0.5	−3.0
80	33	1.7	−7.8
90	56	7.7	−16.7

Notes: [a] Total plants selling permits, 8; total plants buying permits, 44.
         [b] Compared to the competitive permit market abatement cost of $25.5 million annually and price of $3537.24 per ton of pollution, both in 1975 prices.

Source: Maloney and Yandle (1984).

However, at worst (90% cartelisation with monopoly power), the non-competitive permit market achieves a 66% saving over the command and control policy, compared to a 75% saving with a competitive permit market.

6.5.3 The Forth Estuary

As has been noted elsewhere, only seven industrial sources would be involved in a market for BOD permits in the estuary and, whilst thirteen municipal sources (STWs) are involved these are owned by only three regional councils: this makes the maximum market size equal to ten traders (unless consumer groups are permitted to buy-up and withhold permits). For two of the three regional councils (Lothian and Fife), only one STW each, comes within the study area, the rest all being operated by Central Regional Council. These sewage works individually, and collectively, account for a small percentage of total BOD loadings.

If permits in the Forth were auctioned, then the implication of theoretical work is that the permit price would be higher than it would be in a competitive situation *if* price-setting firms emerge. Control costs, and therefore the efficiency properties of the system, are predicted to change by a very small degree. The possibility of a price-setting firm emerging can be judged by inspecting the BOD outputs and control costs of the seven industrial sources. As was noted in Chapter 4, two sources (A & E) have large emissions relative to total emissions (industry plus STWs), being 29% and 24% respectively. Their individual potential demands for permits thus could impact on permit price in an auction system. Moreover, source E faces relatively low marginal control costs, implying that it might benefit from increasing emission control, cutting its demand for permits and so driving down the permit price to reduce its financial burden. All other sources would then also enjoy a reduction in financial burden, but in line with theoretical findings we would not expect control costs to rise significantly over the least-cost solution.

With respect to the, arguably more attractive, grandfathered-system, predictions on non-competitive behaviour are much more difficult to make. Firms must offer both a supply schedule of permits, with supply price varying accordingly to quantity given up; and a demand schedule. The institution through which trade occurs has been shown to be important (McAfee and McMillan, 1987). If the FRPB acts as a clearing house for permit trades, every discharger would indicate its supply and demand for a range of permit prices. Here, as McAfee and McMillan have shown, the number of traders is immaterial, but the system will not converge to a competitive outcome. If trades are bilateral, then the number of traders becomes important, but no general result seems to exist in the literature.

6.6 Distributional Effects

We calculated the distributional effects of both grandfathered and auctioned permit markets. This section describes our methods and results. In 6.6.1 and 6.6.2 we show the payments and receipts that would result for individual firms from auctioned and grandfathered permits, and in 6.6.3 we present some measures of how equitable these payments allow marketable permits to be in comparison to 'flexible regulation'. In 6.6.4 we show the total transfer costs for the industry in different cases.

6.6.1 Auctioned Permit Market

The Economic Optimisation model was re-written to explicitly include an activity representing the bidding of firms for permits in an auction. We know the price that would clear the fixed supply, in any scenario, from the dual value analysis in the least-cost runs. To illustrate the distributional effects between firms, we use the 'industry only, 25% reduction in BOD loading, long run' version of the model. This, as described above, gives a shadow price of £48 kg BOD/day. A new tie-line forces firms to acquire one permit for each kg of BOD they wish to continue discharging, whilst a new constraint fixes the total quantity of permits available at 46,513 (ie. 75% of existing emissions). The model minimises the sum of permit expenditures and control costs. The model run produces the correct degree of

Table 6.7   Transfer Costs to Individual Firms of Auctioned Tradeable Permits (Industry only, long run, 25% cut in BOD)

Source	Permit Purchases	Permit Expenditure (£)
A	14,023	673,104
B	1,990	95,520
C	6,000	288,000
D	3,000	144,000
E	20,000	960,000
F	1,500	72,000
	46,513	2,232,624

Notes:
1. If permit price was increased to £49, source F would purchase 500 more permits.
2. The policy achieves a reduction in total emissions of 15,497 kg day.

abatement (as it must do, being quantity constrained) and indicates the following post-auction holding of permits, with associated permit expenditures:

6.6.2   A Grandfathered Market

Here, conclusions over distributional effects are very much affected by what degree of competitiveness rules in the permit market. We discussed the reasons for this, and the likely direction of effects extensively in Section 6.5.

In the results reported here, we have assumed price-taking behaviour, as at this stage we have not yet modelled non-competitive behaviour. If all agents are price-takers, then the permit market will clear at a price given by the dual value analysis of the least-cost solution. Subsequent trades are also dependent on the initial allocation of permits. For the 'industry only, long-run' version here, we look at the situation where all sources receive an initial (free) allocation equal to 75% of their current consented discharge. We also make the simplifying assumption that all sources are currently discharging at their consented levels.

Our results are given in the following table:

Table 6.8   Trades of Permits Resulting from Grandfathered Permits (Industry only, long run, 25% cut in BOD)

Source	Post-Trade Emission Level	Permits Sold	Permits Purchased	Revenue or Cost(–) from buying/selling
A	14,023	4,737	0	£227,376
B	1,990	0	498	–£23,904
C	6,000	1,500	0	£72,000
D	3,000	0	740	–£35,520
E	20,000	0	5,000	–£240,000
F	1,500	0	0	£0
Totals		6,237	6,238	–£48

Note: Assumes permit price of £48 kg BOD/day

As can be seen, permit sales and purchases are out by a one-permit excess demand. The most important observation we make from the above is the market is dominated by one large seller and by one large buyer. Source F receives, by chance, a cost-minimising initial allocation.

The strong seller (A) would presumably wish to offer rather less permits than predicted above, and so hold up the price. The large buyer (B) would presumably wish to reduce permit purchases as their lower net demand will hold down the price they must pay. The net effect on price is thus unclear, but fewer trades than those suggested in the table above seem inevitable.

6.6.3   Equity Aspects of Tradeable Permits

Section 6.3 noted that, for eliminating the DO sag around Alloa, the least cost solution is in fact no different from the FRPB's current 'flexible' (i.e. cost-sensitive) regulatory plan in terms of which firm controls effluent, and by how much. It may therefore be asked, why should one bother with new market mechanism schemes when they may be no more cost effective than existing, flexible regulatory systems? One answer is that Section 6.3 covers only one case; there might still be a difference between market mechanisms and flexible regulation in the case of more stringent environmental targets, such as raising DO levels throughout the estuary. Another, important answer explored now is that market mechanisms may in fact be fairer in determining which firms pay for effluent control. Table 6.9 shows how the total financial costs of the actions which cost-minimising firms would take in a tradeable permit scheme, i.e. the sum of the resource costs of any BOD control measures and the transfer payments for permits (if any), vary considerably between flexible regulation, auctioned permits and grandfathered permits. All costs in the table have been divided by the original amount of a firm's discharge, to allow for the different sizes of the firms in the industry. It is striking how tradeable permits result in a much more even distribution of financial costs among firms than flexible regulation, under which costs are incurred solely by the firms with low-cost options for effluent control. The costs are of course much higher with auctioned permits than with grandfathered permits because the former include the payments made by firms at auction to the regulatory authority; but they are still very evenly spread, even though A's and C's costs comprise high control costs offset by spare permit sales; B's, D's and E's costs comprise permit purchases, and F's costs comprise just control costs.

Table 6.9 Equity Aspects of Tradeable Permits, Industry only, long run, 25% cut in BOD

Firm	Proportional cut in BOD discharge	Resource cost of cut per unit of original discharge, under perfect flexible regulation £/kg	Resource + permit trade costs of cut per unit of original discharge, under **auctioned** tradeable permits £/kg	Resource + permit trade costs of cut per unit of original discharge, under **grandfathered** tradeable permits £/kg
A	44%	20	47	11
B	–	0	48	12
C	40%	19	48	12
D	–	0	48	12
E	–	0	48	12
F	25%	3	39	3
Total	25%	11	47	11

Whether or not this even spread of total financial costs is viewed as an advantage of tradeable permits, depends very much whether or not the existing effluent control efforts on the Forth Estuary are regarded as fairly distributed among firms. If they are, then it is clearly preferable to spread out the costs of further effluent control evenly among firms, and tradeable permits have a strong advantage over flexible regulation. If they are not, and if the only reason that firms A and C have low marginal costs of effluent control is because they have had in some sense an 'easy ride' for several years and have not installed basic control equipment that other firms already have, then spreading out the cost of further control may actually be unfair. For firms A and C alone to pay for further control may be fair if, in a historical sense, it is 'their turn' to install a certain level of control equipment; in this case, flexible regulation is preferable to tradeable permits.

6.6.4 Total Transfer Costs for Different Cases

For completeness, Table 6.10 lists the industry's total resource costs of control and transfer payments made for auctioned permits (for granted permits, the transfer payments are of course zero) in a range of cases using the 'industry only' model. (The control cost figures have already appeared in Tables 6.3 and 6.4.) Note how sharply both the control costs and transfer payments rise for the last case, where the BOD cut is a full 50%. Transfer payments on this scale will obviously not be popular with those who have to pay them.

6.7 Administration Costs

One argument typically raised against the introduction of market mechanisms for the control of pollution is that they involve increased administration costs for control agencies. Instances where simulation studies have attempted to estimate such costs are relatively few, an exception being Seskin, Anderson and Reid (1983). We have estimated *additional* administrative costs falling on the Forth River Purification Board (FRPB) for the permit system described in Section 6.4. This was done by describing the system to senior FRPB officers, and getting them to work out the extra resources necessary to administer the scheme.

The FRPB's view is that the scheme could be difficult and costly to administer. Trades would, in their expectation, occur infrequently, but setting of Transfer Co-efficients ('Weighting Factors', as the FRPB refer to them), and agreeing these with dischargers, would be expected to be contentious. The extra costs of the scheme would be one high-grade modeller, with data, hardware and software backup. This is expected to cost £40,000–£50,000 *per annum*.

How large these costs are, relative to the resource savings of flexible emission reductions, depends on which scenarios one compares them with. If we take the 10% reduction, long run figure of (£1,340,560 − 275,445), or £1,065,105, then the extra administration costs are small relative to the cost-saving produced by a *competitive* permit market. A much better picture of the *net* cost-saving will emerge once we are able to run the economic model with FEDS derived Transfer Co-efficients, and a 4.5 mg/l DO target for water quality under low flow conditions.

Table 6.10 Resource Costs to and Transfer Payments by Industry for Tradeable Permits, industry only model

Time scale	Target cut in BOD load,	Actual cut in BOD load kg BOD/Day,	Cost using auctioned or grandfathered tradeable permits	
			Resource cost of control (auctioned or grandfathered permits)	Transfer payments by firms (auctioned permits only)
			£k/year	£k/year
Short run	10%	6,199 (10%)	256	2670
	25%	14,247 (23%)	739	2720-3430
	50%	18,495 (30%)	920	2480
Long run	10%	6,499 (10%)	275	2490
	25%	15,497 (25%)	692	2230
	50%	30,970 (50%)	4210	11820

References

DE LUCIA, R. J. (1974) *An Evaluation of Marketable Effluent Permit Systems*, Report EPA600/5-74-030 to US EPA, September 1974.

HAHN, R. W. (1984) 'Market Power and Transferable Property Rights', *Quarterly Journal Of Economics,* November 1984.

HAHN, R. W. AND NOLL, R. G. (1982) 'Designing a Market for Tradeable Emissions Permits', *Reform of Environmental Regulation,* W. A. Magat (Ed), Cambridge, MA: Ballinger.

LONDON ECONOMICS (1991) *Market Mechanisms and Fresh Water Quality.* Paper for the Royal Commission on Environmental Pollution, January.

KRUPNICK, C., OATES, W. & VAN DE VERG, E., (1983) 'On the Design of a Market for Air Pollution Permits', *Journal of Environmental Economics and Management,* 10, 233-247.

MALONEY, M. T. AND YANDLE, B. (1984) 'Estimation of the Cost of Air Pollution Control Regulation', *Journal of Environmental Economics and Management,* 11,244-263.

MCAFEE, R. P. & MCMILLAN J. (1987) 'Auctions and Bidding', *Journal of Economic Literature,* 25 (2), 699-754.

MCGARTLAND, A. M. AND OATES, W. E. (1985) 'Marketable Permits for the Prevention of Environmental Deterioration', *Journal of Environmental Economics and Management,* 12, 207-228.

MONTGOMERY, W. (1972) 'Markets in Licenses and Efficiency Pollution Control programmes', *Journal of Economic Theory,* 5, 395-418.

TIETENBERG, T. (1984) 'Marketable Emission Permits in Principle and Practice', *DP123 Resources for the Future,* Washington DC.

7 Charges and Charge-Subsidies on BOD Emissions

Table of Contents

List of Tables

List of Figures

Chapter 7 reports the results of our simulations of two policies: a uniform charge, or tax, on BOD emissions; and a uniform charge-subsidy on BOD emissions and reduced emissions. In line with Chapter 6, we work with all Transfer Co-efficients set at unity.

7.1 A Uniform Charge on BOD

In this section, we report the results of a uniform charge on BOD. By 'uniform', we mean that all dischargers pay the same rate of charge per Kg of BOD discharged per day irrespective of their location on the estuary. This is equivalent to setting all Transfer Coefficients at one, and treating the whole estuary as one reach. Such a scheme could be expected to be preferred by dischargers according to their location on the estuary on two grounds:

1. It might be argued to be more equitable.

2. It would be easier to administer than a differentiated scheme.

   There are, however, two problems with such a uniform charge:

1. We expect from the literature (for example, Seskin, Anderson and Reid, 1983) that the resource cost of a uniform scheme would exceed that of a differentiated scheme.

2. The discharge pattern resulting from a uniform charge scheme might cause pollution 'hotspots' to occur.

To answer point (l) in the 'problems' section, we need to compute resource costs under both charge schemes. This is only possible if Transfer Co-efficients exist for all stretches Administration cost differences are addressed in Section 7.4. To preview our conclusions on the emergence of 'hotspots', we find that the charge solutions all involve sources which have large discharges to sensitive points on the estuary making proportionately large reductions in BOD loadings. This is because they are faced with relatively low marginal control costs, and find it cheaper to cut emissions than to pay the charge and carry on emitting.

7.1.1 Efficiency Properties of a Uniform Charge on BOD Emissions

To investigate the efficiency properties of a uniform charge on BOD, we ran the 'industry only' version of the model with an activity added to cover charge payments, and a charge-tie line inserted to enforce these payments for each Kg of BOD still discharged. This was to enable the resource costs of the charge policy to be compared with those of both the uniform regulation runs, and the least-cost runs, both of which were reported in Chapter 6.

It is well known from economic theory (Baumol and Oates, 1988) that the correct least-cost charge rate to achieve a given reduction in emissions, for a uniform charge, is equivalent to the shadow price of the emission constraint in the least-cost solution. In all charge runs in our model, however, we encountered a problem similar to that found by the Newcastle study of the Tees estuary, reported by Walker and Storey (1977). This is known as the 'existence problem', and arises when the aggregate marginal control cost function for the industry being controlled is not smooth - but segmented. In Figure 7.1 below, a stylised Marginal Control Cost function with indivisibilities is

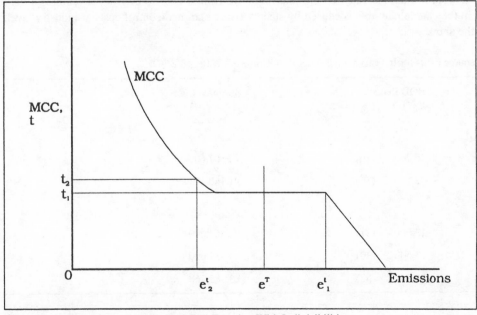

Figure 7.1 Stylised Marginal Control Cost Function With Indivisibilities

shown. The target level of emissions equal to e^T is not achievable at charge rate t_1, as emissions equal to e_1^t are forthcoming. Increasing the charge rate to t_2, however, produces an excess of control, as emissions of e_2^t result.

7.1.2 Industry Only Version, 10% Reduction BOD Loading

Here, in the *short run*, the target reduction in emissions to be comparable to the uniform regulation/least-cost solutions is 6,199 Kg BOD/day. Setting a charge of £48/Kg results in only 2,200 units of BOD reduction, at a resource cost of £63,000. However, increasing the charge to the trip value[1] of £49/Kg produces excess emission control, with a total cut of 10,200 Kg/day. This has a resource cost of £507,600.

In the *long run*, the appropriate target is 6,499 Kg/day. At the charge rate of £45 this gives only 500 units of emission reduction. Raising the charge over to the trip value £46 gives 13,000 units of emission reduction at a resource cost of £568,000. It is therefore the case that a charge on BOD will either drastically overshoot or undershoot the target.

7.1.3 Industry Only Version, 25% Reduction BOD Loading

The comparable target here in the *short run* is 14,247 Kg/day. The shadow price in the least cost run is £72. Introducing a charge on BOD at this rate gives a massive 22,700 unit reduction in emissions, at a resource cost of £1,160,100. The charge rate can be reduced to £58 and still achieve this solution (at, obviously, a lower financial burden). Cutting the charge to £57 returns us to the 10% short run solution: a reduction of 10,200 Kg BOD/day. Thus, again, it is not possible to hit our target in the short run with a charge policy.

In the *long run*, the comparable target is 15,497 Kg BOD/day. The closest we can approach this with a charge policy is to set the charge at £49 Kg/BOD, which yields a reduction of 18,500 Kg/day. The resource cost is £832,000.

7.1.4 Industry Only Version, 50% Reduction BOD Loading

In the *short run*, the target cut in BOD emissions is 18,495 Kg/day. However, as we saw above, this can be over achieved at a resource cost of £1,160,100 at a charge rate of £58. Cutting the charge rate to £57 brings us back to the 10,200 Kg/day reduction also reported above. Both the 25% and 50% targets, in the short run, lie within the charge trip values of £57 and £58.

In the *long run,* the target of 30,970 Kg/day can be achieved almost exactly at a charge £381, which yields 32,165 Kg/day abatement at a resource cost of £3,985,260.

7.1.5 Uniform Charge, Industry Only Scenario

As can be seen from the results reported above, the principal problem from the charge policy from an efficiency point of view is that for all target/period combinations, it is impossible to hit exactly the desired reductions in emissions. In some cases, this inaccuracy is more marked than others, the 25% and 50% short-run reduction scenarios being cases in point. Taking the situation across all targets, we note that increasing the severity of emission reduction requirements by 150% from 10% to 25% requires a charge increase of 47%; in the long run the same increase in reduction requirement requires only a 6.5% increase in the charge rate. The 25% and 50% solutions are identical in the short run, but in the long run we note that the move from a 25% to a 50% cut requires a very large percentage increase in the charge rate: this is caused by steeply rising marginal control costs at industry level. Table 7.1 summarises all the above results.

Table 7.1   Summary of Resource Costs for Industry Only Model Run, Uniform Charge on BOD.

Charge Rate	BOD Reduction Kg/day	(%)	Resource Cost
Short Run:			
£49	10,200	(16)	£507,600
£58	22,700	(36)	£1,160,100
Long Run:			
£46	13,000	(21)	£568,000
£49	18,500	(30)	£832,000
£381	32,165	(52)	£3,985,260

[1] Trip value: the value of a variable at which the optimal solution to the LP changes.

7.2   A Uniform Charge-Subsidy on BOD

As explained in Section 1.3, a charge-subsidy scheme is defined by a baseline level of effluent (say B) and a charge rate (say R) per unit of effluent; if the firm's effluent (say E) exceeds the baseline, it pays a charge for each unit in excess of the baseline, i.e. (E-B) x R; if its effluent is less than the baseline, it receives a subsidy for each unit by which its effluent is beneath the baseline, i.e. (B-E) x R. From economic theory, we know that this scheme has the same short run effect on emissions as a charge on emissions set at the same unit rate (Baumol and Oates, 1988). This is because firms treat the two instruments identically: at the margin, firms set the costs of reducing emissions against either the charge payment saved or the subsidy to be earned. A charge-subsidy on BOD emissions, set at the least-cost charge rate, should therefore be capable of achieving any target reduction in emissions at least-cost. Assuming that firms' baselines are always set correctly, so that for each charge rate the total of the baselines ΣB equals the total effluent ΣE that the industry will wish to discharge at the given charge rate, the total charge revenues equal the total subsidy payments, and the whole scheme results in zero transfer payments between the industry and the control authority.

The simplest way to calculate the effect of a charge-subsidy is actually to do calculations for a pure subsidy (which is equivalent to a charge-subsidy with a baseline set at the effluent a firm would choose to discharge in the absence of any regulatory constraint), and then ignore the total subsidy payments from the authority to the industry. We therefore ran the economic model (in this instance, in "industry only" mode due to time constraints) with a subsidy on emission instead of a charge. This was done for the same target reductions in total BOD loading as are reported in Sections 6.1 and 7.1. The subsidy runs identically replicate the charge runs, in that they produce identical patterns of emission reduction. This is, of course, as we would predict. (The existence problem noted for the charge scheme applies here too.) *Resource costs of control under charge-subsidies are therefore exactly as in Table 7.1.*

As discussed in Chapter 1, there are a number of ways in which charge-subsidies may be regarded as controversial:

1. They may be at odds with a strict interpretation of the Polluter Pays Principle. Whether this matters or not is largely a political rather than an economic judgement (see Pezzey, 1990). Grandfathered permits have very similar financial properties but are not usually regarded as breaking the PPP.

2. Managing the baselines and the unit rates so that the scheme is revenue-neutral overall may be a difficult financial balancing act for the control agency to achieve.

3. If new firms entering the industry are entitled to non-zero baseline effluents, this would probably lead to increasing emissions in an area, relative to a charge scheme, as polluting firms move to the area to take advantage of the entitlement to free baseline effluent; but we would propose that baselines are not available to new firms, so this problem need not arise. This would be because charge-subsidy baselines are effectively property rights in the same way that freely distributed tradeable permits are (see discussion in Section 1.3).

4. Firms operating inefficiently may be given the option of staying in business by a charge subsidy scheme, even though it may be financially irrational to do so because more money could be made by going out of business and claiming permanent subsidy payments for not discharging. The possibility of permanent subsidies may itself be regarded as a problem, even though the net present value of these subsidies will remain finite and could no doubt be compulsorily purchased by a lump sum equivalent. In contrast, a pure charging scheme would force an inefficient firm out of business, and any question of permanent subsidies does not arise.

5. Every time any factor affecting firms' control costs changes significantly, the control authority ideally should know about it so it can recalculate the optimal charge-subsidy rate.

6. The subsidy will only achieve the target level of emission reduction, even if set correctly, if firms know their MCC functions, or actually minimise costs.

7. Charge-subsidy schemes of the type proposed here (as opposed to redistributive charging) are almost completely untried.

Objections 5 and 6 apply equally to emission charge regimes.

7.3   Distributional Effects

According to many authors, the distributional effects of emission charges constitute one of the major barriers to the implementation of such schemes. Under the Baumol and Oates charge scheme, firms pay a standard charge rate for each unit of pollution emitted, in addition to the control costs associated in moving to their cost-minimising level of emissions. This point is emphasised by Pezzey (1988) and the relevant literature is summarised in Hanley *et al*, (1990). Frequently, authors have found that the charge payment element of the total *financial burden* falling on firms dominates the control cost element. For example, a study of a charge on halocarbon emissions in the USA found that the resource cost (control cost) of the scheme was $110 million, whilst the transfer payments amounted to $1,400 million (Palmer *et al*, 1980). Charge payments were thus more than ten times bigger than resource costs.

This tendency for high transfer payments can be reduced by either:

1. Adopting a scheme similar to the German one, where charge payments are refunded if performance exceeds consent standards. However, this eliminates the continuing incentive to reduce effluent beyond consent standards;

2. Returning all or some of the charge taken to the polluters as lump-sum capital grants (as in France), the disadvantage being that these grants may distort pollution abatement efforts in favour of capital-intensive rather than labour-intensive methods;

3. Using a pure charge/subsidy scheme, as described in Section 7.2 above. Provided the charge rates and effluent baselines are properly calculated, this will result in zero transfer payments. As with grandfathered tradeable permits, the other revenue-neutral market mechanism (see section 6.6.3), charge-subsidies may have equity advantages in comparison to flexible regulation. If existing discharge levels are regarded as fair, then charge-subsidies almost certainly result in a more equitable distribution of the costs of a reduction in total BOD than flexible regulation. Some firms pay effluent treatment costs and get subsidies because their effluent falls below their baseline, while other firms do not spend on extra effluent treatment, but pay charges instead. However, we have not done the firm-by-firm calculations for charge-subsidies, which would prove our point by producing figures analogous to those in Table 6.9.

As expected, the standard Baumol and Oates emissions charge, described in Section 7.1.1 above, has high transfer costs. In the *short run*, a charge rate of £49 gave a 10,200 Kg BOD/day reduction for a resource cost of £507,600. The charge payment associated with this policy is £3,095,036. The transfer payment is thus about 6 times greater than the resource cost. Increasing the charge to £58 gave a loading reduction of 22,700 Kg/day at a resource cost of £1,160,100. The transfer payment is £2,938,512, which is only about 2.5 times as great as the resource cost. The charge rate has risen, tending to push up charge payments, but the number of emissions still made has fallen by almost the same proportion, resulting in a total charge payment slightly less than before (£2.9 million instead of £3.1 million).

In the *long run*, a charge rate of £46 produces a 13,000 Kg/day reduction in BOD loading at a resource cost of £568,000. The charge revenue collected would be £2,776,744, five times greater than the resource cost. Pushing the charge up to £49 elicits a greater reduction in emissions, which fall by 18,500 Kg/day. This has a resource cost of £832,000, and a charge take of £2,688,336. Finally, increasing that charge to £381 produces a loading reduction of 32,165 Kg/day. The resource cost is £3,985,260, the transfer payment is £15,696,819: again, five times greater than the resource cost.

We summarise the results reported above in the table below, which is the same as Table 7.1 but with an extra column added.

Table 7.2   Summary of Resource Costs and Charge Revenues for Industry Only Model Run, Uniform Charge on BOD.

Charge Rate	BOD Reduction Kg/day	(%)	Resource Cost	Charge Revenue
Short Run:				
£49	10,200	(16)	£507,600	£3,095,035
£58	22,700	(36)	£1,160,100	£2,938,510
Long Run:				
£46	13,000	(21)	£568,000	£2,776,745
£49	18,500	(30)	£832,000	£2,688,335
£381	32,165	(52)	£3,985,260	£15,696,82

The distributional effects of the simple emissions charge policy described above are therefore very significant, as transfer payments exceed resource cost flows. This is in line with the results of previous empirical work, and constitutes a very significant barrier to the adoption of such a scheme.

7.4 Administration Costs

Following the same procedure as that outlined for tradeable permits, we estimated the additional administrative costs (relative to the existing systems) likely to result from moving to either a charging or a subsidy system, as described in the sections above.

For an *incentive charge* system, the FRPB see two type of costs being incurred. Firstly, a fixed-cost in calculating an appropriate charge rate, which the FRPB would like to be differentiated according to a firm's location along the estuary. This fixed-cost is estimated at £10,000, although may in our view be greater than this (and closer to the £50,000 figure for tradeable permits), as both systems require an accurate working water quality model to be combined with an economic model of the estuary. Also excluded is the cost of re-calculating the charge rate(s) if marginal control costs change. It should be recognised here that the FRPB prefer a charge system backed up by consent regulation. If such a scheme were in operation, then getting the charge(s) correct would not be so crucial (since emissions are quantity constrained).

In addition to this fixed cost, the FRPB estimate that an annual expenditure of around £2,000 (equivalent to one clerk-month) would be necessary to collect charge payments. This is for a system where firms monitor and report their emission levels themselves, with the FRPB performing un-announced 'spot checks'. The enforcement incurs no additional cost over the present system, as it is already an established practice.

For the charge-subsidy scheme, the FRPB foresee considerable problems in getting such a scheme accepted, because of the numerous equity problems raised such as settling each firm's level of baseline effluent. As noted in Section 8.1, FRPB's preference would be for a redistributive charging scheme[2]. However, with regard to administration costs, our estimate is that the charge-subsidy scheme would involve a similar set-up cost (fixed cost) as the charge scheme above, but would incur higher annual costs due to a greater amount of senior management effort being necessary to 'placate' dischargers concerned about equity issues. This effort might also be necessary in the initial stages of the scheme, as an additional set-up cost. This results in an estimated set-up cost of £20,000, with annual administrative costs thereafter of about £5,000.

References

BAUMOL, W. J. AND OATES, W. E. (1988) *The Theory of Environmental Policy*, Cambridge University Press, Cambridge.

HANLEY, N., HALLETT, S. AND MOFFATT, I. (1990) 'Why is more notice not taken of Economists Prescriptions for the Control of Pollution?', *Journal of Environmental Economics and Management*, 22, 1421-1439.

PALMER, A. *et al* (1980) *Economic Implications of Regulating Chlorofluorocarbon Emissions from Non-aerosol Applications*, The Rand Corporation, Santa Monica, California.

PEZZEY, J. C. V. (1988). Market Mechanisms of Pollution Control: 'Polluter Pays', Economic and Practical Aspects. In Turner, R. K., ed., *Sustainable Environmental Management - Principles and Practice*. London: Belhaven Press.

PEZZEY, J (1990) *Charge Subsidies Versus Marketable Permits as Efficient and Acceptable Methods of Effluent Control: a Property Rights Analysis*. Discussion Paper 90/271, Economics Department, University of Bristol.

SESKIN, E., ANDERSON, R. AND REID, R. (1983) 'An Empirical Analysis of Economic Strategies for Controlling Air Pollution', *Journal of Environmental Economics and Management*, 10, 112-124.

WALKER, M. AND STOREY, D. (1977) 'The Standards and Prices Approach to Pollution Control: Problems of Iteration', *Scandinavian Journal of Economics*, 79, 99-109.

---

[2] Although the FRPB were expressing a view on a pure subsidy, rather than a charge subsidy, scheme.

8 Comparisons of BOD Control Systems, and Conclusions

Table of Contents

List of Tables

This report has considered the scope for market based mechanisms in the control of water pollution in the Forth estuary. We restricted our attention primarily to BOD as a measure of polluting potential, and DO as a measure of water quality, as (i) DO levels are, as shown in Chapter 3, the major problem on the estuary; and (ii) BOD is one of the few measures of pollution with sufficient sources of discharge on the estuary to even begin discussing a permit market. Here we collect and compare the key results of Chapters 6 and 7, and consider their implications for pollution control policy.

8.1 Uniform Regulation Versus Least Cost Solutions, Including Flexible Regulation

Table 8.1 shows the main cost results from Sections 6.1 (uniform regulation solutions), 6.2 (least cost solution), and 6.6.1 (transfer payments under auctioned tradeable permits). It is clear that least cost solutions offer substantial (70-90%) savings in resource costs when compared to uniform percentage reductions in discharges. This is an important conclusion: if one is concerned with achieving reductions in BOD loading to the estuary, necessary for improvements in DO, then uniform emission reduction requirements are very inefficient. Since marginal control

Table 8.1   Costs of reducing total BOD discharges into the Forth estuary using uniform percentage cuts or tradeable permits

Industry or full version of model	Time-scale	Actual (target[1]) reduction in total BOD load	Cost of using uniform percentage reductions	Cost using auctioned or granted tradeable permits	
				Extra admin. costs: £0.05M/year	
			Resource cost of control[2]	Resource cost of control (auctioned or granted permits)	Transfer payments by firms (auctioned permits only)
			£M / year[3]	£M / year	£M / year
Industry only (not including STWs)	Short run	10% (10%)	1.08	0.26	2.67
		23% (25%)	3.55	0.74	2.72
		30% (50%)	4.76	0.92	2.48
	Long run	10% (10%)	1.34	0.28	2.49
		25% (25%)	7.38	0.69	2.23
		50% (50%)	15.06	4.21	11.82

costs (MCC) vary greatly across sources, the *least-cost* way of achieving these loading reductions involves a non-uniform pattern of emission reduction, with some sources engaging in high levels of extra treatment, and other (high cost) sources engaging in no extra treatment.

The question is therefore if this least-cost solution can be hit by a pollution control policy. Flexible, as opposed to uniform, regulations for emission reductions can approach the least cost solution and within the limit, achieve it if the Pollution Control Authority (PCA) has knowledge of the least-cost solution. Whilst the FRPB clearly do not

---

[1] The actual reduction achieved is the first figure, and the target reduction is the figure in brackets; the two are different because of indivisibilities in effluent control equipment. All cost figures quoted are for actual, not target, reductions.

[2] Transfer payments are zero for uniform percentage cutbacks, since firms do not pay for the consented discharges that remain after cutbacks.

[3] All costs include both running and capital costs, with the latter annualised using a 6% real discount rate, and lifespans of 4 yr for industrial plant and 15 yr for STWs (Section 4.3).

know the least-cost pattern of emission reductions, our work in Section 6.3, summarised here by Table 8.2, shows that in some cases they would get very close to it.

Table 8.2   Costs of Using Flexible Regulation or Least Cost Solution to Eliminate DO sag in Upper Estuary

Industry or full version of model	Time-scale	Actual reduction in total BOD for reaches 1–10	Cost using FRPB's 'flexible regulation' scheme to eliminating DO sag	Cost using least cost solution to achieve same percentage reduction for reaches 1–10	
				Extra admin. costs: £0.01–0.05M/year?	
			Resource cost of control	Resource cost of control	Transfer payments imposed by least cost restriction
			£M / year	£M / year	
Full (i.e. including STWs) but restricted to reaches 1–10	Long run	43%	1.184	1.016 (1.184[4])	0 or n.c.[5]

n.c. = not calculated

Another consideration when comparing regulation with alternative control mechanism is that when the discharge reductions necessary to hit EQS levels are very close to the maximum technically feasible level, the cost difference between a regulatory system and a tradeable permit system diminishes. This is because, to have cost-saving trades, it is necessary for some firms to reduce emissions more than others: but if all are very close to the maximum reduction technically feasible, then the number of potential trades declines (Hahn and Noll, 1982). So the question arises of whether market mechanisms such as tradeable permits and charges can do any better than flexible regulation, and Section 8.2 now discusses this issue.

8.2   Tradeable Permits Versus Charges Versus Flexible Regulation

According to economic theory, outlined in Chapter 1, market mechanisms such as tradeable emission reduction permits, or a charge on emissions, should be able to hit the least-cost solution. In particular, tradeable permits also have the advantage that in principle the control authorities do not need to calculate any prices or charge rates for the market mechanism to work efficiently. However, Chapters 6 and 7 showed that market mechanisms have various drawbacks, which we summarise in Sections 8.2.1 and 8.2.2. Section 8.2.3 briefly discusses the alternative of redistributive charging, an option we have not studied in this report; and Section 8.2.4 concludes by comparing market mechanisms with flexible regulation.

8.2.1   Tradeable Permits

The scope for, and design of, a tradeable permit market for permits to discharge BOD were discussed in Chapter 6. The problems that emerged are:

i.   Given that the marginal damage costs (MDCs) vary between different locations, only an Ambient Permit System can exactly hit the least-cost solution. Yet the transaction costs implicit in such a system make it unappealing for almost all cases of practical pollution control (Tietenberg, 1984). An Emission Permits System backed up by trading rules, such as that proposed here, can, however, get very close to the least-cost outcome *if* all gains from trade are fully exploited *and* if the permit market is competitive (no price-making behaviour).

---

[4] Considered to be the more practical result, for reasons explained at the end of Section 6.3.

[5] The transfer payment is zero for a granted tradeable permit scheme, and not calculated (n.c.) for an auctioned tradeable permit scheme.

452

ii. With respect to the possibility of unexploited gains from trade existing, it seems that such a situation is quite likely. Given that permits will have a fixed lifespan (we suggest three years), then firms may hoard permits to increase their likely allocation in the next round, if permits are grandfathered (as this would increase their potential revenue from permit sales). Also, evidence from the permit market currently in operation for BOD emission rights in the Fox River, Wisconsin, has been characterised by hoarding due to many of the firms being in competition for output market share (most dischargers are paper mills). In the Forth, we have two paper mills and two chemical works who are in product market competition with each other; transfers between these sources seem unlikely.

iii. With respect to price making behaviour, the market in the estuary consists of six firms and three regional councils. Two of these firms might well become price setters, since they have large discharges, relatively low control costs, and thus have the potential to control much of the supply side of the market once trade commences. However, as we saw in Chapter 6, theoretical and empirical evidence from previous studies suggests that, while noncompetitive behaviour may have a big impact on financial burdens (through its impact on permit prices), it will probably have a much smaller impact on control costs, and is unlikely to bring the resource cost of a tradeable permit market up to that of a command and control system.

8.2.2 Charges and Charge-subsidies

Table 8.3 summarises the results obtained in Chapter 7 for charges and charge-subsidies. Again it is clear that charging schemes can in principle achieve savings in the order of 70-90% in comparison with uniform regulation. However, the problems with charging are:

Table 8.3   Costs of reducing total BOD discharges into the Forth estuary using charges and charge-subsidies

Time-scale	*Actual* reduction in total BOD load	Costs using uniform percentage reductions	Cost using charges or charge subsidies	
			Extra admin. costs: £0.01–0.05M/year	
		Resource cost of control[6]	Resource costs (using charges or charge-subsidies)	Transfer payments of firms (using charges *only*)
		£M/year	£M/year	£M/year
Short run	16%	n.c. (1.08–3.55)	0.51	3.10
	36%	n.c (>4.76)	1.16	2.94
Long run	21%	n.c. (1.34–7.38)	0.57	2.78
	30%	n.c. (7.38–15.06)	0.83	2.69
	52%	n.c. (>15.06)	3.99	15.70

(n.c. = not calculated)

---

[6] The figures in brackets in this column give what information can be obtained about the range of costs from results in Table 8.1. For example, the first entry shows 1.08 and 3.55 as the costs of 10% and 23%, cutbacks respectively, which must therefore span the cost of a 16% cutback.

[7] This problem is rather different to the gradual raising of the charge rate in Germany, as (i) firms in Germany knew the direction and magnitude of changes before they were made, thus could plan their investments taking this into account; as (ii) the German system did not involve using the tax as the principle quantity control: consents were retained.

1. With a uniform charge, it is impossible to hit exactly the loading reduction targets, due to indivisibilities ('lumpiness') in pollution treatment. It may well be that the way in which we obtained data from firms has exaggerated this phenomena, but no doubt should obtain about the existence of such indivisibilities. This was confirmed by follow up research on a sample of firms responding to our survey. Indivisibilities might also have been exaggerated since firms appear to have discounted output reductions as a way of cutting emissions, but concentrated on process changes, input substitution and end-of-pipe technologies. Alternatively, firms responding to our questionnaires were asked to report on the *cost-minimising* way of meeting emission reduction targets, and would not suggest output reductions if these were relatively costly.

   However, these very indivisibilities make one question whether rigid target reductions in BOD loadings are desirable in themselves. We have already commented that, due to the current state of the FEDS Environmental Water Quality Model, we are currently unable to relate these precisely to DO levels. However, the existence of indivisibilities in pollution control, particularly where there are relatively few discharges to a river, lake or estuary, and particularly where these indivisibilities are sizeable, may mean that achieving a marginal improvement in DO levels (or environmental quality levels measured in some other way) is very costly. This will be the case when the marginal improvement is only possible if an extra treatment plant is 'switched in', which is then under-utilised if the target DO level, for example, is to be exactly met. A tradeable permit scheme aimed at rigid effluent targets may therefore result in unjustifiably high control costs being required of the industry. Such a situation calls for a flexible iterative approach to *target setting*, in conjunction with flexible means of meeting these targets.

2. A stand alone charge policy would also have very high transfer payments associated with it, greatly increasing the financial burden on dischargers.

3. Such a charge policy would also suffer from the well-known problems that (i) every change in MCC functions necessitates a re-calculation in the charge rate: this will also be necessary if the number of sources increases; (ii) the control agency must either know these MCC functions, or else engage in an iterative process, which may have high resource costs associated with it[7]; and (iii), the correct charge rate will only achieve the desired reduction in emissions if firms both know their MCC functions *and* cost-minimise.

4. We have modelled a uniform charge, which studies such as that by Seskin *et al* have shown can be very inefficient when marginal damage costs (MDC) vary significantly. To calculate the necessary differentiated charge vector would require the transfer co-efficients from the FEDS environmental water quality model of the Forth Estuary; as explained in Chapter 5, these are not yet achievable at satisfactory confidence levels. However, the section in Chapter 6 on removing the DO sag in the upper estuary does effectively calculate the required differentiated charge rates if we assume that the transfer co-efficients for all sources in that part of the estuary equal unity, whereas those for all sources downstream equal zero. This, according to the FRPB, is probably not at all that far from the actual state of affairs.

8.2.3 Redistributive Charging as an Alternative?

Finally, we turn to 'redistributive charging', the existence of which was discussed in a footnote in Section 1.2, but which has not been discussed elsewhere in this report. However, redistributive charging is well-established in various continental countries (ERL, 1990) and has attracted recent attention in the UK. The FRPB has said it would like charge revenues, net of administrative costs, to be returned to dischargers as grants for improvement of pollution treatment. Furthermore, the FRPB would wish for the charge rate to be reduced for any source as it cuts its emissions below an 'agreed threshold' - presumably less than currently consented levels.

This idea is very similar to what already happens with the German waste-water charge, which has been much studied and receives considerable attention in the Royal Commission's current report. Here, a charge is levied on emissions, but it is combined with regulation by consent. Charge rebates are given when reductions, in emissions below the consented levels are made. This provides an incentive as, although the charge is not set as high as marginal control costs for the lowest cost source, firms save on charge payments by over-achieving their consents. However, the precise details of this rebate scheme remain unclear; it may amount to using financial incentives in a discontinous way to reinforce regulatory targets, which then loses the continual incentive that a pure charging scheme creates for continuing reductions in effluent.

There are two reasons why redistributive charging has not been considered in this report. Firstly, using charge revenues for subsidies for investments in abatement equipment requires a different approach to economic modelling in that capital costs must be modelled separately from operating costs and activities introduced to allow for emission related capital grants to feed through into actual capital expenditure. Secondly, subsidies of the sort usually involved in redistributive charging schemes tend to involve high administrative costs, to add to bureaucratic power, and to distort pollution abatement efforts in favour of visible, capital intensive projects, at the expense of labour-intensive, 'housekeeping' alternatives. They therefore cannot achieve a least cost solution, and it is this reasoning that lies behind the traditional UK stance of being opposed to 'earmarking' or 'hypothecating' tax revenues for particular expenditures. So while redistributive charging clearly has political and administrative appeal and a considerable body of experience, we have not taken the debate about it any further forward, and cannot make any convincing recommendation in favour of it.

8.2.4 Advantages of Market Mechanisms over Flexible Regulation

Given the way in which, for the special case of the summertime DO sag in the Forth estuary, Section 8.1 has shown that flexible regulation can achieve a least cost solution, and given the various drawbacks about different market mechanisms outlined in Sections 8.2.1–3, one may well ask whether market mechanisms offer any notable advantages compared with flexible regulation. They do, and the first may still be a saving in current control costs in achieving other policy goals: little is known about what the cost comparison between flexible regulation and market mechanisms may look like for a tougher environmental goal such as raising DO levels throughout the estuary.

Secondly, flexible regulation cannot match the ability of market mechanisms, mentioned at the start of Chapter 6, to create a continual incentive to discover better effluent treatment techniques, although no new evidence has been gathered for this innovation incentive so to some extent it remains an article of faith in the power of market forces.

Thirdly, and less well known, market mechanisms almost certainly result in a much more even distribution of the financial costs of an effluent control programme between different firms. To put it simplistically, this is because under a market mechanism, firms either reduce effluent a great deal and pay little in the way of transfer payments (e.g. with permits, their effluent is greatly reduced and they either need to buy fewer permits, or can in fact sell off spare permits); or they don't reduce effluent, and therefore pay higher transfer payments. So if the existing firms' effluent control efforts are seen as being fairly distributed, this 'evening out' ability of market mechanisms will maintain the fair distribution of financial burdens, and so is to be regarded as an advantage. But if existing control efforts are in some sense unfairly distributed, and it is the historical 'turn' of specific firms to install new abatement equipment next because they have 'got away' with too generous a discharge consent for several years, then evening out the financial costs of such abatement is not desirable, and flexible regulation which requires the firms in question to pay all their abatement costs will in fact be fairer. Section 6.6.3 and Table 6.9 discussed this issue in some detail.

Fourthly, market mechanisms require less information to be collected by the control authority. Flexible regulation only works if the authority knows a lot about each firm's control costs; under tradeable permits, the authority need not know anything about control costs (although, as suggested in Section 8.2.2, it would be a good idea if the authority did know something, to avoid setting unjustifiable effluent targets), and under charging, the authority may be able to find out all it needs to know about costs simply by starting with a low charge rate and gradually increasing it, while noting firms' responses.

8.3 Conclusions for BOD in the Forth Estuary

Despite the limitations of this study, we would argue that we have demonstrated that, while the least-cost solution to water quality improvements does indeed represent a considerable cost saving over uniform emission controls, actually hitting this least-cost pattern of abatement for the resource cost indicated in the optimal solution may be difficult for the reasons summarised in Section 8.2. What is more, existing control mechanisms in the Forth estuary do not correspond to the textbook idea of 'uniform regulation', but are rather more flexible than this (although this would no longer be the case if the UK is pushed along the uniform standards route favoured by most other members of the EEC). We have shown that market mechanisms offer no immediate control cost advantage over flexible regulation as a means of eliminating the summertime DO sag in the estuary; and the extra administrative costs of a market mechanism, while hard to judge accurately, may be significant in relation to the savings made by a market mechanism compared to flexible regulation.

So as long as eliminating the DO sag remains the only goal of environmental policy, there seems little reason to change from the existing regulatory system, unless the ability of market mechanisms to even out the financial costs of effluent abatement between firms is seen as a substantial equity advantage. But for tougher environmental goals, which we have not modelled, market mechanisms are likely to have significant cost advantages over flexible regulation; only further research, using a full developed environmental water quality model, will, however, show this empirically.

Should market mechanisms have a strong cost advantage, the choice between the three main types available – tradeable permits, incentive charges and charge-subsidies, and redistributive charging - is not a simple one; tradeable permits raise problems such as market domination by a single firm; incentive charging has problems such as not being able to hit a given effluent target easily because of indivisibilities in abatement technologies; redistributive charging involves the bureaucracy of an abatement subsidy scheme, which may distort control efforts in favour of capital-intensive projects. Whichever mechanism is chosen, it seems likely that a revenue-neutral version (i.e. grandfathered permits instead of auctioned permits, and charge-subsidies instead of pure charges) will have to be chosen to secure public acceptance; but this choice is ultimately a political one, and so not one on which an economic report such as this can advise conclusively.

8.4 Applications to Other Pollutants and Locations

We have looked at flow pollutants exerting a BOD in the Forth estuary in this report, and a few thoughts about how our conclusions may or may not apply to other pollutants and geographical location may be useful.

1. If a tradeable permit market was aimed at *stock* pollutants (for which no assimilative capacity exists), then a permit market is still possible (given sufficient traders), but permits now represent a non-renewable resource. A once and for all allocation of permits could be issued, the number of which would depend on the maximum total emissions of, for instance, cadmium, before the EQS is violated. Once a permit is 'used' to legalise a 'one unit' discharge in cadmium, it cannot be reused. Cost minimisation over time requires the rate of increase in marginal control costs to be equal to the discount rate, with emissions declining through time until they reach zero.

2. Sewage treatment works (STWs) turned out to play an relatively unimportant role on the Forth, but in other rivers and estuaries (for example, the Clyde) they may be very important.

3. To include a wide range of pollutants an effective water quality index would need to be developed. Such an index might be somewhat imprecise, but it would increase the number of firms that could be included in (say) a permit scheme and so would reduce the chance of any one firm dominating the permit market.

4. A prerequisite for any market mechanism to work is a water quality model of the river or estuary in question. These take both time and money to develop: about 2.5 years and £65,000 in the case of the Stirling team's investigation, a cost which would be considerably greater had all labour costs and overheads been included. However, one must remember that, to be effective, existing regulatory schemes require a detailed knowledge of water quality, so not all of this cost could be ascribed as a specific cost of market mechanism schemes.

References

ERL (1990) 'Market Mechanisms: Charging and Subsidies', *Environmental Resources Ltd*, 106 Gloucester Place, London W1.

HAHN, R. W. & NOLL, R. G. (1982) 'Designing a Market for Tradeable Emissions Permits', *Reform of Environmental Regulation,* W. A. Magat (Ed) Cambridge, MA: Ballinger.

SESKIN, E., ANDERSON, R. AND REID, R. (1983) 'An Empirical Analysis of Economic Strategies for Controlling Air Pollution', *Journal of Environmental Economics and Management,* 10, 112-124.

TIETENBERG, T. (1982) 'Marketable Emission Permits in Principle and Practice' DP123 *Resources for the Future,* Washington DC.

Printed in the United Kingdom for HMSO
Dd 294965 6/92 C10 531/3 12521